PREDICTABILITY AND FLEXIBILITY IN THE LAW OF MARITIME DELIMITATION

This fully revised new edition offers a comprehensive picture of the law of maritime delimitation, incorporating all new cases and State practice in this field. As with all types of law, the law of maritime delimitation should possess a degree of predictability. On the other hand, as maritime delimitation cases differ, flexible considerations of geographical and non-geographical factors are also required in order to achieve equitable results. How, then, is it possible to ensure predictability while taking into account a number of diverse factors in order to achieve an equitable result? This is the question at the heart of the law of maritime delimitation. This book explores a well-balanced legal framework that reconciles predictability and flexibility in the law of maritime delimitation by looking at three aspects of the question: first it reviews the evolution of the law of maritime delimitation; second, it undertakes a comparative study of the case law and State practice; and third, it critically assesses the law of maritime delimitation in its current form.

Predictability and Flexibility in the Law of Maritime Delimitation

Second Edition

Yoshifumi Tanaka

•HART•
OXFORD • LONDON • NEW YORK • NEW DELHI • SYDNEY

HART PUBLISHING

Bloomsbury Publishing Plc

Kemp House, Chawley Park, Cumnor Hill, Oxford, OX2 9PH, UK

HART PUBLISHING, the Hart/Stag logo, BLOOMSBURY and the Diana logo are trademarks of Bloomsbury Publishing Plc

First edition published in 2006

This edition first published in Great Britain 2019

A catalogue record for this book is available from the British Library.

Library of Congress Cataloging-in-Publication data

Names: Tanaka, Yoshifumi, author.

Title: Predictability and flexibility in the Law of Maritime Delimitation / Yoshifumi Tanaka.

Description: Second edition. | Oxford ; Chicago, Illinois : Hart, an imprint of Bloomsbury, 2019. | Series: Studies in international law | Includes bibliographical references and index.

Identifiers: LCCN 2019021107 (print) | LCCN 2019022293 (ebook) | ISBN 9781509912117 (hardback : alk. paper) | ISBN 9781509912094 (ePDF) | ISBN 9781509912100 (EPub)

Subjects: LCSH: Territorial waters. | Maritime boundaries.

Classification: LCC KZA1450 .T36 2019 (print) | LCC KZA1450 (ebook) | DDC 341.4/5—dc23

LC record available at https://lccn.loc.gov/2019021107

LC ebook record available at https://lccn.loc.gov/2019022293

ISBN: HB: 978-1-50991-211-7
ePDF: 978-1-50991-209-4
ePub: 978-1-50991-210-0

Typeset by Compuscript Ltd, Shannon
Printed and bound in Great Britain by TJ International Ltd, Padstow, Cornwall

To find out more about our authors and books visit www.hartpublishing.co.uk. Here you will find extracts, author information, details of forthcoming events and the option to sign up for our newsletters.

Preface to the Second Edition

SINCE THE FIRST edition of this book was published in 2006, there have been several developments in the law of maritime delimitation. Indeed, the cases on this subject have approximately doubled. Treaties relating to maritime delimitation have also increased. In light of the new development, it became necessary to fully revise the first edition of this book. While maintaining the framework for analysis, in this second edition, all chapters were revised, updated and, where necessary, rewritten. In particular, an analysis of some eleven cases was newly added in chapter five. The analysis of the new cases was also incorporated into chapters seven and eight. The two chapters also refer to recent treaties in this field. Furthermore, in chapter three, a new subsection was added to analyse obligations concerning provisional arrangements set out in Articles 74(3) and 83(3) of the UN Convention on the Law of the Sea. Moreover, chapter five includes a new section concerning the delimitation of the continental shelf beyond 200 nautical miles. Chapters nine and ten were significantly revised. In addition, the Appendix was updated as much as possible. By incorporating all new cases and State practice, like the first edition, this second edition seeks to pursue a legal framework that reconciles predictability and flexibility in the law of maritime delimitation. The manuscript of this new edition was completed in February 2019 in Copenhagen. All websites were current as of that date.

Y.T.

Foreword to the First Edition

OVER THE LAST 50 years, international lawyers have found themselves in effect called upon to re-draw the map of the world. The 1945 Truman Proclamation marked the beginning of a period during which vast areas outlined in atlases without any indication of sovereign affiliation were suddenly required to be criss-crossed with lines of division indicating, first the claims of adjacent States, and subsequently their agreed or judicially determined entitlements. First the sea-bed, and then, with the coming of the concept of the EEZ, the superjacent waters had to be partitioned out. This division of the oceans and the seas in some respects resembled the 'scramble for Africa' of the previous century, but with important differences. In the first place, the sea offered no convenient landmarks (ridges, hills, watersheds) that might suggest themselves as reference points or lines for the fixing of convenient boundaries. Secondly, while the lines drawn on the map of Africa reflected the realities of State occupation or control (or at least 'spheres of interest'), it was realised almost at once that the application of such notions to claims to areas of sea and seabed would inevitably lead to anarchy and conflict.

Some other criterion or regulatory system was therefore required; and the accumulation of State practice and (in particular) judicial and arbitral jurisprudence has led to the creation of a real body of accepted maritime delimitation law. It is this construction that is the subject of Dr Tanaka's magisterial survey, compilation and analysis. Its principal pillars were established early on, with the 1958 Geneva Conventions and the pioneer ruling in the *North Sea Continental Shelf* case: the inherent and *ab initio* rights of the coastal State, the requirement for delimitation by agreement, and the emphasis on the role of equity. But much remained to be worked out by State practice and by jurisprudence; and in such a novel field, it is perhaps not surprising that there have been many inconsistencies and reversals. There could be no better guide through this labyrinth than Dr Tanaka, whose sureness of direction is based on very detailed study.

Furthermore, the new law of the sea has (appropriately enough) its own Scylla and Charybdis. Law is something to live by: the subjects of law are entitled to arrange their affairs on the basis of a reasonable knowledge of which actions of theirs would be open to legal challenge, and which would not, in any circumstances; and this is equally true in a legal system, like the international legal order, in which there is no obligation to submit legal disputes for settlement to a standing tribunal, and to accept its rulings. On the other hand, no system of law can be expected to regulate legal relations in all their variety; there must be provision for the unexpected and the unforeseen. Thus no system of law can be rigid, at least not in its details.

It is a particular merit of Dr Tanaka's study that he has set his analysis of the law of maritime delimitation against the background of these two competing imperatives: the need for predictability of the law, and the need for flexibility in the application of the law. The need for flexibility is evident: no two coasts, and the geographical relationship between them, can be matched point for point with any other pair of coasts, so that a rule appropriate for the one situation is valid in all respects for the other. Predictability signifies, as in other fields of law, the possibility of assessing in advance, with some degree of accuracy, the delimitation that would be likely to be arrived at by a tribunal or arbitrator, on the basis of existing customary law. It goes further than that, however: it must also be possible, when a new maritime boundary is to be negotiated, to have some idea what claims may be advanced consistently with international law, and what circumstances, geographical or other, should properly be taken into account. Without some basis of this kind, such a negotiation can be no more than a test of diplomatic pressure and strength, or more probably will break down without achieving any agreed line.

Dr Tanaka makes extremely clear in what ways the armoury of concepts that have become familiar to experts in maritime delimitation serves to advance these twin aims: eg, equidistance, special circumstances, relevant circumstances, proportionality, coastal fronts, the general direction of the coast, and above all the idea of equity. His analysis is based on a thorough knowledge, and detailed analysis, of the judicial and arbitral case law, the importance of which he rightly emphasises. But he has also made the fullest use of the materials that have increasingly become available indicating the circumstances in which delimitation agreements between States have been arrived at, and the considerations that contributed to their making: in other words, the evidence of State practice contributing to the growth of custom. Dr Tanaka's observations and conclusions of a general nature are the more to be valued because they are clearly based on a wide and intimate knowledge of this material.

So long as the parcelling-out of the seas and oceans has not been completed, and maritime boundaries remain to be determined, the present work will be invaluable to all those concerned in this branch of the law of the sea. It may well however have a broader value and usefulness, as a study of the possibilities of reconciling predictability with flexibility in a particularly difficult context, that will, it is to be hoped, serve as a guide when such a reconciliation is required in other fields of law.

Hugh Thirlway
Principal Legal Secretary, International Court of Justice,
Professor of International Law, University of Bristol.
The Hague, January 2006.

Acknowledgement

THE FIRST EDITION of this book was a revised version of my doctoral thesis submitted to the Graduate Institute of International Studies, Geneva (currently the Graduate Institute of International and Development Studies, Geneva) in 2002. I would like to express my deepest gratitude to three eminent professors of international law: Professor Hugh Thirlway and Professor Lucius Caflisch, both of the Graduate Institute of International Studies, Geneva and Professor Tetsuo Sato at Hitotsubashi University, Tokyo. They were my supervisors when I was a graduate student in Geneva and Tokyo and I owe much to them.

I am grateful to the University of Copenhagen, Faculty of Law and its Library for support with the completion of this book. My thanks are also due to Sinead Moloney, Sasha Jawed and other Hart Publishing staff for their professional assistance. I thank Ms Claire Banyard for her thorough copy-editing. Finally, I am grateful to my wife, Akiko, for all her support and prayers throughout my work.

Y.T.

Brief Contents

PART III
BALANCE BETWEEN PREDICTABILITY AND FLEXIBILITY IN THE LAW OF MARITIME DELIMITATION

Detailed Contents

PART III
BALANCE BETWEEN PREDICTABILITY AND FLEXIBILITY IN THE LAW OF MARITIME DELIMITATION

List of Abbreviations

AFDI	*Annuaire français de droit international*
AJIL	*American Journal of International Law*
ASDI	*Annuaire suisse de droit international*
BYIL	*British Yearbook of International Law*
CJIL	*Chinese Journal of International Law*
CYIL	*Canadian Yearbook of International Law*
EEZ	Exclusive Economic Zone
EFZ	Exclusive Fishery Zone
FZ	Fishery Zone
ICJ	International Court of Justice
ICLQ	*International and Comparative Law Quarterly*
IJECL	*International Journal of Estuarine and Coastal Law*
IJMCL	*International Journal of Marine and Coastal Law*
ILC	International Law Commission
ILM	*International Legal Materials*
ILR	*International Law Reports*
IMB	*International Maritime Boundaries*
LJIL	*Leiden Journal of International Law*
LOSC	*UN Convention on the Law of the Sea*
NILR	*Netherlands International Law Review*
ODIL	*Ocean Development and International Law*
RCADI	*Recueil des cours de l'Académie de droit international*
RGDIP	*Revue générale de droit international public*
UNCLOS	United Nations Conference on the Law of the Sea
YILC	*Yearbook of International Law Commission*

List of Illustrations

The author wishes to thank the American Society of International Law, the Hague Academy of International Law, Nijhoff/Brill Academic Publishers, the Netherlands International Law Review, Permanent Court of Arbitration, and Professor L Caflisch for their permissions to reproduce the illustrations. The author should also like to thank Columbia University Press and the British Yearbook of International Law for their permissions to reproduce the figures.

Table of Cases

Table of Treaties and National Legislation

1996	Agreement between the Dominican Republic and the United Kingdom of Great Britain and Northern Ireland Concerning the Delimitation of the Maritime Boundary between the Dominican Republic and the Turks and Caicos Islands	287, 494
1996	Agreement between the Government of the Republic of Estonia and the Government of the Republic of Latvia on the Maritime Delimitation in the Gulf of Riga, the Strait of Irbe and the Baltic Sea	431, 494
1996	Agreement on Maritime Delimitation between the Government of the French Republic and the Government of the United Kingdom Concerning Guadeloupe and Montserrat	272, 494
	Art 3	322
1996	Agreement on Principle between Eritrea and Yemen	287
	Art 2	91
	Art 2(2)	91
	Art 2(3)	91
	Art 2(3)(a)	91
	Art 9(3)	91
1997	Agreement between the Government of the Kingdom of Thailand and the Government of the Socialist Republic of Vietnam on the Delimitation of the Maritime Boundary between the Two Countries in the Gulf of Thailand	240, 270, 289, 495
1997	Agreement between the Government of the Kingdom of Denmark along with the Local Government of Greenland on the one hand and the Government of the Republic of Iceland on the other hand on the Delimitation of the Continental Shelf and Fishery Zone in the Area between Greenland and Iceland	269, 333, 382, 494
1997	Agreement between the Government of the Republic of Estonia, the Government of the Republic of Latvia and the Government of the Kingdom of Sweden on the Common Maritime Boundary Point in the Baltic Sea	289, 321, 501
1997	Treaty between the Government of Australia and the Government of the Republic of Indonesia Establishing an Exclusive Economic Zone Boundary and Certain Seabed Boundaries (Perth Treaty)	150, 269, 298, 455, 481, 500
	Preamble	456

2010	Agreement between Trinidad and Tobago and Venezuela	385, 506
2011	Agreement between Bahamas and Cuba	289, 498
2011	Agreement between Comoros and Mozambique	289, 499
2011	Agreement between Comoros and Tanzania	289, 434, 499
2012	Agreement between Comoros and Seychelles	289, 434, 499
2012	Agreement between Comoros, Seychelles, and Tanzania	322, 501
2012	Agreement between the Cook Island and Kiribati	385, 498
2012	Agreement between the Cook Islands and Niue	385, 498
2012	Agreement between Kiribati and Marshall Islands	385, 498
2012	Agreement between Kiribati and Nauru	385, 499
2012	Agreement between Kiribati and Tuvalu	385, 499
2012	Agreement between Kiribati, Marshall Islands and Nauru	321, 501
2012	Agreement between Mexico and the United States	385, 506
2014	Treaty between the Republic of Singapore and the Republic of Indonesia Relating to the Delimitation of the Territorial Sea of the Two Countries in the Eastern Part of the Strait of Singapore	289, 478
2014	Agreement between Indonesia and Philippines	289
2018	Treaty between Australia and the Democratic Republic of Timor-Leste Establishing Their Maritime Boundaries in the Timor Sea (the Timor Sea Treaty)	301, 323, 388, 500

National Legislation

1904	Tunisian Instruction of the Director of Public Works of 31 December 1904	394
1928	Straits Settlement and Johore Territorial Waters (Agreement) Act (United Kingdom)	24
1945	Proclamation by President Truman of 28 September 1945 on Policy of the United States with Respect to the Natural Resources of the Subsoil and Sea Bed of the Continental Shelf	vii, 53
1951	Decree 1951 (Tunisia)	394
1972	Decree No.1069 of 23 August 1972 (Venezuela)	433
1976	Royal Decree of 17 December 1976 relating to the establishment of the Economic Zone of Norway	478, 482

* With respect to a comprehensive list of treaties relating to maritime delimitations, see Appendix.

1

Preliminary Considerations

I. NATURE OF THE PROBLEM

A. Importance of Maritime Delimitation in International Law of the Sea

MARITIME SPACES IN international law of the sea are, in essence, defined in relation to the coastal State jurisdiction over each maritime space.[1] Thus, coastal State jurisdiction is the in primary criterion in characterising maritime spaces. The ambit of coastal State jurisdiction is in principle defined *spatially,* based on distance from the coast.[2] Under the 1982 UN Convention on the Law of the Sea (hereafter the LOSC), the territorial sea in which a coastal State exercises territorial sovereignty shall not exceed 12 nautical miles measured from the relevant baseline.[3] The contiguous zone over which a limited jurisdiction is exercised by the coastal State may not extend beyond 24 nautical miles from that line.[4] The Exclusive Economic Zone (EEZ), where the coastal State may exercise sovereign rights regarding the exploration and exploitation of natural resources, shall not extend beyond 200 nautical miles.[5] The same is in principle true for continental shelves of less than 200 nautical miles.[6] It would seem safe to say that these rules have now become customary law.[7]

[1] T Kuwahara, *International Law of the Sea* (in Japanese, Tokyo, Kokusai Shoin, 1992) 26. In fact, the 1982 UN Convention on the Law of the Sea defines each category of maritime space from the viewpoint of coastal State jurisdiction. See for instance, Arts 1(1), 2, 3, 33, 49(1), 56(1), 76(1) and 86. This seems to be logical on account of the fact that the regime of each maritime space has been formulated concomitantly with the extension of coastal State jurisdiction. The UN Convention on the Law of the Sea was adopted 10 December 1982 and entered into force on 16 November 1994. Text in 1833 *UNTS* 3.

[2] Yet internal waters and archipelagic waters constitute exceptions. The former are located on the landward side of the baseline of the territorial sea (Art 8 of the LOSC), and the latter consist of the waters enclosed in the archipelagic baselines drawn in accordance with Art 47 (Art 49 of the LOSC). Thus the two institutions do not rely on the spatial distance from the baseline. Furthermore, the high seas are defined residually as 'all parts of the sea that are not included in the exclusive economic zone in the territorial sea or in the internal waters of a State, or in the archipelagic waters of an archipelagic State' (Art 86 of the LOSC).

[3] LOSC, Art 3.

[4] LOSC, Art 33.

[5] LOSC, Art 57.

[6] LOSC, Art 76(1).

[7] The ICJ held in the *Libya/Malta* case that the EEZ has become a part of customary law. Furthermore, it ruled that the development of the law enables a State to claim a continental shelf up to as far as 200 miles independently of the geological character of the seabed. The *Libya/Malta* case,

The definition of the spatial extent of coastal State jurisdiction is at the heart of the international law of the sea.

In deciding on the spatial extent of coastal State jurisdiction, a problem that may arise is the situation in which the jurisdiction of two or more coastal States overlaps. In particular, owing to the emergence of the continental shelf and EEZ, which generate a vast amount of economic resources for coastal States, States attempt to acquire the largest maritime spaces possible. Accordingly, the extension of coastal State jurisdiction over these resource-oriented zones may give rise to international disputes regarding maritime delimitation. Indeed, the ever-growing use of the oceans by coastal States for living and non-living resources will lead to heightened efforts to delimit maritime spaces.[8] Without rules on maritime delimitation in spaces where coastal State jurisdictions overlap, the legal uses of maritime spaces cannot be enjoyed effectively. Thus, the law of maritime delimitation plays an essential role in the international law of the sea. It is against this background that one should consider the law of maritime delimitation.

B. Development of the Studies on Maritime Delimitation

Since 1945, in particular, many studies have been written in the field of maritime delimitation. Some writers examined the subject starting in the 1980s. So far as monographs are concerned, studies by Jagota,[9] Johnston,[10] Weil,[11] Evans,[12] Tanja[13] and Lucchini/Vœlckel[14] are in particular pioneers in this field. In the 2000s, several monographs on this subject were published by writers, including: Kolb,[15] Nuno Sérgio Marques Antunes,[16] Cottier,[17] Paul von Mühlendahl,[18] Fietta/Cleverly,[19] and

ICJ Reports 1985, 33, para 34; p 35, para 39. See also T Treves, 'Codification du droit international et pratique des Etats dans le droit de la mer' (1990) 223 *RCADI* 69, 87 and 91.

[8] JI Charney and LM Alexander (eds), *International Maritime Boundary*, vol I (Dordrecht, Nijhoff, 1993) xxii.

[9] SP Jagota, *Maritime Boundary* (Dordrecht, Nijhoff, 1985).

[10] DM Johnston, *The Theory and History of Ocean Boundary-Making* (Kingston, McGill-Queen's University Press, 1988).

[11] P Weil, *Perspectives du droit de la délimitation maritime* (Paris, Pedone, 1988).

[12] MD Evans, *Relevant Circumstances and Maritime Delimitation* (Oxford, Clarendon Press, 1989).

[13] GJ Tanja, *The Legal Determination of International Maritime Boundaries* (Deventer, Kluwer, 1990).

[14] L Lucchini and M Vœlckel, *Droit de la mer*, tome 2, vol 1: délimitation (Paris, Pedone, 1996).

[15] R Kolb, *Case Law on Equitable Maritime Delimitation: Digest and Commentaries* (The Hague, Brill/Nijhoff, 2003).

[16] Nuno Sérgio Marques Antunes, *Towards the Conceptualisation of Maritime Delimitation: Legal and Technical Aspects of a Political Process* (Leiden, Nijhoff, 2003).

[17] T Cottier, *Equitable Principles of Maritime Delimitation: The Quest for Distributive Justice in International Law* (Cambridge University Press, 2015).

[18] P von Mühlendahl, *L'équidistance dans la délimitation des frontière maritimes: étude de la jurisprudence internationale* (Paris, Pedone, 2016).

[19] S Fietta, S and R Cleverly, *A Practitioner's Guide to Maritime Boundary Delimitation* (Oxford University Press, 2016).

Lando.[20] A recent joint study of the KG Jebsen Centre for the Law of the Sea at the University of Tromsø also merits mention.[21] Most of them have focused primarily on the case law. In addition to monographs, as is shown in the bibliography, there are a considerable number of articles regarding the jurisprudence in this field. Since the law of maritime delimitation has developed through international jurisprudence, it was only natural that writers turned to the analysis of case law in this field.

By contrast, State practice concerning maritime delimitation has not been sufficiently studied until recently. This situation seems to be understandable due to the difficulties of systematic research in State practice on maritime delimitation and the lack of information regarding the negotiation processes necessary to reach agreements. Recently, however, studies on worldwide and regional State practice concerning maritime boundaries are developing. Regarding the world-wide study of State practice, the publication of *International Maritime Boundaries* by the American Society of International Law is the most important development.[22] With respect to regional State practice on maritime delimitation, regional maritime areas in the world have been examined by regional experts. These areas include: South-East Asia,[23] the China Seas,[24] the Mediterranean Sea,[25] the Russian region,[26] the Persian Gulf,[27] the Caribbean Sea;[28] the Pacific,[29]

[20] M Lando, *Maritime Delimitation as a Judicial Process* (Cambridge University Press, 2019). At the time of writing, the author could not refer to this study.

[21] Alex G Oude Elferink, T Henriksen, and SV Busch (eds), *Maritime Boundary Delimitation: The Case Law Is It Consistent and Predictable?* (Cambridge University Press, 2018).

[22] JI Charney et al (eds), *International Maritime Boundaries*, 7 Vols (Dordrecht, Nijhoff, 1993, 1998, 2002, 2005, 2011, 2016). For another important source relating to worldwide State practice, see United States Department of State, Bureau of Oceans and International Environmental and Scientific Affairs, *Limits in the Seas*. Furthermore, Prescott and Schofield also made worldwide research regarding State practice in this field. V Prescott and C Schofield, *The Maritime Political Boundaries of the World*, 2nd edn (Leiden and Boston, Brill/Nijhoff, 2005).

[23] K Kittichaisaree, *The Law of the Sea and Maritime Boundary Delimitation in South-East Asia* (Oxford, OUP, 1987); CH Park, East Asia and the Law of the Sea (Seoul, Seoul National University Press, 1983); CH Park and JK Park, *The Law of the Sea: Problems from the East Asian Perspective* (Honolulu, University of Hawaii, The Law of the Sea Institute, 1987); VL Forbes, *Indonesia's Delimited Maritime Boundaries* (Berlin, Springer, 2014).

[24] Z Wu, *Maritime Delimitation in the China Seas* (Thesis, Geneva, IUHEI, 1992); J Greenfield, *China's Practice in the Law of the Sea* (Oxford, Clarendon Press, 1992).

[25] FA Ahnish, *The International Law of Maritime Boundaries and the Practice of States in the Mediterranean Sea* (Oxford, Clarendon Press, 1993); U Leanza (ed), *Mediterranean Continental Shelf: Delimitation and Regimes* (New York, NY, Oceana Publications, 1988).

[26] Alex G Oude Elferink, *The Law of Maritime Boundary Delimitation: A Case Study of the Russian Federation* (Dordrecht, Nijhoff, 1994).

[27] A Razavi, *Continental Shelf Delimitation and Related Maritime Issues in the Persian Gulf* (Dordrecht, Nijhoff, 1997); CG MacDonald, *Iran, Saudi Arabia, and the Law of the Sea* (Westport, CT, Greenwood Press, 1980); A El-Hakim, *The Middle Eastern States and the Law of the Sea* (Manchester, MUP, 1979).

[28] E Gold (ed), *A New Law of the Sea for the Caribbean: An Examination of Marine Law and Policy Issues in the Lesser Antilles* (New York, NY, Springer-Verlag, 1988).

[29] DM Johnston and MJ Valencia, *Pacific Ocean Boundary Problems: Status and Solutions* (Dordrecht, Nijhoff, 1991); HI Llanos Mardones, *The Delimitation of Maritime Areas between Adjacent States in the Southeastern Pacific Region* (Thesis, Geneva, IUHEI, 1996). In addition, for

and West Africa.[30] Owing to the development of studies regarding worldwide and regional State practice, it becomes possible, to a certain extent, to examine State practice systematically. Therefore, at present, it is essential to specify the present-day law of maritime delimitation by studying not only the case law but also State practice.

C. Analytical Framework

The principal aim of this study is the quest for a well-balanced legal system that reconciles predictability and flexibility in the law of maritime delimitation. As with all types of law, that which relates to maritime delimitation should have a certain degree of predictability. As Sir Robert Jennings has stated, '[n]o reasonable litigant expects the decision of a court to be predictable, but the range of considerations used for a decision and the procedures for their application should certainly be predictable.'[31] At the same time, as each maritime delimitation case differs, flexible consideration of relevant factors is also required in order to achieve equitable results. How, then, is it possible to ensure predictability while taking into account a diversity of factors in order to achieve an equitable result? This question is, in the author's view, the heart of the law of maritime delimitation. The quest for a well-balanced legal system reconciling predictability and flexibility should thus be the essential element in the law of maritime delimitation.

Predictability versus flexibility of law is a classical dilemma in the legal field.[32] It is of particular concern in the field of maritime delimitation owing to the infinite variety of geographical and non-geographical situations, and to the requirement of a degree of predictability.[33] In order to overcome this difficulty, it is necessary to clarify as much as possible the predictable and flexible aspects of the law of maritime delimitation. With respect to the predictability of the law of maritime delimitation, the sole method that would seem to ensure predictable

a monograph regarding regional issues in general, see DM Johnston and PM Saunders (eds), *Ocean Boundary Making: Regional Issues and Developments* (London, Croom Helm, 1988).

30 M Kamga, *Délimitation maritime sur la côte atlantique africaine* (Brussels, Bruylant, 2006).

31 Sir Robert Jennings, 'Equity and Equitable Principles' (1986) 42 *ASDI* 38. Cottier also stressed that: 'Predictability and stability are among the most important functions of law.' Cottier, *Equitable Principles of Maritime Delimitation* 386.

32 HWA Thirlway, 'The Law and Procedure of the International Court of Justice, Part Six' (1994) 65 *BYIL* 78. See also C de Visscher, *De l'équité dans le règlement arbitral ou judiciaire des litiges de droit international public* (Paris, Pedone, 1972) Préface, i.

33 Related to this, Judge Juménez de Aréchaga, in the *Tunisia/Libya* case of 1982, indicated the fundamental dilemma arising in all cases of continental shelf delimitation, that is to say, 'the need to maintain consistency and uniformity in the legal principles and rules applicable to a series of situations which are characterized by their multiple diversity'. Separate Opinion of Judge Jiménez de Aréchaga, [1982] ICJ Rep 106, [26].

results is that of equidistance.[34] The legal validity and value of the equidistance method is thus one of the principal issues.[35] Regarding the element of flexibility, the examination of relevant circumstances is essential.[36] In fact, such circumstances have been highly important in the search for an equitable result, the goal of the law of maritime delimitation.[37] Thus, the law of maritime delimitation should provide an interesting example of the legal philosophy concerning the classical dilemma in the legal field.

This book contains three parts. In Part One, basic approaches to maritime delimitations will be considered by retracing the evolution of the law of maritime delimitation. Chapter two will examine State practice and writers' views prior to 1958. In Chapter three, the 1958 Geneva Conventions and the 1982 LOSC will be considered. Chapters four and five will then analyse the development of the case law relating to maritime delimitations. Particular focus will be on the two basic approaches taken by the international courts and tribunals.

In Part Two, we will turn to the examination of the elements of predictability and flexibility in the law of maritime delimitation. The analysis will be effected through a comparative study of case law and State practice. The question of interest here is whether the law identified by international courts and tribunals and the law extrapolated from State practice coincide. As will be shown below, since the case law on maritime delimitation tends to rely solely on precedent without regard to State practice and *opinio juris*, it is worth examining the issue in order to clarify the existing law. Thus, chapter six will examine the requirement of predictability in the law of maritime delimitation by focusing on the applicability of the equidistance method at the first stage of delimitation. In chapters seven and eight, the requirement of flexibility of the law will be considered by examining geographical and non-geographical factors.

On the basis of the research presented in Part Two, Part Three will consider a legal framework reconciling predictability and flexibility in the law of maritime delimitation. In this connection, chapter nine examines, in particular, some theoretical issues concerning relevant circumstances and problems with the

[34] HWA Thirlway, 'The Law and Procedure of the International Court of Justice, Part Five' (1993) 64 *BYIL* 41. This does not mean that the requirement of predictability is achieved only by the equidistance method. A certain degree of predictability would also be necessary when taking into account the relevant circumstances. See ch 6, s I.

[35] Equidistance is a line every point of which is equidistant from the nearest points of the baselines from which the breadth of the territorial sea of each State is measured. See Art 12(1) of the Geneva Convention on the Territorial Sea and the Contiguous Zone and Art 6 of the Geneva Convention on the Continental Shelf.

[36] The concept of 'relevant circumstances' is a legal notion, which is indicated, for the first time, in the *North Sea Continental Shelf* judgment. [1969] ICJ Rep 53, [101(C)(1)].

[37] *Delimitation of the Maritime Boundary in the Gulf of Maine Area* (Canada/United States of America), Judgment, [1984] ICJ Rep 299–300, [112]; *Dispute concerning Delimitation of the Maritime Boundary between Bangladesh and Myanmar in the Bay of Bengal* (Bangladesh/Myanmar), Judgment, [2012] ITLOS Rep 67, [235].

three-stage approach to maritime delimitations. Finally, a general conclusion will be drawn in chapter ten.

II. CONCEPT OF MARITIME DELIMITATION

A. Legal Nature of Maritime Delimitation

i. Definition

Maritime delimitation may be defined as the process of establishing lines separating the spatial ambit of coastal State jurisdiction over maritime space where the legal title overlaps with that of another State. This definition calls for five comments:

First, the maritime delimitation is to be effected where there is an overlap of legal titles between States over the same maritime space. Hence, the maritime delimitation does not relate to separating maritime spaces under coastal State jurisdiction from the high seas or the international Seabed Area, to which no State has legal title.

Secondly, a distinction should be made between maritime *limits* and maritime *delimitation*.[38] The establishment of maritime 'limits' consists of drawing lines that define the maritime spaces of a *single* State, that is to say, spaces that are not in contact with those of another coastal State. Accordingly, the objective of maritime *limits* is to delineate maritime spaces under coastal State jurisdiction, considered in isolation. In that sense, the act of establishing 'limits' is a *unilateral* one. In contrast, 'maritime delimitation' is an operation to be effected between two or more States, as its object is to separate overlapping areas where legal titles of coastal States compete and each State attempts to exercise spatial jurisdiction over the same maritime space. This fact highlights an essential characteristic of maritime delimitation: *international character*. The Chamber of the ICJ in the *Gulf of Maine* case affirmed this view as an element of the 'fundamental norm' of the law of maritime delimitation: 'No maritime delimitation between States with opposite or adjacent coasts may be effected unilaterally by one of those States.'[39] Thus maritime delimitation has always had an international character in the sense that it is not a unilateral act, but must be effected between a plurality of States.[40]

Thirdly, according to the definition given, the phenomenon of maritime delimitation is confined to States. Hence delimitation problems among the

[38] Regarding the distinction between delimitation and limits, see L Caflisch, 'The Delimitation of Marine Spaces between States with Opposite and Adjacent Coasts' in R-J Dupuy and D Vignes (eds), *A Handbook on the New Law of the Sea* (Dordrecht, Nijhoff, 1991) 426–27. The maritime delimitation in our definition includes both conventional and jurisdictional delimitations, but it rules out unilateral delimitation.

[39] The *Gulf of Maine* case, [1984] ICJ Rep 299, [112].

[40] Cottier, *Equitable Principles of Maritime Delimitation*, 357–58.

members of federations are excluded from the present study. Furthermore, international organisations, inter alia, the International Sea-Bed Authority, are not subjects of maritime delimitation. In fact, having fixed the outer limit of the continental shelf beyond 200 nautical miles from the baselines, the duty of a coastal State is restricted to filing a copy of a chart or list of geographical co-ordinates with the Secretary-General of the Authority.[41]

Fourthly, the delimitation of maritime spaces relates to the separation of spatial ambits of State jurisdiction. The State jurisdiction to be delimited is of a *spatial nature;* it can be regarded as spatial,[42] as it differs from personal or any other type of jurisdiction. In fact, coastal State jurisdiction over internal waters and the territorial sea is undoubtedly of territorial, ie, spatial character. In addition, jurisdiction over the EEZ and the continental shelf may also be considered as spatial in the sense that it can be exercised solely within the space in question, although it must be distinguished from territorial sovereignty proper. It is true that coastal State jurisdiction over the EEZ and the continental shelf is limited to the matters defined by international law. However, in these matters, the coastal States may exercise sovereign rights, *regardless of the nationality* of the objects within the EEZ and the continental shelf. In addition, such sovereign rights are exercised exclusively. Jurisdiction over the EEZ and the continental shelf can be understood only as spatial jurisdiction, not as personal or any other type.[43]

[41] Art 84(2) of the LOSC. In accordance with Art 76(1) of the LOSC, the continental shelf of a coastal State comprises the seabed and subsoil of the submarine areas that extend beyond its territorial sea throughout the natural prolongation of its land territory to the outer edge of the continental margin, or to a distance of 200 nautical miles from the baselines from which the breadth of the territorial sea is measured where the outer edge of the continental margin does not extend up to that distance. Thus, the coastal State has legal title over the continental shelf up to 200 nautical miles regardless of geological and geomorphological features of the sea-bed. On the other hand, the outer limit of the continental shelf beyond the 200-mile limit is to be fixed in accordance with criteria embodied in Art 76(4) of the Convention. The outer limits of the continental shelf either shall not exceed 350 nautical miles from the baselines from which the breadth of the territorial sea is measured or shall not exceed 100 nautical miles from the 2,500 metre isobath. In this respect, the coastal State shall present information on the limits of the continental shelf beyond 200 miles to the Commission on the Limits of the Continental Shelf set up under Annex II (Art 76(8) of the LOSC).

[42] 'Spatial jurisdiction' may be defined as a jurisdiction that relates to a certain space and can be exercised solely within the space in question. Territorial jurisdiction is a typical example of spatial jurisdiction, but the concept of spatial jurisdiction is wider than territorial jurisdiction. While it has been argued that territorial jurisdiction is equal to territorial sovereignty, spatial jurisdiction includes not only territorial sovereignty but also jurisdiction over the continental shelf and EEZ/FZ.

[43] Y Tanaka, *The International Law of the Sea*, 3rd edn (Cambridge University Press, 2019) 154–55 and 172–73. Teruji Kuwahara clarifies the nature of the jurisdiction in question by calling it 'compétence territoriale limitée' or 'compétence territoriale mineure,' which has been discussed in French theory of international law. T Kuwahara, 'Territorial Jurisdiction and the EEZ' (in Japanese), (1987) 98 *The Hitotsubashi Review* 499–523. See also by the same author, *International Law of the Sea*, 95–96; J Combacau, *Le droit international de la mer* (Paris, PUF, 1985) 21. At the same time, however, as the jurisdiction in question over the EEZ and the continental shelf is in principle limited to economic exploration and exploitation, it becomes necessary to stress that this jurisdiction must be distinguished from territorial sovereignty, which is comprehensive unless international law provides otherwise.

Finally, it may be relevant to touch on an issue of terminology relating to 'delimitation line' and 'boundary'. According to Caflisch, while the expression 'boundary' is reserved for land territory and other spaces under full sovereignty, regarding maritime spaces where coastal States exercise functional powers, not full sovereignty, the terms 'limits' or 'lines of delimitation' are appropriate.[44] The Chamber of the ICJ in the *Gulf of Maine* case appears to support this view.[45] On the other hand, the Arbitral Tribunal in the *Guinea/Guinea-Bissau* case held that practice has not always accurately reflected the distinction.[46] In fact, in the *North Sea Continental Shelf* cases, the ICJ used the expressions 'boundary' or 'boundary line' in the authentic English text, while the words 'limites' or '*lignes de délimitation*' were used in the French translation.[47] In the *Greenland/Jan Mayen* case, the ICJ referred to 'boundary' for the continental shelf and fishery zone in the authentic English text, while the word '*délimitation*' was used in the French translation.[48] In the *Anglo-French Continental Shelf* case, the Court of Arbitration used the term 'boundary' in the English text.[49] In the *Guinea/Guinea-Bissau* award, the term 'frontière' was adopted in the authentic text in French,[50] and the *Guinea-Bissau v Senegal* award referred to 'frontières maritimes'.[51] In treaty practice, the expression 'maritime boundary' tends to be used for the delimitation of the continental shelf and/or the EEZ/Fishery Zone (FZ). This cursory review shows, as Caflisch himself accepted, that the distinction between 'delimitation line' and 'boundary' has not been clearly made. In particular, a delimitation line for the continental shelf and the EEZ/FZ is often called a 'single maritime boundary' in the case law and writers' views. Thus, in this study, the words 'delimitation line' and 'boundary' will be used interchangeably.

To better understand the legal nature of maritime delimitation, two issues need to be examined: the distinction between delimitation and apportionment and the distinction between declaratory and constitutive delimitation.

ii. Arguments on the Distinction between Delimitation and Apportionment

It was the ICJ which, in the *North Sea Continental Shelf* cases of 1969, stressed the distinction between delimitation and apportionment. In examining the

[44] Caflisch, 'The Delimitation of Marine Spaces,' 426. See also, by the same author, 'Essai d'une typologie des frontières' (1990) 63 *Relation internationales* 272–73.

[45] The *Gulf of Maine* case, [1984] ICJ Rep 246, [19]. But the French title of this case is 'affaire de la délimitation de la *frontière* maritime dans la région du golfe du Maine'.

[46] The *Guinea/Guinea-Bissau* case, (1985) 89 *RGDIP* 509, [50].

[47] See the *North Sea Continental Shelf* cases, [1969] ICJ Rep14, [4] and [5]; 17, [8]; 20, [13], respectively.

[48] The *Greenland/Jan Mayen* case, [1993] ICJ Rep 58, [46]; 61, [51].

[49] The *Anglo-French Continental Shelf* case, 18 United Nations, *Reports of International Arbitral Awards* 119, [255].

[50] The *Guinea/Guinea-Bissau* case, (1985) 89 *RGDIP* 502, [37].

[51] The *Guinea-Bissau v Senegal* case, (1990) 94 *RGDIP* 252–57, [63–66].

notion of 'a just and equitable share' referred by the Federal Republic of Germany, the Court clearly distinguished between delimitation and apportionment, stating that:

> [I]ts task in the present proceedings relates essentially to the delimitation and not the apportionment of the areas concerned, or their division into converging sectors. Delimitation is a process which involves establishing the boundaries of an area already, in principle, appertaining to the coastal State and not the determination *de novo* of such an area.[52]

Nevertheless, it seems that the distinction so defined is in reality tenuous.[53] In fact, in the same judgment, the Court ruled that: '[I]f, in the application of the preceding sub-paragraph [which postulated the application of equitable principles], the delimitation leaves to the Parties areas that overlap, these are to be divided between them in agreed proportions or, failing agreement, equally.'[54] However, the very idea of a division in agreed proportions or of an equal division will lead to the idea of apportionment. The same is true for the recourse to proportionality between the extent of the continental shelf areas appertaining to the coastal State and the length of its coast measured in the general direction of the coastline.[55] By its very definition, the idea of proportionality is linked to the concept of the apportionment of the continental shelf.[56] Hence, it may have to be admitted that the concept of maritime delimitation includes some aspects of apportionment.[57]

iii. Arguments on the Distinction between Declaratory and Constitutive Delimitation

The second question to be examined is the distinction between 'délimitation déclarative' (declaratory delimitation) and 'délimitation constitutive' (constitutive or man-made delimitation). This distinction also has its roots in

[52] The *North Sea Continental Shelf* cases, [1969] ICJ Rep 22, [18].

[53] Bouchez points out that apportionment and the delimitation would lead in this case to the same result, although he accepts the theoretical distinction. LJ Bouchez, 'The North Sea Continental Shelf Cases' (1969) 1 *Journal of Maritime Law and Commerce* 118. Indeed, the Court itself accepted that 'in a number of cases the results may be comparable, or even identical'. [1969] ICJ Rep 22, [18].

[54] ibid, 53 [101].

[55] ibid, 54 [101].

[56] Thirlway, 'The Law and Procedure, Part Six,' 56; SC Chaturvedi, 'The North Sea Continental Shelf Cases Analysed' (1973) 13 *Indian Journal of International Law* 484; TM Franck, *Fairness in International Law and Institutions* (Oxford, Clarendon Press, 1995) 65.

[57] This view is supported by several commentators. MD Blecher, 'Equitable Delimitation of Continental Shelf' (1979) 73 *AJIL* 64. See also Chaturvedi, 'The North Sea Continental Shelf Cases Analysed', 484; DM Johnston, *The Theory and History of Ocean Boundary-Making* (Kingston, McGill-Queen's University Press, 1988) 139–40; Bouchez, 'The North Sea Continental Shelf Cases' 118; E Grisel, 'The Lateral Boundaries of the Continental Shelf and the Judgment of the International Court of Justice in the North Sea Continental Shelf Cases' (1970) 64 *AJIL* 585–86. Nevertheless, the ICJ maintains the distinction between the delimitation and apportionment, see the *Tunisia/Libya* case [1982] ICJ Rep 60, [71]; the *Libya/Malta* case [1985] ICJ Rep 40, [46]; the *Greenland/Jan Mayen* case [1993] ICJ Rep 67, [64].

the *North Sea Continental Shelf* cases. Having specified the fundamental principle governing the continental shelf – natural prolongation – the Court ruled that this principle was inconsistent with the notion of 'a just and equitable share':

> More important is the fact that the doctrine of the just and equitable share appears to be wholly at variance with what the Court entertains no doubt is the most fundamental of all the rules of law relating to the continental shelf, enshrined in Article 2 of the 1958 Geneva Convention, though quite independent of it – namely that the rights of the coastal State in respect of the area of continental shelf that constitutes a natural prolongation of its land territory into and under the sea exist *ipso fact* and *ab initio*, by virtue of its sovereignty over the land, and as an extension of it in an exercise of sovereign rights for the purpose of exploring the seabed and exploiting its natural resources. In short, there is here an inherent right.[58]

Some argue that, according to the Court's theory, the boundary of the continental shelf is already fixed by the geological fact of the natural prolongation, since delimitation involves establishing the boundaries of an area already appertaining to the coastal State and not the determination *de novo* of such an area. If this is so, the delimitation simply consists of discovering how far the natural prolongation of each State extends under the sea. Weil called this view 'declaratory delimitation'. In criticising this conception,[59] Weil contrasts it with the idea of constitutive or man-made delimitation, which regards the maritime delimitation as the fruit of the will of States or of decisions of international courts. Having noted these two conceptions of maritime delimitation, Weil argues that the concept of declaratory delimitation has transformed itself into one of constitutive delimitation.[60]

It is doubtful, however, whether the ICJ, in the *North Sea Continental Shelf* cases, considered maritime delimitation as declaratory. The concept of the declaratory delimitation presupposes natural prolongation as a geophysical and geological fact. Yet it is not evident that the Court accepted such a concept of natural prolongation.[61] In fact, the Court affirmed that 'a median line divides equally between the two opposite countries' areas that can be regarded as being the natural prolongation of the territory between them.'[62] This shows that the Court did not consider the natural prolongation as a purely geophysical and geological concept, since it is inconceivable that the natural prolongation of each State always ceases in the middle. Furthermore, the concept of declaratory delimitation is hard to reconcile with the Court's judgment itself. In fact, the operative part of the judgment solely requires that the natural prolongation of

[58] The *North Sea Continental Shelf* cases [1969] ICJ Rep 22, [19].

[59] P Weil, *Perspectives du droit de la délimitation maritime* (Paris, Pedone, 1988) 30–38.

[60] ibid, 25–50.

[61] In addition, the use of the adjective 'natural' by the Court is problematical. W Friedmann, 'The North Sea Continental Shelf Cases – A Critique' (1970) 64 *AJIL* 237.

[62] The *North Sea Continental Shelf* cases [1969] ICJ Rep 37, [58].

each Party should be preserved 'as much as possible'.[63] This indicates that the delimitation of the continental shelf is not effected exclusively by resorting to natural prolongation, although the latter plays an important role. Moreover, as pointed out, the Court held that overlapping areas were to be divided in agreed proportions. In addition, it mentioned natural resources and a reasonable degree of proportionality as elements to be taken into account. In so doing, it is clear that the Court considered the continental shelf delimitation to be constitutive, and not declaratory, ie, based solely on natural prolongation.

In this connection, some doubts can be expressed regarding whether a delimitation could be a declaratory in the sense that there is only one 'correct' delimitation line for each set of geographical and non-geographical circumstances.[64] As will be discussed in this book, the core of the law of maritime delimitation is the achievement of an equitable result. By its very nature, an interpretation of the concept of equity may be variable and there is no single 'correct' interpretation of that concept. In fact, as will be illustrated in this book, international courts and tribunals exercise a large degree of discretion when drawing maritime boundaries. It could be contended, thus, that maritime delimitation is a man-made process of identifying and evaluating a delimitation method and relevant circumstances. In other words, it is always constitutive. In this regard, the view of the Special Chamber of the ITLOS in the *Ghana/Côte d'Ivoire* case deserves quoting:

> Only a decision on delimitation establishes which part of the continental shelf under dispute appertains to which of the claiming States. This means that the relevant judgment gives one entitlement priority over the other. Such a decision accordingly has a *constitutive nature* and cannot be qualified as merely declaratory.[65]

B. Typology of Maritime Delimitations

i. Typology in the 1958 Geneva Conventions

The various types of maritime delimitation exist. The 1958 Geneva Conventions define three types of the maritime delimitation: (i) delimitation of the territorial sea,[66] (ii) delimitation of the contiguous zone,[67] and (iii) delimitation of the continental shelf.[68] No provision was made regarding the delimitation of

[63] ibid, 53 [101].

[64] Separate Opinion of Judge Oda in the *Qatar v Bahrain* case (Merits), [2001] ICJ Rep 134, [26].

[65] Emphasis added. *Dispute Concerning Delimitation of the Maritime Boundary between Ghana and Côte d'Ivoire in the Atlantic Ocean* (Ghana/Côte d'Ivoire), Judgment. Not yet reported, [591], available at: www.itlos.org/en/cases/list-of-cases/case-no-23/.

[66] Article 12 of the Convention on the Territorial Sea and the Contiguous Zone. Text in 516 *UNTS*, 205. Entered into force 10 September 1964.

[67] ibid, Article 24.

[68] Article 6 of the Convention on the Continental Shelf. Text in 499 *UNTS*, 311. Entered into force 10 June 1964.

internal waters, although that problem may arise, for instance, in the case of a bay with several riparians.[69]

ii. Typology in the 1982 UN Convention on the Law of the Sea

The LOSC explicitly refers to three types of maritime delimitation: (i) delimitation of the territorial sea,[70] (ii) delimitation of the EEZ,[71] and (iii) delimitation of the continental shelf.[72] As with the Geneva Conventions, there is no provision for the delimitation of internal waters. Unlike the Geneva Convention on the Territorial Sea and the Contiguous Zone, the LOSC makes no reference to the delimitation of the contiguous zone.

A particular issue that arises in this context concerns the single maritime boundary, which would delimit the continental shelf and the EEZ/FZ by one line. As the relevant factors relating to the sea-bed and to superjacent waters may be different, the delimitation lines of the continental shelf and the EEZ/FZ may not necessarily coincide. For example, while the localisation of fisheries resources may be relevant for the EEZ boundary, a continental shelf boundary may require consideration of the location of mineral deposits. In that case, a delimitation line that is equitable for the superjacent waters does not necessarily have that same quality for the seabed. A divergence of factors relevant for the sea-bed and the superjacent waters produces the risk of creating two competing lines dividing coincident areas and creates a situation in which part of the EEZ belonging to one State may overlap part of another State's continental shelf. Such a situation would give rise to complex problems regarding jurisdiction.[73] This is not a hypothetical question. In drawing a coincident maritime boundary both for the continental shelf and the FZ, the ICJ in the *Greenland/Jan Mayen* case considered equitable access to fisheries, which relates only to superjacent waters, as a relevant circumstance.[74] As shown in this case, the issue of a single maritime boundary may actually arise in the jurisprudence.[75]

[69] Caflisch, 'The Delimitation of Marine Spaces' 431.
[70] LOSC, Art 15.
[71] LOSC, Art 74.
[72] LOSC, Art 83.
[73] For instance, who would have jurisdiction over artificial islands, installations and structures, or over maritime scientific research where there is an overlap? Caflisch, 'The Delimitation of Marine Spaces' 482.
[74] See ch 5, s IV.
[75] As shown in Appendix of this book, in State practice, there is a clear trend in favour of single maritime boundaries. See also D Anderson, 'Developments in Maritime Boundary Law and Practice' in DA Colson and RW Smith (eds), *International Maritime Boundaries*, vol V (Leiden Brill/Nijhoff, 2005) 3209.

Part I

The Evolution of the Law of Maritime Delimitation: Opposition of Two Basic Approaches

2

Law of Maritime Delimitation Prior to the 1958 Geneva Conventions: Emergence of Two Approaches

IN CONSIDERING THE law of maritime delimitation, it is necessary, first of all, to focus on the essential concepts which would characterise the law and the basic approaches which would substantiate these concepts. In order to examine these items, Part One of this book will retrace the evolution of the law of maritime delimitation focusing on two basic approaches. Maritime delimitation as defined here began to take place from the nineteenth century to the beginning of the twentieth century. During this period, there were five basic systems of maritime delimitation:[1] The median-line system; the drawing of a line perpendicular to the general direction of the coast; the prolongation of the land boundary; reference to the *thalweg*; and a common-zone system. In Section I, the five systems will be considered from the angle of State practice, case law, and theory. The examples quoted in examining the basic features and problems of each system will be only illustrative. Section II then reviews the discussion at the 1930 Hague Conference for the Codification of International Law, before offering summary in Section III.

I. FIVE PRINCIPAL SYSTEMS OF MARITIME DELIMITATION

A. Median-Line System

i. State Practice and Opinions of Writers

The median-line system is a method of delimiting maritime spaces by a median-line drawn between two coasts. It is possible to identify a relatively large number

[1] For a general analysis of State practice in this period, see DP O'Connell in IA Shearer (ed), *The International Law of the Sea,* vol II (Oxford, Clarendon Press, 1984) 663–73; GJ Tanja, *The Legal Determination of International Maritime Boundaries* (Boston, MA, Kluwer Law and Taxation Publishers, 1990) 1–20; SM Rhee, 'Sea Boundary Delimitation between States before World War II' (1982) 76 *AJIL* 555. However, the latter confuses national and international instances.

of maritime delimitation treaties adopting this system. For instance, the Peace Treaty of Fredrikshamn of 1809 between Sweden and Russia established a maritime boundary which ran a median course from the Bay of Bothnia to the Aaland Sea.[2] Furthermore, the 1846 Treaty of Limits, Westward of the Rocky Mountains, between the United States of America and the British Government provided that from the point on the forty-ninth parallel of north latitude, the boundary line 'shall be continued westward along the said forty-ninth parallel of north latitude, to the middle of the channel which separates the continent from Vancouver's Island; and thence southerly, through the middle of the said channel, and of Fucas Straits to the Pacific Ocean.'[3] The 1924 Convention between Finland and Norway Concerning the Frontier between the Province of Finmark and the Territory of Petsamo provided that:

> From the point where the channel ends in the Arctic Ocean beyond the mouth of the Jakobselv (Vuoremajoki), the dividing line between the territorial waters of the two Contracting States shall be situated at an equal distance from the coasts of the two States, measured from the nearest point on the mainland, island, islets or reefs which is [sic] not perpetually submerged.[4]

On this point, the words 'an equal distance from the coasts', which imply equidistance, should be noted. In addition, the 1932 Convention between Italy and Turkey Settling the Sovereignty over Certain Islets off the Anatolian Coast delimited the territorial sea by a median line.[5] The median-line system was also adopted in several other agreements, such as the 1893 Treaty between Great Britain and Mexico,[6] the 1864 Treaty of Vienna Concerning the Boundary

[2] Art 5.

[3] Art I. (1845–46) 34 *British and Foreign State Papers* 14. The electronic text is available at: http://avalon.law.yale.edu/19th_century/br-1846.asp. Later, with regard to the choice of the channel in coastal archipelagos, a dispute arose between the parties. The dispute was submitted to the arbitration of German Emperor William I. In 1871, the latter decided upon a median line in the Haro Channel as the boundary between the United Kingdom and the United States. The *San Juan Water Boundary* case, JB Moore, *History and Digest of the International Arbitrations to which the United States Has Been a Party*, vol I (Washington, Government Printing Office, 1898) 196–236.

[4] Art III. (1924–25) 30 *League of Nations Treaty Series* 61.

[5] Art 5. (1937) 135 *British and Foreign State Papers* 629–31. In addition, another treaty frequently quoted in this context is the Treaty of Nanking of 1842 in which the UK acquired Hong Kong. See for instance L Oppenheim, *International Law*, vol I Peace (London, Longman, 1905) 241; Tanja, above n 1, p 4; Rhee, above n 1, p 560. Under this Treaty, the median line bisecting the strait separating Hong Kong from the mainland formed the boundary between British and Chinese territories, but there was no provision regarding maritime delimitation. Gidel held that the Parties accepted tactically the median line as a rule of international law. G Gidel, *Le droit international public de la mer, Le temps de paix*, tome III, La mer territoriale et la zone contigue, fascicule II (Paris, Libraire Edouard Duchemin, 1981) 749. In the meantime, the situation changed when Great Britain acquired the territory of Kowloon in 1860, and the entire strait became British territory. O'Connell, *The International Law of the Sea* 671. The text of the Treaty of Nanking can be found in (1841–42) 30 *British and Foreign State Papers* 389 ff.

[6] Art I. (1892–3) 85 *British and Foreign State Papers* 59.

between Denmark and Germany in the Little Belt,[7] and the 1932 Declaration between Denmark and Sweden Concerning the Boundary of their Territorial Waters in the Sound.[8]

Furthermore, it is of particular interest to note that various codification projects put forward the median-line system as a principle suitable for the delimitation of territorial seas. In 1894, the *Institut de droit international* adopted rules regarding the definition and regime of the territorial sea. Article 10(1) stated that: 'Les détroits dont les côtes appartiennent à des Etats différents font partie de la mer territoriale des Etats riverains, qui y exerceront leur souveraineté jusqu'à la ligne médiane.'[9] At the 17th Conference of the International Law Association (ILA) in 1895, it adopted a formula similar to that proposed by the *Institut* regarding delimitation in straits.[10] The ILA reaffirmed this formula in the 1924 Draft Convention on the Law of Maritime Jurisdiction in Time of Peace.[11] Furthermore, in the 1926 'Rules Concerning the Extent of Littoral Waters and Concerning Powers Exercised Therein by the Littoral State', the Japanese Association of International Law and the Japanese Branch of the ILA suggested the median line system for establishing boundaries in both bays and straits.[12] In addition, Article 9 of the 1929 Draft Convention drawn up by the Research in International Law of Harvard Law School singled out the median-line system with respect to delimitations in straits.[13]

Many scholars supported the use of the median line, notably in the case of straits involving opposite coasts. For instance, Oppenheim stated that: '[I]f such a narrow strait divides the land of two different States, it belongs to the territory of both, the boundary line running, failing a special treaty making another arrangement, through the mid-channel.'[14] Furthermore, relying on Pufendorf, T Twiss stated that: '[I]n case the opposite sides of a bay or strait are inhabited by different Nations, then under the general principle of the Law of Nations, each Nation has a right to go to the central line, drawn at low water

[7] Art V. (1869) 54 *British and Foreign State Papers* 523.

[8] (1937) 135 *British and Foreign State Papers* 474. For other examples, see MM Whiteman, *Digest of International Law*, vol 4, (Washington, Department of State Publication, 1965) 310.

[9] (1904) 20 *Annuaire de l'Institut de droit international* 344.

[10] The International Law Association, *Report of the 17th Conference* (Brussels, 1895) 116.

[11] Art 13. The International Law Association, *Report of the 33rd Conference* (Stockholm, 1924) 264. See also 287.

[12] Art 2 and 3. (1926) 25 *The Journal of International Law and Diplomacy* 635.

[13] 'In the absence of special agreement to the contrary, where two or more States border upon a strait, the territorial waters of each state extend to the middle of the strait in those parts where the width does not exceed six miles.' It should be noted that in Art 12, the following provisions were added: 'The provisions of this Convention relating to the extent of territorial waters do not preclude the delimitation of territorial waters in particular areas in accordance with established usage' (1929) 23 *AJIL* Special Number 243–44.

[14] Oppenheim, *International Law* 249.

mark, as the limit of its maritime territory.'[15] Other scholars, such as Hershey,[16] Martens,[17] Despagnet,[18] Bonfils,[19] Gidel[20] and Guerra,[21] also supported the use of the median-line system.

ii. Emergence of Two Prototypes

In light of the relatively large support provided by State practice, codification projects and scholars, there appears to be a clear tendency in favour of the median-line system as a guiding principle to be followed for the delimitation of the territorial sea, notably in straits. In this connection, two points should be noted.

First, there was not yet a precise method for drawing a median line at that time. Accordingly, the term 'median line' did not necessarily have the strict geometrical meaning it has today.

Secondly, some writers recognised that, in certain cases, recourse to the median-line concept would have inequitable results. For instance, at the 21st Conference of the ILA held at Buenos Aires in 1922, R Storni stated that: 'La ligne médiane n'est pas dans tous les détroits celle qui donne une ligne équitable de séparation de juridiction.' The word 'équitable' should be noted here. Thus, Storni suggested the following provision concerning straits: 'Si les côtes, dans ce cas, appartenaient à deux ou plusieurs Etats, la séparation des juri-dictions serait fixée par convention entre lesdits Etats riverains.'[22] According to Storni's formula, delimitation should be effected only by mutual agreement between States; apart from agreement between States, this formula contains no specific rule applicable to territorial sea delimitation. Here one finds a prototype of maritime delimitation: *the case-by-case solution based solely on the agreement of the parties.*

[15] T Twiss, *The Law of Nations Considered as Independent Political Communities* (Oxford, Clarendon Press, 1861) 251.

[16] AS Hershey, *Essentials of International Public Law* (New York, NY, Macmillan Co, 1912) 201–2.

[17] F de Martens, *Traité de droit international public* (Paris, A Marescq, 1883) 506.

[18] F Despagnet, *Cours de droit international public* (Paris, Librairie de la Société du Recueil général des lois et des arrêts, 1903) 498.

[19] H Bonfils, *Manuel de droit international public (droit des gens),* 4th edn (Paris, Librairie nouvelle de droit et de jurisprudence, 1905) 277.

[20] Gidel, *Le droit international public de la mer* 747, 768.

[21] JG Guerra, 'Les eaux territoriales dans les détroits spécialement dans les détroits peu larges' (1924) 31 *RGDIP* 242. Contrary to the delimitation of straits, few doctrines referred to the lateral delimitation of the territorial sea. Yet, Twiss and Gidel considered that the median line system was also applicable to the lateral delimitation of the territorial sea.

[22] Art 8. International Law Association, *Report of the Thirty-First Conference Held at the Palace of Justice (Buenos Aires)* vol 2 (London, Sweet & Maxwell, 1923) 99. But this view was criticised by Guerra, who contended that one should return to the median line. Guerra, 'Les eaux territoriales,' 232–54 (in particular, at 234, 253–54).

By contrast, while accepting that the median-line system might cause inequitable results, Gidel followed a different line of argument. In his view, it was the median-line system which would provide the general rule for both opposite and lateral territorial sea delimitation.[23] At the same time, he accepted the existence of situations which would require an adjustment of the median line to ensure an equitable division.[24] As an example, Gidel refers to serious inequalities in the field of navigation. In such a case, in his view, navigational considerations, ie, the *thalweg*,[25] should be taken into account. Yet the *thalweg* would come into play solely as an exception to the principal system of the median line.[26] Accordingly, with regard to the situation existing after the Hague Codification Conference in 1930, he concluded that, concerning delimitation of the territorial sea in straits, in the absence of conventions to the contrary, and except for geographical configurations where the system of the median line would cause an excessive disproportion for coastal States with respect to diverse uses, including those of watercourses, the delimitation line should be effected according to that system.[27] The same was to be true for lateral territorial sea delimitation.[28] In short, in the absence of agreement to the contrary, Gidel considered the median-line system to be the general rule, and the *thalweg* as an exception. The theory of that author thus presented another prototype of maritime delimitation: *the model of a solution based on a median-line system as a general rule*. It should be noted that that model also aspired to assure an equitable delimitation of the territorial sea.

It follows that two important aspects of the law of maritime delimitation revealed themselves: first, two prototypes on the maritime delimitation emerged. One was the model of case-by-case solutions without specifying a general rule, the other was the solution based on the median-line system as a general rule. Secondly, at the centre of both models, it is possible to find traces of the notion of 'equity', which would later be at the core of the law of maritime delimitation.[29] In fact, in their discussions, both Storni and Gidel used the word 'équitable'. In these two respects, it appears that the arguments about the median-line system provide a glimpse into the future development of the law of maritime delimitation.

[23] Gidel, *Le droit international public de la mer* 747 and 768. More precisely, regarding lateral delimitations, Gidel contended that the preferable solution was that of a line perpendicular to the general direction of the coast. In his view, the latter is a variety of the median line. ibid, 768–69.

[24] ibid, 756–57. On this point, Gidel also referred to the word 'équitable'.

[25] As will be pointed out later, the concept of the *thalweg* is ambiguous, and several definitions are possible.

[26] Gidel, *Le droit international public de la mer* 756 and 772.

[27] ibid, 759. It should be noted that this conclusion was made after analysis of the Hague Codification Conference in 1930.

[28] ibid, 772.

[29] O'Connell, *The International Law of the Sea* 662.

B. The System of a Line Perpendicular to the General Direction of the Coast

i. The Grisbadarna Case (Norway/Sweden, 1909)[30]

Regarding lateral territorial sea delimitation, there were a few instances where lines perpendicular to the general direction of the coast were drawn.[31] The most important example is the *Grisbadarna* case. This case involved Norway and Sweden and concerned the delimitation of the territorial sea from a point located in the mouth of the Idefjard to the high seas. As both States sought to establish a territorial sea boundary including the sandbar of Grisbadarna which provides good fishing grounds within their territorial seas, a dispute arose.

In 1908, the parties instituted proceedings before the Arbitral Tribunal and requested the latter to determine: (i) the boundary line to be drawn from a point marked XVIII on a map annexed to the draft of a mixed committee of 1897 up to the limit of the territorial sea; and (ii) whether the boundary line had been fixed by a treaty of 1661, and, if it had not, to draw that line, taking into account the facts and the principles of international law.[32] Regarding the second question, the Tribunal answered in the negative, at least with respect to the boundary line beyond the point A of the map annexed to the 1661 Convention.[33] Thus, the Tribunal was to determine the boundary line from a point A to the limit of the territorial sea. As the parties had agreed on the line between points XVIII to XIX, the first question was the position of point XX. Having determined the latter to be Heieknub rather than Heiefluer, claimed by Norway,[34] the Tribunal examined the issue of delimitation from the point XX to the limit of the territorial sea (see Illustration 1).

In delimiting the maritime space in question, the principal issue was to specify the law applicable to the maritime delimitation. In this case, both States agreed that the Norwegian land territory of Bohuslan had been ceded to Sweden by the Peace of Roskilde in 1658. Considering that maritime territory is subordinate to land territory in accordance with a fundamental principle of international law, in the Tribunal's view, the maritime territory had to be divided together with the cession of the land territory. Accordingly, in order to confirm the dividing line which had appeared automatically in 1658, it was necessary to resort to the principles of international law effective at that time.[35] In this respect, the arbitral award accepted neither the median-line system nor that of the *thalweg* as having

[30] (1961) 11 United Nations, *Report of International Arbitral Awards (RIAA)* 147–62. The members of the Arbitral Tribunal were: JA Loff; FVN Beichmann; L de Hammarskjold. For an English translation of the award, see (1910) 4 *AJIL* 226.

[31] As an example, Gidel pointed to the 1926 Protocol of Delimitation between Albania and Yugoslavia. Gidel, *Le droit international public de la mer,* 768.

[32] Art II and III of the 1908 Convention on Arbitration. 11 *RIAA* 155–56.

[33] ibid, 158.

[34] ibid.

[35] ibid, 159.

been the effective rule in the seventeenth century. Hence the Tribunal ruled that it was the line perpendicular to the general direction of the coast which constituted the rule of international law in the seventeenth century.[36]

ii. Evaluation

The Court's view calls for three comments. First, it is doubtful whether any effective rule regarding territorial sea delimitation existed in the seventeenth century, as the institution of territorial sea in the modern sense had not been well-established at that time.

Secondly, while rejecting the median-line and *thalweg* systems, the Arbitral Tribunal failed to specify the legal grounds for identifying the line perpendicular to the general direction of the coast as the effective rule in the seventeenth century. In this respect, the Court stated that 'la division automatique du territoire en question a dû s'effectuer d'après la direction générale du territoire terrestre duquel le territoire maritime formait une appartenance.'[37]

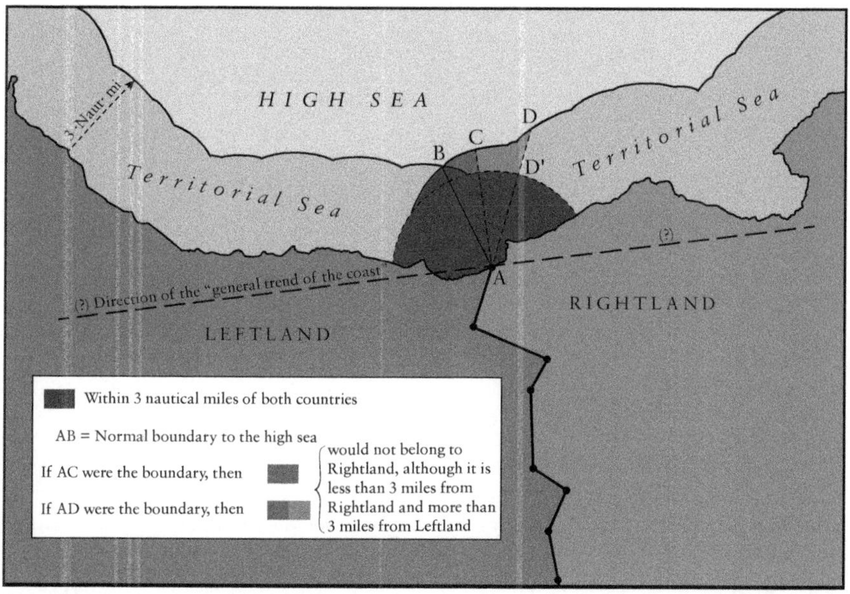

Figure 1 The line A–D is the extension of the last section of the land boundary. The line A–C is a line perpendicular to the general trend of the coasts.

Source: SW Boggs, *International Boundaries – A Study of Boundary Functions and Problems* (New York, Colombia University Press, 1940), 188. Copyright © 1940 Columbia University Press. Reprinted with permission of the Publisher.

[36] ibid, 160.

[37] ibid. The Arbitral Tribunal distinguished lines perpendicular to the general direction of the coast from median lines, although, relying on Münch, Gidel regarded the former as special type of

However, there was no evidence that the line perpendicular to the general direction of the coast was a binding rule.[38]

Thirdly, it should be noted that in certain cases, the establishment of lines perpendicular to the general direction of a coast produces curious results. As indicated in Figure 1, should line A–C be established, the shaded area between points B and C would belong to Leftland, despite the fact that the latter has no legal title over the area, beyond the breadth of the territorial sea permitted in international law.[39] In light of these problems, it is doubtful that the use of lines perpendicular to the general direction of a coast was a general rule applicable to the delimitation of the territorial sea.[40]

Figure 2

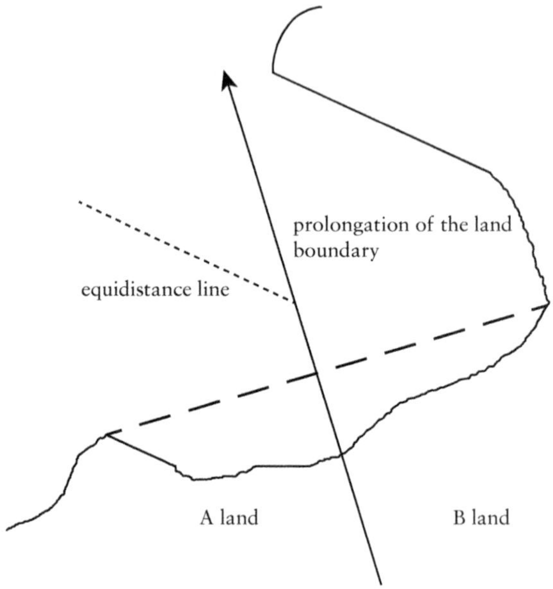

median line. Gidel, *Le droit international public de la mer* 769. In fact, the line perpendicular to the general direction of the coast does not necessarily coincide with the median line, depending on how the general direction of the coast is defined.

[38] R Kolb, *Case Law on Equitable Maritime Delimitation: Digest and Commentaries* (The Hague, Brill/Nijhoff, 2003) 14.

[39] SW Boggs, *International Boundaries – A Study of Boundary Functions and Problems* (New York, NY, Columbia University Press, 1940) 188.

[40] At the stage of tracing the boundary line, the Arbitral Tribunal modified the line perpendicular to the general direction of the coast in view of the passing of the boundary line between the bank of the Grisbadarna and that of Skjottegrunde. This shift was based mainly on an agreement between the Parties which was intended to avoid great unsuitability and to respect practices of the Parties. *Report of International Arbitral Awards*, above n 30, pp 160–62. However, this study does not take this part concentrating on the analysis of the law applicable to the delimitation of the territorial sea. On this issue, see Kolb, *Case Law on Equitable Maritime Delimitation* 15–18.

C. Prolongation of the Land Boundary

The prolongation of the land boundary may be suggested as another system of maritime delimitation.[41] This system is, however, open to objection in cases where a land boundary meets a coast at something other than a right angle. Should a line of prolongation of the land boundary be drawn, the shaded area between points B–D would go to Leftland despite the fact that it is located beyond the breadth of the territorial sea of Leftland (Figure 1). Accordingly, this system may produce inequitable results where a land boundary does not cross a coast at a right angle.[42] Furthermore, the validity of this system depends on the configuration of the coast. For instance, in the geographical situation illustrated in Figure 2, a line of prolongation of the land boundary may not create equitable results.

D. *Thalweg* System

i. State Practice and the Case Law

The fourth system to be examined is that of the *thalweg*, developed in the context of the delimitation in rivers,[43] but not clearly defined. According to Dipla, it is possible to suggest at least three definitions regarding the *thalweg*.[44]

According to the first definition, a *thalweg* simply means navigable channel. It appears that the 1920 Treaty between the Principal Allied Powers and Denmark with regard to Slesvig adopted the first definition in making the boundary line partly coincide with the principal channel of navigation.[45]

According to the second definition, a *thalweg* consists of the median line of the navigable channel. For example, in 1887, Article 3 of 'Projet de réglement international de navigation fluviale' of the *Institut de droit international*

[41] Gidel pointed to two examples: Boundary between France and Belgium, and boundary between France and Italy. Gidel, *Le droit international public de la mer* 767. With respect to France and Belgium, although no delimitation line is fixed within their territorial seas, the customs administrations admit that the separation was made by prolonging the land boundary. UN Doc A/CN 4/71 and Add. 1, (1953) 2 *YILC* 89. Yet in 1990, France and Belgium drew a territorial sea boundary. For the text of the Agreement, see JI Charney and LM Alexander (eds), *International Maritime Boundary,* vol II (Dordrecht, Nijhoff, 1993) 1898–99.

[42] Gidel, *Le droit international public de la mer* 767–68.

[43] Gidel pointed to two meanings of concept in river law: (i) the deepest water line, which coincides with the line of the strongest current; (ii) the centre of the most appropriate channel for navigation by the largest ship. Gidel, *Le droit international public de la mer* 772.

[44] H Dipla, 'Les régles de international en matière de délimitation fluviale: remise en question?' (1985) 89 *RGDIP* 598. See also L Caflisch, 'Régles générales du droit des cours d'eau internationaux' (1989) 219 *RCADI* 71; JHW Virzijl, *International Law in Historical Perspective, Part III, State Territory* (Leyden, Sithoff, 1970) 563–64.

[45] Art I. (1920–21) 2 League of Nations, *Treaty Series* 244. In addition, the *Grisbadarna* judgment identifies the *thalweg* by referring to the most important channel. (1961) 11 *RIAA* 160.

provided that: 'La frontière des Etats séparés par le fleuve est marquée par le thalweg, c'est-à-dire par la ligne médiane du chenal.'[46]

The third definition of *thalweg* is 'the deepest water line'. For instance, The 1893 Treaty between Great Britain and Mexico with Respect to the Boundary between Mexico and British Honduras defined the *thalweg* as the deepest channel.[47]

In addition, the 1928 Straits Settlement and Johore Territorial Waters (Agreement) Act adopted another definition referring to the centre of the deep-water channel.[48] It follows from the above that the concept of the *thalweg* is not uniformly defined.[49] In any event, there are only a few agreements using a *thalweg* system in maritime delimitation.

Regarding the case law, the *Alaska Boundary* arbitration between Great Britain and the United States in 1903 has some bearing on the *thalweg* system, though it did not concern delimitation per se.[50] The issue may be summarised as follows. Regarding the boundary between Alaska and British Columbia, the Treaty of 1825 between Great Britain and Russia provided that the demarcation line between the two Parties ran from the most meridional point of Prince of Wales Island to the north, along the Portland Channel as far as 56 degrees north Latitude. After the division of Pearse Island, however, the question arose as to whether Portland Channel meant the channel south of Pearse and Wales Islands or the one to the north of those two islands.

[46] H Wehberg, *Tableau général des résolutions (1873–1956)* (Bâle, Editions juridiques et socilogiques SA, 1957) 71.

[47] Art I. (1892–93) 85 *British and Foreign State Papers* 59. This Treaty, in a certain part of the boundary, adopted the median line as well (Art I).

[48] The 1928 Act provided that: 'The boundary between the territorial waters of the settlement of Singapore and those of the State and Territory of Johore shall, …, be an imaginary line following the centre of the deep-water channel in Johore Strait, ….' Whiteman, above n 8, p 311. As another agreement adopting the *thalweg* system, Rhee points to the 1900 Convention between France and Spain Concerning the Coast of the Sahara and that of the Gulf of Guinea. Yet the *thalweg* was referred to in order to identify a starting point of the limit between the parties in the Gulf of Guinea. Furthermore in the Convention, a boundary line following the *thalweg* was adopted for the rivers Mouni and Outemboni, not for the ocean (Art IV). GF Martens, (1905) 32 *Nouveau Recueil Général de Traités,* 2ème série, 60.

[49] The ambiguous definition of *thalweg* gives rise to a dispute even today. Indeed, recently, the meaning of '*thalweg*' is discussed by the ICJ in the *Kasikili/Sedudu Island* case (Botswana *vs.* Namibia) of 1999. The Court accepted that there are various definitions of the term '*thalweg*' in delimitation treaties. According to the Court, '[t]he word "thalweg" has variously been taken to mean "the most suitable channel for navigation" on the river, the line "determined by the line of deepest soundings", or "the median line of the main channel followed by boatmen travelling downstream."' [1999] ICJ Rep 1061–62, [24]. In that case, the Court treated the words 'centre of the main channel' in Article III(2) of the 1890 Treaty, which defined a boundary between Botswana and Namibia in the Chobe River, as having the same meaning as the words 'Thalweg des Hauptlaufes' used in the German version of the treaty. ibid, 1062, [25]. In any case, the real dispute between Botswana and Namibia concerned the location of the main channel where the boundary lies, not the definition or application of *thalweg* as a delimitation method. See also Dissenting Opinion of Vice-President Weeramantry, ibid, 1172–74, [58–66].

[50] (1966) 15 United Nations, *RIAA* 481–540. Regarding the summary of the award, see in particular, O'Connell, *The International Law of the Sea* 664–65; Gidel, *Le droit international public de la mer* 753–55.

While Great Britain contended that Portland Channel was, in fact, the western channel on the basis of historical antecedents, the United States founded its arguments on the *thalweg*. According to the United States, although Portland Channel actually includes two different channels, in applying the theory of the *thalweg* as a channel appropriate for navigation, the boundary should be presumed to be in the channel of maximum convenience. The United States thus asserted that the boundary should be in the eastern arm of the channel because it was larger, deeper, and more easily accessible than the western arm. It should be noted that the United States' argument regarding the *thalweg* system was being used for identifying the Portland Channel rather than a boundary line. Great Britain opposed the argument of the United States by contending that the theory of the *thalweg* was applicable solely to navigable rivers and not to maritime areas.

The Arbitral Tribunal accepted the contention of Great Britain that the channel west of Pearse and Wales Islands constituted the Portland Channel. With respect to a boundary line, both Parties considered that the boundary should be the median line, despite the different identification of Portland Channel. The Tribunal took the same view, accepting the median line as the boundary. Thus, despite the intriguing argument based on the *thalweg* system, it may be contended that the *Alaska Boundary* case resulted in the acceptance of the median-line system.

Furthermore, another case related to the *thalweg* system, the Beagle Channel dispute between Chile and Argentina, should be recalled. The Beagle Channel, situated near the southern extremity of South America, about 70 miles (112 km) north of Cape Horn, is a narrow seaway, averaging about 3 to 3.5 miles (4.8 to 5.6 km) in breadth: Its length is approximately 120 to 150 miles (192 to 240 km). It is separated into two waterways by Picton Island. On 23 July 1881, Chile and Argentina had concluded a boundary treaty which provided that the Beagle Channel was to form the boundary between the two States towards the south through Tierra del Fuego.[51] Later, however, with respect to Article 3, which defined the boundary line, a territorial dispute concerning Nueva, Picton, and Lennox Islands arose (see Illustration 2).

Chile argued that the channel mouth was the Bay of Moat lying between the mainland and Picton and Nueva Islands, and that the boundary line should follow the median line. Argentina asserted that the boundary was the line of

[51] Art III provided that: 'In Tierra del Fuego a line shall be drawn, which starting from the point called Cape Espiritu Santo, at parallel 52°40', shall be prolonged to the south along the meridian 68°34' west of Greenwich until it touches Beagle Channel. Tierra del Fuego, divided in this manner, shall be Chilean on the western side and Argentine on the eastern. As for the islands, to the Argentine Republic shall belong Staten Island, the small islands next to it, and the other islands there may be on the Atlantic to the east of Tierra del Fuego and of the eastern coast of Patagonia; and to Chile shall belong all the islands to the south of Beagle Channel up to Cape Horn, and those there may be to the west of Tierra del Fuego.' For the award, see (1997) 21 *RIAA* 53.

greatest depth which would pass Picton and Richmond, not the Bay of Moat.[52] In so doing, Argentina attempted to apply the *thalweg* system, referring to the deepest waterway.

Having failed to resolve the territorial dispute by negotiation, in 1971, both States resorted to arbitration by Britain's Queen Elizabeth II, on the basis of the 1902 Treaty of Arbitration.[53] During the proceedings, however, Argentina no longer invoked the *thalweg* system, but argued that the median line running past Picton and Navarino Islands should be the boundary line.[54] The real issue of the case, then, was that of determining what was meant by 'Beagle Channel.' In 1977, the Arbitral Tribunal ruled that all three geographic features belonged to Chile. At the same time, the Tribunal drew a territorial sea boundary which was 'in principle a median line, adjusted in certain relatively unimportant respects for reasons of local configuration or of better navigability for the Parties.'[55]

ii. Evaluation

In light of the limited State practice available and the small number of cases, the usefulness of the *thalweg* in the context of maritime delimitation is not evident. In addition, few writers support this system as a general rule for maritime delimitation.[56] Furthermore, it should be noted that use of the *thalweg* system creates several problems. First, one will wonder whether a permanent *thalweg*, in the sense either of the deepest water line or the median line of the main channel of navigation, always exists. Where there is no *thalweg*, the system will not function. Secondly, even where a *thalweg* can be found, it may follow a highly complicated line and hence be inconvenient as a boundary. Thirdly, the applicability of the system is usually limited to the particular geographical situation, ie, where the delimitation takes place in the neighbourhood of a channel.

[52] Guerra, 'Les eaux territoriales,' 243–48; Gidel, *Le droit international public de la mer* 755–56; O'Connell, *The International Law of the Sea* 666.

[53] The members of the Arbitral Tribunal were: HC Dillard, Sir Gerald Fitzmaurice, André Gros, CD Onyeama, and S Petrén.

[54] 21 *RIAA* 75–76.

[55] Annex IV, ibid, 262, [4]. See also 185, [110]. The *Beagle Channel* arbitration related to the delimitation of the territorial sea, but only to some extent. Thus, in this study, we will not touch on this award in detail. Regarding the *Beagle Channel* arbitration, see in particular, K Oellers-Frahm, 'Beagle Channel Arbitration' in R Bernhardt, (ed), *Encyclopedia of Public International Law,* vol I (Amsterdam, North-Holland, 1992) 363–65; J Dutheil de la Rochère, 'L'affaire du canal de Beagle (Sentence rendu par la reine d'Angleterre, le 22 avril 1977)' (1977) 23 *AFDI* 408; DM Johnston, *The Theory and History of Ocean Boundary-Making* (Kingston, McGill-Queen's University Press, 1988) 192–96; G Despeux, *Droit de la délimitation maritime: Commentaire de quelques décisions plutoniennes* (Frankfurt am Main, Peter Lang, 2000) 45–85. The award of 1977 was, however, rejected by Argentina on 25 January 1978. The resulting situation between Chile and Argentina was resolved by the Treaty of Peace Friendship on 29 November 1984, thanks to the mediation of the Holy See.

[56] However, Moore supported the application of the *thalweg* system with regard to straits. JB Moore, *A Digest of International Law,* vol I (Washington, Government Printing Office, 1906) 658.

Owing to the insufficiency of State practice and these practical problems, the *thalweg* system appears to be too unstable to serve as a general rule.[57]

E. Common-Zone System

Finally, there is a treaty which identifies an overlapping band as a common zone. The 1879 Treaty between France and Spain divides the Bay of Figuier into three distinct, equal zones, one reserved for France, one for Spain, and a third for common use.[58] According to this system, where there are overlapping territorial seas, the latter are common to both States. Doctrinally, Bluntschli[59] and Rivier[60] promoted this common-zone approach, which transforms an overlapping area into a kind of *condominium,* thus avoiding the delimitation problem.[61] Strictly speaking, however, the common-zone system is not a delimitation technique, precisely because it does not delimit the area of overlap but simply designates it as common.[62]

II. DISCUSSION AT THE HAGUE CONFERENCE FOR THE CODIFICATION OF INTERNATIONAL LAW IN 1930

A. Delimitation of Territorial Sea between States with Adjacent Coasts

The 1930 Hague Conference wrestled with the codification of the law of maritime delimitation. The discussion began in the League of Nations Committee of Experts in 1925. In the 1926 Report of the Sub-Committee, regarding the lateral delimitation of the territorial sea, M Schücking, *Rapporteur*, stated that:

> In the case of existing States, the matter will be settled by historical considerations. In the event of a political change in the existing frontiers between riparian States, it

[57] In this respect, the words of Gidel are worth quoting: '[I]l est nécessaire qu'une règle de principe permette d'échapper aux incertitudes'. Gidel, *Le droit international public de la mer* 758.

[58] Art I. GF De Martens, (1879) 4 *Nouveau Recueil Général de Traités,* 2ème série, 364–65.

[59] J Bluntschli, *Le droit international codifié*, translated by MC Lardy (Paris, Librairie Guillaumin, 1881) 190.

[60] A Rivier, *Principes du droit des gens*, vol I, (Paris, Librairie de droit et de jurisprudence, 1896) 158. In addition, it seems that Latour took the same view. JI Latour, *La mer territorial au point vue théorique* (Paris, G Pedone-Lauriel, 1889) 64. In this quotation, the reference to the median line was made as a secondary option. Thus, although Guerra and Rhee categorised Latour's view as supportive of the median-line system, it seems to be appropriate to assimilate this view with Bluntschli's.

[61] Gidel, *Le droit international public de la mer,* 751. Gidel criticised this system for its practical inconvenience and asserted that the common-zone system was inadequate to provide a rule of general international law. ibid, 752.

[62] This does not imply, however, that the common-zone system is less important. In fact, later in the *North Sea Continental Shelf* cases, the ICJ suggested joint exploitation of the overlapping areas. [1969] ICJ Rep 52, [98]. Furthermore in State practices, there are many instances which established a joint exploitation zone.

> would be advisable to establish special rules in each case having regard to the special geographical circumstances which have led to the fixing of a new frontier. It would be better to arrange for the conclusion of a special agreement between the State concerned, or for the settlement of the matter by arbitration or an ordinary tribunal, than to lay down an immutable principle.[63]

In the proposal, no delimitation system was suggested.

Barbosa de Magalhaes, however, criticised this view, saying: 'What I do not see, however, is why these rules could not be embodied in the Convention. I think this ought to be done.'[64] He then proposed the following clause:

> The limit between the territorial waters of a State and those of another contiguous State is constituted by a line drawn perpendicular to the coast from the point at which the frontier between the two States meets that coast.[65]

Wickersham also affirmed the existence of a general rule applicable to the lateral delimitation of the territorial sea, although in substance his view was different from that of Barbosa de Magalhaes.[66]

In summary, while Schücking considered it inappropriate to lay down a general rule on the lateral delimitation of territorial seas, Barbosa de Magalhaes and Wickersham argued in favour of the existence of such a rule, despite their difference of views on the latter's content. The important point to bear in mind is that these contrasting views reflect a contrast similar to that emerging from the controversy between Storni and Gidel, ie, between the model based on a case-by-case solution, avoiding the formulation of a general rule, and the one based on the need for a general rule. In any event, owing to the differences of views, no provision was formulated regarding the rule applicable to the lateral delimitation of territorial seas.

B. Delimitation of the Territorial Sea between States with Opposite Coasts

The contrast between these two models can also be found in the arguments regarding the delimitation of opposite territorial seas. In Article 6 of the draft

[63] Memorandum by M Schücking, League of Nations C 44 M 21 1926, V Questionnaire No 2, Territorial Waters Annex, Report of the Sub-Committee in S Rosenne, (ed), *League of Nations Committee of Experts for the Progressive Codification of International Law 1925–1928*, vol II (New York, NY, Oceana Publications, 1972) 68.

[64] ibid, 91.

[65] ibid.

[66] Wickersham advanced three different rules. First, where the boundary lines of the States run over land, and terminate at the shore-line, they naturally would be prolonged across the territorial sea. Secondly, where the boundary line between States is a river which empties into the sea, and where it runs into a bay, the rule regarding bays applies. If it does not, the boundary line is drawn in the middle of the navigable channel. Thirdly, if the strait is more than six miles in width and the land on either side belongs to a different State, the general rule is that the boundary line runs through the middle of the stream. If the stream is less than six miles in width, the principle of the *thalweg* would ordinarily apply. ibid, 97.

Convention, Schücking suggested that: 'Straits not exceeding 10 miles in width whose shores belong to different States shall form part of the territorial sea as far as the middle line.'[67] Contrary to what was the case for lateral territorial sea delimitations, he considered it possible to lay down a general rule using the median line for the delimitation of territorial seas in situations of opposite coasts. On the strength of this proposal, Basis of Discussion No 16, prepared for the Hague Conference, formulated the following rule: 'When two States border on a strait which is not wider than twice the breadth of territorial waters, the territorial waters of each State extend in principle up to a line running down the center of the strait.'[68]

At the Hague Conference, however, Basis of Discussion No 16 was criticised by several delegates. An important criticism was made by M Raestad (Norway) who stated: 'I think that Basis No 16 would be more in place in a special convention and is less suited to appear in a general convention.'[69] This view reflects a preference for the case-by-case approach. Later, Basis of Discussion No 16 was re-examined by the Legal Sub-Committee, where a *rapporteur* proposed: 'Si la largeur est inférieure à l'étendue des deux zones de mer territoriale, la ligne de démarcation entre ces deux zones, quand il s'agit de deux Etats riverains, sera fixée de commun accord entre ces Etats.'[70] This view also relied on the case-by-case solution. The discord between the two models was thus repeated. In the end, the Hague Conference failed to adopt an overall rule governing the delimitation of territorial seas between States with opposite coasts.[71]

III. SUMMARY

Before 1930, at least, it seems difficult to identify the law applicable to the delimitation of the territorial sea, although there was a tendency to favour the median line, especially in the context of delimitations in straits. In fact, the failure of the Hague Conference to lay down a delimitation rule shows the uncertainty of the legal situation in this field. Yet the above analysis appears to throw some light on the basic aspects of the question. In this regard, two points can be made.

First, at the early stage of the development of the law, two contrasting models of the law of maritime delimitation were developed by writers as well as within the Committee of Experts and the Hague Conference. The case-by-case solution model was meant to achieve equitable results by agreement and aimed

[67] Draft Convention amended by M Schücking in Consequence of the Discussion in the Committee of Experts, ibid, 98.

[68] League of Nations, *Acts of the Conference for the Codification of International Law,* Meetings of the Committees, vol III, Territorial Waters, (1930) 180.

[69] ibid, 17.

[70] Quoted by Gidel, *Le droit international public de la mer* 758.

[71] It should not be forgotten that at the Hague Conference, no agreement was achieved with respect to the breadth of the territorial sea.

at preventing inequitable results produced by the application of the median-line rule. In other words, it attempted to maintain maximum flexibility. Another model, based on the median-line technique, was typically advocated by Gidel. It aimed at ensuring equitable results by resorting to the median-line system with necessary modifications. This model stresses stability and predictability. Thus, it appears that the difference of the two models consists in the different emphasis given to flexibility and predictability.

Secondly, despite the differences in the two models, it is possible to find a *trace* of a common fundamental concept: the quest for equitable results. In this respect, it is worth noting that, as early as the 1920 and 1930s, both Gidel and Storni drew attention to the concept of equity in maritime delimitation. It may be said that a *hint* of the concept of equity, later to be at the core of the law of maritime delimitation, had already shown itself at the beginning of the twentieth century.

3

The 1958 Geneva Conventions and the 1982 UN Convention on the Law of the Sea

I. THE 1958 GENEVA CONVENTIONS

THE EFFORTS TO codify the law of maritime delimitation bore fruit at the first UN Conference on the Law of the Sea (UNCLOS I) in 1958. UNCLOS I differed from the Hague Conference of 1930 at least in two respects. First, the Conference dealt with the delimitation not only of the territorial sea but also of the contiguous zone and the continental shelf. Secondly, UNCLOS I succeeded in adopting delimitation rules for territorial seas, contiguous zones, and continental shelves. We will now briefly examine the relevant provisions of the Geneva Conventions. Those provisions are: Articles 12 and 24 of the Convention on the Territorial Sea and the Contiguous Zone, and Article 6 of the Convention on the Continental Shelf.

A. Rules Regarding Delimitation of Territorial Sea and the Continental Shelf

i. Basic Structure of the Rules

On account of the similarity in structure of the rules to be examined, it would be appropriate to analyse together Article 12 of the Convention on the Territorial Sea and the Contiguous Zone and Article 6 of the Convention on the Continental Shelf. Paragraph 1 of Article 12 of the former provides that:

> Where the coasts of two States are opposite or adjacent to each other, neither of the two States is entitled, failing agreement between them to the contrary, to extend its territorial sea beyond the median line every point of which is equidistant from the nearest points on the baselines from which the breadth of the territorial seas of each of the two States is measured. The provisions of this paragraph shall not apply, however, where it is necessary by reason of historic title or other special circumstances to delimit the territorial seas of the two States in a way which is at variance with this provision.

In short, the triple rule of 'agreement–equidistance–special circumstances' is applicable to the delimitation of the territorial seas. That triple rule can also be found in Article 6 of the 1958 Convention on the Continental Shelf. Paragraph 1 of Article 6, which governs the delimitation of opposite coasts, provides that:

> Where the same continental shelf is adjacent to the territories of two or more States whose coasts are opposite each other, the boundary of the continental shelf appertaining to such States shall be determined by agreement between them. In the absence of agreement, and unless another boundary line is justified by special circumstances, the boundary is *the median line*, every point of which is equidistant from the nearest point of the baselines from which the breadth of the territorial sea of each State is measured.[1]

Paragraph 2 of Article 6 of the same Convention, which concerns the delimitation of adjacent coasts, stipulates:

> Where the same continental shelf is adjacent to the territories of two adjacent States, the boundary of the continental shelf shall be determined by agreement between them. In the absence of agreement, and unless another boundary line is justified by special circumstances, the boundary shall be determined by application of *the principle of equidistance* from the nearest point of the baselines from which the breadth of the territorial sea of each State is measured.[2]

Except for using the words of 'the median line' for opposite coasts and 'the principle of equidistance' for adjacent coasts, paragraphs 1 and 2 of Article 6 contain the same rule, that is, 'agreement–equidistance (median line)–special circumstances.'[3]

It is true that there are some differences between Article 12 of the Convention on the Territorial Sea and the Contiguous Zone and Article 6 of the Convention on the Continental Shelf. In contrast to Article 6 of the Convention on the Continental Shelf, Article 12 of the Convention on the Territorial Sea and the Contiguous Zone emphasises equidistance by negative prescription by stating 'failing agreement between them to the contrary.'[4] Furthermore, while Article 6 of the Convention on the Continental Shelf distinguishes the terms 'equidistance' and 'median line' as corresponding to situations of adjacent and opposite coasts, respectively, Article 12(1) of the Convention on the Territorial Sea and the Contiguous Zone uses the same words, ie, 'the median line every point of which is equidistant from the nearest points on the baselines,' for the delimitation of

[1] Emphasis added.

[2] Emphasis added.

[3] See also P von Mühlendahl, *L'équidistance dans la délimitation des frontières maritimes: Etude de la jurisprudence internationale* (Paris, Pedone, 2016) 76, [107].

[4] According to Judge Sørensen, a more adequate formulation would have been a negative one, based on the model of Art 12 of the Convention on the Territorial Sea and the Contiguous Zone: '[N]o State is entitled to extend its area of the continental shelf beyond a line every point of which is equidistant from [the coasts].' Dissenting Opinion of Judge Sørensen in the *North Sea Continental Shelf* cases, [1969] ICJ Rep 252.

adjacent and opposite coasts. In addition, in Article 6, no reference is made to historic title as a special circumstance.[5] Despite these differences, however, the applicable rule is essentially the same,[6] namely, the triple rule of 'agreement–equidistance–special circumstances.'[7]

Concerning the salient features of these provisions, two points can be made. First, by establishing the triple rule, the two Geneva Conventions adopted a model based on the general rule of 'equidistance–special circumstances', which was to apply in the absence of an agreement. Thus, the case-by-case solution model was not fully supported by participants in UNCLOS I, although there were arguments favouring delimitation based solely on agreement in the *travaux préparatoires*.[8]

Secondly, it would appear that the concept of equity forms the basis of these two provisions.[9] In this respect, attention should be drawn to the fact that both provisions refer to special circumstances. This reference is clearly meant to correct inequitable results that might result from a mechanistic application of the equidistance method.[10] This is the *raison d'être* of the concept of special

[5] Some writers argued that, as the rights of coastal States over the continental shelf 'do not depend on occupation, effective or notional, or on any express proclamation' (Art 2(3) of the Convention on the Continental Shelf), historic title may well be irrelevant as a circumstance. L Caflisch, 'The Delimitation of Marine Spaces between State with Opposite and Adjacent Coasts' in R-J Dupuy and D Vignes (eds), *A Handbook on the New Law of the Sea* (Dordrecht, Nijhoff, 1991) 447; E Grisel, 'The Lateral Boundaries of the Continental Shelf and the Judgment of the International Court of Justice in the North Sea Continental Shelf Cases' (1970) 64 *AJIL* 583. This issue will be discussed in ch 8.

[6] The ILC saw a parallelism between the rules on delimitation of the territorial sea and those on delimitation of the continental shelf since the beginning of the discussion. (1951) 1 *YILC* 289; (1952) 1 *YILC* 183–84. In addition, in the *North Sea Continental Shelf* cases, Judge Sørensen stated that Art 12 of the Convention on the Territorial Sea and the Contiguous Zone and Art 6 of the Convention on the Continental Shelf, were substantially the same. [1969] ICJ Rep 252.

[7] The triple rule first appeared in 1953. In 1952, the ILC decided to consult with a committee of experts. The Committee of Experts favoured recourse to the equidistance method for the delimitation of the territorial sea between States with opposing or adjoining coasts. At the same time, the Committee of Experts accepted the existence of exceptions which would justify a departure from an equidistance line. On this point, the equidistance method was contended with a set of special circumstances. (1953) 2 *YILC* 79. The view of the Committee of Experts was reflected exactly in the draft provisions regarding the delimitation of the continental shelf. ibid, 216.

[8] Regarding the delimitation of the continental shelf, the delegation of Venezuela proposed an Article according to which the boundary of the continental shelf was to be determined by agreement between States or by other means recognised in international law. (1958) 6 *United Nations Conference on the Law of the Sea, Official Records*, Fourth Committee (Continental Shelf), Geneva, 94, para 9. Concerning the Venezuelan proposal, see Doc A/CONF 13/C4/L42, *ibid,* 138. However, Venezuela's view was criticised by several delegations. For instance, the delegation of the Netherlands declared that: 'It was generally accepted that the best method of delimiting the continental shelf was by agreement among the States concerned, but in the absence of such agreement there should be some principle laid down according to which the boundary could be determined.' ibid, 94, para 14. As the delegation of Colombia pointed out in the proposal of Venezuela, wherever there was no agreement, the problem would remain unsolved. ibid, [11].

[9] L Lucchini and M Vœlckel, *Droit de la mer,* tome II, *Délimitation* (Paris, Pedone, 1996) 53.

[10] Caflisch, 'The Delimitation of Marine Spaces,' 441, 459.

circumstances. In that sense, it would be safe to say that the reference to special circumstances is intended to achieve equitable results.[11]

ii. Comments on the Triple Rule

The triple rule formulated above calls for three comments. First, one may argue that the reference to 'agreement' could have been omitted as self-evident. Indeed, unless they act contrary to *jus cogens*, States are always free to conclude or not to conclude an agreement.[12] Even so, the reference to 'agreement' may be at least useful to imply the lack of validity of unilateral delimitation.[13]

Secondly, the relation between 'equidistance' and 'special circumstances' in each provision is in issue. There appear to be two opposing views on this issue.

The first view finds a hierarchy in these two elements. Theoretically, there are two possibilities: equidistance as a principle and special circumstances as an exception, or, by contrast, special circumstances as a principle and equidistance as an exception. In light of the *travaux préparatoires,* the former possibility would seem reasonable.[14] In the commentary on Article 12, which defines the rule of the territorial sea delimitation, the ILC mentioned that: 'Although the Commission noted that special circumstances would probably necessitate frequent departures from the mathematical median line, it thought it advisable to adopt, *as a general rule*, the system of the median line as a basis for delimitation.'[15] Furthermore, regarding the delimitation of the continental shelf, the ILC stated in 1953 that it 'now felt in the position to formulate a general rule, based on the principle of equidistance, applicable to the boundaries of the continental shelf both of adjacent States and of States whose coasts are opposite each other.'[16]

According to the second view, the relation between 'equidistance' and 'special circumstances' cannot be viewed as a hierarchical one. Two interpretations may be possible regarding this second view. First, some argue that where there are any special circumstances, there may be no room for equidistance. By contrast, where there are no special circumstances, the equidistance method would apply.[17] In other words, this view considers equidistance and special circumstances as mutually exclusive. According to another view, equidistance and special circumstances are not two separate rules, but one combined rule

[11] See the *Anglo-French Continental Shelf* arbitration, (1980) 18 United Nations, *Reports of International Arbitral Awards (RIAA)* 45, [70].

[12] Caflisch, 'The Delimitation of Marine Spaces' 440.

[13] See this study, ch 1, s II. See also the *Gulf of Maine* case, [1984] ICJ Rep 299, [112]. In addition, the ICJ in the *North Sea Continental Shelf* case also stated that delimitation must be the object of agreement between States concerned. [1969] ICJ Rep 46, [85].

[14] M Miyoshi, 'Transition of Legal Principles on Delimitation of Continental Shelf' (in Japanese) (1982) 5 *Kaiyōhō to Kaiyōseisaku* (Law of the Sea and Ocean Policy), (Ministry of Foreign Affairs, Japan) 41.

[15] Emphasis added. (1956) 2 *YILC* 271.

[16] (1953) 2 *YILC* 216.

[17] Caflisch, 'The Delimitation of Marine Spaces,' 441.

intended to achieve an equitable result. As will be explained later, this is the view of the Arbitral Court in the *Anglo–French Continental Shelf* case in 1977.[18] This view would lead to a two-stage method of maritime delimitation, ie, after applying the equidistance method at the first stage, the line provisionally drawn would then be adjusted, taking into account special circumstances. Theoretically, all these interpretations appear possible, and it is difficult to find an authoritative answer in the framework of the Convention.[19] The more important question, however, to bear in mind is to consider how these provisions have been applied in case law and State practice, and what the relation is between treaty provisions and customary law.

The third point to be examined is the concept of special circumstances. In light of the discussion in the ILC as well as in UNCLOS I, it is obvious that the concept of special circumstances is intended to avoid inequitable results resulting from a mechanical application of the equidistance method.[20] The problem is, however, that the specifics of special circumstances are far from clear.[21] It is true that some examples considered to be special circumstances can be found in the discussion in the ILC and in UNCLOS I. For instance, with respect to the territorial sea delimitation, the report of the Committee of Experts consulted by the ILC pointed to the interests of navigation and fishing as examples.[22] During UNCLOS I, the delegation of the United Kingdom mentioned, as examples of special circumstances, the configuration of particular coasts, navigable channels, and islands.[23] In addition, the German delegation proposed to add historical rights.[24] In the context of the delimitation of the continental shelf, the ILC enumerated exceptional configuration of the coast and the islands and navigable channels as examples.[25] During UNCLOS I, the United Kingdom

[18] See this study, ch 4, s II.

[19] D McRae, 'The Applicable Law: The Geneva Convention on the Continental Shelf, the LOSC, and Customary International Law' in Alex G Oude Elferink, T Henriksen and SV Busch (eds) *Maritime Boundary Delimitation: The Case Law Is It consistent and Practicable?* (Cambridge University Press, 2018) 93.

[20] See, for instance, (1956) 2 *YILC* 271; ibid, 1953, vol II, 216. Caflisch, 'The Delimitation of Marine Spaces,' 441.

[21] As early as 1953, Lauterpacht criticised the reference to special circumstances, contending that specific exceptions should be clarified. In his view, 'to state generally that arbitrators should take exceptions into consideration was tantamount to giving them the power to judge *ex aequo et bono*.' (1953) 1 *YILC* 131, para 17. On the other hand, Sir Gerald Fitzmaurice, the United Kingdom delegate, stated that '[i]t was admittedly a weakness that there was no definition of special circumstances so that their existence might be disputed. Nevertheless, special circumstances did exist which, for reason of equity or because of the configuration of a particular coast, might make it difficult to accept the true median line as the actual line of delimitation between two territorial seas.' (1958) 3 *United Nations Conference on the Law of the Sea, Official Records*, First Committee (Territorial Sea and Contiguous Zone) 189, [36].

[22] (1953) 2 *YILC* 79.

[23] (1958) 3 *United Nations Conference on the Law of the Sea, Official Records*, First Committee (Territorial Sea and Contiguous Zone), Geneva, 189, [36].

[24] Doc A/CONF 13/C1/L 121, L 129. *Ibid*, 187, [9]. The delegation of Norway took the same view. ibid, 190, [46]. See also, Doc A/CONF 13/C1/L97, ibid, 239.

[25] (1953) 2 *YILC* 216.

delegation suggested that the presence of small or large islands, special mineral exploitation rights or fishery rights, and the existence of navigable channels were examples of special circumstances.[26] Nevertheless, these features were merely illustrative, and it remains true that there was no authoritative definition of special circumstances.

B. Rules on the Delimitation of Contiguous Zones and Internal Waters

With respect to rules on delimitation of contiguous zones and internal waters, two points should be noted. First, regarding delimitation of contiguous zone, Article 24(3) of the Geneva Convention on the Territorial Sea and the Contiguous Zone provides a delimitation rule different from that governing the territorial sea and the continental shelf:

> Where the coasts of two States are opposite or adjacent to each other, neither of the two States is entitled, failing agreement between them to the contrary, to extend its contiguous zone beyond the median line every point of which is equidistant from the nearest points on the baselines from which the breadth of the territorial sea of the two States is measured.

Thus, the *pure* equidistance method is applicable to the delimitation of contiguous zones. The omission of any reference to special circumstances is likely to be explained by the limited powers attributed to coastal States in such zones.[27]

Secondly, the Geneva Conventions are silent on the delimitation of internal waters. Considering that coastal States possess even larger powers in their internal waters than in their territorial sea, it appears to be possible to apply by analogy or *a fortiori* the same triple rule.[28]

II. THE 1982 UN CONVENTION ON THE LAW OF THE SEA

A. Analysis of Articles 74(1) and 83(1)

i. Legislative History of Articles 74(1) and 83(1)

The 1982 UN Convention on the Law of the Sea (LOSC) differs from the 1958 Geneva Conventions in three respects. First, the law applicable to the continental

[26] (1958) 6 *United Nations Conference on the Law of the Sea, Official Records* 93.

[27] Caflisch, 'The Delimitation of Marine Spaces' 443.

[28] ibid, 442. Lucchini and Vœlckel support this view. Lucchini, and Vœlckel, *Droit de la mer* 63–64. In the *Croatia/Slovenia* arbitration, however, the Annex VII Arbitral Tribunal delimited the 'Bay of Savudrija/Piran' (Croatia) or 'Bay of Piran' (Slovenia) on the basis of the *effectivités* at the date of independence. This issue will be discussed in ch 5, s XVI of this book.

shelf was separated from that of territorial sea delimitation. While the delimitation of the territorial sea is governed by the traditional triple rule under Article 15,[29] that of the continental shelf is to follow a different rule. Secondly, the delimitation of the contiguous zone is no longer mentioned in the Convention text[30] and, consequently, the rule applicable to the contiguous zone remains unclear.[31] Thirdly and most important, Articles 74(1) and 83(1) of the LOSC formulate identical rules for the delimitation of the continental shelf and of the EEZ:

> The delimitation of the exclusive economic zone [the continental shelf] between States with opposite or adjacent coasts shall be effected by agreement on the basis of international law, as referred to in Article 38 of the Statute of the International Court of Justice, in order to achieve an equitable solution.

Thus, the delimitation of the EEZ and the continental shelf is governed by the same rule.[32]

Before analysing Articles 74(1) and 83(1), it would be appropriate to touch briefly on a legislative history of these provisions.[33] It is well known that, from

[29] The adoption of Art 15 as a rule identical to Art 12 of the Convention on the Territorial Sea and the Contiguous Zone was not challenged at UNCLOS III. Caflisch considers the equidistance-special circumstances rule to be customary law as regards the delimitation of the territorial sea. Caflisch, above n 2, p 442. Vukas takes the same view. B Vukas, 'The LOS Convention and Sea Boundary Delimitation' in B Vukas, (ed), *Essays on the New Law of the Sea,* (Zagreb, Sveucilisna Naklada Liber, 1985) 152. See also H Chiu, 'Some Problems Concerning the Application of the Maritime Boundary Delimitation Provisions of the 1982 United Nations Convention on the Law of the Sea Between Adjacent or Opposite States' (1985) 9 *Maryland Journal of International Law and Trade* 7.

[30] Caflisch finds an explanation in the wish of the participants not to complicate the difficult and infinitely more important negotiations on the delimitation of EEZ and the continental shelf. Caflisch, 'The Delimitation of Marine Spaces,' 443. Vukas supports this view. Vukas, above n 25, p 161. For a lengthy analysis of the discussions regarding the delimitation of contiguous zone, see Vukas, ibid, pp 153–64. See also by the same author, 'Possible Role of the International Tribunal for the Law of the Sea in Interpretation and Progressive Development of the Law of the Sea' in D Vidas and W Østreng, (eds), *Order for the Oceans at the Turn of the Century* (The Hague, Kluwer, 1999) 100–1; Nuno Sérgio Marques Antunes, *Towards the Conceptualisation of Maritime Delimitation: Legal and Technical Aspects of a Political Process* (Leiden, Brill/Nijhoff, 2003) 100–2.

[31] According to Caflisch, the possible solutions are: (1) to apply, by analogy, either Art 15 or Arts 74/83 of the LOSC; (2) to resort to the equidistance method of Art 24(3) of the Convention on the Territorial Sea and the Contiguous Zone; (3) allow for the joint exercise of the attributions provided for in Art 33 by the State concerned. Caflisch, 'The Delimitation of Marine Spaces,' 442–45. In the light of the close link between the contiguous zone and the territorial sea, Vukas favours the application of rule of territorial sea delimitation prescribed in Art 15 of the LOSC. Vukas, above n 25, pp 163–64. Nuno Sérgio Marques Antunes is supportive of this view. Nuno Sérgio Marques Antunes, *Towards the Conceptualisation of Maritime Delimitation* 101–2. On the other hand, Symonides advocates the application of Art 74 of the Convention where the economic zone and the contiguous zone are to be delimited. J Symonides, 'Delimitation of Maritime Areas between the States with Opposite or Adjacent Coasts' (1984) 13 *PYIL* 25.

[32] In the *travaux préparatoires*, the rules on the delimitation of the EEZ and on the continental shelf have always been discussed as a set. GJ Tanja, *The Legal Determination of International Maritime Boundaries* (Deventer, Kluwer 1990) 92.

[33] For a legislative history of these provisions, see SN Nandan and S Rosenne, (eds), *United Nations Convention on the Law of the Sea 1982: A Commentary*, vol II (Dordrecht, Nijhoff, 1993) 796–819, and 948–85; SP Jagota, *Maritime Boundary* (Dordrecht, Nijhoff, 1985) 219–72; Tanja,

the outset, there was a disagreement between the supporters of 'equidistance' and the supporters of 'equitable principles.' In particular, this confrontation was clearly shown by the two contrasting proposals made in Negotiating Group 7 (NG7) during the seventh session in 1978. One was based on equidistance as a general rule, and it was presented by 20 States:

> 1. The delimitation of the exclusive Economic Zone/Continental Shelf between adjacent or opposite States shall be effected by agreement employing, as a general principle, the median or equidistance line, taking into account any special circumstance where this is justified.[34]

The other proposal relied on agreements concluded in accordance with equitable principles, and it was supported by 27 States:

> 1. The delimitation of the exclusive economic zone between adjacent or/and opposite States shall be effected by agreement, in accordance with equitable principles taking into account all relevant circumstances and employing any methods, where appropriate, to lead to an equitable solution.[35]

While the first formula adopted the 'equidistance–special circumstance' model in favour of ensuring predictability, the second one followed the case-by-case solution model stressing flexibility. In this sense, it may be said that the marked difference between two groups reflected the dilemma between predictability and flexibility of law. Although, in this session, the Chairman of NG7, Ero J Manner, prepared an informal proposal,[36] no compromise materialised between those in support of the 'equidistance' and those favouring 'equitable principles.'[37] On this point, it should be noted that the confrontation between two groups

The Legal Determination of International Maritime Boundaries 81–116; S Oda, *Chukai Kokuren Kaiyohojyoyaku* (*The Commentary on the UN Convention on the Law of the Sea*, in Japanese) (Tokyo, Yûhikaku, 1985) 235–44 and 272–74; Dissenting Opinion of Judge Oda in the *Tunisia/Libya* case, ICJ Reports 1982, 234–47, para 131–45; A Prölss (ed), *United Nations Convention on the Law of the Sea: A Commentary* (Beck/Oxford, Hart Publishing/Baden-Barden, Nomos, München: 2017) 566–69 and 654–55; P von Mühlendahl, *L'équidistance dans la délimitation des frontières maritimes*, 81–91, [119–36].

[34] UN Doc NG 7/2, 20 April 1978, R Platzöder, *Third United Nations Conference on the Law of the Sea: Documents*, vol IX (New York, NY, Oceana, 1986) 392–93. Members of the NG 7/2 (pro-equidistance) group were: Bahamas, Barbados, Canada, Columbia, Cyprus, Democratic Yemen, Denmark, Gambia, Greece, Guyana, Italy, Japan, Kuwait, Malta, Norway, Spain, Sweden, the United Arab Emirates, the United Kingdom and Yugoslavia. ibid.

[35] UN Doc NG 7/10, 1 May 1978, *ibid*, 402. Members of the NG 7/10 (pro-equitable principles) group were: Algeria, Argentina, Bangladesh, Benin, Congo, France, Iraq, Ireland, Ivory Coast, Kenya, Liberia, Libya, Madagascar, Mali, Mauritania, Morocco, Nicaragua, Nigeria, Pakistan, Papua New Guinea, Poland, Romania, Senegal, Syria, Somalia, Turkey and Venezuela. ibid.

[36] 'The delimitation of the exclusive economic zone/continental shelf between opposite or adjacent States shall be effected by agreement with a view of reaching a solution based upon equitable principles, taking account of all the relevant circumstances, and employing, where local conditions do not make it unjustified, the principle of equidistance.' NG 7/11, 2 May 1978, ibid, 405.

[37] Report be the Chairman of Negotiating Group 7 on the Work of the Group, NG 7/21, 17 May 1978, ibid, 425.

was linked to another hard-core issue – that of peaceful settlement of disputes.[38] The supporters of 'equidistance' were, as part of the package, in favour of establishing a compulsory, third-party system for the settlement of delimitation disputes. By contrast, the supporters of 'equitable principles' have generally rejected the idea of a compulsory judicial procedures.[39] The confrontation between two groups was not solved during the eighth session in 1979. Neither of the differences relating to peaceful settlement mechanism could be resolved.[40]

In the ninth session of 1980, the Chairman of NG 7 suggested a proposal:

> The delimitation of the exclusive economic zone [continental shelf] between States with opposite or adjacent coasts shall be effected by agreement in conformity with international law. Such an agreement shall be in accordance with equitable principles, employing the median or equidistance line, where appropriate, and taking account of all circumstances prevailing in the area concerned.[41]

The proposal was included as Articles 74/83 of the Informal Composite Negotiating Text (ICNT)/Revision 2 of 11 April 1980. Nevertheless, the text remained controversial and no consensus was reached on this matter. For the pro-equitable principles group, these provisions were unacceptable because they leaned towards equidistance.[42] Pro-equidistance States were not satisfied with the texts since, according to ICNT/Revision 2, disputes relating to sea boundary delimitations may, by declaration, be excluded from compulsory procedure, although such conflicts may be submitted to conciliation.[43]

[38] Three issues – delimitation criteria, interim measures and settlement of delimitation disputes – were to be settled together as parts of a 'package' solution. Report of the Chairman of Negotiating Group 7, Document A/CONF 62/L 47, UNCLOS III, *Official Records*, vol XIII, 76, [2].

[39] AO Adede, *The System for Settlement of Disputes under the United Nations Convention on the Law of the Sea* (Dordrecht, Nijhoff, 1987) 182; PC Irwin, 'Settlement of Maritime Boundary Dispute: An Analysis of the Law of the Sea Negotiations' (1980) 8 *ODIL* 110.

[40] UNCLOS III, *Official Record*, vol XI, 60, [40].

[41] Annex: Suggestions by the Chairman of negotiating group 7, UNCLOS III, *Official Records*, vol XIII, 77. The Chairman believed that 'the formulation may have contained the main elements for a solution of a substantive nature' and 'useful to be taken into account in the completion of the final consensus package of the Conference.' ibid, [7(c)].

[42] The delegate for Argentina said that his delegation opposed the wordings of para 1 of Arts 74 and 83 because 'the median or equidistance line was presented in a manner which appeared to accord to it a greater importance than to other criteria for the delimitation of the exclusive economic zone or of the continental shelf between States with opposite or adjacent coasts.' UNCLOS III, *Official Records*, vol XIV, 37, para 96. See also statements made on behalf of Romania, ibid, 18, [86]; Venezuela, ibid, 20, [17]; Senegal, ibid, 26, [84]; Ireland, ibid, 47, [70]; Turkey, ibid, 79, [53]. Jagota, *Maritime Boundary* 239; Tanja, *The Legal Determination of International Maritime Boundaries* 112.

[43] Art 298(1)(a) (i) of ICNT/Rev2. On this point, delegation on behalf of Spain stated that: '[h]is delegation advocated a comprehensive system based on the simple and objective principle of equidistance, corrected where necessary to take account of the special circumstances of each case and supplemented by a system for the binding settlement of disputes. However, none of those wishes was met in the existing text of Arts 74 and 83, which, to be acceptable, must contain a sufficiently precise formula based on the reference to international law'. UNCLOS III, *Official Records,* vol XIV, 53, para 35. See also statement by the delegation of Spain dated 26 August 1980, Document A/CONF62/WS/12, ibid, 150, para 16. See also statements on behalf of Greece, ibid, 38, para 112; United Arab Emirates, ibid, 65, [60]; Cyprus, ibid, 69, [111]; Colombia, ibid, 74, [199].

Owing to the confrontation between the two schools of thought,[44] even one year before the adoption of the new Convention, no agreement had yet been reached regarding the rule applicable to the delimitation of EEZ and to the continental shelf. In order to break this deadlock, in 1981, President Koh proposed a draft article which would bring about a compromise.[45] On 28 August 1981, the draft was incorporated into the Draft Convention,[46] which became the LOSC adopted on 30 April 1982. With a few modifications suggested by the Drafting Committee and approved by the Plenary Conference on 24 September 1982, the texts became, finally, Articles 74(1) and 83(1) in the LOSC. As will be seen next, however, the two provisions leave some room for discussion with regard to its contents.

ii. Problems with Articles 74(1) and 83(1)

The most serious deficiency with these provisions is their lack of specificity. Articles 74(1) and 83(1) omit any reference to a method of delimitation. In the absence of any method of delimitation, these provisions are likely to remain meaningless in specific situations.[47] Furthermore, the use of the terms 'in order to achieve an equitable solution' in conjunction with 'agreement' contradicts the rule of international law according to which States may freely determine the content of agreements in the absence of *jus cogens*. No contention was made that Articles 74(1) and 83(1) were *jus cogens*.[48] Accordingly, States may freely conclude any agreements even if they are not equitable.[49] Moreover, as the concept of 'equitable solution' is highly obscure, this reference may be considered to make little sense. At first sight, Articles 74 and 83 suggest that delimitation shall be effected solely by agreement, but this interpretation does not conform to reality. In reality, relatively many disputes of maritime delimitation were brought before the ICJ or courts of arbitration, and case law plays

[44] See also FA Ahnish, *The International Law of Maritime Boundaries and the Practice of State in the Mediterranean Sea* (Oxford, Clarendon Press, 1993) 73.

[45] A/CONF62/WP11, Platzöder, *Third United Nations Conference on the Law of the Sea*, vol IX, 474. The President explained that 'he had gained the impression that the proposal enjoyed widespread and substantial support in the two most interested groups of delegations, and in the Conference as a whole.' UNCLOS III, *Official Records*, vol XV, 39, para 3. See also Tanja, *The Legal Determination of International Maritime Boundaries* 114–15.

[46] Doc A/CONF62/L78.

[47] In fact, Judge Gros in the *Gulf of Maine* case, called these provisions 'an empty formula.' Dissenting Opinion of Judge Gros, ICJ Reports 1984, 365, [8]. Furthermore, the Court of Arbitration in the *Eritrea/Yemen* arbitration stated that Arts 74 and 83 'were consciously designed to decide as little as possible'. (2001) 40 *ILM* 1003, [116]. See also Ahnish, *The International Law of Maritime Boundaries* 78; and Caflisch, 'The Delimitation of Marine Spaces' 480.

[48] Caflisch, 'The Delimitation of Marine Spaces' 484; P Weil, *Perspective du droit de la délimitation maritime* (Paris, Pedone, 1988) 120–21.

[49] Caflisch, 'The Delimitation of Marine Spaces' 484; H Dipla, *Le régime juridique des îles dans le droit international de la mer* (Geneva, PUF, 1984) 221, 225.

an important role in the law of maritime delimitation. On account of these facts, it is reasonable to conclude that Articles 74 and 83 are not intended to rule out judicial settlement in the absence of such an agreement.[50] In addition, it appears that the reference to 'Article 38 of the Statute of the International Court of Justice' does not necessarily provide a useful guidance. Indeed, the reference to Article 38 does not spell out the law applicable to maritime delimitation simply by enumerating the sources of international law. Thus, mention of Article 38 is not of much use in determining the applicable law,[51] although it is not completely meaningless either, since it makes it possible to turn to the 1958 Geneva Convention on the Continental Shelf. It is also debatable whether 'general principles of law recognized by civilized nations' mentioned in Article 38 exist in the context of maritime delimitation.[52] Another question relates to the fact that the text refers to Article 38 of the Statute of the ICJ as a whole. Paragraph 2 of Article 38 of the Statute defines decisions *ex aequo et bono*, ie, extra-legal considerations, while the sources of international law are enumerated in Article 38(1) of the Statute of the ICJ. Consequently, one may argue that the references in Articles 74 and 83 should have been limited to paragraph 1 of Article 38.[53]

With respect to the delimitation of the continental shelf, where a Party of the LOSC has ratified the Geneva Convention on the Continental Shelf, the relation between these two Conventions is at issue. Paragraph 1 of Article 311 of the LOSC provides that '[t]his Convention shall prevail, as between States Parties, over the Geneva Convention on the Law of the Sea of 29 April 1958.' Yet paragraph 5 of the same Article states that '[t]his Article does not affect international agreements expressly permitted or preserved by other Articles of this Convention.' This provision is applicable to Article 6 of the Geneva Convention on the Continental Shelf, since Article 83 of the LOSC refers to Article 38 of the Statute. It would seem to follow that Article 6 of the Geneva Convention on the Continental Shelf applies between Parties to both the Geneva Convention and the LOSC.[54] In light of these points, it would appear that the only advantage of Articles 74 and 83 is that they bring about a compromise between two schools of thought and provide *some* sort of a delimitation rule in the new Convention.

[50] Caflisch, 'The Delimitation of Marine Spaces' 483.

[51] P Cahier, 'Les sources du droit relatif à la délimitation de plateau continental' in *Le droit international au service de la paix, de la justice et du développement, Mélanges Michel Virally* (Paris, Pedone, 1991) 175.

[52] Chiu, 'Some Problems Concerning the Application of the Maritime Boundary Delimitation Provisions' 8.

[53] Caflisch, 'The Delimitation of Marine Spaces' 485.

[54] ibid, 479. Nuno Sérgio Marques Antunes, *Towards the Conceptualisation of Maritime Delimitation* 95.

B. Analysis of Articles 74(3) and 83(3)

i. Obligations under Articles 74(3) and 83(3)

In many parts of the world's oceans, maritime delimitation is not accomplished yet. Accordingly, it is of particular importance to clarify rights and obligations of States in disputed maritime areas.[55] In this connection, it is necessary to briefly examine obligations concerning provisional arrangements under Articles 74(3) and 83(3) of the LOSC.[56] Articles 74(3) and 83(3) provide virtually the same rule:

> Pending agreement as provided for in paragraph 1, the States concerned, in a spirit of understanding and cooperation, shall make every effort to enter into provisional arrangements of a practical nature and, during this transitional period, not to jeopardize or hamper the reaching of the final agreement. Such arrangements shall be without prejudice to the final delimitation.

This provision calls for three comments.

First, under Articles 74(3) and 83(3), States are under a positive obligation to make every effort to conclude provisional arrangements of a practical nature pending agreement on delimitation 'in a spirit of understanding and cooperation'. There may be scope for arguing that the phrase 'in a spirit of understanding and cooperation' reflects the principle of good faith.[57] Pursuant to the obligation, States must enter into negotiations in good faith, even though this does not imply an obligation to reach an agreement.[58] More specifically, the Arbitral Tribunal in the 2007 *Guyana v Suriname* case observed that the inclusion of the phrase 'in a spirit of understanding and cooperation' is thought to indicate the drafters' intent to require of the parties a conciliatory approach to negotiations, pursuant to which they would be prepared to make concessions in the pursuit of a provisional arrangement.[59]

Secondly, under Articles 74(3) and 83(3), States must not jeopardise or hamper the reaching of the final agreement during the transitional period. Articles 74(3)

[55] For a recent study on this subject, see British Institute of International and Comparative Law, *Report on the Obligations of States under Articles 74(30 and 83(3) of UNCLOS in Respect of Undelimited Maritime Areas* (BIICL, London, 2016).

[56] For an analysis of Arts 74(3) and 83(3), see in particular, R Lagoni, 'Interim Measures Pending Maritime Delimitation Agreements' (1984) 78 *AJIL* 349; N Klein, 'Provisional Measures and Provisional Arrangements' in Oude Elferink, Henriksen, and Busch, *Maritime Boundary Delimitation*, 117; Y Tanaka, 'Article 74' in A Prölss (ed), *The United Nations Convention on the Law of the Sea: A Commentary* (Oxford, Hart Publishing, 2017) 576–81; by the same writer, 'Article 83' in ibid, 663–65.

[57] See also Art 300 of the LOSC.

[58] The *North Sea Continental Shelf* cases, [1969] ICJ Rep 48, [87]. See also *Dispute Concerning Delimitation of the Maritime Boundary between Ghana and Côte d'Ivoire in the Atlantic Ocean (Ghana v Côte d'Ivoire)* (the *Ghana/Côte d'Ivoire* case), Judgment. [2017] ITLOS Rep (not yet reported), [604].

[59] Arbitral Tribunal Constituted Pursuant to Article 287, and in Accordance with Annex VII, of the United Nations Convention on the Law of the Sea in the Matter of an Arbitration between Guyana and Suriname (hereafter the *Guyana v Suriname* case), 17 September 2007, (2013) 30 *RIAA* 1, 153, [461].

and 83(3) contain no indication of what is meant by the phrase 'jeopardize or hamper'. As the Arbitral Tribunal ruled in the *Guyana v Suriname* case, the phrase is not intended to preclude some activities by the States concerned within the disputed area, if those activities would not have the effect of prejudicing the final agreement.[60] Considering that the provisional arrangements can be entered into before the relevant States commence negotiating the final delimitation agreement, this provision can even be said to facilitate the provisional utilisation of the area to be delimited.[61]

Thirdly, as for the time frame of Articles 74(3) and 83(4), the ITLOS Special Chamber, in the 2017 *Ghana/ Côte d'Ivoire* case, took the view that the transitional period means 'the period after the maritime delimitation dispute has been established until a final delimitation by agreement or adjudication has been achieved'.[62] The obligation under Articles 74(3) and 83(3) would also arise when one of the parties in dispute refused to enter into negotiation on the maritime delimitation. It continues to apply if the negotiations between the parties reached a deadlock or discontinued.[63]

ii. *The Lawfulness of Unilateral Exploration and Exploitation*

A contentious issue that arises in this context concerns the lawfulness of unilateral exploration and exploitation of natural resources in disputed areas. In this regard, three cases merit discussion.

The first is the 1976 *Aegean Sea Continental Shelf* case between Greece and Turkey.[64] In this case, a dispute arose with regard to the lawfulness of unilateral seismic exploration conducted by Turkey in disputed areas of the continental shelf. Greece requested that the ICJ indicate the provisional measure that requires Turkey to refrain from all exploration activity or any scientific research in disputed areas of the continental shelf.[65] However, the Court declined the request for three reasons. First, while the explosions (seismic activity) aimed to send sound waves through the seabed so as to obtain information regarding the geophysical structure of the earth beneath it, no complaint had been made that this form of exploration involved any risk of physical damage to the seabed or subsoil or to their natural resources. Secondly, the continued seismic exploration activities by Turkey were of the transitory character. Thirdly,

[60] ibid, [460] and [465]; *Virginia Commentary*, vol 2, 815.

[61] Lagoni, 'Interim Measures,' 354.

[62] The *Ghana/Côte d'Ivoire* case, judgment. [2017] ITLOS Rep, [630].

[63] Lagoni, 'Interim Measures' 364. See also British Institute of International and Comparative Law (BIICL), *Report on the Obligations of States under Articles 73(3) and 83(3) of UNCLOS in respect of Undelimited Maritime Areas* (London, British Institute of International and Comparative Law, 2016) 12, [41].

[64] *Aegean Sea Continental Shelf (Greece v Turkey)*, Interim Measures, [1976] ICJ Rep 3.

[65] ibid, 4–5, [2]. Request for the indication of Interim Measures of Protection submitted by the Government of Greece, 10 August 1976, 66.

Turkey embarked upon no operations involving the actual appropriation or other use of the natural resources of the disputed areas of the continental shelf.[66] The Court accordingly found that the circumstances were not such as to require an order of provisional measures.[67] While the Court did not directly examine the legality of the unilateral seismic exploration in a disputed area, the *Aegean Sea Continental Shelf* Order can be interpreted to imply that the seismic exploration of a transitory nature could not be considered as affecting Greece's potential rights to the continental shelf.[68] It would seem to follow that two types of unilateral acts must be distinguished: unilateral acts that may cause permanent damage to the marine environment and those acts that may not cause such damage.

The distinction between the two types of activity was further elaborated by the Arbitral Tribunal in the 2007 *Guyana v Suriname* arbitration. By referring to the *Aegean Sea Continental Shelf* Order, the Arbitral Tribunal distinguished activities of the kind that lead to a permanent physical change, such as exploitation of oil and gas reserves, from those that do not, such as seismic exploration.[69] According to the Arbitral Tribunal, 'acts that do cause physical change would have to be undertaken pursuant to an agreement between the parties to be permissible, as they may hamper or jeopardise the reaching of a final agreement on delimitation'[70] and, consequently, '[i]t should not be permissible for a party to a dispute to undertake any unilateral activity that might affect the other party's rights in a permanent manner.'[71] By contrast, 'seismic activity [...] should be permissible in a disputed area.'[72] In accordance with the Tribunal's interpretation, one can argue that unilateral seismic testing is not *a priori* inconsistent with a party's obligation to make every effort not to jeopardise or hamper the reaching of a final agreement, unless there is an objection made by the other party,[73] whereas unilateral exploitation of natural resources is not permissible because it may jeopardise or hamper the reaching of a final delimitation agreement by physically changing the marine environment.

However, the ITLOS Special Chamber, in the *Ghana/Côte d'Ivoire* Order, took a different view on this subject. In this case, Côte d'Ivoire asked the Chamber to prescribe provisional measures that require Ghana to take all steps

[66] [1976] ICJ Rep 10, [30].

[67] ibid, 14, [46].

[68] N Klein, 'Provisional Measures and Provisional Arrangements in Maritime Boundary Disputes' (2006) 21 *IJMCL* 432.

[69] The *Guyana v Suriname* case, 30 *RIAA* 132, [467–68].

[70] ibid, [467].

[71] ibid, 133, [470].

[72] ibid, 137, [481].

[73] In the *Guyana v Suriname* case, seismic activities did not give rise to objections from either side. *Ibid*. In this connection, it must be noted that the Tribunal added the phrase 'In the circumstances at hand.' ibid. The phrase seems to suggest that seismic testing is not always permissible. Y Van Longehem, 'The Scope for Unilateralism in Disputed Maritime Areas' in CH Schofield, Moon-Sang Kwon, and Seokwoo Lee (eds), *Limits of Maritime Jurisdiction* (Brill/Nijhoff, Leiden, 2013) 185; BIICL, *Report on the Obligations of States under Articles 73(3) and 83(3) of UNCLOS*, 26.

to suspend all ongoing oil exploration and exploitation operations conducted by Ghana in the disputed area and to refrain from granting any new permit for oil exploration and exploitation there.[74] On the one hand, the Special Chamber accepted that the ongoing exploration and exploitation activities conducted by Ghana in the disputed area would result in a modification of the physical characteristics of the continental shelf. In this connection, it held that:

> [T]he exploration and exploitation activities, as planned by Ghana, may cause irreparable prejudice to the sovereign and exclusive rights invoked by Côte d'Ivoire in the continental shelf and superjacent waters of the disputed area, before a decision on the merits is given by the Special Chamber, and that the risk of such prejudice is *imminent*.[75]

On the other hand, according to the Special Chamber, 'the suspension of on-going activities conducted by Ghana in respect of which drilling has already taken place would entail the risk of considerable financial loss to Ghana and its concessionaires and could also pose a serious danger to the marine environment resulting, in particular, from the deterioration of equipment.'[76] The Special Chamber accordingly declined to prescribe the provisional measure requested by Côte d'Ivoire that requires Ghana to suspend all ongoing oil exploration and exploitation operations in the disputed area, while it prescribed the provisional measure which requires Ghana to take all necessary steps to ensure that no new drilling either by Ghana or under its control takes place in the disputed area.[77] At the stage of the merits, the Special Chamber held that the hydrocarbon activities of Ghana in the dispute maritime area did not constitutes conduct that jeopardised or hampered the reaching of the final agreement.[78]

Overall the Special Chamber, in the *Ghana/Côte d'Ivoire* case, seemed to take the view that in appropriate cases, unilateral drillings in disputed areas may be permissible before reaching a final agreement on maritime delimitations. However, with respect this view seems to be open to criticism. Indeed, it is an elementary judicial principle that the judgment of a court should be effective and, thus, either party, or both must restrain from disrupting the situation or attempting to present its adversary with *a fait accompli*.[79] Nonetheless, there is the serious risk that continuing exploitation operations by Ghana may entail the risk of achieving *a fait accompli*.[80] A factor that affected the *Ghana/Côte*

[74] The *Ghana/Côte d'Ivoire* case, Provisional Measures, [2015] ITLOS Rep 146, 152–53, [25].

[75] Emphasis added. ibid, 164, [96].

[76] ibid, [99].

[77] ibid, 166, [108(1)(a)].

[78] Judgment, [2–17] ITLOS Rep, [631–34].

[79] J Merrills, *International Dispute Settlement*, 6th edn. (Cambridge, Cambridge University Press, 2017) 132.

[80] Y Tanaka, 'Unilateral Exploration and Exploitation of Natural Resources in Disputed Areas: A Note on the Ghana/ *Ghana/Côte d'Ivoire* Order of 25 April 2015 before the Special Chamber of ITLOS' (2015) 46 *ODIL* 315, 326.

d'Ivoire Order might have been that the seabed activities of Ghana were carried out on Ghana's side of an equidistance line. However, a provisional equidistance line is not the final maritime boundary. Whether a party in dispute can unilaterally carry out the exploitation of natural resources in disputed marine areas needs careful consideration, even if it is located on what it believes to be its side of an equidistance line. In this regard, Judge Paik's view deserves quoting:

> The obligation not to jeopardize or hamper under article 83, paragraph 3, of the Convention is applicable to the States concerned during the transitional period. It is an obligation to exercise caution and restraint in the area the legal status of which has yet to be decided. Therefore this obligation is breached as long as a State fails to exercise the required caution and restraint pending agreement, regardless of to which State the disputed area is allocated. To exonerate acts that could jeopardize or hamper the reaching of the final agreement for the reason that the area is ultimately attributed to a State undertaking such acts would significantly diminish the value of this obligation.[81]

Given that Article 83(3) is 'the only reliable legal device that can regulate the conduct of states in the area yet to be delimitation,'[82] it seems difficult to disagree with Judge Paik, stating that: '[T]he obligation not to jeopardize or hamper should not be taken lightly.'[83]

[81] Separate Opinion of Judge Paik in the *Ghana/Côte d'Ivoire* case (merits), [17].
[82] ibid, [18].
[83] ibid.

4

The Methodology of Maritime Delimitation in the Jurisprudence I: Continental Shelf Delimitation

CHAPTERS FOUR AND five analyse the evolution of the case law on a maritime delimitation with specific focus on the methodology of international courts and tribunals. The aim of the analysis is not to examine each and every issue of cases concerning maritime delimitation. Rather, it is to focus on two essential aspects: the law applicable to maritime delimitations and the process of its application in drawing a maritime boundary. In examining the two points, we will consider the methodology of maritime delimitation developed by international courts and tribunals.

I. THE *NORTH SEA CONTINENTAL SHELF* CASES (FEDERAL REPUBLIC OF GERMANY/DENMARK, THE NETHERLANDS, ICJ, 1969)

By two Special Agreements of 2 February 1967 between Denmark and the Federal Republic of Germany and between the latter and the Netherlands, the Parties requested the International Court of Justice to declare: 'What principles and rules of international law are applicable to the delimitation as between the Parties of the areas of the continental shelf in the North Sea which appertain to each of them beyond the partial boundary determined by the above-mentioned Convention of 9 June 1965?'[1] Thus the Court was not asked to draw the continental shelf boundaries. These were to be established by the Parties themselves. While Denmark and the Netherlands were Parties to the 1958 Geneva Convention on the Continental Shelf, the Federal Republic of Germany was not.[2] Having examined the contention of the Federal Republic of Germany, to the effect that the delimitation in question should be effected in accordance with the notion of 'a just and equitable share,' as noted in chapter one, the Court dismissed it.[3] It then

[1] *North Sea Continental Shelf (Federal Republic of Germany v Denmark) (Federal Republic of Germany v Netherlands)* (the *North Sea Continental Shelf* cases), [1969] ICJ Rep 6. The Court joined the proceedings in the two cases.

[2] ibid, 25, [26].

[3] ibid, 22–23, [18–20].

examined the applicability of Article 6 of the Convention on the Continental Shelf. Although the case is well known, some of the important arguments of the Court will be identified below.

A. Law Applicable to the Continental Shelf Delimitation (1): Article 6 of the Convention on the Continental Shelf

Regarding the law applicable to continental shelf delimitations, the important issue was the applicability of Article 6 of the 1958 Geneva Convention on the Continental Shelf to the Federal Republic of Germany. The Court addressed this question from the viewpoints of treaty and customary law. With respect to the former, it reached the conclusion that Article 6 could not apply as treaty law between the Parties to the dispute, since an intention could not be established on the part of the Federal Republic of Germany, not a Party to the Convention, unilaterally to assume the obligations defined in the Convention.[4] While the Court's reasoning on this point is beyond the scope of this study, the Court's arguments regarding customary law must be examined in some detail.

i. The Fundamental Aspects of Article 6

The first issue concerns the fundamental aspects of Article 6. To justify the mandatory character of Article 6, Denmark and the Netherlands alleged that the equidistance principle was to be seen as a necessary expression, in the field of delimitation, of the accepted doctrine of the exclusive appurtenance of the continental shelf to the nearby coastal States, and therefore as having an *a priori* character of, so to speak, juristic inevitability.[5] As a test for such appurtenance, the two Kingdoms identified the concept of 'proximity' which, according to them, underlies the equidistance method. For Denmark and the Netherlands, all parts of a continental shelf closer to one coastal State than to another shall be appurtenant to the former. 'Hence,' Denmark and the Netherlands argued, 'delimitation must be effected by a method which will leave to each one of the States concerned all those areas that are nearest to its own coast. Only a line drawn on equidistance principles will do this.'[6] The Court rejected this argument, however, as the concept of proximity was contrary to the fundamental rule of natural prolongation. In the Court's view,

[4] ibid, 25–27, [28–33]. The Federal Republic of Germany was one of the signatories of the Geneva Convention on the Continental Shelf, but has never ratified it.

[5] ibid, 29, [37].

[6] ibid, 29, [39].

> whenever a given submarine area does not constitute a natural – or the most natural – extension of the land territory of a coastal State, even though that area may be closer to it than it is to the territory of any other State, it cannot be regarded as appertaining to that State.[7]

Furthermore,

> [a]s regards equidistance, it clearly cannot be identified with the notion of natural prolongation or extension, since … the use of the equidistance method would frequently cause areas which are the natural prolongation or extension of the territory of one State to be attributed to another.[8]

This argument runs parallel to the rejection of the concept of 'a just and equitable share'.[9]

ii. The Positive Law Aspects of Article 6

Next, the Court examined the positive law aspects of Article 6 by asking (i) whether Article 6 had already been customary law at the time of the Convention, or (ii) whether it had become customary law through subsequent State practice. After examining these two questions, the Court denied the mandatory character of Article 6.

Regarding the first question, the Court touched on the distorting effects of the equidistance method in lateral delimitations. According to the Court, 'whereas a median line divides equally between the two opposite countries' areas that can be regarded as being the natural prolongation of the territory of each of them, a lateral equidistance line often leaves to one of the States concerned areas that are a natural prolongation of the territory of the other.'[10] Furthermore, 'the distorting effects of lateral equidistance lines under certain conditions of coastal configuration are nevertheless comparatively small within the limits of territorial waters, but produce their maximum effect in the localities where the main continental shelf areas lie further out.'[11] To the Court, the distorting effect of the equidistance method was one of the important reasons for rejecting the application of the equidistance method in lateral delimitations. Moreover, having taken into account the legislative history of Article 6, and the faculty of making reservations thereto, the Court concluded that that Article had been proposed by the International Law Commission at most *de lege ferenda*, and not as *lex lata* or as an emerging rule of customary

[7] ibid, 31, [43].
[8] ibid, [44].
[9] Even at this stage, however, several judges affirmed the mandatory character of Art 6 by considering proximity as constituting legal title. *Dissenting* Opinion of Judge Morelli, ibid, 202. See also Dissenting Opinion of Judge Tanaka, ibid, 180–81.
[10] Judgment ibid, 37, [58].
[11] ibid, [59]. See also 49, [89]. See also Illustration 3.

international law.[12] Although the Court's reasoning is problematical on several points, the conclusions appear valid.[13]

As for the second question, the Court specified three conditions whose fulfilment is necessary for turning treaty rules into customary law.

The first condition is the norm-creating character of the rule, which was doubtful as regarded Article 6. The Court denied the norm-creating character of Article 6 for three reasons.[14] First, Article 6 is so framed as to resort to the equidistance method after the primary obligation to effect delimitation by agreement. In the Court's view, such a primary obligation constitutes an unusual preface to what is claimed to be a potential general rule of law. Secondly, the notion of special circumstances embodied in Article 6 raises further doubts as to the potentially norm-creating character of the rule. Thirdly, the faculty of making reservations to Article 6 also adds difficulty on this point.

The second condition is that there must be 'a very widespread and representative participation in the convention.'[15] Regarding Article 6, the Court considered 'the number of ratifications and accessions so far secured [to be], though respectable, hardly sufficient.'[16]

Thirdly, there needs to be an *opinio juris sive necessitatis*. According to the Court, there was no evidence of such a belief among the States having drawn boundaries according to the principle of equidistance,[17] and even less among the States which have drawn no such boundaries. Consequently, the Court refused to recognise that Article 6 had become mandatory for all States through subsequent State practice. However, the reasoning of the Court cannot escape criticism.

First, the Court clarified neither the concept of the norm-creating character itself, nor the criteria for asserting such character. Furthermore, the reasons for rejecting the norm-creating character of Article 6 are not necessarily persuasive. In the first place, the reference to 'agreement' means the lack of validity of unilateral delimitations, which is the fundamental character of maritime delimitation. Thus, that reference does not deprive Article 6 of a potential norm-creating character. It is also inconceivable that the notion of special circumstances is contrary to the norm-creating character of Article 6. On this point, Judge Tanaka contended that: 'The special circumstances clause, therefore, does not

[12] ibid, 38, [62]. However, the Court's argument about the relevance of the permissibility of reservations to Art 6 was questioned by members of the Court itself and has seen by writers as well. See Dissenting Opinion of Judge Lachs, *ibid*, 224; Dissenting Opinion of Judge Sørensen, ibid, 248; Dissenting Opinion of Judge Morelli, ibid, 198, [1]. Regarding criticism by writers on this subject, see in particular, HWA Thirlway, *International Customary Law and Codification* (Leiden, Sijthoff, 1972) 120–24; P Cahier, 'Cours général de droit international public' (1985) 195 *RCADI* 235.

[13] The members of the ILC themselves had accepted that there was no rule applicable to continental shelf delimitations. Statement by MO Hudson, (1950) *YILC* 233. El Khoury was of the same view, see ibid, 1951, 288.

[14] The *North Sea Continental Shelf* cases, [1969] ICJ Rep 42, [72].

[15] ibid, 42, [73].

[16] ibid.

[17] ibid, 44–45, [77–78].

abolish or overrule the main principle, but is intended to make its functioning more perfect.'[18] If this were the case, the reference to special circumstances will not become an element of rejecting the norm-creating character of the rule. Moreover, there is room to reconsider the validity of the Court's argument regarding the relation between reservations and the norm-creating character. Given that reservations have been made with regard to treaty provisions which have codified customary international law, it would be possible for a provision which may be subject to a reservation to become customary law.[19]

Secondly and more importantly, the Court's arguments on State practice and *opinio juris* in the custom-making process must be examined. Regarding States which are Parties to the Convention on the Continental Shelf, the Court stated that '[f]rom their action no inference could legitimately be drawn as to the existence of a rule of customary law in favour of the equidistance principle,' since they were presumably 'acting actually and/or potentially in the application of the Convention'.[20] If this view were right, we would face a paradox. If a sufficient number of States adopt a consistent practice with a corresponding *opinio juris,* customary law can be created and will bind other States. However, if the same group of States concludes a multilateral treaty adhering to the same principle, no customary rule will come into existence, and other States will be able to exclude the rule by relying on the principle *pactum tertiis nec nocet nec prodest*.[21] As Thirlway points out, successive acts of the Parties to the Convention are relevant in an examination of the status of an alleged customary rule, for they show *consistency* of State practice and the presence of an *opinio juris*.[22]

By contrast, concerning States which were not Parties to the Convention, the Court did not regard their behaviour as evidence of the customary nature of the equidistance principle, for there was no evidence that they had acted in conformity with that principle on the basis of an *opinio juris*.[23] In so doing, the Court took a rigid approach to evaluating *opinio juris* in the application of the equidistance method. Such a rigid approach runs the risk, however, of making it difficult to allow for the formation of customary law through treaty practice.[24] In fact, several judges reached a contrary conclusion, affirming the mandatory character of Article 6 after having examined State practice and *opinio juris*.

[18] Dissenting Opinion of Judge Tanaka, ibid, 186.

[19] With respect to the problems with the 'fundamentally law-creating' criterion, see R Kolb, 'Selected Problems in the Theory of Customary International Law' (2003) 50 *NILR* 149.

[20] The *North Sea Continental Shelf* cases [1969] ICJ Rep 43, [76].

[21] HWA Thirlway, 'The Law and Procedure of the International Court of Justice Part Two' (1990) 61 *BYIL* 44; Kolb, 'Selected Problems', 145–50.

[22] Thirlway, *International Customary Law* 91.

[23] The North *Sea Continental Shelf* cases, [1969] ICJ Rep 44–45, [78]. See also, 44, [76].

[24] Dissenting Opinion of Judge Lachs, ibid, 231. Dissenting Opinion of Judge Tanaka, ibid, 176. Thirlway has stated that it was not merely impossible to determine *ab extra* whether the State concerned applied a treaty rule with a belief that it would have been bound to act as it did regardless of the treaty, but also, if ratification may prove *opinio juris* with regard to the ratifying State, any further evidence of *opinio juris* as regards that State is wholly superfluous. Thirlway, *International Customary Law* 91.

For instance, Judge Tanaka stated that the fact '[t]hat 46 States have signed and 39 States ratified or acceded to the Convention [on the Continental Shelf] is already an important achievement towards the recognition of customary international law on the matter of the continental shelf.'[25] Judge Lachs followed the same line of argument, asserting that: 'It may therefore be said that, from the viewpoints both of number and of representativity, the participation in the Convention constitutes a solid basis for the formation of a general rule of law.'[26] Vice-President Koretsky and Judge ad hoc Sørensen reached the same conclusion.[27] The difference of views between the Majority and the Dissenting Opinions appears to lie in the degree of flexibility for evaluating State practice and *opinio juris*.[28]

B. Law Applicable to the Continental Shelf Delimitation (2): Equitable Principles

After rejecting the mandatory character of the equidistance method, the majority found that there was law applicable to the continental shelf delimitations other than the equidistance method. In the Court's view, the rejection of the equidistance method as a mandatory rule of customary law did not mean that there was no rule. It was equitable principles which were applicable to these delimitations. According to the Court, 'delimitation must be the object of agreement between the States concerned, and that such agreement must be arrived at in accordance with equitable principles.'[29]

After this, the equitable principles became the core of the law of maritime delimitation. Concerning these principles, two questions shall now be considered: What is the legal basis of equitable principles, and what is their substance?

i. Legal Basis of Equitable Principles

Equitable principles must be customary in nature since there are no treaty provisions requiring them.[30] In fact, the Court referred to *opinio juris* in this

[25] Dissenting Opinion of Judge Tanaka, [1969] ICJ Rep 174.

[26] ibid, 228. See also 227.

[27] Dissenting Opinion of Vice-President Koretsky, ibid, 158; Dissenting Opinion of Judge ad hoc Sørensen, ibid, 247.

[28] In sum, five judges argued in favour of the equidistance method in their Dissenting Opinions, as against the majority opinion supported by eleven judges. Although there were six votes opposed to the judgment, the sixth judge did not express his dissent. While he opposed the majority opinion, his views on the equidistance method remain unclear. On the other hand, although joining the majority opinion, as shall be seen later, Judge Ammoun considered that the equidistance method was applicable as an expression of equitable principles.

[29] The *North Sea Continental Shelf* cases, [1969] ICJ Rep 46, [85]. See also 53, [101(C)(1)].

[30] The Court stressed the distinction between equitable principles as a rule of law and judging *ex aequo et bono*. ibid, 48, [88]. See also, 47, [85].

context.[31] However, the essential question is: From where did the relevant customary law derive? On this point, the Court relied on the Truman Proclamation which stated that continental shelf boundaries 'shall be determined by the United States and the State concerned in accordance with equitable principles' and on 'various other State proclamations'.[32] According to the Court, the two elements of agreement and equitable principles underlie all the subsequent history of the subject.[33] Nevertheless, the Court failed to find sufficient examples of State declarations.[34] Furthermore, since these proclamations were *unilateral*, they did not constitute State practice in the context of continental shelf delimitations, which are effected between two or more States. How, then, can such unilateral State proclamations be transformed into customary law?[35] The question remains open. In addition, while considering the Truman Proclamation as the starting point of the positive law on the subject in paragraph 47, the Court regarded it as having propounded the rules of law in paragraph 86.[36] These two views are hard to reconcile. In sum, contrary to what it did when examining the equidistance method, the Court did not apply to equitable principles the rigid test of the two elements of custom.[37] This is a double standard.[38] If the rigid test had been applied, it seems doubtful that the customary law character of equitable principles could have been proved.[39] Thus, one reaches the inevitable

[31] ibid, 46, [85].

[32] ibid, 33, [47].

[33] ibid. See also 36, [55].

[34] In fact, it is highly doubtful whether the United States had an intention to state customary law and whether the equitable principles referred to were in reality the customary law at the time. On this point, Brown believes that the US formula on equitable principles was chosen because in 1945, it was not at all clear what the rules of law were even for the lateral delimitation of traditionally recognised maritime areas such as the territorial sea, and that the object was quite simply to provide for the negotiation of a fair and reasonable boundary. ED Brown, *The Legal Regime of Hydrospace* (London, Stevens & Sons, 1971) 48. Furthermore, it should be noted that the United States had ratified the Geneva Convention on the Continental Shelf. Thus in spite of the fact that the Court deduced the equitable principles from the Truman Proclamation, the United States curiously accepted Art 6 as a rule of continental shelf delimitation. In addition, having examined national legislation, the same author contends that 'even the early series of proclamations, following closely behind the Truman Proclamation, adds nothing to the generality of the language of that Proclamation'. ED Brown, 'The North Sea Continental Shelf Cases' (1970) 23 *Current Legal Problems* 201.

[35] T Rothpfeffer, 'Equity in the North Sea Continental Shelf Cases' (1972) 42 *Nordisk Tidsskrift for International Ret* 97.

[36] K Marek, 'Le problème des sources du droit international dans l'arrêt sur le plateau continental de la mer du Nord' (1970) 6 *Revue belge de droit international* 66.

[37] Cahier, 'Cours general' 245.

[38] See R Higgins, *Problem and Process: International Law and How We Use It* (Oxford, Clarendon Press, 1994) 223. See also P-M Dupuy, 'Le juge et la règle générale' (1989) 93 *RGDIP* 569–98 (in particular, 576–78).

[39] In fact, O'Connell stated that '[d]espite what was said to the contrary by the International Court, the practice of States gives little countenance to the use of equitable principles in continental shelf boundary negotiations, and the paucity of precedent at the time the Court gave its decision in the North Sea Continental Shelf Case has not been redeemed by any significant practice since.' DP O'Connell in IA Shearer (ed), *The International Law of the Sea*, vol II (Oxford, Clarendon Press, 1984) 696. See also Nuno Sérgio Marques Antunes, *Towards the Conceptualisation of Maritime Delimitation: Legal and Technical Aspects of a Political Process* (Leiden, Brill/Nijhoff, 2003) 95–97.

conclusion that the legal grounds on which equitable principles may be viewed as customary law are highly uncertain.[40]

ii. Substance of Equitable Principles

The next questions are what the substance of equitable principles are and how the Court applied the latter to the present cases. In this connection, the Court ruled that:

> Equity does not necessarily imply equality. There can never be any question of completely refashioning nature, and equity does not require that a State without access to the sea should be allotted an area of continental shelf, any more than there could be a question of rendering the situation of a State with an extensive coastline similar to that of a State with a restricted coastline. Equality is to be reckoned within the same plane, and it is not such natural inequalities as these that equity could remedy.[41]

According to the Court, the application of the equidistance method in the present case would create an inequity, however, denying one of these States treatment equal or comparable to the other two States owing to a convex coastline.[42]

Even if one accepts the existence of inequity in the case at issue, a question does arise: what is the actual method for applying equitable principles? On this point, the Court rejected the existence of any obligatory method of continental shelf delimitation, asserting that 'there [is] no other single method of delimitation the use of which is in all circumstances obligatory.'[43] Thus, 'it is necessary to seek not one method of delimitation, but one goal.'[44] In so doing, the Court indicated solely the factors to be taken into account in a negotiation, without specifying a concrete method. Such factors are the general configuration of the coasts of the Parties, the physical and geological structure, the natural resources, the unity of deposits, and a reasonable degree of proportionality.[45] In this respect, one of the approaches regarding equitable principles did appear, namely, the rejection of any obligatory method and the emphasis on the results. According to this approach, it is the goal which should be stressed, and the law of maritime delimitation should be defined only by this goal, ie, the achievement of equitable results. In this sense, one could speak of a *result-oriented-equity approach*. It seems that this approach follows the same line of argument as the case-by-case solution model.

Regarding equitable principles formulated by the Court, it is necessary, however, to point to the following problems. First, several judges stressed the

[40] Rothpfeffer, 'Equity' 101.
[41] Judgment [1969] ICJ Rep 49–50, [91].
[42] ibid.
[43] ibid, 53, [101]. See also 49, [90].
[44] ibid, 50, [92].
[45] ibid, 53–54, [101].

danger of destabilising the system of continental shelf delimitation by introducing equitable principles, owing to their vagueness. For instance, Vice-President Koretsky harboured misgivings about equitable principles, saying that:

> I feel that to introduce so vague a notion into the jurisprudence of the International Court may open the door to making subjective and therefore at times arbitrary evaluations, instead of following the guidance of established general principles and rules of international law in the settlement of disputes submitted to the Court.[46]

Judge Sørensen also stated that if 'the delimitation is to be governed by a principle of equity only, considerable legal uncertainty will ensue.'[47] In fact, despite the theoretical distinction between equitable principles and judging *ex aequo et bono*, it is, in reality, difficult to differentiate the two.[48] Consequently, equitable principles will severely amplify the danger of subjectivity – which has unfortunately been proven in subsequent cases – while ruling out the objective method of equidistance.

Secondly, because of the lack of any specific method of delimitation, if the Parties cannot reach agreement, equitable principles do nothing but re-open the question.[49] In reality, Parties disagree over the very question of what equitable delimitation is and of how to establish an equitable delimitation line.[50]

Thirdly, the Court based its approach on the separation of the equidistance method from special circumstances. In so doing, it completely neglected the role of special circumstances, which is to justify the departure from equidistance lines with a view to achieving equitable results. As Article 6 is composed of the three elements 'agreement–equidistance–special circumstances', however, the Court should have considered the legal effects created by these three elements as a unit. On this point, it is worth noting the argument of Judge Ammoun, who asserted that:

> [T]he Geneva Convention on the Continental Shelf did not depart from the notion of equity in adopting the equidistance line accompanied by the condition referring to special circumstances. It is therefore as a solution based on equity that recourse may be had to the equidistance–special circumstances rule for the purpose of determining the lateral boundaries of the continental shelf as between the Parties to the dispute.[51]

[46] Dissenting Opinion of Vice-President Koretsky, ibid, 166. In addition, with respect to the factors to be considered in the framework of equitable principles, Judge Tanaka stated: '[I]t appears extremely doubtful whether the negotiations could be expected to achieve a successful result, and more likely that they would engender new complications and chaos.' Dissenting Opinion of Judge Tanaka, ibid, 196.

[47] Dissenting Opinion of Judge Sørensen, [1969] ICJ Rep 257. See also Brown, 'The North Sea Continental Shelf Cases'184.

[48] Friedmann states that '[t]he Court's principles of delimitation constituted therefore in effect, an *ex aequo et bono* decision'. W Friedmann, 'General Course in Public International Law' (1969) 127 *RCADI* 161. See also, by the same writer, 'The North Sea Continental Shelf Cases – A Critique' (1970) 64 *AJIL* 235–36.

[49] Dissenting Opinion of Judge Tanaka, [1969] ICJ Rep195–96.

[50] Separate Opinion of Judge Ammoun, ibid, 145, [45]. See also 132, [32].

[51] ibid, 151, [56]. In addition, he also mentioned that: 'This method [the equidistance method], which was rejected as not being a rule of treaty law or customary law, may be re-adopted by virtue of a general principle of law, namely equity.' ibid, 148, [52]. Furthermore, Judge Tanaka stresses

However, the Court did not follow this course, refusing to combine the equidistance method with special circumstances.[52]

II. THE *ANGLO-FRENCH CONTINENTAL SHELF* CASE (FRANCE/UNITED KINGDOM, ARBITRATION, 1977)

The next case that needs consideration is the *Anglo-French Continental shelf* case.[53] On 10 July 1975, the French Republic and the United Kingdom requested the ad hoc Court of Arbitration to decide the following question: 'What is the course of the boundary (or boundaries) between the portions of the continental shelf appertaining to the United Kingdom and the Channel Islands and to the French Republic, respectively, westward of 30 minutes west of the Greenwich Meridian as far as the 1000 metre isobath?'[54] Contrary to the *North Sea*

the significance of the special circumstances clause in Article 6 as correcting the harsh effect produced by the equidistance method. Dissenting Opinion of Judge Tanaka, ibid, 186. In addition, Vice-President Koretsky stated that three elements of Art 6 are intimately interconnected in constituting a normal procedure for the determination of a boundary line on the continental shelf as between adjacent States. Dissenting opinion of Vice-President Koretsky, ibid, 163. Ahnish also criticised this point. FA Ahnish, *The International Law of Maritime Boundaries and the Practice of States in the Mediterranean Sea* (Oxford, Clarendon Press, 1993) 59. See also R Kolb, *Case Law on Equitable Maritime Delimitation: Digest and Commentaries* (The Hague, Brill/Nijhoff, 2003) 27.

[52] After the judgment, by two Agreements between Denmark and the Federal Republic of Germany, and between the latter and the Netherlands, both of which were signed in 28 January 1971, and which entered into force on 7 December 1972, the three States succeeded in establishing their continental shelf boundaries. These two boundaries are pragmatic lines giving the Federal Republic of Germany a continental shelf extending towards the centre of the North Sea. Consequently, the Federal Republic of Germany received 35,600 square kilometres, approximately 12,000 square kilometres more than it would have been entitled to under to the equidistance method. The Danish and the Dutch shares amounted to approximately 46,000, respectively 56,000 square kilometres (see Illustration 4). Rothpfeffer, 'Equity' 129. Both the 1971 Agreement between FRG and the Netherlands and between FRG and the Denmark refers to straddling resources (Art 2(1), respectively). This reference might result from the judgment, which mentions the unity of deposits as a factor to be taken into account in negotiations. It seems that the physical and geological structure of the continental shelf did not influence the course of the boundary in the absence of major distinguishing physical features between the Parties. Furthermore, concerning other factors listed by the Court, ie, the general configuration of the coastlines and proportionality, it is difficult to demonstrate their effect on the boundary established. Regarding the text of the Agreements and a short analysis, see JI Charney and LM Alexander (eds), *International Maritime Boundary,* vol II (Dordrecht, Nijhoff, 1993) 1801–4; 1835–50. For a detailed analysis of the negotiation process following the 1969 *North Sea Continental Shelf judgment*, see AG Oude Elferink, *The Delimitation of the Continental Shelf between Denmark, Germany and the Netherlands: Arguing Law, Practicing Politics?* (Cambridge University Press, 2013) 342 et seq. For an illustration of the final continental shelf boundary, see also S Fietta and R Cleverly, *A Practitioner's Guide to Maritime Boundary Delimitation* (Oxford University Press, 2016), 173–74.

[53] The *Anglo-French Continental Shelf* arbitral award, (1980) 18 United Nations, *Reports of International Arbitral Awards (RIAA)* 1–129. The English text of the arbitral award published in *RIAA* referred to the term 'the Court of Arbitration', while the French text of the arbitral award referred to the term 'le Tribunal arbitral'. Following the English text, this book uses the term 'the Court of Arbitration' when examining the *Anglo-French Continental Shelf* case. The Court of Arbitration consisted of: Erik Castren (President); Herbert Briggs, André Gros, Endre Ustor, and Sir Humphrey Waldock.

[54] ibid, 5.

Continental Shelf cases, the Court was here requested to draw a boundary line. Both Parties had ratified the 1958 Geneva Convention on the Continental Shelf.

A. Law Applicable to the Continental Shelf Delimitation

i. Preliminary Considerations on Reservations

The French Government had made reservations to Article 6 of the Convention on the Continental Shelf,[55] and the United Kingdom had objected to them. On this point, the Court concluded that the combined effect of the French reservations and their rejection by the United Kingdom rendered Article 6 inapplicable between the two countries to the extent – but only to the extent – of the reservations.[56] This did not mean, however, that there were no legal rules to govern continental shelf delimitation in areas where the reservation was in effect. According to the Court of Arbitration, in such areas, the rules and principles of general international law, that is, equitable principles were applicable.[57] In stating this, the legal basis of these principles was no longer examined. Consequently, in the Channel Islands region, owing to the effect of the reservations, delimitation had to be effected according to customary law. In other regions, ie, the Western part of the Channel and the Atlantic areas, nothing prevented the application of the Continental Shelf Convention; accordingly, Article 6 of that Convention was held to apply.[58] In this respect, the Court presented an intriguing view, stating that: '[I]n the circumstances of the present case, the rules of customary law lead to much the same result as the provisions of Article 6.'[59] The relation between Article 6 and the customary law shown in the arbitral award is one of the crucial points addressed by the latter, which will be examined next.

ii. Relationship between Article 6 and Customary Law

Examining the relationship between Article 6 and customary law, the Court first interpreted Article 6 considering the latter as a single rule combining the

[55] The French reservation to Art 6 stated that:

> In the absence of a specific agreement, the Government of the French Republic will not accept that any boundary of the continental shelf determined by application of the principle of equidistance shall be invoked against it:
>
> – if such boundary is calculated from baselines established after 29 April 1958;
> – if it extends beyond the 200-meter isobath;
> – if it lies in areas where in the Government's opinion, there are 'special circumstances' within the meaning of Art 6, para 1 and 2, that is to say: the Bay of Biscay, the Bay of Granville, and the sea areas of the Straits of Dover and of the North Sea off the French coast. ibid, 29, [33].

[56] ibid, 42, [61].
[57] ibid, 42, [62].
[58] ibid, 47, [75].
[59] ibid, 44, [65].

equidistance method with special circumstances. In its view, 'Article 6, as both the United Kingdom and the French Republic stress in the pleadings, does not formulate the equidistance principle and "special circumstances" as two separate rules. The rule there stated in each of the two cases is a single one, a combined equidistance–special circumstances rule.'[60]

Furthermore, the award equated Article 6, as a single combined rule, to the customary law of equitable principles:

> In short, the role of the 'special circumstances' condition in Article 6 is to ensure an equitable delimitation; and the combined 'equidistance–special circumstances rule', in effect, gives particular expression to a general norm that, failing agreement, the boundary between States abutting on the same continental shelf is to be determined on equitable principles.[61]

Thus, the Court of Arbitration assimilated Article 6 to equitable principles *qua* customary law by considering the former as containing a single combined equidistance–special circumstances rule.[62]

The assimilation of Article 6 to customary law leads to an important consequence: the incorporation of the equidistance method into customary law. However, the Court of Arbitration did not follow directly that line of argument. Rather, it drew attention to the fact that, as pointed out in the *North Sea Continental Shelf* cases, there was a material difference between the situation of opposite and adjacent coasts. As for the former, the ICJ itself had accepted that no method other than that of equidistance presented the same combination of practical convenience and certainty of application, and the Court of Arbitration supported this view from the angle of State practice.[63] By contrast, in the case of adjacent coasts, the equidistance method tends to produce inequitable results. In short, according to the Court of Arbitration, the important point was that:

> [T]he validity of the equidistance method, or of any other method, as a means of achieving an equitable delimitation of the continental shelf is always relative to the particular geographical situation. In short, whether under customary law or Article 6, it is never a question either of complete or of no freedom of choice as to

[60] ibid, 44–45, [68].

[61] ibid, 45, [70].

[62] This view was also shared by the *Dubai/Sharjah Border* Arbitration rendered on 19 October 1981. In applying equitable principles of customary law, the Court of Arbitration considered the island of Abu Musa as a 'special circumstance'. At the same time, it held that the equidistance method is generally appropriate to the delimitation of the maritime boundary where that boundary is unaffected by the presence of Abu Musa. (1993) 91 *ILR* 672–73, [256]. On this point, see also L Caflisch, 'The Delimitation of Marine Spaces between State with Opposite and Adjacent Coasts' in R-J Dupuy and D Vignes (eds), *A Handbook on the New Law of the Sea* (Dordrecht, Nijhoff, 1991) 459; H Dipla, *Le régime juridique des îles dans le droit international de la mer* (Geneva, PUF, 1984) 198–200. Furthermore, one should recall in this context the view of Judge Ammoun in the *North Sea Continental Shelf* cases.

[63] The Court of Arbitration stated that 'a large proportion of the delimitations of the continental shelf have been effected by the application either of the equidistance method or, not infrequently, of some variant of that method.' 18 *RIAA* 51, [85].

method; for the appropriateness – the equitable character – of the method is always a function of the particular geographical situation.[64]

In this respect, it seems that the Court attempted to subordinate the equidistance method to special circumstances.[65] As will be discussed below, however, the Court of Arbitration relied considerably on the equidistance method in the application of the law.

B. Application of the Law Identified

i. Establishment of the Continental Shelf Boundary

The delimitation of the continental shelf in the *Anglo-French Continental Shelf* case was divided into three segments. First, regarding the English Channel, where the coasts are opposite each other, both States agreed that the boundary should be the median line. France based its position on customary law, while the United Kingdom relied on Article 6. The result was the same. Furthermore, in the Court's view, the Hurd Deep-Fault Zone did not lead to discarding the equidistance method because of the essential continuity of the continental shelf in the region. Accordingly, the Court concluded that the boundary in the English Channel was to be an equidistance line (see Illustration 5).[66]

Secondly, with respect to the Channel Islands region, where customary law was applicable, the Court ruled that: '[I]t is clear both from the insertion of the "special circumstances" provision in Article 6 and from the emphasis on "equitable principles" in customary law that the force of the cardinal principle of "natural prolongation of territory" is not absolute, but may be subject to qualification in particular situations.'[67] On this point, contrary to the 1969 judgment of the ICJ, the Court of Arbitration downgraded the role of natural prolongation in the delimitation of the continental shelf.[68] As a result, it concluded that the question of delimiting the continental shelf in the Channel Islands areas was

[64] ibid, 51, [84]. See also 111–12, [239].

[65] This appears to be compatible with the ICJ's view of rejecting any obligatory method. E Zoller, 'L'affaire de la délimitation du plateau continental entre la Républic Française et le Royaume-Uni de Grande Bretagne et d'Irelande du Nord' (1977) 23 *AFDI* 374. On this point, however, Zoller criticises the arbitral award as 'impressionnistic'. ibid, 397. Quéneudec took the same view. JP Quéneudec, 'L'affaire de la délimitation du plateau continental entre la France et le Royaume-Uni' (1979) 83 *RGDIP* 82.

[66] 18 *RIAA* 61–62, [108–9]. In addition in this region, there was a problem relating to a base-point on Eddystone Rock. In dismissing a French argument, which rejected Eddystone as a base-point, the Court of Arbitration recognised it as such, since France had previously accepted the Rock as a base-point under the 1964 European Fisheries Convention and in the 1971 negotiations on the continental shelf delimitation. ibid, 72–74, [139–43].

[67] ibid, 91, [191]. See also 92, [194].

[68] DW Bowett, 'The Arbitration between the United Kingdom and France Concerning the Continental Shelf Boundary in the English Channel and South-Western Approaches' (1978) 49 *BYIL* 16; Zoller, 'L'affaire de la délimitation du plateau continental,' 392.

not resolved merely by referring to the principle of natural prolongation.[69] Once again the Court resorted to the equidistance method in the Channel Islands region. In so doing, it adopted a twofold solution. In the central part of the Channel, the boundary line was to be formed by an equidistance line drawn westwards from two accepted Points, D and E, and disregarding the Channel Islands.[70] In addition, a second boundary was drawn which enclaved the Channel Islands within a 12-mile radius.[71] Thus, even in the controversial area of the Channel Islands, the equidistance method was applied under customary law for drawing one of the two boundaries.

Thirdly, regarding the Atlantic region, where Article 6 was applicable, the Court of Arbitration viewed the geographical situation of the Atlantic region as one akin to a lateral delimitation. It began by pointing out that a strict application of the equidistance method would tend to produce inequitable results. In this region, the Scilly Isles also constituted a special circumstance. Accordingly, it was necessary to find a method of remedying the distorting effect of those islands. However, the Court did not consider that the existence of a special circumstance gave 'it carte blanche to employ any method that it [chose] in order to effect an equitable delimitation of the continental shelf.'[72] It held that:

> The Court notes that in a large proportion of the delimitations known to it, where a particular geographical feature has influenced the course of a continental shelf boundary, the method of delimitation adopted has been some modification or variant of the equidistance principle rather than its total rejection. In the present instance, the problem also arises precisely from the distorting effect of a geographical feature in circumstances in which the line equidistant from the coasts of the two States would otherwise constitute the appropriate boundary. Consequently, it seems to the Court to be in accord not only with the legal rules governing the continental shelf but also with State practice to seek the solution in a method modifying or varying the equidistance method rather than to have recourse to a wholly different criterion of delimitation (emphasis added).[73]

Thus, in the Court's view, the equidistance method is applied as a starting point even where a 'special' geographical situation exists in a lateral delimitation.[74] In this phase, the relation between special circumstances and the equidistance method was reversed in favour of the latter. In so doing, it seems that the Court of

[69] 18 *RIAA* 91, [192].

[70] ibid, 94, [201], and 95, [203].

[71] ibid, 95, [202]. The delimitation on the 'French side' of the Channel Islands was considered outside the competence of the Court of Arbitration, since this issue amounted to a delimitation of the territorial sea between the English territory of the Channel Islands and the French Republic. ibid, 24, [20–21].

[72] ibid, 114, [245].

[73] ibid, 116, [249].

[74] The Court have taken into account the fact that in the Atlantic region, Art 6 was applicable. Yet, as Art 6 is the particular expression of a customary law of equitable principles, the result would be the same as if customary law had been applied.

Arbitration considered equity to be a corrective element. This *corrective-equity approach* is related to the model based on the median-line system. Applying this *dictum*, the Court gave half effect to the Scilly Isles by drawing a line mid-way between two equidistance lines, one constructed without using the Scilly Isles as a basepoint, and the other using the Scillies as a base-point.[75]

ii. Comparison between the 1969 and 1977 Decisions

The 1977 arbitral award followed a line of argument different from that adopted in the *North Sea Continental Shelf* judgment in at least three respects. First, contrary to the 1969 judgment, which dealt with the equidistance method independently of special circumstances, the Court of Arbitration considered Article 6 as embodying a single combined rule of equidistance/special circumstances. Secondly, contrary to the *North Sea Continental Shelf* judgment which rejected the customary legal character of Article 6, the award assimilated Article 6 and the customary law of equitable principles. This lead to the consequence of incorporating the equidistance method into customary law. This is one of the important points of the award.[76] Thirdly, despite the emphasis it placed on geographical features, the Court of Arbitration accepted the applicability of the equidistance method at a first stage, even where a particular geographical element exists in a situation of lateral delimitation. On this point, it took *the corrective-equity approach*, in contrast to the result-oriented equity resorted to in the *North Sea Continental Shelf* cases. It could thus be contended that the arbitral award set another starting point for the case law.

In summary, based on the same fundamental concept of equity, two different approaches appeared in the 1969 and 1977 decisions. One is the result-oriented equity approach, which reflects the case-by-case model. The other is the corrective-equity approach, which follows the model of a solution based on the median-line system. How, then, were the two different approaches to develop in the future case law?

III. THE *TUNISIA/LIBYA* CASE (ICJ, 1982)

In 1978, Tunisia and Libya instituted proceedings requesting the ICJ to render a decision on the following issues: What are the principles and rules of international law applicable to the delimitation of the continental shelf? In this connection, the Special Agreements asked the Court to take account of equitable

[75] The 'half effect' technique will be examined in ch 7 s IV.

[76] Quéneudec, 'L'affaire de la délimitation du plateau continental entre la France et le Royaume-Uni,' 72; JG Merrills, 'The United Kingdom-France Continental Shelf Arbitration' (1980) 10 *California Western International Law Journal* 357; Caflisch, 'The Delimitation of Marine Spaces' 459; Kolb, *Case Law on Equitable Maritime Delimitation* 93, 107–8.

principles and the relevant circumstances which characterised the area, as well as recent trends admitted at the Third UN Conference on the Law of the Sea. Furthermore, the Court was asked to 'specify precisely' the practical way enabling the experts of the two countries to delimit those areas without any difficulties.[77] Thus, while requesting the Court to specify 'the practical way' to be used for identifying the delimitation line, it was left to the two Parties to draw the actual line following the Court's judgment.[78] Regarding the scope of the Court's task, however, a disagreement arose between Tunisia, which requested the Court to 'specify precisely' ('clarifier avec précision') this practical way,[79] and Libya, which did not ask the Court to set out the specific method of delimitation, merely using the word 'clarify.'[80] Having examined the pleadings and arguments of both Parties, the Court concluded that the degree of precision required would be made apparent when it had indicated a practical method for application of the relevant principles and rules.[81] In the end, the Court drew an illustrative line to demonstrate the precise direction, including the latitude and longitude, of the delimitation line.[82]

A. Law Applicable to the Continental Shelf Delimitation

i. Relationship between Equitable Principles and Natural Prolongation

While each Party asked the Court to determine the delimitation in accordance with equitable principles, they both relied heavily on the concept of the natural prolongation of the coasts for justifying their contentions. Thus, the relationship between the concept of natural prolongation of the coast and the equitable principles had to be considered.

For Libya, a delimitation determined by the natural prolongation was necessarily in accordance with equitable principles, since it would respect the inherent rights of each State.[83] According to Libya, 'once the natural prolongation of a State is determined, delimitation becomes a simple matter of complying with the dictates of nature.'[84] Libya then contended that the natural prolongation determining the

[77] Art 1 of the Special Agreement submitted by Tunisia (English translation by the Registry), *Continental Shelf (Tunisia v Libyan Arab Jamahiriya)* (the *Tunisia/Libya* case) [1982] ICJ Rep 18, 21, [1].

[78] Art. 2 of the Special Agreement of 1977. Regarding this provision, Judge Gros doubted whether the Parties had the intention of being bound by the judgment. Dissenting Opinion of Judge Gros, [1982] ICJ Rep 144, [3].

[79] Judgment ibid, 39, [27].

[80] ibid, [28].

[81] ibid, 39–40, [29–30].

[82] ibid, 93–94, [133]. Yet Zoller doubts that the Court exceeded the scope of the request by the Parties. E Zoller, 'Recherche sur les méthodes de délimitation du plateau continental: A propos de l'affaire Tunisi-Libye' (1982) 86 *RGDIP* 666–67.

[83] Judgment, [1982] ICJ Rep 44, [39].

[84] ibid, 47, [44].

boundary of the continental shelf with Tunisia consisted in the area in front of its coast, constituting the Pelagian Block, on account of geological considerations. On the other hand, Tunisia argued that the satisfaction of equitable principles in a particular geographical situation was part of the process of the identification of the natural prolongation.[85] Furthermore, based on geomorphological and bathymetric considerations, Tunisia suggested that the Tripolitanian Furrow, an eastward natural prolongation of Tunisia and a continuum northward or north-eastward of Libya, was 'a true natural submarine frontier'[86] (see Illustration 6).

The Court dismissed both arguments, however. With respect to the Libyan arguments, it held that:

> [W]hile the idea of the natural prolongation of the land territory defined, in general terms, the physical object or location of the rights of the coastal State, it would not necessarily be sufficient, or even appropriate, in itself to determine the precise extent of the rights of one State in relation to those of a neighbouring State.[87]

The Tunisian argument had to be discarded as well, since the satisfaction of equitable principles and the identification of the natural prolongation were not to be placed on an equal level.[88] The Court thus concluded that:

> The principle that the natural prolongation of the coastal State is a basis of its legal title to continental shelf rights does not in the present case, as explained above, necessarily provide criteria applicable to the delimitation of the areas appertaining to adjacent States.[89]

As with the award of 1977, the role of natural prolongation in the delimitation process was reduced, although the possibility of taking it into account as a relevant circumstance was left open.[90] Having discarded natural prolongation as a criterion, the Court unveiled its approach to equitable principles, which was a highlight of the present case.

ii. Approach to Equitable Principles

The Court's approach to equitable principles was summarised in the following passage of the judgment:

> The result of the application of equitable principles must be equitable. [...] It is, however, the result which is predominant; the principles are subordinate to the goal. The equitableness of a principle must be assessed in the light of its usefulness for the purpose of arriving at an equitable result.[91]

[85] ibid, 44, [39].
[86] ibid, 56, [64].
[87] ibid, 46, [43].
[88] ibid, 47, [44].
[89] ibid, 48, [48].
[90] ibid, 58, [68].
[91] ibid, 59, [70].

The Court thus emphasised the predominance of the result over the rule of law. The Court accepted neither the mandatory character of equidistance, nor some privileged status of equidistance in relation to other methods.[92] It seems that the Court further developed the result-oriented equity approach set out in the *North Sea Continental Shelf* judgment. Judge Jiménez de Aréchaga, who joined the majority opinion in the present case, explained this view in more detail:

> To resort to equity means, in effect, to appreciate and balance the relevant circumstances of the case, so as to render justice, not through the rigid application of general rules and principles and of formal legal concepts, but through an adaptation and adjustment of such principles, rules and concepts to the facts, realities and circumstances of each case. [...] Equity is here nothing other than the taking into account of a complex of historical and geographical circumstances the consideration of which does not diminish justice but, on the contrary, enriches it.[93]

In his view, the application of the equitable principles is thus broken down into 'a complex of historical and geographical circumstances' in individual situations, ruling out any predetermined method.[94] Thus, in the result-oriented equity approach, all that remains is an 'equitable result' in specific situations.

Several judges, however, disagreed with this result-oriented equity approach in at least three respects. First, contrary to the *North Sea Continental Shelf* cases, the Court in the present instance had to draw the delimitation line 'without any difficulties'. Yet, without a specific method, how was it possible to establish such a delimitation line, applying equitable principles? This was the main question raised by several judges in their dissenting opinions.[95]

Secondly, the lack of method elicited another criticism regarding the *a priori* rejection of the equidistance method. In this connection, Judge Evensen stated that:

> In paragraph 109 of the Judgment, the Court states, after having noted that equidistance 'has been employed in a number of cases' in the practice of States that: 'equidistance may be applied if it leads to an equitable solution; if not, other methods should be employed.' But the Court has not attempted to use this test in the present case. Nor has it examined whether the equidistance principle could be fruitfully used, adjusted by principles of equity and the relevant circumstances characterizing the region concerned to bring about an equitable solution.[96]

[92] ibid, 79, [110].

[93] Separate Opinion of Judge Jiménez de Aréchaga, ibid, 106, [24].

[94] ibid. According to Judge Jiménez de Aréchaga, the concept of equity is 'the one which solves the fundamental dilemma arising in all cases of continental shelf delimitation: the need to maintain consistency and uniformity in the legal principles and rules applicable to a series of situations which are characterized by their multiple diversity.' ibid, [26]. Regarding his views on equitable principles, see also E Jiménez de Aréchaga, 'The Concept of Equity in Maritime Delimitation' in *International Law at the Time of Its Codification, Essays in Honour of Roberto Ago* (Milan, Giuffrè, 1987) 229–39.

[95] See for instance Dissenting Opinion of Judge Oda, [1982] ICJ Rep 255, [155].

[96] Dissenting Opinion of Judge Evensen, ibid, 297, [15]. See also 319, 'Conclusions'.

Judge Gros also criticised the Court on this point: 'The Court's first task was thus to see what an equidistance line would produce in order to identify the "extraordinary, unnatural or unreasonable" result to which, it is said, this method might lead.'[97] In short, the Court failed to clarify its reasoning for rejecting equidistance. It may be inevitable to conclude that the equitableness presumed by the majority opinion is insufficiently explained.

Thirdly, the vagueness of the concept of equity produces a serious problem of distinguishing judgments based on equitable principles as law on the one hand and judgments rendered *ex aequo et bono* under Article 38, paragraph 2, of the Court's Statute on the other hand. In this respect, the Court held that: '[T]he legal concept of equity is a general principle directly applicable as law. [...] Application of equitable principles is to be distinguished from a decision *ex aequo et bono*.'[98] In reality, however, without criteria for judging the equitableness of results, the distinction becomes questionable.[99] In fact, Judge Evensen observed that:

> If applied in a legal void as entirely self-sufficient, equity may easily change the character of a decision from being a legal decision under Article 38, paragraph 1, of the Statute to becoming an *ex aequo et bono* decision governed by the provisions of paragraph 2 of Article 38 of the Statute. The Court has no such authority in the present case.[100]

According to the learned judge, 'equitable principles cannot operate in void.'[101] In so arguing, Judge Evensen, like Judge Oda, favoured the application of the equidistance method.[102] In summary, it may be said that the principal criticism of the dissenters regarding the Court's approach concerned the lack of a delimitation method.[103] How, then, did the Court draw the delimitation line on the continental shelf without specifying any method?

B. Application of the Law Identified

i. Establishment of an Illustrative Continental Shelf Boundary

The Court drew an illustrative delimitation line on the continental shelf by dividing the area into two zones. In the first zone, the Court relied on three

[97] Dissenting Opinion of Judge Gros, ibid, 149, [12]; See also Dissenting Opinion of Judge Oda, *ibid*, 270, [182].

[98] Judgment, [1982] ICJ Rep 60, [71].

[99] Kolb, *Case Law on Equitable Maritime Delimitation* 174.

[100] Dissenting Opinion of Judge Evensen, [1985] ICJ Rep 294, [14].

[101] ibid, 291, [12].

[102] ibid, 296, [15]. As Judge Evensen himself stated next, this view would lead to the corrective-equity approach taken in the arbitral award of 1977. Regarding Judge Oda, see ibid, 267, [176]. See also 261, [166–67].

[103] Writers also criticise this point. See for instance, Zoller, 'Recherche sur les méthodes' 677; LL Herman, 'The Court Giveth and the Court Taketh Away: An Analysis of the *Tunisia-Libya Continental Shelf* Case' (1984) 33 *ICLQ* 857; Kolb, *Case Law on Equitable Maritime Delimitation* 217–23.

relevant circumstances. The first and the most important factor was the conduct of the Parties. When each Party granted successive petroleum concessions, no actual overlapping claims appeared until 1974. The exploration activities were authorised by one Party without protests by the other until 1976. These activities created a *de facto* straight line dividing concessions areas at a bearing of approximately 26° to the meridian.[104] In the Court's view, thus, it must take into account line or lines which the Parties themselves may have considered equitable if only as an interim solution.[105] Secondly, there was a *modus-vivendi* line of delimitation concerning fisheries jurisdiction, which coincided with a *de facto* line similarly directed.[106] Although Tunisia claimed historic fishing rights, she could not oppose them to Libya east of the *modus-vivendi* line.[107] Thirdly, in the Court's view, the idea of drawing a line perpendicular to the coast and following the general direction of a land boundary provided relevant criteria.[108]

In summary, the *de facto* line being at an angle of 26° to the meridian was found to coincide with the *modus-vivendi* line concerning fisheries jurisdiction, which is perpendicular to the coast. In the Court's view, thus, the 26° line reflected all appropriate factors.[109] Accordingly, the Court suggested that line as a boundary of the continental shelf in the first sector. Having examined how far the 26° line should extend, the Court held that the line would turn at the height of the most westerly point of the shoreline (low-water mark) of the Gulf of Gabes on account of a marked change in direction of the coast (see Illustration 7).[110]

In the second zone, the major change of direction of the coast transforms, although not the whole way, the relation between Tunisia and Libya from one of adjacent States into one of opposite States. According to the Court, the relevant circumstances in the second zone consist in the general change in the direction of the Tunisian coast and in the existence and position of the Tunisian Kerkennah Islands. In its view, a line drawn from the most westerly point of the Gulf of Gabes seaward of and tangent to the outer Kerkennah Islands would run at angle of approximately 62° to the meridian. However, the Court considered that selecting such a line as the boundary of the continental shelf would give excessive weight to the Kerkennah Islands. Hence, it decided to give the latter a 'half-effect' by drawing a line bisecting the angle between the line of the Tunisian coast (42°) and the line along the seaward coast of the Kerkennah Islands (62°). Consequently, the line of delimitation in the second sector runs at an angle of 52° to the meridian.[111] Finally, having applied the test

[104] Judgment, [1982] ICJ Rep 83–84, [117].
[105] ibid, 84, [118].
[106] ibid, 84–85, [119].
[107] ibid, 70–71, [95]; 86, [121].
[108] ibid, 85, [120].
[109] ibid, 86, [121].
[110] ibid, 87, [124].
[111] ibid, 89, [129].

of proportionality to the line thus drawn, the Court concluded that that line met the requirements of the test.[112]

ii. Problem of the Illustrative Boundary

By taking a result-oriented equity approach, this case contrasts with the arbitral award of 1977. In fact, the Court, in the present case, never even used the equidistance method for beginning to draw the illustrative line of delimitation. In this regard, two comments are called for.

First, in the first zone, the *de facto* line of 26° played an important role. But it is not evident how this line can be justified as a continental shelf boundary from the viewpoint of international law. The Court failed to clarify the process of transforming mere facts into a legally binding line. In fact, as asked by Judge Oda, was it not a fact that this case was brought before the Court because the *de facto* line was not mutually satisfactory?[113] In addition, after having rejected any obligatory method, including that of equidistance, would it not be absurd to hold that the factors of perpendicularity to a coast and of prolongation of the general direction of the land boundary constitute relevant criteria?[114]

Secondly, the Court's reliance on geographical elements also invites criticism. Indeed, no reason was given for disregarding completely the island of Jerba, the low-tide elevations surrounding both the Kerkennah Islands and of Jerba, and the promontories of Zarzis.[115] Furthermore, as Judge Oda pointed out, the line of 52° in the second zone is highly problematical because this line completely neglects the Libyan coastline by relying solely on the Tunisian coast.[116] No explanation was given as to why the delimitation line should run parallel to the coast of Tunisia rather than to that of Libya.

Overall the Court exercised a large discretion in the process of illustrating the line of delimitation. This discretion generates a problem parallel to that of the lack of a specified method, which is the main feature of the result-oriented equity approach. As several judges noted, too much discretion carries the risk of assimilating judgments based on international law to *ex aequo et bono* decisions. Furthermore, as it relies extensively on the facts peculiar to the case in hand, this judgment is unlikely to provide a precedent for subsequent cases. As the facts are different in each case, it becomes difficult to formulate predictable

[112] ibid, 91, [131]. The judgment was given by 11 votes to 4.

[113] Dissenting Opinion of Judge Oda, ibid, 268, [177]. See also Kolb, *Case Law on Equitable Maritime Delimitation* 191.

[114] Furthermore, Judge Gros asked why the Court had not made any scientific use of the method of drawing a line perpendicular to the coast. Dissenting Opinion of Judge Gros, [1982] ICJ Rep 155, [21].

[115] Judge Evensen criticised this as a refashioning of nature. Dissenting Opinion of Judge Evensen, ibid, 300, [17].

[116] Dissenting Opinion of Judge Oda, ibid, 268–69, [179]. Kolb also criticised the judgment on this point. Kolb, *Case Law on Equitable Maritime Delimitation* 194. See also Herman, 'The Court Giveth and the Court Taketh Away' 830.

rules of maritime delimitation. This is another weak point of the result-oriented equity approach taken in this case.

IV. THE *LIBYA/MALTA* CASE (ICJ, 1985)

The fourth case that needs to be examined is the *Libya/Malta* case. In 1982, the Governments of Libya and Malta asked the ICJ to adjudge and declare:

> What principles and rules of international law are applicable to the delimitation of the area of the continental shelf which appertains to the Republic of Malta and the area of continental shelf which appertains to the Libyan Arab Republic, and how in practice such principles and rules can be applied by the two Parties in this particular case in order that they may without difficulty delimit such areas by an agreement as provided in Article III (Article I of Special Agreement)?[117]

As a preliminary question, there was divergence between the Parties with respect to the second part of the request, relating to the way in which in practice such principles and rules could be applied. While Malta had wished the Court to draw the delimitation line, Libya had asked it only to pronounce on the principles and rules of international law applicable without constructing a delimitation line. In considering this question, the Court noted that it was asked to show how principles and rules can ensure a delimitation of areas 'without difficulty'. In order to accomplish this task, the Court decided to indicate an appropriate method or methods and to draw an illustrative approximate line so as to show how such a method or methods should be applied.[118]

A second preliminary problem was the existence of specific claims of a third State, Italy. In 1984, the ICJ had dismissed Italy's request to intervene under Article 62 of the Statute of the Court. In this regard, the two Parties had agreed that the Court should not feel inhibited from extending its decision to all areas which were claimed by them. The Court held, however, that the decision must be limited to a geographical area in which no third State claims exist, since the Special Agreement requested only a definition of the principles and rules applicable to a delimitation of the continental shelf 'which appertains' to each Party.[119] Consequently, the Court confined its jurisdiction to an area between 13°30' E Longitude and 15°10' E Longitude (see Illustration 8).[120] It then turned to the substance of the case.

[117] *Continental Shelf (Libyan Arab Jamahiriya v Malta)* (the *Libya/Malta* case), [1985] ICJ Rep 13, 16, [2]. Unlike what had occurred in the *Tunisia/Libya* case, the Special Agreement contained no reference to the indication of a method or methods of delimitation.

[118] ibid, 24, [19].

[119] ibid, 25–26, [21].

[120] ibid, 26, [22]. Regarding the problems claimed by third States in the *Libya/Malta* case, see below, ch 7, s VII.

A. Law Applicable to the Continental Shelf Delimitation

i. The Court's Approach to Equitable Principles

In the present case, while Malta was a Party to the 1958 Geneva Convention on the Continental Shelf, Libya was not. Thus, as both Parties agreed, the dispute was to be governed by customary law. There was no doubt that the law applicable was the customary law of equitable principles. According to the Court, 'judicial decisions are at one – and the Parties themselves agree (paragraph 29 above) – in holding that the delimitation of a continental shelf boundary must be effected by the application of equitable principles in all the relevant circumstances in order to achieve an equitable result.'[121] The real issue was, however, the Court's approach to equitable principles. In considering this issue, it is necessary to examine, first, the contentions of the Parties.

Libya based its arguments on the concept of natural prolongation. According to Libya, there existed a fundamental discontinuity in the sea-bed and subsoil, a so-called 'rift zone', which divided the areas of continental shelf into two distinct natural prolongations. Accordingly, in Libya's view, the delimitation of the continental shelf between Libya and Malta should follow the 'rift zone'.[122] The Court, however, rejected this argument:

> [S]ince the development of the law enables a State to claim that the continental shelf appertaining to it extends up to as far as 200 miles from its coast, whatever the geological characteristics of the corresponding sea-bed and subsoil, there is no reason to ascribe any role to geological or geophysical factors within that distance either in verifying the legal title of the State concerned or in proceeding to a delimitation as between their claims.[123]

In this context, the Court took into account the emergence of the EEZ. In fact, the Court stated that, since there cannot be an EEZ without a corresponding continental shelf, the distance criterion must be applied to the continental shelf as well as the EEZ.[124] In this regard, the decline of the role of natural prolongation in the delimitation of the continental shelf may prove definitive.

Basing itself on the distance criterion, Malta asserted that the delimitation of the continental shelf should be effected by recourse to the equidistance method. At first sight, the Maltese view appears to follow the argument of the Court, stressing as it does the use of the distance criterion within a distance of 200 miles from the baselines from which the breadth of the territorial sea is measured. Nevertheless, the Court rejected Malta's argument as well:

> The Court is unable to accept that, even as a preliminary and provisional step towards the drawing of a delimitation line, the equidistance method is one which

[121] [1985] ICJ Rep 38, [45].
[122] ibid, 34, [36].
[123] ibid, 35, [39].
[124] ibid, 33, [34].

> *must* be used, or that the Court is 'required, as a first step, to examine the effects of a delimitation by application of the equidistance method' (ICJ Reports 1982, page 79, paragraph 110). Such a rule would come near to an espousal of the idea of 'absolute proximity', which was rejected by the Court in 1969 (see ICJ Reports 1969, page 30, paragraph 41), and which has since, moreover, failed of acceptance at the Third United Nations Conference on the Law of the Sea.[125]

Furthermore, having touched on the State practice embodying the equidistance method, the Court held that that practice fell short of proving the existence of a rule characterising the equidistance method as obligatory.[126] Thus, rejecting the obligatory force of the equidistance method even at the preliminary stage, the Court discarded the corrective-equity approach taken in the 1977 arbitral award and followed the same approach as the 1969 and 1982 judgments, ie, result-oriented equity. In fact, having noted that, as had been held in the *Tunisia/Libya* case, the term 'equitable' characterised both the result to be achieved and the means to be applied, the Court put the accent on the former, stating that: 'It is however the goal – the equitable result – and not the means used to achieve it, that must be the primary element in this duality of characterisation.'[127] The emphasis on the goal to be achieved is in line with the *Tunisia/Libya* judgment.

ii. Contents of Equitable Principles

As already pointed out by the dissenters in the *North Sea Continental Shelf* cases, the main disadvantage of equitable principles is the vagueness of their substance. In response, the Court, in the *Libya/Malta* case, attempted to clarify these principles:

> [T]he justice of which equity is an emanation, is not abstract justice but justice according to the rule of law; which is to say that its application should display consistency and a degree of predictability; even though it looks with particularity to the peculiar circumstances of an instant case, it also looks beyond it to principles of more general application.[128]

The stress on 'consistency and a degree of predictability' shows a desire of surmounting the subjectivity of the concept of equitable principles. The Court then illustrated 'some well-known examples':

(i) there is to be no refashioning of geography nor compensation for the inequalities of nature;
(ii) one party should not encroach on the natural prolongation of the other Party;
(iii) all relevant circumstances must be considered;

[125] ibid, 37, [43].
[126] ibid, 38, [44].
[127] ibid, 38–39, [45].
[128] ibid, 39, [45].

(iv) equity does not necessarily imply equality; and
(v) there can be no question of distributive justice.[129]

These items call for at least three comments. First, with respect to the second element, it is not evident how one is to reconcile the principle of non-encroachment and the distance criterion on a continental shelf of less than 200 miles. Secondly, the rejection of distributive justice would be difficult to justify even in the *North Sea Continental Shelf* cases, as was shown in the previous chapter. Thirdly, the other three sub-principles are anything but self-evident, and they do not seem to be helpful in specific delimitation processes owing to their highly abstract character.[130] The fundamental weakness of the Court's approach is that, as was shown in the *Tunisia/Libya* case, no method is included within the framework of equitable principles. However, the line of argument by the Court was to change radically at the stage of delimitation.

B. Application of the Law Identified

i. Establishment of the Illustrative Continental Shelf Boundary

At the stage of establishing the boundary of the continental shelf, the Court affirmed the existence of a link between legal title and method of delimitation.[131] The Court then examined the equities of the distance criterion, which is regarded as a legal title to a continental shelf of less than 200 miles, and of the results to which its application may lead. Having noted that the appropriateness of a median line for delimitation between opposite coasts had already been admitted in the *North Sea Continental Shelf* cases, the Court accepted the application of the equidistance method at a provisional stage. In the words of the Court:

> It is clear that, in these circumstances [delimitation between States with opposite coasts], the tracing of a median line between those coasts, by way of a provisional step in a process to be continued by other operations, is the most judicious manner of proceeding with a view to the eventual achievement of an equitable result.[132]

This shows a clear contrast to the *Tunisia/Libya* case, in which the equidistance method was completely discarded. It appears that the Court now gave special prominence to the equidistance method.[133] However, it immediately added that

[129] ibid, 39–40, [46].
[130] Several authors agree. E Decaux, 'L'arrêt de la Cour international de Justice dans l'affaire du plateau continental (Libye/Malte), Arrêt du 3 juin 1985' (1985) 31 *AFDI* 307; TL McDorman, 'The Libya-Malta Case: Opposite States Confront the Court' (1986) 24 *Canadian Yearbook of International Law* 348.
[131] [1985] ICJ Rep 46–47, [61]. The relationship between legal title and methods of delimitation will be examined in ch 6, s III of this book.
[132] [1985] ICJ Rep 47, [62].
[133] McDorman, 'The Libya-Malta Case' 351.

the equidistance method is neither the only method applicable to the present dispute, nor does it even benefit from a presumption in its favour.[134]

In any event the Court began the delimitation process by drawing a provisional median line as a first stage, without regard to the uninhabited Maltese island of Filfla. Then, at a second stage, the Court turned to the question of modifying this provisional line. According to the Court, the median line was to be adjusted by pushing it northward in favour of Libya on the basis of three factors: the considerable disparity between the coastal lengths of the two Parties,[135] the general geographical context, in which Malta appears as a relatively small feature in a semi-enclosed sea,[136] and the considerable distance between the coasts.[137] On account of these factors, as a second step, the Court would consider the extent of the required northward shift of the delimitation line. This is the very approach of corrective equity followed in the *Anglo–French Continental Shelf* case. In this respect, one may find a change in the approach from the result-oriented equity approach to the corrective-equity approach, even though the Court did not explicitly say so.

In this connection, the Court first examined the limits of the extent of the northward shift. In so doing, it raised the hypothetical question of delimitation between Libya and Italy if the Maltese islands were a part of Italy. If a median line were to be drawn between Libya and Sicily, without giving any effect to the islands of Malta, such a line would be at 15°10' E Longitude at 34°36' N Latitude. Nevertheless, as Malta is in reality an independent State, it is inconceivable that a continental shelf boundary between Malta and Libya would be located to the north of the notional median line. Thus, in the Court's view, the outside limit of the northward shift consists of the notional median line.[138]

The equidistance line between Malta and Libya, which would be adjusted northward, was located at 15°10' E Longitude and approximately 34°12' N Latitude. Accordingly, an equitable boundary between Malta and Libya had to be located between the outside limit of 15°10' E Longitude at 34°36' N Latitude and the median line between Libya and Malta at 34°12' N Latitude of the same meridian. At this point, there is a 24' difference of latitude. The Court then concluded that the equitable boundary would be a line produced by translating the median line northwards by 18', which amounts to three-quarters of that difference (see Illustration 9).[139] Finally, having applied the proportionality test, the Court reached the conclusion that the line thus found resulted in no evident disproportion.[140] Nevertheless, a question which arises is why the provisional

[134] [1985] ICJ Rep 47, [63].
[135] ibid, 50, [68].
[136] ibid, 50, [69].
[137] ibid, 52, [73].
[138] ibid, 51–52, [72].
[139] ibid, 52, [73]. See also Fietta and Cleverly, *A Practitioner's Guide* 294.
[140] [1985] ICJ Rep 55, [75]. The Judgment was handed down by a vote of 14 to 3.

median line had to be shifted by 18' northward.[141] The Court failed to explain this matter. Were the extent of a shift of the equidistance line to be decided without reasonable legal basis,[142] as is the case with the result-oriented equity approach, the corrective-equity approach would run the risk of subjectivity.

ii. Evaluation

The Court, in the *Libya/Malta* case, explicitly rejected the obligatory character of the equidistance method and stressed the goal of equitable results rather than the means of achieving such a result. In so doing, the judgment took the result-oriented equity approach, following the line of argument in the *Tunisia/Libya* case. It is true that the Court, in the present case, attempted to clarify equitable principles by illustrating some sub-principles. Yet these sub-principles led to no method of delimitation. In this sense, the Court's attempt still remains within the framework of the result-oriented equity approach.

At the stage of establishing the continental shelf boundary, however, the Court applied the equidistance method as a first provisional step, and the equidistance line was adjusted in a second stage on account of relevant circumstances. In so doing, the Court adopted, at the operational stage, the corrective-equity approach for the delimitation of opposite coasts, while following the result-oriented-equity approach in principle. In this sense, the *Libya/Malta* case has a hybrid character since two approaches were used.

[141] Separate Opinion of Judge Mbaye, ibid, 100; Dissenting Opinion of Judge Schwebel, 181–84; In addition, on this point, Judge Oda drew attention to the curious coincidence that the northern latitude of the shifted line, at 34°30'N Latitude, is at the same point as the southwestern corner of the Italian claim in the Ionian Sea. ibid, 137, [23]. Decaux supposes that the location of the adjustment had already been predetermined when the Court limited its jurisdiction in order not to prejudice the Italian claim. Decaux, 'L'arrêt de la Cour international de Justice dans l'affaire du plateau continental (Libye/Malte)' 320.

[142] Judge Schwebel criticised the majority opinion, saying that: 'In my view, the Court shows no such relevant circumstances; ... Rather, the Court's judgment conspicuously fails to invoke and objectively apply relevant circumstances which specifically or measurably justify, still less require, correction of the median line.' Dissenting Opinion of Judge Schwebel, [1985] ICJ Rep 179. Furthermore, Judge Mosler considered that in the present case, if one discarded island of Filfla, there was no other factor which called for a correction of the median line. Dissenting Opinion of Judge Mosler, ibid, 120.

5

The Methodology of Maritime Delimitation in the Jurisprudence II: Single/Coincident Maritime Boundaries

I. THE *GULF OF MAINE* CASE (UNITED STATES/CANADA, ICJ, 1984)

THE FIRST INSTANCE involving a single maritime boundary is the *Gulf of Maine* case of 1984. By Special Agreement of 29 March 1979, Canada and the United States requested a Chamber of the ICJ to establish a single maritime boundary dividing the continental shelf and the exclusive fishery zone (EFZ) of the two countries.[1] The *Gulf of Maine* case is different from preceding maritime delimitation cases brought before the ICJ for five reasons. First and most importantly, this was the first time that an international court was ever asked to determine a 'single maritime boundary' applicable both to the seabed and to the superjacent water column beyond the limits of the territorial sea.[2] Secondly, the Chamber was requested not only to indicate the applicable principles and rules of international law, but also to determine the delimitation line.[3] Thirdly, contrary to what had happened in the preceding cases submitted to the ICJ, both Canada and the United States had ratified the 1958 Convention on the Continental Shelf. This would raise the issue of the applicability of the Convention to the single maritime boundary. Fourthly, in this case, an EFZ rather than an EEZ was involved. Finally, this was the first case in the history of the ICJ in which the Chamber of the Court was being used.[4]

[1] *Delimitation of the Maritime Boundary in the Gulf of Maine Area (Canada v United States of America)* (the *Gulf of Maine* case), [1984] ICJ Rep 246, 253–55. It should be noted that the Special Agreement fixed an exact starting point for the line (point A) and requiring that the boundary should end at the Atlantic coast somewhere within a predetermined triangle. ibid, 253.

[2] According to the Special Agreement, 'the single boundary line to be drawn should be applicable to all aspects of the jurisdiction of the coastal State, not only jurisdiction as defined by international law in its present state, but also as it will be defined in the future.' ibid, 267, [26].

[3] Art II(2) of the Special Agreement, ibid, 253.

[4] The Chamber was composed as follows: Judge Ago, President; Judges Gros, Mosler and Schwebel; Judge ad hoc Cohen.

A. Law Applicable to the Single Maritime Boundary

i. Three Levels of Structure in the Chamber's Reasoning and its Problems

In accepting the Parties' request for the delimitation of a single maritime boundary, the Chamber stated that it '[was] of the opinion that there is certainly no rule of international law to the contrary, and, in the present case, there is no material impossibility in drawing a boundary of this kind. There can thus be no doubt that the Chamber can carry out the operation requested of it.'[5] The essential issue was, however, whether there existed in international law any rule prescribing *how* such a single maritime boundary should be established. In this connection, the Chamber referred to a 'fundamental norm' applicable to *every* delimitation between neighbouring States, including single maritime boundaries:

> (1) No maritime delimitation between States with opposite or adjacent coasts may be effected unilaterally by one of those States. Such delimitation must be sought and effected by means of an agreement, following negotiations conducted in good faith and with the genuine intention of achieving a positive result. Where, however, such agreement cannot be achieved, delimitation should be effected by recourse to a third party possessing the necessary competence.
>
> (2) In either case, delimitation is to be effected by the application of equitable criteria and by the use of practical methods capable of ensuring, with regard to the geographic configuration of the area and other relevant circumstances, an equitable result.[6]

As the fundamental norm is highly abstract, there was a need to further explore the specific international law applicable. The starting point was an examination of the Geneva Convention on the Continental Shelf, which both States had subscribed to. If the dispute had been limited to the delimitation of the continental shelf, there would have been no doubt as to the mandatory application of Article 6 of the relevant Geneva Convention. The purpose in this case was, however, to identify a single maritime boundary for the continental shelf and the EFZ. Thus, according to the Chamber, the Geneva Convention on the Continental Shelf 'cannot have such mandatory force even between States which are Parties to the Convention, as regards a maritime boundary concerning a much wider subject-matter than the continental shelf alone.'[7]

Furthermore, the Chamber examined whether a specific method of delimitation could be deduced from the conduct of the Parties, and answered this question negatively.[8] Consequently, there was neither treaty law nor any other rule to apply certain criteria or to use certain particular methods for the

[5] [1984] ICJ Rep 267, [27].
[6] ibid, 299–300, [112].
[7] ibid, 303, [124].
[8] ibid, 303–12, [126–54].

establishment of a single maritime boundary.[9] Thus, at the second stage, the Chamber resorted to equitable criteria.

The most important fact to bear in mind is that the single maritime boundary in this case has a twofold objective. Accordingly, there is a possibility that a criterion suitable to the delimitation of continental shelf is different from one appropriate for that of the EFZ.[10] To avoid this problem, the Chamber adopted 'neutral' criteria:

> In reality, a delimitation by a single line, such as that which has to be carried out in the present case, ie, a delimitation which has to apply at one and the same time to the continental shelf and to the superjacent water column can only be carried out by the application of a criterion, or combination of criteria, which does not give preferential treatment to one of these two objects to the detriment of the other, and at the same time is such as to be equally suitable to the division of either of them.[11]

Consequently, the application of any criteria derived from, for instance, ecological or geological elements was excluded because such criteria would only relate to the water column or to the seabed, respectively.

The last stage consists in examining the practical method. According to the Chamber, just as the criteria are basically founded upon geography, the practical methods can likewise only be methods appropriate for use against a background of geography. Furthermore, like the underlying criteria, the methods must be suitable for the delimitation of both the seabed and the superjacent waters. Hence, the Chamber adopted a 'geometrical method'.[12]

In summary, the Chamber extrapolated the law applicable to the single maritime boundary at three levels: (i) fundamental norm, (ii) equitable criteria, and (iii) practical method. However, three issues arise with respect to the three-levelled reasoning of the Chamber.

The first issue is that of ascertaining where the fundamental norm derives from. In this regard, the Chamber held that: 'A more useful course is to seek a better formulation of the fundamental norm on which the Parties were fortunate enough to be agreed, and whose existence in the legal convictions not only of the Parties to the present dispute, but of all States, is apparent from an examination of the realities of international legal relations.'[13] In light of its formulation, the

[9] ibid, 312, [155].

[10] In this connection, Judge Ago, President, put the following question to both Parties: '[i]n the event that one particular method, or set of methods, should appear appropriate for the delimitation of the continental shelf, for that of the exclusive fishery zones, what do the Parties consider to be the legal grounds that might be invoked for preferring one or the other in seeking to determine a single line?' In its reply, the United States mentioned that circumstances relevant to the functional effectiveness of a boundary relating to both the water column and the sea-bed should be given greater weight than circumstances relating to only one of them. On the other hand, Canada stated that preference as to method should be dictated by the relevant circumstances on each of the two areas. ibid, 314–15, [161].

[11] ibid, 327, [194]. See also 326, [193].

[12] ibid, 329, [199].

[13] ibid, 299, [111].

fundamental norm is nothing but customary law. It is questionable, however, whether there was sufficient State practice and *opinio juris* to assert such a fundamental norm as customary law.[14]

The second issue lies in the rejection of the Geneva Convention on the Continental Shelf. In this regard, the question to be examined was the intention of the Parties when they asked for a single maritime boundary in their Special Agreement. They could have meant that, in the area concerned, the Geneva Convention in question was to be wholly ignored by the application of the *lex posterior* principle. Conversely, as a second interpretation, it was possible that they meant that the Special Agreement and the Geneva Convention were to be read together. If the parties intended that, the Chamber should have applied the Geneva Convention regarding the continental shelf delimitation, and as a next step, have examined whether the FZ delimitation also pointed to the 'equidistant–special circumstances' rule.[15] Yet the Chamber rejected the application of the Geneva Convention without clarifying the relationship between the latter and the Special Agreement. The obligation to apply the Geneva Convention, in force between the Parties, cannot be evaded on the pretext that it would not be applicable to the EFZ. The Special Agreement requesting the single maritime boundary did not exclude explicitly the application of the Geneva Convention.[16]

Thirdly, the validity of 'neutral' criteria should be examined. The Chamber adopted criteria which do not give preferential treatment to one of the two delimitation objects because of the twofold character of the single maritime boundary. The question is, however, where the criteria are derived from. In fact, there is no positive law and little State practice to support the existence of 'neutral' criteria.[17] Another question is how one is to consider the relationship between 'neutral' criteria and economic considerations concerning natural resources which are at the core of the continental shelf and the EFZ concepts. As we shall see later, the Chamber tested the equitableness of an established line from the viewpoint of, in particular, fishery resources on Georges Bank. Consequently, the Chamber observed that there were absolutely no conditions of an exceptional kind which might justify any correction of the delimitation line it had drawn.[18] This appears to suggest that, if there are 'conditions of an exceptional kind', the delimitation line resulting from 'neutral' criteria might be corrected.

[14] HWA Thirlway, 'The Law and Procedure of the International Court of Justice 1960–89: Part Six' (1994) 65 *BYIL* 67.

[15] ibid, 66.

[16] See also Dissenting Opinion of Judge Gros, [1984] ICJ Rep 369, [14]; R Kolb, *Case Law on Equitable Maritime Delimitation: Digest and Commentaries* (The Hague, Brill/Nijhoff, 2003) 246.

[17] Thirlway, 'The Law and Procedure: Part Six,' 69.

[18] [1984] ICJ Rep 344, [241].

ii. The Chamber's Approach to the Law Applicable to Single Maritime Boundary

The next issue relates to the Chamber's approach to the law governing to the single maritime boundary. As has been seen, the second part of the fundamental norm includes three elements: (i) equitable criteria, (ii) a practical method, and (iii) an equitable result.[19] In the Chamber's formulation, 'an equitable result' should be achieved by resort to 'equitable criteria' and a 'practical method'. According to the Chamber, there has been no systematic definition of equitable criteria because of their highly variable adaptability to different concrete situations.[20] The essential fact is that:

> [T]he criteria in question are not themselves rules of law and therefore mandatory in the different situations, but 'equitable', or even 'reasonable', criteria, and that what international law requires is that recourse be had in each case to the criterion, or the balance of different criteria, appearing to be most appropriate to the concrete situation.[21]

In the Chamber's view, 'equitable criteria' are, thus, excluded from the legal domain. The same is true regarding the 'practical method', since the latter would be selected on a case-by-case basis, relying on actual situations.[22] Consequently, according to the Chamber, the law defines neither the equitable criteria nor the practical method, simply advancing the idea of 'an equitable result'. In so doing, it could be contended that the Chamber followed the result-oriented equity approach.

The Chamber's arguments run parallel to its rejection of the customary-law character of Article 6 of the Convention on the Continental Shelf. Canada had advocated the application of Article 6 of the Convention of the Continental Shelf as a particular expression of a general norm. Yet, the Chamber rejected the Canadian argument by stating that: 'To accept this idea would amount to transforming the "combined equidistance–special circumstances rule" into a rule of general international law, and thus one capable of numerous applications, whereas there is no trace in international custom of such a transformation having occurred.'[23] Thus the Chamber clearly rejected the corrective-equity approach used in the *Anglo–French Continental Shelf* case. One should note that the Chamber's argument in favour of the result-oriented equity approach calls for the same criticisms as those advanced by the dissenters in the *Tunisia/Libya* case.[24]

[19] However, the distinction between equitable criteria and practical methods appears to be artificial.
[20] [1984] ICJ Rep 312, [157].
[21] ibid, 313, [158].
[22] The Chamber stated that 'there is no single method which intrinsically brings greater justice or is of greater practical usefulness.' ibid, 315, [162]. 'Nor is there any method of which it can be said that it must receive priority.' ibid, [163].
[23] ibid, 302, [122].
[24] See Dissenting Opinion of Judge Gros, ibid, 377, [26].

B. Application of the Law Identified

The Chamber proceeded in two steps for drawing the delimitation line. The first was the establishment of the single maritime boundary in three distinct segments; the second was the testing of the equitable character of the boundary.

i. Operational Stage

The Parties selected the obligatory starting-point (44°11′12″ north, 67° 16′ 46″), called point A. According to the Parties, this point was the first point of intersection of the two lines representing the limits of the fishing zones claimed by Canada and the United States, respectively.[25] In the first segment (points A to B), the Chamber adopted the method of drawing, from point A, two perpendiculars to the two basic coastlines, namely, a line from Cape Elizabeth to the international boundary terminus and a line running thence to Cape Sable. At point A, those two perpendiculars form an acute angle of approximately 82° and a reflex angle of approximately 278°. It is the bisector of this second angle which forms the first segment of the delimitation line.[26]

In the second segment, the Chamber drew an equidistance line, and subsequently adjusted it on account of relevant circumstances. In this sector, the coasts of the two States are opposite each other. 'In such a geographical situation,' the Chamber stated, 'the application of any method of geometrical origin, no matter which, including that pronounced in paragraph 1 of Article 6 of the 1958 Convention, can in practice only result in the drawing of a median delimitation line.'[27] Thus the Chamber drew a median line between the line which links Cape Ann to the elbow of Cape Cod and the line which joins up Brier Island and Cape Sable. Then, it adjusted the median line provisionally drawn taking into account relevant circumstances. The first factor to be considered was the different length of coastlines. The ratio between the coastal fronts of the United States and Canada was 1.38 to 1. In the Chamber's view, the median line should be shifted toward the Canadian coast in such a way as to reflect this ratio. But, there was another factor to be taken into consideration, namely, Seal Island located off Nova Scotia. The Chamber ruled that it was appropriate to give the island half effect. As a result, the ratio to be applied would be approximately 1.32 to 1. Thus, the Chamber corrected the median line by shifting it toward the Canadian coast in accordance with the above-mentioned ratio.[28] This line, beginning where it intersects with the end of the first segment,

[25] Judgment, ibid, 265, [20].

[26] ibid, 333, [213].

[27] ibid, 334, [216].

[28] Kolb indicated that the Chamber must have corrected the line in the second sector as a function of the desired arrival point of the line in light of its prolongation into the third sector. If this was the case, the triangle imposed by the parties as an end-point had a heavy influence on this state of affairs. Kolb, *Case Law on Equitable Maritime Delimitation*, 268.

ends at the closing line of the Gulf of Maine (points B to C).[29] It is worth noting that, in the second segment of opposite coasts, the Chamber took the corrective-equity approach, regardless of its rejection when it had dealt with the applicable law.

Finally, in the third sector, the Chamber drew a delimitation line which coincided with a line perpendicular to the closing line of the Gulf of Maine. This line reaches the last point of the overlapping area of the 200-mile zone claimed by the Parties (points C to D) (see Illustration 10).[30]

ii. Verification Stage

As a verification stage, the Chamber examined non-geographical factors, which had been excluded at the operational stage, to test whether the result could be considered as intrinsically equitable. The question was whether the result might 'unexpectedly be revealed as radically inequitable, that is to say, as likely to entail catastrophic repercussions for the livelihood and economic well-being of the populations of the countries concerned.'[31] The Chamber concluded that this was not the case.[32]

II. THE *GUINEA/GUINEA-BISSAU* CASE (ARBITRATION, 1985)

The second instance to be examined is the *Guinea/Guinea-Bissau* case of 1985.[33] This arbitration first raised the question of whether the Convention of 1886 entered into by France and Portugal established the maritime boundary between Guinea and Guinea-Bissau in West Africa. The Arbitral Tribunal decided that a Convention of 1886 had not established a general maritime boundary. Thus, in the second part, the Tribunal had to answer the following question: '[W]hat is the course of the boundary between the maritime territories appertaining respectively to the Republic of Guinea-Bissau and the People's Revolutionary Republic of Guinea?'[34] Accordingly, the Tribunal was to draw the precise course of a single maritime boundary between the territorial sea, the continental shelf and the EEZ appertaining to each State.[35]

[29] [1984] ICJ Rep 334–37, [217–23].

[30] ibid, 337–39, [224–29]. For an illustration of the construction of the single maritime boundary by the Chamber, see S Fietta and R Cleverly, *A Practitioner's Guide to Maritime Boundary Delimitation* (hereinafter *A Practitioner's Guide*) (Oxford University Press, 2016) 257.

[31] [1984] ICJ Rep 342, [237].

[32] ibid, 344, [240].

[33] Case concerning the delimitation of the maritime boundary between Guinea and Guinea-Bissau, Decision of 14 February 1985. For the text of the decision, see (1990) 19 *RIAA* 149; (1985) 89 *RGDIP* 484. The French text is the authentic one. English translation is available in (1986) 25 *ILM* 251. In this book, quotations of this decision are in the English language text to enhance comprehension. The Tribunal was composed of: Manfred Lachs, President, Kéba Mbaye, and Mohammed Bedjaoui.

[34] Art 2. *ILM*, ibid, 256.

[35] ibid, 272, [42]. See also 289, [86].

A. Law Applicable to the Single Maritime Boundary

Although the Parties had not ratified the Geneva Convention on the Continental Shelf, and although the LOSC had not yet entered into force, they invoked the relevant provisions of these two texts as being consistent with the evolution of international custom brought about by the contemporary trends of the law of the sea, which the Tribunal had thus to consider.[36] For the Tribunal,

> the essential objective consists of finding an equitable solution with reference to the provisions of Article 74, paragraph 1, and Article 83, paragraph 1, of the Convention of 10 December 1982 on the Law of the Sea. This is a rule of international law which is recognised by the Parties and which compels recognition by the Tribunal.[37]

The question of interest here was whether the law prescribed the specific method or methods to draw a delimitation line. In reserving the possibility of modification on account of relevant circumstances, Guinea-Bissau advocated recourse to the equidistance method, while Guinea rejected this. Following the *Gulf of Maine* case, the Tribunal denied the obligatory character of the equidistance method.[38] According to the Tribunal,

> [t]he factors and methods referred to result from legal rules, although they evolve from physical, mathematical, historical, political, economic or other factors. However, they are not restricted in number and none of them is obligatory for the Tribunal, since each case of delimitation is a *unicum*, as has been emphasised by the International Court of Justice.[39]

In this statement, it is possible to identify basic features of the result-oriented equity approach, ie, rejection of any obligatory method and recourse to a case-by-case solution to achieve equitable results. Thus the Tribunal in the present case appears to have followed that of the Chamber in the *Gulf of Maine* case.

B. Application of the Law Identified

In the Tribunal's view, the essential factors taken into account were geographical circumstances: the length of the coastlines, the coastal configuration and orientation, and the existence of islands. In considering these geographical factors, the Tribunal established three types of lines (see Illustration 11): (i) a delimitation line following the 'southern limit' of the 1886 Convention, ie, the Pilots' Pass from the mouth of the Cajet River (points 1 to 2); (ii) the parallel of 10° 40′ north latitude as far as 12 miles west of the Guinean island of Alcatraz

[36] ibid, 272, [43].
[37] ibid, 289, [88].
[38] ibid, 294, [102].
[39] ibid, 289–90, [89]. Underline original.

(points 2 to 3); and (iii) a *grosso modo* perpendicular line to the general direction of the coastline, ie, a line joining Pointe des Almadies and Cape Shilling (point 3).[40] Formally, the Tribunal did not refer to the equidistance method in any of the segments. Nevertheless, a perpendicular line to the general direction of the coast is nothing but an equidistance line based on the coast thus simplified.[41] In this sense, it may be said that, in the present award, the equidistance method was partly applied to the delimitation between States with adjacent coasts.

In a next stage, the Tribunal verified whether this delimitation line effectively led to an equitable result. This double-stage approach is a re-run of the *Gulf of Maine* case. In contrast to the former, however, the Tribunal examined the structure and nature of the continental shelf.[42] It then concluded that the natural prolongation factor was irrelevant because the continental shelf in question was one and same.[43] Related to this, it indicated that: '[T]he rule of natural prolongation can be effectively invoked for purposes of delimitation only where there is a separation of continental shelves.'[44] This *dictum* seems to imply that if there had been such a separation, a natural break could determine the extent of the continental shelf. In that case, should the single maritime boundary be shifted according to the natural prolongation or should the maritime boundaries be different for the seabed and the superjacent waters? The question remained open.

III. THE *ST PIERRE AND MIQUELON* CASE (FRANCE/CANADA, ARBITRATION, 1992)

The *Guinea/Guinea-Bissau* case was followed by another arbitration regarding single maritime boundary, that is, *St Pierre and Miquelon* arbitration between France and Canada.[45] On 30 March 1989, Canada and France concluded an agreement requesting the Arbitral Tribunal to establish 'a single (maritime) delimitation which shall govern all rights and jurisdiction which the Parties may

[40] ibid, 298, [111].

[41] Kolb, *Case Law on Equitable Maritime Delimitation*, 302. See also T Cottier, *Equitable Principles of Maritime Boundary Delimitation: The Quest for Distributive Justice in International Law* (Cambridge University Press, 2015) 195.

[42] The *Guinea/Guinea-Bissau* case, (1986) 25 *ILM* 299, [114].

[43] ibid, 300, [117].

[44] ibid, [116].

[45] *Case concerning the Delimitation of Maritime Areas between Canada and France* (hereafter the *St. Pierre and Miquelon* arbitral award), 10 June 1992, (1997) 21 *RIAA* 265. The English text, which was provided by the Canadian Department of Justice, was reproduced in (1992) 31 *ILM* 1145. In this book, quotations of this decision are in the English language text. While the English text referred to the term 'the Court of Arbitration', the French text of the arbitral award published in *RIAA* used the term 'le Tribunal d'arbitrage'. In this book, the term 'the Arbitral Tribunal' will be used when examining the *St Pierre and Miquelon* case.

exercise under international law in these maritime areas,' that is, those around St Pierre and Miquelon. The Arbitral Tribunal '[should] describe the course of this delimitation in a technically precise manner.'[46] This was the third case where a single maritime boundary was to be established for the continental shelf and the EFZ/EEZ. As in the *Gulf of Maine* case, both Parties had ratified the Geneva Convention on the Continental Shelf.

A. Law Applicable to the Single Maritime Boundary

First, the Arbitral Tribunal, as in the *Gulf of Maine* case, referred to the fundamental norm agreed by the Parties. According to that norm, the delimitation should 'be effected in accordance with equitable principles, or equitable criteria, taking account of all the relevant circumstances, in order to achieve an equitable result. The underlying premise of this fundamental norm is the emphasis on equity and the rejection of any obligatory method.'[47] This view echoes the *Gulf of Maine* case, where a result-oriented equity approach had been used.

Secondly, the Arbitral Tribunal had to examine what criteria concretised the fundamental norm. The Parties disagreed on this matter. While Canada invoked the principle of non-encroachment and proportionality, France contended that Article 6 of the Convention on the Continental Shelf was applicable to the present case.[48] In this respect, as in the *Gulf of Maine* case, the Tribunal denied the applicability of the Convention on the Continental Shelf, which both Parties had ratified.[49] It then stressed the principal role of geographical factors. For the Tribunal, '[g]eographical features are at the heart of the delimitation process,'[50] and 'the criteria governing delimitation are to be found primarily in the geographical facts.'[51] In addition, the Tribunal rejected a Canadian argument based on the physical structure of the sea-bed, stating that that structure ceases to be important when the object is to establish a single, all-purpose delimitation of both the sea-bed and the superjacent waters.[52] It could be said that this was the adoption of 'neutral' criteria.

[46] Art 2(1) and (2) of the Agreement Establishing a Court of Arbitration [an Arbitral Tribunal] for the Purpose of Carrying Out the Delimitation of Maritime Areas Between France and Canada. The *St Pierre and Miquelon* arbitral award, (1992) 31 *ILM* 1151–52. The members of the Tribunal were: Eduardo Jiménez de Aréchaga, President; Judges Gaetano Arangio-Ruiz; Oscar Schachter; Prosper Weil, appointed by French Government; Allan E Gotlieb, appointed by the Canadian Government. In 1977, France claimed an EEZ, while Canada declared a FZ. ibid, 1158, [14].

[47] ibid, 1163, [38].

[48] ibid, 1166, [56]; 1163, [39].

[49] ibid, 1163, [40].

[50] ibid, 1160, [24].

[51] ibid, 1173, [83].

[52] ibid, 1165, [47].

B. Application of the Law Identified

As in the preceding cases, the Arbitral Tribunal first drew a single maritime boundary and, secondly, verified its equitableness.

i. Operational Stage

The Arbitral Tribunal examined separately two different sectors of the delimitation area (see Illustration 12). In the first sector (points 9 to J), the area west of St Pierre and Miquelon, a straight line ran from point 9 of the delimitation referred to in Article 8 of the 1972 Agreement to point D. This is the equidistance line between the Island of Newfoundland and St Pierre and Miquelon. But the Tribunal offered scant explanation why it applied the equidistance method in this segment. From points D to J, it 'granted' to St Pierre and Miquelon an additional 12 nautical miles from the limit of its territorial sea for its EEZ. As a consequence, a line which links points D to J follows circles of a 24-mile radius centred on the nearest points on the baseline of the French islands. That area was to have the breadth of the contiguous zone referred to in Article 33 of the LOSC.[53] In this regard, the question which arises is why the breadth of the French economic zone was determined with reference to the breadth of the contiguous zone.[54] The two zones are completely different both in origin and content. Moreover, the contiguous zone only exists in the water column; it is thus irrelevant to use it for the establishment of a single maritime boundary.

The second sector was located south of St Pierre and Miquelon. Since St Pierre and Miquelon have a coastal opening towards the south, France was fully entitled to a frontal seaward projection towards the south until it reached the 200-mile limit. Its width, determined by the distance between the meridians passing through the easternmost point of the Island of St Pierre and the westernmost point of Miquelon, is approximately 10. 5 nautical miles. Thus, the Arbitral Tribunal established a 'corridor' 10.5 nautical miles wide, 188 nautical miles in length, from the 12-mile limit measured from the baseline (points I to M, M to N, N to Q).[55] In addition, from the northeastern limit of the second sector, the boundary was to take the form of a 12-mile enclave (points Q to S). In contrast to the western side, the Arbitral Tribunal did not accept any seaward projection east of St Pierre and Miquelon. The Arbitral Tribunal did not explain, however, the reasoning for the differing treatment of the areas east and west of the islands.

[53] ibid, 1170, [69].

[54] Dissenting Opinion of Judge Weil, ibid, 1198, [4]; Dissenting Opinion of Judge Gotlieb, ibid, 1195, [61].

[55] The *St Pierre and Miquelon* arbitral award, (1992) 31 *ILM* 1170–71, [70–74].

The aforementioned decision rests on two elements: The theory of frontal projection and the principle of non-encroachment.[56] These elements invite several criticisms, however. According to the frontal-projection theory, coasts project solely in the direction perpendicular to the general direction of the coastal front, and that projection takes place for a breadth corresponding to that of the coastal front. Nevertheless, it is doubtful whether positive law supports this theory.[57] By applying the frontal-projection theory, the French projections were minimised. This runs contrary to the reciprocity of the non-encroachment principle, which requires that the mutual cut-off and encroachment must be shared in a balanced and reasonable manner.[58] Furthermore, as both Judges Weil and Gotlieb indicated, the approach of the Arbitral Tribunal is itself contradictory. Indeed, while depending on the frontal-projection theory in the second sector, in the first sector, the Arbitral Tribunal established an additional 12-mile belt around the west of St Pierre and Miquelon. In other words, on the one hand, the Court made a frontal projection in the south and, on the other, a radial one in the west. This is hardly reconcilable.[59]

All in all, the Arbitral Tribunal established a single maritime boundary by mixing three categories of 'effect': 'partial effect' in the west by applying the concepts of the contiguous zone and of radial projection, 'enclaving with no effect' in the east, and 'full-effect' in the northwest (points 9 to D), and the south based upon the frontal projection theory and the principle of non-encroachment.[60] Yet the mixing of these modes completely lacks theoretical consistency, which is one of the disadvantages of a case-by-case solution.

ii. Verification Stage

At the verification stage, the Arbitral Tribunal attempted to test whether the solution reached was 'radically inequitable'.[61] Again this approach is a re-run of the *Gulf of Maine* case. At this stage, mineral resources were not taken into account, since no drilling had been undertaken.[62] Only fisheries were at issue. In this regard, the Arbitral Tribunal concluded that: '[T]he proposed demarcation [would] not have a radical impact on the existing pattern of fishing in the area';[63] and that '[T]he delimitation decided upon by [it] [would] not have

[56] Dissenting Opinion of Judge Weil, ibid, 1199, [8].

[57] ibid, 1199–1201, [9–13].

[58] Dissenting Opinion of Judge Weil, ibid, 1202–03, [16–19].

[59] ibid, 1202, [14]. Dissenting Opinion of Judge Gotlieb, ibid, 1189–91, [38–48]. H Ruiz-Fabri, 'Sur la délimitation des espaces maritimes entre le Canada et la France, sentence arbitrale du 10 juin 1992' (1993) 97 *RGDIP* 100.

[60] GP Politakis, 'The French–Canadian Arbitration Around St. Pierre and Miquelon: Unmasked Opportunism and the Triumph of the Unexpected' (1993) 8 *IJMCL* 119.

[61] The *St Pierre and Miquelon* arbitral award, (1992) 31 *ILM* 1173, [84].

[62] ibid, 1175, [89].

[63] ibid, 1173, [85].

the effect of depriving either Party of its existing fishing rights under the 1972 Agreement.'[64]

In summary, the Court of Arbitration in *St Pierre and Miquelon* re-affirmed the principal aspects of the *Gulf of Maine* case: (i) the fundamental norm of an equitable result, (ii) the denial of the applicability of the Convention on the Continental Shelf, (iii) the primary role of geographical criteria and their predominance in the process of delimitation, and (iv) the distinction between the operational and verification stages. In these respects, it may be said that this award is in line with the *Gulf of Maine* case.[65]

IV. THE *JAN MAYEN* CASE (*DENMARK v NORWAY*, ICJ, 1993)

The three decisions above examined related to the cases where there was agreement to request a single maritime boundary for the continental shelf and the superjacent waters. By contrast, when there is no agreement on a single maritime boundary, but a third Party is asked to delimit the continental shelf and the superjacent waters, should the two lines coincide? This was the question which the ICJ had to examine in the *Jan Mayen* case.

On 16 August 1988, the Government of Denmark filed an application with the Registry of the Court instituting proceedings against Norway with respect to a dispute concerning maritime delimitation between the Danish territory of Greenland and the Norwegian Island of Jan Mayen. Unlike what had happened in the *Gulf of Maine* case, where there was a special agreement of the Parties, the application in the present case relied on Article 36(2) of the Statute of the ICJ.

The Parties differed on the question whether one delimitation line or two were required. Denmark asked the Court for 'a single line of delimitation of the fishery zone and continental shelf.'[66] Norway contended that the median line constituted the boundary for the delimitation of the continental shelf and also for the fishery zone (FZ).[67] The important point is that, in Norway's view, the two lines would coincide but would remain conceptually distinct. Hence, there was no agreement on a single maritime boundary in the present case. In fact, the Court affirmed this and rejected Denmark's request by stating that the Court was 'not empowered or constrained by any such agreement for a single dual-purpose boundary.'[68] In this respect, the situation is quite different from that of the preceding cases. In addition, both Parties had ratified the 1958 Geneva Convention on the Continental Shelf.

[64] ibid, 1174, [87].

[65] L De La Fayette, 'The Award in the Canada-France Maritime Boundary Arbitration' (1993) 8 *IJMCL* 96.

[66] *Maritime Delimitation in the Area between Greenland and Jan Mayen (Denmark v Norway)* (the *Jan Mayen* case), [1993] ICJ Rep 38, 42, [9].

[67] ibid, 43, [9].

[68] ibid, 57, [43].

A. The Law Applicable to the Maritime Delimitation

i. Law Applicable to the Continental Shelf

As there was no joint request for a single maritime boundary, the law applicable to the continental shelf and to the FZ must be examined separately.[69] For the continental shelf, the applicable law was Article 6 of the Geneva Convention on the Continental Shelf. In this respect, the decision in *Jan Mayen* differs from the *Gulf of Maine* and the *St Pierre and Miquelon* cases, in which the applicability of the 1958 Convention was negated since there was an agreement for single maritime boundaries. However, the Court referred to customary law at the same time, observing that:

> [T]he fact that it is the 1958 Convention which applies to the continental shelf delimitation in this case does not mean that Article 6 thereof can be interpreted and applied either without reference to customary law on the subject, or wholly independently of the fact that a fishery zone boundary is also in question in these waters.[70]

Quoting a passage of the 1977 award of the Court of Arbitration in the *Anglo–French Continental Shelf* case, which regarded the 'combined equidistance–special circumstances rule' as a particular expression of a general norm, the Court further noted that:

> If the equidistance–special circumstances rule of the 1958 Convention is, in the light of this 1977 Decision, to be regarded as expressing a general norm based on equitable principles, it must be difficult to find any material difference at any rate in regard to delimitation between opposite coasts between the effect of Article 6 and the effect of the customary rule which also requires a delimitation based on equitable principles.[71]

For the Court,

> in respect of the continental shelf boundary in the present case, even if it were appropriate to apply, not Article 6 of the 1958 Convention, but customary law concerning the continental shelf as developed in the decided cases, it is in accord with precedents to begin with the median line as a provisional line and then to ask whether 'special circumstances' require any adjustment or shifting of that line.[72]

[69] ibid, 58, [44].
[70] ibid, [46].
[71] ibid.
[72] ibid, 61, [51]. Subsequently, the ICJ's view was echoed by the 2002 *Newfoundland and Labrador/Nova Scotia* arbitral award (the Second Phase). When applying the corrective-equity approach under Art 6 of the Geneva Convention on the Continental Shelf, a three-member arbitral tribunal, which was a national tribunal established to decide the maritime boundary between the two Canadian provinces, noted that: '[I]ts approach would have been precisely the same in applying customary international law or Article 83 of the *1982 Law of the Sea Convention*' (emphasis original). *Arbitration between Newfoundland and Labrador and Nova Scotia Concerning Portions of the Limits of Their Offshore Areas as Defined in the Canada-Nova Scotia Offshore Petroleum Resources Accord Implementation Act and the Canada-Newfoundland Atlantic Accord Implementation Act*, Award of the Tribunal in the Second Phase, 26 March 2002, [5.2]. Text in: (2002) 128 *International law Reports* 504. The electronic text is available at www.cnsopb.ns.ca/sites/default/files/pdfs/

Thus, at least where delimitation between opposite coasts is concerned, the Court assimilated Article 6 of the Geneva Convention in question with customary law based on equitable principles (first assimilation). Considering the fact that the Court had rejected Article 6 as customary law, this represents a turning point in terms of the relationship between treaty law and customary law.[73]

ii. Law Applicable to the FZ

As the Court observed, no international tribunal has ever rendered a decision concerning only an FZ. In the Court's view, however, the Parties had no objection to the boundary of the FZ being determined by the law governing that of the EEZ, that is to say, by customary law.[74] The Court thus equated the customary law applicable to the FZ with that governing the EEZ on the basis of the agreement of the Parties (second assimilation).

The next issue is the relationship between the law applicable to the FZ and that governing the continental shelf. The Court, referring to the words 'an equitable solution' in Articles 74 (1) and 83(1) of the LSOC, ruled that:

> That statement of an 'equitable solution' as the aim of any delimitation process reflects the requirements of customary law as regards the delimitation both of continental shelf and of exclusive economic zones.[75]

This is the first step towards an assimilation of the law applicable to the continental shelf with the law applicable to the FZ at the customary law level. Furthermore, based on the *Gulf of Maine* and the *Libya/Malta* cases, the Court ruled that:

> It thus appears that, both for the continental shelf and for the fishery zones in this case, it is proper to begin the process of delimitation by a median line provisionally drawn.[76]

Moreover, quoting the *Anglo-French* arbitral award, the Court held that:

> It cannot be surprising if an equidistance–special circumstances rule produces much the same result as an equitable principles-relevant circumstances rule in the case of opposite coasts, whether in the case of a delimitation of continental shelf, of fishery zone, or of *an all-purpose single boundary*.[77]

phaseii_award_english.pdf. See also J Currie, J 'Maritime Boundary Delimitation in a Federal Domestic Setting: The Newfoundland and Labrador v. Nova Scotia Arbitration' (2007) 17 *LJIL* 169; P von Mühlendahl, *L'équidistance dans la délimitation des frontière maritimes: étude de la jurisprudence internationale* (Paris, Pedone, 2016) 168–69, [280].

[73] In addition, Judge Oda indicated that the area in dispute was not the 'continental shelf' within the meaning of the Geneva Convention on the Continental Shelf, but arguably the continental shelf referred to in the LOSC or in the customary law which may now be reflected in that Convention. In other words, it was the continental shelf as a transformed concept that was at issue. See Separate Opinion of Judge Oda, [1993] ICJ Rep 99, [35–38].

[74] The *Jan Mayen* case, Judgment, ibid, 59, [47].

[75] ibid, 59, [48].

[76] ibid, 62, [53].

[77] Emphasis added. ibid, [56].

Thus, the Court assimilated the law of continental shelf delimitation with that of the FZ at the customary law level (third assimilation).

In summary, the Court attempted to achieve assimilation at three levels. First, the assimilation of Article 6 of the Convention on the Continental Shelf to customary law; second, assimilation between the law applicable to the EEZ delimitation and that governing the FZ delimitation in customary law; and finally, the assimilation of customary law for the continental shelf delimitation and for an EEZ/FZ delimitation. The essential idea of the Court was the assimilation of customary and treaty law, and the assimilation between the law on the sea-bed and that applicable to the water column.

The Court's view is significant in the sense that, so far as the coasts face each other, the law of maritime delimitation is to be unified under a triple rule of 'agreement–equidistance–special circumstances.' Consequently, so far as opposite coasts are concerned, the equidistant (median) line is to be drawn at a first stage, and relevant circumstances are to be considered at a second stage. Thus, for the first time in the case law of the ICJ, the corrective-equity approach was adopted as customary law.

B. Application of the Law Identified

i. Consideration of the Special/Relevant Circumstances

After having provisionally drawn the median line for both zones, the Court considered several factors which might necessitate an adjustment or shifting of that line. The factors which the Court enumerated were: (i) the disparity in the length of the coastlines (the question of proportionality), (ii) access to resources, (iii) the presence of ice, (iv) population and economy, (v) security, and (vi) the conduct of the Parties involved. It was the disparity between the relevant coasts and access to fishery resources which the Court took into consideration as special/relevant circumstances. In the Court's view, the disparity between the lengths of the coasts constituted, for a continental shelf delimitation, a 'special circumstance' under Article 6 of the Geneva Convention on the Continental Shelf and, for a fishery zone delimitation, a 'relevant circumstance' under customary law.[78] Furthermore, both Parties emphasised the importance of their interests in fisheries. Having examined their arguments, the Court concluded that the median line had to be adjusted eastward in order to assure an equitable access to the capelin stock.[79] It is notable that contrary to the *Gulf of Maine* and the *St Pierre Miquelon* cases, fishing resources were being considered as special/relevant circumstances, not as a test of the equitable nature of the result.[80]

[78] ibid, 69, [68].
[79] ibid, 72, [76].
[80] This issue will be examined in ch 8 s I of this book.

Having concluded that the provisional median line for both the continental shelf and for the FZ must be shifted eastwards so as to attribute a larger maritime space to Denmark,[81] the Court determined the precise position of the delimitation line. In this respect, it held that the lines for the continental shelf and the FZ had to coincide with each other.[82]

In light of the above considerations, the Court divided the area into three zones (see Illustration 13). The southernmost zone, zone 1, which is the principal fishing area, was divided into two parts of equal surface, so as to allow the two Parties to enjoy equitable access. In the two northern areas, zones 2 and 3, the special/relevant circumstances to be considered were a marked disparity in coastal lengths. Taking into account the equal division of zone 1, the Court divided zone 2 between point N and point O, which corresponded to two-thirds of the line I-K. Finally, zone 3 was divided between point O and point A, which is the intersection of the median line and the 200-mile limit from Greenland.[83] Thus, the Court drew a coincident maritime boundary for the continental shelf and the FZ. While in fact this line constitutes a single maritime boundary for both zones, it must be emphasised that it is not a single maritime boundary per se, as in the *Gulf of Maine* case, but a coincidence of two individual lines, one for the continental shelf and one for the FZ. Thus, to prevent confusion, the term 'coincident maritime boundary' is used here.

ii. Balancing the Special/Relevant Circumstances

Theoretically, two different lines were conceivable, particularly in the southernmost area (zone 1), where the equitable access to fishery resources is the core of the issue, since that access cannot be relevant to the continental shelf delimitation.[84] Nonetheless, the Court decided to establish a coincident maritime boundary. An issue at point in this regard is how factors relevant for the delimitation of the continental shelf and for the delimitation of the FZ should be balanced.

In the present case, the only special/relevant circumstance concerning the continental shelf was the disparity of coastal lengths. On the other hand, relevant circumstances for the FZs were both the disproportion of the coasts

[81] The *Jan Mayen* case, Judgment, [1993] ICJ Rep 79, [90].

[82] ibid.

[83] ibid, 79–81, [91–93]. In the Agreement of 18 December 1995 drawing the delimitation lines between the FZs and the continental shelf, the Parties adjusted slightly three of four points indicated by the Court. Report by Anderson in JI Charney and LM Alexander (eds), *International Maritime Boundary*, vol II (Dordrecht, Nijhoff, 1993) 2519. For the text of the 1995 Agreement, see ibid, 2524–25.

[84] R Churchill, 'The Greenland-Jan Mayen Case and Its Significance for the International Law of Maritime Delimitation' (1994) 9 *IJMCL* 26; H Dipla, 'L'arrêt de la Cour internationale de Justice en l'affaire de la délimitation maritime dans la region située entre le Groenland et Jan Mayen' (1994) 98 *RGDIP* 920; ED Evans, 'Case Concerning Maritime Delimitation in the Area between Greenland and Jan Mayen (*Denmark v Norway*)' (1994) 43 *ICLQ* 701.

and the equitable access to the FZ. Hence, the question lies in interpreting the relationship between the disproportionality of the coastal lengths as a common special/relevant circumstance and the equitable access to fisheries resources as a circumstance relevant only for FZs. As pointed out, the Court divided zone 1 into two equal parts in order to achieve equitable access to the fishing resources of that zone without considering this question. As a matter of theory, the adjustment of a provisional median line on the basis of proportionality is possible in an infinite number of ways. Accordingly, it is possible to conclude, in the present case, that a specific adjustment to fishery requirements was effected to make them coincide with the consideration of proportionality. However, a difficult question will arise: If the special/relevant circumstances for the continental shelf were to pull one direction and those for the FZ in the other, would it be possible to establish a coincident maritime boundary?[85] In the present case, the special/relevant circumstances for both the continental shelf delimitation and the FZ delimitation required, by accident, an eastward shift of the median line. Yet this will not happen in all cases. Therefore, some doubts might be expressed regarding whether the solution adopted by the Court can be universally applied.[86]

V. THE *ERITREA/YEMEN* CASE: THE SECOND STAGE (ARBITRATION, 1999)

The next case to be examined is the 1999 *Eritrea/Yemen* case (the Second Stage).[87] On 3 October 1996, Eritrea and Yemen concluded the Arbitration Agreement by which they requested an arbitral tribunal to be established to render an award regarding a dispute on territorial sovereignty and maritime delimitation.[88] Under Article 2 of the Arbitration Agreement, the Tribunal was requested to provide rulings, in accordance with international law, in two stages. 'The first stage shall result in an award on territorial sovereignty and on the definition of the scope of the dispute between Eritrea and Yemen' (paragraph 2), and '[t]he second stage shall result in an award delimiting maritime boundaries' (paragraph 3). Regarding the latter, 'the Tribunal [was to] describe the course of the delimitation in a technically precise manner' (paragraph 3 (a) of Article 2). Pursuant to the Arbitration Agreement, the award in the

[85] Thirlway, 'The Law and Procedure: Part Six' 76.

[86] On this point, Judge Shahabudeen pointed out that 'two lines drawn independently for each area would coincide along their entire lengths only exceptionally.' Separate Opinion of Judge Shahabudeen, [1993] ICJ Rep 201.

[87] For the text of the Award, (2001) 22 *RIAA* 335; (2001) 40 *ILM* 983.

[88] The Arbitral Tribunal was composed of the following members: Sir Robert Jennings, President; Stephen Schwebel; AS El-Kosheri; Keith Highet; and Rosalyn Higgins. The arbitration took place in London. The Tribunal fixed its Registry at the International Bureau of the Permanent Court of Arbitration, The Hague. All written pleadings and verbatim transcripts of the oral proceedings and all the deliberations of the Tribunal were confidential (Art 9(3) of the Arbitration Agreement).

first stage regarding territorial sovereignty was rendered on 9 October 1998.[89] Next, on 17 December 1999, the Tribunal rendered an award on the second stage relating to maritime delimitation, which will be examined below.[90]

In this connection, attention should be drawn to the fact that the Arbitration Agreement did not clearly identify the type of maritime boundary to be drawn. It simply referred to 'maritime boundaries'. The Arbitral Tribunal stated, however, that the boundary line in the northern stretch were 'boundaries between the Yemen and the Eritrean continental shelves and EEZ.'[91] Furthermore, 'after careful consideration of all the cogent and skilful arguments put before them by both Parties,' the Tribunal decided that 'the international boundary shall be a single all-purpose boundary.'[92] Hence, the Tribunal drew a single maritime boundary between the continental shelf and EEZ. It should be noted that the territorial sea boundary was also involved in the middle part of the area to be delimited.

A. Law Applicable to the Single Maritime Boundary

Regarding the law applicable to the single maritime boundary in the present case, Article 2(3) of the Arbitration Agreement provided that: 'The Tribunal shall decide taking into account the opinion that it will have formed on questions of territorial sovereignty, the United Nations Convention on the Law of the Sea, and any other pertinent factor.' This provision calls for three comments. First, as the Tribunal pointed out, the reference to the LOSC was important because Eritrea had not become a party to that Convention.[93] On the basis of the Arbitration Agreement, the LOSC would also be applicable to Eritrea. Secondly, there was no reference to customary law in that Agreement. Nonetheless, the Tribunal considered many of the relevant elements of customary law to be incorporated in the provisions of the Convention.[94] Thirdly, the phrase 'any

[89] For the award after the first stage, see G Distefano, 'La sentence arbitrale du 9 octobre 1998 dans l'affaire du différend insulaire entre le Yemen et l'Erythrée' (1999) 103 *RGDIP* 851; *Chronique des faits internationaux, ibid*, pp 189–92; WM Reisman, 'Award of the Arbitral Tribunal in the First Stage of the Proceedings (Territorial Sovereignty and Scope of the Dispute)' (1999) 93 *AJIL* 668; B Kwiatkowska, 'Current Legal Development: Red Sea, Award of the Arbitral Tribunal in the First Stage of the Eritrea/Yemen Proceedings' (1999) 14 *IJMCL* 125.

[90] For a commentary on the award by the author, see Y Tanaka, 'Reflections on the *Eritrea/Yemen* Arbitration of 17 December 1999 (Second Phase: Maritime Delimitation)' (2001) 48 *NILR* 197.

[91] The *Eritrea/Yemen* arbitral award (the Second Phase), 22 *RIAA* 362, [116]. Curiously, however, Eritrea has never claimed an EEZ. A writer thus argued that the Tribunal delimited a 'potential maritime boundary'. Nuno Sérgio Marques Antunes, 'The 1999 *Eritrea-Yemen* Maritime Delimitation Award and the Development of International Law' (2001) 50 *ICLQ* 333. According to the present award of 1999, Eritrea indicated that the maritime boundary in the northern sector was between respective continental shelves and EEZ. The *Eritrea/Yemen* arbitral award (the Second Phase), 22 *RIAA* 340, [23]. Furthermore in its arguments, Eritrea stressed the importance of fisheries and historic rights regarding fisheries. Accordingly, it would appear that Eritrea might have presupposed its EEZ, although there was no official claim on this matter.

[92] ibid, 365, [132].

[93] ibid, [130].

[94] ibid.

other pertinent factors' is a broad concept. The Tribunal held that it included various factors generally recognised to be relevant to the process of delimitation, such as proportionality, non-encroachment, the presence of islands, and any other factor that might affect the equities of the particular situation.[95]

The Tribunal then clarified the contents of the law applicable in the present case. The view of the Tribunal is worth quoting in full:

> It is a generally accepted view, as is evidenced in both the writings of commentators and in the jurisprudence, that between coasts that are opposite to each other the median or equidistance line normally provides an equitable boundary in accordance with the requirements of the Convention, and in particular those of its Articles 74 and 83 which respectively provide for the equitable delimitation of the EEZ and of the continental shelf between States with opposite or adjacent coasts. Indeed both Parties to the present case have claimed a boundary constructed on the equidistance method, although based on different points of departure and resulting very different lines.[96]

Furthermore,

> The Tribunal has decided, after careful consideration of all the cogent and skilful arguments put before them by both Parties, that the international boundary shall be a single all-purpose boundary which is a median line and that it should, as far as practicable, be a median line between the opposite mainland coastlines. This solution is not only in accord with practice and precedent in the like situations but is also one that is already familiar to both Parties.[97]

Hence the Tribunal expressly ruled that, so far as the maritime delimitation between States with opposites coasts was concerned, a median or an equidistance line would provide an equitable maritime boundary under Articles 74 and 83 of the LOSC. The reference to 'practice and precedent' and 'jurisprudence' is also noteworthy.

At the same time, it should be stressed that the Tribunal did not consider a median line as the end product. Indeed, as will be seen below, the Tribunal applied a proportionality test to examine the equitableness of the median line drawn by it. This means that if there is disproportionality, such a line should be modified, which will lead to the corrective-equity approach.

B. Application of the Law Identified

The Tribunal then turned to the establishment of a single maritime boundary as well as a territorial sea boundary, which was a median line between the coasts. The important feature in the present case was that although both

[95] ibid.
[96] ibid, [131].
[97] ibid, [132].

Parties claimed a median line as being a maritime boundary, their claimed lines followed very different courses owing to differences as to base points.[98] Thus, a question regarding the effects given to islands as base points becomes the core of the delimitation process.[99]

Yemen's line was divided into three sectors by lines of latitude: 16°N (northern sector); 14°25′N (central sector); and 13°20′N (southern sector). In the northern sector, the line claimed by Yemen was a median line measured from the Eritrean Dahlak islands and the Yemeni mid-sea islands of the Jabal al-Tayr and Jabal al-Zubayr group. In the central sector, the boundary proposed by Yemen was an equidistance line between the high-water line on the Eritrean mainland coasts and the low-water line on the westernmost coasts of Yemen's Hanish Island group. The South-West Rocks and the Three Haycocks, which belong to Eritrea, were ignored and placed in limited enclaves. Finally, in the southern sector, the Yemeni line is a simple median between opposite mainland coasts. In this sector, Yemen recognised the Bay of Assab as Eritrean internal waters.[100]

Eritrea's 'historic median line' was drawn as a median between the mainland coasts and ignored the existence of the mid-sea islands of Yemen, but took into account the Eritrean islands, such as South-West Rocks and The Haycocks. Furthermore, Eritrea proposed 'joint resource areas' in view of maintaining the traditional fishing regime.[101]

Both Parties relied on several factors in order to justify their respective median lines. Those factors were: fishing, the traditional fishing regime, petroleum agreements, security, navigation, and proportionality. Among these factors, the Tribunal took only navigation and proportionality into account. As it turned out, the Tribunal discarded both lines proposed by the Parties and constructed its own median line.

In the northern sector, the Tribunal drew an equidistance line, using as base points the Dahlaks, which are subject to Eritrea's sovereignty, and the Kamaran Island and its satellite islets as well as the Uqban and Kutama islets, which belong to Yemen. No effect was given to the single island of al-Tayr and the island group of al-Zubayr, which are subject to Yemen's sovereignty (see Illustration 14).[102]

The middle sector is followed by the narrow sea between the southwest extremity of the Yemen Hanish group on the one hand and the Eritrean islands of the Mohabbakahs, High Island, The Haycocks and the South-West Rocks.

[98] It should be noted that once the base points are fixed, only one possible equidistance line can be objectively determined.

[99] The question concerning the effects given to islands will be examined in ch 7.

[100] The *Eritrea/Yemen* arbitral award (the Second Phase), 22 *RIAA* 338–40, [12–21].

[101] ibid, 340–41, [22–30].

[102] ibid, 367–369, [138–53].

This sector involved not only the drawing of a single maritime boundary for continental shelves and EEZs, but also the delimitation of the territorial seas. Pursuant to Article 15 of the LOSC, the Tribunal drew a median line in the overlapping territorial seas taking into account the Eritrean South-West Rocks and The Haycocks, and the Yemeni island in the Hanish group. In this regard, the Tribunal found that no modification of the equidistance line on the basis of historic title or other special circumstances was necessary.[103]

A question remained between points 13 and 15. In this area, it was necessary to respect the territorial seas of the islands group of Zuqar-Hanish. At the same time, however, the Tribunal hesitated to follow the sinuosities of the Zuqar territorial sea boundary until it turned southward again in order to join the median point pursuant to Article 15 of the LOSC. Accordingly, the Tribunal connected point 13, where it meets a 12-mile territorial sea extending from Zuqar Island with point 14, taking the necessary turn to the South-West to join the territorial sea median line, ie, point 15. From there onwards, the southward part of the delimitation line was drawn, joining point 14 and point 15 where it becomes the median line pursuant to Article 15 of the LOSC.[104]

In the southern part, the Tribunal connected point 20, which is the southernmost turning point of the median line in the overlapping territorial seas, and point 21, which is the intersection of the above-mentioned territorial sea median line. Hence, the Tribunal drew a median line, which was controlled by the two mainland coasts. Having considered the Bay of Assab as internal waters of Eritrea, the Tribunal decided the low-water line of the bay was to be used as the controlling base point of the boundary.[105]

In fixing the northern and southern end points of the boundary, a problem which arose was the presence of third States. The Tribunal believed that 'it [had] neither competence nor authority to decide on any of the boundaries between either of the two Parties and neighbouring States.'[106] In order to avoid areas where third States might be involved, the Tribunal stopped the boundary line at point 1 for the northern end and point 29 for the southern end.[107] Finally, the Tribunal applied the proportionality test in order to verify the equitableness of the delimitation line, and concluded that there was no disproportionality between the ratio of coastal lengths of each Party (1 (Yemen): 1.31 (Eritrea)) and the ratio of waters areas (1 (Yemen): 1.09 (Eritrea)).[108]

[103] ibid, 369–374, [154–59].
[104] ibid, 371, [160–62].
[105] ibid, 371–372, [163].
[106] ibid, 366, [136].
[107] ibid, 372, [164]. The problem of third States in this award will be reconsidered in ch 7, s IV.
[108] ibid, 372–73, [165–68].

VI. THE *QATAR v BAHRAIN* CASE (MERITS, ICJ, 2001)

The next case that needs consideration is the *Qatar v Bahrain* case concerning maritime delimitation and territorial questions.[109] On 8 July 1991, Qatar instituted proceedings before the ICJ against Bahrain regarding certain disputes between two States relating to 'sovereignty over the Hawar islands, sovereign rights over the shoals of Dibal and Qui'at Jaradah, and the delimitation of the maritime areas of the two States.' The application was based on two 'agreements' between Qatar and Bahrain in December 1987 and 'Minutes' of December 1990, respectively.

An important feature of this case is that the dispute concerned both territorial questions and maritime delimitation. On the one hand, Qatar requested the Court adjudge and declare in accordance with international law:

> A. (1) That the State of Qatar has sovereignty over the Hawar islands;
> (2) That Dibal and Qit'at Jaradah shoals are low-tide elevations which are under Qatar's sovereignty;
> B. (1) That the State of Bahrain has no sovereignty over the island of Janan;
> (2) That the State of Bahrain has no sovereignty over Zubarah;
> (3) That any claim by Bahrain concerning archipelagic baselines and areas for fishing for pearls and swimming fish would be irrelevant for the purpose of maritime delimitation in the present case.[110]

Furthermore, Qatar asked the Court to draw a single maritime boundary between the maritime areas of sea-bed, subsoil and superjacent waters appertaining respectively to the State of Qatar and the State of Bahrain so as to follow points indicated by Qatar on the basis that the Hawar islands and the island of Janan appertained to Qatar.

On the other hand, Bahrain asked the Court to adjudge and declare that: Bahrain was sovereign over Zubarah, the Hawar Islands, including Janan and Hadd Janan and that the maritime boundary between Bahrain and Qatar was as described in Part Two of Bahrain's Memorial, Part Two of Bahrain's Counter-Memorial and in its Reply (see Illustration 15).[111]

In this subsection, only part of the maritime delimitation will be examined for the purposes of this study. In the southern part of the delimitation area, where the coasts of the Parties are opposite each other, the distance between the coasts is nowhere more than 24 miles wide and thus the delimitation of the territorial sea was in issue. In the northern part, where the coasts of the two States are comparable to adjacent coasts, the delimitation to be carried out was to be a single maritime boundary between the continental shelf and EEZ. Therefore,

[109] *Maritime Delimitation and Territorial Questions between Qatar and Bahrain (Qatar v Bahrain)* (the *Qatar v Bahrain* case), Judgment (Merits), [2001] ICJ Rep 40. For a commentary on the *Qatar v Bahrain* case by the author, see Y Tanaka, 'Reflections on Maritime Delimitation in the *Qatar v Bahrain* Case of 16 March 2001 (Merits)' (2003) 52 *ICLQ* 53.

[110] The *Qatar v Bahrain* case (Merits), [2001] ICJ Rep 50, [33].

[111] ibid.

the type of delimitation line to be effected is different between the southern and the northern sectors.[112]

A. Law Applicable to Maritime Delimitation

Neither Bahrain nor Qatar was a party to the 1958 Geneva Conventions, including the Convention on the Territorial Sea and the Contiguous Zone and the Convention on the Continental Shelf. While Bahrain had ratified the LOSC, Qatar was only a signatory to it. Thus, it was customary law which was applicable to this case.[113] As the present case simultaneously included the delimitation of both territorial sea and single maritime boundaries, it is relevant to consider the law applicable to the territorial sea delimitation and to a single maritime boundary, respectively.[114]

i. Law Applicable to Territorial Sea Delimitation

The first task of the Court was to identify customary law relating to the delimitation of the territorial sea. The Parties agreed that Article 15 of the LOSC was part of customary law. The Court also held that that provision, which is virtually identical to Article 12(1) of the 1958 Convention on the Territorial Sea and the Contiguous Zone, was to be regarded as having a customary character. Hence the Court held that: 'The most logical and widely practised approach is first to draw provisionally an equidistance line and then to consider whether that line must be adjusted in the light of the existence of special circumstances.'[115] In so stating, the Court clearly adopted the corrective-equity approach for a territorial sea delimitation.

ii. Law Applicable to a Single Maritime Boundary

Regarding the law applicable to a single maritime boundary, it should be recalled that customary law was applicable in the northern sector. In this context, the Court first referred to the *dictum* in the *Libya/Malta* case. In that case, the Court had held that 'greater importance must be attributed to elements, such as distance from the coast, which are common to both concepts.'[116] Furthermore, referring to the approach taken by the *Jan Mayen* case, that is, the corrective-equity approach, the Court in the *Qatar v Bahrain* case clearly stated that

[112] ibid, 91–93, [169–70].

[113] ibid, 91, [167]. It should be noted that both Parties agree that most of the provisions of the 1982 Convention which are relevant for the present case reflect customary law. ibid.

[114] ibid, 111, [231].

[115] ibid, 94, [176].

[116] The *Libya/Malta* case, [1985] ICJ Rep 33, [33].

it would follow the same approach in the present case.[117] Thus, according to the Court, 'it will first provisionally drawn an equidistance line and then consider whether there are circumstances which must lead to an adjustment of that line.'[118] In so doing, the Court explicitly adopted the corrective-equity approach.

In this regard, it is important to note that in the area where a single maritime boundary was to be drawn, 'the coasts of the two States [were] rather comparable to *adjacent coasts*.'[119] Accordingly, the ICJ explicitly accepted, for the first time in the case law of the Court, the applicability of the corrective-equity approach as customary law in the delimitation between States with adjacent coasts. This is a welcome development in view of enhancing the predictability of the law of maritime delimitation. In this connection, Judge Gilbert Guillaume's view, as expressed in the Sixth Committee of the General Assembly of the United Nations, deserves quoting:

> [I]t is encouraging to note that the law of maritime delimitations, by means of these developments in the Court's case law, has reached a new level of unity and certainty, whilst conserving the necessary flexibility. [...] In all cases, the Court, as States also do, must first determine provisionally the equidistance line. It must then ask itself whether there are special or relevant circumstances requiring this line to be adjusted with a view to achieving equitable results.[120]

Moreover, the Court noted that:

> [T]he equidistance/special circumstances rule, which is applicable in particular to the delimitation of the territorial sea, and the equitable principles/relevant circumstances rule, as it has been developed since 1958 in case law and State practice with regard to the delimitation of the continental shelf and the exclusive economic zone, are closely interrelated.[121]

This appears to suggest the assimilation between the law applicable to a territorial sea delimitation and a single maritime boundary delimitation.

B. Application of the Law Identified

i. Territorial Sea Delimitation

a. Identification of Relevant Coasts

In drawing a provisional equidistance line at the first stage of the delimitation, it was necessary to identify baselines. However, neither Party had specified the

[117] The *Qatar v Bahrain* case (Merits), [2001] ICJ Rep 111, [230].
[118] ibid.
[119] Emphasis added. ibid, 91, [170].
[120] Speech by His Excellency Judge Gilbert Guillaume, President of the International Court of Justice, to the Sixth Committee of the General Assembly of the United Nations, 31 October 2001, 10.
[121] The *Qatar v Bahrain* case (Merits), [2001] ICJ Rep 111, [231].

baselines to be used for the determination of the breadth of the territorial sea, nor did they produce official maps or charts reflecting such baselines.[122] Accordingly, the Court had to determine first the relevant coasts from which it would determine the location of baselines and then the pertinent basepoints generating an equidistance line.[123]

Maritime rights derive from the coastal State's sovereignty over the land ('the land dominates the sea'). It is thus necessary to determine the situation on land before effecting maritime delimitation. In this connection, the Court stated that, in accordance with Article 121(2) of the LOSC, which reflects customary law, islands generate the same maritime rights as other land territory.[124] Accordingly, the Court had to establish which islands came under Bahraini sovereignty. On this point, the Court concluded that the Hawar Islands belonged to Bahrain and that Janan belonged to Qatar.[125] Furthermore, Qatar did not contest that Bahrain had sovereignty over Jazirat Mashtan and Umm Jalid islands in the southern sector. Nevertheless, the Parties were divided with respect to the status concerning some islands or low-tide elevations and legal effects to be given to them.[126]

The first issue to produce a dispute was the status of Fasht al Azm. Qatar argued that Fasht al Azm was a low-tide elevation that has always been separated from Sitrah Island by a natural channel which remained navigable even at low tide. According to Qatar, this natural channel was filled during 1982 construction works.[127] By contrast, denying Qatar's arguments, Bahrain claimed that Fasht al Azm was part of Sitrah Island. The main question was whether or not Fasht al Azm was divided from Sitrah by a natural and permanent channel at low tide. On this point, Bahrain maintained that there was no permanent channel at low tide between Sitrah Island and Fasht al Azm.[128] Regarding this question, the Court could not establish whether a permanent passage separating Sitrah Island from Fasht al Azm existed before the reclamation works of 1982 were undertaken. The Court held, however, that it was able to undertake the requested delimitation in this sector without determining the status of Fasht al Azm.[129]

Another issue concerned the question of whether Qit'at Jaradah, which was a maritime feature situated north-east of Fasht al Azm, was an island or

[122] ibid, 94, [177].
[123] ibid, 94, [178].
[124] ibid, 97, [185].
[125] ibid, [187]. For territorial questions concerning those islands, see 70–91, [98–165].
[126] Regarding an analysis on those features, see in particular, E Decaux, 'Affaire de la délimitation maritime et des questions territoriales entre Qatar et Bahreïn, fond arrêt du 16 mars 2001 (*Qatar c Bahreïn*)' (2001) 47 *AFDI* 225–29.
[127] The *Qatar v Bahrain* case (Merits), [2001] ICJ Rep 98, [189]. See also, presentation by Quéneudec, Counsel of Qatar, Verbatim Record, CR 2000/9, [24–26].
[128] Presentation by Reisman, Counsel of Bahrain, Verbatim Record, CR 2000/14, [12–25]; Judgment, [2001] ICJ Rep 98, [189].
[129] ibid, 98, [190].

a low-tide elevation. By referring to a number of eyewitness reports, Bahrain contended that there were strong indications that Qit'at Jaradah was an island that remained dry at high tide.[130] By contrast, Qatar maintained that Qit'at Jaradh was always reflected on nautical charts as a low-tide elevation.[131] Having carefully analysed the evidence submitted by the Parties and the conclusions of experts, the Court concluded that Qit'at Jaradah was an island which should be taken into consideration for the drawing of the equidistance line.[132] At the same time, taking into account the smallness of Qit'at Jaradah, the Court ruled that the activities carried out by Bahrain on that island must be considered sufficient to support Bahrain's claim that it has sovereignty over it.[133]

The third issue was the legal effect to be given to the low-tide elevation Fasht ad Dibal, which was located in the overlapping territorial sea of the Parties. In this respect, the Court concluded that, for the purposes of delimitation, the competing rights of the Parties would neutralise each other and, consequently, such low-tide elevations must be disregarded.[134]

The last issue in this context was Bahrain's straight baselines. Bahrain contended that, as a multiple-island State characterised by a cluster of islands off the coast of its main islands, it was entitled to draw a line connecting the outermost islands and low-tide elevations. In this connection, the Court stressed that the method of straight baselines must be applied restrictively, and such a method may be applicable only where a number of conditions are met.[135] Having examined the geography of Bahrain, the Court found that Bahrain was not entitled to apply the method of straight baselines.[136]

b. Special Circumstances

Having identified basepoints generating a provisional equidistance line, the Court turned to the question of whether special circumstances existed. In this regard, two issues must be examined. The first issue relates to Fasht al Azm. In this connection, the Court presented two hypotheses.

First, if Fasht al Azm were to be regarded as part of Sitrah Island and used as a basepoint creating an equidistance line, this would place the boundary in disproportionate proximity to Qatar's mainland coat. In the Court's view, it would thus not be appropriate to take the equidistance line as the maritime boundary. Secondly, if Fasht al Azm was to be regarded as a low-tide elevation, the equidistance line would brush Fasht al Azm, and, consequently, would be

[130] ibid, 98–99, [192]; presentation by Reisman, Counsel of Bahrain, Verbatim Record, CR 2000/14, [26–31].
[131] The *Qatar v Bahrain* case (Merits), Judgment, [2001] ICJ Rep 99, [193]. See also, presentation by Quéneudec, Counsel of Qatar, Verbatim Record, CR 2000/9, [32–39].
[132] The *Qatar v Bahrain* case (Merits), Judgment, [2001] ICJ Rep 99, [195].
[133] ibid, 99–100, [197].
[134] ibid,102–3, [209].
[135] ibid, 103, [212].
[136] ibid, 103–4, [213–15].

equally inappropriate. The Court thus considered that, in either hypothesis, there were special circumstances prompting a delimitation line passing between Fasht al Azm and Qit'at ash Shajarah.[137]

The second issue concerns Qit'at Jaradah. As explained earlier, the Court observed that Qit'at Jaradah was a very small island, uninhabited and without any vegetation. This tiny island is situated about midway between the main island of Bahrain and the Qatar peninsula. According to the Court, if its low-water line were to be used for determining a basepoint in the construction of the equidistance line, a disproportionate effect would be given to an insignificant maritime feature. Thus, on the basis of the *North Sea Continental Shelf* and *Libya/Malta* cases, the Court found that there was a special circumstance warranting the choice of a delimitation line passing immediately to the east of Qit'at Jaradah.[138]

The Court provisionally drew two equidistance lines. On the one hand, if no effect was given to Qit'al Jaradah, and if Fash al Azm were to be considered part of Sitrah island, the adjusted equidistance line would cut through Fasht ad Dibal, leaving the greater part of it on the Qatari side. On the other hand, if Fasht al Azm were seen as a low-tide elevation, the adjusted equidistance line would run west of Fasht ad Dibal. In either hypothesis, Fasht ad Dibal was largely or entirely on the Qatari side of the adjusted equidistance line. Accordingly, the Court concluded that it was 'appropriate to draw the boundary line between Qit'at Jaradah and Fasht ad Dibal.' 'As Fasht ad Dibal is thus situated in the territorial sea of Qatar,' the Court continued, 'it falls for that reason under the sovereignty of that State.'[139] Based on the above considerations, the Court drew the territorial sea boundary in the southern sector as shown in Illustration 16.[140]

ii. Single Maritime Boundary

Applying the corrective-equity approach, the Court drew, provisionally, an equidistance line at the first stage of delimitation. It then examined whether there were circumstances which would require any adjustment of the equidistance line. The factors to be examined were: (i) pearling, (ii) the 1947 line described by a British decision, (iii) proportionality, and (iv) and Fasht al Jarim. Having examined each and every element, the Court took only Fasht al Jarim into consideration as a special/relevant circumstance. According to the Court, it could not ignore the location of Fasht al Jarim, which was a sizable maritime feature partly situated in Bahrain's territorial sea. In this respect, the Court recalled the *Libya/Malta* case, which stated that: '[T]he equitableness of an equidistance line depends on whether the precaution is taken of eliminating the disproportionate effect of

[137] ibid, 104, [218].
[138] ibid, 104–9, [219].
[139] ibid, 109, [220].
[140] ibid, 109, [222].

certain "islets, rocks and minor coastal projections", to use the language of the Court in its 1969 Judgment.'[141]

The coasts of the Parties in the northern sector were comparable to adjacent coasts abutting on the same maritime areas extending seawards into the Gulf. The northern coasts of the territories concerned are flat and have a gentle slope, and there is no marked difference in character or extent. Thus, in the Court's view, Fasht al Jarim is the only noticeable element. Having noted the above geographical situation, the Court held that, if full effect were given to Fasht al Jarim, it would 'distort the boundary and have disproportionate effects,' to quote the *Anglo–French Continental Shelf* award. On the basis of considerations of equity, the Court thus held that Fasht al Jarim should have no effect in determining the boundary line in the northern sector.[142] Accordingly, it decided that the single maritime boundary was to be formed by a line which, from a point situated to the northwest of Fasht ad Dibal, would meet the equidistance line as adjusted to take account of the absence of effect given to Fasht al Jarim. The boundary then followed this adjusted equidistance line until it met the delimitation line between the respective maritime zones of Iran, on the one hand, and of Bahrain and Qatar, on the other (see Illustration 16).[143]

VII. THE *CAMEROON v NIGERIA* CASE (MERITS, ICJ, 2002)

On 29 March 1994, the Republic of Cameroon (hereafter Cameroon) instituted proceedings before the ICJ against the Federal Republic of Nigeria (hereafter Nigeria) concerning a dispute which related to the question of sovereignty over the Bakassi Peninsula (see Illustration 17). At the same time, Cameroon requested that, as the delimitation of the maritime boundary between the two States has remained a partial one, the Court determine the course of the maritime boundary between the two States beyond the line fixed in 1975 in order to avoid further incidents between the respective parties. The Application relied on the declarations made by the two Parties accepting the jurisdiction of the Court under Article 36(2) of the Statute of the Court. Thus, as with the *Qatar v Bahrain* case of 2002, the *Cameroon v Nigeria* case involved a dispute regarding territorial sovereignty as well as maritime delimitation at the same time. This judgment is important in the sense that this is the first instance in the case law of the ICJ where Articles 74 and 83 of the LOSC were applicable to a dispute concerning maritime delimitations. Thus the interpretation of these provisions by the Court is worth noting.[144]

[141] ibid, 114, [246]. The *Libya/Malta* case, [1985] ICJ Rep 48, [64].

[142] The *Qatar v Bahrain* case (Merits), [2001] ICJ Rep 114–15, [247–48].

[143] ibid, 115, [249].

[144] *Land and Maritime Boundary between Cameroon and Nigeria (Cameroon v Nigeria: Equatorial Guinea intervening)* (the *Cameroon/Nigeria* case), Judgment (Merits), [2002] ICJ Rep 303. For a commentary on the *Cameroon v Nigeria* case by the author, see Y Tanaka, 'Reflections on Maritime Delimitation in the *Cameroon/Nigeria* Case' (2004) 53 *ICLQ* 369.

A. Law Applicable to Maritime Delimitation

According to Cameroon, the maritime boundary between Cameroon and Nigeria was divided into two sectors. The first area was up to point G and the second sector was beyond that point (see Illustration 18). The Court first addressed the first sector of the maritime delimitation where delimitation of the territorial seas was involved. The central issue in this sector was whether a maritime boundary had already been established on the basis of three international legal instruments, ie, the Anglo–German Agreement of 11 March 1913, the Cameroon–Nigeria Agreement of 4 April 1971 including the Yaoundé II Declaration and the appended Chart 3433, and the Maroua Declaration of 1 June 1975.[145] On this issue, the Court concluded, by 13 votes to three, that the Maroua Declaration as well as the Yaoundé II Declaration had to be considered as binding on both Parties. Hence the maritime boundary between Cameroon and Nigeria up to and including point G had to be considered to have been established on a conventional basis by the Anglo–German Agreement, the Yaoundé II Declaration and the Maroua Declaration.[146] The line followed the course indicated in Illustration 18.[147] The Court then addressed the maritime delimitation beyond point G.

The areas to be delimited here lie beyond the outer limit of the respective territorial seas of the Parties.[148] In this respect, Cameroon regarded that this was a classic case of maritime delimitation of EEZs and continental shelves between States with adjacent coasts.[149] Furthermore, the Parties agreed in their written pleadings that the delimitation should be effected by a single line.[150] Accordingly, the Court was to determine a single line of delimitation for the coincident zones of jurisdiction within the restricted area in respect of which it was competent to give a ruling.[151]

[145] See also OO Sholanke, 'Delimiting the Territorial Sea between Nigeria and Cameroon: A Rational Approach' (1993) 42 *ICLQ* 398.

[146] The *Cameroon v Nigeria* case, Judgment, [2002] ICJ Rep 431, [268]. The Marouna Declaration was reproduced in Sholanke, 'Delimiting the Territorial Sea' 410–11.

[147] For a description of the course of the single maritime boundary, see [2002] ICJ Rep 431, [268].

[148] Judgment, [2002] ICJ Rep 440, [285]. Nigeria has claimed 30 nautical miles territorial sea while Cameroon claimed that of 50 nautical miles. According to Cameroon, however, these claims were withdrawn when the LOSC entered into force. Cameroon stated that the two States had accepted territorial seas of 12 nautical miles since 1975. Memorial of Cameroon, 535, [5.79–5.80]. Furthermore, Professor Pellet, Counsel of Cameroon, indicated the fact that the 'assemblée nationale' of Cameroon adopted law No 2000/2 in 17 April 2000, and Art 4 of the law fixed the breath of its territorial sea at 12 nautical miles. Argument of Professor Pellet, Counsel of Cameroon, Verbatim Record, CR 2002/5, 42, [12].

[149] Argument of Professor Pellet, Counsel of Cameroon, Verbatim Record, CR 2002/1, 42, [6].

[150] Rejoinder of Nigeria, January 2001, [10.7]. Reply of Cameroon, 389–92, [9.08–9.19]. Yet Cameroon has not formally proclaimed an EEZ. Counter-Memorial of Nigeria, vol I, May 1999, 562, [20.9].

[151] Judgment, [2002] ICJ Rep 440–41, [286].

With respect to the law applicable to the maritime delimitation, both Cameroon and Nigeria were parties to the LOSC.[152] Accordingly, the relevant provision, in particular Articles 74 and 83 of the Convention were applicable to the maritime delimitation.[153] In this regard, Cameroon argued that the law of maritime delimitation was dominated by the fundamental principle that any delimitation must lead to an equitable solution. Furthermore, it alleged that there was no single method of maritime delimitation and the choice of method depended on the circumstances specific to each case.[154] According to Cameroon, the equidistance method was not a principle of customary law that was automatically applicable in every maritime delimitation between States with adjacent coasts.[155] Nigeria contested, however, that Cameroon's rejection of any reliance on the criteria of appurtenance, equidistance and natural prolongation were inconsistent with modern methods of delimitation. According to Nigeria, international tribunals generally start from an equidistance line, which is then adjusted to take into account other relevant circumstances.[156]

In this regard, the Court referred, above all, to the neutral criteria that were indicated in the *Gulf of Maine* judgment.[157] Furthermore, having referred to the *Libya/Malta* judgment, which stressed the link between continental shelf and EEZ, the Court stated that it had on various occasions made clear the applicable criteria, principles and rules of delimitation of a single maritime boundary. In the Court's view,

> [t]hey are expressed in the so-called equitable principles/relevant circumstances method. This method, which is very similar to the equidistance/special circumstances method applicable in delimitation of the territorial sea, involves first drawing an equidistance line, then considering whether there are factors calling for the adjustment or shifting of that line in order to achieve an 'equitable result'.[158]

Moreover, on the basis of the *Jan Mayen* and *Qatar v Bahrain* cases where the Court drew a provisional equidistance line at the first stage of delimitation and, next considered whether there were relevant circumstances which must lead to an adjustment of that line, the Court concluded that it would 'apply the same method in the present case.'[159] In stating this, the Court took a two-tiered

[152] Cameroon ratified the LOSC on 19 November 1985 and Nigeria ratified the Convention on 14 August 1986.

[153] Judgment, [2002] ICJ Rep 440, [285]. See also Memorial of Cameroon, 533–34 [5.75–5.78]; presentation by Kamto, Counsel of Cameroon, Verbatim Record, CR 2002/22, 43, [24].

[154] Memorial of Cameroon, 533–34, [5.76–5.77]; reply of Cameroon, 409, [9.63]. See also argument of Professor Pellet, Verbatim Record, CR 2002/5, 43–46, [15–25].

[155] Judgment, [2002] ICJ Rep 432–33, [271]. Cameroon used the words 'equidistance principle'. Generally, this is not considered a principle but a method for delimitation.

[156] ibid, 436–37, [280]; presentation by Crawford, Verbatim Record, CR 2002/13, 53–59 [6–30].

[157] The *Gulf of Maine* case, [1984] ICJ Rep 327, [194].

[158] The *Cameroon v Nigeria* case, Judgment, [2002] ICJ Rep 441, [288].

[159] ibid, 442, [290].

approach, that is to say, an equidistance line was drawn at the first stage of the delimitation and, if necessary, this was to be adjusted it by taking relevant circumstances into account. Hence, as with the *Jan Mayen* and *Qatar v Bahrain* cases, the corrective-equity approach was applied in the *Cameroon v Nigeria* case. It is important that the Court applied the corrective-equity approach under Articles 74 and 83 of the LOSC. According to the Court's interpretation, a specific method, ie, the equidistance method, should be incorporated into Articles 74 and 83.[160] It could be said that the Court's approach in this matter is a landmark which will enhance the predictability of the law of maritime delimitation.

B. Application of the Law Identified

i. Identification of Relevant Coasts and Base Points

To construct an equidistance line at the first stage of delimitation, the Court had to define the relevant coastlines of the Parties from which the equidistance line would be calculated. Cameroon contended that the relevant area within which the maritime delimitation was to be undertaken might include the coastlines of third States. According to Cameroon, the relevant area consisted of that part of the Gulf of Guinea bounded by a straight line running from Akasso in Nigeria to Cap Lopez in Gabon. Thus Cameroon presented to Nigeria and to the Court an equitable line, subtended by 'projection lines' connecting points on the 'relevant coasts,' a number of which were situated in third States.[161]

Nevertheless, Nigeria rejected Cameroon's line. In the view of Nigeria, the relevant coasts must be coasts of the Parties, not those of a third States. Nigeria considered that its relevant coast was that which runs west from its boundary with Cameroon as far as Akasso, and that of Cameroon was the coast which runs east from the boundary between the two States and then south, as far as Debundsha Point, which marks the beginning of the blocking effect of Bioko Island.[162]

[160] It should be noted that the Arbitral Tribunal in the *Eritrea/Yemen* arbitration (the Second Phase) considered that, so far as the maritime delimitation between States with opposite coasts is concerned, an equidistance line would provide an equitable maritime boundary under Arts 74 and 83 of the LOSC. Y Tanaka, 'Reflections on the *Eritrea/Yemen* Arbitration of 17 December 1999 (Second Phase: Maritime Delimitation)' (2001) 48 *NILR* 200.

[161] Judgment, [2002] ICJ Rep 433, [272]; presentation by Kamto, Counsel of Cameroon, Verbatim Record, CR 2002/17, 50–60, [20–48].

[162] Judgment, [2002] ICJ Rep 435, [278]; presentation by Abi-Saab, Counsel of Nigeria, Verbatim Record, CR 2002/20, 40–45, [4–28] (in particular, 43–44, [18–20]). See also presentation by Crawford, Counsel of Nigeria, ibid, 53, [15].

The Court discarded Cameroon's contention for two reasons. First, the maritime boundary between Cameroon and Nigeria could only be determined by reference to points on the coastlines of these two States and not of third States. Secondly, the presence of Bioko, which is a constituent part of a third State, Equatorial Guinea, makes itself felt from Debundsha at the point where the Cameroon coast turns south-south-east. The part of the Cameroon coastline beyond Debundsha Point faces Biokko. It cannot, therefore, be treated as facing Nigeria so as to be relevant to the maritime delimitation between Cameroon and Nigeria.[163]

As indicated in the *Qatar v Bahrain* judgment, the equidistance line should be drawn by connecting 'every point of which is equidistant from the nearest points on the baselines from which the breadth of the territorial seas of each of the two States is measured.' The Court determined the land-based anchorage points to be used in the construction of the equidistance line as West point (8°16′38″ east and 4°31′59″ north) and East point (8°30′14″ east and 4°30′06″ north). These two points correspond to the most southerly points on the low-water line for Nigeria and Cameroon to either side of the bay formed by the estuaries of the Akwayafe and Cross Rivers. In the Court's view, no other base point was necessary for the Court to undertake maritime delimitation in this area.[164] Once the base points have been established, it is possible to determine the equidistance line between the relevant coastlines of the two States.

ii. Considerations on Relevant Circumstances

The Court considered next whether there were circumstances that might make it necessary to adjust the equidistance line in order to achieve an equitable result. The elements to be examined were: (i) the concavity of the Gulf of Guinea in general and of Cameroon's coastline in particular, (ii) the Bioko Island, (iii) proportionality, and (iv) the oil concessions of the Parties. Having considered these factors, the Court rejected all elements of them. Hence, the Court concluded unanimously that, in the present case, the equidistance line represented an equitable result for the delimitation of the area where it had jurisdiction to give a ruling. It should be noted that point G does not lie on the equidistance line between Cameroon and Nigeria, but to the east of that line. Thus the Court considered that from point G, the delimitation line should directly join the equidistance line at a point with co-ordinates 8°21′20″ east and 4°17′00″ north, which will be called point X. The maritime boundary therefore continues beyond point G in a westward direction until it reaches point X at the above-mentioned co-ordinates. Then the boundary turns at point X and

[163] Judgment, [2002] ICJ Rep 442–43, [291].
[164] ibid, 443, [292].

continues southwards along the equidistance line (see Illustration 18). However, as the Court could not take any decision that might affect the rights of Equatorial Guinea, it could do no more than indicate the general direction, from point X, of the maritime boundary, which would follow a loxodrome having an azimuth of 187°52′27″.[165]

VIII. THE *BARBADOS v TRINIDAD AND TOBAGO* CASE (ARBITRATION, 2006)

By a Notice of Arbitration dated 16 February 2004, Barbados initiated arbitration proceedings concerning the delimitation of a single maritime boundary between the EEZs and the continental shelves appertaining to Barbados and Trinidad and Tobago respectively, pursuant to Article 286 as well as Annex VII to the LOSC.[166] This is the first award drawing a single maritime boundary by the Arbitral Tribunal constituted in accordance with Article 287 and Annex VII of the LOSC. A particular issue in this arbitration was whether the Tribunal had jurisdiction over the delimitation of the extended continental shelf. In this regard, the Tribunal considered that the dispute to be dealt with by the Tribunal included the outer continental shelf for three reasons: (i) it either formed part of, or was sufficiently closely related to the dispute submitted by Barbados; (ii) the record of the negotiations showed that it was part of the subject-matter on the table during those negotiations, and (iii) there was in law only a single 'continental shelf.'[167] In its Award of 2006, however, the Tribunal did not deal with the problems posed by the relationship in that maritime area of continental shelf and EEZ rights since there was no single maritime boundary beyond 200 nm.[168] Accordingly, the Tribunal effectuated the delimitation of a single maritime boundary within 200 nm only.

[165] ibid, 448, [307]. In the operative part of the judgment, the Court did not refer to any datum. The omission of datum will make the coordinates indicated in the decision difficult to implement from a technical point of view. Furthermore, it became apparent that point X was not a strict equidistant point, but was a point 315 metres west of a strict equidistance point in Cameroon's favour. Fietta and Cleverly, *A Practitioner's Guide* 415–16.

[166] Arbitration between Barbados and the Republic of Trinidad and Tobago, relating to the delimitation of the exclusive economic zone and the continental shelf between them, decision of 11 April 2006, 27 *RIAA* 147, 155, [1]. The Arbitral Tribunal was composed of five members: Stephen M Schwebel (President), Judges Vaughan Lowe, Ian Brownlie, Francisco Orrego Vicuña, and Sir Arthur Watts. For a commentary on the arbitral award, see Y Tanaka, 'Award of the Arbitral Tribunal Constituted Pursuant to Article 287, and in Accordance with Annex VII, of the UN Convention on the Law of the Sea: the *Barbados and the Trinidad and Tobago* Case (11 April 2006)' (2006) 21 *IJMCL* 523; by the same writer, 'Barbados/Trinidad and Tobago Maritime Delimitation' (2007) 2 *Hague Justice Journal* 54.

[167] The *Barbados v Trinidad and Tobago* arbitral award, (2007) 27 *RIAA* 208–09, [213].

[168] ibid, 242, [368].

A. Law Applicable to Maritime Delimitation

Barbados and Trinidad and Tobago have been Parties to the LOSC.[169] Accordingly, Articles 74(1) and 83(1) of the Convention applied to the delimitation of a single maritime boundary. In this regard, the Annex VII Arbitral Tribunal, in its Award of 2006, held that:

> The determination of the line of delimitation thus normally follows a two-step approach. First, a provisional line of equidistance is posited as a hypothesis and a practical starting point. While a convenient starting point, equidistance alone will in many circumstances not ensure an equitable result in the light of the peculiarities of each specific case. The second step accordingly requires the examination of this provisional line in the light of relevant circumstances, which are case specific, so as to determine whether it is necessary to adjust the provisional equidistance line in order to achieve an equitable result.[170]

'[W]hile no method of delimitation can be considered of and by itself compulsory, and no court or tribunal has so held,' the Tribunal continued, 'the need to avoid subjective determinations requires that the method used start with a measure of certainty that equidistance positively ensures, subject to its subsequent correction if justified.'[171] It thus adopted the corrective-equity approach in the operation of maritime delimitation under Articles 74 and 83 of the LOSC. In this connection, the Tribunal stressed the 'need to avoid subjective determination' and 'certainly' of the equidistance method. It also stated that the quest for neutral criteria of a geographical character prevailed in the end over area-specific criteria such as geomorphological aspects or resource-specific criteria such as the distribution of fish stocks.[172] This view seemed to echo the recent trend of the case law in the field of maritime delimitation.

B. Application of the Law Identified

Next, the Tribunal was to establish maritime delimitation line by dividing overlapping marine space into three areas, ie, west, central, and east segments.

i. Delimitation in the West and Central Segment of the Line

It was common ground between the Parties that the delimitation line in the west was provisionally to be found in the equidistance line between their opposite coasts. Nonetheless, claims of the Parties were divided as to whether the

[169] Barbados ratified the Convention on 12 October 1993; Trinidad and Tobago ratified the Convention on 25 April 1986.
[170] 27 *RIAA* 214–15, [242].
[171] ibid, 230–31, [306].
[172] ibid, 211–12, [228].

provisional equidistance line should be shifted taking relevant circumstances into account. While Trinidad and Tobago maintained that the equidistance line should be the delimitation line in the west, Barbados claimed that the provisional line should be adjusted taking account of, inter alia, critical dependence of Barbadian fisherfolk on the maintenance of access to that fishery.[173] However, this claim was rejected by the Tribunal because of the absence of evidence.[174] The Tribunal thus concluded that the equidistance line in the west shall be the delimitation line between Barbados and Trinidad and Tobago.[175] Referring to the *Lac Lanoux* case,[176] the Tribunal also held that Trinidad and Tobago was under the obligation to negotiate in good faith an agreement with Barbados that would give Barbados access to fisheries within the EEZ of Trinidad and Tobago.[177]

The central segment extends from Point D of Barbados' claim to Point A of Trinidad and Tobago's claim. In this short segment of approximately 16 nm, the Parties did not argue for any adjustment of the provisional equidistance line. Consequently, the Tribunal concluded that the equidistance line was agreed to in this segment.[178]

ii. Delimitation in the East

In the East area, the Parties have not agreed to request delimitation by means of a single maritime boundary. Although Barbados has requested the Tribunal to determine a single maritime boundary for the EEZs and continental shelves of the Parties,[179] Trinidad and Tobago contended that the continental shelf and the EEZ are separate and distinct institutions, and that there may therefore be different lines of delimitation for each.[180] In this regard, the Arbitral Tribunal stated that it would firstly determine a single boundary line for the delimitation of both the continental shelf and the EEZ to the extent of the overlapping claims, without prejudice to the question of the separate legal existence of the EEZ and the continental shelf.[181] As pointed out earlier, the Tribunal made it clear that it applies the two-step approach. It thus determined the location of the maritime delimitation line by adjusting a provisional equidistance line taking account of relevant circumstances: (i) the relevant coasts and their projection, (ii) proportionality, and (iii) regional considerations.[182]

[173] ibid, 215–216, [246–47]. See ch 8, s I of this book.
[174] 27 *RIAA* 221, [265].
[175] ibid, 223, [271].
[176] *Lac Lanoux Arbitration* (France v Spain), (1957) 24 ILR 101, 128.
[177] The *Barbados v Trinidad and Tobago* arbitral award, 27 *RIAA* 227, [292].
[178] ibid, 228, [294].
[179] Reply of Barbados, 84–93, [154–173].
[180] The *Barbados v Trinidad and Tobago* arbitral award, 27 *RIAA* 228–29, [296]; Counter-Memorial of Trinidad and Tobago, 91–102, [261–290]. See also Presentation of Professor Crawford, 21 October 2005, 88–109; ibid, 28 October 2005, 32–59.
[181] The *Barbados v Trinidad and Tobago* arbitral award, 27 *RIAA* 229, [298].
[182] ibid, 236, [334]; 237, [337]; 238–39, [347–48].

The geodetic lines of the maritime boundary were specified in the Award,[183] and it was shown in Map V annexed to the Award (see Illustration 19).[184] Finally, the Tribunal applied the proportionality test and concluded that the bending of the equidistance line reflected a reasonable influence of the coastal frontages on the overall area of delimitation, with a view to avoiding reciprocal encroachments which would otherwise result in some form of inequity.[185]

Overall it can be observed that the Arbitral Tribunal, in the *Barbados v Trinidad and Tobago* case, attempted to maintain the consistency with judicial precedents in the field of maritime delimitation. In particular, it is noteworthy that, as with the *Cameroon v Nigeria* case, the Arbitral Tribunal applied that corrective-equity approach under Articles 74 and 83 of the LOSC.

IX. THE *GUYANA v SURINAME* CASE (ARBITRATION, 2007)

In 2007, two decisions were rendered in relation to the delimitation of a single maritime boundary: the *Guyana v Suriname* arbitral award of 17 September 2007[186] and the *Nicaragua v Honduras* judgment of the ICJ.[187] The *Guyana v Suriname* award sharply contrasts with the *Nicaragua v Honduras* judgment on an important point, namely the application of the equidistance method in the process of maritime delimitation. While the ICJ, in one part of the *Nicaragua v Honduras* case, refused to apply the equidistance method and applied the bisector method, the Annex VII Arbitral Tribunal in the *Guyana v Suriname* case applied the equidistance method by rejecting the use of the bisector method. This section examines the 2007 *Guyana v Suriname* arbitral award.

A. Law Applicable to Maritime Delimitation

i. Law Applicable to Delimitation of the Territorial Sea

Both Guyana and Suriname are parties to the LOSC.[188] Accordingly the delimitation of the territorial sea between the Parties was governed by Article 15 of

[183] ibid, 245, [382].

[184] For the verbal description of the maritime boundary, ibid, 244–45, [381].

[185] ibid, 244, [379]. The application of the proportionality test by the Arbitral Tribunal is open to criticism. See ch 7, s III of this book.

[186] Arbitral Tribunal Constituted Pursuant to Article 287, and in Accordance with Annex VII, of the United Nations Convention on the Law of the Sea in the Matter of an Arbitration between Guyana and Suriname, 17 September 2007, 30 *RIAA* 1. The Arbitral Tribunal was composed of five members: Dolliver M Nelson (President), Kamal Hossain, Thomas M Franck, Ivan Shearer and Hans Smit. The Permanent Court of Arbitration served as Registry for the proceedings. For a commentary on this arbitration, see Y Tanaka, 'The *Guyana/Suriname* Arbitration: A Commentary' (2007) 2 *Hague Justice Journal* 28–33.

[187] See s X of this chapter.

[188] Guyana and Suriname ratified the Convention on 16 November 1993 and 9 July 1998, respectively.

the Convention. Nonetheless, Suriname argued that the delimitation of the territorial sea should proceed along an azimuth of N10°E from the 1936 Point/Point 61. This claim was based mainly on the existence of *de facto* agreement between the Netherlands and the United Kingdom, acquiescence or estoppel and consideration of navigation.[189] However, Guyana contended that the delimitation line should follow an 'historical equidistance line' along an azimuth of N34°E from Point 61 for a distance of 12 nautical miles to a point at the outer limit of the territorial sea.[190] In this connection, Guyana argued that there was no justification admissible under Article 15 of the Convention for departing from the provisional equidistance line in Suriname's favour.[191] In this regard, the Tribunal ruled that: 'Article 15 of the Convention places primacy on the median line as the delimitation line between the territorial seas between opposite or adjacent States.'[192]

ii. Law Applicable to Delimitation of the Continental Shelf and EEZ

The delimitation of the continental shelf and EEZ in the *Guyana v Suriname* case was governed by Articles 74 and 83 of the LOSC. In this respect, the Tribunal ruled that:

> In the course of the last two decades international courts and tribunals dealing with disputes concerning the delimitation of the continental shelf and the exclusive economic zone have come to embrace a clear role for equidistance.[193]

The Tribunal further stated that in addition to maritime delimitation between opposite coasts, the presumption in favour of equidistance applied in maritime delimitations between States with adjacent coasts.[194] In view of the Tribunal,

> The case law of the International Court of Justice and arbitral jurisprudence as well as State practice are at one in holding that the delimitation process should, in appropriate cases, begin by positing a provisional equidistance line which may be adjusted in the light of relevant circumstances in order to achieve an equitable solution. The Tribunal will follow this method in the present case.[195]

The Tribunal thus adopted the corrective-equity approach under Articles 74(1) and 83(1) of the Convention. By contrast, the Tribunal clearly discarded the 'angle bisector methodology' claimed by Suriname because, according to the

[189] The *Guyana v Suriname* arbitral award, (2013) 30 *RIAA* 77, [281–82]. See also Counter-Memorial of Suriname, 15–23, [3.1–3.26].
[190] The *Guyana v Suriname* arbitral award, 30 *RIAA* 79, [288]. See also Memorial of Guyana, 105, [8.56].
[191] Guyana Reply, 111, [6.23]; The *Guyana v Suriname* arbitral award, 30 *RIAA* 81–2, [294].
[192] ibid, 82, [296].
[193] ibid, 93, [335].
[194] ibid, 94, [338].
[195] ibid, 95, [342].

Tribunal, 'the general configuration of the maritime area to be delimited does not present the type of geographical peculiarities which could lead the Tribunal to adopt a methodology at variance with that which has been practised by international courts and tribunals during the last two decades.'[196]

B. Application of the Law Identified

i. Delimitation of the Territorial Sea

In delimiting the territorial sea between the Parties, the Tribunal ruled that special circumstances of navigation may justify deviation from the median (equidistance) line. According to the Tribunal, 'the record amply supports the conclusion that the predecessors of the Parties agreed upon a N10°E delimitation line for the reason that all of the Corentyne River was to be Suriname's territory and that the 10° Line provided appropriate access through Suriname's territorial sea to the western channel of the Corentyne River' and Suriname presented evidence of navigation in the western channel.[197] The Arbitral Tribunal thus considered that the 10° Line claimed by Suriname was established between the Parties from the starting point to the three nautical mile limit.[198] It is notable that the Tribunal explicitly regarded navigation as a special circumstance in the delimitation of the territorial seas.[199]

A particular issue that arose in this context was whether and how, in the absence of an agreement to do so, the 10° Line should be extended from the previous limit of territorial sea (three nautical miles) to a newly established limit (12 nautical miles). In this regard, the Tribunal did not support the view that there should be automatic extension of the territorial sea from the previously accepted limit of three nautical miles to the current limit of 12 nautical miles.[200] In the view of the Tribunal, an automatic extension of the line would 'rapidly cease to have relevance to the special circumstances of navigation and control that brought it about.'[201] It was also necessary to find a principled method by which the 10° Line could be connected to the single maritime boundary line to delimit the continental shelves and EEZ of the Parties. Taking these elements into account, the Tribunal concluded that the delimitation line of the territorial sea must be drawn from the point at which the N10°E line intersects the three nautical mile limit to the point at which the equidistance line drawn by the Tribunal in chapter VI of this Award intersects the 12 nautical mile limit.[202]

[196] ibid, 103, [372].
[197] ibid, 85, [306]. The Corentyne River is navigable inland for about 50 miles. ibid, 33, [134].
[198] ibid, 86, [307].
[199] See ch 8, s V of this book.
[200] The *Guyana v Suriname* arbitral award, 30 *RIAA* 87–8, [311].
[201] ibid, 88, [314].
[202] ibid, 91, [325]. For the verbal description of the delimitation line, ibid, [327].

ii. Delimitation of the Continental Shelf and EEZ

In order to draw a provisional equidistance line, there is a need to identify relevant coasts. In this regard, the Tribunal ruled that the relevant coast of Guyana extends from Devonshire Castle Flats to a point just seaward of Marker 'B,' and that the relevant coast for Suriname extends from Bluff Point, the point on the east bank of the Corentyne River used in 1936 as the mouth of the river, to a point on Vissers Bank.[203]

The next issue was whether there were relevant circumstances which might justify the departure from the provisional equidistance line. In this regard, by referring to the *Gulf of Maine* and *Barbados v Trinidad and Tobago* cases, the Arbitral Tribunal focused on neutral criteria of geographical character. Such criteria relates to coastal geography.[204] Having examined the coastal geography, the Tribunal held that the relevant coastlines did not present any marked concavity or convexity; and that the relevant coastlines did not represent a circumstance that would justify any adjustment of the provisional equidistance line.[205] In this connection, it is notable that the Tribunal relied on the assessment of the coastal geography made by the independent expert appointed by Guyana.[206]

By contrast, '[h]aving carefully examined the practice of the Parties with regard to oil concessions and oil wells,' the Tribunal ruled that the oil practice of the Parties could not be taken into account in this case since there was no evidence of any agreement between the Parties regarding such practice.[207] The Tribunal's view was in line with the judicial precedents, in particular, the *Cameroon v Nigeria* case.[208]

After applying the proportionality test, the Tribunal ruled that there were no distortions caused by coastal geography. The Tribunal therefore concluded that the equidistance line, which commences at Point 3, should be the delimitation line of the continental shelf and the EEZ between the Parties (see Illustration 20).[209]

X. THE *NICARAGUA v HONDURAS* CASE (ICJ, 2007)

After the *Guyana v Suriname* arbitral ward, another decision regarding the delimitation of a single maritime boundary, that is, the *Nicaragua v Honduras* judgment, was rendered in 2007.[210] The ICJ, in its judgment, resolved a difficult

[203] ibid, 97, [352].
[204] ibid, [355].
[205] ibid, 105, [377].
[206] ibid.
[207] ibid, 108, [390].
[208] Further, see ch 8, s II of this book.
[209] 30 *RIAA* 109, [392]. See also ch 7, s III of this book.
[210] *Territorial and Maritime Dispute between Nicaragua and Honduras in the Caribbean Sea (Nicaragua v Honduras)*, Judgment, [2007] ICJ Rep 659, 663, [1].

dispute concerning the territorial sovereignty over islands and maritime delimitation in the disputed area in a single judgment.[211] The *Nicaragua v Honduras* case was submitted to the ICJ by Nicaragua on 8 December 1999. In its Application, Nicaragua found the jurisdiction of the Court on Article XXXI of the Pact of Bogotà as well as Article 36(2) of the Statute of the ICJ.[212] As both Nicaragua and Honduras are State Parties to the LOSC,[213] the delimitation of the territorial sea, the EEZ and the continental shelf between the Parties is governed by Articles 15, 74 (1) and 83 (1) of the LOSC, respectively.

A. Law Applicable to Maritime Delimitation

i. The Existence of the Traditional Maritime Boundary Line

The first issue to be addressed in the *Nicaragua v Honduras* case was whether or not there was a traditional maritime boundary line as claimed by Honduras. A pivotal issue in this regard was the applicability of the principle of *uti possidetis juris* to maritime boundaries.[214] Honduras claimed that the *uti possidetis juris* principle referred to in the Gámez-Bonilla Treaty and the 1906 Award of the King of Spain was applicable to the maritime area off the coasts of Honduras and Nicaragua, and that the line of 15th parallel constitutes the line of maritime delimitation resulting from that application.[215] Notably, the ICJ considered that the *uti possidetis juris* principle 'might in certain circumstances, such as in connection with historic bays and territorial seas, play a role in a maritime delimitation.'[216] According to the Court, however, no persuasive case had been made by Honduras as to why the maritime boundary should extend from the

[211] For a commentary by the author, see Y Tanaka, 'Reflections on Maritime Delimitation in the *Nicaragua/Honduras* Case' (2008) 68 *ZaöRV/Heidelberg Journal of International Law* 903; Y Tanaka, 'Case Concerning the Territorial and Maritime Disputes between Nicaragua and Honduras in the Caribbean Sea' (2008) 23 *IJMCL* 327.

[212] The *Nicaragua v Honduras* case, Judgment, [2007] ICJ Rep 664, [1]. During the oral proceedings, Nicaragua further requested that the Court pronounce on sovereignty over islands located in the disputed area to the north of the boundary line claimed by Honduras and running along 14° 59.8′ North latitude. ibid, 699–700, [127]. The ICJ accepted the Nicaraguan claim relating to sovereignty over the islands in the maritime area. ibid, 697, [115].

[213] Nicaragua ratified the LOSC on 3 May 2000 and Honduras on 5 October 1993. ibid, 738, [261].

[214] For an analysis of the application of the principle of *uti possidetis juris* in the *Nicaragua/Honduras* case, see Tanaka, 'Reflections on Maritime Delimitation in the *Nicaragua/Honduras* Case,' 907–9. Concerning the application of the principle of *uti possidetis juris* in maritime delimitations, see G Nesi, '*Uti possidetis juris* e delimitazioni maritime' (1991) 74 *Rivista di diritto internazionale*, 534–70; MG Kohen, *Possession contestée et souveraineté territoriale* (Paris, PUF, 1997) 461–64; S Lalonde, 'Uti Possidetis: Its Colonial Past Revisited' (2001) *Revue belge de droit international* 84.

[215] [2007] ICJ Rep 727–28, [229]; Counter-Memorial submitted by Honduras, Vol. I, 25–27, [2.25–2.28]; 144–46, [7.38–7.45]; presentation by Sands, Verbatim Record, CR 2007/9, 10–39, [1–57].

[216] [2007] ICJ Rep 728, [232].

Cape along the 15th parallel. The Court had already denied the relevance of the principle of *uti possidetis juris* in relation to sovereignty over the disputed islands in the present case. Nor had it been shown that Spanish Crown divided its maritime jurisdiction between the colonial provinces of Nicaragua and Honduras even within the limits of the territorial sea. Furthermore, the 1906 Award did not deal with the maritime delimitation between Nicaragua and Honduras. The Court thus concluded that the *uti possidetis juris* principle cannot be said to have provided a basis for a maritime delimitation along the 15th parallel.[217]

When considering the application of the principle of *uti possidetis juris* to maritime delimitations, intertemporal law should be considered.[218] It seems logical to consider that the principle is not applicable to marine spaces which were unknown in the colonial period. Therefore, the principle will have no role to play in the delimitation of the EEZ, which was crystallised in the post-colonial period.[219] If the principle of *uti possidetis juris* can be applied to the delimitation of the territorial sea, an issue arises with regard to the extension of the delimitation line since there was no agreement on the maximum breadth of the territorial sea in the colonial period. Currently the maximum breadth of the territorial sea is 12 nautical miles under Article 3 of the LOSC. However, it is not suggested that the delimitation line on the basis of the principle of *uti possidetis juris* will automatically extend until 12 nautical miles. The *Guyana v Suriname* arbitration is a case in point. After the examination of the question of whether and how a delimitation should extend from the previous limit of the territorial sea (three nautical miles) to a newly established limit (12 nautical miles), the Arbitral Tribunal did not support automatic extension of the territorial sea from the previously accepted limit of three nautical miles to the current limit of 12 nautical miles.[220]

In any case it appears that the role of this principle remains slim in the field of maritime delimitation. In addition, even though Honduras contended that there was a '*de facto* boundary based on the tacit agreement of the Parties' at the 15th parallel,[221] the Court did not uphold the contention of Honduras.[222]

[217] ibid, 728–29, [232–36]. However, Judge ad hoc Torres Bernárdez considered that on the basis of the principle of *uti possidetis juris*, the 15th parallel constituted the boundary of the territorial sea with a breadth of six nautical miles. Dissenting Opinion of Judge Torres Bernárdez, ibid, 804–06, [75–83]; 812–13, [102–10].

[218] Lalonde, 'Uti Possidetis,' 85; Tanaka, 'Reflections on Maritime Delimitation in the *Nicaragua/Honduras* Case,' 908–9.

[219] Yet Judge Jiménez de Aréchaga was supportive of the application of the principle *uti possidetis juris* to the colonial delimitation of sponge fisheries. Separate Opinion of Judge Jiménez de Aréchaga in the *Tunisia/Libya* case, [1982] ICJ Rep 131–32, [100–02].

[220] The *Guyana v Suriname* arbitral award, 30 *RIAA* 99, [311]. See also s IX of this chapter.

[221] The *Nicaragua v Honduras* case, Judgment, [2007] ICJ Rep 729–33, [237–46].

[222] ibid, 736–37, [257–58]. This issue will be discussed in ch 8, s II of this book.

ii. The Methodology of the Court

a. The Rejection of the Equidistance Method

Next, the Court moved on to establish a single maritime boundary. Concerning the methodology of maritime delimitation, the Court observed that because of the very active morpho-dynamism of the relevant area, 'continued accretion at the Cape might render any equidistance line so constructed today arbitrary and unreasonable in the near future.'[223] Furthermore, there were no viable base points claimed or accepted by the Parties themselves at Cape Gracias a Dios.[224] In the view of the Court, the difficulty in identifying reliable base points was compounded by the differences between the Parties as to 'the interpretation and application of the King of Spain's 1906 Arbitral Award in respect of sovereignty over the islets formed near the mouth of the River Coco and the establishment of "[t]he extreme common boundary point on the coast of the Atlantic"'.[225] In addition, any base points used for the drawing of an equidistance line would be uncertain within a short period of time because of the unstable nature of the relevant coasts. Given the set of circumstances, the Court considered that it was impossible to identify base points and construct a provisional equidistance line for the single maritime boundary delimiting maritime areas off the Parties' mainland coasts. Hence the Court found itself within the exception provided for in Article 15 of the LOSC, namely facing special circumstances in which it cannot apply the equidistance principle.[226] As discussed elsewhere, however, there may be some scope to reconsider the question whether the difficulty in the instability of base points can be a decisive reason to preclude the application of the equidistance method.[227]

First, as suggested by Judge Ranjeva and Judge ad hoc Torres Bernárdez, it appears that the difficulty in the instability of base points may not be insurmountable.[228] In fact, during the oral proceedings, Honduras showed its provisional equidistance line.[229] Similarly, Nicaragua attached an illustration identifying an approximate median line in its Memorial.[230] During the

[223] The *Nicaragua v Honduras* case, Judgment, [2007] ICJ Rep 742, [277].

[224] ibid, 743, [278].

[225] ibid, [279].

[226] ibid, 743–45, [280–81].

[227] Tanaka, 'Reflections on Maritime Delimitation in the *Nicaragua/Honduras* Case,' 924–26.

[228] Separate Opinion of Judge Ranjeva in the *Nicaragua v Honduras* case, Judgment, [2007] ICJ Rep 768–69, [10]; Dissenting Opinion of Judge Torres Bernárdez, 818, [128].

[229] Presentation by Colson, Verbatim Record, CR 2007/10, 24–28, [123–141]. The equidistance line proposed by Honduras was constructed on the basis of Bobel Cay, Port Royal Cay and South Cay on the Honduran side, and Edinburgh Cay and Edinburgh Reef on the Nicaraguan side. The first segment of the provisional equidistance line extends in an east-south-east direction from the mainland to a point which is a trijunction point that is equally distant from Bobel Cay, Edinburgh Cay and the point fixed by the 1962 Mixed Commission. *Ibid*, 25, [127] and 26, [132]. See also Memorial submitted by Nicaragua, vol I, 83, [23]; Reply of Nicaragua, 197, [10.5]; Judgment, [2007] ICJ Rep 742, [276]; 745–46, [285].

[230] Memorial submitted by Nicaragua, 197.

oral proceedings, Nicaragua also showed its provisional median line dividing Nicaraguan and Honduran waters.[231] Hence it appeared to be possible to draw a provisional equidistance line in the *Nicaragua v Honduras* case.

Secondly, Article 7(2) of the LOSC explicitly recognises that the straight baselines remain effective notwithstanding changes in the coastline.[232] Where, as the Court stated, the configuration of the coastlines of Nicaragua and Honduras is highly unstable, Article 7(2) would have provided a solution for identifying reliable basepoints.[233]

Thirdly, in reality, the configuration of coastlines is more or less changeable owing to erosion, accretion, and sea-level rise resulting from global warming. Considering the requirement for stability of maritime boundaries, however, there may be scope for arguing that in principle, changes in basepoints or baselines resulting from natural causes will not affect maritime boundaries already established between States concerned, unless those States agree otherwise.[234] In this connection, it must be recalled that under Article 62 (2) of the Vienna Convention on the Law of Treaties, treaties establishing a boundary – which must be deemed to include treaties establishing maritime boundaries – are excluded from invocation of a fundamental change of circumstances.[235] For the same reasons, arguably boundaries established through international adjudication will not be automatically affected by subsequent changes in the configuration of the coasts.[236]

Fourthly, the Court appeared to consider that an equidistance line may automatically become 'arbitrary and unreasonable' if the location of the basepoints was changed because of the shift of coastlines. If this is the case, the equitableness

[231] Presentation by Brownlie, Verbatim Record CR 2007/12, 45, [28–30].

[232] See Separate Opinion of Judge Ranjeva in the *Nicaragua v Honduras* case, [2007] ICJ Rep 767, [7]. See also Dissenting Opinion of Judge Torres Bernárdez, ibid, 818–19, [131]. With respect to Article 7(2) of the LOSC, see S McDonald and V Prescott, 'Baselines along Unstable Coasts: An Interpretation of Article 7 (2)' (1990) 8 *Ocean Yearbook*, 70–89; V Prescott and E Bird, 'The Influence of Rising Sea Levels on Baselines from Which National Maritime Claims are Measured and an Assessment of the Possibility of Applying Article 7(2) of the 1982 Convention on the Law of the Sea to Offset Any Retreat of the Baseline' *International Boundaries and Boundary Conflict Resolution, Proceedings of the IBRU Conference held at the University of Durham 14–17 September 1989* (International Boundaries Research Unit, University of Durham, 1989) 279–300.

[233] Dissenting Opinion of Judge Torres Bernárdez in the *Nicaragua v Honduras* case, [2007] ICJ Rep 818–19, [131]; 825–26, [161].

[234] Soons has examined the question whether changes in basepoints or baselines resulting from sea level rise may affect existing maritime boundaries, and answered in the negative. AHA Soons, 'The Effects of a Rising Sea Level on Maritime Limits and Boundaries' (1990) 37 *NILR*, 226–29. The answer will be the same with respect to changes in basepoints resulting from erosion or accretion. In practice, for instance, Art 3(3) of the 2000 Agreement on the Delimitation of the Territorial Sea, Exclusive Economic Zone and Continental Shelf in the Beibu Gulf (Gulf of Tonkin) between the People's Republic of China and the Socialist Republic of Vietnam makes clear that no topographical change shall change the demarcation line for the territorial seas of the two countries unless otherwise agreed by the Parties. Text in: DA Colson and RW Smith (eds), *International Maritime Boundaries*, vol V, (Leiden and Boston, Brill/Nijhoff, 2005) 3755–58.

[235] Soons, 'The Effects of a Rising Sea Level,' 228.

[236] ibid, 229.

of an equidistance line will rely solely on the choice of the basepoints. This argument is too simplistic, however. The equitableness of a provisional equidistance line must be envisaged by taking all relevant circumstances into account. Having constructed a provisional equidistance line, the international courts and tribunals are required to examine whether there are any circumstances which necessitate its adjustment. Where an equidistance line was established as a maritime boundary by international courts and tribunals, the line was considered as equitable in relation to all relevant circumstances. Should an equidistance line today be equitable with regard to all relevant circumstances, the shift of coastlines alone will not *automatically* make the equidistance line inequitable.[237]

Finally, the Court stated that 'the pair of base points to be identified on either bank of the River Coco at the tip of the Cape would assume a considerable dominance in constructing an equidistance line.'[238] As Judges Ranjeva and Torres Bernárdez pointed out, however, it is inconceivable that the use of a single pair of base points would become an obstacle requiring a complete rejection of the application of the equidistance line.[239] In fact, the Court, in the *Cameroon v Nigeria* case, constructed the equidistance line on the basis of only two points of the mouth of the Akwayafe and Cross Rivers, West Point and East Point, as determined on the 1994 edition of British Admiralty Chart 3433.[240] Accordingly, the limited number of base points cannot be a decisive factor for one to discard the application of the equidistance line at the first stage of maritime delimitation.

b. The Bisector Method

After having rejected the application of the equidistance method, the ICJ found that the bisector method was to be applied in the present case. For the Court, '[i]n instances where, as in the present case, any base points that could be determined by the Court are inherently unstable, the bisector method may be seen as an approximation of the equidistance method.'[241] At the same time, the Court added that: '[E]quidistance remains the general rule.'[242] This statement appears to suggest that the non-application of the equidistance method in the *Nicaragua v Honduras* dispute is only exceptional. In fact, with respect to the delimitation around the islands in the dispute area, the Court applied, without any problem,

[237] I am obliged to Professor Hugh Thirlway for drawing my attention to this point.

[238] Judgment, [2007] ICJ Rep 742, [277].

[239] Separate Opinion of Judge Ranjeva in the *Nicaragua v Honduras* case, ibid, 768–69, [10]; Dissenting Opinion of Judge Torres Bernárdez, 819, [132]. See also presentation by Quéneudec, Verbatim Record, CR 2007/14, 24–29, [1–25]; HWA Thirlway, *The Law and Procedure of the Intrnational Court of Justice: Fifty Years of Jurisprudnce*, vol II (Oxford University Press, 2013) 1395, footnote 486.

[240] [2002] ICJ Rep 443, [292].

[241] [2007] ICJ Rep 746, [287].

[242] ibid, 745, [281].

the corrective-equity approach by referring to the *Qatar v Bahrain* case.[243] Furthermore, the angle-bisector line may be regarded as a simplified equidistance line since the equidistance line is created from simplified coasts.[244] In fact, ITLOS, in the *Bangladesh/Myanmar* case, clearly stated that the angle-bisector method is 'in effect an approximation of the equidistance method'.[245] It can be argued, therefore, that the departure from the previous jurisprudence is only partial.[246]

B. Application of the Law Identified

i. Establishment of a Single Maritime Boundary

Unlike the equidistance method, this method relies on the macro-geography of a coastline as represented by a line drawn between two points on the coast. In the Court's view, a Honduran coastal front running to Punta Patuca and a Nicaraguan coastal front running to Wouhnta are the relevant coasts for the purposes of drawing the bisector. It follows that the bisector line is an azimuth of 70° 14′41.25″ (see Illustration 21).[247]

The next issue concerns the delimitation around the islands in the disputed area. Nicaragua argued that these islands should be enclaved within only a three-nautical mile territorial sea, since a full 12-nautical mile territorial sea would result in giving a disproportionate amount of the maritime areas in dispute to Honduras.[248] By rejecting this argument, the Court ruled that the Honduran islands of Bobel Cay, Savanna Cay, Port Royal Cay and South Cay shall be accorded a territorial sea of 12 nautical miles.[249] It follows that the territorial seas attributed to the Honduran islands and the Nicaraguan island of Edinburgh Cay would lead to an overlap in the territorial seas of the Parties. Following the

[243] ibid., 751–52, [303–04].

[244] SD Murphy, 'International Law Relating to Islands' (2017) 386 *RCADI*, 184; Cottier, *Equitable Principles of Maritime Boundary Delimitation*, 191; NM Antunes and V Becker-Weinberg, 'Entitlement to Maritime Zones and Their Delimitation: In the Doldrums of Uncertainty and Unpredictability' in Alex G Oude Elferink, T Henriksen and SV Busch (eds) *Maritime Boundary Delimitation: The Case Law Is It consistent and Practicable?* (Cambridge University Press, 2018) 80; D McRae, 'The Applicable Law: The Geneva Convention on the Continental Shelf, the LOSC, and Customary International Law' in ibid, 109.

[245] *Dispute concerning Delimitation of the Maritime Boundary between Bangladesh and Myanmar in the Bay of Bengal* (Bangladesh/Myanmar), Judgment (hereafter the *Bangladesh/Myanmar* case), [2012] ITLOS Rep 66, [234]. See also Dissenting Opinion of Judge Lucky, ibid, 279.

[246] R Churchill, 'Dispute Settlement under the UN Convention on the Law of the Sea: Survey for 2007' (2008) 23 *IJMCL* 622–24.

[247] The *Nicaragua v Honduras* case, Judgment, [2007] ICJ Rep 749, [298].

[248] ibid, 751, [300]. This is a response to the question posed by Judge Simma during the oral proceedings. Judge Simma's question was: 'What are the reasons for the indication by Nicaragua of 3-mile territorial seas around these cays while both Parties to the present dispute in general claim 12-mile territorial seas?' Verbatim Record, CR 2007/12, 54.

[249] The *Nicaragua v Honduras* case, Judgment, [2007] ICJ Rep 751, [300–02].

precedent, the Court applied the equidistance method in the delimitation of the territorial seas between the Parties. It then examined the existence of special circumstances. In this regard, the Court did not consider there to be any legally relevant 'special circumstances' in this area that would warrant adjusting this provisional line.[250] Thus it can be said that the Court applied the corrective-equity approach.

ii. Starting-point and Endpoint of the Maritime Boundary

Finally, the starting-point and endpoint of the maritime boundary must be examined. As for the starting-point, both Nicaragua and Honduras agreed that the appropriate starting-point should be located three nautical miles seaward from the 'mouth' of the River Coco; and that for the first three nautical miles a negotiated solution should be found. Yet there was no agreement from where on the River Coco these three nautical miles should be measured and in what direction.[251] In this respect, the Court set, by 15 votes to two, the starting-point three miles out to sea (15° 00′ 52″N and 83° 05′58″W) from the point already identified by the 1962 Mixed Commission along the azimuth of the bisector.[252] It is of particular interest to note that the starting-point is located at sea.[253] At the same time, the Court found, by 16 votes to one, that the Parties must negotiate in good faith with a view to agreeing on the course of the delimitation line which links the end of the land boundary as fixed by the 1906 Award and the point of departure of the maritime delimitation in accordance with this judgment.[254]

Concerning the endpoint, the Court did not specify the precise location of the point. Instead, it merely stated that it extends beyond the 82nd meridian without affecting third-state rights.[255] Curiously the proportionality test was not applied in the *Nicaragua v Honduras* judgment, even though Nicaragua argued this point.[256] On this point, the *Nicaragua v Honduras* judgment contrasted with the precedents in this field. In conclusion, by 14 votes to three, the Court established the single maritime boundary as shown in Illustration 22.[257]

[250] ibid, 752, [304].

[251] ibid, 755, [307]. On this issue, see Memorial submitted by Nicaragua, vol I, 75–86, [1–30]; Counter-Memorial submitted by Honduras, vol I, 136–37, [7.9–7.14]; 144–46, [7.38–7.45]; Reply of Nicaragua, vol I, 195–206, [10.1–10.30]; Rejoinder of Honduras, vol I, 125–27, [8.02–8.06].

[252] [2007] ICJ Rep 756, [311]; 760, [321(2)]. See Sketch-map No. 6 attached to the judgment. ibid, 757.

[253] In the *Gulf of Maine* case as well, the starting-point, ie, point A, was situated in the Golf, not land. Unlike the *Nicaragua v Honduras* case, the point A was fixed by the Parties. See s I of this chapter.

[254] 2007] ICJ Rep 756, [311] and 763, [321(4)].

[255] ibid, 759, [319].

[256] Reply of Nicaragua, vol I, 193, [9.53–9.54]; presentation by Brownlie, Verbatim Record, CR 2007/5, 39–40, [64–66]; presentation by Brownlie, Verbatim Record, CR 2007/12, 51–52, [63–66].

[257] Judgment, [2007] ICJ Rep 760–61, [321(3)].

XI. THE *BLACK SEA* CASE (ROMANIA v UKRAINE, ICJ, 2009)

The *Black Sea* case, which will be discussed below, was a landmark of the jurisprudence concerning maritime delimitations. On 16 September 2004, Romania instituted proceedings before the ICJ against Ukraine concerning the delimitation of the continental shelf and the EEZs in the Black Sea. Romania founded the jurisdiction of the Court on Article 36(2) of the Statute of the ICJ and paragraph 4*(h)* of the Additional Agreement.[258] Both Romania and Ukraine are Parties to the LOSC.[259]

A. Law Applicable to Maritime Delimitation

The *Black Sea* case relates to the delimitation of a single maritime boundary dividing the EEZ and the continental shelf between Romania and Ukraine in the Black Sea.[260] The first enquiry in this case was whether there is an agreed maritime boundary around Serpents' Island for all purposes.[261] By examining the 1949 instruments and the subsequent agreements, the Court concluded that there is no agreement in force between the Parties with regard to the delimitation of the EEZ and the continental shelf;[262] and that under Article 1 of the 2003 State Border Régime Treaty,[263] the endpoint of the State border between the Parties was fixed at the point of intersection where the territorial sea boundary of Romania meets that of Ukraine. The Court referred to this point as 'Point 1'.[264] The single maritime boundary between Romania and Ukraine begins at this point.

The *Black Sea* case marked the landmark in the sense that the ICJ explicitly formulated the so-called three-stage approach to maritime delimitations. According to the Court, the process of maritime delimitation will be divided into three stages. At the first stage, a provisional delimitation line is to be established. In this regard, the Court held that:

> These separate stages, broadly explained in the case concerning *Continental Shelf (Libyan Arab Jamahiriya/Malta) (Judgment, I.C.J. Reports 1985*, p. 46, para. 60), have in recent decades been specified with precision. First, the Court will establish

[258] *Maritime Delimitation in the Black Sea (Romania v Ukraine)* (the *Black Sea* case) Judgment, [2009] ICJ Rep 64, [1]; 70–71, [17–20]. For a commentary on the *Black Sea* case by the author, see Y Tanaka, 'Reflections on Maritime Delimitation in the *Romania/Ukraine* Case before the International Court of Justice' (2009) 56 *NILR*, 397–427.

[259] Romania ratified the Convention on 17 December 1996 and Ukraine on 26 July 1999. [2009] ICJ Rep 74, [31].

[260] ibid, 70, [17].

[261] ibid, 78–9, [43].

[262] ibid, 86–9, [67–76].

[263] Treaty between Romania and Ukraine on the Romanian-Ukrainian State Border Regime, Collaboration and Mutual Assistance on Border Matters, 2277 *UNTS* 43 (English translation).

[264] [2009] ICJ Rep 86, [66]. See also Sketch-map No 8 annexed to the judgment.

> a provisional delimitation line, using methods that are geometrically objective and also appropriate for the geography of the area in which the delimitation is to take place. So far as delimitation between adjacent coasts is concerned, an equidistance line will be drawn unless there are compelling reasons that make this unfeasible in the particular case (see *Territorial and Maritime Dispute between Nicaragua and Honduras in the Caribbean Sea (Nicaragua* v. *Honduras)*, Judgment of 8 October 2007, para. 281). So far as opposite coasts are concerned, the provisional delimitation line will consist of a median line between the two coasts. No legal consequences flow from the use of the terms 'median line' and 'equidistance line' since the method of delimitation is the same for both.[265]

According to the Court, the provisional equidistance line 'is plotted on strictly geometrical criteria on the basis of objective data.'[266] At the second stage, the Court will examine whether there are relevant circumstances calling for the adjustment of the provisional equidistance line in order to achieve an equitable result. At the final and third stage, the Court will verify whether the delimitation line does not lead to an inequitable result by applying the disproportionality test.[267] The methodology adopted by the ICJ in the *Black Sea* case requires three comments.

First, the Court made clear that it would first draw a provisional equidistance line and, next, examine whether the line must be adjusted taking relevant circumstances into account in order to achieve an equitable result. Considering that the ICJ regarded the disproportionality test as a 'check for an equitable outcome,'[268] the disproportionality test can also be considered as an element for achieving an equitable result. It may be argued, therefore, that in essence, the three-stage approach can be regarded as a variation of the corrective-equity approach developed through jurisprudence.

Secondly, the ICJ, in the *Black Sea* case, applied the equidistance method at the first stage of the maritime delimitation under Articles 74(1) and 83(1) of the LOSC. According to the interpretation of the Court, a specific method, namely, the equidistance method is to be incorporated into Articles 74(1) and 83(1) of the LOSC. Given that those provisions contain no reference to a specific delimitation method, the ICJ's interpretation can be regarded as a creative interpretation.

Thirdly, the Court's delimitation methodology was prudently qualified by the phrase, 'unless there are compelling reasons that make this unfeasible in the particular case'. Although the Court did not make further precision with regard to the 'compelling reasons', as suggested in the *Nicaragua v Honduras* judgment, such reasons may include the serious instability of the relevant coasts. In paragraph 116 quoted above, the 'compelling reasons' was mentioned

[265] ibid, 101, [116].
[266] ibid, [118].
[267] ibid, 101–3, [120–22].
[268] ibid, 103, [122].

only in the context of delimitation between adjacent coasts. The language of paragraph 116 of the *Black Sea* judgment appears to suggest that the qualification relates only to the delimitation between States with adjacent coasts.

B. Application of the Law Identified

i. Construction of the Provisional Equidistance Line

a. Identification of Relevant Coasts and Maritime Area

To draw a provisional equidistance line at the first stage of the maritime delimitation, it is necessary to identify the relevant coasts.[269] In this regard, the Court held that:

> [T]he coast, in order to be considered as relevant for the purpose of the delimitation, must generate projections which overlap with projections from the coast of the other Party.[270]

As a consequence, 'the submarine extension of any part of the coast of one Party which, because of its geographic situation, cannot overlap with the extension of the coast of the other, is to be excluded from further consideration by the Court.'[271] The Court accordingly considered that whole coast of Romania abuts the area to be delimited, and, consequently, constitutes the relevant coast,[272] whilst the Ukraine's coasts of Karkinits'ka Gulf do not form part of the relevant coast because these coasts face each other and their submarine extension cannot overlap with the extensions of Romania's coast. For the same reason, the Ukraine's coast of Yahorlyts'ka Gulf and Dnieper Firth is excluded from relevant coasts.[273] The Court's view appears to contrast with the *Gulf of Maine* judgment which included the Bay of Fundy into the calculation of the length of Canadian coasts.[274] Yet some doubt can be expressed whether it was relevant to preclude the coasts of Karkinits'ka Gulf from consideration since some parts of the coasts of the Gulf, such as the coast at the back of the Gulf, seem to generate projections that overlap with the seaward projections of Romania.[275] The Court also considered that the coast of Serpents' Island is so short that it makes no real difference to the overall length of the relevant coasts of the Parties.[276]

[269] For an overview of the delimitation process in the *Black Sea* case, see Tanaka, 'Reflections on Maritime Delimitation in the *Romania/Ukraine* Case,' 403 et seq.

[270] The *Black Sea* case, [2009] ICJ Rep 97, [99].

[271] ibid. This passage is a dictum of the *Tunisia/Libya* judgment. [1982] ICJ Rep 61, [75].

[272] ibid, 93, [88].

[273] ibid, 97, [100].

[274] The *Gulf of Maine* case, Judgment, [1984] ICJ Rep 336, [221].

[275] Alex G Oude Elferink, 'Relevant Coasts and Relevant Area: The Difficulty of Developing General Concepts in a Case-Specific Context' in Oude Elferink, Henriksen and Busch, *Maritime Boundary Delimitation*, 187.

[276] The *Black Sea* case, Judgment, [2009] ICJ Rep 97–98, [102].

On the other hand, the Court took the view that Ukraine's south-facing coast between the point where southern bank of the Nistru/Dniester Firth meets the coast (referred to by Romania as 'Point S') and Cape Tarkhankut generates projections which overlap with the maritime projections of the Romanian coast. Accordingly, the Court considered these sectors as relevant coasts of Ukraine.[277]

Next, the Court identified the relevant area. According to the Court, 'the legal concept of the "relevant area" has to be taken into account as part of the methodology of maritime delimitation' in two respects. First, it determines the scope of marine spaces to be dealt with by the Court in a particular case. Secondly it is pertinent to checking disproportionality.[278] With regard to the former, the Court stated that: '[T]he relevant area may include certain maritime space and excluded others which are not germane to the case in hand.'[279] The *dictum* of the Court seems to imply the discretionary nature of the identification of relevant area.[280] Specifically, concerning the limit of the north maritime area, the Court ruled that as the section of the Ukrainian coast between Point S and Cape Tarkhankut is regarded as a relevant coast, the area lying immediately south of this coast falls within the delimitation area, while the area of the Karkinits'ka Gulf inside the closing line drawn by the Court is to be excluded from the relevant maritime area.[281] With regard to the southern limit of the relevant maritime area, an issue arises with regard to entitlement of third parties in the south-western triangle as well as in the small area in the western corner of the south-eastern triangle.[282] In this regard, the Court held that:

> However where areas are included solely for the purpose of approximate identification of overlapping entitlements of the Parties to the case, which may be deemed to constitute the relevant area (and which in due course will play a part in the final stage testing for disproportionality), third party entitlements cannot be affected. Third party entitlements would only be relevant if the delimitation between Romania and Ukraine were to affect them.[283]

The Court accordingly found it appropriate to include both the south-western and south-eastern triangles in its calculation of the relevant maritime area,

[277] ibid, 97, [101]. Point S is identified in Figure 30 in Memorial Submitted by Romania, 224. See also S Touzé, 'Affaire relative à la Délimitation maritime en mer Noire (Roumanie c. Ukraine): une clarification didactique de la règle de l'équidistance circonstances pertinentes' (2009) 55 *AFDI* 229–31.

[278] [2009] ICJ Rep 99, [110].

[279] ibid.

[280] Touzé, 'Affaire relative à la Délimitation maritime en mer Noire (Roumanie c. Ukraine)' (2009) 55 *AFDI* 232.

[281] [2009] ICJ Rep 100, [113]. The closing line runs from Cape Priboiny, which is located in slightly north of Cape Tarkhankut, to the point that marks the eastern end of the portion of the Ukrainian northern coast that faces the area to be delimited. ibid, 97, [100].

[282] ibid, 100, [114]. See also Sketch-map No. 5 attached to the Judgment. ibid, 102.

[283] ibid, 100, [114].

without prejudice to the position of any third State concerning its entitlement in this area.[284]

b. Construction of a Provisional Equidistance Line

The ICJ then turned to identify base points for constructing a provisional equidistance line. With regard to the Romanian coast, the Court considered it appropriate to use the landward end of the Sulina dyke as a base point for drawing the provisional equidistance line.[285] As the Ukrainian coast consists of two portions – one adjacent to the Romanian coast, the other opposite to it – there is a need to select the base points in each portion.[286] Concerning the Ukraine's coast adjacent to the Romanian coast, the Court considered it appropriate to use the south-eastern tip of Tsyganka Island, which is the counterpart of the landward end of the Sulina dyke on the Romanian side. On the other hand, the Court regarded the island of Kubansky as irrelevant as a base point because this island does not produce any effect on the equidistance line plotted by reference to Tsyganka Island and the landward end of the Sulina dyke.[287] With regard to the section of Ukraine's coast opposite Romania's coast, the Court deemed it appropriate to use Cape Tarkhankut and Cape Khersones as a relevant base point.[288] In this connection, the Court considered it inappropriate to select any base points on Serpents' Island.[289]

In summary, the Court ruled that the base points for drawing a provisional equidistance line are those situated on the Sacalin Peninsula and the landward end of the Sulina dyke on the Romanian coast, and Tsyganka Island, Cape Tarkankut and Cape Khersones on the Ukrainian coast. By using these base points, the Court constructed the provisional equidistance line between Romania and Ukraine.[290]

ii. Considerations on Relevant Circumstances and the Disproportionality Test

The Court then ascertained whether relevant circumstances of the case call for adjustment of the provisional equidistance line. In this regard, the following factors were examined: (i) Disproportion between lengths of coasts, (ii) the enclosed nature of the Black Sea, (iii) the presence of Serpents' Island, (iv)

[284] ibid, 100, [113–14]. See Sketch-map No. 4 attached to the judgment. ibid, p 94. The influence of third States on relevant areas will be discussed in ch 7, s VII.

[285] [2009] ICJ Rep 108, [138–41]. The issue of Sulina dyke will be discussed in ch 7, s V of this book.

[286] [2009] ICJ Rep 105, [128].

[287] ibid, 109, [143–44].

[288] ibid, [145–48].

[289] ibid, 109–10, [149]. Serpents' Island belongs to Ukraine. Memorial of Romania, 5, [1.2]; Counter-Memorial of Ukraine, vol I, 2, [1.6]. The issue of base points will be discussed in ch 7, s V of this book.

[290] [2009] ICJ Rep 111–12, [154]. See also Sketch-map No. 6 annexed to the judgment.

the conduct of the Parties, (v) any cutting effect, (vi) the security considerations.[291] As pointed out, the Court examined Serpents' Island when selecting base points for constructing a provisional equidistance line. It follows that Serpents' Island was considered twice at the first and second stages of maritime delimitation. The Court concluded that there was no need to adjust the provisional equidistance line on the basis of these factors. The Court then applied the disproportionality test at the third stage of maritime delimitation. In this regard, the ICJ referred to the negative formula of *dis*proportionality on the basis of the *dictum* of the 1977 *Anglo-French Continental Shelf* arbitration.[292]

By referring to the 1985 *Guinea/Guinea-Bissau* arbitration, the Court regarded disproportionality as an *ex post facto* test of equitableness of the delimitation line it has constructed.[293] According to the Court, the length of the relevant coast of Romania is approximately 248 km,[294] while the length of the relevant Ukrainian coast is approximately 705 km.[295] The ratio for the coastal lengths between Romania and Ukraine is approximately 1:2.8, while the ratio of the relevant area between Romania and Ukraine is approximately 1:2.1.[296] The Court thus held that the equidistance line as constructed requires no alteration.[297]

Specifically the maritime boundary begins at Point 1 and follows the arc of the 12-nautical mile territorial sea of Serpents' Island until the arc intersects at Point 2 with a line equidistant from the adjacent coasts of Romania and Ukraine (see Illustration 23).[298] The fact that the 15 eminent judges of the ICJ were unanimous on the maritime delimitation will ensure that the *Black Sea* judgment has considerable influence on any subsequent cases. Indeed, as will be discussed in the next section, the *Black Sea* judgment did affect the *Bangladesh/Myanmar* case in relation to the maritime delimitation of the Bay of Bengal.

XII. THE *BANGLADESH/MYANMAR* CASE (ITLOS, 2012)

Concerning maritime delimitation of the Bay of Bengal, two decisions were given by International Tribunal for the Law of the Sea (ITLOS) and the Anne VII

[291] ibid, 112–28, [155–204]. These factors will be discussed in chs 7 and 8 of this book.

[292] [2009] ICJ Rep 129, [210]. See also United Nations, (1980) 18 *RIAA* 58, [101].

[293] [2009] ICJ Rep 129, [211]. See also ibid, 99–100, [110]; 103, [122].

[294] ibid, 93, [88].

[295] ibid, 98, [103]. The Court drew a line across the entrance of Karkinits'ka Gulf in order to make clear the relevant coasts and areas. However, this line is not taken into account in the calculation of the total length of the Ukrainian relevant coasts. ibid, 97, [100].

[296] ibid, 130, [215].

[297] ibid, [216].

[298] When considering the endpoint of the single maritime boundary, the Court bore in mind the agreed maritime delimitations between Turkey and Bulgaria, as well as between Turkey and Ukraine. ibid, 120, [177]. For the description of the maritime boundary, ibid, 130–31, [218]; 131, [219]. The geographical co-ordinates for Points 2, 3, 4, and 5 are given by reference to WGS 84 datum. ibid,131, [218].

Arbitral Tribunal, respectively: The *Bangladesh/Myanmar* and *Bangladesh v India* cases. This section examines the *Bangladesh/Myanmar* case.[299] This was the first case concerning maritime delimitation in the jurisprudence of ITLOS. At the same time, this was the first international case where the delimitation of the continental shelf beyond 200 nautical miles was effectuated by an international tribunal.[300] Even though Bangladesh contended that the territorial sea boundary shall be the line first agreed between them in 1974 and reaffirmed in 2008,[301] ITLOS declined the Bangladesh's claim.[302] Nor did the Tribunal accept the existence of a tacit or *de facto* agreed line between the parties.[303] ITLOS also found that Bangladesh's claim of estoppel cannot be upheld since there was no indication that Myanmar's conduct caused Bangladesh to change its position to its detriment in reliance on such conduct.[304] The Tribunal thus turned to establish a single maritime boundary for the territorial sea, the EEZ and the continental shelf in the Bay of Bengal.

A. Law Applicable to Maritime Delimitation

i. Law Application to the Single Maritime Boundary

Both Bangladesh and Myanmar are State Parties to the LOSC.[305] Accordingly, the delimitation of the territorial sea, EEZ and continental shelf is governed

[299] *Dispute concerning delimitation of the maritime boundary between Bangladesh and Myanmar in the Bay of Bengal (Bangladesh v Myanmar)* (the *Bangladesh/Myanmar* case), Judgment, [2012] ITLOS Rep 4.

[300] BM Magnússon, 'Judgment in the Dispute Concerning Delimitation of the Maritime Boundary between Bangladesh and Myanmar in the Bay of Bengal (14 March 2012)' (2012) 27 *IJMCL* 623; DH Anderson, 'Delimitation of the Maritime Boundary in the Bay of Bengal (Bangladesh/Myanmar. Case No. 16' (2012) 106 *AJIL* 823; Alex G Oude Elferink, 'ITLOS's Approach to the Delimitation of the Continental Shelf beyond 200 Nautical Miles in the *Bangladesh/Myanmar* Case: Theoretical and Practical Difficulties' in R Wolfrum, M Seršić, and T Šošić (eds), *Contemporary Developments in International Law: Essays in Honour of Budislav Vukas* (Leiden, Brill/Nijhoff, 2015) 230. It is relevant to note that in the *Newfoundland and Labrador/Nova Scotia* case (the Second Phase), an arbitral tribunal undertook the continental shelf boundary beyond 200 nautical miles between the two Canadian provinces of Nova Scotia and Newfoundland and Labrador. In this connection, the tribunal stressed that unlike the *St Pierre and Miquelon* case, 'it is a national and not an international tribunal, so that there is no question of any decision which might be opposable to any international processes for the determination of the outer edge of the Canadian continental shelf.' The *Newfoundland and Labrador/Nova Scotia* case (the Second Phase), [2.31]. See also SV Busch, 'The Delimitation of the Continental Shelf beyond 200 nm: Procedural Issues' in Oude Elferink, Henriksen and Busch, *Maritime Boundary Delimitation*, 326; Fietta and Cleverly, *A Practitioner's Guide*, 388–91 and 397; Oude Elferink, 'ITLOS's Approach,' 236–37; P von Mühlendahl, *L'équidistance dans la délimitation des frontière maritimes*, 379, [593].

[301] [2012] ITLOS Rep 28–29, [60–64]; Bangladesh's Memorial, vol I, 64, [5.18].

[302] [2012] ITLOS Rep 35–6, [88–98].

[303] ibid, 41, [118]. See also ch 8, s II of this book.

[304] ibid, 42, [125].

[305] Bangladesh ratified the Convention on 27 July 2001. Myanmar ratified the Convention on 21 May 1996. ibid, 22, [46].

by Articles 15, 74 and 83 of the LOSC, respectively.[306] However, the claims of the Parties presented a sharp contrast with regard to the methodology of maritime delimitation. Bangladesh argued that the Tribunal should apply the angle-bisector method, specifically the 215° azimuth line, in delimiting the maritime boundary between the parties in the exclusive economic zone (EEZ) and on the continental shelf.[307] However, Myanmar requested the Tribunal to apply the 'equidistance/relevant circumstances' method to draw an all-purpose line for the delimitation of the maritime boundary between the parties.[308]

ITLOS refused to apply the angle-bisector method in the present case because '[t]he resultant bisector fails to give adequate effect to the southward projection of the coast of Bangladesh.'[309] It thus decided that the appropriate method to be applied to delimit the EEZ and the continental shelf between Bangladesh and Myanmar was the 'equidistance/relevant circumstances method' under the LOSC.[310] In this regard, the Tribunal noted that:

> [J]urisprudence has developed in favour of the equidistance/relevant circumstances method. This is the method adopted by international courts and tribunals in the majority of the delimitation cases that have come before them.[311]

The Tribunal specified 'the equidistance/relevant circumstances method' as follows:

> In applying this method to the drawing of the delimitation line in the present case, the Tribunal, taking into account the jurisprudence of international courts and tribunals on this matter, will follow the three stage-approach, as developed in the most recent case law on the subject. Accordingly, the Tribunal will proceed in the following stages: at the first stage it will construct a provisional equidistance line, based on the geography of the Parties' coasts and mathematical calculations. Once the provisional equidistance line has been drawn, it will proceed to the second stage of the process, which consists of determining whether there are any relevant circumstances requiring adjustment of the provisional equidistance line; if so, it will make an adjustment that produces an equitable result. At the third and final stage in this process the Tribunal will check whether the line, as adjusted, results in any significant disproportion between the ratio of the respective coastal lengths and the ratio of the relevant maritime areas allocated to each Party.[312]

[306] ibid, 42, [127]; 55, [182].

[307] ibid, 62, [213] and 63, [217]. For a construction of the 215° azimuth line, see Bangladesh's Memorial, vol. I, 1 July 2010, 91–94, [6.68–6.78].

[308] [2012] ITLOS Rep 63–4, [219–22]. For Myanmar's delimitation method, see Myanmar's Counter-Memorial, vol. I, 1 December 2010, 121, [5.76 et seq]. The term 'the equidistance/relevant circumstances method' is a new vocabulary in the jurisprudence concerning maritime delimitation. Hyun Jung Kim, 'La délimitation de la frontière maritime dans le golfe du Bengale: courir deux lièvres à la fois avec succès dans le règlement de la délimitation maritime' (2012) 58 *AFDI* 453.

[309] [2012] ITLOS Rep 67, [237].

[310] ibid, [239].

[311] ibid, [238].

[312] ibid, 67–68, [240].

It can be said that the Tribunal's approach is essentially the same as that followed by the ICJ in the *Black Sea* case.[313] The Tribunal's approach was echoed by Judges Nelson, Chandrasekhara Rao and Cot. In their Joint Declaration, the three judges stated that: 'Priority is given today to the equidistance/relevant circumstances method'; and that: '[I]t is only if there are compelling reasons that make this unfeasible on objective geographical or geophysical grounds, such as the instability of the coastline, that one should contemplate another method of delimitation, for instance the angle bisector method.'[314]

ii. Law Applicable to the Delimitation of the Continental Shelf Beyond 200 Nautical Miles

ITLOS, in its judgment of 2012, held that it had an obligation to delimit the continental shelf between the Parties beyond 200 nautical miles.[315] In this regard, the Tribunal came to wrestle with key issues of the delimitation of the continental shelf beyond 200 nautical miles.[316] Among other things, a particular issue that arose in this context was whether the same delimitation method applicable to the delimitation of the continental shelf within 200 nautical miles should be employed in the delimitation of the continental shelf beyond 200 nautical miles. On this issue, ITLOS took the view that Article 83 of the LOSC applies equally to the delimitation of the continental shelf both within and beyond 200 nautical miles.[317] For the Tribunal,

> the delimitation method to be employed in the present case for the continental shelf beyond 200 nautical miles should not differ from that within 200 nm. Accordingly, the equidistance/relevant circumstances method continues to apply for the delimitation of the continental shelf beyond 200 nm.[318]

As will be discussed, however, whether the *dictum* of the Tribunal can be generalised needs further consideration.

B. Application of the Law Identified

i. Delimitation of the Territorial Sea Boundary

As noted, the delimitation of the territorial sea is governed by Article 15 of the LOSC. In this regard, ITLOS stated that: '[B]efore the equidistance principle

[313] [2009] ICJ Rep 101–03, [118–22]. The Tribunal's formulation of the three-stage approach does not refer to 'compelling reasons that make this [approach] unfeasible in the particular case.' However, the Tribunal referred to the 'compelling reasons' in para 233. [2012] ITLOS Rep 66, [233].
[314] Joint Declaration of Judges Nelson, Chandrasekhara Rao and Cot, ibid, 134.
[315] [2012] ITLOS Rep 103, [394].
[316] This issue will be discussed in s XIX of this chapter.
[317] [2012] ITLOS Rep 117, [454].
[318] ibid, [455].

is applied, consideration should be given to the possible existence of historic title or other special circumstances relevant to the area to be delimited.'[319] By reversing the order of the equidistance and special circumstances, the Tribunal seemed to take an approach that differs from the corrective-equity approach taken by the ICJ in the *Qatar v Bahrain* case. Yet it is less clear why ITLOS had to deviate from the precedent of the ICJ. In any case the Tribunal found no evidence of an historic title in the area to be delimitation.[320] The only issue was whether St Martin's Island should be regarded as a special circumstance. In this regard, it found that there were no compelling reasons that justify treating St Martin's Island as a special circumstance for the purpose of Article 15 of the LOSC.[321] Thus the territorial sea of the Parties was to be delimited by an equidistance line.[322] As Judges ad hoc Mensah and Oxman observed, this line is 'essentially the same as the contemplated by the Agreed Minutes of 23 November 1974.'[323]

ii. Delimitation of the EEZ and the Continental Shelf

a. The Application of the Three-stage Approach

Under Articles 74 and 83 of the LOSC, ITLOS applied the three-stage approach to the delimitation of the EEZ and the continental shelf in the Bay of Bengal. First, the Tribunal constructed a provisional equidistance line. The line relied on the five base points selected by Myanmar and a new base point selected by the Tribunal. In this connection, ITLOS held that:

> [B]ecause it [St. Martin's Island] is located immediately in front of the mainland on Myanmar's side of the Parties' land boundary terminus in the Naaf River, the selection of a base point on St. Martin's Island would result in a line that blocks the seaward projection from Myanmar's coast. In the view of the Tribunal, this would result in an unwarranted distortion of the delimitation line ...[324]

Accordingly, St Martin's Island was not used as a base point.[325] This means that the consideration of equity already came into play at the first stage of maritime delimitation.[326] In this connection, some doubts can be expressed regarding

[319] [2012] ITLOS Rep 43, [129].
[320] ibid, [130].
[321] ibid, 47, [152].
[322] ibid, [153].
[323] Joint Declaration of Judges ad hoc Mensha and Oxman, ibid, 147, [2]. See also R Churchill, 'The *Bangladesh/Myanmar* Case: Continuity and Novelty in the Law of Maritime Delimitation' (2012) 1 *Cambridge Journal of International and Comparative Law* 141; Magnússon, 'Judgment in the Dispute Concerning Delimitation of the Maritime Boundary between Bangladesh and Myanmar in the Bay of Bengal,' 625.
[324] [2012] ITLOS Rep 73, [265].
[325] ibid.
[326] Hyun Jung Kim, 'La délimitation de la frontière maritime dans le golfe du Bengale,' 454–55.

whether distorting effect of St Martin's Island was a matter of relevant circumstances at the second stage of maritime delimitation.[327]

At the second stage of maritime delimitation, ITLOS examined whether there were relevant circumstances which called for an adjustment of that line with a view to achieving an equitable result. In this regard, ITLOS observed that Bangladesh's coast, seen as a whole, is 'manifestly concave.'[328] According to the Tribunal, 'the provisional equidistance line it constructed in the present case does produce a cut-off effect on the maritime projection of Bangladesh and that the line if not adjusted would not result in achieving an equitable solution, as required by articles 74 and 83 of the Convention.'[329] It thus concluded that the concavity of the coast of Bangladesh was a relevant circumstance which required an adjustment of the provisional equidistance line.[330] Furthermore, it referred to St Martin's Island again:

> [B]ecause of its location, giving effect to St. Martin's Island in the delimitation of the exclusive economic zone and the continental shelf would result in a line blocking the seaward projection from Myanmar's coast in a manner that would cause an unwarranted distortion of the delimitation line. The distorting effect of an island on an equidistance line may increase substantially as the line moves beyond 12 nm from the coast.[331]

Yet, this is merely a repetition of paragraph 265 quoted above.[332] It follows that St Martin's Island was considered twice at the first and second stages of maritime delimitation.[333] However, it seems that the Tribunal's approach may entail the risk of blurring the first and second stages of maritime delimitation. The Tribunal eventually decided not to give any effect to St Martin's Island in drawing the delimitation of the EEZ and the continental shelf.[334]

ITLOS considered that 'the adjustment of the provisional equidistance line should commence at point X with coordinates 20° 03′ 32.0″ N, 91°50′ 31.8″ E, where the equidistance line begins to cut off the southward projection of the coast of Bangladesh.'[335] In the view of the Tribunal,

> [T]here is reason to consider an adjustment of the provisional equidistance line by drawing a geodetic line starting at a particular azimuth. In the view of the Tribunal

[327] McRae, 'The Applicable Law,'103; Alex G Oude Elferink, 'International Law and Negotiation and Adjudicated maritime Boundaries: A Complex Relationship' (2015) 18 *German Yearbook of International Law* 252.

[328] [2012] ITLOS Rep 81, [291].

[329] ibid, [293].

[330] ibid., 82, [297]; 87, [323–24].

[331] ibid, 86, [318].

[332] Hyun Jung Kim, 'La délimitation de la frontière maritime dans le golfe du Bengale' 454.

[333] Churchill, 'The *Bangladesh/Myanmar* Case' 144.

[334] [2012] ITLOS Rep 86, [319].

[335] ibid, 88–89, [331].

> the direction of any plausible adjustment of the provisional equidistance line would not differ substantially from a geodetic line starting at an azimuth of 215°.[336]

It thus held, by 21 votes to 1, that: 'From point 11(X), the delimitation line continues as a geodetic line starting at an azimuth of 215° until it reaches a point which is located 200 nm from the baselines from which the breadth of the territorial sea of Bangladesh is measured'(see Illustration 24).[337]

Nonetheless, it must be recalled that the 215° azimuth line is the line advocated by Bangladesh on the basis of the angle-bisector method.[338] As explained earlier, that method was clearly rejected by ITLOS itself. Thus the revival of the 215° azimuth line at the second stage of the delimitation process is a contradiction which is hard to justify.[339] In addition, ITLOS offered scant explanation why the adjusted delimitation line should follow the 215°, not, for instance, 214° or 216°, azimuth line. Nor was there any explanation how the 215° azimuth line was to be constructed.[340] Overall there are some doubts as to whether the delimitation line drawn by ITLOS can be considered as an adjusted equidistance line.[341]

As for the delimitation of the continental shelf beyond 200 nautical miles, ITLOS considered that the concavity of the Bangladesh coast as a relevant circumstance has a continuing effect beyond 200 nautical miles. It thus decided that the adjusted equidistance line delimiting both the EEZ and the continental shelf within 200 nautical miles between the Parties continues in the same direction beyond 200-nautical mile limit of Bangladesh.[342] In this context, the Tribunal did not regard the geological and geomorphological factors as relevant circumstances.[343] Accordingly, from point 11, the maritime boundary for the continental shelf beyond the 200 nautical mile limit of Bangladesh continues as a geodetic line starting at an azimuth of 215° direction until it reaches the area where the rights of third States may be affected.[344]

At the third stage of maritime delimitation, ITLOS applied the disproportionality test. According to the Tribunal, the ratio of the length of the relevant coasts of the Parties is 1:1.42 in favour of Myanmar, while the ratio of the allocated areas is approximately 1: 1.54 in favour of Myanmar. It thus concluded

336 ibid, 89, [334].

337 ibid, 90, [340]. From point X, the maritime boundary runs parallel to the 215° azimuth line claimed by Bangladesh. See Fietta and Cleverly, *A Practitioner's Guide*, 499.

338 P von Mühlendahl, *L'équidistance dans la délimitation des frontière maritimes*, 207, [331].

339 Separate Opinion of Judge Cot, [2012] ITLOS Rep 189.

340 Separate Opinion of Judge Gao, ibid., 208–9, [39] and 212, [50]; Declaration of Judge Wolfrum, ibid.,139.

341 Separate Opinion of Judge Cot, ibid., 191–92. See also Hyun Jung Kim, 'La délimitation de la frontière maritime dans le golfe du Bengale,' 455–57; Anderson, 'Delimitation of the Maritime Boundary in the Bay of Bengal,' 823.

342 [2012] ITLOS Rep 118, [461–62].

343 ibid, 118, [460]. See also ch 7, s VI of this book.

344 [2012] ITLOS Rep 118, [462] and 128, [505].

that this ratio did not lead to any significant disproportion that would require the shifting of the adjusted equidistance line.[345]

b. The Grey Area

The maritime boundary established by ITLOS created the so called 'grey area.'[346] According to ITLOS, the grey area 'results when a delimitation line which is not an equidistance line reaches the outer limit of one State's exclusive economic zone and continues beyond it in the same direction, until it reaches the outer limit of the other State's exclusive economic zone.'[347]

The grey area in the *Bangladesh/Myanmar* case is located beyond 200 nautical miles from the coast of Bangladesh but within 200 nautical miles from the coast of Myanmar, yet on the Bangladesh side of the delimitation line.[348] As a consequence, Bangladesh's continental shelf rights overlap Myanmar's EEZ rights in the grey area. In the words of ITLOS,

> [I]n the area beyond Bangladesh's exclusive economic zone that is within the limits of Myanmar's exclusive economic zone, the maritime boundary delimits the Parties' rights with respect to the seabed and subsoil of the continental shelf but does not otherwise limit Myanmar's rights with respect to the exclusive economic zone, notably those with respect to the superjacent waters.[349]

The grey area raises two issues. The first concerns the legal validity of the grey area. On this issue, ITLOS held that:

> [T]he legal regime of the continental shelf has always coexisted with another legal regime in the same area. Initially that other regime was that of the high seas and the other States concerned were those exercising high seas freedoms. Under the Convention, as a result of maritime delimitation, there may also be concurrent exclusive economic zone rights of another coastal State. In such a situation, pursuant to the principle reflected in the provisions of articles 56, 58, 78 and 79 and in other provisions of the Convention, each coastal State must exercise its rights and perform its duties with due regard to the rights and duties of the other.[350]

[345] Judgment, ibid, 126, [498–99].

[346] Generally on this issue, see BM Magnússon, 'The Grey Areas in the Bay of Bengal' (2016) 57 *Indian Journal of International Law* 41; Jin-Hyung Paik, 'The Grey Area in the Bay of Bengal Case' in NH Nordquist *et al* (eds), *International Maritime Economy: Law and Policy* (Leiden, Brill, 2017) 271; Jin-Hyun Paik, 'The Grey Area in the Bay of Bengal Case' in MH Nordquist, JN Moore and R Long (eds), *International Marine Economy: Law and Policy* (Brill/Nijhoff, Leiden: 2017) 271.

[347] [2012] ITLOS Rep 119, [464].

[348] ibid, 119, [463].

[349] ibid, 121, [474].

[350] ibid, [475]. However, Churchill gave his misgivings that: '[I]t may pose challenges to states to act with the necessary due regard when exercising their rights in a grey zone.' 'The *Bangladesh/ Myanmar* Case' 151.

With respect this view leaves some room for discussion. Unlike the rights on the continental shelf, the rights in the high seas are not exclusive rights. Accordingly, there is no conflict between two exclusive rights on the continental shelf and the high seas. In the EEZ and the continental shelf, however, the coastal State enjoys the sovereign rights, which are exclusive rights in the sense that no State can explore and exploit natural resources without the consent of the coastal State. Here conflict arises between two exclusive rights. Therefore it is open to debate whether the analogy of the relationship between the continental shelf and the high seas is relevant in this context.

It must also be stressed that under Article 56(1) of the LOSC, the concept of the EEZ includes the seabed as well. As the ICJ rightly stated in the *Libya/Malta* case, '[a]lthough there can be a continental shelf, where there is no exclusive economic zone, there cannot be an exclusive economic zone without corresponding continental shelf.'[351] Thus, according to the Court, 'the two institutions – continental shelf and exclusive economic zone – are linked together in modern law.'[352] Indeed, the two institutions are linked by Article 56(3) of the Convention, which stipulates: 'The rights set out in this article with respect to the sea-bed and subsoil shall be exercised in accordance with Part VI.' The use of the phrase 'in accordance with' under this provision, not the phrase 'subject to', does seem to imply the integral nature of the two institutions.[353] The assimilation of the EEZ and the continental shelf is also strengthened by the fact that up to 200 nautical miles, the entitlement of the coastal State to the continental self and the EEZ commonly depends on distance criterion.[354] In this regard, Judge Jiménez de Aréchaga clearly stated that: '[A]t least in the case of continental shelves not extending beyond 200 miles, the notion of the continental shelf is in the process of being assimilated to, or incorporated in that of the Exclusive Economic Zone.'[355] More recently, a leading commentary stated that:

> [T]he wording of Art. 56(1), by referring also to 'seabed and its subsoil', clarifies that if and to the extent to which the coastal State has claimed and established an EEZ above its continental shelf, the two zones form part of *an integral regime*.[356]

[351] The *Libya/Malta* case. [1985] ICJ Rep 33, [34].

[352] ibid, 33, [33].

[353] This point was highlighted by Barbados in the *Barbados v Trinidad and Tobago* case, 201, [182]. See also A Prölss, 'Article 57' in A Prölss (ed), *United Nations Convention on the Law of the Sea: A Commentary* (Beck/Oxford, Hart Publishing/Baden-Barden, Nomos, München: 2017) 436.

[354] Art 57 and 76(1) of the LOSC. In this regard, the ICJ clearly stated that: '[T]he distance criterion must now apply to the continental shelf as well as to the exclusive economic zone.' The *Libya/Malta* case, [1982] ICJ Rep 33, [34]. See also Concurring and Dissenting Opinion of Dr PS Rao in the *Bangladesh v India* case, [31].

[355] Separate Opinion of Judge Jiménez de Aréchaga in the *Tunisia/Libya* case, [1982] ICJ Rep100–42, [55].

[356] Emphasis added. Prölss, 'Article 57,' 436. Attard also argued that: '[T]hese provisions [Articles 77(1) and 56(3)] merge the self regime with that of the EEZ regime.' David Attard, *The Exclusive Economic Zone in International Law* (Oxford, Clarendon Press, 1987) 139. See also Joe Verhoeven, *Droit International public* (Bruxelles, Larcier, 2000) 553.

In light of the integral nature of the seabed and its superjacent waters in the EEZ, it may have to be admitted that grey area creates a conceptual difficulty.

The second issue relates to the function of an international tribunal. In practice, grey area may give rise to complex problems with regard to the exercise of jurisdiction. Nonetheless, ITLOS refrained from addressing the question as to which rights would prevail and simply stated that:

> In such a situation, pursuant to the principle reflected in the provisions of articles 56, 58, 78 and 79 and in other provisions of the Convention, each coastal State must exercise its rights and perform its duties with due regard to the rights and duties of the other.[357]

According to the Tribunal,

> There are many ways in which the Parties may ensure the discharge of their obligations in this respect, including the conclusion of specific agreements or the establishment of appropriate cooperative arrangements. It is for the Parties to determine the measures that they consider appropriate for this purpose.[358]

However, there appears to be some scope to consider the question whether it was relevant to leaves room for potential disputes between the parties in the implementation of the judgment.[359] In reality, the situation was complicated further since the grey area was to overlap in part with another grey area created by the Arbitral Tribunal in the *Bangladesh v India* case.[360]

XIII. THE *NICARAGUA v COLOMBIA* CASE (MERITS, ICJ, 2012)

In 2012, after the *Bangladesh/Myanmar* case, another decision was rendered by the ICJ: the *Nicaragua v Colombia* case.[361] This case includes some issues that need particular consideration with regard to the law of maritime delimitation. Preliminary points of the case can be summarised as follows.

On 6 December 2001, Nicaragua instituted proceedings against Colombia in respect of a dispute consisting of 'a group of related legal issues subsisting' between the two States 'concerning title to territory and maritime delimitation' in the western Caribbean. Nicaragua found the jurisdiction of the Court on the provisions of Article XXXI of the Pact of Bogotá as well as on the

[357] [2012] ITLOS Rep 121, [475].
[358] ibid, [476].
[359] Hyun Jung Kim, 'La délimitation de la frontière maritime dans le golfe du Bengale' 465.
[360] See s XV of this chapter.
[361] *Territorial and Maritime Dispute (Nicaragua v Colombia)* (the *Nicaragua v Colombia* case), Judgment, [2012] ICJ Rep 624. For a commentary on the *Nicaragua v Colombia* case by the author, see Y Tanaka, 'Reflections on the Territorial and maritime Dispute between Nicaragua and Colombia before the International Court of Justice' (2013) 26 *LJIL* 909.

declarations made by the Parties under Article 36 of the Statute of the Permanent Court of International Justice, which are deemed to be acceptances of the compulsory jurisdiction of the ICJ under Article 36(5) of its Statute.[362] The *Nicaragua v Colombia* case related to disputes concerning title to territory and maritime delimitation in the western Caribbean at the same time. The ICJ, in its judgment of 19 November 2012, found that the Republic of Colombia has sovereignty over the islands at Alburquerque, Bajo Nuevo, East-Southeast Cays, Quitasueño, Roncador, Serrana and Serranilla.[363] The Court also found that it cannot uphold Nicaragua's final submission I(3) concerning a continental shelf boundary beyond 200 nautical miles since Nicaragua had not established that it has a continental margin that extends far enough to overlap with Colombia's 200-nautical-mile entitlement to the continental shelf.[364] Thus the task of the Court was to effect delimitation between the maritime entitlements of Colombia and the continental shelf and EEZ of Nicaragua within 200 nautical miles of the Nicaraguan coast.[365]

A. Law Applicable to Maritime Delimitation

In the *Nicaragua v Colombia* case, the applicable law was customary law since Colombia is not a party to the LOSC.[366] In this connection, the ICJ recognised that principles of maritime delimitation enshrined in Articles 74 and 83 reflect customary international law.[367] As for the methodology of maritime delimitation, the Court adopted the three-stage approach.[368] According to the Court, it 'has made clear on a number of occasions that the methodology which it will normally employ when called upon to effect a delimitation between overlapping continental shelf and exclusive economic zone entitlements involves proceeding in three stages.'[369] At the same time, referring to the *Nicaragua v Honduras* case, the Court went on to add that it would not be appropriate in every case to begin with a provisional equidistance/median line.[370] However, the Court considered that the maritime delimitation between Nicaragua and Colombia was not a case in which the construction of such a provisional equidistance/median line was not feasible. Hence it held that in the present

[362] [2012] ICJ Rep 630–31, [1].
[363] [2012] ICJ Rep 662, [103]; 718, [251(1)].
[364] ibid, 669–70, [129–31]; 719, [251(3)]. Further, see ML Delabie, 'Le fragile équilibre entre prévisibilité juridique et opportunité judiciarei en matière de délimitation maritime : l'arrêt de la Court internationale de Justice du 19 november 2012 dans l'affaire du *Différend territorial et maritime (Nicaragua c Colombie)*' (2012) 58 *AFDI*, 223, 234 et seq.
[365] [2012] ICJ Rep 671, [136].
[366] ibid, 666, [114]; 673, [137].
[367] ibid, 674, [139].
[368] ibid, 695–96, [190–93].
[369] ibid, 695, [190].
[370] ibid, 696, [194].

case, it would proceed via the three stages in accordance with its standard method.[371] According to the Court,

> In the first stage, the Court establishes a provisional delimitation line between territories (including the island territories) of the Parties. In doing so it will use methods that are geometrically objective and appropriate for the geography of the area. This task will consist of the construction of an equidistance line, where the relevant coasts are adjacent, or a median line between the two coasts, where the relevant coasts are opposite, unless in either case there are compelling reasons as a result of which the establishment of such a line is not feasible ....[372]

By referring to the *Libya/Malta* and *Black Sea* cases, the Court further stated that:

> In the second stage, the Court considers whether there are any relevant circumstances which may call for an adjustment or shifting of the provisional equidistance/median line so as to achieve an equitable result. If it concludes that such circumstances are present, it establishes a different boundary which *usually* entails such adjustment or shifting of the equidistance/median line as is necessary to take account of those circumstances .... Where the relevant circumstances so require, the Court may also employ other techniques, such as the construction of an enclave around isolated islands, in order to achieve an equitable result.[373]

The term 'usually' may be interpreted to imply that in exceptional cases, a maritime boundary other than an adjusted equidistance line may be drawn considering relevant circumstances at the second stage. As will be discussed, however, care should be taken in noting that the construction of a maritime boundary totally detached from a provisional equidistance line entrails the serious risk of undermining the value of predictability at the first stage of maritime delimitation. Finally, the Court held that:

> In the third and final stage, the Court conducts a disproportionality test in which it assesses whether the effect of the line, as adjusted or shifted, is that the Parties' respective *shares* of the relevant area are markedly disproportionate to their respective relevant coasts.[374]

The *dictum* seems to suggest that the concept of disproportionality entails that of shares. However, the ICJ repeatedly stressed the distinction between maritime delimitation and 'apportionment' or 'award of a just and equitable share' of marine spaces.[375] In this regard, serious doubts can be expressed regarding whether the concept of disproportionality does not contradict the rejection of the idea of apportionment in maritime delimitation.[376]

[371] ibid, 696–98, [194–99].

[372] ibid, 695, [191].

[373] Emphasis added. ibid, 695, [192].

[374] Emphasis added. ibid, 696, [193].

[375] The *North Sea Continental Shelf* cases, [1969] ICJ Rep 22, [18]; the *Tunisia/Libya* case, [1982] ICJ Rep 60, [71]; the *Libya/Malta* case, [1985] ICJ Rep 39–40, [46]; The *Jan Mayen* case, [1993] ICJ Rep 67, [64]. See also ch 1, s II of this book.

[376] Y Tanaka, 'Disproportionality Test' in Oude Elferink, Henriksen and Busch, *Maritime Boundary Delimitation*, 291, 316. See also ch 9, s IV of this book.

B. Application of the Law Identified

i. Construction of the Provisional Equidistance/Median Line

a. Identification of Relevant Coasts and Maritime Areas

To draw a provisional equidistance/median line, the Court must define the relevant coastlines of the Parties. In this regard, the Court considered that the relevant Nicaraguan coast is the whole coast which projects into the area of overlapping potential entitlements. Accordingly, with the exception of the short stretch of coast near Punta de Perlas, which faces due south and thus does not project into the area of overlapping potential entitlements, the relevant coast is the entire mainland coast of Nicaragua.[377] On the other hand, a marked difference existed between the Parties concerning the relevant Colombian coast. The Court took the view that since the mainland coast of Colombia does not generate any entitlement in that area, the relevant Colombian coast is confined to the coasts of the islands under Colombian sovereignty. In the view of the Court, since the area of overlapping potential entitlements extends well to the east of the Colombian islands, the entire coastline of these islands, not merely the west-facing coasts, must be taken into account. The Court also considered that the coasts of Alburquerque Cays, East-Southeast Cays, Roncador and Serrana must be considered part of the relevant coast.[378]

As for the relevant maritime area, the Court held that:

> [T]he relevant area comprises that part of the maritime space in which the potential entitlements of the parties overlap. It follows that, in the present case, the relevant area cannot stop, as Colombia maintains it should, at the western coasts of the Colombian islands.[379]

In this context, an issue arose with regard to the interest of third States. As the Court observed, the interests of third States become involved in both the north and the south. In the north, the Court took into account a boundary between Nicaragua and Honduras established by the Court in its 2007 judgment and the 1993 Agreement between Colombia and Jamaica.[380] In the south, the 1976 Colombia-Panama Agreement[381] and the 1977 Colombia-Costa Rica Agreement exist.[382]

[377] [2012] ICJ Rep 678, [145].

[378] ibid, 679–80, [151–52]. The Court has not taken account of the parts of the coast of Providencia and Santa Catalina (in the north-west of Providencia, in the area of San Juan Point, and in the south-east of Santa Catalina), Serranilla and Bajo Nuevo.

[379] ibid, 683, [159].

[380] ibid, 683–84, [160]. Yet, the Court ignored the 1986 Treaty between Honduras and Colombia for the purpose of identifying the relevant area. NB O'Sullivan, 'The Case Law's Handling of Issues Concerning Third States' in Oude Elferink, Henriksen and Busch, *Maritime Boundary Delimitation*, 282.

[381] Text in: JI Charney and LM Alexander (eds), *International Maritime Boundaries*, vol I (Dordrecht, Nijhoff, 1993) 532. Entered into force 20 November 1976.

[382] Text in ibid, 474. Not entered into force.

By referring to the *Black Sea* case, the Court held that the fact that the potential entitlements of the Parties overlapped entitlements of third States 'did not preclude the inclusion of those parts in the relevant area "without prejudice to the position of any third state regarding its entitlements in this area".'[383] At the same time, it must be noted that the relevant area cannot extend beyond the area in which the entitlements of both Parties overlap. Accordingly, as the Court stated, 'if either Party has no entitlement in a particular area, whether because of an agreement it has concluded with a third State or because that area lies beyond a judicially determined boundary between that Party and a third State, that area cannot be treated as part of the relevant area for present purposes.'[384] As Colombia has no potential entitlements to the south and east of the boundaries which it has agreed with Costa Rica and Panama, the relevant area cannot extend beyond those boundaries. Furthermore, Colombia-Jamaica 'Joint Regime Area' falls outside the relevant area.[385] The Court thus identified the relevant area which has a size of approximately 209,280 square kilometres.[386]

b. Construction of a Provisional Equidistance/Median Line

Next, the Court proceeded to construct its provisional equidistance line. In this regard, the selection of base points is crucial. The Court selected the base points which it considered appropriate, without following the Colombian line. Specifically the Court considered that Quitasueño should not contribute to the construction of the provisional median line since placing base points on very small maritime features would distort the relevant geography; and that it was appropriate to disregard them in the construction of a provisional median line. Likewise it disregarded Serrana in drawing a provisional median line because of its comparative smallness and considerable distance from any of the other Colombian islands. It also considered that there should be no base point on Low Cay, a small uninhabited feature near Santa Catalina.[387] While the discretion of the Court to select appropriate base points is confirmed by the previous decisions concerning maritime delimitations, some doubts might be expressed as to whether or not the comparative smallness would provide a convincing reason for disregarding Serrana as a base point.[388]

ii. Considerations of Relevant Circumstances and the Disproportionality Test

After the construction of the provisional equidistance line, the Court turned to consider whether there were factors calling for the adjustment of the line

[383] [2012] ICJ Rep 684, [161]. See also the *Black Sea* case, [2009] ICJ Rep 100, [114].
[384] [2012] ICJ Rep 685, [163].
[385] ibid, 685, [163].
[386] ibid, 686, [164–66]. See Sketch-map No. 7 attached to the Judgment. ibid, 687.
[387] ibid, 699, [202].
[388] See ch 7, s IV of this book.

to achieve an equitable result. The Court determined the course of the maritime boundary taking account of the two relevant circumstances: Considerable disparity in the length of the relevant coats and the overall geographical context. The first circumstance requires that the maritime boundary should be such that the portion of the relevant area accorded to each State takes account of the disparity between the lengths of their relevant coasts. The second circumstance necessitates a solution in which neither Party is cut off from the entirety of any of the areas into which its coasts project.[389]

In the western part of the relevant area, the relevant circumstances call for the provisional median line to be shifted eastwards. When shifting the provisional median line eastwards, the Court constructed a line each point on which is three times as far from the controlling base point on the Nicaraguan islands as it is from the controlling base point on the Colombian islands. Thus the 'weighted line' was constructed using a 3:1 ratio between Nicaraguan and Colombian base points.[390] Furthermore, the Court considered that to extend that line into the parts of the relevant area north of point 1 or south of point 5 would not lead to an equitable result. According to the Court, 'an equitable result which gives proper weight to those relevant considerations is achieved by continuing the boundary line out to the line 200 nautical miles from the Nicaraguan baselines along lines of latitude.'[391] The Court thus drew two horizontal lines along lines of latitude from points 1 and 9 (see Illustration 25).[392] However, the construction of the two horizontal lines is open to controversy since there is no linkage between the provisionally drawn equidistance line and these two horizontal lines.[393] Furthermore, the Court established only a 12-nautical-mile envelope of arcs around Quitasueño and a 12-nautical-mile envelope of arcs measured from Serrana Cay and other cays.[394]

At the third and final stage, the Court ascertained whether there was a significant disproportionality which would require further adjustment. According to the Court, application of the adjusted line has the effect of dividing the relevant area between the Parties in a ratio of approximately 1:3.44 in Nicaragua's favour, while the ratio of relevant coasts is approximately 1:8.2.[395] The Court concluded that there is no disproportionality between the ratio for the coastal lengths and the ratio of the relevant area.[396] Yet it is open to debate whether the ratio is not truly disproportionate.[397]

[389] [2012] ICJ Rep 708, [229].
[390] ibid, 709–10, [233–35].
[391] ibid, 710, [236].
[392] ibid, [237].
[393] Further, see ch 9, s IV of this book.
[394] Judgment, [2012] ICJ Rep 713–15, [238]. See ch 7, s IV of this book.
[395] ibid, 716, [243].
[396] ibid, 717, [247].
[397] Further, see ch 7, s III of this book.

The *Nicaragua v Colombia* judgment could not end the dispute between the Parties. Indeed, Colombia refused to accept the judgment since it considered that the Court had committed serious mistakes.[398] In response, Nicaragua instituted proceedings against Colombia with regard to, inter alia, alleged violation of 'Nicaragua's maritime zones as delimited in paragraph 251 of the ICJ Judgment of 19 November 2012 as well as Nicaragua's sovereign rights and jurisdiction in these zones.'[399] Furthermore, Nicaragua instituted proceedings against Colombia with regard to the delimitation of the continental shelf beyond 200 nautical miles.[400]

XIV. THE *PERU v CHILE* CASE (ICJ, 2014)

The next case that needs to be discussed is the *Peru v Chile* case of 2014.[401] On 16 January 2008, the Republic of Peru (hereafter Peru) instituted proceedings against the Republic of Chile (hereafter Chile) with regard to the maritime delimitation between the two States in the Pacific Ocean. In its Application, Peru found the jurisdiction of the Court on Article XXXI of the Pact of Bogotà.[402]

A. Law Applicable to Maritime Delimitation

i. The Existence of an Agreed Maritime Boundary

The *Peru v Chile* case is unique in the sense that the main question concerned the existence of an agreed maritime boundary between the Parties.[403] Chile claimed that the maritime zones of Chile and Peru had been fully delimited by agreement,[404] while Peru argued that no agreed maritime boundary existed between the two countries.[405] Thus, the ICJ was first of all required to

[398] Statement of Colombian President, Mr Juan Manuel Santos. Application of Instituting Proceedings by Nicaragua, 26 November 2013, 6–7, [4]. See also http://wsp.presidencia.gov.co/Prensa/2012/Noviembre/Paginas/20121119_02.aspx. Colombia also denounced the Pact of Bogotá on 27 November 2012. Application of Instituting Proceedings by Nicaragua, 8, [6].

[399] ibid, 24, [22].

[400] Application of Instituting Proceedings by Nicaragua, 16 September 2013, 8, [12].

[401] *Maritime Dispute (Peru v Chile)*, [2014] ICJ Rep 3.

[402] ibid 10, [1]. See also Application Instituting Proceedings, 16 January 2008, 2, [1] and [5]. For a brief overview of this case, see US Burney, 'International Court of Justice Defines Maritime Boundary Between Peru and Chile' (2014) 18 *ASIL Insights*, available at: www.asil.org/insights/year/2014.

[403] T Scovazzi, 'Maritime Dispute (Peru v. Chile), 2008' in PW Almeida and J-M Sorel, *Latin America and the International Court of Justice: Contributions to International Law* (London, Routledge, 2017) 246.

[404] Chile's Counter-Memorial, vol. I, 9 March 2010, 14–8, [1.29–1.37].

[405] Peru's Memorial, vol. I, 20 March 2009, 164–69, [4.139–4.144]. See also [2014] ICJ Rep 16, [22–3].

ascertain whether an agreed maritime boundary existed as Chile claimed.[406] After examining the competing claims of the parties, the Court ruled that there existed a maritime boundary between the parties that extended up to Point A situated at a distance of 80 nautical miles up to (Point A) along the parallel from its starting-point of the single maritime boundary, namely, the intersection of the parallel of latitude passing through Boundary Marker No. 1 with the low-water line.[407] As will be discussed in chapter eight, Section II of this book, however, the existence of the agreed maritime boundary is not free from controversy. The extent of the agreed boundary is also a matter for debate.[408]

The 1954 Special Maritime Frontier Zone Agreement gives no indication of the nature of the maritime boundary.[409] According to the Court, however, the 1947 Proclamation of Chile and Peru and the 1952 Santiago Declaration expressed claims to the sea-bed and to waters above the sea-bed and their resources. Thus the Court considered that the boundary was an all-purpose one.[410]

ii. Maritime Delimitation from Point A

The Court then turned to determine the course of the maritime boundary from Point A.[411] While Chile is a party to the LOSC, Peru is not. However, the ICJ proceeded with the maritime delimitation on the basis of Articles 74(1) and 83(1) of the LOSC since the Court recognised these provisions as part of customary international law.[412] As for the methodology, the ICJ supported the three-stage approach.[413] Nonetheless, an unusual situation in the *Peru v Chile* case is that the start-point for the delimitation is much further from the coast, ie, 80 nautical miles from the closest point on the Chilean coast and about 45 nautical miles from the closest point on the Peruvian coast. Accordingly, the Court had to draw a provisional equidistance line which starts at Point A, which is the endpoint of the existing maritime boundary.[414]

The construction of an equidistance line from Point A seems to show contrast with the *Gulf of Maine* case. As noted earlier, in the *Gulf of Maine* case, the Parties had chosen point A as the obligatory point of departure for the delimitation line. That point was not a point that can be located on the path of any equidistance line traced by the Chamber or constituted the starting-point

406 ibid, [24].
407 ibid, 58, [151] and 64, [176].
408 See ch 8, s II of this book.
409 [2014] ICJ Rep 39, [92].
410 ibid, 41, [102].
411 ibid, 65, [177].
412 ibid, [179].
413 ibid, [180]. Peru supported the three-stage approach, while Chile advanced no arguments in this matter. ibid, 65–66, [181–82].
414 ibid, 66–67, [183–84].

of any such line. Accordingly, the Chamber renounced the application of the equidistance method.[415] In the *Peru v Chile* case, however, the ICJ decided to construct an equidistance line from Point A, even though that point has no connection with an equidistance line.

B. Application of the Law Identified

i. Construction of the Provisional Equidistance Line

To construct a provisional equidistance line, the Court must first select appropriate base points. According to the Court, only those points on the Peruvian coast which are more than 80 nautical miles from Point A can be matched with points at an equivalent distance on the Chilean coast in light of the location of Point A at a distance of 80 nautical miles from the coast along the parallel.[416] Further base points are situated to the north-west of the initial base point on the Peruvian coast and south of the initial base point on the Chilean coast. It follows that the provisional equidistance line constructed runs in a general south-west direction, almost in a straight line, reflecting the smooth character of the two coasts, until it reaches the 200-nautical-mile limit measured from the Chilean baselines (Point B).[417] After Point B, the 200-nautical-mile limits of the Parties' maritime entitlements delimited on the basis of equidistance no longer overlap. Accordingly, the final segment of the maritime boundary proceeds from Point B to Point C, where the 200-nautical-mile limits of the Parties' maritime entitlements intersect.[418]

ii. Considerations of Relevant Circumstances and the Disproportionality Test

Following the three-stage approach, the Court ascertained whether there were any relevant circumstances calling for an adjustment of the provisional equidistance line. In this regard, it found that no relevant circumstances require such an adjustment.[419] Finally, the Court examined whether the provisional equidistance line drawn from Point A produced a result which is significantly disproportionate in terms of the lengths of the relevant coasts and the division of the relevant area and it found that no significant disproportion was evident. The Court accordingly concluded that the maritime boundary between Chile and

[415] The *Gulf of Maine* case, Judgment, [1984] ICJ Rep 1984, 332, [211–12]. See also F Orrego Vicuña, 'International Law Issues in the Judgment of the International Court of Justice in the Peru-Chile Maritime Dispute Case' in Lilian del Castillo (ed), *Law of the Sea, from Grotius to the International Tribunal for the Law of the Sea: Liber Amicorum Judge Hugo Caminos* (Leiden, Brill/Nijhoff, 2015) 574–75.

[416] This issue will be discussed in ch 7, s V of this book.

[417] [2014] ICJ Rep 66–67, [185–86].

[418] ibid, 67, [190].

[419] ibid, 69, [191].

Peru from Point A runs along the equidistance line to Point B, and then along the 200-nautical-mile limit measured from the Chilean baselines to Point C (see Illustration 26).[420] In view of the particularity of the present case in which the equidistance line begins at a distance of 80 nautical miles from the coast along the parallel, however, the Court's application of the disproportionality test is open to criticism.[421] In any event, unlike the *Nicaragua v Colombia* judgment, the Parties expressed their intention to comply with the ICJ judgment. Thus the *Peru v Chile* judgment successfully put an end to a long-standing dispute.[422]

XV. THE *BANGLADESH v INDIA* CASE (ARBITRATION, 2014)

The *Bangladesh v India* arbitration is the second case concerning the maritime delimitation in the Bay of Bengal. By a Notification and Statement of Claim dated 8 October 2009, Bangladesh initiated arbitral proceedings against India, pursuant to Article 287 of the LOSC and in accordance with Annex VII to the Convention. This case related to a single maritime boundary for the territorial sea, the EEZ and the continental shelf between the Parties within and beyond 200 nautical miles in the Bay of Bengal.[423]

A. Law Applicable to Maritime Delimitation

i. Law Applicable to Delimitation of the Territorial Sea

Both Bangladesh and India have ratified the LOSC.[424] The Parties agreed that delimitation of territorial sea is governed by Article 15 of the Convention. When interpreting this provision, the Arbitral Tribunal referred to the corrective-equity approach adopted by the ICJ in the *Qatar v Bahrain* case. By referring to the second sentence of Article 15, however, the Tribunal immediately assessed the possibility of an alternative solution by reason of historic title or other special circumstances since Bangladesh proposed the use of an angle-bisector line in

[420] ibid, 71, [195]. According to Orrego Vicuña, the dispute area that formed by the 200 nautical mile parallel claimed by Chile and the equidistance lien claimed by Peru amounts to approximately 38.224 square kilometres. The maritime boundary established by the ICJ attributed 16.224 square kilometres to Chile and 22.100 square kilometres to Peru. Orrego Vicuña, 'International Law Issues,' 575.

[421] This issue will be discussed in ch 7, s III of this book.

[422] Scovazzi, 'Maritime Dispute (Peru v Chile), 2008,' 248; MT Infante-Caffi, 'The Decision on the Maritime Boundary between Chile and Peru: International Law Revisited' in Lilian del Castillo (ed), *Law of the Sea*, 544.

[423] *Bay of Bengal Maritime Boundary Arbitration between Bangladesh and India (Bangladesh v India)* (the *Bangladesh v India* arbitral award), Award, 7 July 2014, [190]. The text of the arbitral award is available at: https://pca-cpa.org/en/cases/18/. The members of the Annex VII Arbitral Tribunal were: Rüdiger Wolfrum (President), Jean-Pierre Cot, Thomas A. Mensah, Pemmaraju Sreenivasa Rao and Ivan Shearer.

[424] Bangladesh and India ratified the Convention on 27 July 2001 and 26 June 1995, respectively.

light of the prevailing coastal instability and concavity in the Bay of Bengal.[425] For Bangladesh, the instability of the coastline was a major factor weighting against the use of the provisional equidistance/relevant circumstances method. In this connection, Bangladesh stressed in particular the potential effect of climate change and sea level rise in the Bay of Bengal.[426] However, the Tribunal did not support the Bangladesh's argument. Referring to the *dictum* of the ICJ in the *Black Sea* case,[427] the Tribunal stressed that the matter is the 'physical reality at the time of the delimitation'; and that the Tribunal need not address 'the issue of the future instability of the coastline.'[428] The Tribunal's view is noteworthy when considering the impact of climate change in maritime delimitation.

In the *Bangladesh v India* case, it was possible to identify appropriate base points on the basis of which an equidistance line can be constructed. Bangladesh invoked no further consideration which would justify a deviation from the application of the equidistance method. Accordingly, the Tribunal did not admit the use of an angle-bisector line in the delimitation of the territorial sea.[429] It thus decided to apply the equidistance method to the delimitation of the territorial sea.

ii. Law Applicable to Delimitation of the Continental Shelf and EEZ

The Parties agreed that Articles 74(1) and 83(1) of the LOSC govern the delimitation of the EEZ and the continental shelf within 200 nm. Nonetheless, they disagreed on the centrality of the equidistance method. Bangladesh submitted that there was no presumption in favour of the equidistance method in the international jurisprudence.[430] It then argued for the application of the angle bisector method, relying on the *Nicaragua v Honduras* case.[431] Specifically Bangladesh submitted that the boundary line should be a line on an azimuth of 180°.[432] However, India advocated the three-stage approach, stating that: 'The fact that the ITLOS followed – the three stage-approach, as developed in the most recent case law on the subject‖ reflects the authoritative development of the open-textured language of UNCLOS [LOSC] into a reliable and objective three-stage methodology.'[433]

The Tribunal examined the two methods advocated by the Parties. According to the Tribunal, 'the advantage of the equidistance/relevant circumstances method lies in the fact that it clearly separates the steps to be taken and is thus

[425] Bangladesh's Mermorial, vol I, 79, [5.48]. By contrast, India insisted on the use of the median line. India's Counter-Memorial, 94–98, [5.33–5.45].

[426] Bangladesh's Mermorial,108, [6.77]; the *Bangladesh v India* arbitral award, [213].

[427] [2009] ICJ Rep 61, [131].

[428] The *Bangladesh v India* arbitral award, [215].

[429] ibid, [248].

[430] Bangladesh's Memorial, 88–89, [6.22–6.23].

[431] Bangladesh's Memorial, 111, [6.86–6.87].

[432] Bangladesh's Reply, 107, [4.113].

[433] India's Counter-Memorial, 118–19, [6.12]; Hearing Tr, 392.

more transparent.'[434] 'By contrast,' the Tribunal continued, 'depicting the relevant coasts as straight lines under the angle-bisector method involves subjective considerations.'[435] Related to this, notably the Tribunal stressed that:

> [B]y separating the first and second stages in the application of the equidistance/relevant circumstances method, a high degree of transparency can be achieved.[436]

By contrast, according to the Tribunal, 'even if clearly reasoned, a decision based on the angle-bisector method does not possess the same structure or the same degree of transparency.'[437] The Tribunal also noted that unlike the *Nicaragua v Honduras* case, Bangladesh was able to identify base points on its coast as well as on the coast of India. It thus considered it appropriate to apply the equidistance/relevant circumstances method in the *Bangladesh v India* case.[438] As will be discussed below, after constructing a provisional equidistance line, the Tribunal shifted it taking account of a relevant circumstance. It then applied the disproportionality test. Thus, it can be observed that the Tribunal applied the three-stage approach in the present case. The Tribunal's approach sharply contrasted with the ICJ's approach in the *Nicaragua v Honduras* case. The *Bangladesh v India* arbitral award appears to suggest that if it is possible to identify base points for constructing a provisional equidistance line, the equidistance method can be applied, despite the future instability of the coastline.

A particular issue that needs further consideration concerns the delimitation of the continental shelf beyond 200 nautical miles. Both Parties agreed that the Tribunal had jurisdiction to deal with this matter.[439] The Parties also agreed that they both have entitlement to the continental shelf beyond 200 nautical miles.[440] On this issue, the Tribunal took the same approach taken by ITLOS in the *Bangladesh/Myanmar* case, stating that:

> [T]he appropriate method for delimiting the continental shelf remains the same, irrespective of whether the area to be delimited lies within or beyond 200 nm. Having adopted the equidistance/relevant circumstances method for the delimitation of the continental shelf within 200 nm, the Tribunal will use the same method to delimit the continental shelf beyond 200 nm.[441]

[434] The *Bangladesh v India* arbitral award, [343].

[435] ibid. In this regard, Fietta and Cleverly also argued that: 'A disadvantage of the bisector method … is that the identification of a simplified coastal front is inherently subjective.' Fietta and Cleverly, *A Practitioner's Guide*, 101.

[436] The *Bangladesh v India* arbitral award, [344].

[437] ibid.

[438] ibid, [346].

[439] ibid, [74].

[440] ibid, [78]. In fact, both Parties have made submissions to the Commission on the Limits of the Continental Shelf (CLCS). Bangladesh's Reply, 133–34, [5.13]. See also India's Rejoinder, 169–70, [7.3].

[441] The *Bangladesh v India* arbitral award, [465]. This issue will be discussed in s XIX of this chapter.

B. Application of the Law Identified

i. Establishment of the Territorial Sea Boundary

As for the delimitation of the territorial sea between Bangladesh and India, first the Tribunal was to draw the equidistance line. The line was constructed in two steps: Identification of the base points and that of the median/equidistance line.[442] The Tribunal first decided that it would not rely on base points located on low-tide elevations detached from the coast,[443] and it selected two base points on the coast of Bangladesh and that of India, respectively.[444] The Tribunal then examined whether there were any circumstances that require an adjustment of the equidistance line in the territorial sea. While the Tribunal did not regard the concavity of the coastline of the Bay of Bengal as a special circumstance, it considered that the need to connect the land boundary terminus to the equidistance line constructed by it for the delimitation of the territorial sea constituted a special circumstance.[445] The Tribunal thus decided to shift the provisional equidistance line. As a consequence, 'the boundary should take the form of a 12 nm long geodetic line continuing from the land boundary terminus in a generally southerly direction to meet the median line at 21° 26′ 43.6″N; 89° 10′ 59.2″E.'[446] In summary, the Tribunal applied the corrective-equity approach to the delimitation of the territorial sea at the operational stage.

ii. Establishment of the Boundary of the EEZ and Continental Shelf

a. The Application of the Three-stage Approach

To construct a provisional equidistance line, there is a need to identify appropriate base points. The Tribunal thus examined the validity of base points proposed by Bangladesh and India with a view to establishing the provisional equidistance line. It did not accept some base points proposed by Bangladesh and India. Accordingly, the Tribunal identified appropriate base points combining those proposed by the Parties and those identified by the Tribunal itself. By using the base points, the Tribunal constructed the provisional equidistance line.[447]

The Tribunal then turned to question whether relevant circumstances call for an adjustment of the provisional equidistance line. While Bangladesh claimed three relevant circumstances, ie. coastal instability, a concavity of the coast of Bangladesh and cut-off effects, and its dependence on fish,[448] the Tribunal accepted only a cut-off effect arising from the concavity of the Bangladesh's

[442] ibid, [249].
[443] ibid, [264].
[444] ibid, [268–69].
[445] ibid, [271–74].
[446] ibid, [276].
[447] ibid, [368–70].
[448] ibid, [372–76]; [380–86]; [393].

coast as a relevant circumstance which may require the adjustment of the provisional equidistance line.[449] In this connection, it considered that the provisional equidistance line also required adjustment beyond 200 nautical miles to produce an equitable result.[450]

The next question was to what extent the cut-off effect would require adjustment of that line. In this regard, the Tribunal decided that from point Prov-3, the adjusted line delimiting the EEZ and the continental shelf between Bangladesh and India within and beyond 200 nm is a geodetic line with an initial azimuth of 177° 30′ 00″ until this line meets with the maritime boundary established by ITLOS to delimit the EEZ and the continental shelf between Bangladesh and Myanmar within and beyond 200 nm.[451] However, the Tribunal offered scant explanation with regard to the legal basis for selecting an azimuth of 177° 30′ 00″.[452] As Judge Chandrasekhara Rao pointedly observed, the azimuth chosen by the majority is similar to the azimuth of the bisector line proposed by Bangladesh which was rejected by the Tribunal, ie, an azimuth of 180°.[453] It seems to follow that the azimuth of the bisector line was *de facto* re-introduced at the second stage of maritime delimitation, even though it was rejected by the Tribunal itself.

At the third stage of maritime delimitation, the Tribunal applied the disproportionality test. The ratio between the lengths of the relevant coasts of the Parties is 1: 1.92, while the ration of the allocated areas is approximately 1: 2.81. The Tribunal found that this ration did not produce any significant disproportion.[454] In conclusion, the Tribunal decided, by four votes to one, that the maritime boundary between Bangladesh and India runs as shown in the illustration 27.[455]

b. Grey Area

The Tribunal's delimitation line created an area that lies beyond 200 nm from the coast of Bangladesh and within 200 nm from the coast of India, and yet lies to the east of the Tribunal's delimitation line.[456] The grey area party overlaps with the grey area created by ITLOS in the *Bangladesh/Myanmar* case. As a consequence, three grey areas were created in the Bay of Bengal.[457] The first is

[449] ibid, [408].
[450] ibid, [475].
[451] ibid, [478].
[452] Concurring and Dissenting Opinion of Dr PS Rao, [21].
[453] ibid, [9] and [22].
[454] The *Bangladesh v India* arbitral award, [495–97].
[455] For the verbal description of the maritime boundary, ibid, [509].
[456] ibid, [498].
[457] Magnússon, 'The Grey Areas in the Bay of Bengal,' 43–44; R Mishra, 'The "Grey Area" in the Northern Bay of Bengal: A Note on a Functional Cooperative Solution' (2016) 47 *ODIL*, 33–35; For the location of the grey areas, see Map 11 annexed to the *Bangladesh v India* arbitral award, 161; Fietta and Cleverly, *A Practitioner's Guide*, 567.

the area where Bangladesh's continental shelf rights overlap Myanmar's EEZ rights. The second area is a trilateral or 'double' grey area where the EEZ of Myanmar and India overlap Bangladesh's continental shelf.[458] The third is the area where Bangladesh's continental shelf rights overlap India's EEZ.

However, the creation of grey area was criticised by Judge Chandrasekhara Rao. In this regard, Judge Chandrasekhara Rao stressed the unity of the legal regime of the EEZ, stating that: '[W]ithin 200 nm from the coast, the sovereign rights of a coastal State over the water column and the seabed and its subsoil are considered as two *indispensable and inseparable parts* of the coastal State's rights in the EEZ.'[459] Therefore, according to the learned judge, 'it may not be possible in practice to divide the EEZ and separate the rights of one coastal State in the water column from the rights of another over the seabed and its subsoil.'[460]

The grey areas, in particular, the 'double' grey area creates highly complicated problems with regard to the exercise of jurisdiction. Nonetheless, the Arbitral Tribunal did not address the question. Instead, it merely stated that: 'It is for the Parties to determine the measures they consider appropriate in this respect, including through the conclusion of further agreements or the creation of a cooperative arrangement.'[461] Yet some doubt might be expressed regarding whether the Tribunal's dictum was relevant.[462] In this regard, Judge Chandrasekhara Rao stated his misgivings that: '[I]nviting the Parties to negotiate a solution in the grey area may lead to further problems and may be considered as a failure on the Tribunal's part to delimit the maritime areas in a definitive manner.'[463] It is true that in appropriate cases, an international court or tribunal may direct parties to carry out negotiation.[464] The *North Sea Continental Shelf* cases are a case in point. In this case, the Parties requested the ICJ to only pronounce principles and rules of international law application to the delimitation of the continental shelf between the Parties;[465] and the final solution was left to the Parties at the very outset. In the *Bangladesh v India* case, however, the Arbitral Tribunal seemed to create a new problem that must be

[458] Judge Rao used the term 'double' grey area. Concurring and Dissenting Opinion of Dr PS Rao in the *Bangladesh v India* case, [24].

[459] Emphasis original. Concurring and Dissenting Opinion in the *Bangladesh v India* arbitral award, [31].

[460] ibid, [36].

[461] ibid, [508].

[462] Indeed, Schofield *et al* argued that: 'The Tribunal's perspective may, [...], be overly sanguine and optimistic.' C Schofield, A Telesetsky and Seokwoo Lee, 'A Tribunal Navigating Complex Waters: Implications of the Bay of Bengal Case' (2013) 44 *Ocean Development and International Law* 376.

[463] Concurring and Dissenting Opinion of Dr. P.S. Rao in the *Bangladesh v India* case (n. 113) at para 36.

[464] This is called 'judicially directed negotiation'. Yoshifumi Tanaka, *The Peaceful Settlement of International Disputes* (Cambridge University Press, 2018) 35–36.

[465] The *North Sea Continental Shelf* cases, [1969] ICJ Rep 6.

settled by negotiation between the Parties.[466] Here it may be difficult to disagree with Judge Chandrasekhara Rao's statement:

> [A]s a matter of policy, international courts and tribunals should avoid delimiting boundaries in a way that leaves room for potential conflicts between the parties. The entire purpose of delimitation is to settle inter-State disputes definitively by allocating particular areas where one party can effectively exercise sovereign rights (such as exploitation) without the need for permission of another sovereign. Grey areas do precisely the opposite.[467]

Even though one can find a few instances of grey area in State practice,[468] as a matter of judicial policy, caution will be needed to avoid creating a grey area.

XVI. THE *CROATIA/SLOVENIA* CASE (ARBITRATION, 2017)

The *Croatia/Slovenia* arbitration concerns a territorial and maritime dispute between the Croatia and Slovenia.[469] For the purposes of this chapter, two issues

[466] The same applies to ITLOS in the *Bangladesh/Myanmar* case.

[467] Concurring and Dissenting Opinion of Dr PS Rao in the *Bangladesh v India* case (n. 113) at para 35.

[468] In State practice, there are a few treaties creating grey area. An example is provided by the 1990 Agreement between the United States and Soviet Union. The agreement created three special areas that lie beyond 200 nautical miles from one party but within the 200 nautical miles from another party yet on the side of the former party of the boundary line. Under Art 3 of the Agreement, the parties agreed the manner of exercise of jurisdiction in the special areas. Concerning the eastern special area, the Soviet Union agreed that 'henceforth the United States may exercise the sovereign rights and jurisdiction derived from exclusive economic zone jurisdiction that the Soviet Union would otherwise be entitled to exercise under international law in the absence of the agreement of the Parties on the maritime boundary' (Art 3(1)). Likewise, in the western special area, the United States agreed that 'henceforth the Soviet Union may exercise the sovereign rights and jurisdiction derived from exclusive economic zone jurisdiction that the United Sates would otherwise be entitled to exercise under international law in the absence of the agreement of the Parties on the maritime boundary' (Art 3(2)). Accordingly, the Parties relinquished entitlements in the special areas in the reciprocal manner. For the text of the Agreement, *IMB*, vol I, 454. Another example is the 2010 Cooperation Agreement between Norway and the Russian Federation. The continental shelf boundary established by the Agreement created an area beyond 200 nautical miles from the Russian coast, but within 200 nautical miles from the Norwegian coast. This area is called the 'Special Area' in Art 3 of the Agreement. Under Art 3, the Russian Federation is entitled to exercise 'sovereign rights and jurisdiction derived from exclusive economic zone jurisdiction that Norway would otherwise be entitled to exercise under international law'. Text in: *IMB*, vol VII, 5189. See also Report by Fife, ibid, 5167, 5181–82. Furthermore, the 1997 Perth Treaty between Australia and Indonesia for the Timor and Arafura Sea created an area where the EEZ appertaining to Indonesia overlaps the continental shelf of Australia. Text in: *IMB*, vol IV, 2714. For an analysis of treaties creating grey areas, see Paik, 'The Grey Area in the Bay of Bengal Case,' 280–81. For the Perth Treaty, see ch 9, s III of this book.

[469] PCA Case No. 2012-04. *In the Matter of an Arbitration under the Arbitration Agreement between the Government of the Republic of Croatia and the Government of the Republic of Slovenia*, 29 June 2017. Final Award, available at: https://pca-cpa.org/en/cases/3/. Croatia and Slovenia are successor States to the Socialist Federal Republic of Yugoslavia. Croatia and Slovenia declared independence on 25 June 1991. ibid., [34]. The members of the Arbitral Tribunal were: G Guillaume (President), RE Fife, V Lowe, N Michel and B Simma. The arbitral tribunal was recomposed after the partial award of 30 June 2016. In this regard, see Tanaka, *The Peaceful Settlement of International Disputes*, 112–13.

must be examined. The first is the delimitation of the 'Bay of Savudrija/Piran' (Croatia) or 'Bay of Piran' (Slovenia)[470] and the second is the delimitation of the territorial sea between Croatia and Slovenia.

A. Law Applicable to Maritime Delimitation

i. Law Applicable to the Delimitation of the Bay

The first issue concerns the delimitation of the Bay. According to the Arbitral Tribunal, the Bay was established as a juridical bay.[471] However, subsequently the bay had two coastal States as a result of the dissolution of the Socialist Federal Republic of Yugoslavia. In this regard, the Tribunal took the view that the dissolution did not have the effect of altering the acquired status and that the Bay remained in internal waters.[472] As two coastal States cannot exercise the territorial sovereignty over the same areas at the same time, delimitation of the Bay was needed. The LOSC contains no provision on the delimitation of internal waters. Accordingly, the Arbitral Tribunal considered that delimitation within the Bay is to be made on the basis of the same principles as are applicable to the delimitation of land territories.[473] In the present case, the Parties agreed that there had been no formal division of the Bay between two Republics prior to the dissolution of Yugoslavia. The Tribunal thus ruled that delimitation must be made the delimitation of the Bay on the basis of the *effectivités* at the date of independence.[474] However, the Tribunal's view is open to question at least in two respects.

First, the Tribunal's view relied on the *Case Concerning the Land, Island and Maritime Frontier Dispute*. In this case, the Chamber of the ICJ held that the Gulf of Fonseca was a historic bay the waters whereof were held in sovereignty by El Salvador, Honduras and Nicaragua.[475] Yet it is debatable whether there is a bay bordered by plural States the water of which is internal waters in international law. After the thorough examination of development of rules governing a bay, Judge Oda stated that:

> [T]he simple outcome of this study of the development of the law of the sea is that there did not and still does not (or even, cannot) exist any such legal concept as a 'pluri-State bay' the waters of which are internal waters.[476]

[470] Following the Tribunal, the tem 'Bay' is denoted the body of water that is referred to by the Parties as the 'Bay of Savudrija/Piran' (Croatia) or the 'Bay of Piran' (Slovenia). The *Croatia/Slovenia* arbitral award, [771].

[471] ibid, [881].

[472] ibid, [885].

[473] ibid, [886].

[474] ibid, [888].

[475] *Case Concerning the Land, Island and Maritime Frontier Dispute* (El Salvador/Honduras: Nicaragua intervening), Judgment, [1992] ICJ Rep 616, [432(1)].

[476] Dissenting Opinion of Judge Oda, ibid, 745, [24].

In fact, as territorial sovereignty is exclusive by nature, the internal waters of one State cannot belong to another State at the same time. Thus, that the idea of a bay bordered by more than one State, the waters of which are internal waters, contains a conceptual contradiction. Accordingly, as Judge Oda rightly stated, it seems reasonable to consider that the waters inside a geographical bay which was bordered by two or more States are left as being the territorial sea and the high seas if these States did not claim their EEZ.[477]

Secondly, the absence of a rule governing the delimitation of the internal waters does not automatically means that the delimitation of these waters would be governed by the law of acquisition of territory. Needless to say, the internal waters are governed by the law of the sea. Hence it is logical to consider that the delimitation of the internal waters would be governed by the law of maritime delimitation. As discussed in this chapter, there is a clear trend that international courts and tribunals apply the corrective-equity approach or the three-stage approach to maritime delimitations. Hence it may not be unreasonable to argue that by analogy, the same approach can apply to delimitation of internal waters.[478]

ii. Law Applicable to Delimitation of the Territorial Sea

The next issue pertains to the delimitation of territorial sea in the Adriatic Sea. The rule applicable to the delimitation of territorial sea between Croatia and Slovenia is set out in Article 15 of the LOSC. Related to this, the Arbitral Tribunal held that:

> In relation to the delimitation both of the territorial sea and of the maritime zones beyond the territorial sea, international law thus calls for the application of an equidistance line, unless another line is required by special circumstances. That is reflected in the practice of the ICJ, which has applied the 'equidistance/special circumstances' approach in the drawing of single maritime boundaries without distinguishing between its application to the territorial sea and its application beyond the territorial sea.[479]

According to the Tribunal,

> [t]his convergence of the principles applicable to the territorial sea and to other maritime zones is further evidenced by the fact that a maritime boundary may separate adjacent maritime zones of different juridical character, such as the territorial sea of State A and the exclusive economic zone of State B.[480]

[477] ibid, 738, [13].

[478] Concerning the delimitation of the internal waters, Caflisch argued that it would be preferable to resort, by analogy, to the rules governing the delimitation of the territorial sea. L Caflisch, 'The Delimitation of Marine Spaces between State with Opposite and Adjacent Coasts' in R-J Dupuy and D Vignes, (eds), *A Handbook on the New Law of the Sea* (Dordrecht, Nijhoff, 1991) 442. See also ch 3, s I of this book.

[479] The *Croatia/Slovenia* arbitral award, [1000].

[480] ibid.

The *dictum* of the Tribunal did seem to suggest the unification of the methodology of maritime delimitations under the corrective-equity approach.[481]

B. Application of the Law Identified

i. Establishment of the Boundary in the Bay

In light of various *effectivités*, the Arbitral Tribunal held that the line determined in the agreement contemplated by the Parties in 2001,[482] namely, the line that was drawn to join the end of the land boundary in the mouth of the Dragonja River to a point on the closing line of the Bay, which is at a distance from Cape Madona that is three times the distance from that same point to Cape Savudrija, corresponds to the *effectivités* (see Illustration 28).[483]

ii. Establishment of the Territorial Sea Boundary

When establishing a territorial sea boundary, the question arose whether any special circumstance would render the equidistance line inapposite for the definitive maritime boundary.[484] In this connection, the Tribunal did not consider that the great difference between the lengths of the coastal fronts of Croatia and Slovenia constitutes a special circumstance that calls for a departure from the equidistance line.[485] The Tribunal's view represents a sharp contrast to the jurisprudence that regarded the difference of the coastal lengths as a relevant circumstance that requires adjustment of a provisional equidistance line.[486] Furthermore, the Tribunal denied the existence of historic title that would warrant a departure from the equidistance line.[487]

By contrast, the Tribunal regarded the 'boxing-in' or 'cut-off effect' in relation to Slovenia's waters as a special circumstance. In the words of the Tribunal,

> That special circumstance is the fact that very close to Point A the coastline of Croatia turns sharply southwards around Cape Savudrija, so that the Croatian basepoints that control the equidistance line are located on a very small stretch of coast whose general (north-facing) direction is markedly different from the general (southwest-facing) direction of much the greater part of the Croatian coastline …, and deflect the equidistance line very significantly towards the north, greatly exaggerating the 'boxed-in' nature of Slovenia's maritime zone.[488]

[481] Further, see s XIX of this chapter.
[482] See Art 3 of Treaty between the republic of Slovenia and the Republic of Croatia on Common State Border, signed on 20 July 2001.
[483] The *Croatia/Slovenia* arbitral award, [912].
[484] ibid, [1005].
[485] ibid, [1011].
[486] See the *Libya/Malta, Gulf of Main, Jan Mayen* and *Nicaragua v Colombia* cases.
[487] The *Croatia/Slovenia* arbitral award, [1011].
[488] ibid.

The Tribunal thus held that the equidistance line must be modified in order to attenuate the 'boxing-in' or 'cut-off effect' that results from the geographic configuration. It accordingly decided that the maritime boundary shall proceed northwest from Point A in a direction approximately parallel to the Treaty of Osimo line T2-T3 (see illustration 28).[489] In addition, the Tribunal determined Slovenia's junction to the high seas.[490] When establishing the territorial sea boundary in the Adriatic Sea, the Tribunal did not apply the disproportionality test. The Tribunal's view in the *Croatia/Slovenia* arbitration leaves some room for discussion in three respects.

First, it is less clear why the fact that the Croatian basepoints that control the equidistance line are located on a very small stretch of coast creates the 'boxing-in' or 'cut-off effect'. In fact, the equidistance line drawn by the Tribunal runs almost perpendicular to the closing line of the Bay. This seems to imply that there is no cut-off effect.[491]

Secondly, as the ICJ stated in the *Black Sea* case, 'the coast, in order to be considered as relevant for the purpose of the delimitation, must generate projections which overlap with projections from the coast of the other Party.'[492] The southwest-facing coast of Croatia does not generate projections which overlap with projections from the coast of the other Party.[493] Therefore it is hard to understand why Croatia's southwest-facing coast must be taken into account in this context.

Thirdly, the Tribunal's equidistance line before adjustment line run from Point A. Yet this point was closer to Croatia than Slovenia. It would seem to follow that the Tribunal's line was not a true equidistance line.[494] Accordingly, there appears to be some scope to reconsider the question whether the territorial sea boundary established by the Tribunal can be truly regarded as an adjusted equidistance line.

Under Article 7(3) of the Arbitration Agreement, the Parties shall take all necessary steps to implement the award within six months after the adoption of the award. Yet, Croatia rejected the implementation of the arbitral award, stating that Croatia terminated the arbitral proceedings because of the breach of the Arbitration Agreement by Slovenia.[495]

[489] ibid, [1012–14].

[490] See ch 8, s V of this book.

[491] Alex G Oude Elferink, 'Slovenia/Croatia Arbitration: Is the territorial Sea Delimitation Inconsistent with the Case Law on Maritime Delimitation?' The JCLOS Blog, 16 August 2017, available at: http://site.uit.no/jclos/2017/08/16/sloveniacroatia-arbitration-is-the-territorial-sea-delimitation-inconsistent-with-the-case-law-on-maritime-delimitation/.

[492] [2009] ICJ Rep 97, [99].

[493] Oude Elferink, 'Slovenia/Croatia Arbitration'.

[494] R Churchill, 'One Response to *Slovenia/Croatia arbitration – Is the territorial sea delimitation inconsistent with the case law on maritime delimitation?*' (2 December 2017), available at: http://site.uit.no/jclos/2017/08/16/sloveniacroatia-arbitration-is-the-territorial-sea-delimitation-inconsistent-with-the-case-law-on-maritime-delimitation/.

[495] Republic of Croatia, Ministry of Foreign and European Affairs, Termination of the Arbitration Process between Croatia and Slovenia: Causes and Consequences, available at: www.mvep.hr/en/

XVII. THE *GHANA/CÔTE D'IVOIRE* CASE (ITLOS, 2017)

The *Ghana/Côte d'Ivoire* case which will be discussed in this section is the first case of the ITLOS Special Chamber. By the Special Agreement and Notification dated 3 December 2014, Ghana and Côte d'Ivoire submitted the dispute concerning the single maritime boundary between them in the Atlantic Ocean to a Special Chamber of ITLOS.[496] Having found that no tacit agreement on the maritime boundary between the Parties exists and that the requirements of estoppel have not been met,[497] the Special Chamber turned to the delimitation of the territorial sea, the EEZ and the continental shelf within and beyond 200 nautical miles.[498]

A. Law Applicable to Maritime Delimitation

i. Law Applicable to Delimitation of the Territorial Sea

Since Ghana and Côte d'Ivoire are both States Parties to the LOSC,[499] Article 15 of the Convention is applicable to the delimitation of the territorial sea. Nonetheless, opinions of the Parties were divided with regard to the methodology for the delimitation of the territorial sea. While Ghana argued for the application of the equidistance method pursuant to Article 15,[500] Côte d'Ivoire argued in favour of the application of the angle bisector methodology for the delimitation of the territorial sea.[501]

The Special Chamber stressed that under the LOSC, different rules apply to the delimitation of the territorial sea and that of the EEZ and the continental shelf.[502] At the same time, however, the Special Chamber noted that both Parties had implicitly agreed that the same delimitation methodology be used for the whole delimitation process.[503] On this basis, the Special Chamber considered

other/termination-of-the-arbitration-process/. See also Y Tanaka, *The Peaceful Settlement of International Disputes* (Cambridge University Press, 2018) 112–13.

[496] *Dispute Concerning Delimitation of the Maritime Boundary between Ghana and Côte d'Ivoire in the Atlantic Ocean (Ghana v Côte d'Ivoire)* (the *Ghana/Côte d'Ivoire* case), Judgment. [2017] ITLOS Rep (not yet reported). The electronic text is available at: www.itlos.org/en/cases/list-of-cases/case-no-23/. The composition of the Special Chamber was as follows: Bouguetaia (President), Wolfrum, Paik, Mensah and Abraham.

[497] See ch 8, s II of this book.

[498] The *Ghana/Côte d'Ivoire* case, [2017] ITLOS Rep [247].

[499] Ghana ratified the LOSC on 7 June 1983 and Côte d'Ivoire ratified the Convention on 26 March 1984. ibid, [83].

[500] Ghana's Memorial, vol I, 90–92, [4.4–4.8].

[501] Côte d'Ivoire's Counter-Memorial, vol I, 132, [6.1 et seq].

[502] The *Ghana/Côte d'Ivoire* case, [2017] ITLOS Rep [260].

[503] ibid, [262].

'it appropriate to use the same methodology for the delimitation of the Parties' territorial seas, exclusive economic zones and continental shelves within and beyond 200 nautical miles.'[504]

ii. Law Applicable to Delimitation of the EEZ and the Continental Shelf

a. Delimitation of the EEZ and Continental Shelf within 200 Nautical Miles

Ghana and Côte d'Ivoire agreed that Articles 74(1) and 83(1) of the Convention govern the delimitation of the EEZ and continental shelf. However, they disagreed with regard to two questions: the first question was whether, like the equidistance/relevant circumstances methodology, the angle bisector methodology is equally applicable and the second question was whether the circumstances prevailing in the present case call for the application of the angle bisector methodology.[505] While Ghana claimed that the equidistance/relevant circumstances method is the standard method,[506] Côte d'Ivoire advocated the application of the angle bisector method.[507] However, the Special Chamber did not agree with the Côte d'Ivoire.[508] In this connection, the Chamber made an important statement:

> To conclude, the Special Chamber finds that the international jurisprudence concerning the delimitation of maritime spaces in principle favours the equidistance/relevant circumstances methodology. It further finds that the international decisions which adopted the angle bisector methodology were due to particular circumstances in each of the cases concerned. This international jurisprudence confirms that, in the absence of any compelling reasons that make it impossible or inappropriate to draw a provisional equidistance line, the equidistance/relevant circumstances methodology should be chosen for maritime delimitation … The Special Chamber would consider it to be in contradiction of the principle of transparency and predictability invoked above (para. 281) to deviate, in this case, from a delimitation methodology which has been practised overwhelmingly by international courts and tribunals in recent decades.[509]

The above statement calls for two comments.

[504] ibid, [263].
[505] ibid, [279].
[506] Presentation by Sands, ITLOS/PV.17/C23/2/Rev.1, 7 February 2017, 21. Originally Ghana claimed that the maritime boundary between Ghana and Côte d'Ivoire has been settled by agreement of the Parties. According to Ghana, however, 'if the equidistance/relevant circumstances method were employed, it would result in the establishment of a very similar line to the customary equidistance line that the Parties regarded as the international border for five decades.' Memorial of Ghana, vol I, 4 September 2015, 144, [5.85].
[507] Counter-Memorial of Côte d'Ivoire, vol I, 4 April 2016, 15, [26]. See also ibid, 132 et seq.
[508] The *Ghana/Côte d'Ivoire* case, [2017] ITLOS Rep [282].
[509] ibid, [289].

First, even though the Special Chamber did not make an explicit reference to the three-stage approach in the statement, the Chamber made clear, in another paragraph, that it would follow the three-stage approach as developed in international jurisprudence. The Chamber called this approach the 'internationally established approach'.[510]

Secondly, notably the Special Chamber, in the above statement, explicitly referred to the 'principle of transparency and predictability'. It is noteworthy that transparency and predictability were regarded as the 'principle' by the Chamber. It would seem to follow that the normative level of transparency and predictability are now enhanced to the level of 'principle'. In this connection, the Chamber stressed that: '[T]ransparency and predictability of the delimitation process as a whole are also objectives to be taken into account in this process.'[511]

Next, the Chamber turned to examine the issue of whether there were particular reasons that require an alternative method of maritime delimitation.[512] In this connection, Côte d'Ivoire invoked some factors that support its argument in favour of the angle bisector methodology, ie, insufficiency of reflecting the coastal geography by base points for constructing the equidistance line, location of base points on Jomoro, instability of the coastline, and interests of neighbouring States.[513] However, the Chamber was not persuaded by the argument of Côte d'Ivoire. In particular, the Chamber did not consider that the relevant coasts of the Parties were so unstable that it was difficult or impossible to identify appropriate base points for constructing an equidistance line.[514] The Chamber thus held that it saw 'no convincing reason to deviate in this case from the equidistance/relevant circumstances methodology for the delimitation of the territorial sea, the exclusive economic zone and the continental shelf.'[515]

b. Delimitation of the Continental Shelf beyond 200 Nautical Miles

Ghana and Côte d'Ivoire agreed that the Special Chamber has jurisdiction to decide on the delimitation of the continental shelf beyond 200 nautical miles.[516] The Chamber also confirmed its jurisdiction to this matter.[517] As for the delimitation methodology, the Chamber recalled that there is only one single continental shelf. Thus it considered it 'inappropriate to make a distinction

[510] ibid, [360].
[511] ibid, [281].
[512] ibid, [290].
[513] ibid, [292–322].
[514] ibid, [318].
[515] ibid, [324].
[516] ibid, [489].
[517] ibid, [495].

between the continental shelf within and beyond 200 nm as far as the delimitation methodology is concerned.'[518] As will be discussed in section XVIII of this chapter, 'one single continental shelf' seemed to constitute a key concept to apply the same delimitation methodology to the delimitation of the continental shelf beyond 200 nautical miles.

B. Application of the Law Identified

i. Construction of the Provisional Equidistance Line

As the Special Chamber stated, the first step in the construction of the provisional equidistance line is to identify the Parties' coasts of which the seaward projection overlaps.[519] In this connection, the Chamber made clear that:

> For a coast to be relevant in maritime delimitation it must generate projections which overlap with those of the coast of another party.[520]

This is a re-run of the *dictum* of the *Black Sea* and *Bangladesh/Myanmar* cases.[521] The Chamber further added that the relevant coast is determined by the geographic reality of that coast, not a simplified configuration of the coast.[522] As for the coast of Ghana, the Chamber observed that between BP 55+to Cape Three Points where the coast turns abruptly to the north-east, the coast of Ghana faces directly towards the disputed area. Accordingly, this area is relevant. However, the coast further eastward is not relevant because it faces away from the area to be delimited.[523] Concerning the coast of Côte d'Ivoire, the Chamber considered that the coast from BP 55+ to the north-west until it reaches a bend in the coast near Abidjan and to the west until Sassandra is relevant since this part of the coast of Côte d'Ivoire overlaps with projections of the Ghanaian coast. However, the coast between Sassandra and the boundary with Liberia does not have a projection to the sea in a way that overlaps with the disputed area.[524] Accordingly, this part of the coast is not relevant. Overall the Special Chamber concluded that: '[T]he relevant coasts are, on Ghana's side, from BP 55+ to Cape Three Points and, on Côte d'Ivoire's side, from BP 55+ to Sassandra.'[525]

Next, the Special Chamber identified the relevant area surrounded by three lines, ie, a line running due south starting from Cape Three Points until it

[518] ibid, [526].
[519] ibid, [361].
[520] ibid, [372].
[521] See [2009] ICJ Rep 97, [99]; [2012] ITLOS Rep 58, [198].
[522] The *Ghana/Côte d'Ivoire* case, [2017] ITLOS Rep [378].
[523] ibid, [376].
[524] ibid, [377–78].
[525] ibid, [379]. See Sketch-map No. 2 attached to the Judgment.

reaches the outer limits of the continental shelf of Ghana, a line running due south starting from until it reaches the outer limits of the continental shelf of Ghana, and the outer limits of the continental shelf of Ghana and those of the continental shelf claimed by Côte d'Ivoire.[526] Related to this, Chamber stressed that: '[I]t is only possible to give an approximation of the size of the relevant area since, …, the outer limits of the continental shelf beyond 200 nm have not yet been established.'[527]

The Special Chamber considered it mandatory that the base points used for the construction of a provisional equidistance line be situated at the low-water line.[528] Since the base points suggested by the Parties were not appropriate for various reasons, the Chamber identified base points from Chart BA 1383 on its own.[529] On the basis of these points, a simplified provisional equidistance line was established.[530]

ii. Considerations of Relevant Circumstances and the Disproportionality Test

At the second stage of maritime delimitation, the Special Chamber examined multiple factors suggested by the Parties. These factors were: concavity/convexity, the geography of Jomoro, location of resources, conduct of the Parties.[531] In this regard, the Chamber concluded that there was no relevant circumstance which would justify an adjustment of the provisional equidistance line.[532] Accordingly, the delimitation line follows the equidistance line as described in paragraph 481 of the judgment (see Illustration 29). It also ruled that the delimitation line for the territorial sea, the EEZ and the continental shelf within 200 nautical miles continues in the same direction until it reaches the outer limits of the continental shelf.[533]

The third stage of maritime delimitation is the application of the disproportionality test. According to the Special Chamber, the ratio of the length of the relevant coasts of the Parties is approximately 1:2.53 in favour of Côte d'Ivoire, while the ratio of the allocated areas is approximately 1:2.02 in favour of Côte d'Ivoire. Therefore the Special Chamber found that the disproportionality test was met.[534] Overall it may be said that the *Ghana/Côte d'Ivoire* case is in line with the recent developments of the case law relating to maritime delimitation.

[526] ibid, [382–385]. See Sketch-map No. 3 attached to the Judgment.
[527] ibid, [386].
[528] ibid, [396].
[529] ibid, [399].
[530] ibid, [400–1]. See Sketch-map No. 4 attached to the Judgment.
[531] For an analysis of these factors, see chs 7 and 8 of this book.
[532] The *Ghana/Côte d'Ivoire* case, [2017] ITLOS Rep [480].
[533] ibid, [527].
[534] ibid, [536–37].

XVIII. THE *COSTA RICA* v *NICARAGUA* CASE (ICJ, 2018)

On 25 February 2014, Costa Rica instituted proceedings against Nicaragua with regard to a dispute concerning the establishment of single maritime boundaries between the two States in the Caribbean Sea and the Pacific Ocean, respectively.[535] Subsequently the ICJ, in its Order of 2017, decided to join the proceedings in the case concerning maritime delimitation and the case concerning the land boundary in the Northern Part of Isla Portillos. The Court found that Costa Ria has sovereignty over the whole northern part of Isla Portillos.[536] It thus turned to maritime delimitations in the Caribbean Sea and the Pacific Ocean, respectively.

A. Law Applicable to Maritime Delimitation

i. Law Applicable to Delimitation of the Territorial Sea

As Costa Rica and Nicaragua are Parties to the LOSC,[537] Article 15 of the Convention is applicable to the delimitation of the territorial sea in the present case. In this regard, the relationship between the delimitation method under Article 15 and that under Articles 74 and 83 of the Convention was at issue. Costa Rica stressed the difference between the delimitation of the territorial sea under Article 15 and the delimitation of the EEZ and of the continental shelf under Articles 74 and 83 of the Convention. It thus argued that the Court should delimit the Parties' boundary in the territorial sea first, and thereafter in the EEZ and on the continental shelf, by means of two different methods.[538] However, Nicaragua maintained that there is no practical difference between the delimitation of the territorial sea under Article 15 and that of the EEZ and the continental shelf under Articles 74 and 83 of the Convention.[539] In any event, the Parties agreed that for the delimitation of the territorial sea, it is first necessary to establish the equidistance line.[540] The ICJ, for its part, made clear that it would take the corrective-equity approach to the delimitation of the territorial sea:

[535] *Maritime Delimitation in the Caribbean Sea and the Pacific Ocean (Costa Rica v Nicaragua)* (the *Costa Rica v Nicaragua* case), Judgment, [2018] ICJ Rep (not yet reported), [1]. The ICJ, in its Order of 2017, decided to join the proceedings in the case concerning maritime delimitation and the case concerning the land boundary in the Northern Part of Isla Portillos. *Maritime Delimitation in the Caribbean Sea and the Pacific Ocean (Costa Rica v Nicaragua)*, Order, [2017] ICJ Rep (not yet reported), [18].

[536] [2018] ICJ Rep [205(2)].

[537] Costa Rica and Nicaragua ratified the LOSC in 1992 and 2000, respectively.

[538] [2018] ICJ Rep [91].

[539] ibid, [92]; Counter-Memorial of Nicaragua, 29–30, [2.43].

[540] [2018] ICJ Rep [94].

> In accordance with its established jurisprudence, the Court will proceed in two stages; first, the Court will draw a provisional median line; second, it will consider whether any special circumstances exist which justify adjusting such as line.[541]

The Court applied the same approach to the delimitation of the territorial sea in the Pacific Ocean.[542]

ii. Law Applicable to Delimitation of the EEZ and the Continental Shelf

For the delimitation of the EEZ and the continental shelf in the Caribbean Sea, the Court clearly stated that it would delimit the EEZ and the continental shelf 'pursuant to its established methodology in three stages.'[543] In the words of the Court,

> First, it will provisionally draw an equidistance line using the most appropriate base points on the relevant coasts of the Parties. Second, it will consider whether there exist relevant circumstances which are capable of justifying an adjustment of the equidistance line provisionally drawn. Third, it will assess the overall equitableness of the boundary resulting from the first two stages by checking whether there exists a marked disproportionality between the length of the Parties' relevant coasts and the maritime areas found to appertain to them .... The Court notes that the methodology in three stages set out in its Judgment in *Maritime Delimitation in the Black Sea (Romania* v. *Ukraine)* has also been adopted by other international tribunals requested to delimit maritime boundaries (see e.g. *Delimitation of the Maritime Boundary in the Bay of Bengal (Bangladesh/Myanmar), Judgment, ITLOS Reports 2012*, pp. 64–68, paras. 225–240; *Bay of Bengal Maritime Boundary Arbitration (Bangladesh* v. *India), Award of 7 July 2014, International Law Reports*, Vol. 167, pp. 111–114, paras. 336–346).[544]

It is noteworthy that in the above statement, the ICJ made an explicit reference to the practice of ITLOS and Annex VII Arbitral Tribunal.

B. Application of the Law Identified

i. Establishment of the Territorial Sea Boundary

a. The Caribbean Sea

The Court constructed the provisional median line for delimiting the territorial sea only on the basis of points on the natural coast, including points placed on islands or rocks.[545] An inquiry was whether, as claimed by Nicaragua, the

[541] ibid, [98].
[542] ibid, [172].
[543] ibid, [135].
[544] ibid.
[545] ibid, [100].

convex-concave combination of the configuration of the coast was regarded as a 'special circumstance' requiring an adjustment of the provisional median line.[546] In this regard, the Court held that the combined effect of the concavity of Nicaragua's coast west of the mouth of the San Juan River and of the convexity of Costa Rica's coast east of harbour Head Lagoo is of limited significance and that it does not represent a special circumstance that could justify an adjustment of the median line. However, the Court considered that the high instability and narrowness of the sandspit near the mouth of the San Juan River constitutes a special circumstance affecting maritime delimitation in the territorial sea.[547] It thus set out the fixed point at sea on the median line and connected the point by a mobile line to the point on solid land on Costa Rica's coast which is closest to the mouth of the San Juan River. As a consequence, the delimitation line in the territorial sea follows the median line from the fixed point at sea up to the intersection of the 12-nautical-mile line (see Illustration 30).[548] It is of particular interest to note that unlike the *Nicaragua v Honduras* judgment, instability of the coastline was not regarded as a 'compelling reason' for discarding the application of the equidistance method. The creation of a mobile line seems to be a useful option when considering the impact of change of coastlines with the passage of time, on maritime boundaries.[549]

Another special circumstances relevant for the delimitation of the territorial sea consisted in the instability of the sandbar separating Harbor Head Lagoon from the Caribbean Sea and its situation as a small enclave within Costa Rica's territory. According to the Court, '[s]hould territorial waters be attributed to the enclave,' they would break the continuity of Costa Rica's territorial sea. The Court thus held that the delimitation in the territorial sea would not take into account any entitlement which might result from the enclave.[550] It is notable that the instability of the sandbar of Harbor Head Lagoon did not constitute a compelling reason for rejecting the application of the corrective-equity approach to the delimitation of the territorial sea.

b. The Pacific Ocean

In the context of the delimitation of the territorial sea in the Pacific Ocean, a question was raised whether locating base points on the Santa Elena Peninsula has a significant distorting effect on the provisional median line which would result in a cut-off of Nicaragua's coastal projection within the territorial sea. The Court answered no because the Santa Elena Peninsula cannot be considered

[546] ibid, [101].
[547] ibid, [104].
[548] For specific co-ordinates, see ibid, [106].
[549] Further, see ch 7, s VIII of this book.
[550] [2018] ICJ Rep [105].

to be a minor coastal projection. Furthermore, in the view of the Court, the adjustment proposed by Nicaragua in the territorial sea would significantly cut off Costa Rica's coastal projections in the territorial sea. The Court thus concluded that the territorial sea in the Pacific Ocean shall be delimited by means of a median line.[551]

ii. Establishment of the Boundary of the EEZ and the Continental Shelf

a. The Caribbean Sea

The Court constructed a provisional median line on the basis of the selected base points, including base points placed on the Corn Islands, the Palmenta Cays and Paxaro Bovo.[552] Given their limited size and significant distance from the mainland coast, however, the Court gave only half effect to the Corn Islands (see Illustration 31).[553] To this extent the provisional median line was adjusted in favour of Costa Rica. The Court then applied the disproportionality test. According to the Court, the ratio of coastal length is 1:2.04 in favour of Nicaragua and the ration of the area belonging to the Parties is 1:2.4 in favour of Nicaragua. The Court thus concluded that the comparison of the ratios does not show any 'marked disproportion' (see Illustration 32).[554]

b. The Pacific Ocean

The delimitation of the EEZ and the continental shelf in the Pacific Ocean raised two issues. The first issue was whether the existence of the Santa Elena Peninsula would result in an inequitable cut-off of Nicaragua's coastal projections. The Court considered that beyond the territorial sea, the base points placed on the Santa Elena Peninsula would result in a significant cut-off of Nicaragua's coastal projections. Therefore it found it appropriate to adjust the provisional equidistance line for the EEZ and the continental shelf in the Pacific Ocean. Specifically the Court gave only half effect to the Santa Elena Peninsula in order to achieve an equitable solution.[555] This constitutes a unique precedent that the ICJ gave only half effect to a particular feature *on* a relevant coastline (see Illustration 33). It followed that a different effect was given to the Santa Elena Peninsula in the delimitation of the territorial sea and in the delimitation of the EEZ and the continental shelf.

The second issue was whether the existence of the Nicoya Peninsula creates an inequitable cut-off of Nicaragua's coastal projections. According to the Court,

[551] ibid, [174–75].
[552] ibid, [140–42].
[553] ibid, [154].
[554] ibid, [165].
[555] ibid, [198]. Further, see ch 7, s V of this book.

the Nicoya Peninsula is a prominent part of Costa Rica's mainland. The Court accordingly considered that it cannot be given less than full effect in delimitation the boundary in the EEZ and the continental shelf[556] and that no adjustment is necessary on account of the presence of the Nicoya Peninsula.[557] Finally, the Court applied the disproportionality test. The ratio of coastal lengths is 1:1.42 in favour of Costa Rica and the ratio between the maritime areas appertaining to the Parties is 1:1.30 in Costa Rica's favour. The Court accordingly concluded that, 'taking into account all the circumstances', the maritime boundary between Costa Rica and Nicaragua in the Pacific Ocean does not result in 'gross disproportionality' (see Illustration 34).[558]

XIX. ANALYSIS OF APPROACHES TO THE MARITIME DELIMITATION

A. Evolution of the Methodology of Maritime Delimitation

i. Toward the Unification of the Methodology of the Maritime Delimitation

The above analysis shows that the law of maritime delimitation has evolved with the passage of time. In parallel, international courts' approaches to maritime delimitations have also changed over time. The preceding study reveals that there are two approaches to maritime delimitations.

One is the result-oriented equity approach (ie, *l'équité créatrice*), which rejects any obligatory method by stressing the equitable results to be achieved. This approach corresponds to the method of the case-by-case solution, which was already advocated at the beginning of the twentieth century. According to this approach, it is solely equitableness which the law of maritime delimitation prescribes, and no method of delimitation is provided for by law. Result-oriented equity allows an international court or tribunal to exercise a large measure of discretion in each case. In other words, the courts may decide, case-by-case, on the equitable results to be achieved without being bound by any method. In light of the diversity of the factors to be considered in each case, the merit of flexibility is not negligible. It could be said that the result-oriented equity approach is one which attempts to maintain maximum flexibility.

Another approach is that of corrective equity (ie, *l'équité correctrice*), which uses a two-stage method: the equidistance method is applied at a first stage, and a shift of the equidistance line may then be envisaged if relevant circumstances warrant it.

556 [2018] ICJ Rep [196].

557 ibid, [198].

558 ibid, [203]. With regard to the maritime boundary established in the Caribbean Sea, the Court made no reference to 'all the circumstances in the present case' when applying the disproportionality test. On this point, see ch 7, s III of this book.

Figure 3

Year	Case	Type	Configuration	Approach
1969	The *North Sea Continental Shelf* cases (ICJ)	CS	AC	RE
1977	The *Anglo-French Continental Shelf* case (Arbitration)	CS	AC/OC	CE
1982	The *Tunisia/Libya* case (ICJ)	CS	AC/OC	RE
1984	The *Gulf of Maine* case (ICJ)	SMB	AC/OC	RE/CE
1985	The *Libya/Malta* case (ICJ)	CS	OC	RE/CE
1985	The *Guinea/Guinea-Bissau* case (Arbitration)	SMB	AC	RE
1992	The *St Pierre and Miquelon* case (Arbitration)	SMB	AC	RE
1993	The *Jan Mayen* case (ICJ)	SMB	OC	CE
1999	The *Eritrea/Yemen* case (Arbitration)	SMB	OC	CE
2001	The *Qatar v Bahrain* case (ICJ)	TS/SMB	AC/OC	CE
2002	The *Cameroon v Nigeria* case (ICJ)	TS/SMB	AC	CE
2006	The *Barbados v Trinidad and Tobago* case	SMB/CS	AC/OC	RE/CE
2007	The *Guyana v Suriname* case (Arbitration)	TS/SMB	AC	CE
2007	The *Nicaragua v Honduras* case (ICJ)	TS/SMB	AC	RE/CE
2009	The *Black Sea* case (ICJ)	SMB	AC/OC	Three-stage
2012	The *Bangladesh/Myanmar* case (ITLOS)	TS/SMB/ CS*	AC	Three-stage
2012	The *Nicaragua v Colombia* case (ICJ)	TS/SMB	OC	Three-stage
2014	The *Peru v Chile* case (ICJ)	TS/SMB	AC	Three-stage
2014	The *Bangladesh v India* case (Arbitration)	TS/SMB/ CS*	AC	Three-stage
2017	The *Croatia/Slovenia* case (Arbitration)	TS	AC	CE
2017	The *Ghana/Côte d'Ivoire* case (ITLOS)	TS/SMB/ CS*	AC	Three-stage
2018	The *Costa Rica v Nicaragua* case (ICJ)	TS/SMB	AC	Three-stage

CS: continental shelf CS*: continental shelf beyond 200 nautical miles SMB: single maritime boundary TS: territorial sea

AC: adjacent coast OC: opposite coast RE: result-oriented equity approach CE: corrective-equity approach

Three-stage: the three-stage approach

The corrective-equity approach follows the idea of the median-line system as a general rule, which was advocated, typically, by Gidel in the 1930s. At present, this approach is reformulated as the three-stage approach. According to this approach, a specific method, equidistance, is part of the law. In so doing, this approach stresses the predictability of the law of maritime delimitation.

Overall the development of the law of maritime delimitation presents a vacillation between two contrasting approaches: The result-oriented equity approach emphasising maximum flexibility and the corrective equity or three-stage approach favouring predictability. In this sense, it can be considered that the development of the law is essentially characterised by the tension between flexibility and predictability. The use of the two approaches in the case law is described in Figure 3. While some elements of uncertainty still exist, in broad perspective, it can be observed that the law of maritime delimitation has developed from the co-existence of the two approaches toward the unification of the three-stage approach. The unification of the law can be seen at three levels:

(i) Sources of the law: The unification between customary law and treaty law in the field of maritime delimitation;
(ii) The configuration of the coast: The unification of the law applicable to delimitation between States with adjacent coasts, and those with opposite coasts.
(iii) Maritime spaces: The unification of the law applicable to the delimitation of the territorial sea, the EEZ and the continental shelf.

First, as noted, the ICJ, in the *Qatar v Bahrain* case, declared Article 15 of the LOSC to be part of customary international law.[559] Furthermore, the Court, in the *Nicaragua v Colombia* case, considered that principles of maritime delimitation enshrined in Articles 74 and 83 reflect customary international law.[560] Accordingly, one can argue that provisions of the LOSC concerning maritime delimitations coincide with rules of customary international law.[561]

Secondly, the development of the jurisprudence demonstrates that the distinction between adjacent and opposite coasts is irrelevant to identify the methodology of maritime delimitation and that the corrective-equity approach or the three-stage approach can apply to maritime delimitations regardless of the configuration of the coasts.

Thirdly, there is a clear trend that international courts and tribunals apply the same methodology to the delimitation of the EEZ and the continental shelf.[562] On the other hand, the methodology to the delimitation of the territorial sea leaves some room for discussion. As explained earlier, the ICJ, in the

559 [2001] ICJ Rep 94, [176].
560 [2012] ICJ Rep 674, [139].
561 D Anderson, 'Developments in Maritime Boundary Law and Practice' in DA Colson and RW Smith (eds), *International Maritime Boundaries*, vol V (Leiden, Brill/Njhoff, 2005) 3211–12.
562 ibid, 3212.

Qatar v Bahrain case, adopted the corrective-equity approach under Article 15 of the LOSC.[563] In the *Bangladesh/Myanmar* case, however, ITLOS inverted the order of the equidistance and special circumstances.[564] Likewise, the Arbitral Tribunal, in the *Bangladesh v India* case, examined the possibility of an alternative solution by reason of historic title or other special circumstances before the construction of a provisional equidistance line. However, there is no convincing reason why the tribunals must deviate from the earlier jurisprudence. The inversed approach may even entail the risk of undermining predictability of the law of maritime delimitation, emphasising judicial discretion to the detriment of legal certainty.[565] In any event, the deviation from the orthodox application of the corrective-equity approach should not be overemphasised. In fact, the Arbitral Tribunal, in the *Bangladesh v India* case, applied the corrective-equity approach to the delimitation of the territorial sea at the operational stage. Furthermore, the Arbitral Tribunal, in the *Croatia/Slovenia* case, stressed that the 'equidistance/special circumstances' approach – which is actually the corrective-equity approach – applies to the delimitation of single maritime boundary 'without distinguishing between its application to the territorial sea and its application beyond the territorial sea.'[566] In the *Ghana/Côte d'Ivoire* case, the ITLOS Special Chamber also applied the same methodology for the delimitation of the Parties' territorial seas, EEZs and continental shelves within and beyond 200 nautical miles. Related to this, Judge Crawford stated that: 'Whether or not there is a formal presumption of equidistance in territorial sea delimitation may be debated, but *it is certainly the norm*.'[567] Furthermore, Guillaume, former President of the ICJ, observed that the ICJ has

> unified the law of maritime delimitation – whether the continental shelf, territorial sea or the exclusive economic zone – in holding that in all these cases it was necessary to first draw the line of equidistance, then adjust it to take account of relevant factors related mainly to the coastline. Finally, it generalized this solution in 2001 in *Bahrain/Qatar*, and resumed it in the 2009 case of *Romania/Ukraine*.[568]

[563] [2001] ICJ Rep 94, [176].

[564] [2012] ITLOS Rep 43, [129].

[565] M Lando, 'Judicial Uncertainties Concerning Territorial Sea Delimitation under Article 15 of the United Nations Convention on the Law of the Sea' (2017) 66 *ICLQ* 607. After the thorough examination of Article 15, Lando argued that: '[A]s a general rule, the territorial sea is to be delimited by means of an equidistance line, and that it is only if special circumstances made such a boundary inequitable that it should depart from equidistance.' ibid, 599.

[566] The *Croatia/Slovenia* arbitral award, [1000].

[567] Emphasis added. J Crawford, *Brownlie's Principles of Public International Law* (Oxford University Press, 2012) 285.

[568] G Guillaume, 'The use of Precedent by International Judges and Arbitrators' (2011) 2 *Journal of International Dispute Settlement* 11–12. Anderson, former Judge of ITLOS, also took a similar view. D Anderson, 'Developments in Maritime boundary Law and Practice' in DA Colson and RW Smith (eds), *International Maritime Boundaries*, vol V (Leiden, Brill/Nijhoff, 2005) 3212. See also D Vidas, 'The Delimitation of the Territorial Sea, the Continental Shelf, and the EEZ: A Comparative Perspective' in Oude Elferink, Henriksen and Busch, *Maritime Boundary Delimitation*, 55.

Overall there appears to be good reasons to argue that the methodology of maritime delimitation is unified under the three-stage approach. Under this approach, the equidistance method is to be applied at the first stage of maritime delimitation, unless there are any compelling reasons that make it impossible or inappropriate to draw a provisional equidistance line. A possible compelling reason may be the serious instability of the relevant coasts. As demonstrated by the *Costa Rica v Nicaragua* judgment, however, if the coastline is highly instable, it is possible to apply the three-stage approach to maritime delimitation by establishing a mobile line connecting a fixed point at sea and a starting-point on the coast. Furthermore, as pointed out earlier, the Annex VII Arbitral Tribunal focused on the 'physical reality at the time of the delimitation', not 'the issue of the future instability of the coastline'.[569] Hence the scope of the compelling reasons seems to be highly limited. All in all, it may be safe to argue that in principle, the three-stage approach can apply to all types of maritime delimitation.

ii. Discussion

The unification of the law of maritime delimitation under the corrective-equity approach or the three-stage approach would be significant with a view to enhancing the normative level of the law of maritime delimitation. Indeed, the result-oriented equity approach presents serious problems in three respects.

The first, and the most important difficulty, is its excessive subjectivity. Without any objective criteria for judging equitableness, the result-oriented equity approach runs the risk of producing legal impressionism. As several judges have warned, this blurs the distinction between decisions based on equitable principles and those taken *ex aequo et bono*. In this connection, in the *Jan Mayen* case, Judge Oda took the following view:

> Accordingly, and on the premise that there are in fact no rules of law for effecting a maritime delimitation in the presence of overlapping *titles* (not overlapping *claims*), it follows that if the Court is requested by the parties to decide on a maritime delimitation in accordance with Article 36, paragraph 1, of the Statute, it will not be expected to apply rules of international law but will simply 'decide a case *ex aequo et bono*.'[570]

Furthermore, he continued that:

> Only in a case in which the parties in dispute have asked the Court by agreement to effect a maritime delimitation *ex aequo et bono* is it qualified to examine what factors or elements should be taken into account as relevant, and to what degree such

[569] The *Bangladesh v India* arbitral award, [215].

[570] Separate Opinion of Judge Oda in the *Jan Mayen* case, [1993] ICJ Rep 113, [85]. In addition, referring to the *Libya/Malta* case, he considers it as a decision *ex aequo et bono*, even though the Court never expressly stated as much. ibid, 113, [86].

> factors or elements should be evaluated when it is determining the line to be drawn or indicating a concrete line based on its own evaluation of the relevant factors and elements.[571]

This view is, in essence, equal to refusing the existence of a law of maritime delimitation. Although Judge Oda's opinion is an extreme one, it is undeniable that the law of maritime delimitation does include a subjective aspect.

The second problem is unpredictability. With the result-oriented approach, it is the specific factors characterising any given individual situation which define the equitable result. Consequently, the appreciation of equity is defined by each of the factors of any given case and this makes it difficult to form predictable rules of maritime delimitation. This is contrary to an essential requirement of law: certainty and predictability.[572] As an essential condition, the law of maritime delimitation should have a degree of predictability beyond the reliance on the particular circumstances of each case. Over-individualisation prevents this by undermining the certainty and predictability of law. It is noteworthy that, in the *Libya/Malta* case, the ICJ itself stressed the importance of consistency and a degree of predictability going beyond the circumstances of each case.[573]

Thirdly, since the result-oriented equity approach is nothing but a truisms, it is meaningless in practice. As Judge Oda stated in the *Tunisia/Libya* case, it simply suggests 'the principle of non-principle'.[574] The problem is that of determining which rules of international law should be applied in order to achieve an equitable result.[575] In fact, the point disputed between the Parties is the concrete method to be applied for maritime delimitations. According to the result-oriented equity approach, however, such criteria and methods are considered as outside the realm of law. In sum, because of its excessive subjectivity and unpredictability, the result-oriented equity approach carries the danger of undermining the law of maritime delimitation.[576] Although it is difficult to rule

571 ibid, 114, [88]. See also S Oda, 'The International Court of Justice Viewed from the Bench (1976–1993)' (1993) 244 *RCADI* 151; M Miyoshi, 'Considerations of Equity in Maritime Boundary Cases Before the International Court of Justice' in N Ando, et al, (eds), *Liber Amicorum Judge Shigeru Oda* (The Hague, Kluwer, 2002) 1101.

572 On this point, the argument of Malta in the *Libya/Malta* case is worth noting. In its Counter-Memorial, Malta mentioned that 'an excessive individualisation of the rule of law, which changes from one case to another, would be incompatible with the very concept of law. Every legal rule presupposes a minimum of generality. A rule which is elaborated on a case by case basis rests on the discretionary power of the judge, on conciliation, on distributive justice in brief, on *ex aequo et bono*.' The *Libya/Malta* case, Counter-Memorial of Malta, 293, [111].

573 The *Libya/Malta* case, [1985] ICJ Rep 39, [45].

574 Dissenting Opinion of Judge Oda in the *Tunisia/Libya* case, [1982] ICJ Rep 157, [1].

575 ibid, 255, [155].

576 P Weil, *Perspective du droit de la délimitation maritime* (Paris, Pedone, 1988) 174–75. See also by the same author, 'Le droit international en quête de son identité, Cours général de droit international public' (1992) 237 *RCADI* 245; and 'L'équité dans la jurisprudence de la Cour internationale de Justice: Un mystère en voie de dissipation?' in V Lowe and M Fitzmaurice (eds), *Fifty Years of the International Court of Justice, Essays in Honour of Sir Robert Jennings* (Cambridge University Press, 1996) 121.

out completely the subjectivity and unpredictability derived from equitable principles, an effort must be made to improve the situation.[577]

By contrast, the important advantage of the corrective-equity approach and its variation of the three-stage approach is that it has a certain degree of predictability by incorporating a predictable method of delimitation, ie, the equidistance method, into the legal domain. Indeed, equidistance is the only predictable method of drawing an initial line to be tested for equity.[578] In this connection, ITLOS in the *Bangladesh/Myanmar* case acknowledged 'the objective precision of equidistance'.[579] In the *Black Sea* case, the ICJ also regarded the equidistance method as 'geometrically objective'.[580] In the *Nicaragua v Honduras* case, the Court accepted that the equidistance method 'has a certain intrinsic value because of its scientific character'.[581] According to the corrective-equity or three-stage approach, a consideration of equity may come into play at a second stage, but only in cases in which equidistance lines provisionally drawn produce inequitable results. In this sense, the equidistance method reflects a standard of equitableness.[582] Accordingly, the corrective-equity approach makes it possible to reduce the subjectivity and unpredictability of equitable principles. In addition, by separating the first and second stages in the application of the equidistance/relevant circumstances method, a high degree of transparency can be achieved under this approach.[583] In conclusion, one can argue that the corrective-equity or three-stage approach would provide a better framework for balancing predictability and flexibility. However, the three-stage approach contains at least three issues that need further consideration.

The first issue relates to the legal basis on which the equidistance line should be established in the first place. This issue was not explained persuasively by international courts and tribunals.[584]

The second issue concerns the circumstances to be taken into account at the second stage. Since corrective equity aims at mitigating the effects of the strict application of the equidistance method, recourse to relevant circumstances to modify provisional lines is of critical importance. In fact, the final line is determined by the consideration of relevant circumstances. Accordingly, it is important to examine legal effect of the relevant circumstances on the modification of the line.[585]

[577] Sir Robert Jennings stated that: 'A structured and predictable system of equitable procedures is an essential framework.' Sir Robert Jennings, 'Equity and Equitable Principles' (1986) 42 *ASDI* 38.

[578] See also CG Lathrop, 'The Provisional Equidistance Line: Charting a Course between Objectivity and Subjectivity?' in Oude Elferink, Henriksen and Busch, *Maritime Boundary Delimitation*, 208–9.

[579] [2012] ITLOS Rep 65, [228].

[580] [2009] ICJ Rep 101, [116].

[581] [2007] ICJ Rep 741, [272].

[582] Marques Antunes and Becker-Weinberg, 'Entitlement to Maritime Zones and Their Delimitation' 74.

[583] The *Bangladesh v India* arbitral award, [344].

[584] This issue will be discussed in ch 6 of this book.

[585] See chs 7 and 8 of this book.

The third issue concerns the validity of the disproportionality test. Under the three-stage approach, the disproportionality test performs an important role to check the equitableness of maritime boundaries constructed by an international court or tribunal. Thus there is a need to review the manner of the application of the disproportionality test. In so doing, it becomes possible to consider the question regarding whether and to what extent the disproportionality contributes to enhancing the predictability and transparency of the law of maritime delimitation.[586] Before examining these issues in Part Two of this book, some consideration must be given to an emerging issue of the law of maritime delimitation: a delimitation of the continental shelf beyond 200 nautical miles.

B. Delimitation of the Continental Shelf Beyond 200 Nautical Miles

i. Jurisdiction of an International Court or Tribunal to Delimit a Continental Shelf Beyond 200 Nautical Miles

a. Nature of the Problem

The delimitation of the continental shelf beyond 200 nautical miles is a comparatively novel issue in the law of maritime delimitation. Where the outer edge of the continental margin extends beyond 200 nautical miles, the limit of the continental shelf is to be determined on the basis of the criteria set out by Article 76(4) of the LOSC. The coastal State intending to claim a continental shelf beyond 200 nautical miles must submit information on the limits of the shelf to the Commission on the Limits of the Continental Shelf (CLCS).[587] The Commission performs a dual function under Article 3(1) of Annex II. First, it examines the data and other material submitted by coastal States and makes recommendations to the coastal States in this matter in accordance with Article 76 and the Statement of Understanding adopted on 29 August 1980 by UNCLOS III. Secondly, the Commission provides scientific and technical advice, if requested by the coastal State concerned. In so doing, the Commission ensures that the continental shelf of a coastal State does not extend beyond the limits provided for in Article 76(4), (5) and (6) of the LOSC and thus prevents the continental shelf from encroaching on the 'Area and its resources', which are 'the common heritage of mankind'.[588]

[586] This issue will be discussed in ch 7, s III and ch 9, s IV, of this book.

[587] For the procedure to set out the limits of the continental shelf beyond 200 nautical miles, see Y Tanaka, The International Law of the Sea, 3rd edn (Cambridge University Press, 2019) 167–71. The examination of the law and procedure of the CLCS falls outside scope of this book. On this issue, see, for instance, Ø Jensen, *The Commission on the Limits of the Continental Shelf: Law and Legitimacy* (Leiden, Brill/Nijhoff, 2014).

[588] *Question of the Delimitation of the Continental Shelf between Nicaragua and Colombia beyond 200 Nautical Miles from the Nicaraguan Coast (Nicaragua v Colombia)*, Preliminary Objections, Judgment, [2016] ICJ Rep 136, [109].

In cases where a land or maritime dispute exists, the Commission shall not consider and qualify a submission made by any of the States concerned in the dispute, unless there is prior consent given by all States that are parties to such a dispute.[589] Where one of the parties or a third State raises an objection to the Commission considering and making recommendations on the submission of a State concerning the continental shelf beyond 200 nautical miles, an international court or tribunal will encounter difficulties. On the one hand, without considerations and recommendations by the CLCS with regard to the validity of submissions concerning the continental shelf beyond 200 nautical miles, it may be difficult for an international court or tribunal to judge whether the continental shelf of a party actually extends beyond 200 nautical miles. On the other hand, if the international court or tribunal declines to delimit the continental shelf beyond 200 nautical miles, the dispute on this subject remains unsettled.[590] Here a dilemma arises. In considering this question, three issues that are closely interlinked must be examined: the relationship between the function of the CLCS and that of an international court or tribunal, the existence of overlapping entitlements to the continental shelf beyond 200 nautical miles, and relationship between the natural prolongation and the distance criterion.

b. Delineation and Delimitation

First, the relationship between the function of the CLCS and that of an international court or tribunal must be considered. In the *Bangladesh/Myanmar* case, ITLOS stressed the difference between the delineation under Article 76 and delimitation under Article 83 of the LOSC:

> There is a clear distinction between the delimitation of the continental shelf under article 83 and the delineation of its outer limits under article 76. Under the latter article, the Commission is assigned the function of making recommendations to coastal States on matters relating to the establishment of the outer limits of the continental shelf, but it does so without prejudice to delimitation of maritime boundaries. The function of settling disputes with respect to delimitation of maritime boundaries is entrusted to dispute settlement procedures under article 83 and Part XV of the Convention, which include international courts and tribunals.[591]

For the Tribunal, 'the exercise of its jurisdiction in the present case cannot be seen as an encroachment on the functions of the Commission.'[592] ITLOS accordingly

[589] Para 5(a) of Annex I of the Rules of Procedure of the Commission on the Limits of the Continental Shelf, available at: www.un.org/depts/los/clcs_new/commission_rules.htm. See also SV Busch, *Establishing Continental Shelf Limits Beyond 200 Nautical Miles by the Coastal State: A Right of Involvement for Other States?* (Leiden, Brill/Nijhoff, 2016) 134 et seq.

[590] The *Bangladesh v India* arbitral award, [390]; the *Bangladesh/Myanmar* case, [2012] ITLOS Rep 102, [391].

[591] [2012] ITLOS Rep 99, [376].

[592] ibid, 102, [393].

concluded that in order to fulfil its responsibilities under Part XV, Section 2, of the Convention, it has an obligation to delimit the continental shelf between the Parties beyond 200 nautical miles.[593]

The *dictum* of ITLOS was echoed by the Annex VII Arbitral Tribunal in the *Bangladesh v India* case. For the Arbitral Tribunal,

> [I]n the present case, the outer limits of the continental shelf have not yet been established in accordance with article 76 and Annex II to the Convention, concerning the Commission on the Limits of the Continental Shelf (the "CLCS"). However, recalling the reasoning of the International Tribunal for the Law of the Sea in *Bangladesh/Myanmar* ..., the Tribunal sees no grounds why it should refrain from exercising its jurisdiction to decide on the lateral delimitation of the continental shelf beyond 200 nm before its outer limits have been established.[594]

In the *Ghana/Côte d'Ivoire* case, the ITLOS Special Chamber took the same view. In this case, the CLCS already made its recommendations on Ghana's submission under Article 76(8) of the LOSC. The Chamber thus considered that there was no risk that its judgment might interfere with the functions of the CLCS.[595]

The difference between the delineation of the outer limits of the continental shelf and maritime delimitation was also stressed by the ICJ in the *Question of the Delimitation of the Continental Shelf between Nicaragua and Colombia beyond 200 nautical miles from the Nicaraguan Coast* (hereafter *Nicaragua v Colombia II*). For the Court,

> Because the role of the CLCS relates only to the delineation of the outer limits of the continental shelf, and not delimitation, Article 76 of UNCLOS [LOSC] states in paragraph 10 that "[t]he provisions of this article are without prejudice to the question of delimitation of the continental shelf between States with opposite or adjacent coasts".[596]

The Court thus considered that:

> [S]ince the delimitation of the continental shelf beyond 200 nautical miles can be undertaken independently of a recommendation from the CLCS, the latter is not a prerequisite that needs to be satisfied by a State party to UNCLOS [LOSC] before it can ask the Court to settle a dispute with another State over such a delimitation.[597]

In *Maritime Delimitation in the Indian Ocean* (Preliminary Objections), however, the ICJ appeared to take a more nuanced view, stating that:

> A lack of certainty regarding the outer limits of the continental shelf, and thus the precise location of the endpoint of a given boundary in the area beyond 200 nautical miles, does not, however, necessarily prevent either the States concerned or the Court

[593] ibid, 103, [394].
[594] The *Bangladesh v India* arbitral award, [76].
[595] The *Ghana/Côte d'Ivoire* case, [2017] ITLOS Rep [495].
[596] *Question of the Delimitation of the Continental Shelf between Nicaragua and Colombia beyond 200 Nautical Miles from the Nicaraguan Coast (Nicaragua v Colombia), (Nicaragua v Colombia II)*, Preliminary Objections, Judgment, [2016] ICJ Rep 136, [110].
[597] ibid, 137, [114].

> from undertaking the delimitation of the boundary *in appropriate circumstances* before the CLCS has made its recommendations.[598]

The term 'in appropriate circumstances' can be interpreted to imply that the Court may decide whether it would undertake the delimitation of the continental shelf beyond 200 nautical miles on a case-by-case basis.[599]

As provided in Article 76(10) of the LOSC, '[t]he provisions of this article are without prejudice to the question of delimitation of the continental shelf between States with opposite or adjacent coasts.'[600] Accordingly, as a matter of theory, it is possible to distinguish delimitation from delineation. In practice, States have concluded agreements regarding the delimitation of the continental shelf beyond 200 nautical miles without receiving recommendations from the CLCS or even before making a submission to the Commission.[601]

However, a contentious issue that arises in this context is whether a court or tribunal can proceed with the delimitation of the continental shelf in the situation where the entitlement to the continental shelf beyond 200 nautical miles is not well established. In this regard, ITLOS, in the *Bangladesh/Myanmar* case made an important statement:

> Notwithstanding the overlapping areas indicated in the submissions of the Parties to the Commission, the Tribunal would have been hesitant to proceed with the delimitation of the area beyond 200 nm had it concluded that there was *significant uncertainty* as to the existence of a continental margin in the area in question.[602]

As Judge Ndiaye stated, 'unless there are overlapping, equal entitlements to a given area, there is hardly any call for maritime delimitation.'[603] The existence of overlapping entitlements should be a necessary precondition to maritime delimitation.[604] Accordingly, as ITLOS held in the *Bangladesh/Myanmar* case, 'the question the Tribunal should first address in the present case is whether the

[598] Emphasis added. *Maritime Delimitation in the Indian Ocean (Somalia v Kenya)*, Preliminary Objection, Judgment, 2 February 2017, [2017] ICJ Rep [94].

[599] G Vega-Barbosa, 'The Admissibility of Outer Continental Shelf Delimitation Claims Before the ICJ Absent a Recommendation by the CLCS' (2018) 49 *ODIL* 111.

[600] See also LOSC, Annex II, Art 9.

[601] BM Magnússon, *The Continental Shelf Beyond 200 Nautical Miles: Delineation, Delimitation and Dispute Settlement* (Leiden, Brill/Nijhoff, 2015) 210. See also Bjarni M. Magnússon, 'Outer Continental Shelf Boundary Agreement' (2013) 62 *ICLQ* 345.

[602] Emphasis added. [2012] ITLOS Rep 115, [443]. The *dictum* of ITLOS can be called the 'lack of significant uncertainty' test. According to Treves, '[t]he Tribunal was able to overcome its hesitation because of the consideration that "the Bay of Bengal presents a unique situation as acknowledged in the course of negotiations at the Third United Nations Conference on the Law of the Sea"' (footnote omitted). Presentation by Treves in *Nicaragua v. Colombia II*, Verbatim Record, CR 2015/28,33, [16].

[603] Separate Opinion of Judge Ndiaye in the *Bangladesh/Myanmar* case, [2012] ITLOS Rep 179, [98].

[604] See definition of maritime delimitation in ch 1, s II of this book. See also M Lando, 'Delimiting the Continental Shelf Beyond 200 Nautical Miles at the International Court of Justice: The *Nicaragua v Colombia* Cases' (2017) 16 *CJIL* 140; Oude Alferink, 'ITLOS's Approach,' 247.

Parties have overlapping entitlements to the continental shelf beyond 200 nm. If not, it would be dealing with a hypothetical question.'[605] The question is whether an international court or tribunal can always decide the existence of overlapping entitlements to the continental shelf beyond 200 nautical miles, without recommendations of the CLCS.

c. Overlapping Entitlements

The *Bangladesh/Myanmar* case raised the question of whether the parties had the entitlement to a continental shelf beyond 200 nautical miles. In this case, Bangladesh presented geological and geomorphological evidence to demonstrate that the continental shelf beyond 200 nautical miles in the Bay of Bengal is the natural prolongation of Bangladesh, but is not the natural prolongation of Myanmar.[606] However, Myanmar contended that Myanmar's continental margin satisfies the appurtenance test of Article 76 (4) of the LOSC, ie, the edge of Myanmar's continental margin established in accordance with the Convention is situated beyond 200 nautical miles measured from its baseline.[607]

In examining the issue, the Tribunal stressed the unique feature of the Bay of Bengal. According to the Tribunal, the thick layer of sedimentary rocks covers practically the entire floor of the Bay of Bengal.[608] 'In view of uncontested scientific evidence regarding the unique nature of the Bay of Bengal and information submitted during the proceedings', the Tribunal considered that: '[T]here is a continuous and substantial layer of sedimentary rocks extending from Myanmar's coast to the area beyond 200 nm.'[609] According to the Tribunal, '[t]he scientific data and analyses presented in this case, which have not been contested, do not establish that Myanmar's continental shelf is limited to 200 nm under article 76 of the Convention, and instead indicate the opposite.'[610] The Tribunal thus concluded that: 'The submissions of Bangladesh and Myanmar to the Commission clearly indicate that their entitlements overlap in the area in dispute in this case.'[611] In this regard, two comments can be made.

First, it must be noted that the *Bangladesh/Myanmar* case was decided on the exceptional condition, that is, the unique feature of the Bay of Bengal.[612]

605 The *Bangladesh/Myanmar* case, Judgment, [2012] ITLOS Rep 105, [399].

606 Bangladesh's Memorial, vol I, 18–28.

607 Myanmar's Counter-Memorial, vol I, 190, para A.28 et seq.

608 [2012] ITLOS Rep 115, [444–45].

609 ibid, [446].

610 ibid, 116, [448].

611 ibid,116, [449].

612 The ICJ in the *Nicaragua v Colombia* case accepted the exceptional nature of the *Bangladesh/Myanmar* case, stating that: '[I]n view of the fact that a thick layer of sedimentary rocks covers practically the entire floor of the Bay of Bengal, the Bay presents a unique situation and that this fact had been acknowledged in the course of negotiations at the Third United Nations Conference on the Law of the Sea.' [2012] ICJ Rep 668, [125]. See also Lando, 'Delimiting the Continental Shelf Beyond 200 Nautical Miles,' 160 et seq.

Yet, the circumstance as shown by the unique nature of the Bay of Bengal will not exist in other regions.[613] Accordingly, whether the *dictum* of the *Bangladesh/Myanmar* judgment can be generalised needs careful consideration.

Secondly, if the scientific evidence was uncontested by the Parties, this does not automatically relieve ITLOS of the need to verify the validity of the evidence.[614] The agreement of the Parties cannot be a valid substitute for evidence to prove the entitlement to the continental shelf beyond 200 nautical miles.[615] Nonetheless, the Tribunal did not review the scientific evidence on its own. The *Bangladesh/Myanmar* case is not an isolated example on this matter. In the *Bangladesh v India* case, the Annex VII Arbitral Tribunal noted the Parties' agreement that both States had entitlements beyond 200 nautical miles, and both had made submissions to the CLCS.[616] Hence, it did not verify the scientific evidence with regard to the entitlements to the continental shelf beyond 200 nautical miles.[617] Likewise, the ITLOS Special Chamber, in the *Ghana/Côte d'Ivoire* case, did not investigate scientific evidence on its own since it considered that there is no doubt that a continental shelf beyond 200 nautical miles exists in respect of the two Parties since the Parties in dispute had made their submission to the CLCS.[618]

In reality, there is no guarantee that there is always an agreement between the Parties in dispute with regard to the existence of overlapping entitlements to the continental shelf beyond 200 nautical miles. Where there is a dispute regarding the existence of overlapping entitlements, an international court or tribunal encounters a considerable challenge. The *Nicaragua v Colombia* case is an example. In this case, Colombia argued that: '[T]here are no areas of extended continental shelf within this part of the Caribbean Sea given that there are no maritime areas that lie more than 200 nautical miles from the nearest land territory of the coastal States.'[619] At the time of the 2012 Judgment, Nicaragua submitted to the Commission only 'Preliminary Information'. According to the Court, however, it 'falls short of meeting the requirements for information on the limits of the continental shelf beyond 200 nautical miles' under Article 76(8) of the LOSC.[620] Accordingly, the Court, in its judgment of 2012, concluded that:

> [S]ince Nicaragua, in the present proceedings, has not established that it has a continental margin that extends far enough to overlap with Colombia's 200-nautical-mile

613 Xuexia Liao, 'Evaluation of Scientific Evidence by International Courts and Tribunals in the Continental Shelf Delimitation Cases' (2017) 48 *ODIL* 148. See also Churchill, 'The *Bangladesh/Myanmar* Case,' 149–50.

614 Liao, 'Evaluation of Scientific Evidence,'145–46.

615 Lando, 'Delimiting the Continental Shelf Beyond 200 Nautical Miles,' 162–63.

616 The *Bangladesh v India* arbitral award, [457]. See also [78].

617 Liao, 'Evaluation of Scientific Evidence by International Courts and Tribunals,'147.

618 The *Ghana/Côte d'Ivoire* case, [2017] ITLOS Rep [491] and [496].

619 The *Nicaragua v Colombia* case, [2012] ICJ Rep 667, [122].

620 ibid, 669, [127]. This point was amplified by Judge Donoghue. According to the learned Judge, '[i]f the information falls short of what is needed to permit factual conclusions by expert scientists, surely it cannot be a sufficient basis for the Members of this Court to reach factual conclusions about

> entitlement to the continental shelf, measured from Colombia's mainland coast, the Court is not in a position to delimit the continental shelf boundary between Nicaragua and Colombia, as requested by Nicaragua, even using the general formulation proposed by it.[621]

In 2013, however, Nicaragua newly instituted proceedings against Colombia with regard to the delimitation of the continental shelf beyond 200 nautical miles from the Nicaraguan coast.[622] The Court, in its judgment of 2016 (Preliminary Objections), made clear that: 'Nicaragua had to submit such information as a prerequisite for the delimitation of the continental shelf beyond 200 nautical miles by the Court.'[623] Nicaragua provided the CLCS with 'final' information required in Article 76(8) of the LOSC.[624] In the view of the Court, a recommendation from the CLCS 'is not a prerequisite that needs to be satisfied by a State party to UNCLOS [LOSC] before it can ask the Court to settle a dispute with another State over such a delimitation.'[625] The Court thus admitted Nicaragua's request concerning the precise course of the maritime boundary between Nicaragua and Colombia in the areas of the continental shelf which appertain to each of them beyond the boundaries determined by the Court in its judgment of 19 November 2012.[626]

The Court seemed to consider that, once a coastal State submitted the information to the CLCS, this will automatically prove the entitlement to the continental shelf beyond 200 nautical miles.[627] This is not the case, however. In fact, the CLCS can reject, whether partially or entirely, the validity of a coastal State's submission. Hence, filing the full information with the CLCS does not automatically prove a coastal State's entitlement to a continental shelf beyond 200 nautical miles.[628] As Evans stated, 'just because a State claims that it has an entitlement does not mean that it does.'[629] The submission of information to

the location of the outer limits of the continental shelf beyond 200 nautical miles of Nicaragua's coast.' Separate Opinion of Judge Donoghue, ibid, 754, [12].

[621] Judgment, ibid, 669, [129].

[622] Application instituting proceedings, 16 September 2013.

[623] *Nicaragua v Colombia II*, Preliminary Objections, Judgment, [2016] ICJ Rep 136, [105].

[624] ibid, 132, [86].

[625] ibid, 137, [114].

[626] ibid,139–40, [126]. In this case, *res judicata* of the judgment of 2012 constituted an essential issue. On this issue, see M Sarzo, '*Res Judicata*, Jurisdiction *Ratione Materiae* and Legal reasoning in the Dispute between Nicaragua and Colombia before the International Court of Justice' (2017) 16 *The Law and Practice of International Courts and Tribunals* 224; N Ridi, 'Precarious Finality – Reflections on Res Judicata and the Question of the Delimitation of the Continental Shelf Case' (2018 31 *LJIL* 383.

[627] Lando, 'Delimiting the Continental Shelf Beyond 200 Nautical Miles' 153.

[628] ibid, 154. See also B Kunoy, 'The Delimitation of an Indicative Area of Overlapping Entitlement to the Outer Continental Shelf' (2013) 83 *BYIL* 81.

[629] MD Evans, 'Maritime Boundary Delimitation' in D Rothwell, Alex G Oude Elferink, K Scott and T Stephens (eds), *Oxford Handbook on the Law of the Sea* (Oxford University Press, 2015) 261.

the CLCS is required because the data must be validated by the Commission. Therefore, it is hard to understand why the recommendation of the CLCS is not a prerequisite, while the submission of information to the Commission is a prerequisite.[630]

In this connection, Judge Donoghue took the view that: '[T]he proposed delimitation methodology would require the Court to reach conclusions about the same question of fact that the technical experts comprising the Commission would also address after receiving a complete submission from Nicaragua.'[631] However, the members of the Court are not technical experts. It seems debatable whether the Court is well-equipped to assess scientific evidence with a degree of credible certainty.[632] Furthermore, as Judge Donoghue pointedly observed, the delimitation of the continental shelf beyond 200 nautical miles without the recommendation of the Commission may create 'a variety of institutional and legal difficulties' in the future. In this regard, Judge Donoghue gave her misgivings that: '[T]he Court's conclusions regarding the location of the outer limits, in a judgment that is binding on the parties, might differ from recommendations that later emerge from the Commission.'[633] Hence, great caution will be needed in deciding whether an international court or tribunal should proceed with the delimitation of the continental shelf beyond 200 nautical miles when there is 'significant uncertainty as to the existence of a continental margin in the area in question'.[634]

ITLOS, in the *Bangladesh/Myanmar* case, did not furnish any further precision with regard to the standard for deciding the existence or non-existence of 'significant uncertainty'. It is clear that the submission of information to the CLCS is a necessary condition for effecting the delimitation of the continental shelf beyond 200 nautical miles. However, it is debatable whether the submission itself is a sufficient condition.[635] Given that the two *Bay of Bengal* cases and the *Ghana/Côte d'Ivoire* case were rather unique and exceptional cases where the

[630] Joint Dissenting Opinion of Vice-President Yusuf, Judges Cançado Trindade, Xue, Gaja, Bhandari, Robinson and Judge ad hoc Brower, [2016] ICJ Rep 159, [58].

[631] Separate Opinion of Judge Donoghue in the *Nicaragua v Colombia* case, [2012] ICJ Rep 758, [25].

[632] Lando, 'Delimiting the Continental Shelf Beyond 200 Nautical Miles,' 156. In this regard, ITLOS, in the *Bangladesh/Myanmar* case, noted that: '[A]s this article contains elements of law and science, its proper interpretation and application requires both legal and scientific expertise.' [2012] ITLOS Rep 107, [411].

[633] Separate Opinion of Judge Donoghue in the *Nicaragua v Colombia* case, [2012] ICJ Rep 757, [23].

[634] Busch, 'The Delimitation of the Continental Shelf beyond 200 nm' 349–50. See also Churchill, 'The *Bangladesh/Myanmar* Case' 149–50; Liao, 'Evaluation of Scientific Evidence' 148. Lando argued that: '[I]n most cases it would seem more appropriate for international tribunal to establish boundaries beyond 200 nm only after the CLCS's recommendation ascertaining that entitlement to a continental shelf beyond 200 nm actually exist.' Lando, 'Delimiting the Continental Shelf Beyond 200 Nautical Miles' 173. Furthermore, Judge Ndiaye stated that: 'Good sense required terminating the delimitation line at the 200-nautical-mile limit, not beyond.' Separate Opinion of Judge Ndiaye in the *Bangladesh/Myanmar* case, [2012] ITLOS Rep 179, [98].

[635] Ø Jensen, 'Maritime Boundary Delimitation Beyond 200 Nautical Miles: The International Judiciary and the Commission on the Limits of the Continental Shelf' (2015) 84 *NJIL* 587–88.

existence of the continental shelf beyond 200 nautical miles in respect to the Parties could be adequately proved, it may not be unreasonable to consider that the standard for the 'lack of significant uncertainty' test may be high.[636]

d. Relationship Between the Natural Prolongation and the Distance Criterion

A further issue concerns the relationship between the natural prolongation and distance as legal title to the continental shelf beyond 200 nautical miles.[637] As typically shown in the *Nicaragua v Colombia* case,[638] this issue arises in the situation where the distance between the two opposite coasts is beyond 400 nautical miles and the claimed continental shelf beyond 200 nautical miles of one coastal state intruded into the 200 nautical mile limit of another coastal State.[639] As a matter of theory, three possible interpretations exist.

According to the first interpretation, natural prolongation prevails over the distance criterion. As the ICJ stated in the *Libya/Malta* case, however, 'there cannot be an exclusive economic zone without corresponding continental shelf.'[640] As shown in the *dictum*, the concept of the EEZ comprises the seabed and its subsoil. Furthermore, there is no doubt that the coastal State is entitled to a 200 nautical mile continental shelf under customary international law. Accordingly, there is no convincing reason why natural prolongation prevails over the distance criterion within an EEZ of a coastal State.

By contrast, according to the second interpretation, distance criterion prevails over natural prolongation. This interpretation was advocated by Judge Chandrasekhara Rao in the *Bangladesh v India* case. Judge Chandrasekhara Rao, in his Concurring and Dissenting Opinion, contrasted the entitlement to the EEZ with the entitlement to the continental shelf beyond 200 nautical miles:

> It is clear from the Convention that the entitlement to the EEZ is based solely on distance from the coast and does not depend on other factors. By contrast, the entitlement to the continental shelf beyond 200 nm is based on natural prolongation which is in turn explained and conditioned with reference to the foot of the continental slope. Having calculated the outer limits of its continental shelf, the coastal

[636] Lando, 'Delimiting the Continental Shelf Beyond 200 Nautical Miles' 162.

[637] Generally on this issue, see Xuexia Liao, 'Is There a Hierarchical Relationship between Natural Prolongation and Distance in the Continental Shelf?' (2017) 32 *IJMCL* 1.

[638] Nicaragua claimed that its continental shelf beyond 200 nautical miles overlaps with Colombia's 200-nautical mile shelf. The *Nicaragua v Colombia* case [2012] ICJ Rep 667, [121].

[639] Where distance between the opposite coasts is less than 400 nautical miles, this issue will not arise since only the distance criterion applies. In fact, the ICJ, in the *Libya/Malta* case, held that: '[A]t least in so far as those areas are situated at a distance of under 200 miles from the coasts in question, title depends solely on the distance from the coasts of the claimant States of any areas of sea-bed claimed by way of continental shelf, and the geological or geomorphological characteristics of those areas are completely immaterial.' [1985] ICJ Rep 35, [39]. Given that the coastal State has the continental shelf in a legal sense up to 200 nautical miles regardless of the configuration of the seabed by virtue of Art 76(1) of the LOSC as well as customary international law, there will be no room for a coastal State to claim its continental shelf beyond 200 nautical miles in this case.

[640] The *Libya/Malta* case, [1985] ICJ Rep 33, [34].

> State shall submit details of the calculation to the Commission of the Limits of the Continental Shelf, the role of which is to examine the submission and to make recommendations to the coastal State. The coastal State will then establish the outer limits of the continental shelf on the basis of such recommendations, which limits shall be final and binding.[641]

The learned judge thus considered that:

> This complicated method to calculate the outer limits of the continental shelf suggests that the entitlement to the continental shelf beyond 200 nm depends on different factors and is not as absolute as the entitlement to the EEZ. It follows that the entitlement to the EEZ takes priority over the entitlement to the continental shelf beyond 200 nm.[642]

In this connection, it must be noted that while the distance criterion became customary law, the same is not true of the detailed provisions of Article 76(2)–(8).[643] Furthermore, it is of particular interest to note that in State practice, there is a clear tendency to deliberately refrain from encroaching on neighbouring States' 200 nautical mile limit when submitting information on the continental shelf beyond 200 nautical miles to the CLCS.[644] The same approach is also taken by parties in relation to non-parties to the LOSC.[645] If State practice may be short of subsequent practice under Article 31(3)(b) of the Vienna Convention on the Law of Treaties, nevertheless it should contribute to the interpretation pursuant to Article 32 of the Vienna Convention.[646] In light of its uniformity and consistency, it may not be unreasonable to consider that State practice might give rise to an emerging rule of customary international law.[647] According to the second interpretation, the continental shelf beyond 200 nautical miles of a coastal State should give way to the 200 nautical mile EEZ/continental shelf in cases where they meet. While distance provides a clear criterion, it would be less easy for an international court or tribunal to verify whether the continental shelf of one of the disputing parties truly extends

[641] Concurring and Dissenting Opinion in the *Bangladesh v India* arbitral award, [39]. Footnotes omitted.

[642] ibid, [40].

[643] In the 2012 *Nicaragua v Colombia* case, the ICJ considered that the definition of the continental shelf set out in Art 76(1) of the LOSC forms part of customary international law. [2012] ICJ Rep 666, [118]. However, the ICJ did not state that the detailed provisions of Art 76(2)–(8) were also rules of customary international law. MD Evans, 'Maritime Boundary Delimitation: Whatever Next' in J Barrett and R Barnes (eds), *Law of the Sea: UNCLOS as a Living Treaty* (London, British Institute of International and Comparative Law, 2016), 75, footnote 133. In addition, at the 193rd meeting of UNCLOS III, Mr Koh, President of the Conference, stated that: '[A] State which is not a party to this Convention [LOSC] cannot invoke the benefits of Art 76.' TTB Koh, 'Closing Statement by President on 10 December 1982' in R Platzöder, (ed), *Third United Nations Conference on the Law of the Sea: Documents* (New York, NY, Oceana, 1988) 426. See also, L Caflisch, 'La convention des Nations Unies sur le droit de la mer adoptée le 30 avril 1982' (1983) 39 *ASDI* 89.

[644] Liao, 'Is There a Hierarchical Relationship,' 17 et seq.

[645] ibid, 25.

[646] ibid, 23–4.

[647] ibid, 37.

beyond 200 nautical miles. Hence, as an alternative, this interpretation has some merits.

According to the third interpretation, there is no hierarchical relationship between natural prolongation and distance as a legal title over the continental shelf. Following this view, entitlements to the continental shelf overlap and there is a need to effectuate maritime delimitation.[648] Given that the LOSC contains no clear rule with regard to the relationship between natural prolongation and distance as a legal title, this interpretation may be arguable. However, the interpretation raises another difficult issue with regard to method of delimitation.[649] Furthermore, if delimitation of the continental shelf could be effectuated, part of the EEZ belonging to one State overlaps part of another State's continental shelf. Such a situation would give rise to complex problems associated with jurisdiction. In any event, in light of paucity of the jurisprudence in this matter, the relationship between natural prolongation and distance in the delimitation of the continental shelf beyond 200 nautical miles still remains a matter for discussion.

ii. Methodology of the Delimitation of the Continental Shelf Beyond 200 Nautical Miles

As regards the methodology of the delimitation of the continental shelf beyond 200 nautical miles, ITLOS held that Article 83 of the LOSC applies equally to the delimitation of the continental shelf both within and beyond 200 nautical miles;[650] and that the delimitation method to be employed in the present case for the continental shelf beyond 200 nautical miles should not differ from that within 200 nautical miles.[651] As noted, the ITLOS's approach was echoed by the Annex VII Arbitral Tribunal in the 2014 *Bangladesh v India* arbitration[652] and the ITLOS Special Chamber in the *Ghana/Côte d'Ivoire* case.[653]

In deciding the methodology of the delimitation of the continental shelf beyond 200 nautical miles, the concept of 'one single continental shelf' is the key. In this regard, the Arbitral Tribunal in the *Barbados v Trinidad and Tobago* case held that: 'There is in law only a single "continental shelf" rather than an inner continental shelf and a separate extended or outer continental shelf.'[654] The concept of 'one single continental shelf' was confirmed in the *Bangladesh/Myanmar*,[655] *Bangladesh v India*,[656] and *Ghana/Côte d'Ivoire* cases.[657] This concept

[648] ibid, 5.
[649] ibid, 33.
[650] The *Bangladesh/Myanmar* case, [2012] ITLOS Rep 117, [454].
[651] ibid, [455].
[652] The *Bangladesh v India* arbitral award, [465].
[653] The *Ghana/Côte d'Ivoire* case, [2017] ITLOS Rep [526].
[654] The *Barbados v Trinidad and Tobago* arbitral award, 208–09, [213].
[655] The *Bangladesh/Myanmar* case, [2012] ITLOS Rep 96–7, [362].
[656] The *Bangladesh v India* arbitral award, [77].
[657] The *Ghana/Côte d'Ivoire* case, [2017] ITLOS Rep [490].

seems to provide a legal basis for the application of the same method to the delimitation of the continental shelf beyond 200 nautical miles. In the words of the ITLOS Special Chamber,

> As far as the methodology for delimiting the continental shelf beyond 200 nm is concerned, the Special Chamber recalls its position that there is only one single continental shelf. Therefore it is considered inappropriate to make a distinction between the continental shelf within and beyond 200 nm as far as the delimitation methodology is concerned.[658]

From a legal viewpoint, however, it should not be forgotten that the continental shelf beyond 200 nautical miles differs from that within 200 nautical miles in some respects.

First, the coastal State is unconditionally entitled to extend its continental shelf up to 200 nautical miles under Article 76(1) of the LOSC. By contrast, the extension of continental shelf beyond 200 nautical miles is possible on the condition that stringent legal and scientific conditions were to be met. In other words, it is conditional.[659]

Secondly, according to the ICJ, the submission of relevant information to the CLCS pursuant to Article 76(8) of the LOSC is a prerequisite for the delimitation of the continental shelf beyond 200 nautical miles.[660] This requirement does not apply to the delimitation of the continental shelf within 200 nautical miles.

Thirdly, unlike the continental shelf within 200 nautical miles, the coastal State is obliged to make payments or contributions in kind in respect of the exploitation of the non-living resources of the continental shelf beyond 200 nautical miles pursuant to Article 82 of the LOSC. It may be said that the principle of the common heritage of mankind counterbalances overexpansion of the exclusive interests of coastal States.[661]

Fourthly, the legal title to the continental shelf beyond 200 nautical miles relies on the concept of natural prolongation, while the legal title to the continental shelf within 200 nautical miles rests on the distance criterion. As will be discussed in chapter six, the distance criterion as legal title and the equidistance method are intimately intertwined in the context of maritime delimitation within 200 nautical miles.[662] However, such a linkage does not exist with regard to the delimitation of the continental shelf beyond 200 nautical miles. Accordingly, as a matter of theory, there appears to be scope to argue that the delimitation methodology of the continental shelf beyond 200 nautical miles may differ from

[658] ibid, [526].

[659] Presentation by Treves in *Nicaragua v. Colombia II*, Verbatim Record, CR 2015/28, 31, [6]. See also Vega-Barbosa, 'The Admissibility of Outer Continental Shelf Delimitation Claims Before the ICJ' 109.

[660] In *Nicaragua v Colombia II*, the Court held that: 'Nicaragua had to submit such information as a prerequisite for the delimitation of the continental shelf beyond 200 nautical miles by the Court.' [2016] ICJ Rep 136, [105].

[661] S Oda, *International Control of Sea Resources* (Dordrecht, Nijhoff, 1989) xxxii.

[662] See ch 6, s III of this book.

that of the continental shelf within 200 nautical miles.[663] In this regard, the 2002 Report of the International Law Association (ILA) Committee stated that:

> Entitlement to the EEZ and a continental shelf extending up to the 200 nautical mile limit is based on distance from the coast. This makes the distance criterion also an important consideration in the delimitation of these areas. Distance does not play the same role in the establishment of entitlement over and the outer limit of the outer continental shelf. This may have an impact on the rules applicable to the delimitation of this part of the continental shelf.[664]

If, as ITLOS and the Annex VII Arbitral Tribunal stated, the three-stage method is applicable to the delimitation of the continental shelf beyond 200 nautical miles, three issues arise. First, the Annex VII Arbitral Tribunal, in the *Bangladesh v India* case, held that base points for the construction of the provisional equidistance line within 200 nautical miles continue to affect the equidistance line beyond 200 nautical miles and remain appropriate.[665] Furthermore, the Tribunal identified an additional base point on the Indian coast for construction of the provisional equidistance line beyond 200 nautical miles.[666] It would seem to follow that the provisional equidistance line for the continental shelf beyond 200 nautical miles is also controlled by the base points on the coast. If this approach may be relevant in the delimitation between adjacent coasts, in the delimitation of the continental shelf beyond 200 nautical miles between States with opposite coasts, a question arises from where a provisional equidistance line should be measured.[667]

Secondly, at the second stage of maritime delimitation, the Arbitral Tribunal, in the *Bangladesh v India* case, adjusted the provisional equidistance line to ameliorate the excessive negative consequences the provisional equidistance line would have for Bangladesh in the areas within and beyond 200 nautical miles. This means that the provisional equidistance line within and beyond 200 nautical miles was shifted taking account of the *same* relevant circumstance, namely, a cut-off effect arising from the concavity of Bangladesh's coast. In the *Bangladesh/Myanmar* case, ITLOS considered that the concavity of the Bangladesh coast as a relevant circumstance has a continuing effect beyond

[663] ILA, *New Delhi Conference (2002), Committee on Legal Issues of the Outer Continental Shelf*, 9, available at: www.ila-hq.org/index.php/committees.

[664] ibid. See also Oude Alferink, 'ITLOS's Approach' 246 et seq.

[665] The *Bangladesh v India* arbitral award, [462].

[666] ibid, [463].

[667] As an option, Schofield *et al* suggested that an equidistance line should be constructed between opposing foot of slope points. In their view, '[t]he advantage of this approach would be that a boundary line delimited would have a stronger relationship to the basis for entitlement to and delineation of areas of outer continental shelf – something that an equidistance-based line between coastal baselines lacks.' Schofield, Telesetsky and Lee, 'A Tribunal Navigating Complex Waters' 375. In any event it seems that in the particular context of the delimitation of the continental shelf beyond 200 nautical miles, the delimitation between States with opposite coasts is more difficult than that between States with adjacent coasts. See P von Mühlendahl, *L'équidistance dans la délimitation des frontière maritimes*, 383–84, [600].

200 nautical miles. It thus extended the line of single maritime boundary beyond 200-autical mile-limit until it reaches the area where the rights of third States may be affected.[668] The *Bangladesh/Myanmar* case seems to suggest that the configuration of the coasts may be a relevant circumstance both for the delimitation of the continental shelf boundary within and beyond 200 nautical miles.[669] On the other hand, the relevance of geological and geomorphological factors needs careful consideration. In the *Bangladesh/Myanmar* and *Bangladesh v India* cases, geological and geomorphological factors were not considered as relevant circumstances. While the exclusion of these factors may be relevant in the two cases, one cannot *a priori* preclude the possibility that geological and geomorphological factors may be taken into account as relevant circumstances in future cases on the delimitation of the continental shelf beyond 200 nautical miles.[670]

Thirdly, in the *Bangladesh/Myanmar*,[671] *Bangladesh v India*,[672] and *Ghana/Côte d'Ivoire* cases,[673] the relevant area for the disproportionality test encompasses the potential areas of the continental shelf beyond 200 nautical miles, even though the outer limits of the continental shelf beyond 200 nautical miles remain undetermined. In this regard, the ITLOS Special Chamber admitted that:

> [U]nder the particular circumstances of this case this figure [of the relevant area] can only be an approximation. This is due to the fact that the outer limits of the continental shelf beyond 200 nm have not yet been finally established under article 76, paragraph 8, of the Convention.[674]

According to the Chamber, however, 'this figure is sufficient to conduct the disproportionality test.'[675] Given that the extent of the continental shelf between the Parties is yet to be determined, however, it may be less easy to apply the disproportionality test properly.[676]

All in all, it can be observed that the rules governing the delimitation of the continental shelf beyond 200 nautical miles are still fluid. The number of cases on this subject remains limited and, at the time of writing, all cases relate to the delimitation between States with adjacent coasts only. Thus further accumulation of case law is required to clarify the rules governing the delimitation of the continental shelf beyond 200 nautical miles.

[668] The *Bangladesh/Myanmar* case, [2012] ITLOS Rep 118, [462].

[669] Ø Jensen, 'The Delimitation of the Continental Shelf beyond 200 nm' in Oude Elferink, Henriksen and Busch, 369; Oude Alferink, 'ITLOS's Approach,' 242–43.

[670] See Churchill, 'The *Bangladesh/Myanmar* Case,' 150; Schofield, Telesetsky and Lee, 'A Tribunal Navigating Complex Waters,' 375.

[671] The *Bangladesh/Myanmar* case, [2012] ITLOS Rep 96–7, [362].

[672] The *Bangladesh v India* arbitral award, [77].

[673] The *Ghana/Côte d'Ivoire* case, [2017] ITLOS Rep [383–85].

[674] ibid, [534].

[675] ibid.

[676] MD Evans, 'Maritime Boundary Delimitation: Whatever Next,' 76. See also ch 9, s IV of this book.

Part II

Comparative Analysis between the Case Law and State Practice

6

Predictability in the Law of Maritime Delimitation: The Applicability of the Equidistance Method at the First Stage of Delimitation

I. METHOD OF ANALYSIS

A. Importance of Comparative Analysis between the Case Law and State Practice

PART TWO OF this book aims to examine the existing law of maritime delimitation by comparing case law and State practice. In the author's view, a comparative analysis between the case law and State practice is significant for two reasons.

First, in appropriate cases, international courts and tribunals have applied customary law to maritime delimitation disputes. As customary law derives from State practice and *opinio juris*, one may argue that, at least theoretically, there is no divergence between the case law and State practice when international courts and tribunals apply such rules. Nevertheless, the practice of the courts does not necessarily reflect this. In fact, normally international courts and tribunals do not examine State practice and *opinio juris* in detail when applying customary law to maritime delimitation disputes. Hence, there is a need to address whether and to what extent the jurisprudence coincides with State practice.

Secondly, in the particular field of maritime delimitation, State practice has not been sufficiently studied due to the paucity of information. Consequently, most studies regarding maritime delimitation have tended to focus only on case law. Owing to the development of world-wide and regional studies on State practice regarding maritime delimitation, however, it has become possible, to a certain extent, to examine State practice systematically. Thus, on the basis of these new studies, it is necessary to examine development of State practice in the field of maritime delimitation. Indeed, an analysis of State practice will further enrich contemporary studies regarding the law of maritime delimitation. It is against the above background that we will analyse both case law and State practice in this Part.

As shown in the Appendix to this study, at present a large number of agreements on maritime delimitations relate to the delimitation of the continental shelf and single maritime boundaries. Since the two types of maritime delimitation have been the principal subjects of the case law, it will be appropriate to focus our analysis on these points. Thus, in this Part, we will examine the case law and State practice particularly in relation to the delimitation of both the continental shelf and single maritime boundaries in a framework of predictability and flexibility.

B. Concept of Predictability

The concept of predictability has two meanings. The first is predictability as ensured by the application of the equidistance method. Indeed, this method is the only method of ensuring predictability of results in the sense that, once the base-points are fixed, the delimitation line is mathematically determined.[1] Thus, the equidistance method plays a tangible role in maintaining a certain degree of predictability in this field. This may be termed predictability in a strict sense.[2]

[1] HWA Thirlway, 'The Law and Procedure of the International Court of Justice Part Five' (1994) 64 *BYIL* 41. See also P von Mühlendahl, *L'équidistance dans la délimitation des frontières maritimes: Etude de la jurisprudence internationale* (Paris, Pedone, 2016) 37–39, [34–36]. To be absolutely accurate, one may point to the equiratio method as another predictable method. According to Langeraar, that method may be defined as follows: 'A boundary line between the offshore areas under the jurisdiction of two coastal States, either adjacent or opposite, will be called an equiratio line when every point of it will be defined by a constant ratio of its distances from the nearest points of the baselines from which the breadth of the territorial sea of each State is measured.' W Langeraar, 'Maritime Delimitation: The Equiratio Method – A New Approach' (1986) *Marine Policy* 7. For instance, one may draw a line every point on which is at a distance from the nearest points of the baseline of State A which is $\frac{9}{10}$ of the distance to the nearest points on the baseline of State B. This is a 0.90 equiratio line. An equidistant, which is the most well-known kind, is a line equiratio of 1.00. In that sense, it may be said that the equidistance method is a variation of the equiratio method.

[2] This does not mean, however, that the equidistance method is completely free from technical defects. There are several factors which will affect the drawing of an equidistance line. In this respect, Hodgson and Cooper point to seven possible elements: Choice of (1) map projections; (2) scales; (3) spheroids; (4) horizontal datums; (5) tidal datums; (6) nature of the line utilised for the boundary; (7) baselines and the tolerances. RD Hodgson and EJ Cooper, 'The Technical Delimitation of a Modern Equidistant Boundary' (1976) *ODIL* 371. For instance, the location of an equidistance line is different depending on the use of a Mercator projection or a conic one such as the Lambert Conformal projection. Furthermore, the degree of accuracy depends on the scale of the maps used. Moreover, a three-dimensional line in the spherodial earth shall become two-dimensional when drawing a line. According to Hodgson and Cooper, there are at least nine different ways of doing so. The results differ according to the types of lines used. In addition in some cases, the validity of the base-points or straight base-lines selected may be controversial. Thus, there are uncertainties even relating to the equidistance method. Nevertheless, one should not exaggerate these technical problems. Considering that they are present in every method of maritime delimitation, it remains true that the mathematical character of equidistance ensures predictability. In fact, if computers are used, strict equidistance lines can be determined to a degree of accuracy consistent with the quality of the baseline data available. ibid, pp 383–87. For techniques of maritime delimitation, see in particular Nuno Sérgio Marques Antunes, *Towards the Conceptualisation of Maritime Delimitation: Legal and Technical Aspects of a Political Process* (Leiden, Nijhoff, 2003) 585–625; L Lucchini and

The second is predictability *lato sensu* which can be ensured through clarification of the factors to be taken into account in the case law and in State practice. As will be discussed later, the Parties usually insist on variety of relevant circumstances being put before the international courts and tribunals. In this regard, it is necessary for the courts to maintain a certain degree of predictability with regard to considerations of relevant circumstances. Various factors to be considered in the process of maritime delimitations will be examined in chapter seven and chapter eight of this book. This chapter thus considers predictability in the first sense, that is, the applicability of the equidistance method.

II. ANALYSIS OF STATE PRACTICE

As outlined in chapters four and five, the applicability of the equidistance method in customary law has been controversial. Nevertheless, the real problem is not so much the customary-law character of the equidistance method per se, but that of the combined rule of 'equidistance–special/relevant circumstances'. According to the result-oriented equity approach, the obligatory character of the equidistance method is rejected even for the first and provisional stage of maritime delimitation. By contrast, under the corrective-equity approach or three-stage approach, the equidistance method is applied at the provisional stage under Articles 74(1) and 83(1) of the LOSC as well as customary law, unless there are compelling reasons that make it impossible or inappropriate to draw a provisional equidistance line. Thus, the fundamental difference between the two approaches consists in the question of whether the equidistance method is applicable at the first stage of the delimitation process as *a norm*. Noting the above-mentioned points, we will now consider the applicability of the equidistance method at the first stage of delimitation in examining both State practice and case law.

A. The Equidistance Method in State Practice

i. Method of Analysis

This survey attempts to present the current situation of bilateral treaty practice incorporating the equidistance method. It is mainly based on data included in

M Vœlckel, *Droit de la mer*, tome 2, *Délimitation* (Paris, Pedone, 1996) 317–96; P Beazley, 'Technical Considerations in Maritime Boundary Delimitations' in JI Charney and LM Alexander, *International Maritime Boundaries*, vol I (Dordrecht, Nijhoff, 1993) 243–62; SW Boggs, 'Delimitation of Seaward Areas Under National Jurisdiction' (1951) 45 *AJIL* 240; and, by the same author, 'Problems of Water-Boundary Definition: Median Lines and International Boundaries Through Territorial Waters' (1937) 27 *The Geographical Review* 445. The last article was reproduced in the next book written by the same author: *International Boundaries. A Study of Boundary Functions and Problems* (New York, NY, Cambridge University Press, 1949) 176–92; M Thamsborg, 'Geodetic Hydrography as Related to Maritime Boundary Problems' (1974) 51 *International Hydrographic Review* 157.

the seven volumes of the *International Maritime Boundaries* published by the American Society of International Law.[3] In addition, other sources are available, such as the *Law of the Sea Bulletin, International Legal Materials* and current developments as presented by the *International Journal of Marine and Coastal Law*. So far as the present writer knows, at the end of the year 2018, there were approximately 300 agreements concerning maritime delimitation (see Appendix). Although comprehensive research on treaty practice goes beyond the scope of this book, the sample should illustrate the general trend of maritime delimitation.

Regarding the method of delimitation, many agreements do not specify the method applied in drawing a boundary. In such cases, the method can be identified by comparing the delimitation to the equidistance line hypothetically drawn in the maps annexed in the above-mentioned *International Maritime Boundaries*. Furthermore, equidistance lines drawn in agreements are, to a certain extent, simplified or modified. Thus, there is room for doubt as to the degree to which a line may depart from strict equidistance and still be regarded as a simplified or adjusted equidistance line.

In analysing treaty practice on this subject, it is of interest to note the distinction between delimitation involving opposite and adjacent coasts. In some cases it is difficult to classify the configurations of the coasts within the category of opposite or adjacent delimitations.[4] In this survey, for practical purposes, the doubtful cases are categorised into a group of hybrid character.[5] Agreements following decisions of the ICJ are excluded when assessing the evidence favourable to the equidistance method. The ratio of the equidistance method is rounded off to the third decimal place. Finally, because of inevitable subjectivity in some respects, it should be stressed that this survey is intended to present merely a general tendency of treaty practice rather than to provide perfectly objective information.

ii. The Results

When considering maritime delimitations as a whole, including delimitations relating to the territorial sea or the continental shelf, or to single maritime

[3] JI Charney and LM Alexander, (eds), *International Maritime Boundaries*, 7 vols (The Hague, Nijhoff, 1993, 1998, 2002, 2005, 2011, 2016 (Editors of vol IV are JI Charney, and RW Smith; vol V and vol VI were edited by DA Colson and RW Smith; vol VII was edited by CG Lathrop)). Hereafter the volumes will be quoted as *IMB*.

[4] Regarding adjacency of coasts, the *dictum* of the *Anglo-French Continental Shelf* award should be recalled. In that case, the Court of Arbitration regarded the Atlantic region as an adjacent situation, although the coasts in the English Channel are opposite each other. Following the award, even where delimitation concerns the area between two opposing islands, such as the Scilly Islets and Ushant Island in the Atlantic sector of the 1977 award, there may be a situation which could be regarded as in an adjacent relationship. Our interpretation concerning adjacency in this survey follows that of the *Anglo-French Continental Shelf* award.

[5] That problem concerns in particular, bays which are surrounded by two neighbouring States. Usually, their coasts transform the relationship from adjacent to opposite. Yet it is hard to determine precisely the point where such transformation begins. It would be practical to categorise such bays into mixed geographical relationships.

boundaries, one finds that approximately 84 per cent of agreements have recourse to the equidistance method for all or part of maritime boundaries between opposite coasts. On the other hand, with respect to delimitations between States with adjacent coasts, around 56 per cent of the maritime delimitation agreements use the equidistance method for all or part of their maritime boundaries. In addition, nearly 87 per cent of the maritime boundaries involving coasts with a hybrid character are based on the equidistance method.

The results of our survey are not surprising. Previous writers have affirmed the same trend.[6] For instance, Caflisch presented an anonymous document of 1 April 1979 in an article. According to the data, 29 of 34 agreements (85 per cent) drawing maritime boundaries between States with opposite coasts used equidistance for all or part of their boundaries. On the other hand, with respect to delimitation between States with adjacent coasts, only 9 of 23 agreements (39 per cent) had recourse to the equidistance method for all or part of boundaries.[7] A study of treaty practice by Legault and Hankey reached a similar conclusion in 1993, although the analytical method was not the same. According to their study, 89 per cent of the maritime boundaries separating opposite coasts are based on the equidistance method. Furthermore, 86 per cent of the boundaries involving mixed coastal relationships flow from the equidistance method. On the other hand, regarding the delimitations in cases of adjacent coasts, only 40 per cent of the boundaries rest on the equidistance method.[8] Hence, broadly speaking, it could be contended that our survey proves a similar trend.

B. Evaluation

i. Extensive and Virtually Uniform State Practice

The above survey shows that the frequency with which treaties use the equidistance method varies depending on whether the delimitations involve opposite or adjacent coasts. In this regard, two points can be made.

First, with respect to the former, treaty practice shows, to a large extent, uniformity in favouring the equidistance method for drawing maritime

[6] See also T Cottier, *Equitable Principles of Maritime Boundary Delimitation: The Quest for Distributive Justice in International Law* (Cambridge University Press, 2015) 242–50.

[7] L Caflisch, 'Les zones maritimes sous juridiction nationale, leurs limites et leur délimitation' in D Bardonnet and M Virally (eds), *Le nouveau droit international de la mer* (Paris, Pedone, 1983) 60–61.

[8] L Legault and B Hankey, 'Method, Oppositeness and Adjacency, and Proportionality in Maritime Boundary Delimitation' in *IMB*, vol I, pp 203–41. It appears that their research was done before 1992. (But, within the list annexed to their study, agreements after 1990 are not included.) The number of agreements which they analysed was 134. In some cases, their interpretation of oppositeness or adjacency of the coasts and the use of the equidistance method is different from ours.

boundaries.[9] In fact, more than 80 per cent of the treaties on these matters have adopted the method of equidistance exclusively or for part of the delimitation line. This seems to be an impressive State practice.[10]

Secondly, in relation to delimitation between adjacent States, however, the treaties using the equidistance method for all or part of the delimitation remain, at best, around 56 per cent. It would be difficult to regard them as attesting to an extensive and virtually uniform practice. On the other hand, the fact that more than 50 per cent of the agreements relating to delimitation between adjacent coasts use the equidistance method wholly or in part appears to suggest that the equidistance method is not *a priori* excluded even in delimitations between adjacent coasts.

ii. Existence of Opinio Juris

As some writers have noted, *opinio juris* has been a controversial issue in customary law-making.[11] One of the main difficulties regarding *opinio juris* is to find evidence for it.[12] The difficulty ought to arise in the present context, for explicit evidence of *opinio juris* is difficult to find in treaty practice. However, the two elements of State practice and *opinio juris* are usually inseparable.[13]

[9] In 1985, Judge Valticos in his Separate Opinion in the *Libya/Malta* case, explicitly pointed to the fact that an overwhelming majority of opposite-coast delimitations derived from the median line. Separate Opinion of Judge Valticos, [1985] ICJ Rep 107, [10]. See also P Weil, 'A propos du droit coutumier en matière de délimitation maritime' in *International Law at the Time of Its Codification: Essays in Honour of Roberto Ago*, vol II (Milan, Giuffrè, 1987) 549.

[10] In this respect, on the one hand, Charney considers that 'no normative principle of international law has developed that would mandate the specific location of any maritime boundary line' through State practice. On the other hand, he accepts that '[i]f State practice has any influence on the positive law for maritime boundary delimitations, equidistance must have a place'. JI Charney, 'Introduction' in *IMB*, vol I, p xlii.

[11] B Stern, 'La coutume au cœur du droit international. Quelques réfletions' in *Le droit international: unité et dicersité, Mélanges offerts à Paul Reuter* (Paris, Pedone, 1981) 485. See also Thirlway, 'The Law and Procedure of the International Court of Justice Part Five' 40–54.

[12] M Sørensen, 'Principles de droit international public' (1960) 101 *RCADI* 49. See also, by the same author, *Les sources de droit international, Etude sur la jurisprudence de la Cour permanente de Justice internationale* (Copenhagen, Einar Munksgaard, 1946) 108–11. In fact, for some writers, this was one of the principal reasons for questioning the necessity of *opinio juris* in the formation of customary law. Typical examples were Kelsen and Guggenheim. H Kelsen, 'Théorie du droit international coutumier' (1939) 1 *Révue internationale de la théorie du droit* 264; P Guggenheim, *'Les deux éléments de la coutume en droit international' in Mélanges G Scelle tome I* (Paris, Librairie générale de droit et de jurisprudence, 1950) 280; *Traité de droit international public, tome I* (Geneva, Librairie de l'Université, 1953) 47–48. Yet later, the two authors changed their views by accepting the need of *opinio juris*. H Kelsen, *Principles of International Law* (New York, NY, Rinehart and Company Inc, 1952) 307; P Guggenheim, *Traité de droit international public, tome I*, 2nd edn (Geneva, Librairie de l'Université, 1967) 101–5. It is not suggested, however, that the difficulty was resolved. In addition, some recent studies attempt to exclude the element of *opinio juris*, for instance, P Haggenmacher, 'La doctrine des deux éléments du droit coutumier dans la pratique de la Cour internationale' (1986) 90 *RGDIP* 5; and M Mendelson, 'The Subjective Element in Customary International Law' (1995) 66 *BYIL* 177.

[13] Concerning this point, Stern said that 'les deux «éléments constitutifs» de la coutume ne sont pas deux entités juxtaposées, mais ne sont que deux aspects d'un même phénomène.' Stern,

With respect to delimitations between States with opposite coasts, considering the high degree of uniformity of treaty practice in favour of the equidistance method, it would be unrealistic to neglect such 'impressive' treaty practice in the formulation of customary law on the grounds that *opinio juris* is not clearly expressed. In fact, as some writers have pointed out, the Court itself has not always required expressed evidence of *opinio juris*.[14] Rather, as Rousseau explains, owing to the difficulty of demonstrating the existence of *opinio juris* in a positive way, international case law has deduced it from the circumstances surrounding relevant State practice as a whole, such as the succession of similar facts, the existence of a uniform and constant practice, the number and importance of the States participating in a multilateral treaty creating new law, etc.[15] In the context of maritime delimitation as well, the ICJ has not required strict evidence of *opinio juris* with respect to equitable principles. Accordingly, it would be absurd to apply a rigid test of *opinio juris* when it comes to the equidistance method. In this context, one should note the view of Judge Valticos in the *Libya/Malta* case:

> It would at all events be highly unfortunate if, on a point of such importance, a divorce were to set in between the treaty practice of States, to which Article 38 of the Statute of the Court refers, and the Court's jurisprudence.[16]

Different considerations should apply to delimitations between adjacent coasts, however. Owing to the less extensive treaty practice, one cannot lightly presume the existence of an *opinio juris* in favour of equidistance.

Overall it can be observed that in State practice, the application of the equidistance method to maritime delimitations considerably differs according to the configuration of coasts. While State practice shows uniformity in favouring the equidistance method for delimitation between States with opposite coats, it is less favourable to that method in delimitation between States with adjacent coasts.

'La coutume au cœur du droit international' 482. For the same view, P-M Dupuy and Y Kerbrat, *Droit international public,* 12e edn (Paris, Dalloz, 2014) 368–69; Thirlway, 'The Law and Procedure of the International Court of Justice Part Five' 41; Haggenmacher, 'La doctrine des deux éléments' 114.

[14] On this point, Virally mentioned that: 'The truth is that the Court, though it pays lip-service to the concept of the *opino juris* and though it has had occasion to speak of the "consciousness of a legal duty", is concerned less with analysis of mental states than with the examination and assessment of the facts proved. What it seeks to determine is whether or not they disclose an effective exercise by a state of a right, coupled with a recognition by another state of a corresponding obligation.' M Virally, 'Sources of International Law' in M Sørensen, *Manual of Public International Law* (New York, NY, St Martin's Press, 1968) 134. Furthermore, as early as 1939, Kelsen pointed out that, where international tribunals applied customary law generated from treaties, they had not attempted to examine *opinio juris*. Kelsen, 'Théorie du droit international coutumier' 264.

[15] C Rousseau, *Droit international public*, tome I, *Introduction et sources* (Paris, Sirey, 1970) 325.

[16] Separate Opinion of Judge Valticos, [1985] ICJ Rep 108, [11]. He also said that '[l]ike the Court, I tend to the view that the States which conclude those bilateral agreements to which reference has been made did not have the impression that they were following a binding rule of law, and were not guided by any *opinio juris*. But, at the very least, they did conclude these agreements in the light of the legal background, and in the belief that the median line was the most widespread and convenient method and that is reflected what might be called an *opinio aequitatis*.' ibid.

If one can find a sign of emergence of customary law concerning the application of the equidistance method to delimitation between opposite coasts, the same will not hold true in delimitation between adjacent coasts. As described in chapter five, however, there is a clear trend that the recent jurisprudence relating to maritime delimitation adopted the corrective-equity or three-stage approach under the LOSC and customary law, regardless of configuration of the coasts. In light of the difference between State practice and case law, it may be said that the three-stage approach is 'judge-made law.'[17] An issue that arises in this context concerns the legal basis for applying the equidistance method at the first stage of delimitation. When considering this issue, it is necessary to address the idea of linking the delimitation method with legal title.

III. INTERLINKAGE BETWEEN LEGAL TITLE AND METHOD OF DELIMITATION

A. Concept of Legal Title in Maritime Delimitation

Before turning to the discussion concerning the relation between legal title and delimitation method, it will be relevant to examine the concept of legal title in maritime delimitation. Legal title has to do with defining the basis on which a State is legally empowered to exercise rights and jurisdiction over the maritime areas adjacent to its coasts.[18] The legal title in the strict sense, which constitutes the ultimate source of all legal title over maritime space, is condensed in the phrase 'the land dominates the sea.' In this respect, the ICJ, in the *Fisheries* case of 1951, stated that: 'It is the land which confers upon the coastal State a right to the waters off its coasts.'[19] In the *North Sea Continental Shelf* judgment, the Court, quoting this *dictum*, said that: '[T]he land is the legal source of the power which a state may exercise over territorial extensions to seaward.'[20] The *dictum* was echoed again by the Court in the *Aegean Sea Continental Shelf* case: '[I]t is solely by virtue of the coastal State's sovereignty over the land that rights of exploration and exploitation in the continental shelf can attach to it, *ipso jure*, under international law.'[21] This *dictum* has thus been accepted by the ICJ and there is no longer any challenge on this point.

As will be shown later, the substance of this phrase has been complicated by references to the concepts of adjacency, proximity, natural prolongation

[17] In fact, international courts and tribunals have rarely examined State practice concerning maritime delimitations.

[18] P Weil, *Perspective du droit de la délimitation maritime* (Paris, Pedone, 1988) 53.

[19] *Fisheries (United Kingdom v Norway)*, Judgment, [1951] ICJ Rep 116, 133.

[20] [1969] ICJ Rep 51, [96].

[21] [1978] ICJ Rep 36, [86].

of the coasts, etc. At present, however, the substance of the legal title is expressed as the distance criterion. On this point, the ICJ held in the *Libya/Malta* case that:

> [I]n so far as those areas are situated at a distance of under 200 miles from the coasts in question, title depends solely on the distance from the coasts of the claimant States of any areas of sea-bed claimed by way of continental shelf, and the geological or geomorphological characteristics of those areas are completely immaterial.[22]

Furthermore, with respect to the exclusive economic zone, the Court held that:

> [T]he institution of the exclusive economic zone, *with its rule on entitlement by reason of distance,* is shown by the practice of States to have become a part of customary law. ... Although there can be a continental shelf where there is no exclusive economic zone, there cannot be an exclusive economic zone without a corresponding continental shelf. It follows that, for juridical and practical reasons, the distance criterion must now apply to the continental shelf as well as to the exclusive economic zone.[23]

Accordingly, the distance criterion, which is in essence of a *spatial* nature, is the common denominator of jurisdiction of coastal States over maritime spaces. In this sense, the concept of natural prolongation, which has been regarded as legal title over the continental shelf, has been downgraded with the emergence of the distance criterion.[24]

The legal title of coastal States is equal and has the same potential for generating jurisdiction over maritime spaces.[25] There is no discrimination between States. Nor is there discrimination between coasts. In this connection, it will be noted that the Chamber in the *Gulf of Maine* case, rejected arguments of the United States according to which coasts are divided into primary and secondary coasts, the former prevailing over the latter.[26]

On the basis of the legal title of the distance criterion, jurisdiction of coastal States is generated by their coasts. The ICJ in the *Libya/Malta* case ruled that: 'The juridical link between the State's territorial sovereignty and its rights to certain adjacent maritime expanses is established *by means of its coast*. The concept of adjacency measured by distance is based entirely on that of the coastline, and not on that of the landmass.'[27] A coastline constitutes an essential element in the seaward projection of coastal State jurisdiction.[28] Accordingly, it is self-evident that land-locked States, which have no coastline, will not generate

[22] [1985] ICJ Rep 35, [39].

[23] Emphasis added. ibid, 33, [34].

[24] This does not mean that the concept of natural prolongation plays no role as a legal title over the continental shelf. Insofar as the continental shelf which is located beyond 200 miles is concerned, that concept will still serve as a legal title under Art 76 of the LOSC.

[25] Lucchini and Vœlckel, *Droit de la mer*, 211.

[26] [1984] ICJ Rep 271, [36].

[27] Emphasis added. [1985] ICJ Rep 47, [49].

[28] Weil, *Perspective du droit de la délimitation maritime,* 58.

jurisdiction over maritime spaces. At the same time, this is why the size of the landmass is irrelevant to maritime delimitation.[29]

In this connection, a question which arises is the direction of the projection. According to Weil, such projection is omni-directional, ie, radial. In other words, coastal State jurisdiction will extend not only to the frontage but also in all directions over a distance determined by international law.[30] That view appears to have much force. Nevertheless, the Arbitral Tribunal in the *St Pierre and Miquelon* case partly adopted a frontal projection theory. As explained already, the Tribunal established a 'corridor' 10.5 nautical miles wide and 188 nautical miles in length, from the 12-mile limit measured from the baseline in the second sector on the basis of the French frontal seaward projection towards the south.[31] As pointed out, however, that judgment invited criticism by Weil.[32] In any event, there is no doubt that the legal title over maritime spaces is, in principle, the distance criterion. Thus, the next issue to be examined is the relationship between the distance criterion as legal title and the method of delimitation. This includes two questions: (i) whether legal title over maritime space has legal effects upon the method of delimitation; and (ii) if so, what is the legal consequence of the effects. The case law of the ICJ will shed some light on these questions.

B. Relationship between Legal Title and Delimitation Method in the Case Law

When considering the relationship between legal title and delimitation method, four decisions of the ICJ merit discussion: the *North Sea Continental Shelf*, *Tunisia/Libya*, *Gulf of Maine*, and *Libya/Malta* cases.

In the *North Sea Continental Shelf* cases, Denmark and the Netherlands contended that the test of appurtenance was 'closer proximity' and that all those parts of the continental shelf were appurtenant to a coastal State which was closer to them than to the territory of another State. 'Hence', the two Kingdoms claimed 'delimitation must be effected by a method which will leave to each one

[29] On this point, the ICJ in the *Libya/Malta* case held that: '[t]he capacity to engender continental shelf rights derives not from the landmass, but from sovereignty over the landmass; and it is by means of the maritime front of this landmass in other words by its coastal opening, that this territorial sovereignty brings its continental shelf rights into effect.' [1985] ICJ Rep 41, [49].

[30] For the notion in general, see Weil, *Perspective du droit de la délimitation maritime*, 68–75. In this part, Weil explained that the idea of radial projection was already reflected in the cannon-shot rule. Considering that a cannon shoots in all directions, the cannon-shot rule had in essence a radial character. ibid, 69. Furthermore, according to Weil, that idea is connected to the method of envelop of arcs of circles technique determining a limit of a territorial sea. ibid, 70. For the genesis of the method in some detail, see DP O'Connell, *The International Law of the Sea*, vol I (Oxford, Clarendon Press, 1982) 230–35.

[31] The *St Pierre and Miquelon* arbitral award, (1992) 31 *ILM* 1170–71, [70–74].

[32] Dissenting Opinion of Judge Weil, ibid, 1199–201, [9–13].

of the States concerned all those areas that are nearest to its own coast. Only a line drawn on equidistance principles will do this.'[33] However, the majority of the ICJ refused to accept the argument which justified the equidistance method based on the legal title of proximity. Having held that the legal title over the continental shelf was not proximity but the concept of natural prolongation of the coasts, it ruled that: 'The conclusion drawn by the Court from the foregoing analysis is that the notion of equidistance as a logical necessity, in the sense of being an inescapable *a priori* accompaniment of the basic continental shelf doctrine, is incorrect.'[34] In this respect, appearances notwithstanding, it is less clear whether the Court discarded, in a general way, the argument combining legal title and the method of delimitation. Indeed, from other parts of the judgment, it appears that the Court gave, to a certain extent, legal effect to the legal title of natural prolongation when choosing a method of delimitation. As discussed elsewhere in this book, it held that delimitation was to be effected by agreement in accordance with equitable principles, taking account of all the relevant circumstances, in such a way as to leave to each Party as much as possible of all those parts of the continental shelf that constitute a natural prolongation of its land territory into and under the sea.[35] While the expression 'as much as possible' implies that the natural prolongation is not identical with a delimitation line, it implies at the same time that the delimitation method should not contrast with natural prolongation as a legal title. This is illustrated by the fact that one of the principal reasons for rejecting the obligatory character of the equidistance method is that the latter is incompatible with the fundamental notion of natural prolongation of the coasts as legal title.[36]

However, Judges Tanaka and Morelli upheld the customary-law character of the equidistance method, asserting that the method of delimitation should be derived from legal title over the continental shelf. In this connection, Judge Tanaka stated that: 'The equidistance principle constitutes the method which is the result of the principle of proximity or natural continuation of land territory, which is inseparable from the concept of continental shelf.'[37] It is true that there appears to be some confusion between the principle of proximity and that of the natural continuation of land territory.[38] Yet an important point is that Judge

[33] [1969] ICJ Rep 29, [39].
[34] ibid, 32, [46].
[35] ibid, 53, [101].
[36] ibid, 31, [44].
[37] Dissenting Opinion of Judge Tanaka, ibid, 181.
[38] With respect to legal title, Judge Tanaka argued that: 'The criterion of adjacency – or proximity, propinquity, contiguity – seems a most reasonable one if one adopts the principle of the sovereign rights of the coastal State, excluding the régime of *res nullius* or *res communis*. The idea that the continental shelf constitutes the natural continuation or extension of the coastal State is most natural and reasonable from the geographical and economic viewpoints.' ibid, 180. On this point, the meaning of 'natural continuation of land territory' is at issue as compared to 'natural prolongation of the coasts' used by the majority opinion. The precise meaning of Judge Tanaka's words is difficult to understand. Yet in the other part of his opinion, as the only condition of enabling a coastal State

Tanaka deduced the equidistance method from legal title over the continental shelf. This is illustrated by the following statement:

> The equidistance principle is integrated in the concept of the continental shelf. The former is inherent in the latter, being inseparably connected with it. Therefore, if the law of the continental shelf were devoid of the provision concerning delimitation by means of the equidistance principle, satisfactory functioning of the institution of the continental shelf could not be expected.[39]

Judge Morelli followed a similar line of argument. Regarding the legal title over the continental shelf, he considered that it was the contiguity or adjacency of that area to the territory of the State concerned. Furthermore, he contended that: 'The criterion for determining the extent of the continental shelf which, starting from that line, appertains to a State, by comparison with the continental shelves appertaining to other States, can only be inferred indirectly from the concept of contiguity itself.'[40] In his view, although the criterion of contiguity postulates the line from which the continental shelf of the State commences, it cannot, in itself, be used to determine the extent of the continental shelf. Nevertheless, the criterion of contiguity leads to that of proximity. Thus, Judge Morelli concluded that:

> On the basis of this criterion, there must be considered as appertaining to a given State all points on the continental shelf which, although not situated on the line delimiting the territory of any other State, are nearer to that line than to the line delimiting the territory of any other State. In my view, there is nothing arbitrary about this deduction; it is, on the contrary, a wholly logical one. From the criterion of proximity, the passage is almost automatic to that of equidistance, so that it could be said that the two criteria merge.[41]

In saying this, Judge Morelli deduced the applicability of the equidistance method from three levels of reasoning, ie, contiguity → proximity → equidistance.

The aspect distinguishing the majority opinion from that of the two dissenters was their differing views over legal title over the continental shelf. In so far as one regards the natural prolongation of the coast as legal title over the continental shelf, it is impossible to deduce the equidistance method from the latter, for the two elements conflict.

The second instance to be examined is the *Tunisia/Libya* case. With respect to legal title over the continental shelf, the ICJ confirmed its 1969 judgment and held that the notion of natural prolongation was already a part of existing customary law.[42] Concerning a method of delimitation, both Parties

to exercise sovereign rights over the continental shelf, he stated that 'the existence of the relationship of adjacency between the continental shelf and the coastal State is required'. ibid. In this respect, he appeared to stress the criterion of proximity as legal title over the continental shelf.

[39] ibid.

[40] Dissenting Opinion of Judge Morelli, ibid, 202.

[41] ibid, 202.

[42] [1982] ICJ Rep 46, [43].

based their argument upon the *North Sea Continental Shelf* judgment. Libya contended that 'once the natural prolongation of a State is determined, delimitation becomes a simple matter of complying with the dictates of nature'.[43] Tunisia asserted that the satisfaction of equitable principles was as much a part of the process of the identification of the natural prolongation.[44] The ICJ rejected both arguments, however. In the Court's view, the notion of natural prolongation of the coasts 'would not necessarily be sufficient, or even appropriate, in itself to determine the precise extent of the rights of one State in relation to those of a neighbouring State.'[45] In this regard, one will note the term 'not necessarily,' which appears to suggest that perhaps there may be cases where natural prolongation will be sufficient in itself for delimiting the continental shelf.

The Court continued that the *North Sea Continental Shelf* judgment, which both Parties relied on, did not regard an equitable delimitation and a determination of the limits of the 'natural prolongation' as synonymous.[46] In fact, the Court, in 1969, clearly distinguished between a principle which affords justification for the appurtenance of an area to a State and a rule for determining the extent and limit of such an area. Thus, the argument of Libya, which equated natural prolongation as a legal title with delimitation, was not warranted.[47] At the same time, the Tunisian contention was also unacceptable since the satisfying of equitable principles and the identification of the natural prolongation were not to be placed on a plane of equality.[48]

As the Court indicated, it is true that legal title and method of delimitation are conceptually distinct. However, the above argument does not reveal whether the Court generally rejected the link between a method of delimitation and legal title. In this connection, one should note that at this stage another legal title based on the distance criterion was already provided for under Article 76(1) of the draft UN Convention on the Law of the Sea. Yet the Court did not examine this question, since the Parties relied solely on the notion of natural prolongation without advancing any arguments regarding the distance criterion. In any case, the Court adopted neither a method related to natural prolongation nor the equidistance method in the *Tunisia/Libya* case.

By contrast, Judge Evensen was of the view that the equidistance method should be applicable on account of the legal title resulting from the distance criterion. In the view of the learned judge,

> When neighbouring States claim functional sovereign rights up to 200 miles – be they opposite or adjacent States – their claims are based on a distance criterion.

[43] ibid, 47, [44].
[44] ibid.
[45] ibid, 46, [43].
[46] ibid, [44].
[47] ibid.
[48] ibid.

> This very fact seems to strengthen the equidistance/median line principle as an equitable approach for delimiting overlapping areas.[49]

As with the earlier opinions of two of the Judges in the 1969 judgment, however, Judge Evensen remained in the minority.

In the *Gulf of Maine* case, which related to a single maritime boundary, Canada advocated the application of the equidistance method based on the distance criterion. The Canadian arguments may be summarised as follows. With respect to legal title, adjacency is the fundamental legal foundation for a 200-mile zone, for it is the spatial relationship between the land and the sea, expressed in terms of the 200-mile distance principle, that provides the sole and exclusive criterion of coastal State title. The importance given to the distance criterion cannot fail to exert an influence on the law of continental shelf delimitation. That influence must be all the more profound for a single maritime boundary.[50]

The distance criterion includes the double parameter of 'distance' in relation to 'coasts.' Equidistance is the method which incorporates that double parameter. Indeed, regarding the parameter of the coasts, the equidistance method reflects precisely the configurations of 'coasts.' With respect to the parameter of distance, this method, by its definition, traces a line every point of which is equidistant from the nearest points of the baseline. This constitutes the essence of the principle of distance.[51] Thus, the emergence of the distance principle as a primary basis of coastal State title lends new weight to equidistance as a method of delimitation.[52]

Nevertheless, the Chamber of the ICJ rejected the Canadian argument. According to the Chamber, international law confers on the coastal State a legal title to an adjacent continental shelf or a maritime zone adjacent to its coasts. Yet this does not mean that international law recognises the title conferred on the State by the adjacency of the shelf or that zone as if the mere natural fact of adjacency produced legal consequences. There is a logical gulf between recognising the above-mentioned legal realities and an idea based solely on the distance criterion.[53] The Chamber concluded that the equidistance method 'has not thereby become a rule of general international law, a norm logically flowing from a legally binding principle of customary international law, neither has it been adopted into customary law simply as a method to be given priority or preference.'[54] Thus, the Chamber accepted neither the distance criterion as legal title nor the link between the latter and the equidistance method. In the next

[49] Dissenting Opinion of Judge Evensen, ibid, 296, [15].
[50] Memorial of Canada, vol I, 124. See also, Counter-Memorial of Canada, vol III, 209–12.
[51] Plaidoirie de M Weil, Conseil du Governement canadien, Verbatim Record 1984, Pleadings, vol VI, 177–78.
[52] Counter-Memorial of Canada, vol III, 211.
[53] [1984] ICJ Rep 296–97, [103–06].
[54] ibid, 297, [107].

year, however, the Chamber's view was to be changed, to a large extent, by the full Court in the *Libya/Malta* case.

In the *Libya/Malta* case concerning the delimitation of the continental shelf, Malta attempted to deduce the equidistance method from the legal title of the distance criterion. The argument of Malta was essentially the same as that of Canada in the *Gulf of Maine* case. In short, according to Malta, the equidistance method should be applicable at the first provisional stage of maritime delimitation.[55]

In this connection, the full Court made two important points. First, as pointed out, it accepted that the distance criterion constitutes the common legal title for both the continental shelf and the EEZ.[56] Secondly, the Court supported, to a certain extent, the existence of a link between the legal title and a method of delimitation by saying that:

> The criterion is linked with the law relating to a State's legal title to the continental shelf. … It therefore seems logical to the Court that the choice of the criterion and the method which it is to employ in the first place to arrive at a provisional result should be made in a manner consistent with the concepts underlying the attribution of legal title.[57]

For the Court, 'the legal basis of that which is to be delimited cannot be other than pertinent to the delimitation.'[58] Having examined the equities of the distance criterion and of the results of its application, the Court affirmed the validity of the approach consisting in tracing a median line at the provisional stage.[59] Thus, it would appear that it put forward deductive arguments combining the legal title of distance criterion and a method of delimitation.

Nevertheless, as already pointed out, the Court did not accept the obligatory character of the equidistance method even at the first and provisional stage.[60] Should a method of delimitation be combined with the distance criterion, the equidistance method should logically be singled out, as advocated by Malta. In fact, where the legal title based on the distance criterion is based on customary law, the method derived from the legal title would be customary law as well. On this point, there appears to be a logical gap in the Court's judgment. One explanation may be that the Court attempted to emphasise that the equidistance method is subject to the consideration of equitableness and that the application of that method must be examined in the context of equitable principles, taking into account relevant circumstances.

[55] Plaidoirie de M Weil, Verbatim Record 1984, Pleadings, vol III, 421–27.
[56] [1985] ICJ Rep 33, [34]; 35, [39].
[57] ibid, 46–47, [61].
[58] ibid, 34, [34].
[59] ibid, 47, [62].
[60] ibid, 37–38, [43]; 47, [63].

As the Court itself ruled, there are good reasons to argue that the method of delimitation should be connected to the legal title. Weil explicitly advanced this view, stating that:

> [I]l est tout aussi évident, faut-il le rappeler, que la délimitation est étroitement liée à la base juridique du titre. La délimitation ne peut pas être comprise en dehors du titre; elle est fille du titre.[61]

This view was echoed by Lucchini and Voelckel. In their words,

> Le titre est, en effet, l'élément fondamental de base. La délimitation ne peut avoir lieu qu'à partir de lui et en s'appuyant sur lui.[62]

In light of the linkage between equidistance and the basis of entitlement, ie, distance, Marques Antunes and Becker-Weinberg also stated that: 'Equidistance is inherent in delimitation.'[63] Likewise Lathrop considered that: 'With distance from the coast as the criterion, equidistance [is] the logical method.'[64]

Since the legal title over maritime spaces is attributed by virtue of distance, it is logical that the method of delimitation should reflect this element. The criterion of distance is spatial in nature. Equidistance is the only method which reflects the spatial nature of the distance criterion, for it comes nearest to an equal division of overlapping area by relying on the distance from the coasts.[65] Should a method of delimitation be combined with the distance criterion, the equidistance method should logically be singled out. Currently, as the ICJ ruled in the *Libya/Malta* case, there is no doubt that the distance criterion as the common legal title for the continental shelf and the EEZ has become customary law. Where the legal title based on the distance criterion reflects customary law, the method derived from the legal title would also have a customary nature. Hence much can be said for the view that the equidistance method applies at the first stage of maritime delimitation as a normative standard.[66]

[61] Weil, *Perspective du droit de la délimitation maritime*, 53. The translation by MacGlashan, which differs slightly from the original text, is as follows: '[I]t must be remembered that delimitation is nonetheless closely linked with the legal basis of title. Delimitation cannot be understood without title, which lies at its very heart.' P Weil, *The Law of Maritime Delimitation – Reflections* (translated by M MacGlashan, Cambridge, Grotius, 1989) 48–49.

[62] Lucchini and Vœlckel, *Droit de la mer* 211.

[63] NM Antunes and V Becker-Weinberg, 'Entitlement to Maritime Zones and Their Delimitation: In the Doldrums of Uncertainty and Unpredictability' in Alex G Oude Elferink, T Henriksen and SV Busch (eds), *Maritime Boundary Delimitation: The Case Law Is It consistent and Practicable?* (Cambridge University Press, 2018) 74–75.

[64] CG Lathrop, 'The Provisional Equidistance Line: Charting a Course between Objectivity and Subjectivity?' in ibid, 206.

[65] Weil, *Perspective du droit de la délimitation maritime*, 53 and 86.

[66] Marques Antunes and Becker-Weinberg, 'Entitlement to Maritime Zones and Their Delimitation' 81.

If the equidistance line is to be drawn at the first stage of the delimitation, however, this does not consecrate the equidistance line as an end product. As the delimitation should be effected in order to reach an equitable result, the equitable character of the delimitation needs to be examined in each and every case, taking account of multiple factors. Thus, the consideration of relevant circumstances becomes essential.

7

Flexibility in the Law of Maritime Delimitation I: Geographical Factors

I. INTRODUCTION

REGARDING THE REQUIREMENTS of flexibility, we will now examine the principal factors considered in maritime delimitations. The relevant factors to be examined are divided into two groups: geographical and non-geographical factors. In relation to the former, eight elements must be examined: configurations of coasts, proportionality, presence of islands, baselines, geological and geomorphological considerations, presence of third States, the position of land boundaries and drift ice. Regarding non-geographical factors, the seven elements to be considered are: economic factors, the conduct of parties, historic rights, security considerations, navigation, environmental factors and cultural factors. Although the above may not be a complete list, these elements are the principal factors discussed before international courts and tribunals. Thus, they will furnish sufficient material to analyse attitudes of the courts and of States concerning the main factors in maritime delimitation.[1]

II. CONFIGURATION OF THE COAST

It is beyond question that geographical factors play an important role in maritime delimitations.[2] The first geographical factor to be considered is the configuration of the coast. In this regard, three elements must be

[1] Our analysis is mainly based on data included in the seven volumes of the *International Maritime Boundaries* published by the American Society of International Law (hereafter *IMB*). With respect to recent agreements, other sources were also used, such as the *Law of the Sea Bulletin*, *International Legal Materials* and current developments as presented by the *International Journal of Marine and Coastal Law*.

[2] The case law has clearly stressed the importance of geographical factors. See [1969] ICJ Rep 53–54, [101]; [1982] ICJ Rep 82, [114]; The *Anglo-French Continental Shelf* arbitral award, (1980) 18 *RIAA*, 51, [84]. See also 57, [97]; [1985] ICJ Rep 57, [79]; [1984] ICJ Rep 327, [195]; the *Guinea/Guinea-Bissau* arbitral award, (1986) 25 *ILM* 293 [98]; the *St Pierre and Miquelon* arbitral award, (1992) 31 *ILM* 1160, [24]. For general considerations concerning geographical factors, see P Weil, ‘Geographic Considerations in Maritime Delimitation’ in *IMB*, vol I, 115–30.

examined: opposite or adjacent coasts, concavity or convexity of coasts and the general direction of coastlines.

A. Opposite or Adjacent Coasts

i. Analysis of the Case Law

In the early jurisprudence, international courts and tribunals have attached great importance to the distinction between opposite and adjacent coasts when evaluating the appropriateness of the equidistance method. For instance, the Court of Arbitration, in the *Anglo-French Continental Shelf* case, stated that:

> [I]n appreciating the appropriateness of the equidistance method as a means of achieving an equitable solution, regard must be had to the difference between a 'lateral' boundary between 'adjacent' States and a 'median' boundary between 'opposite' States.[3]

A reason for this distinction may consist in the fact that, according to the courts, the risks of inequity arising from the equidistance method are different between opposite and adjacent coasts. On this point, the ICJ in the *North Sea Continental Shelf* cases held that:

> [W]hereas a median line divides equally between the two opposite countries areas that can be regarded as being the natural prolongation of the territory of each of them, a lateral equidistance line often leaves to one of the States concerned areas that are a natural prolongation of the territory of the other.[4]

This *dictum* was echoed by the ICJ in the *Libya/Malta* case. In the words of the Court,

> [I]t is well to recall the precise reason why the Court in its 1969 Judgment contrasted the effect of an equidistance line between opposite coasts and the effect between adjacent coasts. In the latter situation, any distorting effect of a salient feature might well extend and increase through the entire course of the boundary; whilst in the former situation, the influence of one feature is normally quickly succeeded and corrected by the influence of another, as the course of the line proceeds between more or less parallel coasts.[5]

However, this dichotomy is not always free from difficulties.

First, in some cases, the distinction between opposite and adjacent coasts is not obvious. Rather, as confirmed in international decisions, the relation between coasts is, in reality, often hybrid.[6] In the *Anglo-French*

[3] The *Anglo-French Continental Shelf* arbitral award, 18 *RIAA* 57, [97].
[4] *The North Sea Continental Shelf* cases, [1969] ICJ Rep 37, [58].
[5] The *Libya/Malta* case, [1985] ICJ Rep 51, [70].
[6] P Weil, *Perspective du droit de la délimitation maritime* (Paris, Pedone, 1988) 261; MD Evans, *Relevant Circumstances and Maritime Delimitation* (Oxford, Clarendon Press, 1989) 124.

Continental Shelf award, for instance, the Court of Arbitration regarded the Atlantic region as a situation of adjacent coasts, while in the English Channel region there was considered to be a relationship of opposite coasts. In the *Tunisia/Libya* case, the Tunisian coast transformed the relationship between Libya and Tunisia from one of adjacency to one of oppositeness. In the *Gulf of Maine* case, the configuration of coasts presented a hybrid nature of adjacent (the first and third sectors) and opposite (the second sector) coasts. In the *Guinea/Guinea-Bissau* case, Guinea-Bissau contended that, to a certain extent, the two States were situated opposite each other, while Guinea saw them as adjacent States. On this point, the Arbitral Tribunal accepted that the two States had coasts which were partially adjacent and partially opposite each other.[7] The *St Pierre and Miquelon* case might provide another example of a situation where it was doubtful whether the coasts were opposite or adjacent. Since there is no objective criterion to draw the distinction between adjacency and oppositeness, there may be differences of opinion concerning the interpretation of the relationship between the relevant coasts.

Secondly, the coasts of a State may comprise a segment which is adjacent to its neighbouring State's coast, and another segment which is opposite another neighbour's coasts which are in issue. Accordingly, in following the above dichotomy, different approaches toward equitable principles will be applicable to the same State according to the sections of its coasts. The ICJ, in the *Jan Mayen* case, appears to follow that line of argument, by stating that:

> In the particular case of maritime delimitation, international law does not prescribe, with a view to reaching an equitable solution, the adoption of a single method for the delimitation of the maritime spaces on all sides of an island, or for the whole of the coastal front of a particular State, rather than, if desired, varying systems of delimitation for the various parts of the coasts.[8]

Yet such a view runs the risk of impeding the unity of the law of maritime delimitation. As discussed in chapter five, presently there is a clear trend that international courts and tribunal apply the three-stage approach to maritime delimitations regardless of the configuration of the coasts.[9] Therefore it can be said that the importance of the distinction between opposite and adjacent coasts has been reduced in the case law.[10]

ii. Analysis of State Practice

As pointed out in chapter six, State practice tends to distinguish between opposite and adjacent coasts. The oppositeness or adjacency of the coasts has had

[7] The *Guinea/Guinea-Bissau* arbitral award, (1986) 25 *ILM* 290, [91].

[8] [1993] ICJ Rep 77, [86].

[9] See ch 5, s XIX of this book. See also Y Tanaka, 'Reflections on Maritime Delimitation in the *Qatar/Bahrain* Case' (2003) 52 *ICLQ* 76.

[10] See also R Kolb, *Case Law on Equitable Maritime Delimitation: Digest and Commentaries* (The Hague, Brill/Nijhoff, 2003) 548.

an important bearing upon the choice of the method of delimitation. The distinction between oppositeness and adjacency is, however, often a matter of degree. Accordingly, as in the case law, there is room for doubting whether, in concluding an agreement regarding maritime delimitation, the dichotomy in question will always provide an adequate criterion for determining the method of delimitation.

B. Concave or Convex Coasts

i. Analysis of the Case Law

Since the *North Sea Continental Shelf* cases, it has been argued that the concavity or convexity of coasts constitutes a relevant circumstance. In those cases, the ICJ has regarded the equidistance method as inequitable where coasts are concave on account of the distorting effect produced by that method (see Illustration 3). It stated that:

> [W]here two such lines are drawn at different points on a concave coast, they will, if the curvature is pronounced, inevitably meet at a relatively short distance from the coast, thus causing the continental shelf they enclose to take the form approximately of a triangle with its apex to seaward and, as it was put on behalf of the Federal Republic, 'cutting off' the coastal State from the further areas of the continental shelf outside of and beyond this triangle.[11]

The Court in the *Libya/Malta* case echoed this view by stating that the equidistance line 'may yield a disproportionate result where a coast is markedly irregular or markedly concave or convex.'[12]

In the context of single maritime boundaries, the concavity or convexity of coasts played, once again, an important role in the *Guinea/Guinea-Bissau* case. In that case, there was concavity of the coastline from Guinea-Bissau and Sierra Leone, and this affected Guinea. In the view of the Arbitral Tribunal,

> When … there are three adjacent States along a concave coastline, the equidistance method has the other drawback of resulting in the middle country being enclaved by the other two and thus prevented from extending its maritime territory as far seaward as international law permits.[13]

[11] [1969] ICJ Rep 17, [8]. However, some members of the Court questioned this view. For instance, Judge Tanaka refused to accept concavity as a special circumstances for three reasons. First, there is no lack of examples where a large State has gotten a very small portion of continental shelf because of a special geographical configuration. Secondly, the smallness of the area attributed to the FRG was not only the result of the two equidistance lines, but also of relationships between other States, such as the Denmark and Norway, the Netherlands and Belgium and the United Kingdom. Thirdly, the above view of the Court would be the equivalent of accepting the idea of a just and equitable share, which was rejected by the Court itself. Dissenting Opinion of Judge Tanaka, ibid, 189. Judges Lachs and Sørensen also refused to accept the majority opinion in this matter. Dissenting Opinion of Judge Lachs, ibid, 239; Dissenting Opinion of Judge Sørensen, ibid, 255.

[12] [1985] ICJ Rep 44, [56]. See also, 51, [70].

[13] The *Guinea/Guinea-Bissau* arbitral award, (1986) 25 *ILM* 295, [104].

The Tribunal accordingly rejected the equidistance method and adopted the 'limite sud' referred to in the final paragraph of Article 1 of the 1886 Convention.[14]

In the *Cameroon v Nigeria* dispute, Cameroon contended that the concavity of the Gulf of Guinea in general and of Cameroon's coastline in particular constituted special circumstances to be taken into account.[15] Although the Court did not deny that the concavity of the coast may be a relevant circumstance, it stressed that: '[T]his can only be the case when such concavity lies within the area to be delimited.'[16] In the Court's view, the concavity of Cameroon's coastline is apparent primarily in the sector where it faces Equatorial Guinea's territory of Bioko. Yet this area is not relevant to the maritime delimitation of the present case. The sectors of coastline relevant to the present delimitation exhibit no particular concavity. Consequently, the Court rejected the fact that the configuration of the coasts represented a relevant circumstance in the present case.[17]

Subsequently, ITLOS, in the *Bangladesh/Myanmar* case, elaborated the effect of concavity or convexity of coasts on maritime delimitation. According to the Tribunal, a cut-off effect arising from concavity of the coast, not concavity per se, constitutes a relevant circumstance. In the words of the Tribunal,

> in the delimitation of the exclusive economic zone and the continental shelf, concavity *per se* is not necessarily a relevant circumstance. However, when an equidistance line drawn between two States produces a cut-off effect on the maritime entitlement of one of those States, as a result of the concavity of the coast, then an adjustment of that line may be necessary in order to reach an equitable result.[18]

Given that the coast of Bangladesh is 'manifestly concave',[19] ITLOS considered that the provisional equidistance line produces a cut-off effect on the maritime projection of Bangladesh.[20] It thus found that the concavity of the coast of Bangladesh is a relevant circumstance requiring an adjustment of the provisional equidistance line.[21]

[14] ibid, 298, [111].

[15] [2002] ICJ Rep 445, [296]. Memorial of Cameroon, 545, [5.98]; 549, [5.110]; reply of Cameroon, 403–9, [9.54–9.60]; presentation by Professor Kamto, Counsel of Cameroon, Verbatim Record, CR 2002/6, 39–41, [41–45]; presentation by Professor Mendelson, Counsel of Cameroon, Verbatim Record, CR 2002/6, 46–49, [5–10]; presentation by Professor Cot, Counsel of Cameroon, Verbatim Record, CR 2002/22, 28–29, [5–9]; presentation by Professor Kamto, Counsel of Cameroon, Verbatim Record, CR 2002/17, 56–58, [37–39]. Yet Nigeria contested that the Court's task was not to compensate Cameroon for any disadvantages suffered by it as a direct consequence of the geography of the area. See Judgment, the *Cameroon v Nigeria* case, [2002] ICJ Rep 445, [296]; Counter-Memorial of Nigeria, 575–81, [21.14–21.23].

[16] [2002] ICJ Rep 445, [297].

[17] ibid, 445–46, [297].

[18] [2012] ITLOS Rep 81, [292]. This *dictum* was confirmed by ITLOS Special Chamber in the *Ghana/Côte d'Ivoire* case. *Dispute Concerning Delimitation of the Maritime Boundary between Ghana and Côte d'Ivoire in the Atlantic Ocean (Ghana/Côte d'Ivoire)*, Judgment of 23 September 2017, [2017] ITLOS Rep (not yet reported), [421].

[19] [2012] ITLOS Rep 81, [291].

[20] ibid, [293].

[21] ibid, 82. [297].

The *dictum* of the *Bangladesh/Myanmar* judgment was amplified by the Annex VII Arbitral Tribunal in the *Bangladesh v India* case.[22] In this case, a question arose whether the concavity of the coast of Bangladesh constituted a relevant circumstance warranting an adjustment of the provisional equidistance line.[23] According to the Arbitral Tribunal, 'the existence of a cut-off effect should be established on objective basis and in a transparent manner.'[24] In this connection, the Tribunal specified two criteria to warrant adjustment of the provisional equidistance line in light of a cut-off effect:

> First, the line must prevent a coastal State from extending its maritime boundary as far seaward as international law permits. Second, the line must be such that – if not adjusted – it would fail to achieve the equitable solution required by articles 74 and 83 of the Convention. This requires an assessment of where the disadvantage of the cut-off materializes and of its seriousness.[25]

Yet, the Tribunal offered scant explanation with regard to the standard to decide the 'seriousness' of a cut-off effect. Accordingly, it may have to be admitted that 'seriousness' of a cut-off effect is a matter of subjective appreciation. In any event, in light of a cut-off effect arising from concavity of the coast of Bangladesh, the Arbitral Tribunal adjusted the provisional equidistance line in order to avoid an unreasonable cut-off effect to the detriment of Bangladesh.[26]

In the *Croatia/Slovenia* case, Slovenia claimed that the concave nature of its coast constituted a special circumstance under Article 15 of the LOSC.[27] However, Croatia countered that concavity had no legal significance in the territorial sea delimitation pursuant to Article 15.[28] As explained earlier, the Arbitral Tribunal shifted the equidistance line in order to attenuate the 'boxing-in' or 'cut-off effect' that results from the geographic configuration.[29] However, the 'boxing-in' or 'cut-off effect' seemed to derive from the configuration of the Croatian coast line of Cape Savudrija,[30] not the concavity of the Slovenian coast.

Finally, the *Ghana/Côte d'Ivoire* case must be examined. After having confirmed the *dicta* of the *Bangladesh/Myanmar* judgment and the *Bangladesh v India* judgment,[31] the ITLOS Special Chamber held that:

> [T]he existence of a cut-off effect should be established on *an objective basis* and that the decision as to the existence of a cut-off effect must take into account the relevant area in which competing claims have been made.[32]

[22] The *Bangladesh v India* arbitral award, [402].
[23] ibid, [400].
[24] ibid, [404].
[25] ibid, [417].
[26] See ch 5, s XV of this book.
[27] The *Croatia/Slovenia* arbitral award, [970].
[28] ibid, [974].
[29] See ch 5, s XVI of this book.
[30] The *Croatia/Slovenia* arbitral award, [1014].
[31] The *Ghana/Côte d'Ivoire* case, [2017] ITLOS Rep [421–22].
[32] Emphasis added. ibid, [423].

The *dictum* is similar to that of the *Bangladesh v India* arbitral award quoted above. However, the Chamber offered no further detail respecting the 'objective basis'. While the Special Chamber accepted that the coast of Côte d'Ivoire is concave, it considered that: '[T]he cut-off effect to the detriment of Côte d'Ivoire is in itself not so *significant* as to require adjustment of the provisional equidistance line.'[33] An issue that arises in this regard is how it is possible to judge the degree of 'significance' of the cut-off effect. In this connection, the Chamber noted that: '[T]he cut-off effect only comes into being at a distance of approximately 163 nm from BP 55+ along the provisional equidistance line.'[34] Following the Chamber's view, there may be scope for arguing that if concavity of the coasts would affect only a short segment of the provisional equidistance line, the cut-off effect is not considered as significant. If this is the case, arguably the scope of the provisional equidistance line that would be affected by the cut-off effect may provide a criterion to judge whether that effect is significant as to require adjustment of the provisional equidistance line. In any event, the Chamber also considered that: '[A]djusting the provisional equidistance line for the benefit of Côte d'Ivoire and to the detriment of Ghana would in fact cut off the seaward projection of the coast of Ghana.'[35] Therefore the Chamber did not regard concavity of the Côte d'Ivoire's coast as a relevant circumstance requiring adjustment of the provisional equidistance line. In summary, one can argue that when an equidistance line produces a cut-off effect as a result of the concavity of the coast, the coastal configuration of concavity constitutes a relevant circumstance. In this connection, three points must be noted.

The first lies in the difficulty of defining concavity and convexity of the coast. The following paragraph of the *Guinea/Guinea-Bissau* award typically presents this difficulty:

> If the coasts of each country are examined separately, it can be seen that the Guinea-Bissau coastline is convex, when the Bijagos are taken into account, and that that of Guinea is concave. However, if they are considered together, it can be seen that the coastline of both countries is concave and this characteristic is accentuated if we consider the presence of Sierra Leone further south.[36]

This statement suggests that the evaluation of concavity or convexity is up to the courts. In considering the configuration of the coast, various interpretations may be possible according to the scale of the map or micro- or macro-geography, ie, the question of whether coasts of third neighbouring States will be taken into account in appreciating the configuration of the coasts concerned.[37]

[33] ibid, [425].
[34] ibid, [426]. See also [424].
[35] ibid.
[36] The *Guinea/Guinea-Bissau* arbitral award, (1986) 25 *ILM* 294–95, [103].
[37] In this connection, the ICJ held in the *Tunisia/Libya* case: 'the relative importance of a geographical feature, and judgment whether it constitutes a norm or an exception, may vary – or appear to

Thus, international tribunals may exercise large discretion in this matter but thereby run the risk of subjectivity.

Secondly, under the corrective-equity approach or three-stage approach, it is possible to remedy the distorting effect at the second stage of the delimitation process in order to achieve an equitable result. It appears thus that the concavity of the coast alone may not be a decisive reason to reject the equidistance method at the first stage of maritime delimitation.

Thirdly, there is no established standard to judge 'seriousness' or 'significance' of cut-off effects in the jurisprudence concerning maritime delimitation. Following the *dictum* of the ITLOS Special Chamber in the *Ghana/Côte d'Ivoire* case, the extent of the provisional equidistance line affected by the cut-off effect may provide a criterion to decide 'seriousness' or 'significance' of cut-off effects.

ii. Analysis of State Practice

In State practice, it is difficult to evaluate the effect of the concavity or convexity of coasts upon the delimitation process. In fact, there are only some instances in which this factor was explicitly considered. As a relatively clear example, one may mention the 1987 agreement establishing a single maritime boundary between Dominica and the French territory of Guadeloupe and Martinique. In this case, the Dominican coast toward the Atlantic Ocean turns concave, sandwiched as it is between the French islands of Marie-Galante and Guadeloupe, on the one hand, and Martinique, on the other. Accordingly, as in the cases of the *North Sea Continental Shelf*, two equidistance lines would enclose Dominica's EEZ within a triangle which would extend less than 55 miles east of the island. With a view to avoiding this result, in the 1987 Agreement, the Parties drew *quasi*-parallel lines to points 8 and 9, giving each party a full 200-mile seaward extension.[38] The issue of concavity also arose in the delimitation between Monaco and the French Republic. The very short coast of Monaco enclosed by the coasts of France and, to a minor extent of Italy, is concave. Were 12-mile equidistance lines be drawn for the territorial sea of France, they would intersect less than 12 miles from Monaco, forming a small triangle. Thus, the 1984 Agreement between the Parties established a full 12-mile limit corridor for Monaco. Furthermore, the corridor extends beyond the 12-mile limit in order to give Monaco a continental shelf.[39]

In other cases, however, the effect of the concavity or convexity of coasts is less clear.[40] An explanation may be that, as pointed out above, the coastal

vary – according to the cartographic scale employed, and according to whether the observer contemplates such feature in a much wider context or concentrates upon it in its immediate surroundings.' [1982] ICJ Rep 34, [17]. Several writers also highlighted this point. Weil, *Perspective du droit de la délimitation maritime*, 236; Evans, *Relevant Circumstances and Maritime Delimitation*, 129.

[38] See Report by Nweihed in Charney and Alexander in *IMB*, vol I, 709.

[39] Report by Scovazzi and Francalanci in ibid, 1584.

[40] Weil, 'Geographic Considerations in Maritime Delimitation' 129.

configuration is, in itself, hard to determine. Furthermore, even when this factor appears to have been considered, it is probable that other factors contributed to the establishment of a non-equidistance line.[41] Thus, although there are some agreements which have taken this factor into account in the course of the negotiations, a specific conclusion on this matter should be postponed.

C. General Direction of the Coast

i. Analysis of the Case Law

The general direction of the coast is closely linked to two methods of maritime delimitation: the perpendicular method and the bisector method.

a. The Establishment of a Line Perpendicular to the Coast

Concerning the inter-relationship between the general direction of the coast and the perpendicular method, three cases must be examined. First, in the *Tunisia/Libya* case, the ICJ ruled that a line perpendicular to the coast was relevant for determining the location of a delimitation line.[42] It considered that any margin of disagreement relating to the perpendicularity to the 'general direction' of the coast would centre around the 26° *de facto* line. Yet no specific line of the general direction of the coast was identified.

Secondly, in the *Gulf of Maine* case, the United States proposed the 'adjusted perpendicular' method. The core of the US argument was the idea of representing the general direction of the coast by a continuous horizontal line formed by the coasts designated as the principal coasts of Maine and New Brunswick. According to the United States, first, the line perpendicular to the general direction of the coast should be drawn at point A. Next, the line would be adjusted in order to leave Canada the two fishing banks (German Bank and Browns Bank) and to award Georges Bank to the United States.[43] On the one hand, the Chamber of the ICJ discarded this proposal. In its view, an essential condition for using the proposed method was that the territories of the two States form a more or less rectilinear coast.[44] In the present case, however, this condition was absent, for the starting point of the line was situated in one of

[41] For instance, Weil asserts that in the 1974 Agreement between France and Spain relating to the delimitation of the continental shelf, the concavity of the French coast was certainly a relevant factor. ibid. As will be shown later, however, the Agreement considered proportionality in establishing the boundary of the continental shelf. Thus, it is not evident to what extent the concavity had an impact upon the location of the boundary.

[42] [1982] ICJ Rep 85, [120]. In that case, the Court confined its attention to the sea-bed area which was closer to the coast at Ras Ajdir, disregarding the Island of Jerba.

[43] [1984] ICJ Rep 318–19, [170–72].

[44] ibid, 320, [176].

the angles of the rectangle in which the delimitation was to be effected. The Chamber found that such a situation could not be remedied by the abstract concept of the 'general direction' of the coast, since 'the real geographical configuration differs so markedly from such general direction'.[45] On the other hand, the Chamber established, in the third segment of the single maritime boundary, a line perpendicular to the closing line of the Gulf. In so doing, the Chamber pointed out that: 'The direction of the closing line of the Gulf, with which that line would form a right angle, corresponds generally to the direction of the coastline at the back of the Gulf, and it will be recalled that the United States had proposed …, a perpendicular to the direction of that coast.'[46] Nonetheless, the revival of the idea of the general direction of the coast is hard to reconcile with the preceding rejection of the argument of the United States.

Thirdly, the most dramatic impact of the general direction of the coast may be found in the *Guinea/Guinea-Bissau* case. In that case, the Arbitral Tribunal drew a line *grosso modo* perpendicular to the general direction of the coastline joining Pointe des Almadies (Senegal) and Cape Schilling (Sierra Leone), arguing that the overall configuration of the West African coastline should be taken into account.[47] The point to be noted is that, when specifying the general direction of the coasts, the Arbitral Tribunal selected two points located in third States, and that it rejected a line joining two points on the territory of the Parties, ie, the line between Cap Roxo and Pointe Sallatouk.[48] It expressly referred to the need to take into account the present and future delimitations in West Africa as a whole. It thus ruled that:

> In order for the delimitation between the two Guineas to be suitable for equitable integration into the existing delimitations of the West African region, as well as into future delimitations which would be reasonable to imagine from a consideration of equitable principles and the most likely assumptions, it is necessary to consider how all these delimitations fit in with the general configuration of the West African coastline, and what deductions should be drawn from this in relation to the precise area concerned in the present delimitation.[49]

In so doing, the Tribunal relied on a macro-geographic perspective. The Tribunal's reliance on macro-geography is open to objection, however. In fact, the line connecting Pointe des Almadies and Cape Schilling cuts almost all the coast of Guinea-Bissau for nearly 350 km and runs approximately 70 km inside of the latter's territory.[50] The line selected by the Court is clearly unfavourable to

[45] ibid.

[46] ibid, 338, [225]. On this point, see the criticism by Judge Gros in his dissenting opinion. ibid, 379–80, [32].

[47] The *Guinea/Guinea-Bissau* arbitral award, (1986) 25 *ILM* 298, [111].

[48] ibid, 297–98, [109–10] See Illustration 11 of this book.

[49] ibid, 297, [109].

[50] In the *Tunisia/Libya* case, Judge Evensen criticised the general direction of the Tunisian coast as determined by the majority on the grounds that it was drawn inland, some 11 kilometres from

Guinea-Bissau. On this point, the Arbitral Tribunal might have given the impression of refashioning nature, something that was rejected in other cases.[51]

b. The Application of the Angle-bisector Method

The general direction of the coasts needs to be identified when applying the bisector method. Unlike the equidistance method, this method relies on the macro-geography of a coastline as represented by a line drawn between two points on the coast. As explained earlier, the ICJ applied this method in the *Nicaragua v Honduras* case.[52] After the examination of multiple options for selecting the relevant coastal front,[53] the Court ruled that a Honduran coastal front running to Punta Patuca and a Nicaraguan coastal front running to Wouhnta were the relevant coasts for the purposes of drawing the bisector.[54] Given that the coastlines of Nicaragua and Honduras are unstable, however, the line connecting two points on the coast is also subject to change with the passage of time. If this is the case, the question arises why a current bisector line between the general directions of two coastlines remains reasonable regardless of the change of coastlines, while an equidistance line so constructed today suddenly becomes unreasonable in the future.

In summary, a deficiency of the angle-bisector method is that it lacks a scientific means for identifying the general direction of coastlines.[55] In this connection, the statement of the Annex VII Arbitral Tribunal in the *Bangladesh v India* case deserves quoting:

> In the view of the Tribunal, the advantage of the equidistance/relevant circumstances method lies in the fact that it clearly separates the steps to be taken and is thus more transparent. The identification of a provisional equidistance line is based on geometrically objective criteria, while at the same time account is taken of the geography of the area through the selection of appropriate base points. By contrast, depicting the relevant coasts as straight lines under the angle-bisector method involves subjective

the actual sea-coast. Judge Evensen regarded this as a refashioning of nature. Dissenting Opinion of Judge Evensen, [1982] ICJ Rep 303, [19]. Considering that in the *Guinea/Guinea-Bissau* case, the line of general direction of the coast departed more radically from the actual sea-coast, the problem of the refashioning of nature is more serious than in the *Tunisia/Libya* case. On this point, see E David, 'La sentence arbitrale du 14 février 1985 sur la délimitation de la frontière maritime Guinée-Ginée Bissau' (1985) 31 *AFDI* 385.

[51] ibid. Weil also criticises this as arbitrary. Weil, *Perspective du droit de la délimitation maritime*, 238–39.

[52] See ch 5, s X of this book.

[53] [2007] ICJ Rep 82, [295–97].

[54] ibid, 81, [298].

[55] M Pratt, 'Commentary: Case Concerning Territorial and Maritime Dispute between Nicaragua and Honduras in the Caribbean Sea (Nicaragua v Honduras,' (2007) 2 *Hague Justice Journal*, 38; Y Tanaka, 'Reflections on Maritime Delimitation in the *Nicaragua/Honduras* Case' (2008) 68 *ZaöRV/Heidelberg Journal of International Law* 932–33; S Fietta and R Cleverly, *A Practitioner's Guide to Maritime Boundary Delimitation* (Oxford University Press Oxford 2016) 101.

considerations. As the present case demonstrates, there may be more than one way of depicting the relevant coast with straight lines.[56]

It thus clearly supported the application of the equidistance/relevant circumstances method, unless there are factors which make the application of the equidistance method inappropriate.[57] In reality, it is rare that such factors exist. Indeed, apart from the *Nicaragua v Honduras* case, there is no case that applied the angle-bisector method to maritime delimitations in the jurisprudence.

ii. Analysis of State Practice

In State practice, there are only a few agreements creating lines perpendicular to the general direction of the coast. One available example is the 1972 Agreement between Brazil and Uruguay,[58] in which the Parties established a single maritime boundary consisting of a rhumb line nearly perpendicular to the general direction of the coast. Another example is the 1976 Agreement between Portugal and Spain. The two territorial sea boundaries established by the Agreement were approximately perpendicular to the general direction of the coasts.[59] Experience shows that, owing to the difficulty of defining the general direction of the coast, the method of the perpendicular tends to be adopted where a coastline is simple and straight.[60]

D. Summary

The above considerations seem to reveal three conclusions.

First, in the case law, the configuration of the coast is always subject to interpretation by the international courts and tribunals. Owing to the infinite variety of configurations, however, it is on occasion difficult to distinguish between opposite and adjacent, or concave and convex coastlines. The identification of the general direction of the coast is difficult as well. On this point, there is room for subjectivity.[61]

Secondly, the real issue is not the configuration of the coast per se, but its impact upon the maritime delimitation. As has been seem, it is well established in the jurisprudence that normally the equidistance method is to be applied at

[56] The *Bangladesh v India* arbitral award, [343].

[57] ibid, [345].

[58] Report by Jiménez de Aréchaga in *IMB*, vol I, 788. A rhumb line (or a loxodrome line) is a true straight line on a Mercator chart. *A Manual on Technical Aspects of the United Nations Convention on the Law of the Sea-1982, Special Publication No. 51*, 4th edn (Monaco, International Hydrographic Bureau, 2006) [3.9.3].

[59] Report by Anderson, ibid, vol II, 1794.

[60] L Legault and B Hankey, 'Method, Oppositeness and Adjacency, and Proportionality in Maritime Boundary Delimitation' in Charney and Alexander in *IMB*, vol I, 213.

[61] Weil, *Perspective du droit de la délimitation maritime*, 239. See also 264.

the first stage of maritime delimitation. One can argue that the adjacency and concavity of the coasts cannot provide the legal basis for rejecting the equidistance method at the first stage of maritime delimitation in the jurisprudence.

Thirdly, State practice appears to suggest that to a certain extent, the distinction between oppositeness and adjacency of the coasts may affect the choice of the method of delimitation. Even so, it is not decisive since the dichotomy is often a matter of degree. Likewise, the impact of the concavity or convexity of coasts on the process of maritime delimitation is obscure in State practice. Overall it would be fair to say that in State practice, the configuration of the coast does not provide an adequate criterion for determining the method of delimitation.

III. PROPORTIONALITY

The concept of (dis)proportionality holds an important position in the case law, having been taken into account in almost every judgment on maritime delimitation.[62] The concept of (dis)proportionality in the law of maritime delimitation has been elaborated through the jurisprudence. In a broad perspective, this process can be divided into two phases. A first phase is devoted to the emergence and development of the concept of (dis)proportionality and the second phase concerns the establishment of the (dis)proportionality test as an *ex post facto* test at the third stage of maritime delimitation.[63]

A. Analysis of the Case Law

i. The First Phase (1969–2007): Development of the Concept of Proportionality in the Jurisprudence Concerning Maritime Delimitation

a. Emergence of the Concept of (Dis)proportionality

The concept of proportionality in maritime delimitations was originally formulated by the Federal Republic of Germany (FRG) in the *North Sea Continental Shelf* cases. The FRG contended that each State concerned should

[62] As early as 1946, Sir Francis Vallat suggested an idea of proportionality in the context of a bay by saying that: 'where a bay or gulf is bounded by several states …, the most equitable solution would be to divide the submarine area outside the territorial waters among the contiguous states in proportion to the length of their coastline.' Sir Francis Vallat, 'The Continental Shelf' (1946) 23 *BYIL* 336.

[63] In the early cases concerning maritime delimitations, the terminology of 'proportionality' or 'disproportionality' has not been used consistently. In principle, this chapter will follow the terminology adopted in each decision. For an analysis of the jurisprudence concerning (dis)proportionality by the author, see also Y Tanaka, 'Reflections on the Concept of Proportionality in the Law of Maritime Delimitation' (2001) 16 *IJMCL* 433–63; Y Tanaka, 'Disproportionality Test' in Alex G Oude Elferink, T Henriksen, and SV Busch (eds), *Maritime Boundary Delimitation: The Case Law Is It Consistent and Predictable?* (Cambridge University Press, 2018) 291–318.

receive a 'just and equitable share' of the available continental shelf, proportionate to the length of its coastline or sea-frontage.[64] According to the FRG, '[t]he breadth of the coastal front of each State facing the North Sea is an appropriate objective standard of evaluation with respect to the equitableness of a proposed boundary'.[65] Although the ICJ rejected the idea of a 'just and equitable share', it held that:

> [I]n the present case there are three States whose North Sea coastlines are in fact comparable in length and which, therefore, have been given broadly equal treatment by nature except that the configuration of one of the coastlines would, if the equidistance method is used, deny to one of these States treatment equal or comparable to that given the other two. ... What is unacceptable in this instance is that a state should enjoy continental shelf rights considerably different from those of its neighbours merely because in the one case the coastline is roughly convex in form and in the other it is markedly concave, *although those coastlines are comparable in length*.[66]

Thus it did accept the concept of proportionality as a final factor to be taken into account:

> A final factor to be taken account of is the element of a reasonable degree of proportionality which a delimitation effected according to equitable principles ought to bring about between the extent of the continental shelf appertaining to the States concerned and the lengths of their respective coastlines – these being measured according to their general direction *in order to establish the necessary balance between States with straight, and those with markedly concave or convex coasts, or to reduce very irregular coastlines to their truer proportions*.[67]

The *dicta* in the *North Sea Continental Shelf* judgment suggest three geographical features which justified the recourse to proportionality: (i) the coasts of the three States concerned were adjacent to each other; (ii) the coastlines of the FRG were concave; and (iii) the coastlines of the three States abutting on the North Sea were comparable in length (see Illustration 3). In cases where concavity or convexity exists in adjacent coasts that are comparable in length, a distorting effect would be produced by the application of the equidistance method. For the Court, such a result was unacceptable.[68] As Higgins rightly observed, it was in this particular geographical situation that proportionality came into play.[69]

[64] [1969] ICJ Rep 20, [15].

[65] Reply of the Federal Republic of Germany, 433, [99]. Professor Oda, Counsel for the FRG, called the idea 'the façade approach'. Verbatim Record 1968, Pleadings, vol II, 62–63; see also Reply of Professor Oda, ibid, 195–96.

[66] Emphasis added. ibid, 50, [91].

[67] Emphasis added. Judgment, [1969] ICJ Rep 52, [98]. Judge *ad hoc* Sørensen refused to accept the concept of proportionality on the ground that it lacked any basis in law. Dissenting Opinion of Judge Sørensen, ibid, 255.

[68] Judgment, ibid, 50, [91].

[69] R Higgins, *Problems and Process: International Law and How We Use It* (Clarendon Press Oxford 1994) 229. See also R Ida, 'The Role of Proportionality in Maritime Delimitation Revisited: The Origin and Meaning of the Principle from the Early Decisions of the Court' in N Ando et al (eds), *Liber Amicorum Judge Shigeru Oda* (Kluwer The Hague 2002) 1039; Kolb, *Case Law on*

In this regard, Judge Oda, who advocated the concept of proportionality as Counsel for Germany in *North Sea Continental Shelf*, stated that:

> [W]hat the Court intended to say in 1969 was that in such specific circumstances, in which the States concerned were located as adjacent States in similar situations, but where the existence of a marked concave or convex coastline produced a somewhat distorting effect, the proportion of the length of the coast as rectified by its general direction ... was in principle useful in the verification of geographical equity ....[70]

The learned Judge further stated that:

> The 1969 Judgment nowhere implied the possibility of generally applying the concept of proportionality in other cases, particularly in cases of delimitation between opposite States.[71]

In interpreting the *North Sea Continental Shelf* judgment, Bowett also argued that:

> Indeed, it would seem that the proportionality factor might only be applied, or be meaningful, in the case of adjacent States (not 'opposite') where the existence of a markedly concave or convex coastline will produce a cut-off effect if the equidistance principle is applied.[72]

It must also be noted that in the *North Sea Continental Shelf* judgment, proportionality was suggested merely as a final factor to be taken into account in the course of the negotiations between the three States concerned. Overall there may be room for the view that originally the role of proportionality was limited to a particular geographical situation, even though the paragraphs of the judgment concerning proportionality seemed to be formulated in somewhat general terms.

The above considerations were confirmed in the 1977 *Anglo-French Continental Shelf* arbitration. In this case, the Court of Arbitration seems to have limited recourse to proportionality in particular geographical situations such as that of the North Sea coast. In this regard, the Court of Arbitration asserted that:

> In particular, this Court does not consider that the adoption in the *North Sea Continental Shelf* cases of the criterion of a reasonable degree of proportionality

Equitable Maritime Delimitation, 257–58; P von Mühlendahl, *L'équidistance dans la délimitation des frontières maritimes: Etude de la jurisprudence internationale* (Paris, Pedone, 2016) 325–26, [512].

[70] Dissenting Opinion of Judge Oda in *Libya/Malta*, [1985] ICJ Rep 134, [18].

[71] ibid, 135, [18]. Judge Oda's view was echoed by Judges Schwebel and Valticos. Dissenting Opinion of Judge Schwebel, ibid, 184; Separate Opinion of Judge Valticos, ibid, 110, [19].

[72] DW Bowett, *The Legal Regime of Islands in International Law* (Oceana Publications New York 1979) 164. Similar views were taken by writers, including: Higgins, *Problems and Process* 229. Jin-Hyun Paik, 'The Role of Proportionality in Maritime Delimitation: State of Jurisprudence' in HP Hestermeyer et al (eds), *Coexistence, Cooperation and Solidarity, Liber Amicorum Rüdiger Wolfrum*, vol I (Nijhoff Leiden 2012), 201. See also Fietta and Cleverly, *A Practitioner's Guide*, 608.

> between the areas of continental shelf and the lengths of the coastlines means that this criterion is one for application in all cases. On the contrary, it was *the particular geographical situation of three adjoining States situated on a concave coast* which gave relevance to that criterion in those cases.[73]

Furthermore, the Court clarified the function of proportionality in two respects.

First, proportionality is regarded as a *criterion* of evaluating the equitableness of equidistance lines. In the words of the Court, '[t]he concept of "proportionality" merely expresses the criterion or factor by which it may be determined whether such a distortion results in an inequitable delimitation of the continental shelf as between the coastal States concerned.'[74] Since proportionality is merely a criterion, it does not constitute an independent source of rights over the continental shelf. This is made clear in the next paragraph of the award:

> Proportionality, therefore, is to be used as a criterion or factor relevant in evaluating the equities of certain geographical situations, not as a general principle providing an independent source of rights to areas of continental shelf.[75]

Secondly, proportionality is a criterion for evaluating *disproportions* in particular geographical situations:

> In short, it is disproportion rather than any general principle of proportionality which is the relevant criterion or factor. [...] there can never be a question of completely refashioning nature, [...]; it is rather a question of remedying the disproportionality and inequitable effects produced by particular geographical configurations or features.[76]

In *Anglo-French Continental Shelf*, proportionality only plays a role in appreciating whether the Scilly Isles are to be considered a 'special circumstance' having distorting effects on the equidistance boundary as between the French Republic and the United Kingdom and, if so, the extent of the adjustment appropriate to abate the inequity.[77]

b. Development of the Concept of Proportionality

A change relating to the concept of proportionality was perceptible in the *Tunisia/Libya* case. The ICJ stated that: '[T]he Court considered that that

[73] Emphasis added. The *Anglo-French Continental Shelf* arbitral award, 18 *RIAA* 57, [99].

[74] ibid, 58, [100]. The Court of Arbitration seems to have linked proportionality to the equidistance method. In fact, it stated that proportionality 'may also appear, and more usually does, as a factor for determining the reasonable or unreasonable – the equitable or inequitable – effects of particular geographical features or configurations upon the course of an equidistance-line boundary.' ibid, 58, [100]. See also 57, [99].

[75] ibid, 58, [101].

[76] ibid. In this case, proportionality came into account only in appreciating whether the Scilly Isles were to be considered a special circumstances having distorting effects on the equidistance line between France and the UK. *Ibid*, 116–17, [250].

[77] ibid, 116–17, [250].

element [of proportionality] is indeed required by the fundamental principle of ensuring an equitable delimitation between the States concerned.'[78] By using the term 'fundamental principle', the Court appeared to highlight proportionality at the level of a general rule. In this judgment, no reference was made to the particular geographical conditions.[79] In fact, although the geographical circumstances were different from those in the *North Sea Continental Shelf* cases,[80] the Court decided to consider the element of proportionality. In so doing, it appeared to discard the rigorous interpretation of that element, which limited its own application to particular geographical circumstances.[81]

In the *Tunisia/Libya* case, the Court saw the role of proportionality as an *ex-post-facto* check of the equitableness of a delimitation line. In applying the test of proportionality, the ICJ made a sophisticated calculation. It held that the ratio between the relevant coastlines of Libya and Tunisia was approximately 31:69. The ratio between the coastal front of Libya, represented by a straight line drawn from Ras Tajoura to Ras Ajdir, and that of Tunisia, represented by straight lines connecting Ras Kaboudia to the most westerly point of the Gulf of Gabes and from that point to Tas Ajdir, was about 34:66.[82] The areas of the continental shelf *below the low-water mark* appertaining to Libya and to Tunisia stood in a proportion of approximately 40:60. The Court, accordingly, found that the result met the requirements of the test of proportionality.[83] Nevertheless, the method used for calculating proportionality cannot escape criticism.

First, while reaffirming that the continental shelf in the legal sense did not comprise the sea-bed areas below the internal and territorial waters,[84] the Court considered these zones as parts of the continental shelf for the purpose of calculating proportionality.[85] It may appear more appropriate to compare the Parties' continental shelves in the legal sense.[86] Indeed, the results of the proportionality

[78] [1982] ICJ Rep 75, [103].

[79] HWA Thirlway, *The Law and Procedure of the International Court of Justice: Fifty Years of Jurisprudence*, vol I (Oxford University Press, 2013), 500.

[80] In the *Tunisia/Libya* case, the coastline of the Parties was neither concave nor comparable to that of the North Sea.

[81] In this respect, Judge Gros stated: 'The present judgment drastically alters the restricted role which properly belongs to the proportionality factor, and the justice of the calculations it employs it not borne out by any of the precautions taken in a delimitation which took account of the proportionality of the areas concerned.' Dissenting Opinion of Judge Gros in the *Tunisia/Libya* case, [1982] ICJ Rep 152, [17]. For a similar view, see the Dissenting Opinion of Judge Evensen, ibid, 314, [23].

[82] ibid, 91, [131]. The judgment, thus, presented two different methods for calculating the coast.

[83] ibid. Yet Ida wonders whether the difference between the relation of 31:69 (length of the coasts) and the relation of 40: 60 (attributed continental shelf) was negligible from the viewpoint of the proportionality. Ida, 'The Role of Proportionality' 1048.

[84] [1982] ICJ Rep 76, [104].

[85] ibid, 91, [131].

[86] Ida, 'The Role of Proportionality,' 1042. Judge Evensen criticised the inclusion of internal and territorial waters into the calculation, as this runs counter to the very concept of the continental shelf, and lacks any basis in law. Dissenting Opinion of Judge Evensen in the *Tunisia/Libya* case, [1982] ICJ Rep 313, [23].

test may be different depending on whether internal and territorial waters are included in the calculation.

Secondly, it is unclear how the coastal lengths and relevant areas were calculated. On this point, the Court stated in a general way that only the coasts of overlapping maritime areas were deemed relevant.[87] In the process of calculation, however, no explanation was given for the fact that the Kerkennah Archipelago was totally disregarded.[88] The question is more complex when considering the presence of third States. As the outer limits of the delimitation area remain indeterminate owing to the existence of third States, the size of the relevant area will change. Thus the result of the proportionality test appears questionable.[89]

The scope of the proportionality test was enlarged again in the *Libya/Malta* case. While the earlier instances related, although not exclusively, to delimitations between adjacent coasts, this case was one where proportionality was applied to a delimitation between States with opposite coasts. In this case, Libya alleged that: 'In the particular geographical situation of this case, the application of equitable principles requires that delimitation should take account of the significant difference in lengths of the respective coastlines which face the area in which the delimitation is to be effected.'[90] However, the Court refused to accept this argument on the grounds that the use of the ratio of coastal lengths as a determinative of the coastal State's seaward reach and area of the continental shelf went beyond the use of proportionality as a test of equity. 'If such a use of proportionality were right', the Court stated, 'it is difficult indeed to see what room would be left for any other consideration.'[91] Nevertheless, the Court did take into account the difference of coastal lengths in the delimitation process itself. It held that: 'This difference is so great as to justify the adjustment of the median line so as to attribute a larger shelf area to Libya.'[92] The Court thus adjusted a provisional median line by shifting it 18' to the north (see Illustration 9).

However, two problems arose. First, the Court took into consideration the different lengths of the coasts because it was 'so great'. Yet the term 'so great' is so ambiguous as to be devoid of objective content.[93] Secondly, it is unclear

[87] Judgment, ibid, 61, [75].

[88] Dissenting Opinion of Judge Evensen, ibid, 313, [23].

[89] ibid.

[90] Counter-Memorial of Libya, vol II, 174. See also Memorial of Libya, vol I, 132–35; Reply of Libya, vol III, 87–95. By contrast, Malta rejected the application of the concept of proportionality. Memorial of Malta, vol I, 492–93; Counter-Memorial of Malta, vol II, 331–45; Reply of Malta, vol III, 214–25.

[91] [1985] ICJ Rep 45, [58].

[92] ibid, 50, [68]. According to the Court, the coast of Libya from Ras Ajdir to Ras Zarruq is 192 miles long, while the coast of Malta from Ras il-Wardija to Delimara Point, excluding the islet of Filfla, measures 24 miles. ibid.

[93] According to Judge Oda, the ratio between the coastal length was 1: 8 in Libya's favour. The ratio of the area of the continental shelf was 1:3.8 in Libya's favour. Dissenting Opinion of Judge Oda, ibid,134, [16]. See also Fietta and Cleverly, *A Practitioner's Guide* 605.

Figure 4

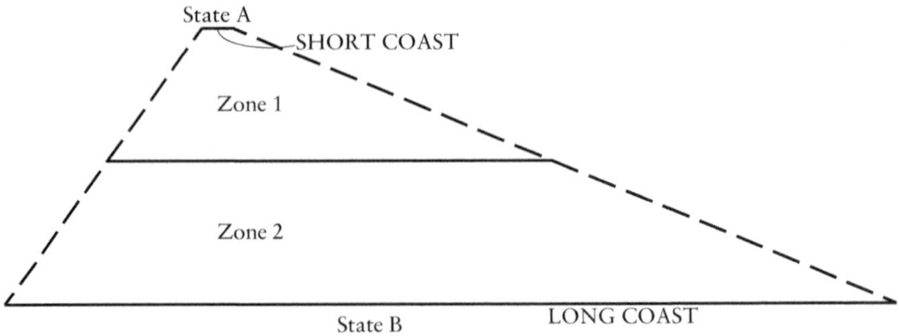

Source: The *Libya/Malta* case, Pleadings, Maps, Charts and Illustrations, vol V, Figure B, The Trapezium, 13.

(This figure is simplified and intended for illustrative purposes only. In fact, the line dividing zone 1 and zone 2 is not a strict median line. As a result, zone 1 as actually shown is too large.)

how the disproportion of the coastal lengths was reflected in the drawing of the delimitation line. A northward shift of 18' on the 15°10' E meridian resulted in a delimitation line intersecting the reference line at 34°30' N. Even though the ICJ did not mention it, this point was the same as the southwestern corner of the Italian claim in the Ionian Sea. It would seem to follow that the line was dictated by a third party claim.[94] In summary, the Court specified neither a criterion for judging a disparity of coastlines nor the way in which to shift the median line.

At the final stage, the Court applied proportionality as a test for the equitableness of the result of the delimitation. In this respect, the problem was that the area to be delimited was a small one owing to the presence of a third State. As the Court itself accepted, it would be unrealistic to apply the test of proportionality to such a limited area, as future delimitations with third States would change the situation. According to the Court, however, this did not debar it from applying the test of proportionality, and it was possible to make a broad assessment of the equitableness of the result. Having checked the equitableness of the result from the angle of proportionality, the Court concluded that there was no evident disproportion in this case.[95] It is debatable, however, that this is the proper conclusion. Before applying the test of proportionality, it is essential to define the relevant area.[96] But the Court refrained from doing so owing to the presence of Italy. How, then, was it possible to verify the equity of the result? Furthermore, the Court delimited the continental shelf in a very narrow

[94] For a criticism on this point, see Dissenting Opinion of Judge Oda in the *Libya/Malta* case, [1985] ICJ Rep 137–38, [23–25].

[95] ibid, 53–55, [74–75].

[96] Separate Opinion of Judges Ruda, Bedjaoui and Jiménez de Aréchaga, ibid, 92, [40]; Dissenting Opinion of Judge Oda, ibid, 133, [15].

geographical context excluding areas related to the potential claim of the third State. Considering that the continental shelf area of each Party was subject to change as a result of a subsequent delimitation with a third State, the validity of the Court's calculation of proportionality was questionable.[97] Moreover, the application of proportionality in a delimitation between opposite coasts was criticised by the members of the Court and commentators. In this regard, four points can be made.

First, where an extreme disproportion between two coastal lengths comes into play, a State with a short coastline, such as Malta, might have no continental shelf at all.[98] This is particularly true where the distance between the States with opposite coasts is relatively short.[99] In the *Libya/Malta* case, there was a 'considerable distance' between them, but this is not true for everywhere.[100]

Secondly, it should be noted that the difference of coastal lengths was already reflected in the surfaces of the two zones separated by the median line (Figure 4). In fact, the northern part of the area delimited by the median line was considerably smaller than the southern part because of the much shorter coasts of Malta and the much longer coast of Libya.[101] This is a geometrical truth.[102] The present geographical situation constitutes a trapezium, surrounded by the short coastline of Malta (apex) and by the longer coast of Libya (base). If a median line is drawn within the trapezium, the area of continental shelf appertaining to Libya is much larger than that of Malta.[103] Thus it would appear that there was no decisive reason to give an additional area to Libya because its coastlines were

[97] Dissenting Opinion of Judge Oda, ibid. Jaenicke and Kolb too criticised the Court's view. G Jaenicke, 'The Role of Proportionality in the Delimitation of Maritime Zones' in A Bos and H Siblesz (eds), realism in Law-Making, Essays on International Law in Honour of Willem Riphagem (Dodrecht, Nijhoff, 1986) 60; Kolb, *Case Law on Equitable Maritime Delimitation*, 350–54. In addition, Judges Ruda, Bedjaoui and Jiménez de Aréchaga stated that the triangular area which was excluded from the delimitation by the Court had to be included when determining the areas to be attributed to each Party. According to the three judges, this area was to be adjudicated to Malta. Joint Separate Opinion of Judges Ruda, Bedjaoui and Jiménez de Aréchaga, [1985] ICJ Rep 91–92, [39].

[98] Dissenting Opinion of Judge Schwebel, ibid, 186.

[99] Reply by Professor Brownlie, Verbatim Record 1984, Oral Argument *(concluded)*, Correspondence, vol IV, 288 and 300.

[100] One may ask whether the disproportion in coastal lengths is an independent relevant circumstance or whether it may be taken into account only where a considerable difference exists between two coasts. Separate Opinion of Judge Mbaye, [1985] ICJ Rep 102.

[101] Dissenting Opinion of Judge Mosler, ibid, 121.

[102] Fietta and Cleverly rightly argued that: '[I]f the relevant area is defined as a trapezium, a strict equidistance lien automatically allocates a larger area to the longer State. For these and other reasons, […], it is highly questionable whether the proportionality principle has any place in delimitation between opposite coasts.' Fietta and Cleverly, *A Practitioner's Guide*, 605.

[103] Dissenting Opinion of Judge Mosler, ibid, 121. See also presentation by Brownlie, Verbatim Record 1984, Oral Argument *(concluded)*, Correspondence, vol III, 475–76. But, Libya criticised the argument regarding the trapezium put forward by Malta. Counter-Memorial of Libya, vol II, 175–81. One of the criticisms was that, whatever the length of the Libyan coast, Malta would always get approximately one-third of the trapeze. Nevertheless, as the theory of proportionality does not attribute maritime zones to States in proportion to coastal lengths, this criticism is unconvincing.

longer than Malta's.[104] In fact, as the Court admitted, an equitable delimitation does not mean that shelf areas should be attributed to States in proportion to their coastal lengths.[105]

Thirdly, as already pointed out, the theory of proportionality was originally intended for delimitations between States with adjacent coasts of *quasi*-equal length in order to establish a balance between regular and irregular configurations of coasts.[106] However, the Court, in the *Libya/Malta* case, applied the test of proportionality to a completely different situation. In so doing, the Court departed radically from the original concept. On this point, Judge Valticos questioned the majority opinion by stating that:

> The aim of proportionality, where adjacent coasts are concerned, is to avoid solutions which, in some instances, owing to the particular configuration of the coasts in question, may seem contrary to equity. Here, in my opinion, there are neither adjacent coasts nor any abnormal configuration, and no part should be played by proportionality.[107]

Fourthly, in this case, proportionality has played a double role as a factor for adjusting a provisionally drawn median line and as a test of the equitableness of the result. This double use of proportionality smacks of circular reasoning. In light of the above, there is room for doubting whether proportionality is relevant in delimitation between opposite coasts.[108]

c. The Concept of (Dis)proportionality in the ICJ Jurisprudence Concerning Single Maritime Boundaries

In the *Gulf of Maine* case, the Chamber of the ICJ took proportionality into account for the second segment, where the situation was one of opposite coasts. In the words of the Chamber:

> [A] maritime delimitation can certainly not be established by a direct division of the area in dispute proportional to the respective lengths of the coasts belonging to the parties in the relevant area, but it is equally certain that a substantial disproportion to the lengths of those coasts that resulted from a delimitation effected on a

[104] Dissenting Opinion of Judge Schwebel, [1985] ICJ Rep 182–83. According to Judge Oda, the genuine equidistance line would produce an area divided the ratio of 1:2.3 or slightly higher. Dissenting Opinion of Judge Oda, ibid, 134, [16].

[105] The *Anglo-French Continental Shelf* arbitral award, 18 *RIAA* 58, [101].

[106] See presentation by Brownlie, Verbatim Record 1984, Oral Argument *(concluded)*, Correspondence, vol III, 456–60; reply by Brownlie, Verbatim Record 1984, Oral Argument *(concluded)*, Correspondence, vol IV, 295–96.

[107] Separate Opinion of Judge Valticos, [1985] ICJ Rep 110, [19]; for the same view, see Dissenting Opinions of Judge Oda, ibid, 134, [18], and of Judge Schwebel, ibid, 184. In addition, as early as 1979, Bowett already expressed the same view: 'Indeed, it would seem that the proportionality factor might only be applied, or be meaningful in the case of adjacent States (not "opposite") where the existence of a markedly concave or convex coastline will produce a cut-off effect if the equidistance principle is applied.' Bowett, *The Legal Regime of Islands* 164.

[108] Weil, *Perspective du droit de la délimitation maritime*, 258; Fietta and Cleverly, *A Practitioner's Guide* 605.

> different basis would constitute a circumstance calling for an appropriate correction. In the Chamber's opinion, the need to take this aspect into account constitutes a valid ground for correction.[109]

According to the Chamber, as the difference in the coastal lengths was 'particularly notable,'[110] it was necessary to correct the provisional median line in the second segment of delimitation.[111] The ratio between the coastal fronts of the United States and Canada in the Gulf of Maine was 1.38 to 1. According to the Chamber, this ratio should be reflected in the boundary of the second segment. At the same time, the Chamber decided to give half effect to Seal Island off Nova Scotia. Consequently, the ratio became approximately 1.32 to 1. To reflect precisely this ratio in the boundary of the second segment, the Chamber shifted the median line provisionally drawn to the Canadian side.[112] As the second sector constituted a quadrangle, the ratio in question reflected automatically the size of the maritime space of each Party.[113] Thus, proportionality applied, for the first time in the case law, as a factor of correcting a median line for both the continental shelf and the FZ. However, the Chamber did not apply proportionality as an *ex post facto* test to check the equitableness of the single maritime boundary. The judgment in the *Gulf of Maine* case raises another problem concerning the calculation of the coastal fronts of each State. The Chamber included the Bay of Fundy in its calculation,[114] although it is not an area of overlap. As Judge Schwebel indicated, this distorted the calculation of proportionality.[115] Moreover, the Chamber's selection of coasts contrasts with the *dictum* in the *Tunisia/Libya* case, to the effect that non-overlapping areas must be eliminated from the consideration of proportionality. The difficulty of selecting the coasts relevant for proportionality purposes was thus admirably exemplified.

In the *Jan Mayen* case, the parties' views with regard to the role of proportionality were sharply divided. Claiming a maritime zone of 200 nautical miles, Denmark requested the Court to take into account the ratio of the relevant coastal lengths, which was 9.2 to 1 in favour of Greenland. For Denmark, proportionality had to play a double role: as a relevant circumstance in the adoption of an appropriate method, and as a test of equity.[116] By contrast, Norway rejected this view by advocating a median line.[117] Considering the disparity or

[109] [1984] ICJ Rep 323, [185].
[110] ibid, 323, [184].
[111] ibid, 334–35, [218].
[112] ibid, 336, [222].
[113] A map annexed to Cooper's paper is useful in order to understand the process of delimitation. J Cooper, 'Delimitation of the Maritime Boundary in the Gulf of Maine Area' (1986) 16 *ODIL* 82.
[114] [1984] ICJ Rep 336, [221].
[115] Separate Opinion of Judge Schwebel, ibid, 356. See also Ida, 'The Role of Proportionality' 1045.
[116] [1993] ICJ Rep 65, [62]; presentation by Bernhard, CR 93/4, 14 January 1993, 32.
[117] Presentation by Haug, CR 93/11, 27 January 1993, 45; presentation by Weil, CR 93/9, 21 January 1993, 8–31.

disproportion between the lengths of the relevant coasts,[118] the Court held that: '[T]he differences in length of the respective coasts of the Parties are so significant that this feature must be taken into consideration already during the delimitation operation.'[119] It thus concluded that the disparity between the lengths of the coasts constituted, for a continental shelf delimitation, a 'special circumstance' under Article 6 of the Geneva Convention on the Continental Shelf, and, for the delimitation of an FZ, a 'relevant circumstance' under customary law.[120] In light of proportionality, the Court adjusted the median line in the two northern zones in such a way as to draw the delimitation line closer to the coast of Jan Mayen. In this case, the Court did not apply proportionality as an *ex post facto* test.

However, the application of proportionality was loose in two respects.[121] The Court took proportionality into account in the delimitation process because the disparity of the lengths was 'so significant'. Yet the term 'so significant' is so ambiguous as to be devoid of objective content. The Court based its decision on the *Gulf of Maine* case, in which the Chamber had considered a ratio of 1 to 1.38 as sufficient to justify a 'correction' of a median-line delimitation.[122] This cannot, however, be an objective criterion to judge whether there is disparity of coastal lengths. A similar problem of subjectivity arose in relation to the extent of the adjustment. According to figures given by Denmark, the ratio of the lengths of the coastal fronts of Greenland and Jan Mayen, defined as straight lines between points G and H, respectively points E and F, was approximately 9 to 1.[123] This was not disputed by Norway. In considering proportionality, the Court divided zone 2 between points N and O in such a way as to give Norway two-thirds of the distance I–K, and zone 3 was divided by a line drawn from O to A. It is difficult to understand how the ratio of coastal lengths is reflected in the division of zones 2 and 3.

In the 2001 *Qatar v Bahrain* case, Qatar had recourse to proportionality as a test of the equitableness of a single maritime boundary.[124] According to Qatar, the ratio of its mainland coasts to that of Bahrain's principal islands was 1.59:1 and such a significant disparity between the coastal lengths of the Parties constituted a special or relevant circumstance calling for an appropriate correction of an equidistance line provisionally drawn.[125] In applying the proportionality test to the single maritime boundary proposed by Qatar in the northern sector,

[118] [1993] ICJ Rep 65, [61].

[119] ibid, 68, [68].

[120] ibid, 69, [68].

[121] Thirlway, *The Law and Procedure*, vol. I, 503.

[122] [1993] ICJ Rep 68, [68].

[123] ibid, 65, [61].

[124] Memorial submitted by Qatar, 301. See also 279–83; presentation by Quéneudec, Counsel of Qatar, Verbatim Record, CR 2000/10, [17] and [38–39].

[125] The *Qatar/Bahrain* case (Merits), [2001] ICJ Rep 114, [241].

the ratio between the sizes of the maritime areas on either side of the boundary was 1.68 to 1 in favour of Qatar. It thus argued that the proportionality test was sufficient to permit the conclusion that the proposed boundary is equitable.[126] By contrast, Bahrain contended that the above calculation relied on the assumption that the Hawar Islands were under Qatar's sovereignty. It stated that, if these islands were considered as appertaining to Bahrain, the lengths of the relevant coasts would be almost equal.[127] Furthermore, Bahrain refused to admit the result of Qatar's proportionality test because it was arbitrary.[128] The ICJ supported Bahrain's view. With respect to the dispute over the Hawar Islands, the Court decided that Bahrain had sovereignty over those islands. Accordingly, the Court held that: '[T]he disparity in length of the coastal fronts of the Parties cannot be considered such as to necessitate an adjustment of the equidistance line.'[129] The Court's view, which was very condensed on this matter, calls for two comments.

First, proportionality was not regarded as a relevant circumstance in this case. As the Court indicated, however, this was because there was no disparity between the coastal lengths of the Parties which called for an adjustment of an equidistance line. This appears to suggest that, where there is a disproportion between coastal lengths, proportionality may be considered. Hence it may be inadvisable to rush to the conclusion that the ICJ in the *Qatar v Bahrain* judgment reversed the precedents which have given prominence to the concept of proportionality.

Secondly, the Court's reasoning relied on the fact that the lengths of the relevant coasts between the Parties were approximately the same. As Judge *ad hoc* Torres Bernárdez pointed out, however, no precise figures were given in the judgment to support that conclusion.[130] Indeed, the Court identified neither relevant coasts nor areas.

In the 2002 *Cameroon v Nigeria* case, Cameroon invoked the disparity between the length of coastlines of the Parties in the Gulf of Guinea as a relevant circumstance that could justify shifting the delimitation line towards the north-west.[131] In this connection, Cameroon divided the relevant area into three sectors. In the first sector, connecting Bonny (Nigeria) and Campo (Cameroon), Cameroon maintained that the ratio of the relevant coastline is about 2.3:1 in favour of Cameroon. The second sector is the area bounded by the Bonny-Campo line and by a construction line running from Akasso in Nigeria and Cabo San Juan in Equatorial Guinea. According to Cameroon,

[126] Memorial submitted by Qatar, 304–5.
[127] Judgment, [2001] ICJ Rep 114, [242]; Counter-Memorial submitted by Bahrain, [647–49].
[128] ibid, [647]; presentation by Reisman, Counsel of Bahrain, Verbatim Record, CR 2000/16, [17].
[129] Judgment, [2001] ICJ Rep 114, [243].
[130] Dissenting Opinion of Judge *ad hoc* Torres Bernárdez, ibid, 436, [521].
[131] [2002] ICJ Rep 446, [300].

in this sector, the ratio of relevant coastline is approximately 1.25:1 in favour of Cameroon. The third area is subtended by a line running between Akasso in Nigeria and Cap Lopez in Gabon and here the ratio of coastal lengths, 1.25:1, is the same. Applying the above ratios to constructing lines of each sector, Cameroon drew an equitable line.[132] By contrast, Nigeria contended that the ratio of coastal lengths was in favour of Nigeria by a factor of between 1:1.3. and 1:1.2 depending on the precise points used. In Nigeria's view, Cameroon's line was questionable since it failed to take due account of the criterion of proportionality.[133] The Court noted that substantial differences in the lengths of the Parties' coastlines may be a factor to be taken into account in order to adjust the provisional delimitation line. In the present case, however, the Court held that whichever coastline of Nigeria was regarded as relevant, the relevant coastline of Cameroon was not longer than that of Nigeria. The Court therefore denied the relevance of proportionality in this case.[134]

In the 2007 *Nicaragua v Honduras* case, no mention was made of the proportionality test, although Nicaragua argued this point.[135] Nor did the Court define the relevant coast and area of the parties in dispute for the purpose of the proportionality test.

d. Proportionality in the Arbitral Awards

Proportionality was also taken into account in the arbitral awards concerning single maritime boundaries as well. In the 1985 *Guinea/Guinea-Bissau* case, the Arbitral Tribunal considered the proportionality issue at the verification stage. Thus it regarded proportionality as an *ex post facto* test of equitableness. Yet the award is so condensed in this matter as to make it difficult to apprehend the concrete process by which proportionality was applied. In fact, the Arbitral Tribunal compared the coastal lengths of the parties without calculating maritime surfaces. Then, it merely stated that the coastlines of the two States were

[132] In the second sector, the broken part of the construction line corresponding to the Equatorial Guinea coastline was not taken into account. In the third sector, the broken part of the construction line corresponding to Gabon's coastline was not considered. For the method of drawing Cameroon's line, see Memorial of Cameroon, 553–55, [5.119–5.128]; reply of Cameroon, 421–26, [9.81–9.95]; presentation by Mendelson, Counsel of Cameroon, Verbatim Record, CR 2002/6, 51–55, [16–28]; presentation by Kamto, Counsel of Cameroon, Verbatim Record, CR 2002/7, 28–31, [31–42]. Later, however, Cameroon explained that this line was an equidistance line adjusted to take into account the relevant circumstances so as to produce an equitable solution. Presentation by Kamto, Counsel of Cameroon, Verbatim Record, CR 2002/17, 50–60, [20–48]; Judgment, [2002] ICJ Rep 433, [272]. Yet it is hard to understand how these totally different reasons could be compatible. On this issue, see presentation by Crawford, Counsel of Nigeria, Verbatim Record, CR 2002/20, 53–54, [15]; 58–64, [29–48].

[133] Rejoinder of Nigeria, Part IV, Ch 13, [13.13]; [13.41]; The *Cameroon v Nigeria* case (Merits), [2002] ICJ Rep 435, [278].

[134] ibid, 446–47, [301].

[135] Reply of Nicaragua, vol I, 193, [9.53–9.54]; presentation by Brownlie, Verbatim Record, CR 2007/5, 39–40, [64–66]; presentation by Brownlie, Verbatim Record, CR 2007/12, 51–52, [63–66].

the same length, taking the islands into account, and that, therefore, neither party could claim any advantage.[136]

In the 1992 *St Pierre and Miquelon* case, the Arbitral Tribunal used the concept of proportionality to test the equitableness of the delimitation. According to the Tribunal, while the ratio between the Canadian and French coastlines was 15.3 to 1,[137] the ratio of the actual maritime spaces appertaining to the Parties was 16.4 (Canada) to 1 (France).[138] The Tribunal thus concluded that there was no disproportion. Nevertheless, this application of the proportionality test was sharply criticised by two arbitrators: Gotlieb and Weil.[139] The principal difficulty consisted in the definition and calculation of the relevant coasts and area. As Weil indicated, the Parties submitted divergent views concerning the identification and measurement of these coasts and area. For instance, with respect to the coastlines, while Canada contended that the ratio of coastal lengths was 21.4 (Canada):1 (France),[140] France arrived at a ratio of 6.5:1.[141] The Tribunal adopted a ratio of 15.3:1 without giving convincing reasons. The same problem arose regarding the calculation of the relevant area. In this respect, while the Parties submitted divergent figures as to its size, the Court of Arbitration made another identification of the relevant area, which embraced the whole economic zone generated in the south by the southern coast of Newfoundland.[142] This solution was criticised by Gotlieb, as it embraced an excessive amount of ocean space which was not near the areas claimed by France.[143] In short, this award shows that no scientific criterion was used for identifying and measuring the relevant coasts and the area.[144]

In the 1999 *Eritrea/Yemen* case, both Parties had recourse to proportionality by relying on the *dictum* regarding proportionality found in the *North Sea Continental Shelf* cases. Following the *Anglo-French Continental Shelf* case, they agreed that the role of proportionality was a test of equitableness and not a method of delimitation, and that manifest disproportionality must be avoided. Thus, there was little dispute between the Parties regarding the role of proportionality.[145] The Arbitral Tribunal itself also confirmed the *dictum*.[146] However, there was strong disagreement about how to measure the length of the respective coasts and the significance of that operation once executed.[147]

[136] The *Guinea/Guinea-Bissau* arbitral award, (1986) 25 *ILM* 301, [120].
[137] The *St Pierre and Miquelon* arbitral award, (1992) 31 *ILM* 1162, [33].
[138] ibid, 1176, [93].
[139] Dissenting Opinion of Mr Gotlieb, ibid,1181–88, [5–37]; Dissenting Opinion of Mr Weil, ibid, 1204–7, [20–26].
[140] The *St Pierre and Miquelon* arbitral award, (1992) 31 *ILM* 1164, [33].
[141] Dissenting Opinion of Mr Weil, ibid, 1207, [para 24] [check].
[142] Judgment, ibid, 1176, [93].
[143] Dissenting Opinion of Mr Gotlieb, ibid, 1188, [35–37].
[144] Dissenting Opinion of Mr Weil, ibid, 1206, [24]. H Ruiz-Fabri, 'Sur la délimitation des espaces maritimes entre le Canada et la France, sentence arbitrale du 10 juin 1992' (1993) 97 *RGDIP* 95.
[145] The *Eritrea/Yemen* arbitral award (the Second Stage), (2001) 22 *RIAA* 343, [39].
[146] ibid, 372, [165].
[147] ibid, 343, [39].

On the one hand, Yemen suggested that a line dividing the areas concerned into almost equal parts correctly reflected the proportion between the lengths of the respective coasts. On the other hand, Eritrea alleged that its own historic median line between the mainland coasts would produce areas favouring Eritrea by a proportion of 3 to 2. According to Eritrea, this reflected accurately the proportion of the lengths of the coasts.[148] Furthermore, in calculating the areas resulting from the delimitation, Eritrea insisted that account should not be taken of the internal waters within the Dahlaks or the bays along its coast, including the Bay of Assab.[149]

In the Arbitral Tribunal's view, there was no doubt that the calculation of the Eritrean coastal length should follow the outer circumference of the Dahlak group of islands.[150] The issue was, however, how far north the Eritrean coast should go for the purposes of establishing its length. Eritrea wished to include in the proportionality calculation the whole of its mainland coast up to the latitudinal line of 16°N, and that line was also used by Yemen to define its northern sector of the area in question. Yet the Tribunal had doubts regarding the appropriateness of the latitudinal line of 16°N for the purposes of the proportionality test, since the waters of the Red Sea lie at an angle of roughly 45° (see Illustration 14). The Tribunal thus considered the relevant proportion of the Eritrean coast to cease where the general direction of that coast met a line drawn from what seems to be the northern terminus of the Yemen land frontier at right angles to the general direction of the Yemeni coast. In the same way, the Tribunal determined the southern end point to be considered for the computation of the length of the Yemen coast.[151] According to the calculations of the Tribunal, the ratio of coastal lengths, Yemen: Eritrea, was 387,026 meters to 507,110 meters, or 1:1.31. On the other hand, the ratio of water areas, including the territorial seas, Yemen: Eritrea, was 25,535 to 27,944 square kilometres, or 1:1.09. The Tribunal then concluded that the delimitation line it had decided upon engendered no disproportion.[152] Yet the strong dispute between the Parties over the calculation of the lengths of the coastlines revealed once again a disadvantage of the proportionality theory envisaged here: The lack of objective criteria to determine the relevant coasts.

In the 2006 *Barbados v Trinidad and Tobago* arbitration, proportionality was at issue in the delimitation of the eastern part of the area to be delimited. While delimiting this area, the Arbitral Tribunal found that proportionality is a relevant circumstance to be taken into consideration in reviewing the equity of a tentative delimitation line, but not in any way to require the application of ratios or mathematical determinations in the attribution of maritime areas.

[148] ibid, 344, [42].
[149] ibid, [43].
[150] ibid, 372, [166].
[151] ibid, 373, [167].
[152] ibid, [168].

The Tribunal thus decided that it would not resort to any form of 'splitting the difference' or other mathematical approaches or use ratio methodologies that would entail attributing to one Party what as a matter of law might belong to the other.[153] At the operational stage of the maritime delimitation, the Tribunal adjusted the equidistance line in light of the existence of the significant coastal frontage of Trinidad and Tobago. As a consequence, the delimitation line was drawn from this point in a straight line in the direction of its terminal point, which is located at the point of intersection of Trinidad and Tobago's southern maritime boundary with its 200 nm EEZ limit.[154] The Tribunal examined this outcome in the light of proportionality as the ultimate test of the equitableness of the solution. By applying the proportionality test, the Tribunal concluded that the bending of the equidistance line reflects a reasonable influence of the coastal frontages on the overall area of delimitation, with a view to avoiding reciprocal encroachments which would otherwise result in some form of inequity.[155] However, the Arbitral Tribunal did not specify the relevant coastal lengths of the Parties and the relevant areas belonging to each Party.[156] Nor did it determine the validity of the arguments of the Parties with regard to proportionality. Furthermore, it seems that the Tribunal focused on the question whether the adjusted equidistance line reflects *the coastal frontages* on the overall area of delimitation, not the disproportion between the relevant coastal lengths and relevant areas belonging to each Party. This is an original approach of the *Barbados v Trinidad and Tobago* case. In consequence, the proportionality test in this case was not applied on the basis of the ratios of the relevant coastal lengths and the maritime areas attributed to each party.

In the 2007 *Guyana v Suriname* arbitration, Guyana claimed that its relevant coastline is materially longer than Suriname's rather than shorter, as Suriname claimed.[157] In this regard, Guyana explained that the ratio of the lengths of the Parties' relevant coastlines is thus 1.4 to 1 (215 km to 153 km) in its favour.[158] Guyana thus argued that its calculation of the maritime areas appurtenant to the Parties' relevant coasts using the relevant coastal lengths presented by it revealed Guyana to have a larger appurtenant maritime area than Suriname, rather than a smaller one as Suriname claims.[159] However, Suriname contended that the relevant coasts identified by Guyana were excessive in length and that the disparity in relative relevant coastal lengths favoured Suriname in this case. It also disputed the basis on which Guyana calculated appurtenant maritime areas,

[153] The *Barbados v Trinidad and Tobago* arbitral award, (2007) 27 *RIAA* 237 [337–38].

[154] ibid, 243, [373–74].

[155] ibid, 244, [379].

[156] Alex G Oude Elferink, 'Relevant Coasts and Relevant Area: The Difficulty of Developing General Concepts in a Case-Specific Context' in Oude Elferink, Henriksen and Busch, *Maritime Boundary Delimitation*, 185–86.

[157] The *Guyana v Suriname* arbitral award, (2013) 30 *RIAA* 59 [224].

[158] ibid, 96, [346].

[159] ibid, 59, [225].

asserting that the area of overlapping maritime entitlements was to be determined using lines perpendicular to the angles of the States' coastal fronts.[160] The Arbitral Tribunal did not consider that there were any relevant circumstances in the continental shelf or exclusive economic zone which would require an adjustment of the provisional equidistance line.[161] Thus there are no factors which would render the equidistance line determined by the Tribunal inequitable. The Tribunal then checked the relevant coastal lengths for proportionality and concluded that the ratio of the coastal lengths 'comes up with nearly the same ratio of relevant areas (Guyana 51%: Suriname 49%) as it does for coastal frontages (Guyana 54%: Suriname 46%).'[162]

ii. The Second Phase (2009–Present): Disproportionality as an Ex Post Facto *Test at the Third Stage of Maritime Delimitation*

a. The Disproportionality Test in the *Black Sea* Case and After

The *Black Sea* judgment marked an important landmark in the jurisprudence concerning maritime delimitation in the sense that the ICJ clarified what might be called the three-stage approach of maritime delimitation.[163] According to this approach, at the final and third stage, the Court, by applying the disproportionality test, will verify whether the delimitation line does not lead to an inequitable result.[164] Under this approach, notably disproportionality was given an independent status distinct from other relevant circumstances. In this regard, the ICJ clarified the principal elements of the disproportionality test.

First, by referring to the *dictum* of the *Anglo-French Continental Shelf* case,[165] the ICJ used the negative formula of *dis*proportionality. In the Court's view, 'it is disproportion rather than any general principle of proportionality which is the relevant criterion or factor.'[166]

Secondly, according to the Court, the continental shelf and EEZ allocations are not to be assigned in proportion to length of respective coastlines. Rather, the Court is to 'check, *ex post facto*, on the equitableness of the delimitation line it has constructed.'[167]

Thirdly, the disproportionality test is not in itself a method of delimitation. For the Court:

> It is rather a means of checking whether the delimitation line arrived at by other means needs adjustment because of a significant disproportionality in the ratios between the maritime areas which would fall to one party or other by virtue of

[160] ibid, 60, [228].
[161] ibid, 109, [392].
[162] ibid.
[163] See ch 5, s XI of this book.
[164] [2009] ICJ Rep 103, [122].
[165] The *Anglo-French Continental Shelf* arbitral award, 18 *RIAA* 58, [101].
[166] [2009] ICJ Rep129, [210].
[167] ibid, [211].

> the delimitation line arrived at by other means, and the lengths of their respective coasts.[168]

Fourthly, the checking of the equitableness of the delimitation line by the disproportionality test can only be approximate. In this regard, the ICJ admitted a certain degree of flexibility with regard to the calculation of coastal length, stating that:

> Diverse techniques have in the past been used for assessing coastal lengths, with no clear requirements of international law having been shown as to whether the real coastline should be followed, or baselines used, or whether or not coasts relating to internal waters should be excluded.[169]

The Court further stated that:

> The Court cannot but observe that various tribunals, and the Court itself, have drawn different conclusions over the years as to what disparity in coastal lengths would constitute *a significant disproportionality* which suggested the delimitation line was inequitable and still required adjustment. This remains in each case a matter for the Court's appreciation, which it will exercise by reference to the overall geography of the area.[170]

The above passage did seem to imply that currently there is no objective criterion for checking whether there is a significant disproportionality in coastal lengths that requires an adjustment of a provisional line drawn at the second stage of the delimitation.

According to the Court, the length of Romania's relevant coast is approximately 248 km,[171] while the length of the Ukraine's relevant coast is approximately 705 km.[172] The ratio for the coastal lengths between Romania and Ukraine is approximately 1:2.8, while the ratio of the relevant area between Romania and Ukraine is approximately 1:2.1.[173] The Court thus held that the equidistance line as constructed required no alteration.[174]

Subsequently, the disproportionality test was applied as an *ex post facto* test by the ICJ in the *Nicaragua v Colombia*, *Peru v Chile*, and *Costa Rica v Nicaragua* cases.[175] In the *Nicaragua v Colombia* case, the ICJ noted that it was not applying a principle of strict proportionality. In the view of the Court, '[m]aritime delimitation is not designed to produce a correlation between the lengths of the Parties' relevant coasts and their respective shares of the relevant

[168] ibid, 99–100, [110].
[169] ibid, 129, [212].
[170] Emphasis added. ibid,129, [213].
[171] ibid, 93, [88].
[172] ibid, 98, [103]. The Court drew a line across the entrance of Karkinits'ka Gulf in order to make clear the relevant coasts and areas. However, this line is not taken into account in the calculation of the total length of the Ukrainian relevant coasts. ibid, 97, [100].
[173] ibid, 130, [215].
[174] ibid, [216].
[175] See ch 5, ss XIII, XIV and XVIII of this book.

area' and '[t]he Court's task is to check for a significant disproportionality'.[176] The Court clarified its approach to the disproportionality test as follows:

> The Court thus considers that its task, at this third stage, is not to attempt to achieve even an approximate correlation between the ratio of the lengths of the Parties' relevant coasts and the ratio of their respective shares of the relevant area. It is, rather, to ensure that there is not a disproportion so gross as to 'taint' the result and render it inequitable. Whether any disproportion is so great as to have that effect is not a question capable of being answered by reference to any mathematical formula but is a matter which can be answered only in the light of all the circumstances of the particular case.[177]

The ICJ calculated that the length of Nicaragua's relevant coast is approximately 531 kilometres taking the general direction of this coast and that of Colombia's relevant coast is 65 kilometres.[178] According to the Court, the ratio for the coastal lengths is approximately 1:8.2 in Nicaragua's favour and the ratio of the relevant area is approximately 1:3.44 in Nicaragua's favour. In the words of the Court, '[t]he question, therefore, is whether this *disproportion* is so great as to render the result inequitable.'[179] This statement did seem to suggest that in itself the Court admitted the existence of disproportion.[180] Nevertheless, the Court eventually concluded that, 'taking account of all the circumstances of the present case', the result achieved by the application of the provisional line did not entail such a disproportionality as to create an inequitable result.[181] Given that the ratio of the relevant area is over twice as great as the ration between the relevant coastal lengths, however, it is debatable whether there is no disproportionality between the ration of the coastal lengths and that of the relevant area.[182] Furthermore, the phrase 'taking account of all the circumstances of the present case' seems to imply that other circumstances were considered at the stage of the disproportionality test. Yet some doubts can be expressed regarding whether this is a proper manner of application of the disproportionality test.

In the 2014 *Peru v Chile* case, the starting-point for the delimitation was 80 nautical miles from the closest point on the Chilean coast and about 45 nautical miles from the closest point on the Peruvian coast.[183] As the ICJ itself noted, however, the existence of the agreed maritime boundary, which

[176] [2012] ICJ Rep 715, [240].
[177] ibid, 716, [242].
[178] ibid, 680, [153].
[179] Emphasis added. ibid, 716, [243].
[180] MD Evans, 'Maritime Boundary Delimitation: Whatever Next?' in J Barrett and R Barnes (eds) *Law of the Sea: UNCLOS as a Living Treaty* (British Institute of International and Comparative Law London 2016) 62.
[181] [2012] ICJ Rep 717, [247].
[182] Evans, 'Maritime Boundary Delimitation: Whatever Next?' 62. Further, Tanaka, 'The Disproportionality Test' 315.
[183] [2014] ICJ Rep 66, [183].

extends for a significant distance (80 nautical miles), gave rise to novel questions about how to assess proportionality in respect of the area delimited on the basis of equidistance.[184] In fact, the Court admitted that:

> The existence of that line would make difficult, if not impossible, the calculation of the length of the relevant coasts and of the extent of the relevant area, were the usual mathematical calculation of the proportions to be undertaken.[185]

If so, together with Evans, one can ask the question: '[W]here does this leave the third stage of the test?'[186] In this regard, the Court recalled that in some instances in the past, it had not undertaken that calculation because of the practical difficulties arising from the particular circumstances of the case; and that it engaged in a broad assessment of disproportionality. Given the unusual circumstances of this case, the Court decided that it would follow the same approach and concluded that no significant disproportion was evident, such as would call into question the equitable nature of the provisional equidistance line.[187] However, the Court provides scant explanation as to why there is no significant disproportion in this case.[188] Thus the *Peru v Chile* case revealed that the application of the disproportionality test encounters considerable difficulty in a situation where agreed maritime boundary that does not rely on the equidistance method already exists.[189]

Lastly, in the *Costa Rica v Nicaragua* case, the ICJ applied the disproportionality test to the maritime boundaries between Costa Rica and Nicaragua in the Caribbean Sea and in the Pacific Ocean, respectively.[190] With regard to the maritime boundary established between Costa Rica and Nicaragua in the Pacific Ocean, the Court considered that it does not result in gross disproportionality, 'taking into account all the circumstances of the present case'.[191] Yet, as pointed out earlier, a question arises why all relevant circumstances must be considered again at the final stage of the disproportionality test. Concerning the maritime boundary established between Costa Rica and Nicaragua in the Caribbean Sea, curiously the Court compared only the ratio of coastal lengths and the ratio of the relevant area when applying the disproportionality test, without taking into account 'all the circumstances'. However, the Court

[184] See Declaration of Judge Donoghue, ibid, 110.

[185] Judgment, ibid, 69, [193].

[186] Evans, 'Maritime Boundary Delimitation: Whatever Next?' 65.

[187] [2014] ICJ Rep 69–71, [193–94].

[188] MD Evans, 'Maritime Boundary Delimitation' in DR Rothwell, Alex G Oude Elferink, KN Scott and T Stephens (eds), *The Oxford Handbook of the Law of the Sea* (Oxford University Press Oxford 2015), 272. See also Separate opinion, partly concurring and partly dissenting, of Judge ad hoc Orrego Vicuña, 131, [28] and 133, [34].

[189] In this regard, Evans observed that the ICJ in the *Peru v Chile* seemed to have 'thrown in the towel' by admitting that it is 'difficult if not impossible' to calculate the relevant coastal lengths and the extent of the relevant area. Evans, 'Maritime Boundary Delimitation: Whatever Next?'65.

[190] See ch 5, s XVIII of this book.

[191] [2018] ICJ Rep [203].

remained mute why 'all the circumstances' were considered again when applying the disproportionality test to the maritime boundary in the Pacific Ocean, while the 'pure' disproportionality test was applied to the maritime boundary established in the Caribbean Sea.

b. The Disproportionality Test in the ITLOS Jurisprudence

The disproportionality test has been applied in the jurisprudence of ITLOS. In *Bangladesh/Myanmar* case, both Bangladesh and Myanmar invoked the disproportionality test to support the equitableness of their own delimitation lines.[192] When applying the disproportionality test, however, ITLOS used its own figures. According to ITLOS, the length of Bangladesh's relevant coast is approximately 413 kilometres and that of Myanmar's coast 587 kilometres, resulting in a ratio between these coastal lengths of approximately 1:1.42 in favour of Myanmar.[193] According to the Tribunal, the adjusted delimitation line allocates approximately 111,631 square kilometres of the relevant area to Bangladesh and approximately 171,832 square kilometres to Myanmar. The ratio of the allocated areas is approximately 1:1.54 in favour of Myanmar. When calculating the size of the relevant area, an issue arose with regard to a claim of a third State in the same maritime area.[194] In this regard, ITLOS simply stated that: 'The fact that a third party may claim the same maritime area does not prevent its inclusion in the relevant maritime area for purposes of the disproportionality test.'[195] IITLOS concluded that the above mentioned ratio did not lead to any significant disproportion between the respective lengths of the coasts of the Parties and the maritime areas allocated to the Parties.[196]

Likewise the ITLOS Special Chamber applied the proportionality test at the third stage in the *Ghana/Côte d'Ivoire* case. According to the Special Chamber, the length of the relevant Ghanaian coast is approximately 139 kilometres and that of Côte d'Ivoire 352 kilometres.[197] The ratio of the length of the relevant coasts of the Parties is approximately 1:2.53 in favour of Côte d'Ivoire. Furthermore, the delimitation line constructed by the Chamber allocates approximately 65,881 square kilometres to Ghana and 132,842 square kilometres to Côte d'Ivoire. The ratio of the allocated areas is approximately 1:2.02 in favour of Côte d'Ivoire. The Special Chamber thus found that this ratio did not lead to

[192] Memorial of Bangladesh, vol I, 92–93, [6.75–6.76]; Counter-Memorial of the Union of Myanmar, vol I, 1 December 2010, 157, [5.151].

[193] [2012] ITLOS Rep 59, [202–05].

[194] As Churchill pointedly observed, the size of the area appertaining to Bangladesh could be affected by the location of a future maritime boundary with India. R Churchill, 'The *Bangladesh/Myanmar* Case: Continuity and Novelty in the Law of Maritime Boundary Delimitation' (2012) 1 *Cambridge Journal of International and Comparative Law* 145.

[195] [2012] ITLOS Rep 125, [494].

[196] ibid,126, [499].

[197] ibid, [379].

any significant disproportion in the allocation of maritime areas to the Parties relative to the respective lengths of their relevant coasts.[198]

c. Disproportionality Test in the *Bangladesh v India* Arbitral Award

Finally, the disproportionality test in the *Bangladesh v India* arbitral award merits discussion. In this case, the parties agreed that the final step in the delimitation process involves a test to ensure that the delimitation line does not yield a disproportionate result.[199] Yet the parties submitted different figures with regard to the relevant coastal lengths and the size of the relevant area. According to Bangladesh, the length of the relevant coast of Bangladesh and India was 424 kilometres and 708 kilometres respectively, and the ratio of the relevant coasts was 1:1.67 in favour of India, while the Bangladesh's proposed boundary line allocated Bangladesh and India maritime areas of 145,364 square kilometres and 211,490 square kilometres respectively, the ratio of which is 1: 1.52 in favour of India.[200] Bangladesh thus asserted that this result passed the disproportionality test. On the other hand, India submitted that the ratio of relevant coasts of the Parties was 1: 1.015, while the ratio of the relevant areas resulting from India's proposed line as 1: 0.942.[201] Hence India asserted that its proposed line satisfied the disproportionality test.

When applying the disproportionality test, the Arbitral Tribunal confirmed its function as an *ex post facto* test to check the equitableness of the delimitation line it had constructed.[202] In this connection, the Tribunal stressed that:

> [P]roportionality is not a mathematical exercise that results in the attribution of maritime areas as a function of the length of the coasts of the Parties or other such ratio calculations.[203]

According to the Tribunal, to produce a correlation between the relevant coastal lengths and the relevant maritime areas could itself produce inequity. In addition, the Tribunal clearly stated that: 'Whether or not significant disproportionality exists remains a matter for the Tribunal's appreciation, which it will exercise by reference to the overall geography of the area.'[204] According to the Tribunal, the length of the relevant coast of Bangladesh and India was 418.6 kilometres and 803.7 kilometres, respectively. Accordingly, the ratio between the lengths of the relevant coasts of the parties was 1: 1.92. The Tribunal's delimitation line allocates approximately 106,613 square kilometres of the

[198] ibid, [536–37].
[199] The *Bangladesh v India* arbitral award, [481]. See also Reply of Bangladesh, vol I, 125, [4.150]; Counter-Memorial of India, vol I, 195, [6.108].
[200] The *Bangladesh v India* arbitral award, [486].
[201] ibid, [489].
[202] ibid, [492].
[203] ibid, [492].
[204] ibid, [494].

relevant area to Bangladesh and approximately 300,220 square kilometres to India. Thus the ratio of the allocated areas is approximately 1: 2.81. The Tribunal found that this ratio did not produce any significant disproportion in the allocation of maritime areas to the Parties that would require alteration of the adjusted equidistance line to ensure an equitable solution.[205]

B. Analysis of State Practice

i. Agreements Regarding Continental Shelf Boundaries

Contrary to what occurred in the case law, the use of proportionality in State practice remains exceptional. In fact, there are only a few conventions regarding maritime delimitation which rely on that element. Regarding the boundaries of the continental shelf, a typical example is the 1974 Agreement between France and Spain in the Bay of Biscay.[206] While the Parties agreed to apply the equidistance method between points Q and R, beyond the latter point there was no such agreement. In drawing a continental shelf boundary in the area beyond point R, proportionality was taken into account. In order to establish the relevant area, a 'box' was created by construction lines: and a line drawn from the starting point M to Pointe de la Negade and then to Pointe du Raz; a line from point M to Cabo Orgegal. Then a closing line was drawn from Pointe du Raz to Cabo Ortegal. Next, point X was fixed in front of the Spanish coast at a distance from Point M equal to the distance from there to Pointe de la Negade. The latter and point X were joined with point R, where equidistance was no longer used.[207] The location of point R was a negotiated element.[208] Consequently, a 'box' surrounded by the points X, R, Pointe de la Negade, Pointe du Raz and Cabo Ortegal became the relevant area.

The length of the French coastal fronts from Pointe de la Negade to Pointe du Ras was 213 miles long, while the Spanish coast from point X to Cabo Orgegal 138 miles.[209] The ratio was 1.54:1. The continental shelf boundary divides the 'box' so as to leave approximately 22,000 square miles to France and 13,500 square miles to Spain. As the result, the ratio of the maritime spaces

[205] ibid, [495–97].

[206] For a detailed explanation, see Annexes to the Counter-Memorial of the United States in the *Gulf of Main* case, Annex 10, Pleadings, vol IV, 455–57; Legault and Hankey, 'Method,' 219–20; Report by Anderson in *IMB*, vol II, 1723; RD Hodgson, 'The Delimitation of Maritime Boundaries Between Opposite and Adjacent States Through the Economic Zone and the Continental Shelf: Selected State Practice' in TA Clingan, Jr, *Law of the Sea: State Practice in Zones of Special Jurisdiction, Proceedings of the Law of the Sea Institute Thirteenth Annual Conference in 1979* (Honolulu, Law of the Sea Institute, 1982) 297–98; United States Department of State, Office of the Geographer, *Limits in the Seas,* No 83 (1979) 10–15.

[207] Report by Anderson in *IMB*, vol II, 1723.

[208] *Limits in the Seas* No 83 (1979), 14.

[209] Those lines were called 'artificial coast lines' in *Limits in the Seas.* ibid, 14.

allocated was approximately 1.63:1.[210] Hence the ratio of coastal lengths and that of the maritime spaces almost coincide. In this case, the size of the relevant area and the way of calculating the length of the coasts is relatively clear.

Another example is the 1992 Protocol Supplementary to the Agreement between the United Kingdom and Ireland of 7 September 1988 Concerning the Delimitation of the Areas of the Continental Shelf between the Two Countries.[211] Ireland's coast is approximately 30 miles long, while that of the United Kingdom has a length of nearly 17.5 miles. The ratio between the two is 1.71:1.[212] This disparity was taken into account in the course of the negotiation, but it is unclear how. Furthermore, the substantial difference in relevant coastal lengths may be considered in the Indonesia-Viet Nam Agreement of 2003 in drawing the continental shelf boundary in favour to Viet Nam compared to a strict equidistance line.[213] In addition, to some extent, the disparity in overall coastal lengths was considered in the negotiations delimiting the continental shelf beyond 200 nautical miles between Denmark (Greenland) and Iceland to the benefit of Denmark.[214]

ii. Agreements Regarding Single Maritime Boundaries

There are several instances in which proportionality affected the location of single maritime boundaries. The first instance is the 1978 Boundary Delimitation Treaty between Venezuela and the Netherlands. While the length of the coastline of the Netherlands Major Leeward Antilles is 67.5 miles, Venezuela's coast measures 156 miles. Thus, the ratio between the two coasts is 1:2.3, as was stressed by the Venezuelan negotiators. Consequently, the Parties agreed to allocate to the Dutch Antilles 56 per cent of the maritime space which they could have claimed pursuant to strict equidistance. At the same time, it should be noted that elements of political geography, such as the considerable population of the Dutch islands and their autonomy and expectation of independence, contributed to the allocation of a relatively generous amount of maritime space to the Netherlands Antilles.[215]

In the 1988 Treaty between Denmark and the former German Democratic Republic, proportionality was taken into account when adjusting the line in the

[210] Report by Anderson in *IMB*, vol III, 1723.

[211] Text in ibid, 2495.

[212] Report by Anderson in ibid, p 2490. He indicates that ratio of the relevant coastline is 1 (UK):1.72 (Ireland). But if the ratio is rounded off to the second decimal place, it is 1:1.71.

[213] Report by McDorman and Schofield in *IMB*, vol VI, 4307.

[214] Report by Magnússon in ibid, vol VII, 5264.

[215] Hodgson, 'The Delimitation of Maritime Boundaries' 298–99; Legault and Hankey, 'Method' 220; Report by Nweihed in *IMB*, vol I, 621–22. For the text of the Agreement, see ibid, 631–37. In addition, Nweihed suggests that the 1980 Treaty between Venezuela and France might also have taken proportionality into account. But, as the writer admitted, this may not have been the case. ibid, 609.

Adler Grund area.[216] The 1986 Agreement between Burma and India allegedly considered proportionality as one of the reasons for extending Burma's maritime domain beyond a strictly equidistance line. In that case, the ratio of coastal lengths between the Burmese mainland and India's archipelago was 3.5:1. Yet it is unclear whether this disproportion was decisive for drawing the delimitation line. It could also be that partial effect was given to the Indian islands to justify a departure from strict equidistance.[217] It is also suggested that the 1997 Treaty between Thailand and Vietnam on the Delimitation of Maritime Boundary in the Gulf of Thailand took proportionality into account as well.[218] In the 2010 Agreement between Grenada and Trinidad and Tobago, the disparity in coastal lengths that revealed a 2.3:1 in favour of Trinidad and Tobago constituted the principal relevant circumstance for the adjustment of the provisional equidistance line.[219] In the 2010 Treaty between Norway and the Russian Federation, significant differences in length between the relevant Russian coasts of the Kola Peninsula and of Novaya Zemlya and those of the county of Finnmark on the Norwegian mainland contributed to the shift or adjustment of the delimitation line to the west in favour of Russia, as compared to a calculated equidistance line.[220]

Apart from the above-mentioned instances, however, no clear effect of proportionality upon the drawing of maritime boundaries can be established. Furthermore, even in cases where considerations of proportionality may be presumed to have been present, it is difficult to determine its effect on the negotiated boundary with any degree of precision. Indeed, in the field of negotiated settlements, the use of proportionality is often subjective and impressionistic.[221] It is true that owing to the paucity of available information, it is impossible to evaluate the ratio between relevant coasts and areas for each and every agreement relating to maritime delimitation in order to verify the effect of proportionality. Furthermore, the lack of criteria to determine the relevant coasts and areas makes it difficult to examine the role of proportionality in treaty practice. Nevertheless, the above description shows at least that the concept of proportionality is not supported by 'extensive and virtually uniform' State practice and *opinio juris* which can generate customary rules. It could be contended that

[216] Legault and Hankey, 'Method' 220–21. In this respect, the authors stated that the deviation from equidistance could also be justified by the attribution of partial effects to islands. However, Franckx is of the opinion that full effect was given to the Danish island of Bornholm, and that the delimitation line relied on proportionality. Report by Franckx in *IMB*, vol II, 2090–91. For the text of the Agreement, see ibid, 2094–96.

[217] Report by Cooper in ibid, vol II, 1334; Legault and Hankey, 'Method' 220.

[218] Interview with the Ambassador of Vietnam, Nguyen Quy Binh, on 2 March 2001.

[219] Report by Mitchell in *IMB*, vol VII, 4710.

[220] Report by Fife in ibid, 5167, 5185. Joint Statement on Maritime Delimitation and Cooperation in the Barents Sea and the Arctic Ocean explicitly referred to the 'effect of major disparities in respective coastal lengths'. This instrument was reproduced in T Henriksen and G Ulfstein, 'Maritime Delimitation in the Arctic: The Barents Sea Treaty' (2011) 42 *ODIL* 10–11.

[221] Legault and Hankey, 'Method' 219.

the role of proportionality in State practice remains modest and not altogether clear.

C. Summary

On the basis of the above considerations, two points can be made with regard to the concept of (dis)proportionality in the law of maritime delimitation.

The first point pertains to the change of the role of the concept of (dis)proportionality. The above survey reveals that the concept of proportionality first emerged in the particular geographical situation of the *North Sea Continental Shelf* cases. Subsequently, however, the ICJ and arbitral tribunals considered proportionality in every geographical situation. Before the *Black Sea* case, the manner of the application of the concept of proportionality was not consistent. In some cases, international courts and tribunals applied proportionality as an *ex post facto* test. In other cases, however, proportionality was not considered or it was not applied as an *ex post facto* test. In the *Black Sea* case, disproportionality was given a distinct status as an *ex post facto* test at the third stage of maritime delimitation. In subsequent cases, the disproportionality test was consistently applied as an *ex post facto* test. The disproportionality test is not in itself a method of delimitation. Nor does it aim to achieve an approximate correlation between the ratio of their respective shares of the relevant area. The function of the disproportionality test is to avoid a significant disproportionality.[222] Yet, as will be discussed in chapter nine, whether the disproportionality test contributes to enhancing predictability and objectivity of the law of maritime delimitation needs further consideration.

The second point concerns a difference between case law and State practice on this subject.[223] The above survey shows a clear contrast between case law and State practice. While almost all international decisions relating to maritime delimitation took proportionality into account, State practice tends to remain silent on this matter. The indifference of State practice toward proportionality challenges the legal basis for the disproportionality test. In light of the limited State practice, it will be difficult to find evidence to argue that the concept of proportionality is supported by 'extensive and virtually uniform' State practice and *opinio juris* which can generate customary rules. If so, the question arises from where the concept of (dis)proportionality derives. If the disproportionality test can be regarded as an operationalisation of the equitable principles that result in an equitable result, such an operationalisation must be undertaken in the framework of law, not *ex aequo et bono*. However, serious doubts can be expressed regarding whether the disproportionality test

[222] Tanaka, 'The Disproportionality Test' 317.
[223] ibid, 313–14.

developed through the jurisprudence is adequately objective and scientific as a norm of international law.[224] Overall it may have to be admitted that the concept of (dis)proportionality in the field of maritime delimitation is the fruit of judicial creativity, detached from actual State practice.[225]

IV. PRESENCE OF ISLANDS

It is beyond serious argument that the presence of islands may constitute a relevant circumstance in maritime delimitation. In the commentary to draft Article 72, which was to become Article 6 of the Convention on the Continental Shelf, the ILC already had stated that: 'As in the case of the boundaries of the territorial sea, provision must be made for departures necessitated by any exceptional configuration of the coast, as well as *the presence of islands* or of navigable channels.'[226] Furthermore, during the discussion relating to the draft Article, several proposals for eliminating islands from special circumstances were rejected by a majority of the Fourth Committee, which discussed questions of the continental shelf.[227] That rejection suggested that a majority of the Fourth Committee regarded islands as a special circumstance.[228] Moreover, as will be shown below, the case law and State practice clearly demonstrates that the presence of islands could be an important relevant circumstance.[229] Thus, this section examines the effect of islands upon maritime delimitations.[230]

[224] ibid, 314. In the *St Pierre and Miquelon* case, Weil already voiced his misgivings about the uncertainties of the proportionality test in its quantified form. Dissenting Opinion of Mr Weil, 1206, [24]. See also P Weil, *Perspectives du droit de la délimitation maritime* (Pedone, Paris, 1988) 259. The problems with the disproportionality test will be discussed in ch 9, s IV of this book.

[225] Tanaka, 'The Disproportionality Test' 313.

[226] Emphasis added. (1956) 2 *YILC* 300.

[227] Such a proposal was made by Italy and Iran. For the Italian proposition, see A/CONF13/C4/L25/Rev.1. *United Nations Conference on the Law of the Sea, Official Records,* Geneva, vol VI, 1958, 133; for the Iranian proposition, see A/CONF13/C4/L60, *ibid*, 142. The Italian proposal was rejected by 31 votes to three, with 18 abstentions. The Iranian amendment was rejected by 33 votes to two, with 21 abstentions, ibid, 98, [28] and [33]. By contrast, a delegate of the United Kingdom pointed to the presence of islands as an example of special circumstances, ibid, 93, [3].

[228] H Dipla, *Le régime juridique des îles dans le droit international de la mer* (Geneva, PUF, 1984) 148.

[229] For data of maritime features discussed in the jurisprudence, see A Pellet and B Samson, 'La delimitation des espaces marins' in M Forteau and J-M Thouvenin (eds), *Traité de droit international de la mer* (Paris, Pedone, 2017) 611–23.

[230] The examination of legal status of maritime features falls outside scope of this book. In this chapter (and this book), the term 'island' is used in a general manner and the use of the term 'island' does not mean that a maritime feature can be regarded as a fully entitled island pursuant to Art 121 of the LOSC. For an analysis of Art 121 by the author, see Y Tanaka, 'Reflections on the Interpretation and Application of Article 121(3) in the *South China Sea* Arbitration (Merits)' (2017) 48 *ODIL* 365–85.

A. Analysis of the Case Law

i. Islands in the Context of Continental Shelf Delimitations

a. Islands in the *Anglo-French Continental Shelf* Case

In the *Anglo-French Continental Shelf* case, the Court of Arbitration faced the question of whether the Channel Islands and the Scilly Isles were factors justifying a departure from the equidistance method. The Channel Islands, which are under British sovereignty, lie off the French coasts of Normandy and Brittany. At their nearest point, they are only 6.6 miles from the French coast. Accordingly, they are typical example of islands 'on the wrong side,' close to the coast of another State. They are composed of four principal islands. The total land area of the four is approximately 195 square kilometres, and their total population is about 130,000.[231] In addition, the Channel Islands have a high degree of autonomy and economic vitality.[232]

France maintained that the application of the equidistance method in the Channel Islands, as claimed by the United Kingdom, would produce inequitable results. Thus, the French Government proposed a solution giving the Channel Islands a six-mile enclaved zone.[233] The United Kingdom thought that a median line drawn between the Channel Islands and the French mainland should form the boundary. According to the United Kingdom, only very small islands may not be given full effect. However, the Channel Islands cannot be regarded as such in light of their area, population, commerce and degree of autonomy.[234] Furthermore, the United Kingdom questioned the six-mile enclave solution proposed by France. In the view of the United Kingdom, as the 12-mile territorial sea was clearly accepted, the Channel Islands should have a continental shelf of at least that same extent. Indeed, the Channel Islands already possessed a 12-mile fishery zone.[235]

The Court of Arbitration began its examination by clarifying the geographical and legal framework of the area. In the Court's view, owing to a considerable population as well as to their economic activities, the Channel Islands were clearly territorial and political units, which must be distinguished from rocks or small islands. This did not mean, however, that the UK Islands must be treated

[231] The *Anglo-French Continental Shelf* arbitral award, 18 *RIAA* 19–20, [6–7].

[232] ibid, 84, [171]. As indicated earlier, the relevant area to be delimited was the north and northwest of the Channel Islands. The Court of Arbitration did not have jurisdiction to effect delimitation in this region between the Channel Islands and the coasts of Normandy and Brittany, because this area involves the Parties' territorial seas. ibid, 22–25, [14–22].

[233] ibid, 76–77, [150]. See also 81–82, [164–67].

[234] ibid, 84, [171]. The United Kingdom contended that 'for boundary purpose there is no difference between islands and mainland and, therefore, the median line is the proper boundary with any opposite State in the absence of agreement or special circumstances.' ibid, 83, [170].

[235] ibid, 87, [179].

as a semi-independent States. Considering that the Britain was responsible for the foreign relations and maritime jurisdiction of the Channel Islands, the latter should be regarded as islands of the United Kingdom. Thus, the legal framework in this region was that of two opposite States, one of which possessed island territories close to the coast of the other State.[236]

The Court of Arbitration then turned to the second question, ie, the effect of these islands upon the continental shelf boundary. In this respect, the Court declined to accept that the Channel Islands should be considered a projection from the mainland of the United Kingdom constituting its coast 'opposite' *vis-à-vis* France. Accordingly, the question was one of the extent of the Channel Islands' own entitlement to a continental shelf as islands separated from the United Kingdom.[237] Next, the Court examined the question of whether the Channel Islands, if given full effect, would create inequitable results. Noting the approximate equality of the mainland coastlines of the Parties and the equality of their geographical relation to the continental shelf, the Court of Arbitration pronounced that:

> The presence of these British islands close to the French coast, if they are given full effect in delimiting the continental shelf, will manifestly result in a substantial diminution of the area of continental shelf which would otherwise accrue to the French Republic. This fact by itself appears to the Court to be, *prima facie*, a circumstance creative of inequity and calling for a method of delimitation that in some measure redresses the inequity.[238]

Thus, the Court of Arbitration adopted a two-fold solution. First, as the primary boundary, the Court drew a median line between the mainlands of the two States. Secondly, it created a 12-mile enclave to the north and west of the Channel Islands (see Illustration 5).[239] The Court's solution calls for two comments.

The first point to be noted is the novelty of the Court's enclave solution. As will be seen later, *before* this award, there was no precedent adopting the total-enclave solution in State practice. Accordingly, the award of 1977 was the first case of totally enclaving a continental shelf in maritime delimitation.[240]

[236] ibid, 88–89, [184–87].

[237] ibid, 90–91, [189–90].

[238] ibid, 93, [196].

[239] ibid, 94–95, [201–02].

[240] DW Bowett, 'The Arbitration between the United Kingdom and France Concerning the Continental Shelf Boundary in the English Channel and South-Western Approaches' (1978) 44 *BYIL* 8. This article was reproduced in his book, *The Regime of Islands in International Law* (New York, NY, Oceana, 1979). (In this section, the views quoted are those expressed in *BYIL*). It will be noted that the decisive precedent of the enclave solution could be found in the delimitation of lakes. In Lake Nyasa, two Malawian islands, ie, Chizamula and Likoma, are located in the 'wrong side' of a median line. The 1954 Agreement between the United Kingdom and Portugal established a two mile enclave around these islands. At the same time, the United Kingdom's – today Malawi's – unconditional rights concerning access to the islands were accepted by the Agreement. L Caflisch, 'Règles générales du droit des cours d'eau internationaux' (1989) 219 *RCADI* 99; HW Jayewardene, *The Regime of Islands in International Law* (Dordrecht, Nijhoff, 1990) 245–47.

Figure 5

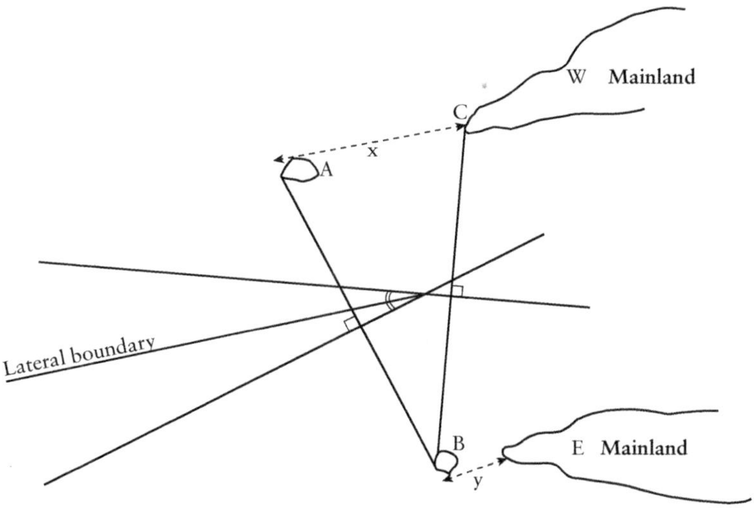

Source: DW Bowett, 'The Arbitration between the United Kingdom and France Concerning the Continental Shelf Boundary in the English Channel and South-Western Approaches,' (1978) 44 *BYIL* 23. Reprinted with permission of the *BYIL*.

The second point to be examined is the question of why the radius of the enclave should be 12 miles. A principal reason may consist in the fact that a 12-mile fishery zone was already established around the Channel Islands. Indeed, the Court stated that the second boundary must not be so drawn as to allow the French continental shelf to encroach upon the 12-mile fishery zone of the islands.[241] Another reason may be that the Channel Islands would possibly extend their territorial seas from three to 12 miles.[242] According to the Court's solution, however, the Channel Islands would have no continental shelf once the territorial sea is extended to 12 miles.[243]

Another issue concerned the Scilly Isles in the Atlantic area. The British territory of the Scilly Isles lies, at the nearest point, some 21 nautical miles, and at their most westerly point, some 31 nautical miles from the mainland

[241] The *Anglo-French Continental Shelf* arbitral award, 18 *RIAA* 95, [202]. On this point, however, Bowett criticised that the Court failed to clarify any reason as to why the 12-mile fishery zone should coincide with the boundary of the continental shelf. Bowett, 'The Arbitration between the United Kingdom and France' 9. The Court of Arbitration might have taken into account the fact that the United Kingdom itself contended that the Channel Islands should have a continental shelf of at least 12 miles.

[242] The *Anglo-French Continental Shelf* arbitral award, 18 *RIAA* 89–90, [187].

[243] DM McRae, 'Delimitation of the Continental Shelf between the United Kingdom and France: The Channel Arbitration' (1977) 15 *CYIL* 190. On the other hand, it is conceivable that the solution of the Court could serve as a guideline for the proposition that the extent of the enclave cannot be inferior to the maximum potential territorial sea. MD Blecher, 'Equitable Delimitation of Continental Shelf' (1979) 73 *AJIL* 80.

Figure 6

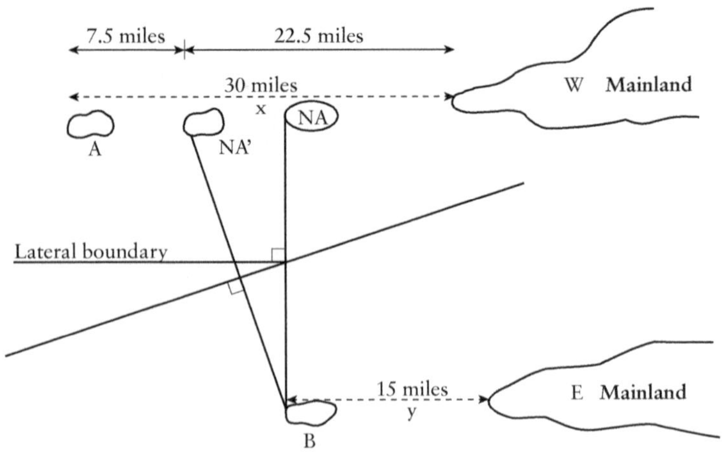

Source: Drawn by the author on the basis of Bowett's article.

of the United Kingdom. The French island of Ushant is, at its nearest point, only about 10 nautical miles and, at its most westerly point no more than 14.1 nautical miles off the coast of Finistère.[244] France alleged that the Scillies and Ushant constituted special circumstances which called for a method other than that of equidistance. As an equitable boundary, France proposed a median line between two straight lines which purported to represent the general direction respectively of the French coast (line DGF) and the British coast (line DGB), respectively. In drawing these straight lines – so-called '*lignes de lissage*' – neither Ushant nor the Scillies were taken into account.[245] However, the United Kingdom contended that France had not discharged the onus of showing the existence of special circumstances in the region.[246] It thus proposed a median line equidistant from the baselines of each State, taking the Scilly Isles and Ushant into account.[247]

The Court of Arbitration found that the projection westwards of the Scilly Isles constituted a special circumstance. In the Court's view, considering that the coasts of the Parties were not markedly different in extent and were broadly similar in their relation to the continental shelf, giving full effect to the Scilly Isles would have produced disproportionate effects.[248] Thus the Court held that: 'The appropriate method, in the opinion of the Court, is to take account of

[244] The *Anglo-French Continental Shelf* arbitral award, 18 *RIAA* 110, [235].
[245] ibid, 98–99, [209].
[246] ibid, 99, [210].
[247] ibid, 100, [212].
[248] ibid, 114, [244].

the Scilly Isles as part of the coastline of the United Kingdom but to give them less than their full effect in applying the equidistance method.'[249] As a specific method, the Court determined to give the Scilly Isles half effect. The distance between the Scilly Isles and the mainland of the United Kingdom is twice that separating Ushant from the French mainland. For the Court, this was 'an indication of the suitability of the half effect method.'[250] Thus, the Court drew, first, an equidistance line without using offshore islands as a base-point and, next, using it as a base-point. A boundary line was then drawn mid-way between those two equidistance lines (Figure 5).[251] According to the Court's solution, Ushant was given full effect.

The method of giving half effect to the Scilly Isles was criticised by Bowett. According to him, the Court's method of half effect was questionable, since it treated the island of Ushant as if it were a mainland.[252] Indeed, following the Court's method, it was more disadvantageous to the United Kingdom than if both islands and groups had been ignored completely. Thus, he suggested an alternative method. Suppose that island A lies 30 miles from W and island B is located 15 miles off the coast of E (Figure 6). In that case, island A is further removed from W than island B is from E by 15 miles. Consequently, the excess distance requiring correction is 15 miles. It is this excess which should be given half effect, not the whole distance from the mainland. According to Bowett, if the inequity brought about by the two islands consists in the fact that the one lies further offshore than the other, it is preferable to apply the ratio of the distance to this 'excess' rather than to the whole distance of island A from its mainland. Thus, according to that formula, the half effect is to be applied to the *excess distance* of 15 miles. Accordingly, one could divide the 'excess' by the ratio 1/2, ie, 7.5 miles. In short, Bowett's proposition may be expressed by the formula $(y/x) \times (x - y)$.

One could then draw back island A by 7.5 miles from the present position to give a notional position. In that case, the notional position for the island A (NA') would be located at 22.5 miles from the mainland W (30 – 7.5 = 22.5 miles). One would then proceed to join NA' and B by a straight line and draw the perpendicular bisector of that line to give lateral boundary. This method would be more favourable to mainland W than the method of the Court, and, according to Bowett, more equitable.[253] In short, the *Anglo-French Continental Shelf* case created two novelties relating to the role of islands in the delimitation of the continental shelf: the enclave solution for the

[249] ibid, 116, [249].

[250] ibid, 117, [251]. But the Court prudently added that it does not attribute 'any special force as a criterion to this ratio of the difference in the distances of the Scillies and Ushant from their respective mainlands.' ibid.

[251] ibid.

[252] Bowett, 'The Arbitration between the United Kingdom and France,' 24; JRV Prescott, *The Maritime Political Boundaries of the World* (London, Methuen, 1985) 290.

[253] Bowett, 'The Arbitration between the United Kingdom and France' 24–26.

Channel Islands and the half effect given to the Scilly Isles. In this respect, the Court of Arbitration broke new ground.[254]

b. Islands in the ICJ Jurisprudence

The issue of islands has been discussed in the ICJ jurisprudence respecting the delimitation of the continental shelf. In the *Tunisia/Libya* case, the Tunisian islands of Jerba and Kerkennah were at issue. The island of Jerba, which has a surface of 514 square kilometres, is separated from the mainland by a very narrow strait. It has a considerable permanent population.[255] The Kerkennah Islands lie some 11 miles from the Tunisian coast. The land area of the islands is approximately 180 square kilometres.[256] In addition, shoals and low-tide elevations also surround the seaward side of the islands, constituting a belt varying from nine to 27 km in width. In its submissions to the ICJ, Tunisia contended that the delimitation should take into account the fact that 'the eastern coastal front of Tunisia was marked by the presence of a body of islands, islets and low-tide elevations which form a constituent part of the Tunisian littoral.'[257] Libya maintained that both the Jerba and the Kerkennah Islands should be excluded from the delimitation of the continental shelf.[258]

With respect to the island of Jerba, the Court stated that:

> [T]he presence of the island of Jerba and of the Kerkennah Islands and the surrounding low-tide elevations is a circumstance which clearly calls for consideration. [...] However that may be, the Court cannot accept the exclusion in principle of the island of Jerba and the Kerkennah Islands from consideration.[259]

At the same time, the Court added that:

> The practical method for the delimitation to be expounded by the Court hereafter is in fact such that, in the part of the area to be delimited in which the island of Jerba would be relevant, there are other considerations which prevail over the effect of its presence; the existence and position of the Kerkennah Islands and surrounding low-tide elevations, on the other hand, are material.[260]

[254] Attention will be drawn to the *Dubai/Sharjah Border* case, although the latter did not lead to an international judgment but rather concerns a dispute between two member States of a federation. Sharjah requested the Court of Arbitration to give the island of Abu Musa half effect. The Court refused to admit this request since it would have produced a distorting effect upon neighbouring shelf areas. Thus, the Court determined to give a full 12-mile territorial sea to Abu Musa. (1993) 91 *ILR* 677 and 680.

[255] Counter-Memorial of Tunisia, vol II, 53. See also Memorial of Tunisia, vol I, 65. In 1984, its population was 92,269. *La grande encyclopedie du monde: Afrique,* vol X (Bruxelle, Edition Atlas, 1988) 4306.

[256] [1982] ICJ Rep 89, [128]. The population of the Kerkennah was 15,000. Counter-Memorial of Tunisia, vol II, 52.

[257] [1982] ICJ Rep 28, [15].

[258] ibid, 63, [79].

[259] ibid, 63–64, [79].

[260] ibid.

The phrase appears to suggest that the effect given to the Jerba and the Kerkennah may be different. In fact, the Court neglected the island of Jerba in drawing a boundary, although the Court took it into account when calculating the Tunisian coastline for the proportionality test.[261] The Court also indicated a delimitation line on the basis of the concession lines drawn by the Parties. To this extent, geographical factors became irrelevant for the Court.

However, the exclusion of Jerba Island from consideration invited criticism by Judge Evensen. In his view, it was difficult to agree with the Court's disregarding of Jerba. In fact, at low tide, it is scarcely an island, since it is separated from the mainland only by a very narrow strait. In that sense, it is actually a continuation of the mainland. Furthermore, the island has a large surface and its economic importance is significant. It has a considerable permanent population. Thus, according to Judge Evensen, the island of Jerba is by no means a small and negligible feature.[262] As the problem regarding the ignoring of Jerba Island relates to the validity of the Court's solution based on the conduct of the Parties, it might be irrelevant to discuss that issue as an isolated question. Yet it appears at least that there is an inconsistency in the Court's arguments which ignored the island of Jerba while simultaneously accepting that it was a relevant circumstance.

Regarding the Kerkennah Islands, the Court found it necessary to take into account not only the islands but also the low-tide elevations. A line drawn from the most westerly point of the Gulf of Gabes along the seaward coast of the islands would run at a bearing of approximately 62° to the meridian. However, the Court considered that the line of 62° to the meridian, which runs parallel to the coastline of the islands, would give excessive weight to the Kerkennahs. For that reason, the Court thought it appropriate to attribute them only partial effect on the basis of 'a number of examples in State practice'. It then decided to attribute 'half effect' to the Kerkennah Islands. It did so by drawing a line bisecting the angle between the line of the Tunisian coast (42°) and the tangent of the seaward coast of the Kerkennah Islands (62°). Consequently, a line of 52° to the meridian was to be the boundary of the continental shelf in this area.[263] On the other hand, the Court ignored the Kerkennah Islands when calculating the length of the coast for the purposes of the proportionality test.

However, the Court's delimitation in this area is open to objections. First and foremost, it is unclear why only half effect should be given to the Kerkennah Islands. It should be recalled that the half effect given to the Scilly Isles in the *Anglo-French Continental Shelf* case had geometrical grounds. Yet there was no such reason in the present instance. Moreover, unlike the Scilly Isles, which are

[261] ibid, 85, [120].

[262] Dissenting Opinion of Judge Evensen, ibid, 300, [17]. Judge Evensen indicated that the Island of Jerba had a surface of some 690 square kilometres, which corresponded to twice the size of Malta. According to Tunisia, however, the surface of Jerba is 514 square kilometres. Counter-Memorial of Tunisia, vol II, 53. See also Dipla, *Le régime juridique des îles* 209.

[263] [1982] ICJ Rep 88–89, [128–29].

located, at its nearest point, approximately 21 nautical miles from the mainland of the United Kingdom, the Kerkennah Islands lie at a distance of only 11 nautical miles from the Tunisian coast. It is doubtful whether such offshore islands could be regarded as an abnormal geographical feature. As pointed out by Judge Evensen, the Court did not prove why attributing full effect to the Kerkennahs would be giving them 'excessive weight'.[264] True, the Court referred, in a general way, to State practice as supporting the proposal to give only partial effect to the Kerkennahs. Yet the specifics of such State practice were not discussed at all.

Secondly, the Court disregarded the low-tide elevations surrounding the Kerkennah Islands without giving any reason. This is hard to reconcile with the view formerly expressed that the Kerkennah Islands *and* the surrounding low-tide elevations were a circumstance clearly calling for consideration.[265]

Thirdly, it will be noted that the method of half effect in this case is different from that used in the *Anglo-French Continental Shelf* award. In the latter, half effect was used to correct equidistance lines. In the 1982 judgment, it was resorted to, not to correct an equidistance line, but to construct a boundary entirely independent of such a line.[266] Furthermore, in the *Tunisia/Libya* case, the line in question relied solely on the Tunisian coast. This is highly questionable, as the other Party's coast was neglected completely.[267] In any event the Court in 1982 created another novelty regarding the half effect method.

Fourthly, it appears that the Court's view regarding the islands lacks consistency. The Court discounted the Kerkennah Islands in the calculation of proportionality but gave them half effect. By contrast, while the Court ignored Jerba in establishing a delimitation line, it took the island into account when calculating the length of the Tunisian coast for the proportionality test. The contradiction regarding the role of islands inherent in the judgment will prove a source of complication for maritime delimitations.[268] In light of those problems, the Court runs the risk of being accused of excessive subjectivity regarding the treatment of islands.[269]

The next case to be examined is the *Libya/Malta* case. The fact that Malta is an island State gave rise to some argument. The Parties agreed that the entitlement to a continental shelf was the same for an island as for mainland territory. However, Libya argued that, as with the Channel Islands

[264] Dissenting Opinion of Judge Evensen, ibid, 304, [19]. See also Dissenting Opinion of Judge Gros, ibid, 150, [14].

[265] On this point, Judge Evensen pointed out '[i]f these low-tide elevations had been taken into account the line drawn from the westernmost point of the Gulf of Gabes to the Kerkennahs would run approximately in the direction of 66 to the meridian and not 62. Even according to the Court's ruling of giving half effect to the Kerkennahs … the veering should in no event be a 52 line but a line running some 57.5 to the meridian.' Dissenting Opinion of Judge Evensen, ibid, 304, [19].

[266] Judgment, ibid, 467.

[267] Dissenting Opinion of Judge Oda, [1982] ICJ Rep 268–69, [179]. See also Kolb, *Case Law on Equitable Maritime Delimitation* 194.

[268] Weil, *Perspective du droit de la délimitation maritime* 247–48.

[269] Dissenting Opinion of Judge Evensen, [1982] ICJ Rep 300, [17].

in the 1977 award, an island may be treated in a particular way in the actual delimitation.[270] Malta emphasised the distinction between island States and islands politically linked to a mainland State. In the Maltese view, it was only in the case of dependent islands that international law gave them less than full effect.[271] In this connection, the ICJ explained that:

> [I]t might well be that the sea boundaries in this region would be different if the islands of Malta did not constitute an independent State, but formed a part of the territory of one of the surrounding countries. This aspect of the matter is related not solely to the circumstances of Malta being a group of islands, and an independent State, but also to the position of the islands in the wider geographical context, particularly their position in a semi-enclosed sea.[272]

This citation appears to suggest that the effect given to an island will depend on the status of the island as an independent State or as part of the territory of a State. In order to determine the extreme limits of a shift of the median line between Libya and Malta, the Court supposed the Maltese islands to be a part of the Italian territory, as if there were a question of the delimitation of the continental shelf between Libya and Italy. In that case, in the view of the Court, the boundary would not be the median line between Libya and Sicily, since at least 'some account would be taken of the islands of Malta.' The Court continued that:

> [E]ven if the minimum account were taken, the continental shelf boundary between Italy and Libya would be somewhat south of the median line between the Sicilian and Libyan coasts. Since Malta is not part of Italy, but is an independent State, it cannot be the case that, as regards continental shelf rights, it will be in a worse position because of its independence.[273]

It is implicit in this citation that, since the islands of Malta form an independent State, they will enjoy a larger continental shelf area than if they were part of the territory of another State.[274] In determining the continental shelf boundary, it was difficult, however, to determine the different effect between the status of an independent State and that of islands which belong to another State.

ii. Islands in the Context of the Single/Coincident Maritime Boundaries

a. Islands in the ICJ Jurisprudence

The issues of islands were raised in many cases before the ICJ. In the *Gulf of Maine* case, the Canadian territory of Seal Island was at issue in the

[270] [1985] ICJ Rep 42, [52].
[271] ibid.
[272] ibid, 42, [53].
[273] ibid, 51, [72].
[274] Yet the Court of Arbitration in the *St Pierre and Miquelon* case said that this paragraph suggested equality of treatment rather than a less favoured status for politically dependent islands. The *St Pierre and Miquelon* case (1992) 31 *ILM* 1165, [50].

delimitation of the second segment. Seal Island is some two and a half miles long, and lies 14.234 km (approximately 7.69 miles) off the coast of Nova Scotia (see Illustration 10). It is inhabited all year round.[275] The Chamber of the Court considered that Seal Island could not be disregarded owing to its position. In the Chamber's view, 'it would be excessive to treat the coastline of Nova Scotia as transferred south-westwards by the whole of the distance between Seal Island and that coast.'[276] Accordingly, the Chamber determined to give the island half effect. At the same time, as explained elsewhere in this study, another factor of proportionality should be considered in the second segment. Applying the ratio of 1.38:1 to the total distance between the half effect position of Seal Island and Cape Cod, the median line provisionally drawn was to be corrected toward Nova Scotia in proportion of 1.32 to 1.38.[277]

The reasoning of the Chamber was very condensed, leaving some ambiguities. Indeed, as with the *Tunisia/Libya* case relating to the Kerkennah Islands, the Chamber failed to specify why giving Seal Island full effect would be excessive. Owing to the fact that Seal Island lies only some 7.69 miles from the Canadian coast, it is doubtful whether a significant distorting effect would be produced. Furthermore, no explanation can be found in the judgment as to why there should be a half effect rather than any other ratio.[278] In addition, the Chamber's technique for giving half effect to Seal Island merits attention. Applying the half effect method, the Chamber drew Seal Island back to half its real distance from the mainland. The distance between Seal Island and Chebogue Point in Nova Scotia was 14,234 meters. Dividing this distance by two, a position of 7,117 meters from Chebogue Point would represent a notional half effect position for Seal Island.[279] This half effect technique is different from that method used in the *Anglo-French Continental Shelf* arbitral award or in the *Tunisia/Libya* case.

The next case to be examined is the *Jan Mayen* case. Greenland is a large island belonging to Denmark. Its total population is approximately 55,000. The Norwegian island of Jan Mayen, about 53 km long and with a maximum width of 16 km, has no settled population and is located approximately 550 miles west of northern Norway.[280] Both Greenland and Jan Mayen could be regarded as detached islands separated from their mother States. Denmark claimed entitlement to a full 200-mile continental shelf and

[275] [1984] ICJ Rep 336–37, [222]. Yet the number of the population in 1984 is unclear. According to Canadian Advisory Services, the island has had a manned light station since 1832. In 1984, there would have been at least two lighthouse keepers and possibly, but not necessarily, their families. Email from Information Officer dated 3 April 2001.

[276] [1984] ICJ Rep 336–37, [222].

[277] ibid. See also s III of this chapter.

[278] A partial explanation given by the Chamber may be that the practical impact of Seal Island was limited. Yet, this could not be a reason for avoiding clarification of the legal motives for the half effect in question.

[279] Technical Report of the *Gulf of Maine* case, [1984] ICJ Rep 350, [13].

[280] [1993] ICJ Rep 46, [14–15].

FZ for Greenland.[281] Norway limited its claim to the area inside the median line. Nevertheless, this did not mean that it considered that Jan Mayen was less entitled to a 200-mile continental shelf and FZ than the coast of Greenland.[282] Thus, Norway called the area between the 200-mile line claimed by Denmark and the 200-mile line potentially claimable by Norway a 'potential area of overlap of claims'. The ICJ referred to it as the 'area of overlapping potential entitlement'.[283] In this respect, there was little doubt that Greenland and Jan Mayen were entitled to 200-mile maritime spaces.[284] As pointed out earlier, the median line provisionally drawn was adjusted so as to attribute larger areas to Greenland on account of proportionality and equitable access to fisheries. It appears that the specific situation of delimitation between two detached islands had no impact upon the process of delimitation.

The *Qatar v Bahrain* case (Merits) raised the issues of legal effects given to three islands: (i) The Hawar Islands, (ii) Janan Island, and (iii) Qit'at Jaradah. There was only a short distance between the islands and the main coastlines of the Parties.[285] Furthermore, with respect to some maritime features, the Parties were divided on the question of whether or not they were islands or low-tide elevations.

The first issue to be examined was the effect to be given to the Hawar Islands. The main island of Hawar group is located at a distance of 21.85 kilometres (approximately 11.8 nautical miles) from the nearest coastal point on Bahrain's main island. At low tide, the distance between the tip of the spit of Hawar Island and the nearest point on the Qatari coast is 250 meters. Approximately half of the Hawar group lies wholly or partially within three miles of Qatar's mainland coast.[286] The Parties disputed sovereignty over the Hawar Islands. Regarding this question, the ICJ found that Bahrain has sovereignty over them.[287] It follows that there are Bahraini islands in the immediate vicinity of the Qatari mainland coast.

When drawing a delimitation line, the Court did not regard the Hawar Islands as a relevant circumstance. This appears to suggest that it gave them full effect when drawing an equidistant boundary line. The Court's solution

[281] However, the claim of Denmark was criticised by Judge Oda on account of the fact that Denmark simply claimed the whole potential area of its entitlement without any regard to the entitlement of Jan Mayen. Separate Opinion of Judge Oda, ibid, 101, [44].

[282] ibid, 47, [19].

[283] ibid.

[284] The Conciliation Commission of 1981, established by Norway and Iceland to settle the delimitation of the continental shelf, suggested that Jan Mayen must be considered an island and, therefore, is entitled to a territorial sea, an EEZ and a continental shelf. *Report and Recommendations to the Governments of Iceland and Norway of the Conciliation Commission on the Continental Shelf Area between Iceland and Jan Mayen*, (1981) 20 *ILM* 803–4.

[285] Accordingly, one should note that arguments to be examined here relate to territorial sea delimitation.

[286] Memorial submitted by Qatar, 50.

[287] Judgment, [2001] ICJ Rep 85, [147]; 116–17, [252].

invited a criticism, however, by Judge *ad hoc* Torres Bernárdez. In his view, the delimitation line drawn by the Court 'leads indeed to an *extraordinary disproportionate effect* in the maritime delimitation of that area *because the Hawar Islands are too close to, indeed, they are in fact part of, the Qatari mainland coast facing them*.'[288] On the basis of the *Anglo–French Continental Shelf* case, Judge *ad hoc* Torres Bernárdez argued that the Court should have applied the enclave method in the Hawar Islands area. According to him, the enclave solution could be achieved by defining to the west of the Hawar islands and area of common territorial sea or by creating a Qatari corridor of territorial sea between the Hawar Islands and Bahrain Island.[289]

It is indeed curious that there was no argument regarding effect to be attributed to the Hawar group in the decision, despite the fact that these islands are very close to Qatar's coastline. In the Hawar Islands area, however, it might be difficult to adopt the enclave solution as had been done for Channel Islands in the *Anglo-French Continental Shelf* case. On the eastern side of the Hawar group, the distance between the islands and Qatar's coastline is partly less than three miles. In such a case, the only realistic solution may be to draw a median line between Hawar group and Qatar's coastline. Furthermore, there is no Qatari territory in the area between the Hawar islands and Bahrain's main island, and consequently, Qatar has no entitlement regarding territorial sea in this area. Accordingly, it might be difficult to create an enclave on the western side of the Hawar Islands.

The next issue related to Janan Island. According to Qatar, it is an island approximately 700 metres long and 175 metres wide situated off the south-western tip of the main Hawar Island. The island is located 2.9 miles, or 5,360 metres, from the nearest point on Qatar's low-water line and 17 miles from the nearest point of Bahrain (Ras al Barr). It is located at a distance of 1.6 miles, or 2,890 metres, from the main Hawar islands.[290] Sovereignty over the island was disputed between the Parties. The Court decided that Qatar had sovereignty over Janan Island, including Hadd Janan.[291]

Janan Island lies near to the Bahrain's Hawar Islands. Yet, the Court made no argument relating to the effect to be attributed to Janan Island. It decided that, from the point of intersection of the respective maritime limits of Saudi Arabia on the one hand and of Bahrain and Qatar on the other, the boundary would follow a north-easterly direction, then immediately turn in an easterly direction, after which it would pass between Jazirat Hawar and Janan.[292] As the boundary is an equidistance line, it could be contended that Janan Island was given full effect.

[288] Dissenting Opinion of Judge *ad hoc* Torres Bernárdez, ibid, 441, [536].
[289] ibid, [543].
[290] Memorial submitted by Qatar, 183.
[291] Judgment, [2001] ICJ Rep 117, [252].
[292] ibid, 109, [222].

The third issue to be considered was Qit'at Jaradah, which is situated within the 12-mile territorial sea of both States. While Qatar argued that it was a low-tide elevation,[293] Bahrain regarded it as an island.[294] As pointed out, the Court found that Qit'at Jaradah is an island which should be taken into consideration for the drawing of the equidistance line.[295] In this connection, an issue arose with regard to the effect to be given to Qit'at Jaradah. This small island is situated nearly midway between the main island of Bahrain and the Qatar peninsula. In this regard, the Court held that: '[I]f its low-water line were to be used for determining a basepoint in the construction of the equidistance line, and this line taken as the delimitation line, a disproportionate effect would be given to an insignificant maritime feature.'[296] In the view of the Court, Qit'at Jaradah constituted a special circumstance. Accordingly, the Court drew a delimitation line passing immediately to the east of Qit'at Jaradah.[297]

In the northern sector, where a single maritime boundary was to be drawn, an issue arose whether Fasht al Jarim, which is partly situated in the Bahraini territorial sea, should be given full effect. Without specifying the legal nature of this maritime feature, the Court held that, given its location, its low-water line might be used as a baseline from which the breadth not only of the territorial sea, but also of the continental shelf and the EEZ, is measured.[298] In the Court's view, however, to use Fasht al Jarim as a baseline would lead to an inequitable result. Thus, the Court decided that Fasht al Jarim should have no effect on the boundary line in the northern sector.[299] An explanation may be that the delimitation in the relevant area was one between adjacent coasts. Considering that the adjacent coasts of the Parties were not markedly different in character or extent, as the Court indicated, the projection northwards of Fasht al Jarim would have produced disproportionate effects.

Overall, owing to the presence of many tiny islands in the limited area, the geographical situation in the *Qatar v Bahrain* case was highly complicated. On account of the complexity of the areas, it would appear that the Court took a pragmatic approach. When disregarding Qit'at Jaradah and Fast al Jarim, for instance, the Court failed to explain why giving full effect to those maritime features would produce a distorting effect. The only criterion was whether or not there was a sufficient distance between the delimitation line and each coast.

[293] Memorial submitted by Qatar, 238–39; presentation by Quéneudec, Counsel of Qatar, Verbatim Record, CR 2000/9, [32–39].

[294] Memorial submitted by Bahrain, 268–69, [622–24]; Counter-Memorial submitted by Bahrain, [511–20]; presentation by Reisman, Counsel of Bahrain, Verbatim Record, CR 2000/14, [26–31].

[295] Judgment, [2001] ICJ Rep 99, [195]. According to Bahrain, at high tide, the length and breadth of Qit'at Jaradah is approximately 12 by four metres, whereas at low tide these distances are 600 and 75 metres. At high tide, its elevation is approximately 0.4 metres. ibid, 99–100, [197].

[296] ibid, 104–9, [219].

[297] ibid.

[298] ibid, 114, [245].

[299] ibid, 114–15, [247–48].

In the *Cameroon v Nigeria* case (Merits), Cameroon asserted that the presence of Bioko Island constituted a relevant circumstance to be taken into account since Bioko Island substantially reduced the seaward projection of Cameroon's coastline. By drawing an analogy with the *Anglo-French Continental Shelf* and *St Pierre and Miquelon* cases, Cameroon argued that Bioko should not necessarily be given its full effect and that a radical and absolute cut-off of the projection of Cameroon's coastal front should be avoided.[300] Nigeria opposed Cameroon's argument. According to Nigeria, Bioko cannot simply be treated as a relevant circumstance since it is a major part of an independent State, possessing its own maritime areas on which the Court is not entitled to encroach. The same is true in regard to the archipelago of São Tomé and Príncipe. Nigeria contended that Cameroon's 'equitable line' gave these islands no effect, taking account only of the mainland coasts. In addition, Nigeria alleged that, since Bioko Island belonged to Equatorial Guinea, their effect could not be reduced in the absence of some other relevant or special circumstance justifying this.[301]

The Court accepted that islands have sometimes been considered as a relevant circumstance when such islands lie within the zone to be delimited and fall under the sovereignty of one of the parties.[302] In the present case, however, Bioko Island is a territory of a third State, Equatorial Guinea. Thus the Court concluded that the effect of Bioko Island on the seaward projection of the Cameroonian coastal front was an issue between Cameroon and Equatorial Guinea and not between Cameroon and Nigeria; consequently, Bioko was not a relevant circumstance in this case.[303]

In the *Black Sea* case, an issue arose whether the presence of Serpents' Island constitutes relevant circumstances calling for an adjustment of the provisional equidistance line.[304] In light of the geographical configuration of Serpents' Island, the Court took the view that any continental shelf and EEZ entitlements possibly generated by Serpents' Island could not project further than the entitlements generated by Ukraine's mainland coast. Any possible entitlements generated by Serpents' Island in an eastward direction are fully subsumed by the entitlements generated by the western and eastern mainland coasts of Ukraine itself. The Court accordingly concluded that: '[T]he presence of Serpents Island does not

[300] ibid, 434, [274]. Memorial of Cameroon, 550, [5.114]; Reply of Cameroon, 409, [9.61–9.62]; presentation by Kamto, Counsel of Cameroon, Verbatim Record CR 2002/6, 41–42, [48–51].

[301] Judgment, [2002] ICJ Rep 435–36, [279]; presentation by Professor Georges Abi-Saab, Counsel of Nigeria, Verbatim Record, CR 2002/13, 36, [33–34]; ibid, Verbatim Record, CR 2000/20, 42, [13–14].

[302] Judgment, [2002] ICJ Rep 446, [299].

[303] ibid.

[304] Serpents' Island is above water at high tide, and has a surface area of approximately 0.17 sq km and a circumference of approximately 2,000 m. [2009] ICJ Rep 70, [16]. See also S Touzé, 'Affaire relative à la Délimitation maritime en mer Noire (Roumanie c. Ukraine): une clarification didactique de la règle de l'équidistance circonstances pertinentes' (2009) 55 *AFDI* 240–41.

call for an adjustment of the provisional equidistance line.'[305] At the same time, it stated that a 12-nautical-mie territorial sea was attributed to Serpents Island pursuant to agreement between the Parties.[306] In consequence, Serpents' Island has only a 12-nautical mile arc of the territorial sea. The Court's solution would seem to produce the same effect that Serpents' Island is treated as a rock under Article 121(3) of the LOSC, even though the Court did not determine the legal status of that Island.[307]

In the *Nicaragua v Colombia* case (Merits), the effect given to Quitasueño and Serrana was at issue. Quitasueño is a large bank approximately 57 kilometres long and 20 kilometres wide. Among multiple marine features at Quitasueño, only one feature named QS 32 is above water at high tide. It is a minuscule feature, barely one square metre in area, and is above water at high tide only by some 0.7 metres.[308] Interestingly the ICJ made clear that: 'Quitasueño is *a rock* incapable of sustaining human habitation or an economic life of its own and thus falls within the rule stated in Article 121, paragraph 3, of UNCLOS [LOSC] ….'[309] The Court accordingly established a 12-nautical-mile envelope of arcs around Quitasueño. Similarly it constructed only a 12-nautical-mile envelope of arcs measured from Serrana Cay and other cays in its vicinity in light of its small size, remoteness and other characteristics. Accordingly, Serrana was given the same effect as Quitasueño.[310] It follows that Serrana was *de facto* treated as a rock, even though the Court refrained from deciding the legal status of Serrana. Yet, Serrana is larger than Quitasueño[311] and Serrana cay has a six-metre-wide well for water supply of the marine infantry corpsmen and fishermen who visit the cay. There are also facilities, solar panels and communication systems for a detachment of the Colombian marine infantry.[312] Hence it is open to debate whether the legal status of, and effect given to, Serrana should be the same as Quitasueño.[313]

Finally, the *Costa Rica v Nicaragua* case raised an issue with regard to legal effect given to the Corn Islands. The Corn Islands, which are Nicaragua's territory, are located approximately 26 nautical miles off the coast of Nicaragua in

[305] [2009] ICJ Rep 122–123, [187].

[306] ibid, 123, [188].

[307] Y Tanaka, 'Reflections on Maritime Delimitation in the *Romania/Ukraine* Case before the International Court of Justice (2009) 56 *NILR* 409.

[308] [2012] ICJ Rep 640, [24]; 645, [37] and 699, [202].

[309] Emphasis added. ibid, 713, [238]. For an analysis of the legal status of Quitasueño, see Y Tanaka, 'Reflectiosn on the Territorial and Maritime Disputes between Nicaragua and Colombia before the International Court of Justice' (2013) 26 *LJIL* 910–11.

[310] [2012] ICJ Rep 713–15, [238].

[311] Serrana consists of several groups of cays. The largest one, Serrana Cay (also known as Southwest Cay), is some 1,000 metres in length and has an average width of 400 metres. ibid, 640, [24]. See also Tanaka, 'Reflection on the Territorial and Maritime Disputes' 921.

[312] Counter-memorial of the Republic of Colombia, vol I, 11 November 2008, 28, [2.22];

[313] Y Tanaka, 'The Mirage of Predictability in the Law of Maritime Delimitation' (2014) 113 *The International Journal of Law and Diplomacy*, 23–4.

the Caribbean Sea. Great Corn Island has an area of 9.6 square kilometres and Little Corn Island has an area of three square kilometres. The total population of Corn Islands is approximately 7,400 inhabitants. According to Nicaragua, they also sustain a vibrant economic life. In fact, while fishing became the economic mainstay during the 1960s and 1970s, more recently tourism has grown considerably.[314] The ICJ considered that the Corn Islands have a significant number of inhabitants and sustain economic life. Therefore it held that they 'amply satisfy the requirements set forth in Article 121 of the LOSC for an island to be entitled to generate an exclusive economic zone and the continental shelf.'[315] Nonetheless, 'given their limited size and significant distance from the mainland coast', the ICJ gave them only half effect when constructing the maritime boundary.[316] However, the Court's reasoning leaves some room for discussion.

First, the size of a maritime feature is not a decisive factor to fulfil the requirements provided by Article 121. In fact, the ICJ in the *Nicaragua v Colombia* case, made clear that: '[I]nternational law does not prescribe any minimum size which a feature must possess in order to be considered an island.'[317] More recently, the Annex VII Arbitral Tribunal, in the *South China Sea* arbitral award (Merits), held that 'size cannot be dispositive of a feature's status as a fully entitled island or rock and is not, on its own, a relevant factor', even though size may correlate to the availability of water, food, living space and resources for an economic life.[318] It follows that if a

[314] Counter-Memorial of Nicaragua, 60, [3.7] and 122, [3.104]; *Maritime Delimitation in the Caribbean Sea and the Pacific Ocean (Costa Rica v Nicaragua)*, Judgment, [2018] ICJ Rep (not yet reported), [49].

[315] [2018] ICJ Rep [140].

[316] ibid, [154].

[317] ibid, 645, [37]. See also the *Qatar v Bahrain* case, [2001] ICJ Rep 97, [185]. In a Judgment of 7 May 1996, the Norwegian Supreme Court held that Abel Island, which is 13.2 square kilometres in area, was too large to be a 'rock' within the meaning of Art 121(3) and that the island would be able to support a significant polar bear hunt, were such hunting not prohibited for conservation reasons. See R Churchill, 'Norway: Supreme Court Judgment on Law of the Sea Issues' (1996) 11 *IJMCL* 576–80, in particular, 579. While the judgment seemed to rely only on the size of the island, it also referred to a sort of economic activity, namely, the polar bear hunt.

[318] PCA Case No. 2013–19. The *South China Sea* arbitration (Merits), Award of 12 July 2016, [538], available at: https://pca-cpa.org/en/cases/. In this regard, Hafetz argued that: 'Proposed guidelines based on size, however, were never adopted, and the text of Article 121(3) neither explicitly mentions size nor provides any guidelines to that effect.' JL Hafetz, 'Fostering Protection of the Marine Environment and Economic Development: Article 121(3) of the Third Law of the Sea Convention' (2000) 15 *American University International Law Review* 590–91. Symmons' view is more nuanced. He argued that: '[S]ize as such has been abandoned as a feasible criterion of insular status, …, but, indirectly size may still be important because the geological phenomenon of a "rock" has been singled out for special treatment.' C Symmons, *The Maritime Zones of Islands in International Law* (The Hague, Nijhoff, 1979) 41. See also Alex G Oude Elferink, 'The Islands in the South China Sea: How Does Their Presence Limit the Extent of the High Seas and the Area and the maritime Zones of the Mainland Coasts?' (2011) 32 *ODIL* 173 and R Kolb, 'L'interprétation de l'article 121, paragraph 3, de la Convention de Montego Bay sur le droit de la mer: les « roches qui ne se prêtent pas à l'habitation humaine ou à une vie économique propre … »' (1994) 40 *Annuaire Français de Droit International* 904.

maritime feature fulfils the requirements under Article 121 of the Convention, it can generate a 200-nautical mile EEZ and continental shelf, regardless of its size. Accordingly, a question arises why the Corn Islands can receive only half effect because of its size.

Secondly, the Court offered no objective standard to judge 'significant distance from the mainland coasts'. It might have been useful if the Court had been able to furnish legal reasons why 26 nautical miles can be regarded as 'significant distance from the mainland coast'.

b. Islands in Arbitral Awards

Effects given to islands were considered in arbitral awards regarding maritime delimitation. Three cases merit discussion. First, the *Guinea/Guinea-Bissau* arbitration raised the issues of three Types of Islands. The coastline considered in the *Guinea/Guinea-Bissau* case was characterised by the presence of numerous islands (see Illustration 11). According to the Arbitral Tribunal, they could fall into three categories: (a) coastal islands, separated from the continent by narrow sea channels or narrow watercourses; (b) the Bijagos, the nearest of which is two miles and the furthest 37 miles from the continent; (c) the more southerly islands scattered over shallow areas (Poilao, Samba, Sene, Alcatraz). The Tribunal considered the islands in categories (a) and (b) to be relevant.[319]

With respect to the islands in category (a), the Tribunal regarded them as forming an integral part of the continent.[320] They did not, in effect, influence the location of the delimitation line, which follows the 'southern limit' of the 1886 Convention, ie, the Pilots' pass from the mouth of the Cajet River and north latitude 10°40', as far as the Guinean island of Alcatraz. Following the above delimitation line, Alcatraz Island would have only 2.25 miles of territorial sea to the north. For that reason, the Court determined to 'grant' a 12-mile maritime zone to the west of Alcatraz.[321] However, the Court failed to explain why the extent of that zone should be 12 miles. In that case, Alcatraz Island has, in reality, no continental shelf or EEZ. Thus, the question discussed in the 1977 award relating to the Channel Island also arose here. Thirdly, in the south-western region, the delimitation line was drawn *grosso modo* perpendicular to the general direction of the coast, represented by the line joining Pointe des Almadies and Cape Schilling.[322] In selecting the general direction of the coast, offlying islands played no role.

In no part of the boundary line did the Arbitral Tribunal give effect to the Bijagos. This is rather surprising, as the Bijagos Archipelago consists of inhabited islands with a close relation to the continent.[323] On the other hand,

[319] The *Guinea/Guinea-Bissau* arbitral award, (1986) 25 *ILM* 291–92, [95].

[320] ibid.

[321] ibid, 298, [111].

[322] ibid.

[323] David, 'La sentence arbitrale du 14 février 1985' 367.

when calculating the coastal lengths of the Parties for applying the proportionality test, the Court took the coastal islands and the Bijagos Archipelago into account.[324] It could be inferred from the above that the impact of islands in that case remained modest or even minimal. In fact, the Tribunal did not consider the coastal islands or the Bijagos Archipelago for the purpose of drawing the delimitation line.[325] Furthermore, the Alcatraz Island has only a 2.25-mile territorial sea to the north. In this sense, the maritime projection of the island was highly limited, despite the sufficient open space available in the northern and westerly directions.

The second case to be examined is the *St Pierre and Miquelon* arbitration. The French territory of St Pierre and Miquelon is located within the concavity formed by the Canadian coasts of Newfoundland and Nova Scotia. It is formed by detached islands, far away from the mother State and close to the coast of another State.[326] It consists of two main islands, Miquelon and St Pierre, and several smaller islands, islets and drying rocks. Its total surface is 237 square kilometres; its population numbers 6500. The island of Miquelon, 21.6 miles long, with a maximum width of seven miles, lies about 27 miles south of the mainland of Newfoundland. It has a surface area of 210 square kilometres. The island of St Pierre is situated approximately 10 miles southwest of the Burin Peninsula. It has a surface of 27 square kilometres and a length of 4.4 miles.[327]

In this case, there was the difference of opinion between the Parties with respect to the effect of the status of St Pierre and Miquelon upon maritime delimitation. While France advanced that the delimitation was to be effected between two equally sovereign States, Canada alleged that the political dependency of the French Islands would justify giving St Pierre and Miquelon a less extensive maritime space than if they constituted an independent island State.[328] The Arbitral Tribunal rejected the view that the extent of the maritime space given to an island was dependent on its political status. In fact, as it indicated, both Article 121(2) of the LOSC and Article 10 of the Geneva Contention on the Territorial Sea and the Contiguous Zone made no distinction according to the political status of islands.[329]

The single maritime boundary established around St Pierre and Miquelon has already been discussed in another part of this book.[330] In this section,

[324] The *Guinea/Guinea-Bissau* arbitral award, (1986) 25 *ILM* 292–93, [97]; 301, [120].

[325] On this point, see David, 'La sentence arbitrale du 14 février 1985' 367.

[326] It is suggested that St. Pierre and Miquelon form part of the 'collectivités d'outre-mer' belonging to France. See www.vie-publique.fr/decouverte-institutions/institutions/collectivites-territoriales/categories-collectivites-territoriales/que-sont-collectivites-outre-mer.html.

[327] The *St Pierre and Miquelon* arbitral award, (1992) 31 *ILM* 1160, [22].

[328] ibid, 1165, [48].

[329] ibid, 1165, [49].

[330] See ch 5, s III of this book.

it will be sufficient to recall that the Arbitral Tribunal gave St Pierre and Miquelon three kinds of effect: 'partial effect' in the west of St Pierre and Miquelon; 'enclaving with no effect' in the east of St Pierre and Miquelon; and 'full-effect' in the northwest (points 9 to D) and the south of St Pierre and Miquelon. The Court's solution leaves some room for discussion at least on three points.

First, with respect to the westward delimitation, the Arbitral Tribunal determined to 'grant' an additional 12 miles for the EEZ. Accordingly, St Pierre and Miquelon would have a contiguous zone of the same extent.[331] However, it is by no means clear why the concept of the contiguous zone should be involved here. Secondly, the Court granted only a 12-mile zone to the east of St Pierre and Miquelon.[332] This means that there is no EEZ or continental shelf in this area. Furthermore, as Weil observed, it is hard to understand why no additional maritime space was attributed to the east of St Pierre and Miquelon, while an additional 12 miles were given in the western part of the latter.[333] Thirdly, as discussed already, the frontal projection theory applied in the south of St Pierre and Miquelon is problematical from the viewpoints of theory and practice. As Weil has pointed out, maritime projections are *not* effected only in a direction perpendicular to the general direction of the coast and over the breadth of that coastline, but radiate in all directions, creating an envelope of ocean around the coastal front.[334]

In sum, the delimitation line drawn by the Court of Arbitration forms a strange mushroom shape. Regarding the cap of the mushroom, the Court established a 24-mile (12-mile territorial sea plus 12-mile zone corresponding to the contiguous zone) enclave around St Pierre and Miquelon on the basis of a radial projection. With respect to the stem of the mushroom, a 200-mile corridor was created based on the theory of frontal projection. In the east of St Pierre and Miquelon, the Court provided for no continental shelf or EEZ. Considering the inconsistency of the methods used in the award and the problems inherent in each method, some doubts might be expressed whether the award has a value as a precedent for delimitation in relation to detached islands.

The third case to be considered is the 1999 *Eritrea/Yemen* arbitration. In this case, the many islands and islets located in the Red Sea gave rise to difficult questions. Although both Parties claimed a median line as being a maritime boundary, their claimed lines follow different courses owing to differing considerations concerning islands in the area. The principal islands to be examined here will be divided into five groups.

[331] The *St Pierre and Miquelon* arbitral award, 1170, [69].
[332] ibid, 1171, [71].
[333] Dissenting Opinion of Judge Weil, ibid, 1199, [7].
[334] ibid, 1199–202, [9–15] in particular, 1200, [11]. See also Weil, *Perspective du droit de la délimitation maritime* 68–75.

The first one is the Dahlaks, a tightly knit group of islands and islets belonging to Eritrea. The largest island, which has a considerable population, is located within 24 miles of the Eritrean coast, but many islets around the island lie more than 24 miles off the mainland of Eritrea. Both Parties agreed that the Dahlaks are an integral part of the Eritrean mainland coast.[335] By supporting the above view, the Arbitral Tribunal held that:

> [The Dahlaks] is a typical example of a group of islands that forms an integral part of the general coastal configuration. It seems in practice always to have been treated as such. It follows that the waters inside the island system will be internal or national waters and that the baseline of the territorial sea will be found somewhere at the external fringe of the island system.[336]

In this connection, two points should be noted. First, the Tribunal considered the offshore and offlying islands of Dahlaks as an integral part of the coasts and gave full effect to them. On this point, the award shows a clear contrast with the *Tunisia/Libya* and *Gulf of Maine* cases where the ICJ ignored offshore islands or gave them only half effect. Secondly, the reference to 'practice' in the above paragraph should be noted. So far as offshore islands which are located within 24 miles, as will be seen below, our research on State practice regarding effects given to islands supports the Tribunal's view. On the other hand, the external fringe of the Dahlaks lie some 40 miles off the coast. There may be room for considering whether those islands could be regarded as integral parts of the general coastal configuration.

The second category is formed by the small single island of al-Tayr and the Zubayr group, which belong to Yemen. They lie more than 24 miles off the coasts of the Parties. Although Yemen used the mid-sea island of Jabal al-Tayr and Jabal al-Zubayr as base points, Eritrea's historic median line was drawn as a median between the mainland coasts, ignoring the existence of the mid-sea island of Yemen.[337] The Tribunal supported Eritrea's view on two grounds: The geographical fact that these islands do not constitute a part of Yemen's mainland coast; and their barren and inhospitable nature and their position well out in the sea. Thus, the Tribunal decided that both the single island of Jabal al-Tayr and the Zubayr group should have no effect upon the delimitation line.[338] According to the Tribunal, this decision was confirmed by the fact that, in any event, these mid-sea islands would enjoy a full territorial sea of 12 miles, even on their western side.[339]

The third group of islands consists of offshore islands on Yemen's coast. This includes the inhabited and important island of Kamaran off this part of

[335] The *St Pierre and Miquelon* arbitral award, 363, [118].
[336] ibid, 367, [139].
[337] ibid, 339, [15] and 341, [28].
[338] ibid, 368, [147–48].
[339] ibid, 363, [119].

the Yemeni coast. Furthermore, to the north of Kamaranm, there is the relatively large islet of Tiqfash and the smaller islands of Kutama and Uqban. As pointed out, Eritrea's historic median line was drawn as a median between the mainland coasts. With respect to the island of Kamaran, the Tribunal held that: '[It] forms an important bay and there can be no doubt that these features are integral to the coast of Yemen and part of it and should therefore control the median line. One significant controlling base point is therefore on the westernmost extremity of Kamaran.'[340] Accordingly, full effect was attributed to Yemen's islands close to the Yemeni mainland. Concerning the relatively large islet of Tiqfash and the smaller islands of Kutama and Uqban, the Tribunal stated that they 'all appear to be part of an intricate system of islands, islets and reefs which guard this part of the coast.'[341] Accordingly, it decided to use as median-line base points not only Kamaran and its satellite islets but also the islets to the northwest named Uqban and Kutama. The fact that these islands and islets 'guard this part of the coast' appears to mean that they constitute an integral part of the coast. It may be said that the integrity of islands and coasts is, once again, a criterion for attributing full effect to them.

Fourthly, when drawing the middle part of the boundary, the question arose with regard to the effects to be given to Yemen's islands of Zuqar and Hanish and to the Eritrean islands of the Mohabbakahs, High Island, the Haycocks and the South West Rocks. Those formations are located within 24 miles from the mainland of each Party. In this area, Zuqar and Hanish generate a territorial sea which overlaps with those of the Haycocks and South West Rocks.[342] Yemen's proposed boundary ignored both the South West Rocks and the three Haycocks as being no more than small rocks, while taking Yemen's Hanish Island group into account. In Yemen's proposal, the Haycocks and South West Rocks were left out, and beyond the Eritrean territorial sea, Eritrean sovereignty over these islets was to be recognised by placing them in its limited enclaves.[343] By contrast, Eritrea took full account of South West Rocks and the Haycocks. In Eritrea's view, there could be no question of these islands being enclaved by application of Article 15 of the UN Convention on the Law of the Sea.[344]

The Tribunal questioned Yemen's solution and preferred the Eritrean argument, which brought into play Article 15. In fact, there is no doubt that an island and even rocks are capable of generating a territorial sea of up to 12 miles. It follows that a chain of islands each of which is less than 24 miles apart, can generate a continuous band of territorial sea. In the Tribunal's view, this is the situation in the case of the Eritrean islands out to, and including,

[340] ibid, 369, [150].
[341] ibid, [151].
[342] ibid, 369–70, [154].
[343] ibid, 339, [16–17].
[344] ibid, 340, [25].

South West Rocks.[345] In addition, according to the Tribunal, the Eritrean solution also had the advantage of avoiding the need for awkward enclaves in the vicinity of a major international shipping route.[346] Consequently, the Eritrean territorial sea, which potentially extends beyond South West Rocks and the Haycock group of island, overlaps with those generated by Yemen's Hanish group of islands. The Tribunal decided that that situation suggested a median-line boundary and found no variance necessary.[347] Thus, full effect was given to those islands when drawing the median line.

With respect to the Yemeni island of Zuquar, a different consideration was necessary. The Tribunal stated that, if the international boundary was to be diverted in order to respect the territorial sea of Zuqar after point 13, where the boundary meets a 12-mile territorial sea extending from the island of Zuqar, it would trace the sinuosities of the Zuqar territorial sea boundary until it has to turn southward again in order to join the Article 15 boundary. Instead of that solution, however, the Tribunal decided that the line should be a geodetic one joining points 13 and 14.[348] A geodetic line was thus drawn joining points 14 and 15. In so doing, the Tribunal itself accepted that the line between points 14 and 15 was very near the putative boundary of Yemen's territorial sea in this area.[349] In short, according to the Tribunal's solution, Zuqar might only have a territorial sea and no EEZ. Thus, it may be said that partial effect was given to Zuqar Island in drawing the maritime boundary in this segment.

Finally, in the most southern sector, Eritrea's offshore islands in the Bay of Assab were at issue. Yemen assumed that that Bay was integral to the Eritrean coast and, thus, the controlling base points would be on the low-water line of the outer coastal islands.[350] Having upheld this view, the Tribunal decided that, as the Bay of Assab was internal waters, the controlling base points of the boundary, ie, a median line, were to found seaward of this bay.[351]

The Tribunal's solutions call for two comments. First, in the award, the integrity of islands and relevant coasts became a criterion in determining the effect given to islands. So far as relevant islands constituted an integral part of a mainland coast, the Tribunal attributed full effect to offshore islands. By contrast, the mid-sea islands of al-Tayr and the Zubayr group were ignored since they did not form a part of Yemen's mainland.

Secondly, when ignoring the mid-sea islands, the Tribunal relied on their barren and inhospitable nature. This is a novelty in the case law. On this point,

[345] ibid, 370, [155].
[346] ibid, 364, [125].
[347] ibid, 370–71, [158].
[348] ibid, 371, [161].
[349] ibid, [162].
[350] ibid, 364, [127].
[351] ibid, 371–72, [163].

there may be room for considering whether the barren and inhospitable nature of islands could be a reason for ignoring them.

In the *Barbados v Trinidad and Tobago* case, the Arbitral Tribunal effectuated maritime delimitation between two island States. As explained earlier, the west and central segments of the maritime boundary is an equidistance line and the eastern segment of the boundary is an adjusted equidistance line.[352] The specific situation of delimitation between two islands States seemed to have no influence on the process of maritime delimitation.

c. Islands in the ITLOS Jurisprudence

In the jurisprudence of ITLOS, the issue of St Martin's Islands in the *Bangladesh/Myanmar* case merits discussion. St Martin's Island, which is part of Bangladeshi territory, is located 6.5 nautical miles southwest of the land boundary terminus and an equivalent distance from the Bangladeshi coast. It has a surface area of some eight square kilometres and sustains a permanent population of about 7,000 people.[353] When establishing a boundary of the territorial sea, ITLOS held that full effect should be given to St Martin's Island.[354] It thus drew an equidistance line delimiting the territorial sea of the Parties giving full effect to that island pursuant to Article 15 of the LOSC. However, ITLOS decided not to give any effect to St Martin's Island when drawing a single maritime boundary for both the EEZ and the continental shelf, since giving effect to that island would cause an unwarranted distortion of the delimitation line.[355] It thus concluded that: 'St. Martin's Island is not a relevant circumstance and, accordingly, decides not to give any effect to it in drawing the delimitation line of the exclusive economic zone and the continental shelf.'[356] Yet, ITLOS did not explain how St Martin's Island would produce a disproportionate result.[357] Nor did it offer any explanation why even a partial effect should not be accorded to that island.[358]

B. Analysis of State Practice

In analysing State practice, it would be appropriate to use an analytical framework categorising islands into several groups. In this respect, the equidistance

[352] See ch 5, s VIII of this book.
[353] [2012] ITLOS Rep 46, [143]. See also Reply of Bangladesh, vol I, 15 March 2011, 87, [3110].
[354] [2012] ITLOS Rep 49, [164].
[355] ibid, 86, [318].
[356] ibid, [319].
[357] See also Declaration of Judge Wolfrum in ibid, 139.
[358] Judge Gao deemed it appropriate to give St Martin's Island half effect. Separate Opinion of Judge Gao, ibid, 223, [82].

line from the coast will provide a good criterion. Based on the equidistance line from the coast, islands may be categorised into four groups:[359]

(i) offshore islands, which lie on 'the right side' of an equidistance line;
(ii) islands 'on the wrong side', which are straddling the equidistance line or lie beyond that line;
(iii) detached islands, which are located far from the mother State and constitute the sole unit of entitlement;
(iv) islands which compose so called 'Island States'.[360]

Based on this categorisation, the effect of islands upon maritime delimitations in State practice will be examined next. In light of the paucity of primary sources regarding the effect given to islands in the course of negotiations, our research depends mainly on reports in *International Maritime Boundaries,* analyses by the US Department of State in *Limits in the Seas* and regional studies. In addition, because of the lack of data regarding the precise distance of each and every island from the relevant coasts, it was inevitable that, in some cases, there were difficulties in categorising islands. Thus this survey is intended to present solely a general tendency of treaty practice rather than perfectly objective information. In addition, this survey does not aim to provide an exhaustive list of relevant agreements, but it refers to typical examples only.

i. Offshore Islands

State practice relating to offshore islands is highly diverse. There are numerous agreements that give full effect to such islands by using the equidistance method.[361] At the same time, it cannot pass unnoticed that many agreements

[359] The hypothetical equidistance line could be identified in the maps annexed in the *IMB* published by the American Society of International Law. Jayewardene categorised islands into nine groups on the basis of the distance from the coast: (i) coastal islands, which are located within 12 miles; (ii) offshore islands falling within the territorial se and contiguous zone envelope; (iii) offlying islands, which lie beyond 24 miles from the mainland; (iv) islands on the right side, which are located within a median zone astride the equidistance line which extends to 12 miles on the same side as that of the parent State; (v) islands astride the median line; (vi) islands on the wrong side, which located within a median zone astride the equidistance line which extends to 12 miles on the seaward side; (vii) detached islands, which lie on the 'wrong side' of an equidistance line, but outside the 12 miles median zone; (viii) detached islands proximate to the coast of the other State; (ix) islands of indeterminate political status (disputed islands). See Jayewardene, *The Regime of Islands in International Law*, 368–71. Because of the paucity of data regarding the precise distance of each and every island from the relevant coasts, however, it appears to be difficult to categorise all relevant islands into nine categories. Thus our survey simplified the typology of islands on the basis of the equidistance line. In addition, the problem of disputed islands may be characterised, in essence, as a territorial dispute rather than one of maritime delimitation. In this section, thus, disputed islands will not be discussed as an independent category.

[360] So called 'island States' are independent States composed of many islands in the mid-ocean, such as Fiji and the Cook Islands. They are *not* equal to 'archipelagic States'. Indeed, the word 'island States' is not a legal regime and is used only for convenience in our research.

[361] JRV Prescott and G Triggs, 'Islands and Rocks and Their Role in Maritime Delimitation' in DA Colson and RW Smith (eds), *International Maritime Boundaries*, vol V (Leiden Brill/Nijhoff, 2005) 3247 et seq.

do not take offshore islands into account.[362] On this point, special attention should be drawn to the delimitation method applied in those agreements. Indeed, where a method other than equidistance is chosen, the relevance of islands diminishes.[363] Hence one should note whether those agreements disregarded offshore islands in the application of the equidistance method or whether no effect was given to those islands because of the nature of the delimitation method, such as an azimuth line or a line parallel to longitude and/or latitude.

In some cases, Parties discounted islands while applying the equidistance method. For instance, in the 1958 Agreement between Bahrain and Saudi Arabia, small offshore islands were disregarded, while the Parties established a continental shelf boundary based on equidistance, giving full effect to Umm Nasan (Bahrain) and Chaschus Island (Saudi Arabia). The turning points of that boundary were located on Bahrain's island of Lubainah Al-Saghirah and Saudi Arabia's island of Lubainah Al-Kabirah. Thus it is suggested that both islands do not even have territorial seas.[364] When the 1969 Agreement between Iran and Qatar established an equidistance line as the boundary of the continental shelf, the Iranian Island of Lavan was not taken into account.[365] In the 1974 Agreement between Iran and UAE (Dubai) establishing a continental shelf boundary, the three islands of Queys, Forur and Bani Forur were disregarded.[366] Furthermore, all offshore islands were disregarded in the 1979 Agreements between Malaysia and Thailand relating to the delimitation of the territorial sea and the continental shelf.[367] Other examples include the 1978 Agreement between Colombia and Haiti drawing a single maritime boundary,[368] and the 1980 Agreement between Costa Rica and Panama, which established a single maritime boundary.[369]

There are some treaties which disregard offshore islands because of the methods of delimitation used. For instance, the 1976 Agreement between Colombia and Panama neglects Coiba Island, which belongs to Panama, by using the parallel of latitude as a single maritime boundary.[370] Furthermore, the 1980 Agreement between Costa Rica and Panama ignores, in the Pacific, the Panamanian Islands of Ladrones and Montuosa and the Costa Rican Island of Coco by establishing a perpendicular to the coast.[371] In the 1976 Agreement

[362] See also, ibid, 3255 et seq.
[363] D Bowett, 'Islands, Rocks, Reefs and Low-Tide Elevations' in *IMB*, vol I, 134.
[364] Report by Pietrowski in ibid, vol II, 1491. See also Jayewardene, *The Regime of Islands in International Law*, 397–98.
[365] Report by Pietrowski, Jr., in ibid, 1513.
[366] Jayewardene, *The Regime of Islands in International Law,* 395; Report by Pietrowski in *IMB*, vol II, 1513.
[367] Report by Alexander in ibid, 1535. Jayewardene, *The Regime of Islands in International Law*, 405.
[368] Report by Park Choon-ho in *IMB*, vol I, 1092 and 1101.
[369] Report by Nweihed in ibid, 494.
Report by Nweihed in ibid, 542.
[370] Report by Nweihed in ibid, 525.
[371] Report by Nweihed in ibid, 542–44. Owing to the adjacent relationship of the coasts, the delimitation line includes a territorial sea boundary.

between Kenya and Tanzania, Tanzania's Pemba Island is disregarded since the single maritime boundary runs along a line of latitude.[372] The same is true for the 1952 Agreement between Ecuador and Peru[373] and the 1975 Agreement between the Gambia and Senegal.[374] The 1981 Agreement between Brazil and French Guyana adopts the loxodromic curve of the true azimuth and disregards the French Island of Le Grand Connétable when drawing a single maritime boundary.[375] The delimitation line drawn in the 1960 Agreement between Senegal and Guinea-Bissau runs at 240°, ignoring the Bijagos Archipelago belonging to Guinea-Bissau.[376]

In some cases, offshore islands have been disregarded because their sovereignty was in dispute. For instance, in the 1977 Agreement between Cuba and Haiti, Navassa Island was discounted in the drawing of a single maritime boundary as both the United States and Haiti claimed sovereignty over it.[377] In the 1969 Agreement between Iran and Qatar, Halul Island was ignored because of its disputed status.[378] In other instances, the Parties have agreed to disregard islands on account of relevant circumstances, without having recourse to the equidistance method. For instance, in creating a single maritime boundary, it is said that the 1989 Agreement between Poland and the former GDR disregarded the islands of Rügen and Greifswalder Oie in order to secure Polish navigational interests.[379] Furthermore, the 1974 Agreement between France and Spain ignored offshore islands off the Spanish coast and French islands north of the Gironde in drawing a continental shelf boundary. In so doing, as explained above, the Parties relied mainly on proportionality.[380]

Furthermore, there are some agreements that give offshore islands only partial effect. It is possible to identify three methods of doing this. The first method is to draw an arc of a determinate distance around an island. For instance, in the context of the delimitation of the continental shelf, the 1968 Agreement between Iran and Saudi Arabia establishes a 12-mile arc around Sirri Island, which belongs to Iran.[381] The 1968 Agreement between Italy and the former Yugoslavia also draws a 12-mile arc around the Yugoslav Islands of

[372] Report by Adede in ibid, 878.
[373] Report by Eduardo Jiménez de Aréchaga in ibid, vol I, 832.
[374] Report by Adede in ibid, 850.
[375] Report by Eduardo Jiménez de Aréchaga in ibid, 779.
[376] Report by Adede in ibid, 869. The delimitation line constitutes the boundary of a territorial sea, contiguous zone, and continental shelf.
[377] Report by Nweihed in ibid, 555.
[378] Report by Pietrowski in ibid, vol II, 1513.
[379] Report by Franckx in ibid, 2012.
[380] In addition, according to Ahnish, the 1968 Agreement between Italy and the former Yugoslavia gives no effect to the Italian Island of Pianosa. FA Ahnish, *The International Law of Maritime Boundaries and the Practice of States in the Mediterranean Sea* (Oxford, Clarendon Press, 1993) 299. At point 32, however, it appears that Pianosa was given to full effect. Report by Scovazzi in *IMB*, vol II,1630. See also, *Limits in the Seas,* No 9, 6.
[381] Report by Pietrowski in *IMB*, vol II, 1521.

Pelagruza and Galijula.[382] In that region, while there are a series of islands off the coast of the former Yugoslavia, there are no such islands off the Italian coast. A series of agreements between Australia and Indonesia also offer interesting examples. In the region to be delimited, offshore islands are located on both sides. In their 1981 Agreement, which creates a provisional fisheries surveillance line, Australia and Indonesia attribute a 12-mile arc to Ashmore and the Cartier Reef of Australia.[383] In 1997, the arc in question was extended to 24 miles, when the Parties concluded a Treaty establishing an EEZ and certain seabed boundaries.[384] In addition, under the 1942 Agreement between Venezuela and Trinidad and Tobago, the delimitation line runs from the three-mile limit of the Island of Patos to a tangent to a three-mile arc measured from Soldado Rock.[385]

The second method consists of attributing half effect to the islands concerned. For example, in the context of the delimitation of the continental shelf, the 1965 Agreement between Iran and Saudi Arabia gave half effect to the Iranian island of Khark (or Kharg). It is suggested that the 1965 Agreement was the first precedent of 'half-effect'.[386] Furthermore, the 1977 Agreement between Greece and Italy gave a half effect to the Greek Island of Strofades.[387] In the area to be delimited, while Greece possesses a series of islands lying off its coast, Italy has virtually none.

In other cases, the effects given to offshore islands are more diverse. For instance, the 1969 Agreement between Indonesia and Malaysia drawing a continental shelf boundary gave some Indonesian islands, including Natuna, partial effect ranging from 0.86 to 0.56.[388] In that area, there were no Malaysian islands to balance them. Furthermore, in their 1997 Agreement creating a single maritime boundary, Iceland and Denmark agreed to give a 70 per cent effect to Kolbeinsey islet belonging to Iceland.[389] There was no island on the Danish side

[382] Report by Scovazzi and Francalanci in ibid, 1630.

[383] Report by Prescott in ibid, 1232.

[384] V Prescott, 'Current Legal Developments: Treaty between the Government of Australia and the Government of the Republic of Indonesia Establishing an Exclusive Economic Zone Boundary and Certain Seabed Boundaries' (1997) 12 *IJMCL* 534. See also Report by the same author in *IMB*, vol IV, 2704.

[385] Report by Nweihed in ibid, vol I, 644–45.

[386] Bowett, 'Islands, Rocks, Reefs and Low-Tide Elevations' 140. A Razavi, *Continental Shelf Delimitation and Related Maritime Issues in the Persian Gulf* (The Hague, Nijhoff, 1997) 132–33; Jayewardene, *The Regime of Islands in International Law*, 403–4; report by RF Pietrowski Jr in *IMB*, vol II, 1521–22. At the time, Khark was sparsely populated. At present, it is a major oil trans-shipment terminal. ibid, 404. This agreement was not ratified by Iran since Iran found out that most of the oil field was located on the Arabian side.

[387] Report by Scovazzi and Francalanci in *IMB*, vol II, 1594.

[388] RD Hodgson, 'Islands: Normal and Special Circumstances' in J Gamble Jr and G Pontecorvo (eds), *Law of the Sea: The Emerging Regime of the Oceans, Proceedings Law of the Sea Institute Eighth Annual Conference in 1973* (Cambridge, MA, Ballinger, 1974) 191; Jayewardene, *The Regime of Islands in International Law*, 419.

[389] While Iceland used the islet of Kolbeinsey to establish the median line, Denmark did not take it into consideration. Thus the differing baselines of Denmark and Iceland produced an overlap. The Parties agreed to divide the disputed area, giving some 70% to Iceland and some 30% to Denmark.

in that region. Moreover, in the 1988 Agreement between Sweden and the former Soviet Union, which created a single maritime boundary, the Swedish islands of Gotland and Gotska Sandön were taken into account for 75 per cent effect.[390] In that case, while the former USSR also had the offshore islands of Hiiumaa and Saaremaa,[391] these were incorporated into a straight baseline. Similarly, in the 1989 Agreement between Poland and Sweden establishing a single maritime boundary, Gotland was given a $\frac{3}{4}$ effect.[392] There were virtually no islands on the Polish side. It is also reported that the 1977 Agreement between Greece and Italy, which drew a continental shelf boundary, attributed a $\frac{3}{4}$ effect to the Greek islands including Othoni in the Channel of Otranto.[393] In that region, Italy had virtually no islands. In addition, it is suggested that the provisional fisheries surveillance line between points 39 and 44, which was established in the 1981 Agreement between Australia and Indonesia, follows an agreed-upon course dividing a disputed zone bounded by an equidistance line ignoring the Australian islands and one that gives them full effect.[394] In addition, it is suggested that, in the 1997 Agreement between Thailand and Vietnam drawing a single maritime boundary, the Vietnamese island of Tho Chu was given only 53 per cent effect.[395] It is possible that different effects are given to a maritime feature in different sectors. For instance, the 2003 Agreement between Oman and Yemen gave Yemen's Socotra full effect when identifying Point 5 and Point 17, respectively, while Socotra was given a half effect in the boundary between Points 5 and 11.[396]

ii. Islands 'on the Wrong Side'

Regarding islands located 'on the wrong side' of an equidistance line, State practice suggests the establishing of an arc of a determinate distance arc as a solution. The 1968 Agreement between Iran and Saudi Arabia, for instance, which creates a continental shelf boundary, draws a 12-mile arc on the Saudi Arabian side of Farshi Island, which belongs to Iran.[397] In the 1969 Agreement regarding the delimitation of the continental shelf, Qatar and the UAE. (Abu Dhabi) drew a three-mile arc around Daiyina, which belongs to Abu Dhabi.[398]

Alex G Oude Elfernik, 'Current Legal Developments: Bilateral Agreements on the Delimitation of the Continental Shelf and Fishery Zones' (1998) 13 *IJMCL* 608.

[390] Report by Franckx in *IMB*, vol II, 2061–63.

[391] At present, they are part of the territory of Estonia.

[392] Report by Franckx in *IMB*, vol II, 2080.

[393] Report by Scovazzi and Francalanci, *ibid*, vol II, 1593–94. See also, *Limits in the Seas,* No 96, 4; Bowett, 'Islands, Rocks, Reefs and Low-Tide Elevations,' 139.

[394] Report by Prescott in *IMB*, vol II, 1232–33.

[395] Report by McDorman in ibid, vol IV, 2687.

[396] Report by Prescott, in ibid, vol V, 3903 and 3905–6.

[397] Report by Pietrowski, Jr in ibid, vol II, 1521. On the other hand, as indicated already, Saudi Arabia's island of Al Arabiyah also was given a 12-mile arc by that treaty.

[398] Report by Pietrowski, Jr in ibid, 1543.

In the 1971 Agreement between Italy and Tunisia drawing a continental shelf boundary, the Italian island of Lampione was surrounded by a 12-mile arc on the Tunisian side. At the same time, the Italian islands of Pantelleria, Lampedusa and Linosa were given a 13-mile arc on their Tunisian side.[399] This 12-mile territorial sea plus one-mile continental shelf formula was unique. The 1993 Agreement between Colombia and Jamaica also provides an intriguing solution in that it creates a 12-mile enclave around Colombia's cays on Serranilla (west circle) and on Bajo Nuevo (east circle).[400] There is little doubt that the enclave solution purports to eliminate the distorting effect of equidistance lines. In so doing, at least three treaties adopted a 12-mile arc. In such cases, the islands have no continental shelf but only a territorial sea.[401]

Where islands of one State are located close to the coast of another State, a difficult question arises regarding their effect. An extreme situation was dealt with in the 1978 Agreement between Australia and Papua New Guinea, where the Australian islands of Boigu and Saibai lie within three and four miles off the coast of Papua New Guinea. On the landward side facing the coast of Papua New Guinea, a simplified equidistance line was established with respect to fisheries jurisdiction.[402] On the seaward side, however, the territorial seas of all 15 Australian islands lying to the north of the seabed jurisdiction line, including Boigu and Saibai, are restricted to a three-mile arc.[403] The second example relates to a boundary for fisheries in the region of the Channel Islands. In the 1992 Exchange of Notes between the United Kingdom and France, the Parties agreed to draw equidistance lines between the United Kingdom's Alderney and Guernsey, respectively, and the French mainland coast.[404]

iii. Detached Islands (Islands as the Sole Unit of Entitlement)

There are numerous examples of maritime delimitations concerning detached islands. Such delimitations may be divided into three types.

The first type is that of maritime delimitations between detached islands and a continental State. The single maritime boundary between Venezuela and the Netherlands Antilles in 1978 offers a typical example. The Netherlands Antilles,

[399] Report by Scovazzi and Francalanci in ibid, 1619.

[400] Report by Nweihed in ibid, vol III, 2191–92.

[401] An exception is furnished by the 1972 Agreement between Canada and France (St Pierre and Miquelon) regarding the territorial sea boundary. If an inter-coastal median line had been drawn disregarding the Canadian Green Islands group, the median line would have placed these islands on the wrong side of the line. However, by placing turning points 4 and 5 in Enfant Perdu and Little Green Island, which belong to the Green Island group, the agreed boundary runs closer to St Pierre and Miquelon. This solution includes the Green islands in the Canadian sector of the water-body eliminating possible administrative difficulties. In so doing, it may be said that those islands were given partial effect. Jayewardene, *The Regime of Islands in International Law,* 378–79.

[402] Bowett, 'Islands, Rocks, Reefs and Low-Tide Elevations'147.

[403] Art 3(1) of the 1978 Agreement. For the text of the Agreement, see *IMB*, vol I, 937–75.

[404] Report by Anderson in ibid, vol III, 2475.

the Netherlands' insular domain in the Caribbean, are situated at an average distance of 30 miles off the Venezuelan mainland in the Major Area. Obviously, the Netherlands Antilles are far away from the mainland of the Netherlands. Thus, the delimitation was to be effected between the Antilles, as the sole unit of entitlement, and Venezuela. Another example is provided by the single maritime boundary between the United Kingdom and Honduras concerning the delimitation of the maritime areas between the Cayman Island and Honduras in 2001. The Cayman Island is the British territory located in the Caribbean Sea.

The second type includes maritime delimitations between two groups of detached islands belonging to different States. A typical example is the 1996 Agreement between the French territories of St Martin and St Barthélemy and the United Kingdom's territory of Anguilla. The French Islands of St Martin and St Barthélemy are located opposite and to the south of the British island of Anguilla in the Caribbean Sea. A single maritime boundary was established between the two groups of detached islands, which constituted the respective units of entitlement.

The third type relates to delimitations between an 'island State' and detached islands. The 1983 Agreement between Fiji and the French territory of New Caledonia, Wallis and Futuna provides a good example of this. In fact, Fiji is an 'island State' without any continental territory. New Caledonia, Wallis and Futuna are French overseas territories in the Pacific Ocean. Accordingly, the delimitation was effected between Fiji, which is a political unit composed of many islands, and French islands detached from the French mainland. Another example is provided by the 2005 Agreement between France (Reunion) and Madagascar.[405]

In either type of situation, the bulk of the treaty practice tends to give full effect to detached islands. Even so, some mention should also be made to agreements giving partial effect to detached islands. Such agreements include: Venezuela and the Netherlands (Antilles); Iceland and Norway (Jan Mayen); Myanmar and India; Colombia and Honduras; Dominica and France (Guadeloupe and Martinique). In the 1978 Agreement between Venezuela and the Netherlands Antilles, the latter were given 56 per cent less area than would have been under a strictly equidistance line.[406] However, the boundary was determined mainly on the basis of proportionality and of geological and geomorphological features. Thus, the detached status of the islands did not in and of itself influence the delimitation process.

Regarding the delimitation between Iceland and Norway (Jan Mayen), the 1980 Agreement attributed a full 200-mile EEZ to Iceland. Consequently, the area given to Jan Mayen was smaller than what it would have received on the basis of an equidistance line. It was Iceland's dependence upon fisheries which

[405] Text in ibid, vol VI, 4412.

[406] Hodgson, 'The Delimitation of Maritime Boundaries' 299.

led to the concession made by Norway.[407] Later, following the recommendation of a conciliation commission, the same Parties, in 1981, agreed to draw a continental shelf boundary which coincided with the previously established EEZ boundary. In its Report and Recommendation, the Conciliation Commission clearly considered Jan Mayen to be an island entitled to a territorial sea, an EEZ and a continental shelf.[408] Furthermore, the recommendation to establish a coincident maritime boundary made by the Conciliation Commission relied on two facts: the already-established 200-mile EEZ of Iceland and uncertainties regarding the resource potential of the area.[409] Accordingly, it could be contended that the status of Jan Mayen played virtually no role in the series of delimitations in that area.

In the 1986 Agreement between Myanmar and India drawing a single maritime boundary, the Parties gave approximately half effect to India's islands of Barren and Narcondam. Although the reasons for adopting this solution remain unclear, Prescott suggests that Narcondam Island is small and detached from India's Andaman Islands; that Myanmar's coast is much longer than that of the Andaman Islands; and that Myanmar's coast is concave.[410] In any event, it appears that the detached status of Narcondam Island was of no consequence. In addition, although some of the islands in the Andaman Sea were disregarded in the delimitation, it appears that this was because they were small and detached from the Andaman Islands.[411] The 1986 Agreement between Honduras and Colombia concerned the establishment of a single maritime boundary between the continental territory of Honduras and the insular territory of Colombia. That boundary follows the parallel of 14°59′08″ N, disregarding Colombia's islands (Providencia) and cays including Roncadorand North Cay. It appears, however, that the reason for disregard of Colombia's islands lay in the fact that a parallel of latitude was followed, and not in the detachment from the Colombian mainland. On the other hand, between points 4 and 5, Colombia's cays of Serranilla were given a 12-mile radius. In addition, Colombia's San Andrés Island was given full effect when determining points 2 and 6.[412] In short, the effect attributed to Colombia's islands varied, though all of them are located in the same Caribbean Sea. It may be said that detachment did not, in itself, provide a decisive reason which would justify the granting of partial or no effect.

Finally, in the 1987 Agreement between Dominica and France (Guadeloupe and Martinique) establishing a single maritime boundary, the French overseas

[407] Report by Anderson in *IMB*, vol II, 1757.

[408] Report and Recommendations to the Governments of Iceland and Norway of the Conciliation Commission on the Continental Shelf Area between Iceland and Jan Mayen, (1981) 20 *ILM* 803–4.

[409] ibid, 825.

[410] Report by Prescott in *IMB*, vol II, 1334.

[411] ibid, 1333. Yet Prescott wonders why India's West Island appears to have been ignored in the Bay of Bengal.

[412] Report by Nweihed in ibid, vol I, 511.

territory was attributed a maritime space smaller than that which would have resulted from an equidistance line. As indicated already, it was the convexity of Dominica's coastline which provided the main reason for attributing a larger maritime area to that State.[413] Thus, it appears that the status of Guadeloupe and Martinique as overseas territory did not influence the maritime delimitation. It follows from the above survey that the geographical detachment of the islands played little, if any, role in maritime delimitations.

iv. Island States

Although this is not a central issue, it may be relevant to touch briefly on 'Island States.' In the Pacific Ocean, especially, there are island States composed of many small islands, such as Fiji, the Solomon Islands, the Cook Islands, Kiribati, Nauru, and Tuvalu, etc. In applying the equidistance method, islands belonging to such States are likely to be given full effect. However, there is no evidence that the islands of those States were given much more effect than other groups of islands on account of their status as States.

C. Summary

On the basis of the above considerations, four observations can be made.

First, judicial practice is so diverse that it is difficult to specify a general rule with respect to the legal effect given to islands. As ITLOS stated in the *Bangladesh/Myanmar* case, 'neither case law nor State practice indicates that there is a general rule concerning the effect to be given to islands in maritime delimitation.'[414]

Secondly, as has been seen, it is possible to identify four modes to give effects to maritime features: (i) full effect, (ii) no effect, (iii) partial (or half) effect, and (iv) enclave solution. The selection of mode is subject to discretion of an international court or tribunal. In the words of ITLOS,

> [T]he effect to be given to an island in the delimitation of the maritime boundary in the exclusive economic zone and the continental shelf depends on the geographic realities and the circumstances of the specific case. There is no general rule in this respect. Each case is unique and requires specific treatment, the ultimate goal being to reach a solution that is equitable.[415]

It is possible to combine multiple modes. For instance, different legal effects were given to the different coasts of St Pierre and Miquelon. In the *Bangladesh/Myanmar* case, even though ITLOS gave full effect to St Martin's Island in delimiting the territorial sea, the Tribunal gave no effect to the island when

[413] Report by Nweihed in Charney and Alexander in *IMB*, vol I, 709. See also s II of this chapter.
[414] [2012] ITLOS Rep 46, [147]. See also 86, [317].
[415] ibid, 86, [317].

drawing a single maritime boundary for both the EEZ and the continental shelf.

Thirdly, State practice reveals that, to a certain extent, the location of islands can provide a criterion for determining the effect of them. Indeed, with respect to islands 'on the wrong side', State practice tends to give them partial effect in order to correct the distorting effects of the equidistance method. Furthermore, detached islands are likely to be given full weight in applying the equidistance method unless there are no relevant circumstances suggesting another solution. Where offshore islands exist on one side only, more often than not, partial effect is to be attributed to such islands. It must be stressed, however, that this is merely a general trend.

Fourthly, it may be contended that the main purpose for giving partial effect to offshore islands is to exclude the distorting effect which would be produced in using the equidistance method. However, the method of eliminating the distorting effect varies from case to case. Some have attributed a 12- or 24-mile arc to the islands concerned, while others have granted a partial effect of varying degrees to them. Regarding other factors such as size, populations and political factors, it is difficult to identify any standard in State practice[416] or in case law.[417] In any case, it should be stressed that the above description shows but a general trend of State practice. In light of the high diversity of that practice, it appears to be difficult and dangerous to extrapolate a general rule regarding the effect of islands.[418]

V. BASELINES AND BASE POINTS

The selection of base points is of critical importance when drawing a provisional equidistance line. However, it is not uncommon that in the case law,

[416] For instance, the Swedish offlying island of Gotland, which has a population of 55,000 and a surface of 3,200 square kilometres, was given only 75% effect in the 1988 Agreement between Sweden and the USSR and in the 1989 Agreement between Poland and Sweden. By contrast, the 1974 Agreement between India and Indonesia gave full effect to Indonesia's offlying islands of Pulau Rond and Pulau Benggala, neither of which is inhibited or has a surface in excess of 1 square kilometre. Furthermore, Kawa, Mata Kawa, Kussa (PNG), Oeno (UK), Pulau Enu (Indonesia), Utklippan (Sweden) were given full effect, although they are uninhabited islands.

[417] In fact, the ICJ gave the same half effect to the Kerkennah Islands, which have a surface area of 180 square kilometres, and to Seal Island, which is much smaller than Kerkennah. The absence of a settled population in Jan Mayen was not at issue in the *Jan Mayen* case. It is true that the Court of Arbitration, in the *Anglo-French Continental Shelf* case, stated that the size and importance of the Channel Islands May properly be taken into account in balancing the equities in this region. The *Anglo-French Continental Shelf* arbitral award, 18 *RIAA* 89, [187]. Nevertheless, it is by no means clear to what extent such factors were essential for establishing the enclave. Bowett, 'The Arbitration between the United Kingdom and France Concerning the Continental Shel Boundary' 17. With respect to the political status of islands, the *Libya/Malta* judgment suggests that a difference in political status might influence the maritime delimitation, but the effect of the difference is far from clear. Furthermore, the Court of Arbitration in the *St Pierre and Miquelon* case discarded such a view.

[418] Bowett, 'Islands, Rocks, Reefs and Low-Tide Elevations'150; L Lucchini and M Vœlckel, *Droit de la mer*, tome 2 vol 1, *Délimitation* (Paris, Pedone, 1996) 170.

the parties disagree with regard to relevant base points. In this context, the validity of straight baseline may also be at issue. Thus, this section addresses the issue of base points and baselines in maritime delimitations.

A. Analysis of the Case Law

i. Arguments in the Context of Continental Shelf Delimitations

a. Baselines/Base Points in the *Anglo-French Continental Shelf* Case

The *Anglo-French Continental Shelf* case raised two issues concerning the validity of baselines. A first issue related to delimitation in the English Channel. In this regard, a dispute arose between the Parties with respect to the use of Eddystone Rock as a basepoint. The United Kingdom maintained that the Rocks were to be regarded as islands and should accordingly be used as a basepoint for determining a median line in the English Channel west of the Channel Islands. By contrast, the French Government contested the use of Eddystone Rock because it was not an island but a low-tide elevation.[419] Regarding this difference of opinion, the Court of Arbitration first made it clear that the question to be decided was not the legal status of Eddystone Rock as an island but its relevance in the delimitation of the median line in the Channel. It then found that France had previously accepted the relevance of Eddystone Rock as a basepoint under the 1964 European Fisheries Convention as well as in the negotiations of 1971 regarding the continental shelf. For that reason, it concluded that it was a relevant basepoint.[420]

A second issue concerned the delimitation of the Atlantic sector, where Article 6 of the Geneva Convention on the Continental Shelf was applicable. France contended that the Atlantic region called for a method of delimitation other than that of equidistance from the nearest points of the baselines from which the territorial sea of each State was measured. It thus proposed a line drawn midway between the two straight lines, which were said to represent the general direction respectively of the French and British coasts on either side of the English Channel. In drawing these straight lines, neither Ushant on the French side nor Scilly on the British side were taken into account.[421] By contrast, the United Kingdom alleged that the boundary in the Atlantic region is 'the median line, every point of which is equidistance from the nearest points of *the baselines from which the breadth of the territorial sea is measured,* unless another boundary is justified by special circumstances'.[422] It also contested the

[419] The *Anglo-French Continental Shelf* arbitral award, 18 *RIAA* 66–72, [122–38].

[420] ibid, 72–74, [139–44]. Further, see Y Tanaka, 'Low-Tide Elevations in International Law of the Sea: Selected Issues' (2006) 20 *Ocean Yearbook*, 189, 193–95.

[421] The *Anglo-French Continental Shelf* arbitral award, 18 *RIAA*, 98–99, [208–9]. France called the straight lines 'lignes de lissage'. ibid, 108, [230].

[422] Emphasis added. ibid, 99, [210].

straight lines suggested by France, since they were purely arbitrary and since other methods could be suggested which would give quite different results.[423]

The Court of Arbitration did not accept the French argument since it 'detaches the delimitation almost completely from the coasts which actually abut on the continental shelf of the Atlantic region and is thus not easily reconciled with the fundamental principle that the continental shelf constitutes the natural prolongation of a State's territory under the sea.'[424] This does not mean, however, that the Court admitted the contention of the United Kingdom. Having considered that the Scilly Isles constituted a special circumstance, as pointed out, the Court drew an adjusted median line giving them only half effect.[425] In so doing, it did not deal with the question of whether the same baselines as those used for measuring the territorial sea should necessarily be used for the delimitation of the continental shelf as well.

b. Baselines/Base Points in the ICJ Jurisprudence

In the *Tunisia/Libya* case, the validity of Tunisia's straight baseline was disputed between the Parties. In 1973, Tunisia had established a straight baseline drawn in the direction of the Shebba shores and to the Kerkennah Islands and the closing lines of the Gulfs of Tunisia and Gabes.[426] However, Libya argued that those lines were not opposable to her and that giving effect to them would be inappropriate and inequitable.[427] In Libya's view, the Tunisian baseline did not observe the conditions established for the drawing of a straight baseline.[428] The dispute regarding Tunisia's straight baseline related to historic rights and proportionality. Regarding proportionality in particular, the question arose whether the internal waters and territorial sea, measured from the baseline of each State, would be included in the calculation of the relevant surfaces. While Libya argued that the entire area of the sea-bed and subsoil beyond the low-water mark of each State must be taken into account, Tunisia contended that internal and territorial waters should be excluded. The ICJ rejected the Tunisian argument and decided to compare all areas of sea-bed below the low-water mark of relevant coasts of the two States.[429] In so doing, it prudently stated that its findings did not amount to any ruling on the validity or opposability of Tunisia's straight baseline.[430] Furthermore, the Court found it unnecessary to examine the question of historic rights as a justification for the baseline.[431] Accordingly, it avoided

[423] ibid, 108, [230].
[424] ibid, 115, [246].
[425] See s IV of this chapter.
[426] [1982] ICJ Rep 74, [101]. For the specific position of Tunisian straight baseline, see Scovazzi et al (eds), *Atlas of the Straight Baselines*, 2nd edn (Milan, Giuffrè, 1989) 225.
[427] [1982] ICJ Rep 75, [101].
[428] Memorial of Libya, vol I, 502–5.
[429] [1982] ICJ Rep 76, [104].
[430] ibid.
[431] ibid. With respect to historic rights in the *Tunisia/Libya* case, see below, ch 8, s III of this book.

going into the problem of the straight baseline at any stage of the judgment. Indeed, the Court's method of delimitation did not rely on Tunisia's straight baseline.

The validity of straight baselines was also at issue in the *Libya/Malta* case. In that case, Malta had drawn such lines from the main island to the uninhabited islet of Filfla. As in the *Tunisia/Libya* case, the ICJ refrained from expressing any opinion on the legality of the Maltese baselines. In drawing a provisional median line, however, the Court found it equitable *not* to take account of Filfla in the calculation.[432] According to the Court, 'the baselines as determined by coastal States are not *per se* identical with the points chosen on a coast to make it possible to calculate the area of the continental shelf appertaining to that State.'[433] In so holding, the Court explicitly accepted that the points used for constructing a continental shelf boundary might be different from those used for measuring the territorial sea. However, the Court did not clarify why the use of Malta's straight baselines would produce an inequitable result.[434]

ii. Arguments in the Context of Single Maritime Boundaries

a. Baselines/Base Points in the ICJ Jurisprudence

The issue of baselines or base points has been discussed in a series of cases concerning single maritime boundaries. The first case that needs consideration is the *Qatar v Bahrain* case. Although both Parties agreed that the equidistance method should be applied at the first stage of the delimitation, they were divided on the question from where such equidistance should be measured. Qatar argued that the mainland-to-mainland method should be applied in order to construct the equidistance line.[435] However, Bahrain contended that, as a multiple-island State characterised by a cluster of islands off the coast of its main islands, it was entitled to draw a line connecting the outermost islands and low-tide elevations.[436] A particular issue was whether Fasht ad Dibal could be used as a basepoint. Both Parties agreed that it was a low-tide elevation.[437] Fasht ad Dibal is situated in the overlapping area of the territorial sea of the

[432] [1985] ICJ Rep 48, [64]. On the other hand, by fixing a notional median line between Libya and Sicily, which was the extreme limit of a shift of the median line between Libya and Malta, the Court calculated the median line from 'the baseline on the coast of Sicily established by the Italian Government'. ibid, 52, [72]. The baseline in question was a straight one. Accordingly, the Court relied on the straight baseline on Sicily in determining a notional median line between Libya and Sicily, while disregarding the Maltese straight baseline. For the straight baseline established for Sicily, see Scovazzi *et al*, *Atlas of the Straight Baselines* 156–57.

[433] [1985] ICJ Rep 48, [64].

[434] Kolb, *Case Law on Equitable Maritime Delimitation* 347.

[435] Counter-Memorial submitted by Qatar, 228 et seq.

[436] Reply submitted by Bahrain, [287–305]. See also presentation by Professor Weil, Counsel of Bahrain, Verbatim Record, CR 2000/15, [12 et seq]; Judgment, [2001] ICJ Rep 103, [210–11].

[437] [2001] ICJ Rep 100, [200]; Memorial submitted by Bahrain, 270, [626]; presentation by Professor Weil, Verbatim Record, CR 2000/15, [41]; Memorial submitted by Qatar, 238, [10.54]; 239, [10.58]; and 245, [10.73]; Counter-Memorial submitted by Qatar, 267, [8.43].

Parties. According to the Court, in such a situation, both States are entitled to use their low-water line for measuring the breadth of their territorial sea.[438] However, the ICJ did hold that: 'For delimitation purposes the competing rights derived by both coastal States from the relevant provisions of the law of the sea would by necessity seem to neutralize each other.'[439] It thus concluded that for the purposes of drawing the equidistance line, such low-tide elevations must be disregarded.[440]

The Court then turned to the question regarding Bahrain's straight baselines. The Court's view on this subject may be worthy of note:

> The Court observes that the method of straight baselines, which is an exception to the normal rules for the determination of baselines, may only be applied if a number of conditions are met. This method must be applied restrictively. Such conditions are primarily that either the coastline is deeply indented and cut into, or that there is a fringe of islands along the coast in its immediate vicinity.[441]

Furthermore, it stated that:

> the fact that a State considers itself a multiple-island State or a *de facto* archipelagic State does not allow it to deviate from the normal rules for the determination of baselines unless the relevant conditions are met. The coasts of Bahrain's main islands do not form a deeply indented coast, nor does Bahrain claim this.[442]

Hence, the Court held that Bahrain was not entitled to apply the method of straight baselines.[443] Finally, the Court concluded that:

> Thus each maritime feature has its own effect for the determination of the baselines, on the understanding that, on the grounds set out before, the low-tide elevations situated in the overlapping zone of territorial seas will be disregarded. It is on this basis that the equidistance line must be drawn.[444]

The statement appears to suggest that the Court rejected the mainland-to-mainland method claimed by Qatar. Indeed, there appears to be no decisive reason why an equidistance line should be measured from any mainland, disregarding maritime features located before the coasts, since islands generate the same maritime rights as any other land territory. In the *Qatar v Bahrain* case, the geographical situation was much more complicated and thus the baselines were difficult to identify.[445] This instance shows that, even when the corrective-equity

[438] Art 13 of the LOSC.

[439] Judgment, [2001] ICJ Rep 101, [202]. See also, 103–4, [215].

[440] ibid, 102–3, [209].

[441] ibid, 103, [212].

[442] ibid, [213].

[443] ibid, 103–4, [215]. On this issue, see also E Decaux, 'Affaire de la délimitation maritime et des questions territoriales entre Qatar et Bahreïn, fond arrêt du 16 mars 2001 (*Qatar c Bahreïn*)' (2001) 47 *AFDI* 220.

[444] Judgment, [2001] ICJ Rep 103–4, [215].

[445] Judge Oda stated that, owing to the extreme difficulty of specifying baselines, this exercise is beyond the competence of the Court; it should have confined itself to describe the method by which the boundary line should be measured and should have ordered that a panel of experts in the fields

approach is applied, a difficult question may arise relating to the identification of baselines from which equidistance lines should be constructed.

The difficulty in identifying baselines or base points was vividly exemplified by the *Nicaragua v Honduras* case. In this case, the ICJ encountered difficulty in identifying base points for constructing an equidistance line since, according to the Court,

> whatever base points would be used for the drawing of an equidistance line, the configuration and unstable nature of the relevant coasts, including the disputed islands formed in the mouth of the River Coco, would make these base points (whether at Cape Gracias a Dios or elsewhere) uncertain within a short period of time.[446]

Hence, the Court decided that the equidistance method cannot be applied in this case. The *Nicaragua v Honduras* judgment suggests that the difficulty in identifying reliable base points can be a 'compelling reason' to deny the application of the equidistance method to maritime delimitation. As pointed out earlier, however, it is open to debate whether the difficulty arising from the instability of coastlines can truly be a decisive reason to preclude the application of the equidistance method.[447] In any event, apart from the *Nicaragua v Honduras* case, there is no instance that an international court or tribunal precluded the application of that method because of the difficulty in identifying reliable base points.

In the *Black Sea* case, the ICJ specified a general guide to select relevant base points:

> [T]he Court will identify the appropriate points on the Parties' relevant coast or coasts which mark a significant change in the direction of the coast, in such a way that the geometrical figure formed by the line connecting all these points reflects the general direction of the coastlines.[448]

It seems that its practical application is less easy, however. Indeed, two issues arose in the *Black Sea* case.[449]

The first issue concerned the Sulina dyke, which is a 7.5 km-long dyke out to sea and is situated on the southern headland of Musura Bay.[450] In this regard, an issue arose whether or not the seaward end of the Sulina dyke should be used as a base point. Romania used the seaward end of the Sulina dyke as a base point for drawing the baseline for its territorial sea, and this choice was not

of geography and hydrography be appointed to determine the mathematical or geometric means. Separate Opinion of Judge Oda, ibid, 135–36, [28].

[446] [2007] ICJ Rep 744, [280].

[447] See ch 5, s X of this book.

[448] [2009] ICJ Rep 105, [127].

[449] On these issues, see also Touzé, 'Affaire relative à la Délimitation maritime en mer Noire (Roumanie c. Ukraine)' (2009) 55 *AFDI* 233–36; Tanaka, 'Reflections on Maritime Delimitation in the *Romania/Ukraine* Case' 404–7.

[450] [2009] ICJ Rep106, [132]. The permanent nature of the Sulina dyke has not been questioned. ibid, [133].

contested by Ukraine.[451] As the ICJ observed, neither the LOSC nor the 1958 Geneva Convention on the Territorial Sea and the Contiguous Zone give clear meaning of the term 'harbour works which form an integral part of the harbour system'. In this regard, the ICJ considered that these works are 'generally installations which allow ships to be harboured, maintained or repaired and which permit or facilitate the embarkation and disembarkation of passengers and the loading or unloading of goods'.[452] According to the Court, however, the functions of a dyke differ from those of a port because the Sulina dyke purports to protect shipping destined for the mouth of the Danube and for the ports situated there.[453] Therefore, the Court considered that the seaward end of the Sulina dyke is not a proper base point for constructing a provisional equidistance line delimiting the continental shelf and the EEZs.[454] In conclusion, it held that the landward end of the Sulina dyke should be used as a base point for drawing the provisional equidistance line.[455] The ICJ's view seemed to contrast with that of the Court of Arbitration in the *Dubai/Sharjah* case where the permanent harbour works of both Dubai and of Sharjah must be treated as a part of the coast for the purpose of drawing the baselines from which the lateral sea boundary between them is constructed.[456]

The second issue relates to the question of whether Serpents' Island should be taken as a base point for constructing the provisional equidistance.[457] On this issue, the Court considered it inappropriate to select any base points on Serpents' Island for the construction of a provisional equidistance line between the Parties for two principal reasons. First, the Arbitral Tribunal, in the 1999 *Eritrea/Yemen* award (the Second Phase), used certain fringe islands, that is, the islands of Dahlaks, as base points since they constitute an integral part of the coasts.[458] According to the Court, however, Serpents' Island, lying alone and some 20 nautical miles away from the mainland, is not 'one of a cluster of fringe islands constituting "the coast" of Ukraine'.[459] Secondly, in the view of the Court, the use of Serpents' Island as a relevant part of the coast would amount to grafting an extraneous element onto Ukraine's coastline and would produce a judicial refashioning of geography, which neither the law nor practice of maritime delimitation authorises.[460] However, the Court's

[451] ibid, 107, [135]; Reply Submitted by Romania, 22 December 2006, 50–53, [3.66–3.73]; Presentation by Mr. Müller, Verbatim Record, CR 2008/30, 65–72, [1–18].

[452] [2009] ICJ Rep 106, [133].

[453] ibid, 106–07, [134].

[454] ibid, 108, [138]

[455] ibid, [140].

[456] (1993) 91 *ILR*, 662.

[457] Tanaka, 'Reflections on Maritime Delimitation in the *Romania/Ukraine* Case' 406–07.

[458] The *Eritrea/Yemen* arbitral award (the second phase), 22 *RIAA*, 367–68, [139–46]. This criterion may be called as the integrity test. Y Tanaka, 'Reflections on the *Eritrea/Yemen* Arbitration of 17 December 1999 (Second Phase: Maritime Delimitation)' (2001) 48 *NILR* 213–14.

[459] [2009] ICJ Rep 109–110, [149].

[460] ibid, 110, [149].

view is open to controversy. The Arbitral Tribunal, in the *Eritrea/Yemen* award, used 'certain of the outer Dahlak islets, Mojeidi and an unnamed islet east of Dahret Segala' as base points generating the Tribunal's equidistance line.[461] These islands lie more than 30 nautical miles from the mainland and 15–20 nautical miles from the larger of the Dahlak Islands.[462] According to the criterion of this award, arguably the location of Serpents Island will not be a bar to using it as a base point. It is also difficult to see the reason why an island must be one of a cluster of 'fringe islands' in order to use it as a base point for the establishment of the provisional equidistance line. Furthermore, the Court did not adequately explain the reason why the use of Serpents' Island as a relevant part of the coast would produce a refashion of geography. In reality, the existence of an offshore island is not an abnormal geographical feature. Given that there is no size criterion in Article 121 of the LOSC, the smallness of Serpents' Island will not provide a convincing reason.[463]

In the *Nicaragua v Colombia* case, Colombia's equidistance line relied on two base points on Alburquerque Cays, several base points on the west coast of San Andrés and Providencia, one base point on Low Cay, a small cay to the north of Santa Catalina, and several base points on Quitasueño.[464] However, the ICJ proceeded to construct its provisional equidistance line by reference to the base points which it considered appropriate, without following the Colombian line. Specifically the Court considered that Quitasueño should not contribute to the construction of the provisional median line since placing base points on very small maritime features would distort the relevant geography; and that it was appropriate to disregard them in the construction of a provisional median line. It also considered that there should be no base point on Low Cay, a small uninhabited feature near Santa Catalina. Likewise, as pointed out earlier, it disregarded Serrana in drawing a provisional median line because of its comparative smallness and considerable distance from any of the other Colombian islands.[465] Yet, some doubts might be expressed as to whether or not the comparative smallness would provide a convincing reason for disregarding Serrana as a base point.

The selection of base points in the *Peru v Chile* case is also open to controversy. As noted, this case is unusual in that the starting-point for the maritime delimitation is Point A, which is 80 nautical miles from the closest point on

[461] The *Eritrea/Yemen* arbitral award (the second phase), 22 *RIAA*, 368, [146].

[462] Report by DA Colson in *IMB*, vol IV, 2745.

[463] In fact, the ICJ, in the 2001 *Qatar v Bahrain* case (Merits), remarked that: 'In accordance with Article 121, paragraph 2, of the 1982 Convention on the Law of the Sea, which reflects customary international law, islands, regardless of their size, in this respect enjoy the same status, and therefore generate the same maritime rights, as other land territory.' Emphasis added. [2001] ICJ Rep 97, [185]. See also L Hafetz, 'Fostering Protection of the Marine Environment and Economic Development: Article 121(3) of the Third Law of the Sea Convention' (2000) 15 *American University International Law Review* 590–91.

[464] [2012] ICJ Rep 698, [200].

[465] ibid, 699, [202]. See also s IV of this chapter.

the Chilean coast.[466] According to the Court, 'for the purpose of constructing a provisional equidistance line, only those points on the Peruvian coast which are more than 80 nautical miles from Point A can be matched with points at an equivalent distance on the Chilean coast.'[467] No points on the Peruvian coast which line to the south-east of that initial point on that coast were used since they are all situated less than 80 nautical miles from Point A.[468] According to the Court's selection of base points, some 120 nautical miles of the Peruvian coast was discounted. As a consequence, the provisional equidistance line was constructed substantially in Chile's favour.[469] It may have to be admitted that the Court's equidistance line is regarded as an imaginative line since the provisional equidistance line constructed by the Court is not a strict equidistance line reflecting actual coasts of the parties.[470]

In the *Costa Rica v Nicaragua* case, a contentious issue in this regard concerns the base points located in the Santa Elena Peninsula. The Santa Elena Peninsula is some 286 square kilometres and it has a permanent population of more than 2,400 inhabitants.[471] Costa Rica selected two base points on a seaward protrusion of the Santa Elena Peninsula called Punta Blanca.[472] However, Nicaragua requested the ICJ to adjust equidistance line by discounting the base points on the Santa Elena Peninsula since that Peninsula would have a distorting effect on the equidistance line.[473] The Court considered that the Santa Elena Peninsula cannot be considered to be a minor coastal projection; and that the adjustment proposed by Nicaragua in the territorial sea would significantly cut off Costa Rica's coastal projections in the territorial sea in the Pacific Ocean. The Court thus drew a median line as territorial sea boundary by using the base points selected by both Parties, including base points on Punta Blanca on Costa Rica's coast.[474]

As for the delimitation of the EEZ and the continental shelf in the Pacific Ocean, the Court constructed a provisional equidistance line, by using the base points selected by the Parties, including base points on the Santa Elena Peninsula, at the first stage of maritime delimitation.[475] At the second stage, however, the

[466] [2014] ICJ Rep 66, [183]. See also ch 5, s XIV of this book.
[467] ibid, 66–67, [185].
[468] ibid.
[469] Fietta and Cleverly, *A Practitioner's Guide* 544.
[470] CG Lathrop, 'The Provisional Equidistance Line: Charting a Course between Objectivity and Subjectivity?' in Oude Elferink, Henriksen and Busch, *Maritime Boundary Delimitation* 219; Alex G Oude Elferink, 'International Law and Negotiated and Adjudicated Maritime Boundaries: A Complex Relationship' (2015) 58 *GYIL* 253–55; Chuanxiang Sun, 'Comments on the Tree-stage Approach of Maritime Delimitation' in MH Nordquist, JN Moore, and R Long (eds), *Challenges of the Changing Arctic; Continental Shelf, Navigation, and Fisheries* (Leiden, Brill/Nijhoff, 2014) 625.
[471] [2018] ICJ Rep [170].
[472] ibid. See also Memorial of Costa Rica, vol I, 38 et seq.
[473] [2018] ICJ Rep [171]. See also presentation by Mr Reichler, Verbatim Record, CR 2017/11, 48 et seq.
[474] [2018] ICJ Rep [173–75].
[475] ibid, [186–88].

Court considered that the base points located on the Santa Elena Peninsula have 'a disproportionate effect on the direction of the provisional equidistance line'.[476] Thus the Court adjusted the provisional equidistance line by giving half effect to the Santa Elena Peninsula. To this end, the Court drew two lines, one giving full effect and one giving no effect to the Santa Elena Peninsula for the EEZ and the continental shelf. It then drew a line whose course lies midway between the two lines.[477] In summary, the base points located on the Santa Elena Peninsula were given full effect when constructing the provisional equidistance line for the EEZ and the continental shelf in the Pacific Ocean at the first stage of maritime delimitation. At the second stage, the provisional equidistance line was adjusted by giving only half effect to the Santa Elena Peninsula. In so doing, one can argue that the Court maintained the structure of the three-stage approach.

b. Baselines/Base Points in Arbitral Awards

In considering the issue of baselines or base points in arbitration, two cases merit discussion. The first is the *Eritrea/Yemen* case. In this case, Eritrea's baseline was at issue in two respects. First, in Eritrean domestic law, enacted by Ethiopia in 1953, its territorial sea is defined as extending from the extremity of the seaboard at maximum annual high tide. Yemen claimed that, by virtue of the 1953 legislation, the Tribunal of Arbitration should measure the median-line boundary from the high-water line instead of the low-water line along the Eritrean coast. The Tribunal ruled, however, that the median line boundary was to be measured from the low-water line in accordance with Article 5 of the LOSC since both Parties had agreed that the Tribunal was to take into account the provisions of that Convention.[478]

The second issue related to Eritrea's straight baseline established in the region of the Dahlaks. The Tribunal stated that it was not called upon to decide on the reality, validity or definition of Eritrea's straight baseline system. However, it had to decide on the base points which controlled the course of the maritime boundary.[479] The question of interest here concerned a feature called the 'Negileh Rock'. Yemen objected to the use of this uninhabited islet as a base point on the grounds that, on the BA Chart 171, it was shown to be a reef and not to be above water at any state of the tide.[480] According to the Tribunal, a reef which is not a low-tide elevation is out of the question as a base point by virtue of Article 6 of the LOSC.[481] Furthermore, the difficulty regarding the Negileh Rock is reinforced if there is indeed

[476] ibid, [193].
[477] ibid, [198–99].
[478] The *Eritrea/Yemen* arbitral award (the Second Phase), 22 *RIAA* 366, [134–35].
[479] ibid, 367, [142].
[480] ibid, 368, [143].
[481] ibid.

a straight baseline system in existence for the Dahlaks, since Article 7(4) of the Convention stipulates that: 'Straight baselines shall not be drawn to and from low-tide elevations, unless light houses or similar installations which are permanently above sea level have been built on them or in instances where the drawing of straight baselines to and from such elevations has received general international recognition.' Although Eritrea was not a Party to the Convention, it had agreed to its application in the present case. Accordingly, the Tribunal held that Eritrea's claims concerning the existence of a straight baseline system seemed to foreclose any right to use a reef that is not proud of the water at low-tide as a baseline of the territorial sea.[482] It then decided that the western basepoints to be employed on this part of the Eritrean coasts shall be on the low-water line of certain of the outer Dahlak islets, Mojeidi, and an unnamed islet east of Dahret Segala.[483]

The second case to be examined is the *Bangladesh v India* arbitration. This case raised the question of whether low-tide elevations should be considered as appropriate base points for use by a court or tribunal in delimiting a maritime boundary between adjacent coasts. In this connection, from 22 to 25 October 2013, the Annex VII Arbitral Tribunal and the Parties visited relevant areas of the Bay of Bengal.[484] The site visit by the Tribunal and representatives of both Parties confirmed the location, visibility and protuberance of the base points located on the respective coastlines of Bangladesh and India identified by the Parties. Yet it could not confirm the visibility of the base points located on low-tide elevations.[485] Related to this, the Annex VII Arbitral Tribunal ruled that: 'If alternative base points situated on the coastline of the parties are available, they should be preferred to base points located on low-tide elevations.'[486] The Tribunal thus decided that it would not rely on base points located on low-tide elevations detached from the coast for the purpose of delimitation of the territorial seas of the two Parties.[487]

c. Baselines/Base Points in the ITLOS Jurisprudence

The issue of baseline or base points was discussed by ITLOS in the *Bangladesh/Myanmar* and *Ghana/Côte d'Ivoire* cases. In the *Bangladesh/Myanmar* case, an issue arose whether St Martin's Island could serve as the source of a base point for constructing a provisional equidistance line. Referring to the *Black Sea* case, ITLOS took the view that:

> [W]hile coastal States are entitled to determine their base points for the purpose of delimitation, the Tribunal is not obliged, when called upon to delimit the maritime

[482] ibid, 368, [144–45].
[483] ibid, [146].
[484] The *Bangladesh v India* arbitral award, [22].
[485] ibid, [263].
[486] ibid, [262].
[487] ibid, [264]. See also [360] and [362].

> boundary between the parties to a dispute, to accept base points indicated by either or both of them.[488]

In the view of the Tribunal, to use St Martin's Islands as a base point would 'result in an unwarranted distortion of the delimitation line, and amount to "a judicial refashioning of geography"'.[489] Accordingly, ITLOS excluded St Martin's Island as the source of any base point in drawing a provisional equidistance line.[490] As pointed out earlier, ITLOS gave no effect to St Martin's Island in drawing the delimitation line of the EEZ and the continental shelf since it does not constitutes a relevant circumstance. In short, the Tribunal, in the *Bangladesh/Myanmar* case, examined St Martin's Island twice at the first and second stage of maritime delimitation.[491]

In the *Ghana/Côte d'Ivoire* case, Côte d'Ivoire contended that the location of base points on Jomoro Peninsula constituted a geographical circumstance requiring the adoption of the angle bisector method. Jomoro Peninsula is a tiny strip of land representing only 0.1 per cent of Ghana's territory.[492] According to Côte d'Ivoire, however, 'this peninsula defines the entire course of the provisional 34 equidistance line up to 220 nautical miles.'[493] The ITLOS Special Chamber dismissed the argument advocated by Côte d'Ivoire for two main reasons. First, since Jomoro does not constitute a peninsula, it cannot be treated like an island or a protruding peninsula which distorts the general direction of the coast or its seaward projection. Secondly, while it is true that only a limited number of base points may be established on Jomoro, this does not mean that these base points are inappropriate.[494] Similarly, the Special Chamber did not consider the geography of Jomoro as a relevant circumstance warranting adjustment of the provisional equidistance line.[495]

B. Analysis of State Practice

i. Straight Baselines Which Did Not Influence the Maritime Delimitation

In approximately 50 agreements at least, straight baselines were not taken into account at all or only partly. First, there are instances where only one Party had established straight baselines. In those cases, a number of agreements disregarded such straight baselines. For instance, with respect to the delimitation

[488] [2012] ITLOS Rep 72, [264].
[489] ibid, 73, [265].
[490] ibid.
[491] See ch 5, s XII of this book.
[492] Rejoinder of Côte d'Ivoire, 42, [2.61].
[493] Presentation by Mr Pitron, Verbatim Record, ITLOS/PV.17/C23/5/Rev.1, 5.
[494] The *Ghana/Côte d'Ivoire* case, [2017] ITLOS Rep [309–10].
[495] ibid, [434].

of the continental shelf between the United Arab Emirates (Dubai) and Iran, only the latter had drawn straight baselines. However, these did not affect the location of the continental shelf boundary.[496] Similarly, with respect to the maritime delimitation between Estonia and Latvia, only Estonia had established straight baselines. In this respect, the straight baseline segments surrounding Ruhnu Island created a disagreement between the Parties. In the 1996 Agreement drawing a single maritime boundary, the Eritorian straight baselines did not influence the location of the boundary line.[497] The Bahrain–Saudi Arabia Agreement of 1958,[498] the Italy–Yugoslavia Agreement of 1968,[499] the Italy–Greece Agreement of 1977,[500] the Iceland–Norway (Jan Mayen) Agreement of 1980,[501] the Australia–France Agreement of 1982,[502] the France–Monaco Agreement of 1984,[503] the Costa Rica–Equator Agreement of 1985,[504] the Myanmar–India Agreement of 1986,[505] the Dominican Republic-UK Agreement of 1996,[506] the Oman–Pakistan Agreement of 2000,[507] and the Norway-Russian Federation Treaty of 2010[508] all provide further examples. Moreover, in a series of Agreements between Australia and Indonesia of 1971, 1972, and 1973, the Indonesian archipelagic baselines played no role in determining the boundaries concerned.[509]

Secondly, even when both Parties had established straight baselines, some agreements disregarded them when drawing boundaries. The Iran-Saudi Arabia Agreement of 1968,[510] the Iran-Oman Agreement of 1974,[511] the UK-Ireland

[496] Report by Alexander in Charney and Alexander in *IMB*, vol II, 1535.

[497] Report by Franckx in Charney and Smith in ibid, vol IV, 3006–8.

[498] Report by Pietrowski in ibid, vol II, 1491.

[499] Report by Scovazzi and Francalanci in ibid, 1630. Only former Yugoslavia had established its system of straight baselines at the time of signature.

[500] Report by Scovazzi and Francalanci in ibid, 1594. Only Italy established its system of straight baselines at the time of signature.

[501] Report by Alexander in ibid,1758. Only Iceland established its system of straight baselines in the area to be delimited.

[502] Report by Prescott in ibid, 1188. Only France established its system of straight baselines at the time of signature.

[503] Report by Scovazzi and Francalanci in ibid, 1584–85. Only France established its system of straight baselines at the time of signature.

[504] Report by Eduardo Jiménez de Aréchaga in ibid, vol I, 821. Only Equator adopted the straight baselines system at the time of signature.

[505] Report by Prescott in ibid, vol II, 1333. Only Myanmar established its system of straight baselines at the time of signature. Myanmar's straight baseline crossing the Gulf of Martaban is the longest single straight baseline in the world, at 222 miles. Its validity is questionable.

[506] Report by Anderson in ibid, vol III, 2238. Only the Dominican Republic established its system of straight baselines at the time of signature.

[507] Both Oman and Pakistan have claimed straight baselines in 1982 and 1996 respectively. Yet, no Omani straight baselines exist in the vicinity of Ra's al Hadd. On the other hand, Pakistan's straight baselines have been drawn along the entire coast of the delimitation area. Report by Prescott in ibid, vol IV, 2813.

[508] Report by Fife, ibid, vol VII, 5183.

[509] Report by Prescott in ibid, vol II, 1198, 1210, and 1221.

[510] Report by Pietrowski in ibid, 1522.

[511] ibid, 1505.

Agreement of 1988,[512] the Albania-Italy Agreement of 1992,[513] and the Finland-Sweden Agreement of 1994[514] offer examples.

Thirdly, in some cases, one of the Parties claimed new or rectified straight baselines during or after concluding an agreement on maritime delimitation. Usually, however, the new or redefined straight baselines did not influence the established maritime boundary. For instance, Japan and South Korea concluded an agreement creating a continental shelf boundary in 1974. Later, in 1978, South Korea established straight baselines along part of its coast. However, these lines did not affect the 1974 boundary.[515] Having ratified the LOSC, the Japanese Government also established straight baselines in 1997. The new baselines did not, however, influence the existing continental shelf boundary. A similar situation may be found in the 1978 Agreement between Australia and Papua New Guinea regarding the Torres Strait. After concluding the Agreement, Australia proclaimed straight baselines in 1983. These did not, however, influence the territorial sea boundary established in the Torres Strait Agreement.[516] Furthermore, in 1985, Finland and the Soviet Union signed an agreement which purported to transform their entire existing maritime boundary, which had been fixed on the basis of the equidistance method, into a single maritime boundary. Less than a month before the signature of the Agreement, the USSR drew a series of straight baselines in the Baltic. These new lines created a situation in which the previously established boundary between the Parties was manifestly not equidistant with respect to the new baselines. The Parties, however, preferred not to reopen the negotiations.[517] Since the conclusion of the delimitation agreements between Finland and the former Soviet Union, Finland readjusted its system of straight baselines in 1995. Estonia – which regained its independence during the early 1990s – established a system of straight baselines in 1993. Thus, substantial changes were made with respect to the baselines on both side of the Gulf of Finland. Yet, these changes had only a negligible impact on the single maritime boundary established in 1996.[518]

A particular issue that arises in this context concerns the impact of land reclamation activities on baselines. Owing to the extensive land reclamation, Singapore's normal baseline have considerably changed and advanced seaward between 1973 and 2014. Concerns were thus raised about the impact of these reclamation activities on Singapore's baselines in the negotiations between Singapore and Indonesia that resulted in the 2009 Treaty extending their 1973

[512] Report by Anderson in ibid, 1770.
[513] Report by Scovazzi and Francalanci in ibid, vol III, 2450.
[514] Report by Franckx in ibid, 2545.
[515] Report by Park Choon-ho in ibid, vol I, 1059.
[516] ibid, 932–33.
[517] Report by Franckx in ibid, vol II, 1991–92.
[518] Report by Franckx in ibid, vol IV, 3029–31.

territorial sea boundary to the west. In the 2009 Treaty between Singapore and Indonesia delimiting the territorial sea, the Parties agreed that the alterations to Singapore's baselines arising from its reclamation would have no impact on the position of the maritime boundary. The same approach was adopted in the negotiation that led to the 2014 Treaty extending the territorial sea boundary between Indonesia and Singapore eastward.[519]

ii. Straight Baselines Which Did Influence the Maritime Delimitation

It is not suggested that agreements taking straight baselines into account do not exist. For example, in applying the equidistance method, the following texts do consider straight baselines or archipelagic baselines in whole or in part: The 1968 Norway-Sweden Agreement,[520] the 1965 Norway-UK Agreement,[521] the 1972 Finland-Sweden Agreement,[522] the 1988 Denmark-German Democratic Republic Agreement,[523] the 2005 Honduras-Mexico Agreement,[524] the 2009 Indonesia-Singapore Treaty,[525] the 2010 Grenada-Trinidad and Tobago Treaty,[526] the 2011 Bahamas-Cuba Agreement,[527] the 2012 Comoros-Seychelles Agreement,[528] the 2014 Indonesia-Philippines Agreement,[529] the 2011 Comoros-Mozambique Agreement,[530] and the 2011 Comoros-Tanzania Agreement.[531]

A question arises in cases where the validity of straight baselines established by one Party is disputed by the other Party. For instance, in the 1997 Agreement between Estonia and Latvia, the Parties preferred another solution to their controversy over an Estonian straight baseline. In 1993, Estonia incorporated Ruhnu Island into her system of straight baselines.[532] Yet Latvia contested that line on the ground that the straight baselines inside the Gulf of Riga did not follow the general direction of the coast. The problem was resolved by enclaving Ruhnu Island within a 12-mile zone.[533] Furthermore, when a single maritime

[519] Report by Schofield, McDorman and Arsana, ibid, vol VII, 4818–19; Report by Schofield and Arsana, ibid, 4830–31.

[520] Report by Anderson in ibid, vol II, 1872–73. Both States had drawn straight baselines.

[521] ibid, I, 1881. Only Norway had a system of straight baselines at the time of signature.

[522] ibid, 1948. Both States had drawn straight baselines.

[523] Report by Franckx in ibid, vol II, 2090. Both States had drawn straight baselines.

[524] Report by Contreras, ibid, vol VI, 4205.

[525] Report by Schifield, Mcdorman and Arsana, ibid, vol VII, 4817.

[526] Report by Mitchell, ibid, 4711.

[527] Report by Saunders, Klein and Turnquest, ibid, 4725.

[528] Text in: ibid, 5046.

[529] Report by Schofield and Arsana, ibid, 4954.

[530] Text in: ibid, 5025.

[531] Text in: ibid, 5066.

[532] Law on the Boundaries of the Maritime Tract of 10 March 1993.

[533] E Franckx, 'Current Legal Developments: Baltic' (1997) 12 *IJMCL* 368. In addition in the course of negotiation drawing a single maritime boundary between Vietnam and Thailand, the legitimacy of the Thailand's straight baselines was disputed. Accordingly, it is suggested that the 1997 Agreement between Vietnam and Thailand on the Delimitation of the Maritime Boundary

boundary between Cuba and the United States was to be drawn, Cuba's straight baselines were questioned by the United States on the ground that the geographical features of the Cuban coast did not meet the conditions for drawing straight baselines under international law.[534] Thus, the Parties calculated, first, an equidistance line from the relevant basepoints on their respective low-water lines, and from the Cuban straight baselines and from comparable hypothetical construction lines along the coast of the United States. The Parties then drew a compromise line running between those two lines, dividing the contested area about equally between them.[535] Such a solution may be called a 'half effect solution regarding straight baselines'.

The half effect solution regarding straight baselines can also be found in the 1975 Agreement between Italy and Yugoslavia. Yugoslavia did not establish straight baselines in the Gulf of Trieste, except for one closing line in the Bay of Piran. During the negotiations over the delimitation of the territorial sea in the Gulf of Trieste, however, Italy announced her intention to establish a system of straight baselines along its coasts. Consequently, an equidistance line measured from straight baselines would have favoured Italy. By contrast, a strict equidistance line from the coasts would have favoured Yugoslavia. The Parties agreed therefore to draw a delimitation line that was generally an intermediate line between the two former baselines.[536] Another example of a half effect solution is provided by the 1984 Agreement between Denmark and Sweden creating a single maritime boundary. In the course of the negotiations, the Parties agreed, as a general rule, to use their straight baselines to compute the delimitation line. In the Southern Kattegat, however, Sweden objected to a particular Danish baseline connecting Hesselo with Sjaelland. By contrast, in the Baltic, Denmark objected to Sweden's basepoint of Falsterborev. It is suggested that, in both instances, the Parties agreed to split in half the area generated by those baselines.[537] The half effect given to straight baselines, suggested in the above agreements, may thus offer a solution when the validity of straight baselines is disputed. There are also cases where third States have contested the validity of the straight baselines of one or both Parties to an agreement. Third States which are not Parties to an agreement on maritime delimitation need not recognise any straight baselines which do not fulfil the requirements of international law. Furthermore, these States are free to protest questionable lines. Nevertheless, in reality, such protests will not affect the boundary created by the Parties, since the Parties are free to

in the Gulf of Thailand did not use the equidistance method in drawing a single maritime boundary. Interview to Ambassador Nguyen Quy Binh on 2 March 2001. Regarding Thailand's straight baselines, see Scovazzi et al, *Atlas of the Straight Baselines*, 223.

[534] For Cuba's straight baselines, see Scovazzi et al, *Atlas of the Straight Baselines*, 113; Report by Smith in *IMB*, vol I, 419.

[535] ibid.

[536] Report by Scovazzi and Francalanci in ibid, vol II, 1642. Yet Italy's straight baseline system was established in 1977. See Scovazzi et al, *Atlas of the Straight Baselines*, 156.

[537] Report by Franckx in *IMB*, vol II, 1935.

divide as they please their overlapping maritime area. The maritime delimitation is, in principle, effected only in the area of overlap where the Parties, and the Parties alone, have legal title. Accordingly, barring infringement of the legal title of a third State over a maritime space, protests will not influence the validity of the maritime boundary between the Parties.[538]

C. Summary

On the basis of the above survey, four points can be made.

First, the weight of any baseline in a maritime delimitation depends on the method of delimitation used. When the Parties prefer methods other than equidistance, the straight baseline will lose its relevance. In this sense, it may be said that the validity of straight baselines is linked to the application of the equidistance method.

Secondly, an inquiry is whether the same baselines or basepoints for measuring *limits* of maritime zones should be used for the purpose of maritime delimitations. Under Article 15 of the LOSC,

> Where the coasts of two States are opposite or adjacent to each other, neither of the two States is entitled, failing agreement between them to the contrary, to extend its territorial sea beyond the median line every points of which is equidistant from the nearest points on *the baselines from which the breadth of the territorial seas of each of the two States is measured*.[539]

Article 6 of the Geneva Convention on the Continental Shelf also stipulates that the median or equidistance line is the line every point of which is equidistant

[538] LB Sohn, 'Baseline Considerations' in ibid, 156. However, this does not mean that such protests have no legal effect. An excessive straight-baseline system may incorporate part of the high seas into zones under coastal State jurisdiction, such as an EEZ. In that case, freedom of high seas, including fisheries, will be affected. Thus, the protest against excessive straight-baselines system plays a certain role in maintaining the right to fish on the high seas. The *Norwegian Fisheries* case provides a classic example. In addition, an excessive straight baseline system will create large areas of internal waters which otherwise would be territorial sea. Accordingly, the right of innocent passage may be affected in such enlarged internal waters. In such a case, however, the right of innocent passage will be protected under Art 8(2) of the LOSC, which provides that: 'Where the establishment of a straight baseline in accordance with the method set forth in Art 7 has the effect of enclosing as internal waters areas which had not previously been considered as such, a right of innocent passage as provided in this Convention shall exist in those waters.' For excessive baseline claims, see JA Roach and RW Smith, *United States Responses to Excessive Maritime Claims,* 3rd edn (Leiden, Brill/Nijhoff, 2012) 72 et seq. For the problem of straight baseline in detail, see WM Reisman and GS Westerman, *Straight Baselines in International Maritime Boundary Delimitation* (London, Macmillan, 1992); LM Alexander, 'Baseline Delimitations and Maritime Boundaries' (1983) 23 *Virginia Journal of International Law* 503; T Scovazzi, 'The Establishment of Straight Baselines Systems: The Rules and the Practice' in D Vidas and W Østreng (eds), *Order for the Oceans at the Turn of the Century* (The Hague, Kluwer, 1999) 445–56; JA Roach and RT Smith, 'Straight Baselines: The Need for a Universally Applied Norm' (2000) 31 *ODIL* 47.

[539] Emphasis added. Art 12 of the Geneva Convention on the Territorial Sea and the Contiguous Zone also provides the same rule.

from the nearest point of the baselines from which the breadth of the territorial sea of each State is measured.[540] By virtue of those provisions, it may be contended that when applying the equidistance method to maritime delimitations, an equidistance line should be, in principle, drawn from the baselines of the territorial sea. In State practice, however, some agreements have not applied the system of straight baselines claimed solely by one Party, while others have disregarded straight baselines altogether.

Thirdly, more often than not, a provisional equidistance line has been constructed on the basis of appropriate base points selected by judges. The selection of base points directly affects the construction of a provisional equidistance line at the first stage of maritime delimitations. The judicial practice demonstrates that at the first stage of the delimitation process, consideration of equity already comes into play in an international court's selecting relevant base points for drawing a provisional equidistance line.[541]

Fourthly, State practice suggests that newly claimed straight baselines or redefinitions of straight baselines do not affect the location of a previously established maritime boundary. An explanation may consist in the postulate of the stability of maritime boundaries and considerations of practical convenience. In this connection, it is worth noting that, in disputes between Parties concerning the validity of straight baselines, some agreements proposed the interesting solution of giving half effect to the baselines concerned.

VI. GEOLOGICAL AND GEOMORPHOLOGICAL FACTORS

The next issue that needs consideration relates to the impact of geological and geomorphological factors on maritime delimitations.[542] The relevance of these factors in maritime delimitation has been discussed in the jurisprudence in this field. In State practice, as will be discussed below, these factors may be at issue particularly in delimiting the continental shelf beyond 200 nautical miles.

[540] Having examined the discussion in the ILC on this matter, Weil pointed out: 'Pas un seul moment la possibilité ne paraît avoir été envisagée au sein de la Commission [du droit international] d'une ligne de délimitation tracée à partir de points côtiers autres que ceux faisant partie des lignes de base de la mer territoriale.' P Weil, 'A propos de la double fonction des lignes et points de base dans le *droit* de la mer' in *Écrits de droit international* (Paris, PUF, 2000) 283.

[541] See ch 9, s IV of this book.

[542] Strictly speaking, geology and geomorphology are different concepts. While the former relates to the composition and structure of the seabed, the latter concerns in its shape and form. Yet in the case law, these two notions have not been strictly distinguished. See for instance, the *Anglo-French Continental Shelf* case, 18 *RIAA*, 60, [107]; the *Libya/Malta* case, [1985] ICJ Rep 35, [38]. Regarding the geological and geomorphological elements in the seabed, see the thorough study by K Highet, 'The Use of Geophysical Factors in the Delimitation of Maritime Boundaries' in *IMB*, vol I, 163–202. See also JI Charney, 'International Maritime Boundaries for the Continental Shelf: The Relevance of Natural Prolongation' in N Ando et al, (eds), *Liber Amicorum Judge Shigeru Oda* (The Hague, Kluwer, 2002) 1011.

A. Analysis of the Case Law

i. Arguments in the Context of Continental Shelf Delimitations

a. Geological and Geomorphological Factors in the *Anglo-French Continental Shelf* Arbitration

As explained earlier, the ICJ in the *North Sea Continental Shelf* cases identified the concept of natural prolongation as the legal title over the continental shelf. Although it was not suggested that the concept of natural prolongation would automatically allow for the fixing of a continental shelf boundary,[543] that concept encouraged States to request an international court or tribunal to determine continental shelf boundaries on the basis of the geological and geomorphological features of the seabed. Thus, in the *Anglo-French Continental Shelf* case of 1977, the United Kingdom proposed the axis of the Hurd Deep and Hurd Deep Fault Zone as an alternative to a median line.[544] However, the Court of Arbitration rejected the British argument:

> The geological faults which constitute the Hurd Deep and the so-called Hurd Deep Fault Zone, even if they be considered as distinct features in the geomorphology of the shelf, are still discontinuities in the seabed and subsoil which do not disrupt the essential unity of the continental shelf either in the Channel or the Atlantic region. Indeed, in comparison with the deep Norwegian Trough in the North Sea, they can only be regarded as minor faults in the geological structure of the shelf; [...] Moreover, to attach critical significance to a physical feature like the Hurd Deep-Hurd Deep Fault Zone in delimiting the continental shelf boundary in the present case would run counter to the whole tendency of State practice on the continental shelf in recent years.[545]

The Court thus concluded that: '[T]here is no intrinsic reason why a boundary along that axis should be the boundary which is justified by the special circumstance under Article 6 or which, under customary law, is needed to remedy the particular inequity.'[546]

b. Geological and Geomorphological Factors in the ICJ Jurisprudence

In the ICJ jurisprudence, two cases merit mention: The *Tunisia/Libya* and *Libya/Malta* cases. First, in the *Tunisia/Libya* case, the Parties relied heavily on geological and geomorphological factors. As indicated already, the ICJ discarded the contentions of the Parties. Regarding the geomorphological factor, however, the Court implied in a general sense that that factor could be viewed as a relevant

[543] On this point, see ch 1, s II. In addition, while the Court touched on the Norwegian Trough, no evaluation was made regarding the status of that feature. The *North Sea Continental Shelf* cases [1969] ICJ Rep 32, [45].

[544] The *Anglo-French Continental Shelf* case, 18 *RIAA*, 21, [12]; 59–60, [104–6].

[545] ibid, 60, [107].

[546] ibid, 61, [108].

circumstance, even though it had no relevance in this particular case.[547] Secondly, in the *Libya/Malta* case, the Court discarded the Libyan argument regarding the 'rift zone', which was based on the concept of natural prolongation in a physical sense. In this regard, the Court made an important statement:

> The Court however considers that since the development of the law enables a State to claim that the continental shelf appertaining to it extends up as far as 200 miles from its coast, whatever the geological characteristics of the corresponding sea-bed and subsoil, there is no reason to ascribe any role to geological or geophysical factors within that distance either in verifying the legal title of the States concerned or in proceeding to a delimitation as between their claims.[548]

It may be said that the rejection of geological and geomorphological factors was total in this case.

ii. Arguments in the Context of Single/Coincident Maritime Boundaries

a. Geological and Geomorphological Factors in the ICJ Jurisprudence

The delimitation of single/coincident maritime boundaries extends to the seabed as well as to the superjacent waters. Accordingly, in the context of the single/coincident maritime boundary, the nature of the arguments concerning geological and geographical factors is different from that of the arguments pertaining to the continental shelf boundary alone. In the *Gulf of Maine* case, the United States originally proposed a line of the greatest depths, thus attributing decisive importance to geomorphological factors.[549] Its purpose was to keep intact the unity of each ecosystem. The Chamber of the ICJ rejected this approach, since it related only to the FZ and thus was unusable for drawing a single maritime boundary for both the continental shelf and the FZ.[550] Furthermore, the Chamber decided to apply geometric methods and neutral criteria which gave preferential treatment to neither the seabed nor the superjacent waters. When applying neutral criteria, as the Chamber indicated, even where a distinctive geological feature is said to exist, such a feature would not be relevant to the drawing of a single maritime boundary since it relates only to the seabed.[551]

In the *Nicaragua v Honduras* case, geological factors were in issue when considering the applicability of the equidistance line. In light of 'a very active morpho-dynamism' of the relevant coastlines, as noted, the Court considered it

[547] [1982] ICJ Rep 58, [68]; 64, [80]. By contrast, the Court did not classify geological factor as relevant circumstances. See Evans, *Relevant Circumstances and Maritime Delimitation* 116.

[548] [1985] ICJ Rep 35, [39]. In this paragraph, geology and geomorphology were not distinguished.

[549] [1984] ICJ Rep 316, [166]. As explained above, however, the United States changed its proposal to the adjusted perpendicular line.

[550] ibid, 317, [168].

[551] ibid, 327, [193].

inappropriate to apply the equidistance method in this case.[552] In other cases, the relevance of geological and geomorphological factors was not in issue.

b. Geological and Geomorphological Factors in Arbitral Awards

In the *St Pierre and Miquelon* arbitration, Canada alleged that St Pierre and Miquelon generate no continental shelf because physically they are superimposed upon the Canadian continental shelf. However, the Court of Arbitration rejected the Canadian argument on two grounds. First, the continental shelf in this area is all one shelf and cannot be considered as exclusively Canadian.[553] Secondly, as had been held by the Chamber in the *Gulf of Maine* case, the structure of the seabed ceases to be important when the object is to establish a single, all-purpose delimitation of both the sea-bed and the superjacent waters.[554] On this point, the Arbitral Tribunal echoed the Chamber's view by following the idea of 'neutral' criteria.

The *Guinea/Guinea-Bissau* case, too, calls for comment. Having drawn a single maritime boundary, the Arbitral Tribunal examined the structure and nature of the continental shelf at the verification stage. In the event, no geological and geomorphological factors were taken into account because the continental shelf concerned was one and the same.[555] As indicated above, however, the argument of the Arbitral Tribunal does raise the question of whether a natural break would affect the delimitation of the superjacent waters. By contrast, in the *Guyana v Suriname* case, the Parties themselves agreed that geological or geophysical factors were of no relevance.[556] Thus these factors had no influence on the location of a single maritime boundary established by the Arbitral Tribunal.

In the *Bangladesh v India* case, geological or geomorphological factors were discussed in the context of delimitation of the continental shelf beyond 200 nautical miles. Both Parties agreed that: '[N]either may claim a superior entitlement based on geological or geomorphological factors in the overlapping area.'[557] As discussed earlier, the Arbitral Tribunal adjusted the provisional equidistance line within and beyond 200 nautical miles taking account of a cut-off effect arising from the concavity of the Bangladesh's coast.[558] Consequently, geological or geomorphological factors did not affect the location of the continental shelf boundary beyond 200 nautical miles.

[552] [2007] ICJ Rep 742, [277]. See also ch 5, s X of this book.

[553] The *St Pierre and Miquelon* arbitral award, (1992) 31 *ILM* 1164–65, [46].

[554] ibid, p 1165, para 47.

[555] The *Guinea/Guinea-Bissau* arbitral award, (1986) 25 *ILM* 300, [116–17].

[556] The *Guyana v Suriname* arbitral award, 30 *RIAA* 97, [354]. See also Memorial of Guyana, 89, [7.35]; Counter-Memorial of Suriname, 7, [2.6].

[557] The *Bangladesh v India* arbitral award, [457]. See also Bangladesh's Reply, [5.11].

[558] See ch 5, s XV of this book.

c. Geological and Geomorphological Factors in the ITLOS Jurisprudence

The consideration of geological and geomorphological factors was at issue in two cases before ITLOS. In the *Bangladesh/Myanmar* case, Bangladesh claimed that the geology and geomorphology of the seabed and subsoil constituted the relevant circumstances in the delimitation of the continental shelf beyond 200 nautical miles since entitlement beyond 200 nautical miles depends entirely on natural prolongation.[559] According to Bangladesh, its claim to the continental shelf beyond 200 nautical miles rests firmly on the underlying Bengal Depositional System, while 'Myanmar can at best point only to geomorphological continuity based on sedimentation and accretion caused by subduction of the Indian tectonic plate.'[560] 'From either perspective', Bangladesh continued, 'the seabed is "the *most natural* extension of the land territory" of Bangladesh'.[561] ITLOS refused to admit the Bangladesh's 'the most natural prolongation' argument, however. In the words of the Tribunal,

> The Tribunal has already determined that natural prolongation is not an independent basis for entitlement and should be interpreted in the context of the subsequent provisions of article 76 of the Convention, in particular paragraph 4 thereof. The Tribunal has determined that both Parties have entitlements to a continental shelf beyond 200 nm in accordance with article 76 and has decided that those entitlements overlap. The Tribunal therefore cannot accept the argument of Bangladesh that, were the Tribunal to decide that Myanmar is entitled to a continental shelf beyond 200 nm, Bangladesh would be entitled to a greater portion of the disputed area because it has 'the most natural prolongation'.[562]

As pointed out earlier,[563] the Tribunal accepted that there was a 'continuous and substantial layer of sedimentary rocks extending from Myanmar's coast to the area beyond 200 nm'.[564] In light of the unique feature of the Bay of Bengal, arguably 'natural prolongation' cannot be regarded as a relevant circumstance in the delimitation of the continental shelf beyond 200 nautical miles in the Bay. Given that the unique feature does not always exist in other parts of the seabed of the world oceans, however, whether the *dictum* of ITLOS in the *Bangladesh/Myanmar* case can be generalised needs careful consideration.[565]

In the *Ghana/Côte d'Ivoire* case, ITLOS Special Chamber accepted that: '[A] continental shelf beyond 200 nm exists for Côte d'Ivoire since its geological

559 [2012] ICJ Rep 117, [457].

560 Reply of Bangladesh, vol I, 144, [4.81].

561 Emphasis original. ibid. In the *Bangladesh v India* case, Bangladesh withdrew the argument that the continental shelf beyond 200 nautical miles was geologically the 'most natural prolongation' of its coast. The *Bangladesh v India* arbitral award, [439]. In this case, the Parties agreed that: '[N]either may claim a superior entitlement based on geological or geomorphological factors in the overlapping area.' ibid, [457].

562 [2012] ICJ Rep 118, [460].

563 See ch 5, s XIX of this book.

564 [2012] ICJ Rep 115, [446].

565 R Churchill, 'The *Bangladesh/Myanmar* Case: Continuity and Novelty in the Law of Maritime Delimitation' (2012) 1 *Cambridge Journal of International and Comparative Law* 150.

situation is identical to that of Ghana, for which affirmative recommendation of the CLCS exits.'[566] The Chamber thus drew a maritime boundary within and beyond 200 nautical miles. As pointed out earlier, the maritime boundary is an equidistance line.[567] Hence geological or geomorphological factors had no influence on the location of the maritime boundary.

B. Analysis of State Practice

i. Agreements Regarding Continental Shelf Delimitations

The impact of geological and geomorphological factors was not unknown in treaty practice relating to continental shelf delimitation within 200 nautical miles. An example is provided by the 1972 Agreement between Australia and Indonesia. The Agreement established a continental shelf boundary in the Timor and Arafura Seas. In the course of negotiations, while Indonesia favoured the equidistance method on the grounds that the seabed in question formed a single unit, Australia asserted that that seabed was interrupted by the Timor Trough.[568] In its deepest part, the Trough is 3,100 metres deep, its width from north to south being nearly 70 nm. Regarding the nature of the Timor Trough, there were differences of opinions among geologists, and neither Party succeeded in achieving its maximum claim. Thus, as a compromise, the boundary of the continental shelf was established in the area between the equidistance line to the south and the axis of the Timor Trough to the north. Finally, the agreed-upon boundary runs closer to the axis of the Timor Trough, and Australia gained about 80 per cent of the area in dispute.[569] In this Agreement, although the agreed-upon line does not precisely follow the axis of the Timor Trough, that feature had an important impact upon the location of the boundary of the continental shelf. It is also suggested that, in the 1975 Agreement between Indonesia and Thailand regarding the delimitation of the continental shelf in the Andaman Sea, geomorphological features were influential so as to justify a boundary deviating from a strict equidistance line.[570] Furthermore, Prescott presumes that, in the 1971 Agreement between Indonesia and Thailand, the morphology of the seabed might have played some role in identifying the terminus of the boundary of the continental shelf, although there is no evidence to this effect.[571]

[566] The *Ghana/Côte d'Ivoire* case, [2017] ITLOS Rep [491].

[567] See ch 5, s XVII of this book.

[568] PG Bassett, 'Australia's Maritime Boundaries' (1984) 55 *Australian Foreign Affairs Record* 186; Report by Prescott in *IMB*, vol II, 1211.

[569] ibid, 1211.

[570] Report by Prescott in ibid, 1466, 1468. See also SP Jagota, *Maritime Boundary* (Dordrecht, Nijhoff, 1985) 84.

[571] Report by Prescott in *IMB*, vol II, 1458.

Where the Parties claim the continental shelf beyond 200 nautical miles, geological and geomorphological factors become important particularly in fixing the terminal point of the continental shelf boundary. For instance, in the 1988 Agreement between Ireland and the United Kingdom, two delimitation lines of the continental shelf were established in two regions. It is suggested that the terminal points of the two boundaries were decided according to the geological and geomorphological criteria defined in Article 76 of the LOSC.[572] It is also reported that the Points A 79 and A 82 of the continental shelf boundary established by the 1997 Treaty between Australia and Indonesia coincides with a line 60 nm seaward of the foot of the Australian continental slope in accordance with Article 76(4)(a)(ii) of the LOSC.[573] Furthermore, the recommendations of the Commission on the Limits of the Continental Shelf (CLCS) may affect the terminal points or the location of the continental shelf boundary beyond 200 nautical miles. In this connection, it is of particular interest to note that some treaties take a flexible approach by leaving the precise location of the terminal points open. By way of example, the precise location of the northernmost terminal point of the maritime boundary between Norway and the Russian Federation, which was established in the 2010 Treaty between Norway and the Russian Federation,[574] is to be identified on the basis of the final recommendations of the CLCS.[575] Likewise the 2009 Agreement between Kenya and Tanzania specified that the maritime boundary is delimited along the parallel of latitude from Point T-C eastwards to a point that 'it intersects the outermost limits of the Continental Shelf', which is beyond 200 nautical miles.[576] Both Kenya and Tanzania submitted the information on the continental shelf beyond 200 nautical miles to the CLCS in 2009 and 2012, respectively.[577] However, the CLCS has not yet issued its recommendations on the submissions. Thus the precise location of the outermost limits of the continental shelf boundary beyond 200 nautical miles is not fixed yet.[578] In addition, the most part of the delimitation line established in the 2004 Agreement between Australia and New Zealand delimits the continental shelf beyond 200 nautical miles. According to commentators, '[i]t is understood that the termini could be adjusted at some future point to reflect the outcomes of both countries' submissions' to the CLCS.[579]

[572] Report by Anderson in ibid, 1770.

[573] Report by Prescott in ibid, vol IV, 2708.

[574] Article 5(2). Text in ibid, vol VII, 5189.

[575] While the CLCS issued its final recommendations to Norway's submission on the continental shelf beyond 200 nautical miles in the North East Atlantic and the Arctic in 2009, the final recommendations for the Russian side are still pending. See Report by Fife, ibid, 5184; www.un.org/Depts/los/clcs_new/submissions_files/submission_nor.htm.

[576] Article 3. Text in: *IMB*, vol VII, 4789.

[577] Report by Pratt, ibid, 4784; www.un.org/Depts/los/clcs_new/commission_submissions.htm.

[578] See also BM Magnússon, *The Continental Shelf Beyond 200 Nautical Miles: Delineation, Delimitation and Dispute Settlement* (Leiden, Brill/Nijhoff, 2015) 200.

[579] Report by Fyfe and French, *IMB*, vol V, 3763. Fyfe and French also indicated that: 'Geomorphological factors played an important role in determining some aspects of the boundary.' ibid, 3764. See also Magnússon, *The Continental Shelf Beyond 200 Nautical Miles* 196–97.

Moreover, the recommendations of the CLCS may affect the scope of the overlapping areas of the continental shelf. In this regard, some countries agreed to adjust the continental shelf boundary in light of the recommendation of the Commission. For instance, Denmark (Faroe Islands), Island and Norway adopted the Agreed Minutes on the Delimitation of the Continental Shelf beyond 200 Nautical Miles between the Faroe Islands, Iceland and Norway in the Southern Part of the Banana Hole of the Northeast Atlantic on 20 September 2006.[580] Paragraph 2 of the Agreed Minutes specifies straight geodetic lines that the bilateral delimitations of the continental shelf will follow. Under paragraph 8, the lines may be adjusted after consideration by the CLCS. Pursuant to paragraph 9, the States are simultaneously to conclude three parallel bilateral agreements on the final determination of the boundary lines in accordance with these Agreed Minutes and their appendices as soon as possible, and no later than three month after the States have concluded the procedure set out in Article 76(8) of the LOSC. A similar solution was adopted in the 2013 Agreed Minutes between Greenland and Iceland in the Irminger Sea.[581] The Agreed Minutes specifies straight geodetic lines as the continental shelf boundary beyond 200 nautical miles. The dividing line divides the overlapping area according to the ratio of 53 (Greenland): 47 (Iceland).[582] Under paragraph 8, if the area of interest is adjusted after consideration by the CLCS, it will be divided according to the same apportioning ratio. These Agreed Minutes seems to provide a practical solution in delimiting the continental shelf beyond 200 nautical miles.

In some cases, differences of opinions regarding features of the seabed may prevent the conclusion of agreements establishing a continental shelf boundary. The dispute between South Korea and Japan regarding the Okinawa Trough provides an important example. The Trough, which lies in the East China Sea, is 630 miles long, its width being over 100 miles and its depth over 2,000 metres.[583] Based on the theory of natural prolongation, South Korea insisted that the Japanese continental shelf terminated on the eastern edge of the Okinawa Trough. Japan proposed a solution based on an equidistance line on the grounds that South Korea and Japan faced one and the same continental shelf. According to Japan, in such a situation, the equidistance method should be applied.[584]

[580] The Agreed Minutes is available at the website of Norway's Ministry of Foreign Affairs www.regjeringen.no/nb/dep/ud/dok/lover_regler/retningslinjer/2006/Agreed-Minutes.html?id=446839. See also Magnússon, *The Continental Shelf Beyond 200 Nautical Miles* 197–99.

[581] For the text of the Agreed minutes, see www.assidmer.net/doc/2013_Agreed_Minutes_(Irminger_Sea).pdf.

[582] Paragraph 3.

[583] Z Wu, *Maritime Delimitation in the China Sea* (Geneva, IUHEI, Thesis, 1992) 117–18; CH Park, 'Continental Shelf Issues in the Yellow Sea and the East China Sea' in *Law of the Sea Institute, University of Rhode Island, Occasional Paper* (No 15, 1972) 32; by the same author, 'China and Maritime Jurisdiction: Some Boundary Issues' in CH Park and JK Oark, (eds), *The Law of the Sea: Problems from the East Asian Perspective* (Honolulu University Hawaii, The Law of the Sea Institute, 1987) 282.

[584] CH Park, 'Oil Under Troubled Waters: The Northeast Asia Sea-Bed Controversy' (1973) 14 *Harvard International Law Journal* 243; C Mizukami, *Nippon to Kaiyoho* (Japan and the Law of

Thus, the negotiation was deadlocked. As a compromise, the two States, in the Agreement of 1974, established a Joint Development Zone in the southern part of the overlapping area of the continental shelf.[585] Another example is provided by Socotra Rock, which is referred to as 'Ieodo' in Korea and 'Suyan Jiao' in Chinese. Socotra Rock, which is located in the East China Sea, is a submerged rock situated 4.6 meters under water, and its surface is 3.7 square kilometres. The Republic of Korea and China claim that Socotra Rock is in their EEZs. In light of its strategic location, Socotra Rock constitutes a critical element in negotiations between Korea and China with regard to maritime delimitation in the East China Sea.[586]

On the other hand, it appears that a majority of agreements did not take geological and/or geomorphological characteristics into account. For instance, the continental shelf in the North Sea is separated by the Norwegian Trough, a feature off Norway's southern coast, which is 20 nm wide and about 700 metres deep in the Skagerrak. However, in the three Agreements establishing continental shelf boundaries between Denmark and Norway (1965),[587] Norway and Sweden (1968),[588] and Norway and the United Kingdom (1965 and 1978),[589] the Norwegian Trough was ignored and equidistance lines were drawn. Nor did the Ionian abyss plain play any role in the 1977 Agreement between Greece and Italy.[590] Other examples may be furnished by the 1971 Agreement between Italy and Tunisia,[591] the 1974 Agreement between Italy and Spain,[592] the 1974 Agreement between France and Spain[593] and the 1978 Agreement between India and Thailand.[594] In fact, apart from the 1974 Agreement between France and Spain, those agreements established continental shelf boundaries on the basis of the equidistance method. In addition, it will be noted that, on the Pacific side of

the Sea, in Japanese) (Tokyo, Yushindo, 1995) 120–21. In relation to the Okinawa Trough, China and Taiwan took the same view as South Korea. Z Wu, *Maritime Delimitation in the China Sea* 131.

585 Agreement between Japan and the Republic of Korea Concerning the Joint Development of the Southern Part of the Continental Shelf Adjacent to the Two Countries. For the text, see *IMB*, vol I, 1073–89. For an analysis of the process of negotiation and the text of the Agreement, see Mizukami, *Nippon to Kaiyoho*, 119–34.

586 Suk Kyoon Kim, 'Maritime Boundary Negotiations between China and Korea: The Factors at Stake' (2017) 32 *IJMCL*, 83. In 2003, Korea constructed an Ocean research Station on Ieodo. ibid, 84. For the location of Ieodo, see Figure 4 annexed to the article. ibid.

587 Report by Anderson in *IMB*, vol II, 1817.

588 Report by Anderson in ibid, 1873.

589 ibid, 1881–82. See also, *Limits in the Sea,* No 10, 1974, 5.

590 Report by Scovazzi in *IMB*, vol II, 1594–95.

591 Report by Scovazzi in ibid, 1617–18. According to Scovazzi, there is a well-marked interruption between the shelves of Africa and Sicily. There is also a well-marked interruption between the shelves of North Tunisia and of Sardinia.

592 ibid, 1603. It is suggested that there is a well-marked separation between the continental shelves adjacent to Sardinia and to the Balearic Islands.

593 Cape Breton Trough was disregarded. On the other hand, the 4500 metres isobath was considered in drawing the continental shelf boundary. Report by Anderson in ibid, 1722–23.

594 Report by Prescott in ibid, 1436. In the relevant area, there is the axis of the Andaman basin, which descends to 4,000 metres.

South America, States have very modest continental shelves in a geological and geomorphological sense. Yet such geological and geomorphological features did not have any effect on the maritime boundaries in this region.[595]

The 2018 Treaty between Australia and the Democratic Republic of Timor-Leste Establishing Their Maritime Boundaries in the Timor Sea (hereafter the Timor Sea Treaty) also provides an interesting instance in this matter.[596] This Treaty was concluded through compulsory conciliation procedures under the LOSC.[597] In the discussion with the *Timor-Leste/Australia* Conciliation Commission, Timor-Leste argued that: '[C]oncepts of natural prolongation and the geology and geomorphology of the seabed were no longer relevant to the delimitation of a continental shelf between two States situated at a distance of less than 400 nautical miles.'[598] By contrast, Australia contended that: '[T]he physical continental shelves of Australia to the south and Timor-Leste and Indonesia to the north are entirely separate, and that these significant factual characteristics geologically, geomorphologically and ecologically remained relevant in maritime boundary delimitation.'[599] Owing to the effort of the Conciliation Commission, Timor-Leste and Australia reached agreement on a comprehensive package of measures including a maritime boundary and a special regime for the joint development of the Sunrise and Troubadour gas field on 30 August 2017 in Copenhagen. The agreement was formalised in a draft treaty in October 2017.[600] The Timor Sea Treaty was signed at the United Nations in New York on 6 March 2018.[601] Under the Timor Sea Treaty, the western segment of the southern continental shelf boundary line partially follows the median line and partially runs to the north of the median line (TA5 to TA-6).[602] As a consequence, it appears that the Timor Trough did not affect the location of the continental shelf boundary.

[595] Report by Jiménez de Aréchaga in ibid, vol I, 289. The 1984 Agreement between Argentina and Chile was, however, an exception.

[596] The electronic text is available at: http://dfat.gov.au/geo/timor-leste/Documents/treaty-maritime-arrangements-australia-timor-leste.pdf.

[597] This was the first case of compulsory conciliation under the LOSC. The members of the Conciliation Commission were: Peter Taksøe-Jensen (Chairman), Rosalie Balkin, Abdul G Koroma, Donald McRae and Rüdiger Wolfrum.

[598] *Report and Recommendations on the Compulsory Conciliation Commission between Timor-Leste and Australia on the Timor Sea* (hereinafter Report of 2018), 9 May 2018, [232], available at: https://pca-cpa.org/en/cases/132/. This was the first case of compulsory conciliation under the LOSC. ibid, [1]. The members of the Conciliation Commission were: Peter Taksøe-Jensen (Chairman), Rosalie Balkin, Abdul G Koroma, Donald McRae and Rüdiger Wolfrum. For a commentary on the conciliation by the author, see Y Tanaka, 'Maritime Boundary Delimitation by Conciliation' (2018) 36 *Australian Year Book of International Law* (forthcoming).

[599] Report of 2018, [234]. See also Presentation by Mr Gleeson, Opening Session Transcript, 92.

[600] Report of 2018, [3–4].

[601] ibid, [219]. The text was reproduced as Annex 28 to the Report of 2018.

[602] ibid, [261] Australian Government, Department of Foreign Affairs and Trade, 'Australia and Timor-Leste Maritime Boundaries Rules-based Order in Action' March 2008.

ii. Agreements Regarding Single Maritime Boundaries

The geological and geomorphological factors play little, if any, role in agreements regarding single maritime boundaries. For instance, in the Caribbean Sea, by drawing a single maritime boundary on the basis of a median line, the 1978 Agreement between Colombia and the Dominican Republic did not consider the Beata Ridge, which clearly divides the eastern (Venezuelan) from the western (Colombian) basin.[603] Furthermore, the single maritime boundary established between Cuba and Haiti in 1977 disregards the Cayman Trench, which is around 2,900 metres deep.[604] Another interesting example will be furnished by the 1980 Agreement between France (Guadeloupe and Martinique) and Venezuela. In the course of the negotiations for the establishment of a single maritime boundary, both Parties proposed methods based on geological or geomorphological considerations. These proposals were, however, dismissed during the negotiations. Accordingly, the factors in question did not affect the location of the boundary.[605] Moreover, with respect to the 1979 Agreement between the Dominican Republic and Venezuela, which establishes a single maritime boundary, it is suggested that Muertos Trough, 5,000 metres deep, did not influence the location of the boundary.[606] In addition, according to Jiménez de Aréchaga, the 1984 Agreement between Argentina and Chile establishes a single maritime boundary leaving the geological continental shelf of the Chilean islands under the jurisdiction of Chile.[607] In reality, however, that boundary runs along parallels of latitude and longitude. Accordingly, it appears that the single maritime boundary does not follow precise geological characteristics.

There are a few agreements, however, in which geological and geomorphological factors did, to a certain extent, affect single maritime boundaries. As with the agreements relating to continental shelf delimitations, geological and geomorphological characteristics may came into play solely for determining the terminal points of a delimitation line. For instance, in the 1982 Agreement drawing a single maritime boundary between France (Kerguelen Islands) and Australia (Heard/McDonald Islands), geological and geomorphological factors were taken into account in identifying the boundary's eastern and western terminus. The eastern terminus is located 240 nm from the coast of each Party, east of a very steep submarine escarpment which marks the eastern limit of

[603] Report by Nweihed in *IMB*, vol I, 482–83.

[604] Report by Nweihed in ibid, 556–57; B Beazley, 'Maritime Boundaries: A Geographical and Technical Perspective' in ED Brown and RR Churchill (eds), *The UN Convention on the Law of the Sea: Impact and Implementation, Proceedings of Law of the Sea Institute 19th Annual Conference* (University of Hawaii, 1987) 328 and 338, n 49.

[605] Report by Nweihed in *IMB*, vol I, 608–9.

[606] Report by Nweihed in ibid, 583.

[607] Report by Jiménez de Aréchaga in ibid, 723.

the Kerguelen-Gaussberg ridge running almost perpendicular to the direction of the boundary. Thus, it appears that the negotiators attempted to identify the terminus of the boundary by reference to the continental margin.[608] On the other hand, the western terminus lies off the well-marked western escarpment of the plateau. It is suggested that the uncertainty of the configuration of the continental shelf southwest of the agreed-upon line contributed to the decision to avoid delimitation in this area.[609]

The terminal point of the single maritime boundary between Trinidad and Tobago and Venezuela, which was established in 1990, was determined on the basis of geological and geomorphological data.[610] The same was true of the 1982 Agreement between Australia and France (New Caledonia),[611] the 1988 Agreement between Australia and Solomon Islands[612] and the 1990 Agreement between Trinidad and Tobago and Venezuela.[613]

In some cases, geological and geomorphological characteristics played some role connected with economic or navigational interests. For example, the single maritime boundary between the Netherlands (Antilles) and Venezuela follows, in the Bonaire–Curacao sector, the contours of the Bonaire Trench. Yet it is suggested that the consideration of geological features stems from their economic potential rather than from the features as such.[614] Another example is the 1988 Treaty between Denmark and the former German Democratic Republic. In drawing a single maritime boundary, Adler Grund, which is less than 10 meters deep, had an important impact upon the location of the middle part of the boundary's eastern segment. Accordingly, the established single maritime boundary deviates from a simplified equidistance line.[615] On this point, the 1988 Treaty presents an interesting example of factors relating only to the seabed and affecting the delimitation of superjacent waters. It should be

[608] Report by Prescott in ibid, vol II,1188.

[609] ibid, 1188–89.

[610] Report by Nweihed in ibid, vol I, 681. The boundary is located nearly 6-nm beyond the 200–nm limit. According to Nweihed, this may be the first agreement in which the edge of the margin was calculated on the basis of the thickness of the sedimentary rocks according to Art 76 of the UN Convention on the Law of the Sea. ibid.

[611] Report by Park in ibid, 908.

[612] ibid, 980.

[613] Report by Nweihed in ibid, 681.

[614] ibid, 625. In the context of territorial sea delimitation, there are some instances where seabed characteristics may influence the location of boundaries connecting navigational interests. In fact in three Agreements regarding delimitation of territorial seas between Indonesia and Singapore (1973), Malaysia and Thailand (Gulf of Thailand, 1979), and Italy and the former Yugoslavia (1975), a geomorphological factor (a *thalweg*) was considered in order to take navigational interests into account. This issue will be discussed later. In addition, the 1974 Agreement between the Federal Republic of Germany and the former German Democratic Republic considered, to a certain extent, navigational factors. But, this treaty is no longer operative owing to the unification of Germany.

[615] Report by Franckx in ibid, vol II, 2091. It should be noted that proportionality also affected the location of the single maritime boundary. ibid.

noted that the fisheries around Adler Grund are an important economic interest for the Parties. Furthermore, the deviation from an equidistance line in the Adler Grund area was based on a proportionality calculation. Accordingly, several factors simultaneously determined the location of the single maritime boundary in the area.

Prescott suggests that, in the 1986 Agreement between Myanmar and India, geological and geomorphological considerations probably influenced the selection of Points 9 and 10, since an equidistance line in this area would have given India part of the submarine delta of the Irrawaddy River.[616] In this respect, it should not be forgotten that that delta might contain fields of natural gas or petroleum. Consequently, it could be contended that such a delta might be a relevant circumstance owing to its economic potential rather than purely geological or geomorphological reasons.[617]

C. Summary

The above considerations may be summarised as follows.

In the context of the maritime delimitation within 200 nautical miles, the case law attributes limited importance to geological and geomorphological factors.[618] This may be explained by two reasons. The first is that, regarding the cases brought before international tribunals, there were no marked features in the seabed. Where the seabed is continuous and undivided, geological and geomorphological factors have no practical relevance. Secondly and more important, in contemporary international law of the sea, coastal States may claim the continental shelf as well as an EEZ/FZ of 200 miles, regardless of the geological or geomorphological characteristics of the area. Consequently, as the ICJ held in the *Libya/Malta* case, geological and geomorphological factors become irrelevant in the process of delimitation. Indeed, within the area of 200 miles from the coast, consideration of seabed characteristics clashes with the distance criterion as legal title. This is the decisive reason for disregarding the characteristics of the seabed.[619] Furthermore, with respect to single maritime boundaries, the application of neutral criteria and geometrical methods

[616] Report by Prescott in ibid, 1333–34.

[617] In addition, according to Prescott, Point 9 is equidistant between Myanmar's mainland and the northern tip of the main Andaman Islands. Point 10 is very close to the equidistance which gives Narcondam island full effect. And the line connecting Point 9 and Point 10 is a parallel of latitude. Owing to those geometric facts, it appears that the delimitation line in this part was not necessarily based only on geological and geomorphological factors. ibid, 1331.

[618] See also T Cottier, *Equitable Principles of Maritime Delimitation: The Quest for Distributive Justice in International Law* (Cambridge University Press, 2015) 470.

[619] Kolb, *Case Law on Equitable Maritime Delimitation* 331 and 333; Magnússon, *The Continental Shelf Beyond 200 Nautical Miles* 184. For a different view, see Evans, *Relevant Circumstances and Maritime Delimitation* 115 and 117.

will contribute to disregarding geological and geomorphological factors. However, these reasons do not apply to the delimitation of the continental shelf beyond 200 nautical miles. Hence there may be some scope to consider that in appropriate cases, geological and geomorphological factors may be taken into account in the delimitation of the continental shelf beyond 200 nautical miles in future cases.[620]

It is true that there are some agreements which considered geological and geomorphological factors when determining maritime boundaries. In a majority of the agreements, however, the characteristics of the seabed did not have a significant effect upon the location of maritime boundaries.[621] Even when those factors are considered, they usually play only a secondary role, either for fixing terminal points of the boundary or together with other elements including economic and navigational interests.[622] One reason may be the scientific difficulty of clarifying the nature of geophysical features in the seabed. In fact, for that very reason, France and Venezuela dismissed reference to such factors during the negotiations for drawing a single maritime boundary. Another reason may be the practical difficulty in drawing a line based on the characteristics of a seabed.[623] A natural discontinuity of the seabed normally creates a zone, not a line.[624] Such a zone cannot, in itself, produce a delimitation line, and there remains the problem of delimiting that zone. It follows from the above discussion that in both case law and State practice, geological and geomorphological factors will not provide a useful criterion for maritime delimitation.

VII. THE PRESENCE OF THIRD STATES

The presence of third States creates particular sensitivity associated with maritime delimitation. In particular, two issues arise. The first concerns legal titles of third States in the area to be delimited and the second relates to the macro-geographical view sometimes adopted when considering configurations of the coastline. The second issue was typically raised in the *Guinea/Guinea-Bissau* case. As the second issue has been examined in the context of the configuration of the coast, this section focuses on the first issue.

[620] Churchill, 'The *Bangladesh/Myanmar* Case,' 150; C Schofield, A Telesetsky and Seokwoo Lee, 'A Tribunal Navigating Complex Waters; Implications of the Bay of Bengal Case' (2013) 44 *ODIL* 375.

[621] In 1993, Highet suggested that the ratio of agreements where those factors were taken into account was nearly 32 to 36% in maritime delimitation as a whole. Highet, 'The Use of Geophysical Factors'186.

[622] ibid, 195.

[623] ibid, 118; Lucchini and Voelckel, *Droit de la mer*, 136–37 and 174.

[624] In the *Libya/Malta* case, Libya noted this problem regarding a rift zone. [1985] ICJ Rep 35, [38].

A. Analysis of the Case Law

i. Arguments in the Context of Continental Shelf Delimitations

a. The Interest of Ireland in the *Anglo-French Continental Shelf* Case

In the *Anglo-French Continental Shelf* case, a problem arose relating to a possible meeting of the continental shelf boundary between the Parties with the boundary between Ireland and the United Kingdom. On this point, the United Kingdom took the position that the Court's power to delimit the Anglo-French continental shelf boundary was questionable westward of a notional meeting point with the Anglo-Irish boundary.[625] The Court of Arbitration, however, rejected this view, holding that:

> The Court's decision, it scarcely needs to be said, will be binding only as between the Parties to the present arbitration and will neither be binding upon nor create any rights or obligations for any third State, and in particular for the Republic of Ireland, for which the Decision will be *res inter alios acta*.[626]

For the Court,

> [I]t is manifestly outside the competence of this Court to decide in advance and hypothetically the legal problem which may then arise. The problem would normally find its appropriate solution by negotiations directly between the three States concerned. …[627]

It may be said that this view conforms to legal orthodoxy.[628] As shall be seen next, however, the Court of Arbitration's view did not survive in the judgments rendered by the ICJ.[629]

b. Third-State Interests in the ICJ Jurisprudence

In the jurisprudence of the ICJ concerning the delimitation of the continental shelf, the issue of third States was raised in the *Tunisia/Libya* and *Libya/Malta* cases.

In the *Tunisia/Libya* case, the interest of Malta was at issue. In 1981, Malta filed an application requesting permission to intervene in the *Tunisia/Libya* case under Article 62 of the Statute. The precise object of the intervention was to enable Malta to submit its views on the issues raised in the case before the

[625] The *Anglo-French Continental Shelf* case, 18 *RIAA*, 26, [26].
[626] ibid, 27, [28].
[627] ibid.
[628] Weil, *Perspective du droit de la délimitation maritime* 269.
[629] In this connection, the *Dubai/Sharjah Border* award should be noted. In that case, the Court of Arbitration held that the maritime boundary between points B to H, which did not concern any third State, were to be considered as definitive. On the other hand, the Court did not specify the end point of the maritime boundary, since the point shall be determined between Iran and the United Arab Emirates. (1993) 91 *ILR* 678.

Court. In so doing, Malta insisted that it had a 'specific and unique interest' in the proceedings by virtue of its geographical location *vis-à-vis* the two parties to the case. In Malta's view, 'its interests will necessarily be affected by the Court's decision in the case notwithstanding Article 59 [of the Statute].'[630] However, the ICJ unanimously dismissed Malta's request. Although its reasoning was complicated, it is possible to highlight two main reasons. The first was that Malta did not have an interest of a legal nature which might be affected by the decision. In the view of the Court, Malta's interest was of the same kind as that of other States within the region.[631] Secondly, Malta's intervention would allow Malta to submit arguments to the Court on concrete issues forming an essential part of the case between Tunisia and Libya.[632] The request to intervene could lead to prejudging the merits of Malta's own claims against Tunisia and Libya in separate disputes with each of those States.[633] According to the Court, such a request fell outside the scope of intervention under Article 62 of the Statute.[634]

The above rejection of Malta's request did not mean that the interest of Malta in the *Tunisia/Libya* case would be disregarded. The Court indirectly accepted 'the circumstance of the existence and interests of other States' as a relevant circumstance.[635] In fact, it attempted to avoid prejudging the rights of Malta. Regarding the northern and northeastern parts of the Pelagian Block, where conflicting claims of the Parties existed, the Court stated that it 'has no jurisdiction to deal with such problems in the present case and must not prejudge their solution in the future.'[636] In the part of the judgment concerning the second sector, namely, the area which extends seawards beyond the parallel of the most westerly point of the Gulf of Gabes, the Court did not indicate the terminal point of the delimitation line. In its view, 'the extension of this line northeastwards is a matter falling outside the jurisdiction of the Court in the present case, as it will depend on the delimitation to be agreed with a third State.'[637] Accordingly, despite the rejection of the request to intervene, the Court, to a certain extent, took Malta's interest into account.

In the *Libya/Malta* case, an issue arose with regard to the interest of Italy. In 1983, Italy submitted to the ICJ a request for permission to intervene under Article 62 of the Statute in the *Libya/Malta* case. In its submissions,

[630] [1981] ICJ Rep 9, [13]. Malta did not intend to be bound by the decision of the Court. ibid, 10, [14]. In addition, both of the original parties were opposed to Malta's application to intervene. ibid,10–12, [15–18].

[631] ibid, 19, [33].

[632] ibid, [32].

[633] ibid, 18, [31].

[634] The Court's view was not to escape criticism. Judge Oda pointed out that the Court imposed an unduly sever test regarding the affirmation of a legal interest by Malta. Separate Opinion of Judge Oda, ibid, 31, [18]. See also Separate Opinion of Judge Schwebel, ibid, 39.

[635] The *Tunisia/Libya* case, [1982] ICJ Rep 64, [81].

[636] ibid, 42, [33].

[637] ibid, 94, [133 C(3)].

Italy alleged that the areas of continental shelf to be delimited between the parties all belonged to one and the same region of the Central Mediterranean, and that Italy had a right over parts of the continental shelf in that region. The legal interest of Italy was not merely an 'interest' but constituted 'sovereign rights' over the appropriate areas of continental shelf.[638] In this connection, it should be noted that Italy's application to intervene was different from that of Malta in two respects. First, while Malta's object was simply to submit its views, Italy would also attempt to defend its legal rights. Secondly, while Malta did not agree to be bound by the decision of the Court, Italy did.[639] However, Italy's request to intervene was rejected by 11 votes to 5. According to the majority, Italy's application to intervene was inadmissible inasmuch as the protection of Italian rights would be equivalent to the introduction of an entirely new case.[640]

In the following year, the Court, in the *Libya/Malta* case of 1985, dealt with the consequences of its rejection of Italy's request to intervene. It did so by limiting the scope of its judgment so as not to infringe upon the rights of Italy in the region. The Court said clearly that: 'The present decision must, as then foreshadowed, be limited in geographical scope so as to leave the claims of Italy unaffected, that is to say that the decision of the Court must be confined to the area in which, as the Court has been informed by Italy, that State has no claims to continental shelf rights.'[641] In so doing, the Court confined itself to areas where no claims by a third State existed, that is to say, to the area between the meridians 13°50'E and 15°10'E, and thus Italy's insistence during the proceedings on its application for permission to intervene was rewarded (see Illustration 8).[642] In short, it simply cut off the line at the limit of the Italian claim rather than identifying the direction of the line with an arrow, as it had done in the *Tunisia/Libya* case.

The Court's approach in the *Libya/Malta* case is highly controversial. The most disputable point is that, while it rejected Italy's intervention in 1984,

[638] Application by Italy for permission to intervene in the *Libya/Malta* case, [1984] ICJ Rep 11, [15]. The original Parties contested the permissibility of the intervention.

[639] ibid, 12–13, [17].

[640] ibid, 19–20, [30–31]. In that case, five dissenting opinions and four separate opinions were annexed to the decision, showing the difficulty of the problem. The principal issue was whether, as the Court ruled, Italy's request would introduce a new case by requiring the Court to recognise or to reject the new claim. Some dissenters considered that the answer should have been in the negative, since to require the safeguarding of one's rights does not amount to requesting a ruling on the validity of those rights. For instance, when criticising the Court's confusion between 'right' and 'claim', Judge Sette-Camara asked '[w]hat is an interest of legal nature but a claim to a right?' Dissenting Opinion of Judge Sette-Camara, ibid, 83, [64]. See also the dissenting opinion of Judge Ago, ibid, 125–26, [17]. Judge Jennings pointed out that if, as the Court had done, the request for the safeguarding of Italy's rights should be rejected because it introduced a new dispute, there was no practical possibility of safeguarding rights by intervention under Art 62. Dissenting Opinion of Judge Jennings, ibid, 154, [19].

[641] The *Libya/Malta* case, [1985] ICJ Rep 26, [21].

[642] ibid, [22].

in 1985 the Court virtually granted Italy what it would have achieved had its request to intervene been granted and its claim been accepted.[643] This contradiction is difficult to justify. In doing what it did, the Court failed to examine the rights of Italy but confined the competence conferred upon it by Libya and Malta to the restricted area between the two meridians suggested by Italy.[644] This leads to a dangerous situation; the determination of the extent of the Court's jurisdiction is placed into the hands of a third State and depends on that State's claims. The danger increases with the extent of that State's claim.[645] As Judge Mosler stated, the competence of the Court to decide on the delimitation area lying between the coasts of the parties could not be made to depend on the pretensions of a third State brought to the Court's notice.[646] Furthermore, this result conforms neither to the Special Agreement between the Parties nor to the terms of Article 36, paragraph 6 of the Statute.[647] In light of this criticism, it may be said that the validity of the Court's approach in the *Libya/Malta* case is doubtful.[648]

ii. Arguments in the Judgments on Single/Coincident Maritime Boundaries

a. Third-State Interests in the ICJ Jurisprudence

The presence of third States created some debatable issues in the ICJ jurisprudence regarding the delimitation of single/coincident maritime boundaries. The *Land, Island and Maritime Frontier Dispute* case between El Salvador and Honduras is a case in point. In this case, the Interest of Nicaragua was at issue. In 1989, by virtue of Articles 36(1) and 62 of the Statue of the Court,

[643] Dissenting Opinion of Judge Schwebel, ibid, 173; Dissenting Opinion of Judge Oda, ibid, 131, [10].

[644] Dissenting Opinion of Judge Mosler, ibid, 116.

[645] Dissenting Opinion of Judge Schwebel, ibid, 177. See also Kolb, *Case Law on Equitable Maritime Delimitation* 326.

[646] Dissenting Opinion of Judge Mosler, [1985] ICJ Rep 117.

[647] ibid, 175.

[648] The Chamber of the ICJ came to a different conclusion in the *Frontier Dispute* case between Burkina Faso and Mari in 1986, which related to a land boundary. In that case, the Chamber faced the question of the rights of Niger *vis-à-vis* either party. The question was whether the Chamber had the power of fixing the tri-point Niger/Mali/Burkina Faso without the agreement of Niger. Mali answered the question in the negative, whilst Burkina Faso did the opposite. The Chamber considered that its jurisdiction was not restricted simply because the end-point of the frontier was located on the frontier of a third State not a party to the proceedings, since the rights of Niger were safeguarded by Art 59 of the Statute. Thus the Chamber concluded that it had a duty to indicate the line of the frontier between the Parties over the entire length of the disputed area. *Frontier Dispute* (Burkina Faso/Republic of Mali) [1986] ICJ Rep 576–80, [44–50]. In the 2005 *Benin/Niger* case, however, the Chamber of the ICJ took a different approach. In this case, the Chamber left the location of the tripoint Benin/Niger/Nigeria and the tripoint Benin/Niger/Burkina Faso open. *Case Concerning the Frontier Dispute* (Benin/Niger), [2005] ICJ Rep 150–51, [146]. See also A Pellet, 'Land and Maritime Tripoints in International Jurisprudence' in H Hestermeyer et al (eds), *Coexistence, Cooperation and Solidarity, Liber Amicorum Rüdiger Wolfrum* (Leiden, Brill/Nijhoff, 2011) 245, 261.

Nicaragua requested from the ICJ permission to intervene in the *Land, Island and Maritime Frontier Dispute* case, which was submitted to a Chamber of the ICJ in 1986.[649] In its application, Nicaragua asserted that it had an interest of a legal nature which must inevitably be affected by a decision of the Chamber relating to the legal situation of the islands and maritime spaces.[650] According to Nicaragua, the object of the intervention was to protect its legal rights in the Gulf of Fonseca and the adjacent maritime areas, and to inform the Court of the nature of its legal rights which were at issue in the dispute between El Salvador and Honduras.[651] Furthermore, Nicaragua clearly stated that it had no intention of intervening in other aspects of the procedure relating to the land boundary between El Salvador and Honduras.[652] In view of determining the scope of permitted intervention, five issues were examined: (i) the matters of islands, (ii) the situation of the waters within the Gulf of Fonseca, (iii) the possible delimitation of the waters within the Gulf, (iv) the situation of the waters outside the Gulf, and (v) the possible delimitation of the waters outside of the Gulf.

The Chamber accepted Nicaragua's intervention solely on the second point, which related to the legal regime of the waters of the Gulf of Fonseca.[653] That decision is the first case in which a request for intervention under Article 62 of the Statute of the Court has been accepted. At the same time, the Court's answers on debatable issues related to this subject were innovative. For the purpose of this subsection, however, it would be appropriate to limit our considerations to points 3, 4 and 5.[654]

With respect to the possible delimitation in the Gulf of Fonseca, Nicaragua invoked, as a consideration supporting its assertion of a legal interest, the 'essential character of the legal principles, including relevant equitable principles, which would be relevant to the determination of the questions placed on the agenda by the Special Agreement' (Application, paragraph 2(d)). Yet the Chamber held that an interest of a third State in the general legal rules and principles likely to be applied by the decision cannot justify an intervention.[655]

Furthermore, Nicaragua alleged that it had an interest of a legal nature owing to the 'leading role of coasts and coastal relationships in the legal regime of maritime delimitation and the consequence in the case of the Gulf of Fonseca

[649] The menders of the Chamber were: Sette-Camara, President of the Chamber; Judges Oda, Jennings; Judges *ad hoc* Valticos, Torres Bernárdes.

[650] [1990] ICJ Rep 108, [37]; 109, [40]. While Honduras did not object to Nicaragua's intervention, El Salvador requested that the Chamber deny the permission sought by Nicaragua. ibid, 99, [16].

[651] ibid, 108–9, [38].

[652] ibid, 109, [40].

[653] ibid, 119–22, [67–73]; 137, [105].

[654] It should be noted that there was a difference between El Salvador and Honduras with respect to the question of whether the Chamber was conferred jurisdiction to delimit within or outside the Gulf. While Honduras was of the view that delimitations should be effected, El Salvador alleged that the Parties had not asked the Chamber to trace a delimitation line. ibid, 105–6, [30–31].

[655] ibid, 124, [76].

that it would be impossible to carry out a delimitation which took into account only the coasts in the Gulf of two of the three riparian States' (paragraph 2(f)).[656] The Chamber discarded that argument as well, stating that:

> It occurs frequently in practice that a delimitation between two States involves taking account of the coast of a third State; but the taking into account of all the coasts and coastal relationships within the Gulf as a geographical fact for the purpose of effecting an eventual delimitation as between two riparian States – El Salvador and Honduras in the instant case – in no way signifies that by such an operation itself the legal interest of a third riparian State of the Gulf, Nicaragua, may be affected. In any case, it is for the Applicant States in the present proceedings to demonstrate to the satisfaction of the Chamber that this would be actually the case in the present instance. This Nicaragua has failed to do.[657]

In the same context, Nicaragua relied on 'the geographical situation in the Gulf of Fonseca and the adjacent maritime areas' as an element supporting the contention that it had a legal interest regarding the delimitation within the Gulf. The Chamber, however, refused to accept that contention on the grounds that Nicaragua did not indicate any maritime spaces in which it might have a legal interest which could be said to be affected by a possible delimitation line between El Salvador and Honduras.[658] It therefore follows that the mere existence of geographical relations is insufficient to prove the existence of a legal interest.

Moreover, Nicaragua argued that the Chamber might have to consider 'navigation routes in a Gulf whose mouth is less than 20 miles wide and the reasonable security interests of the riparians.' Yet the Chamber also refused that contention since it was too general to justify intervention.[659]

Regarding the legal regime of the maritime spaces outside the Gulf, the Chamber denied the existence of Nicaragua's interest of a legal nature as well. In the Chamber's view, an interest in the application of general legal rules and principles, which was invoked by Nicaragua as an element justifying its legal interest, was not the kind of interest which would justify an application for permission to intervene.[660]

Finally, concerning the delimitation of maritime areas outside the Gulf, Honduras had proposed, in its pleadings, a scheme of delimitation. That demonstration called for some indication in response by the State seeking to intervene. But Nicaragua failed to indicate how this delimitation [proposed by Honduras], or any other delimitation regarded by it as a possible one, would affect an actual Nicaraguan interest of a legal nature.[661] Accordingly, the Chamber refused to admit Nicaragua's request to intervene in this matter.

[656] ibid, 124, [77].
[657] ibid, 124–25, [77].
[658] ibid, 125, [78].
[659] ibid.
[660] ibid, 126–27, [82].
[661] ibid, 127–28, [84].

In summary, the Chamber rejected the existence of Nicaragua's legal interest relating to delimitations within and outside the Gulf of Fonseca. According to the Chamber, neither the existence of geographical relations nor an interest in general legal rules is insufficient to show a legal interest which might be affected by the Chamber's decision. Thus, applicant States will be required to show, more positively, maritime spaces which might be affected by a judgment and how they might be influenced.

By contrast, Judge Oda argued that Nicaragua had an interest of a legal nature in those matters. In his view, should the islands of Meanguera and Meanguerita be determined to lie under the sovereignty of El Salvador, a delimitation line between El Salvador and Honduras would not reach any closing line of the Gulf. If this were the case, Judge Oda said, 'Nicaragua would then undoubtedly have a legal interest in the fixing of the point where the delimitation between El Salvador and Honduras terminates – in other words, where its own boundary with Honduras terminates and its own boundary with El Salvador begins.'[662] Furthermore, with respect to delimitation of maritime space outside the Gulf of Fonseca, Judge Oda indicated that Honduras had proposed a delimitation line on the basis of its calculations of its own sea areas on the assumption of the acceptance of a line which would purport to delimit a Honduran boundary with Nicaragua. In the light of this fact, Judge Oda concluded that, if the Chamber were to delimit zones outside the Gulf, Nicaragua could reasonably claim to possess a legal interest which may be affected by a judgment of the Chamber.[663]

In 1992, the Chamber rendered the judgment regarding the *El Salvador/Honduras* dispute. Regarding the issues of delimitation, it decided that the Parties had not conferred upon the Chamber jurisdiction to effect any delimitation of those maritime spaces, whether within or outside the Gulf of Fonseca.[664] Thus, no delimitation was effected by the Chamber, and an occasion to discuss the influence of the third States upon delimitation in the area concerned was lost.

In the *Qatar v Bahrain* case, interests of Saudi Arabia and Iran might have been involved in the determination of the starting and terminal points of the delimitation line. When drawing the territorial sea boundary in the southern sector, the Court found that it could not fix the boundary's southernmost point since its definitive location depended on the limits of the maritime zones of Saudi Arabia and the Parties. The Court therefore simply stated that the delimitation line began from the point of intersection of the maritime limit of Saudi Arabia, on the one hand, and of Bahrain and Qatar, on the other, which could not be fixed.[665]

[662] Separate Opinion of Judge Oda, ibid, 142.

[663] ibid, 143.

[664] The case concerning the *Land, Island and Maritime Frontier Dispute*, [1992] ICJ Rep 617, [430(2)].

[665] Judgment, [2001] ICJ Rep 109, [221–22]. See also 115–16, [250].

Regarding the single maritime boundary in the northern sector, a tri-point between Iran, Bahrain and Qatar was at issue. In that region, agreements relating to the continental shelf delimitation had been concluded between Iran and Qatar in 1969, and between Iran and Bahrain in 1971.[666] Although these agreements purported only to establish continental shelf boundaries, they would affect the Qatar/Iran/Bahrain tri-point. Accordingly, for Bahrain, these agreements were relevant circumstances for the delimitation of the northern sector.[667] On the other hand, Qatar maintained that the Court had no jurisdiction to determine the Qatar/Iran/Bahrain tripoint without the express consent of Iran.[668] As in the southern sector, the Court did not fix the terminal point of the delimitation line. It simply held that the delimitation line followed a certain course 'until it meets the delimitation line between the respective maritime zones of Iran on the one hand and of Bahrain and Qatar on the other.'[669] In summary, the Court did not determine the limits of the delimitation line since they were to be decided by agreements between Saudi Arabia and Iran, on the one hand, and Bahrain and Qatar, on the other.[670]

The *Cameroon v Nigeria* case (Merits) raised the issues of the interest of Equatorial Guinea. The Gulf of Guinea, which is the area to be delimited, concerns five States: Nigeria, Cameroon, Equatorial Guinea, Gabon and São Tomé and Príncipe (see Illustration 17).[671] The island of Bioko is a part of Equatorial Guinea's territory. In addition, in 1999, Equatorial Guinea and São Tomé and Príncipe drew a maritime boundary by agreement. In the present geographical situation, a maritime delimitation between Cameroon and Nigeria beyond

[666] For the text of the 1969 Agreement, *IMB*, 1516–17; Regarding the 1971 Agreement, ibid, 1487–88.

[667] Memorial submitted by Bahrain, 283, [651]. The line proposed by Bahrain terminated in the point 2 of the 1969 Agreement between Qatar and Iran. ibid, 285, [655].

[668] Memorial submitted by Qatar, 287, [12.42]. But, the Qatar's line terminated in the point 2 of the 1971 Agreement between Bahrain and Iran. Counter-Memorial submitted by Qatar, 248, [8.11]. In addition, it argued that the 1958 Agreement between Saudi Arabia and Bahrain relating to the continental shelf delimitation should be taken into account as a relevant circumstances in particular in order to make the calculation of proportionality. ibid, 249, [8.13]. See also Memorial submitted by Qatar, 285, [12.40].

[669] Judgment, [2001] ICJ Rep 115, [249]. See also [250].

[670] Theoretically at least, it may not be impossible to determine a terminal point of the delimitation line. For instance, one might select the point where the delimitation line intersects with the line connecting two continental shelf boundaries between Qatar and Iran, and between Iran and Bahrain.

[671] All five States ratified the UN Convention on the Law of the Sea. In addition, according to the data presented by Division for Ocean Affairs and the Law of the Sea of the United Nations, all those States claimed 12-mile territorial seas and 200-mile EEZ (1999) 39 *Law of the Sea Bulletin* 40. Regarding Cameroon's claims over maritime spaces, however, Nuno Sérgio Marques Antunes points to the fact that no indication could be found in spite of the data of the United Nations. Furthermore, Antunes indicates that Professor Pellet, Counsel of Cameroon, stated that only a 12-mile territorial sea could be claimed by Cameroon. Nuno Sérgio Marques Antunes, 'The Pending Maritime Delimitation in the *Cameroon v Nigeria* Case: A Piece in the Jigsaw Puzzle of the Gulf of Guinea' (2000) 15 *IJMCL* 171.

point G might influence third States, ie, Equatorial Guinea and São Tomé and Príncipe.

Regarding Cameroon's submission to the Court, the Government of Nigeria presented eight preliminary objections, in the eighth of which it was asserted that: 'The question of maritime delimitation necessarily involves the rights and interests of third States and is inadmissible beyond point G.'[672] By contrast, Cameroon alleged that the interests of all other States are preserved by Article 59 of the Statute and by the principle according to which any delimitation between two States is *res inter alios acta*. In this regard, the ICJ accepted that:

> [I]t is evident that the prolongation of the maritime boundary between the Parties seawards beyond point G will eventually run into maritime zones where the rights and interests of Cameroon and Nigeria will overlap those of third States [ie, Equatorial Guinea and Sao Tomé and Príncipe]. It thus appears that the rights and interests of third States will become involved if the Court accedes to Cameroon's request.[673]

Furthermore,

> [T]he Court cannot rule out the possibility that the impact of the judgment required by Cameroon on the rights and interests of the third States could be such that the Court would be prevented from rendering it in the absence of these States, and that consequently Nigeria's eighth preliminary objection would have to be upheld at least in part. Whether such third States would chose to exercise their rights to intervene in these proceedings pursuant to the Statute remains to be seen.[674]

In any event, the Court refused the eighth preliminary objection as it did not have an exclusively preliminary character.[675]

In the merits, the Court found that it could not decide upon legal rights of third States not party to the proceedings. In this connection, notably the ICJ itself accepted the limitations of Article 59, stating that:

> [I]n particular in the case of maritime delimitations where the maritime areas of several States are involved, the protection afforded by Article 59 of the Statute may not always be sufficient. In the present case, Article 59 may not sufficiently protect Equatorial Guinea or Sao Tome and Principe from the effects – even if only indirect – of a judgment affecting their legal rights. ... It follows that, in fixing the maritime boundary between Cameroon and Nigeria, the Court must ensure that it does not adopt any position which might affect the rights of Equatorial Guinea and Sao Tome and Principe.[676]

[672] Case concerning the *Land and Maritime Boundary Between Cameroon and Nigeria*, Preliminary Objections, [1998] ICJ Rep 289, [19]. See also 286, [18].

[673] ibid, 324, [116].

[674] ibid. On this point, Judge Ajibola stated that the Nigeria's eighth preliminary objection ought to be upheld by the Court, since in his view, it cannot decide a dispute between two parties without the consent of those States whose interests are directly affected, unless they intervene in such a matter. Dissenting Opinion of Judge Ajibola, ibid, 415.

[675] Judgment, ibid, 324, [116]; 326, [118(2)].

[676] The *Cameroon v Nigeria* case, Judgment, Merits [2002] ICJ Rep 421, [238].

It also held that, contrary to Cameroon's view, the reasoning in the *Frontier Dispute (Burkina Faso/Mali)* and *Territorial Dispute (Libya/Chad)* cases in regard to land boundaries was not transposable to those concerning maritime boundaries. According to the Court, these were 'two distinct areas of the law, to which different factors and considerations apply.'[677] Related to this, both Parties agreed that it should not fix the tripoint and, indeed, it was not entitled to do so.[678] In light of the above considerations, the Court concluded that it could not rule on Cameroon's claims in so far as they might affect the rights of Equatorial Guinea and São Tomé and Príncipe. At the same time, the Court found that the mere presence of those two States did not in itself preclude the Court from having jurisdiction over a maritime delimitation between the Parties in the case before it.[679] In conclusion, the Court drew a maritime boundary in so far as it did not affect the rights of Equatorial Guinea.

The Court in the *Cameroon v Nigeria* case took the approach cutting off the area where claims of third States may be involved. This approach was in line with the *Tunisia/Libya*, *Libya/Malta* and *Qatar v Bahrain* cases. With respect to the cut-off approach, however, it has been argued that this approach is problematic since, as is demonstrated by the *Libya/Malta* case, the extent of the Court's jurisdiction depends not simply on the entitlement of third States, but on what those States choose to claim. Hence this solution leads to an anomalous situation in which the extent of the Court's jurisdiction is determined by third States. In this respect, the *prima facie* legal credibility test, which was contended by Nigeria, is worth noting. According to this theory, although the Court cannot pronounce the legal validity of the intervener's argument, it nevertheless verifies the credibility of it on the basis of the equidistance method.[680] An advantage of this theory is that, if one applies the legal credibility test on the basis of an objective method, that is, the equidistance method, it is possible to avoid danger of an excessive claim by a third State. Given that the case law tends to draw an equidistance line at the first stage of the maritime delimitation, that test seems to be relevant. According to this approach, however, the spatial extent of

[677] ibid. Nevertheless, the Court's view on this point is not free from controversy. Indeed, it is difficult to find a convincing reason to distinguish disputes concerning maritime boundaries from those regarding land boundaries. Regarding maritime boundaries, usually, territorial sovereignty (territorial sea) and sovereign rights (continental shelf and EEZ) are at issue, while territorial sovereignty is involved in land boundary disputes. Both territorial sovereignty and sovereign rights over a continental shelf and an EEZ have, in essence, spatial nature in the sense that they are related to a certain space and can be exercised solely within that space. Furthermore, sovereignty over land territory is a more comprehensive jurisdiction than sovereign rights over continental shelf and EEZ. One may wonder why the Court should fix the tripoint in the terrestrial area where territorial sovereignty of a third State may be involved, while Court should refrain from drawing a maritime boundary in the area where a third State's sovereign rights are concerned.

[678] Judgment, [2002] ICJ Rep 421, [238].

[679] ibid.

[680] Presentation by Professor George Abi-Saab, Counsel of Nigeria, Verbatim Record, CR 2002/23, 22–23, [19–25].

the Court's jurisdiction will be highly limited in a situation where several third States co-exist in close proximity in the same region. Indeed, in the *Cameroon v Nigeria* case, the Court could indicate merely the direction of the delimitation line from point X.[681]

The influence of third States may be at issue when identifying relevant areas. The *Black Sea* case is an example. In this case, entitlement of third parties may come into play in the south-western triangle as well as in the small area in the western corner of the south-eastern triangle.[682] In this regard, the Court expressed the following view:

> However where areas are included solely for the purpose of approximate identification of overlapping entitlements of the Parties to the case, which may be deemed to constitute the relevant area (and which in due course will play a part in the final stage testing for disproportionality), third party entitlements cannot be affected. Third party entitlements would only be relevant if the delimitation between Romania and Ukraine were to affect them.[683]

The Court accordingly found it appropriate to include both the southwestern and the south-eastern triangles in its calculation of the relevant area.[684] At the operational stage of maritime delimitation, however, the ICJ merely held that the maritime boundary continues along the equidistance line in a southerly direction until the boundary reaches the area where the rights of third States may be affected.[685]

In the *Nicaragua v Honduras* case, it became necessary for the ICJ to consider the potential third-State interests when determining the end point of the maritime boundary. A possible source of third-State interests was the 1986 Treaty between Colombia and Honduras on maritime delimitation. The Treaty established a maritime boundary commencing at the 82nd meridian. Accordingly, any extension of the delimitation line in this case past the 82nd meridian could prejudice Colombia's rights under that treaty. According to the Court, this was not the case since 'any delimitation between Honduras and Nicaragua extending east beyond the 82nd meridian and north of the 15th parallel ... would not actually prejudice Colombia's rights because Colombia's rights under this Treaty do not extend north of the 15th parallel.'[686] If the maritime boundary constructed by the ICJ would cross the delimitation line established in the 1986 Treaty, however, Colombia's rights would seem to be prejudiced.[687]

[681] Further, see Y Tanaka, 'Reflections on Maritime Delimitation in the *Cameroon/Nigeria* Case,' (2004) 53 *ICLQ* 393–402.

[682] [2009] ICJ Rep100, [114].

[683] ibid.

[684] ibid. See also Sketch-map No. 5 attached to the Judgment. ibid,102.

[685] ibid, 131, [218].

[686] [2007] ICJ Rep 758, [316].

[687] NB O'Sullivan, 'The Case Law's Handling of Issues Concerning Third States' in Oude Elferink, Henriksen and Busch, *Maritime Boundary Delimitation*, 269 and 273.

Another possible source of third-State interests related to the joint jurisdictional regime established by Jamaica and Colombia in an area south of Rosalind Bank near the 80th meridian pursuant to their 1993 bilateral Treaty on maritime delimitation. In this regard, the ICJ held that it would not draw a delimitation line that would intersect with this line because of the possible prejudice to the rights of both Parties to that Treaty.[688] It thus considered certain interests of third States in the region. As for the end point, the Court noted that: '[I]t is usual in a judicial delimitation for the precise endpoint to be left undefined in order to refrain from prejudicing the rights of third States.'[689] The Court accordingly ruled that without specifying a precise end-point, the maritime boundary between Nicaragua and Honduras extends beyond the 82nd meridian without affecting third-State rights.[690]

However, the Court's approach in the *Nicaragua v Colombia* case contrasted with the above mentioned precedents.[691] Even though Honduras filed an Application for permission to intervene pursuant to Article 62 of the ICJ Statute, the Court declined the Application.[692] Likewise, the ICJ dismissed Costa Rica's request to intervene under Article 62 of the Statute. In this case, the Court ruled that: '[A] third State's interest will, as a matter of principle, be protected by the Court, without it defining with specificity the geographical limits of an area where that interest may come into play.'[693] As explained earlier, the ICJ, in its judgment of 2012, drew two horizontal lines in the northern and southern parts of the delimitation area, respectively.[694] Colombia had already established maritime boundaries with Panama and Costa Rica in the Caribbean Sea in 1976 and 1977, respectively.[695] It had also constructed the maritime boundary with Honduras in 1986 and Joint Regime Area with Jamaica in 1993. In addition, Costa Rica and Panama had established a delimitation line, without fixing an

[688] [2007] ICJ Rep 759, [317].

[689] ibid, 756, [312].

[690] ibid, 759, [318–319]. See also 759–60, [320].

[691] Tanaka, 'Reflectiosn on the Territorial and Maritime Disputes between Nicaragua and Colombia' 928.

[692] *Territorial and Maritime Dispute (Nicaragua v Colombia), Application by Honduras for Permission to Intervene*, Judgment, [2011] ICJ Rep 444, [76].

[693] *Territorial and Maritime Dispute (Nicaragua v Colombia), Application by Costa Rica for Permission to Intervene*, Judgment (hereafter cited as *Application by Costa Rica*), [2011] ICJ Rep 372, [86]. See also 372, [89].

[694] [2012] ICJ Rep 713, [237].

[695] Treaty on the Delimitation of Marine and Submarine Areas and Associated Matters between the Republic of Panama and the Republic of Colombia of 20 November 1976. Entered into force 30 November 1977. Text in: *IMB*, vol I, 532–35; Treaty on Delimitation of Marine and Submarine Areas and Maritime Cooperation between the Republic of Colombia and the Republic of Costa Rica of 17 March 1977. Not yet in force. Text in ibid, 474–76. In this regard, Colombia stated that: 'Costa Rica has stated on numerous occasions that it has applied the 1977 Treaty in good faith and will continue to do so.' Presentation by Mr Bundy, Verbatim Record, 27 April 2012, CR 2012/12, 21, [52]. See also Counter-Memorial of the Republic of Colombia, vol I, 11 November 2008, 352–63, [8.33–8.56]; Rejoinder of the Republic of Colombia, vol I, 18 June 2010, 192–96, [5.58–5.69].

end point, by the 1980 Treaty.[696] The maritime boundaries constructed by the Court in the northern part of the delimitation area would seem to affect the maritime boundary between Honduras and Colombia for Colombia has only a 12-nautical-mile territorial sea surrounding Quitasueño and Serrana Cay in this area.[697] Furthermore, the southern horizontal line would inevitably affect the existing maritime boundaries between Colombia and Panama, between Colombia and Costa Rica. In this regard, the Court held that the Judgment in the present case 'addresses only Nicaragua's rights as against Colombia and vice versa and is, therefore, without prejudice to any claim of a third State or any claim which either Party may have against a third State.'[698] Yet, Judge Xue expressed her misgivings that:

> The boundary line in the south would virtually produce the effect of invalidating the existing agreements on maritime delimitation that Colombia has concluded with Panama and Costa Rica respectively and drastically changing the maritime relations in the area.[699]

The learned judge was thus of the view that the maritime boundary should stop at Point 8 with an arrow pointing eastward.[700]

The ICJ's approach in the *Nicaragua v Colombia* case seems to rely on the effect of Article 59 of the Court's Statute. In fact, the Court stated that: '[A]s Article 59 of the Statute of the Court makes clear, it is axiomatic that a judgment of the Court is not binding on any State other than the parties to the case.'[701] Yet, the Court's view appears to be too optimistic. In this regard, Judge Xue clearly stated that: 'The principle *res inter alios acta* and Article 59 of the Statute do not help in the present situation.'[702] Judge ad hoc Cot also stated that: 'Article 59 of the Statute of the Court does not afford them [third States] adequate protection in this case.'[703] Likewise Judge ad hoc Mensah gave his misgivings that: 'I am not sure that reliance on Article 59 of the Court's Statute alone would offer adequate protection for the rights of third States, and achieve the objective of stability and practicability, in this case.'[704]

The *Costa Rica v Nicaragua* case also raised the issue of third States. In this case, the relevance of three delimitation treaties was at issue: The 1976 Treaty between Colombia and Panama, the 1977 Treaty between Costa Rica and

[696] Treaty Concerning Delimitation of Marine Areas and Maritime Cooperation between the Republic of Costa Rica and the Republic of Panama of 2 February 1980. Entered into force 11 February 1982. Text in *IMB*, vol I, 547–49.

[697] [2012] ICJ Rep 713–15, [238].

[698] [2012] ICJ Rep 707, [228].

[699] Declaration of Judge Xue in the *Nicaragua v Colombia* case, [2012] ICJ Rep 750, [15]. See also Declaration of Judge ad hoc Cot, ibid, 769, [10].

[700] ibid, 749, [11]. See also O'Sullivan, 'The Case Law's Handling of Issues Concerning Third States,' 274–75.

[701] The *Nicaragua v Colombia* case, Judgment, [2012] ICJ Rep 707, [228].

[702] Declaration of Judge Xue in the *Nicaragua v Colombia* case, ibid, 750, [13].

[703] Declaration of Judge ad hoc Cot, ibid, 769, [9].

[704] Declaration of Judge ad hoc Mensah, ibid, 766–67, [13].

Colombia, and the 1980 Treaty between Costa Rica and Panama. In this regard, the ICJ generally stated that:

> [A] judgment rendered by the Court between one of the Parties and a third State or between two third States cannot per se affect the maritime boundary between the Parties. The same applies to treaties concluded between one of the Parties and a third State or between third States.[705]

Furthermore, the Court held that the 1976 Treaty between Colombia and Panama cannot be considered relevant for the delimitation between Costa Rica and Nicaragua; and that with regard to the 1977 Treaty between Costa Rica and Colombia, there is no evidence that a renunciation by Costa Rica of its maritime entitlements was also intended to be effective with regard to a State other than Colombia.[706] The Court then constructed the maritime boundary by adjusting a provisional equidistance line.[707] Related to this, the Court held that: '[T]he construction of this line is without prejudice to any claims that a third State may have on part of the area crossed by the line.'[708] The Court did not specify the end point of the maritime boundary. However, the boundary appears to have implications for the existing treaties on maritime delimitation that Colombia has concluded with Panama and Costa Rica.

b. Third-States Interests in Arbitral Awards

The issue of the presence of third States has also been discussed in arbitration. In the *Eritrea/Yemen* case, the existence of Saudi Arabia and Djibouti was at issue with respect to the northern and southern ends of the boundary. Regarding the northern end, Saudi Arabia had indicated to the Registrar of the Tribunal, in 1997, that its boundaries with Yemen were disputed, and suggested that the Tribunal restrict its decisions to areas 'that do not extend north of the latitude of the most northern point on Jabal al-Tayr Island'. Although Yemen wished the boundary to extend to the latitude of 16°N, which is the limit in the northern sector, Eritrea did not oppose the Saudi Arabian proposal.[709]

Concerning the southern end, a question arose as to the effect of the Island of Perim upon the maritime boundary (see Illustration 14). That question might involve the interests of Djibouti. In this respect, Eritrea was most concerned about the arrow with which Yemen terminated its claimed line since that arrow pointed in such a direction as to 'slash' the main shipping channel and to place it within the territorial waters of Yemen.[710]

[705] [2018] ICJ Rep [123].
[706] ibid, [134].
[707] See ch 5, s XVIII of this book.
[708] [2018] ICJ Rep [144]. See also [157].
[709] The *Eritrea/Yemen* case (the Second Phase), 22 *RIAA* 344, [44].
[710] ibid, [45].

Regarding that question, the Arbitral Tribunal held that:

> The Tribunal has the competence and the authority according to the Arbitration Agreement to decide the maritime boundary between the two Parties. But it has neither competence nor authority to decide on any of the boundaries between either of the two Parties and neighbouring States. It will therefore be necessary to terminate either end of the boundary line in such a way as to avoid trespassing upon an area where other claims might fall to be considered.[711]

Thus, the Tribunal stopped the boundary line at point 1 for the northern and at point 29 for the southern end. According to the Tribunal, these terminal points are well short of where the boundary line might be disputed by any third State.[712] In fact, point 29 is located short of the place where the influence upon it by Perim Island would begin to take effect.[713] In short, as the ICJ had done in the *Libya/Malta* case, the Tribunal simply cut off the line at the point where a third State might become involved.

In the *Barbados v Trinidad and Tobago* case, Trinidad and Tobago asserted that the delimitation between Trinidad and Tobago and Venezuela in the region south of Barbados and that between France (Guadeloupe and Martinique) and Dominica in the region north of Barbados needed to be considered in this dispute as they entailed a recognition of a departure from the equidistance line in order to avoid a cut-off effect.[714] But Barbados opposed Trinidad and Tobago's argument on the regional implication.[715] The Tribunal ruled that the agreement between France (Guadeloupe and Martinique) and Dominica had no connection at all to the present dispute.[716] On the other hand, the Arbitral Tribunal was bound to take into account the 1990 Trinidad-Venezuela Agreement in so far as it determined what the maritime claims of Trinidad and Tobago might be.[717] The Tribunal thus held that in so far as Trinidad and Tobago's claim was concerned, the maximum extent of overlapping areas between the Parties was determined in part by the treaty between Trinidad and Tobago and Venezuela.[718]

Furthermore, particular attention must be paid to the inter-linkage between the *Bangladesh/Myanmar* and *Bangladesh v India* cases concerning the endpoint of maritime boundaries. ITLOS, in the *Bangladesh/Myanmar* case, decided that the adjusted equidistance line delimiting both the EEZ and the continental shelf within 200 nm between the Parties continues in the same direction beyond the

[711] ibid, 366, [136].
[712] ibid, 372, [164].
[713] ibid, 344, [46].
[714] The *Barbados v Trinidad and Tobago* arbitral award, 27 *RIAA* 237, [340]; Rejoinder of Trinidad and Tobago, 95–100, [193–201]; Counter-Memorial of Trinidad and Tobago, 81, [231–232].
[715] The *Barbados v Trinidad and Tobago* arbitral award, 27 *RIAA* 238, [343]; Reply of Barbados, 97–103, [179–189]; Presentation by Professor Reisman, 18 October 2005, 74–83.
[716] The *Barbados v Trinidad and Tobago* arbitral award, 27 *RIAA* 238, [344].
[717] ibid, 238–39, [347].
[718] ibid, 239, [348].

200 nm limit of Bangladesh until it reaches the area where the rights of third States may be affected.[719] In the *Bangladesh v India* case, the Annex VII Arbitral Tribunal held that the endpoint of the maritime boundary between Bangladesh and India was a point on the line decided by ITLOS in the *Bangladesh/Myanmar* case.[720] It would seem to follow that India is bound by the *Bangladesh/ Myanmar* judgment of ITLOS.[721]

B. Analysis of State Practice

State practice has preferred practical solutions, avoiding the problems of delimitation with third States outside of agreements creating maritime boundaries.[722] In broad terms, such solutions may be categorised into two types. The first solution is to conclude agreements for fixing a tri-point between relevant maritime boundaries. The second solution is to stop a delimitation line before the relevant area, so as to avoid a dispute with a third State.

i. Establishment of a Tri-Junction Point

With respect to the first solution fixing a tri-point, the practice in the Indian Ocean furnishes some examples. In 1971, Indonesia, Malaysia and Thailand determined a tri-point connecting three maritime boundaries between the Parties.[723] Furthermore, a tri-point of three maritime boundaries between India, the Maldives and Sri Lanka was fixed in 1976.[724] Subsequently, in 1978, India, Indonesia and Thailand concluded an agreement determining a tri-junction, which connected already established maritime boundaries between the Parties.[725] Moreover, in 1993, India, Myanmar and Thailand agreed to establish a tri-point connecting three delimitation lines between India and Myanmar, Myanmar and Thailand, and Thailand and India, respectively.[726] In another example, in the Baltic Sea, Poland, Sweden and the Soviet Union determined a tri-point for their maritime boundaries in 1989.[727] Other examples include the 1997 Agreement between Estonia, Latvia and Sweden,[728] the 2001 Agreement between Estonia, Finland and Sweden,[729] the 2012 Agreement between Kiribati,

[719] [2012] ITLOS Rep 118, [462] and 128, [505].
[720] The *Bangladesh v India* case, [509(3)].
[721] O'Sullivan, 'The Case Law's Handling of Issues Concerning Third States,' 271.
[722] For a detailed examination of treaty practice on this matter, see C Lathrop, 'Tripoint Issues in Maritime Boundary Delimitation' in *IMB*, vol V, 3305 et seq.
[723] For the text of the Agreement in ibid, vol II, 1452–54.
[724] For the text of the Agreement, ibid, 1407–8.
[725] For the text of the Agreement, ibid, 1386–88.
[726] For the text of the Agreement, ibid, vol III, 2372–73.
[727] For the text of the Agreement, ibid, vol II, 2103–4.
[728] For the text of the Agreement, ibid, vol IV, 3056.
[729] For the text of the Agreement, ibid, 3138–39.

Marshall Islands and Nauru[730] and the 2012 Agreement between Comoros, Seychelles, and Tanzania.[731]

ii. Agreements Which Provide for Future Delimitation with Third States

There are also agreements which do not determine the end point of the boundary so as to leave room for future negotiations with third States. Examples may be furnished by the following agreements: the 1984 Agreement between Sweden and Denmark, the 1989 Agreement between Poland and Sweden, the 1978 Agreement between Sweden and the German Democratic Republic, the 1988 Treaty between the German Democratic Republic and Denmark and the 1989 Treaty between Poland and the former German Democratic Republic. In relation to this, interestingly, all agreements expressly stated that the end point of the maritime boundary would be determined in future negotiations with the third State. Thus, Article 2(2) of the 1978 Agreement between Sweden and the German Democratic Republic provides: 'West of point 1 and East of point 3 the boundary line shall extend to the outer points which will have to be agreed with the third State concerned.'[732] Article 2 of the 1989 Agreement between Poland and Sweden also stipulates that: 'From point A to the West and point F to the East the delimitation line shall continue to points on which Agreement shall be reached with the third State concerned.'[733] The same is true of Article 5 of the 1984 Agreement between Sweden and Denmark,[734] Article 2 of the 1988 Agreement between Denmark and the German Democratic Republic[735] and Article 4(2) of the 1989 Agreement between the German Democratic Republic and Poland.[736] Accordingly, when the States of a region succeed in determining connecting points between their delimitation lines, a new network of maritime boundaries will be created in that region. Many other examples could be furnished for other regions, including the Caribbean Sea[737] and the Indian Ocean.[738]

[730] For the text of the Agreement, ibid, vol VII, 4933.
[731] The agreed tripoint between Comoros, Seychelles, and Tanzania (Point T) is equidistant from the nearest points on the baselines of all three States. Report by Pratt, ibid, 5042. For the text of the Agreement, ibid, 5056.
[732] ibid, vol II, 2037.
[733] ibid, 2086.
[734] ibid, 1940.
[735] ibid, 2095.
[736] ibid, 2021.
[737] Regarding maritime delimitations in the Caribbean Sea, see Art 2 of the 1979 Agreement between the Dominican Republic and Venezuela; Art 2 of the 1978 Agreement between Venezuela and the United States (Puerto Rico); Art 2(3.2 and 4.2) of the 1978 Agreement between Venezuela and the Netherlands (Antilles); Art 2 of the 1978 Agreement between Colombia and the Dominican Republic; Art 1 of the 1993 Agreement between Colombia and Jamaica; Art 2(2) of the 1994 Agreement between Cuba and Jamaica; Art 3 of the 1996 Agreement between France and the United Kingdom.
[738] In the Indian Ocean, the following agreements are relevant: Art 1(4) of the 1980 Agreement between Myanmar and Thailand; Art 1(3) of the 1978 Agreement between Thailand and India;

In the Mediterranean Sea, all of the endpoints in three agreements, namely, Cyprus-Israel, Cyprus-Egypt, and Cyprus-Lebanon, are subject to provisions whereby the coordinates may be reviewed and/or modified as necessary if all three of the relevant States agree to such modification.[739] This approach is unique in the sense that it incorporates future changes into bilateral delimitation agreements with a view to addressing potential third State interests.[740]

Another example on this matter is provided by the 2018 Timor Sea Treaty between Australia and Timor-Leste. Under Article 3 of the Treaty, 'Should Timor-Leste and Indonesia agree an endpoint to their continental shelf boundary west of point A17 or east of point A16 on the 1972 Seabed Treaty Boundary, the continental shelf boundary between Australia and Timor-Leste shall be adjusted in accordance with paragraphs 2, 3 and 4 of this Article.' Thus Article 2 of the Treaty makes clear that: 'The line connecting points TA-1 and TA-2, and the lines connecting points TA-11, TA-12, and TA-13 are "Provisional", which for the purposes of this Treaty means that they are subject to adjustment in accordance with Article 3 of this Treaty.'

C. Summary

In State practice, the Parties take a flexible approach by concluding agreements relating to a tri-junction point between maritime boundaries or inserting provisions for future delimitation with third States. However, the existence of third States creates a challenge in international adjudication. An essential issue is whether the principle of *res inter alios acta* and Article 59 of the ICJ Statue can provide an adequate safeguard for third States. In this regard, it is of particular interest to note that the ICJ, in the *Cameroon v Nigeria* case (Merits), explicitly accepted that, in the context of maritime delimitation, Article 59 may not be sufficient to protect legal rights of third States.[741]

It is undeniable that, in reality, the delimitation line drawn by the Court might affect legal rights and interests of third States creating a presumption of the finality of the boundary, regardless of the formalistic protection of Article 59.[742] Indeed, the rights over continental shelf exist *ipso facto* and *ab initio* and they are inherent rights.[743] It is a right *erga omnes*. In such a case,

Art 1 of the 1986 Agreement between Myanmar and India; Art 1 of the 1976 Agreement between India and Sri Lanka.

[739] Art 1(e) of the 2010 Agreement between Cyprus and Israel; Art 1(e) of the 2007 Agreement between Cyprus and Lebanon; Art 1(e) of the 2003 Agreement between Cyprus and Egypt.

[740] Report by Srebro, Ma'udi, and Zenonos. *IMB*, vol VII, 5097.

[741] Judgment, [2002] ICJ Rep 421, [238].

[742] Presentation by Professor George Abi-Saab, Counsel of Nigeria, Verbatim Record, CR 2002/23, 18, [3–4]. P-M Dupuy, Counsel of Equatorial Guinea, used the words 'l'effet indirect de chose jugée'. Presentation by Professor P-M Dupuy, Verbatim Record, CR 2002/24, 19, [2].

[743] [1969] ICJ Rep 22, [19].

as the Court's judgment indicated, Article 59 may be insufficient to protect the rights of third States. Moreover, it appears to be difficult for the Court to draw an equitable delimitation line in such an area where rights of third States may be involved since the Court does not have jurisdiction to judge the validity of relevant circumstances relating to third States in that area.[744] Thus the ICJ, in its jurisprudence, has taken the cut-off approach in order to refrain from prejudicing the rights of third States.[745] As the ICJ itself accepted, 'the Court has always taken care not to draw a boundary line which extends into areas where the rights of third States may be affected.'[746]

With respect to the cut-off approach, however, it has been argued that this approach is problematic since, as is demonstrated by the *Libya/Malta* case, the extent of the Court's jurisdiction depends not simply on the entitlement of third States, but on what those States choose to claim. Hence this solution leads to an anomalous situation in which the extent of the Court's jurisdiction is determined by third States. In this respect, the *prima facie* legal credibility test, which was contended by Nigeria, is worth noting. According to this theory, although the Court cannot pronounce the legal validity of the intervener's argument, it nevertheless verifies the credibility of it on the basis of the equidistance method.[747] An advantage of this theory is that, if one applies the legal credibility test on the basis of an objective method, that is, the equidistance method, it is possible to avoid danger of an excessive claim by a third State. At the same time, one should note that, according to this approach, the spatial extent of the Court's jurisdiction will be highly limited in a situation where several third States co-exist in close proximity in the same region. Indeed, in the *Cameroon v Nigeria* case, the Court could indicate merely the direction of the delimitation line from point X.

In the recent jurisprudence, the ICJ seemed to change its approach to this matter. In fact, the Court, in the *Nicaragua v Colombia* case, constructed the maritime boundary in the south, even though it would produce the effect of invalidating the existing agreements on maritime delimitation between Colombia and Panama and between Colombia and Costa Rica, respectively. The maritime boundary established by the ICJ in the *Costa Rica v Nicaragua* case seemed to affect the existing treaties on maritime delimitation. In the *Nicaragua v Colombia* and *Costa Rica v Nicaragua* cases, again the Court appeared to rely on the principle of *res inter alios acta* and Article 59 of

[744] As an example, the result of a proportionality test will be changeable depending on the future delimitation between a party/parties and third State(s).

[745] According to Pellet, 'abstaining from precisely defining tripoints while indicating a direction for the boundary' is 'an elegant, simple and globally satisfactory solution. …' Pellet, 'Land and Maritime Tripoints in International Jurisprudence' 279. See also O'Sullivan, 'The Case Law's Handling of Issues Concerning Third States' 279.

[746] The *Nicaragua v Colombia* case, Judgment, [2012] ICJ Rep 707, [228].

[747] Presentation by Professor George Abi-Saab, Counsel of Nigeria, Verbatim Record, CR 2002/23, 22–23, [19–25].

the Court's Statute. Overall, it can be observed that the ICJ's approach is not consistent on this matter. In light of the *erga omnes* character of the rights over the continental shelf, great caution will be needed when establishing a maritime boundary in the area where the rights of third States might be involved.

VIII. POSITION OF LAND BOUNDARY

The position of land boundaries is at issue when maritime boundaries are established between States with adjacent coasts. This section addresses two issues: The terminus of the land boundary and its direction or prolongation.[748]

A. Analysis of the Case Law

i. Arguments in the Context of Continental Shelf Delimitations

The instance relevant in this context is the *Tunisia/Libya* case. In this case, the ICJ listed 'the position of the land frontier, or more precisely the position of its intersection with the coastline' among the relevant circumstances to be taken into account.[749] There was no dispute between the Parties regarding the fact that the 1910 Convention established a land frontier between them. Thus, they both recognised the relevance of the land boundary as a starting point of the continental shelf boundary. Only in this sense, did the Court regard the undisputed land frontier established by the 1910 Convention to be a relevant circumstance.[750]

Concerning the direction or prolongation of the land boundary, however, the Court's views are not entirely consistent. On the one hand, the Court did not accept the claim of Libya according to which the boundary on the seaward side of Ras Ajdir would continue in the northward direction from the end point of the land frontier.[751] On the other hand, it did mention that the factor of perpendicularity to the coast, and the concept of prolongation of the general direction of the land boundary, were relevant criteria for selecting a line of delimitation to ensure an equitable solution.[752] At this point, the Court appeared to accept the relevance of the prolongation of the general direction of the land boundary. As Judge Evensen noted, however, the Court's view seemed inconsistent with the former view, which rejected Libya's claim regarding the prolongation of the land boundary.[753]

[748] Evans, *Relevant Circumstances and Maritime Delimitation* 161.
[749] [1982] ICJ Rep 64, [81].
[750] ibid, 66, [85].
[751] ibid.
[752] ibid, 85, [120].
[753] Dissenting Opinion of Judge Evensen, ibid, 308, [21].

Furthermore, the idea of prolonging the land boundary in its general direction presents at least two difficulties. The first is the identification of that direction, as land boundaries are frequently irregular and take different directions along their course. The second difficulty relates to the question of what segment or segments of the land boundary shall have a bearing on the direction of the seaward projection. Is it solely the last part, or should the projection be determined by averaging the direction of the whole frontier?[754] There appears to be no positive international law on those issues. Thus, the seaward projection of the land boundary would introduce vagueness into the law of maritime delimitation. In any event, in the *Tunisia/Libya* dispute, the prolongation of the general direction of the land frontier played little, if any, role in situating the continental shelf boundary. Hence, it could be said that the relevance of the land boundary was limited to indicating the starting point of the continental shelf boundary.

ii. Arguments in the Context of Single Maritime Boundaries

a. Land Boundary in the ICJ Jurisprudence

In the ICJ jurisprudence concerning single maritime boundaries, the *Gulf of Maine* and *Costa Rica v Nicaragua* cases merit discussion. In the *Gulf of Maine* case, the United States asserted the relevance of the location of the land boundary in two regards. First, it insisted that, in the Gulf of Maine area,

> Because the international boundary terminates at the northern end of the Gulf, by far the greater part of the concavity is on the United States' side of the international boundary. As recognized in previous international adjudications, such a concavity is a circumstance that may lead to an inequitable delimitation, particularly if the equidistance method is used.[755]

The United States thus suggested an adjusted perpendicular line. In its view, such a line 'respect[ed] the location of the land boundary by taking into account the seaward extension of the coastal front of Maine and New Hampshire, while leaving unimpeded the seaward extension of the primary coastal front of Canada into the Atlantic Ocean.'[756]

By contrast, Canada observed that:

> There is nothing in law, State practice or logic to suggest that the terminal point of the land boundary between States should be any guide to the point of latitude or longitude to which a maritime boundary can reach. On the contrary, the delimitation of offshore zones will, by definition, extend existing boundaries beyond the land territories of the States concerned.[757]

[754] ibid, 309, [21].
[755] Memorial of the United States, vol II, 111, [290].
[756] Counter-Memorial of the United States, vol IV, 123, [292].
[757] Counter-Memorial of Canada, vol III, 257, [690].

According to Canada, '[a] scheme of perpendicularly cannot be applied to an area where two of the relevant coasts [...] are virtually at right angles to each other. The position of Nova Scotia, as well as its importance and extent, therefore rule out this approach *ab initio* in the Gulf of Maine area.'[758] Canada, thus, proposed an adjusted equidistance line as a single maritime boundary.

The Chamber of the ICJ did not attach any importance to the location of the land boundary. First, since it was requested to draw a single maritime boundary from a given point seaward of the land boundary, the latter could not be used as a starting point of the single maritime boundary to be drawn.[759] This constitutes a difference with the *Tunisia/Libya* case. Secondly, the Chamber declined to accept the validity of the 'perpendicular' method claimed by the United States. In its view: '[I]t is hard to imagine a case less conductive to the application of this [adjusted perpendicular] method of delimitation than the *Gulf of Maine* case, in which the starting point of the line to be drawn is situated in one of the angles of the rectangle in which the delimitation is to be effected.'[760] Hence, in neither aspect did the location of the land boundary influence the location of the single maritime boundary established by the Chamber.

In the *Costa Rica v Nicaragua* case, the Parties' views were sharply divided with regard to the starting-point of the maritime delimitation in the Caribbean Sea. This case raised a challenge with regard to the instability of the coast. In this connection, the ICJ invited the Parties to indicate their positions concerning the possibility of 'starting the maritime boundary from a fixed point in the Caribbean Sea some distance from the coast'.[761] While the primary position of Costa Rica was that the Court should select a starting-point on land, it suggested as an alternative a mobile line connecting any fixed point at sea to the mouth of the San Juan River.[762] Nicaragua also agreed the possibility of a mobile line.[763] The Court supported the idea of a mobile line. In the words of the Court,

> [T]he great instability of the coastline in the area of the mouth of the San Juan River [...] prevents the identification on the sandspit of a fixed point that would be suitable as the starting-point of the maritime delimitation. It is preferable to select a fixed point at sea and connect it to the starting-point on the coast by a mobile line. Taking into account the fact that the prevailing phenomenon characterizing the coastline at the mouth of the San Juan River is recession through erosion from the sea, the Court deems it appropriate to place a fixed point at sea at a distance of 2 nautical miles from the coast on the median line.[764]

[758] Reply of Canada, vol V, 28, [79].

[759] Evans, *Relevant Circumstances and Maritime Delimitation*, 161. Indeed, owing to the position of the land boundary, there was a risk that a delimitation line fixed by the Chamber would pass very close to the Canadian coasts. Thus, Kolb stressed that the 'inequitable' position of the land boundary at the point where it reached the sea was one of the most important factors in the *Gulf of Maine* dispute. Kolb, *Case Law on Equitable Maritime Delimitation* 227.

[760] [1984] ICJ Rep 320, [176].

[761] The *Costa Rica v Nicaragua* case, Judgment, [2018] ICJ Rep [82].

[762] ibid, [83].

[763] ibid, [84].

[764] ibid, [86].

It thus connected the fixed point at sea on the median line to the point on solid land on Costa Rica's coast which is closest to the mouth of the river by a mobile line.[765] The fixed point at sea constitutes the starting-point of the maritime boundary. The mobile line appears to be a solution well worth considering in response to the highly instable coastline.

b. Land Boundary in Arbitral Awards

The land boundary terminus was also at issue in arbitration regarding maritime delimitation. In this regard, two cases merit discussion. The first is the *Guinea/Guinea-Bissau* arbitration. Contrary to the Chamber in the *Gulf of Maine* case, the Arbitral Tribunal in the *Guinea/Guinea-Bissau* arbitration held that the land boundary constituted a relevant circumstance on the basis of the *Tunisia/Libya* judgment. In this respect, the Court held that, in the first segment near the coast, the single maritime boundary coincided with the 'southern limit' indicated by the 1886 Convention between France and Portugal.[766] It begins from the end of the land boundary, which is a point on the *thalweg* of the Cajet River, and runs for about 20 miles along the Pilots' Pass, which is the geographical prolongation of the land boundary. Furthermore, it follows the same direction, being roughly perpendicular to the coast at this point.[767] This being so, the land boundary plays a double role. First, it indicates the starting point of the single maritime boundary, and secondly, its prolongation becomes part of the maritime boundary. Thus the land boundary influenced the location of the single maritime boundary in the *Guinea/Guinea-Bissau* case.

The second case to be examined is the *Bangladesh v India* arbitration. The location of the land boundary terminus was to be determined by application of the Radcliffe Award of 1947, which drew the boundaries between India and the new State of Pakistan.[768] The Radcliffe Award adopted the pre-partition district boundary between the districts of Khulna and 24 Parganas.[769] The district boundary had been delimited in 1925 by Notification No. 964 Jur. of the Governor of Bengal as follows:

> [T]he western boundary of district Khulna passes along the south-western boundary of Chandanpur […] till it meets the midstream of the main channel of the river Ichhamati, then along the midstream of the main channel for the time being of the rivers Ichhamati and Kalindi, Raimangal and Haribhanga till it meets the Bay.[770]

However, each Party identifies a different 'midstream of the main channel' for the purpose of identifying the location of the land boundary terminus.[771]

[765] ibid, [104].
[766] The *Guinea/Guinea-Bissau* arbitral award, (1986) 25 *ILM* 298, [111].
[767] ibid, 295–96, [106].
[768] The *Bangladesh v India* arbitral award, [85].
[769] ibid, [87].
[770] ibid, [88].
[771] ibid, [145].

In this regard, the Annex VII Arbitral Tribunal held that it would locate the land boundary terminus as it was decided in 1947 on the basis of the available information at the time and supplemented by more recent information as to the situation at the critical date.[772] Accordingly, the Tribunal determined the land boundary terminus by transporting the ends of the closing line and the land boundary terminus indicated on the Radcliffe Map.[773]

A particular issue in this context concerns the impact of the terminus on the provisional equidistance line for the delimitation of the territorial seas between Bangladesh and India. On this issue, the Tribunal considered that: '[T]he need to connect the land boundary terminus to the median line constructed by the Tribunal for the delimitation of the territorial sea constitutes a special circumstance ....'[774] According to the Tribunal, this circumstance was similar to the *Guyana v Suriname* case where the seaward terminus of a previous delimitation of the three-nautical mile wide territorial sea was not on the median line in the sense of Article 15 of the LOSC and had to be connected to the Tribunal's delimitation line based on equidistance.[775] Thus the Tribunal shifted the provisional equidistance line so that the maritime boundary forms a 12-nautical mile long geodetic line continuing from the land boundary terminus in a generally southerly direction to meet the median line at 21° 26′ 43.6″N; 89° 10′ 59.2″E.[776]

c. Land Boundary in the ITLOS Jurisprudence

In the ITLOS jurisprudence, the position of land boundary was at issue in the *Bangladesh/Myanmar* and *Ghana/Côte d'Ivoire* cases. In the *Bangladesh/Myanmar* case, the Parties were in agreement as to the starting point of the delimitation line. This point, which is marked as Point 1 in Tribunal's sketch-map No. 9, corresponds to the land boundary terminus as agreement between Burma and Pakistan in 1966.[777] Thus the territorial sea boundary in this case runs from this point.

The impact of land boundary on the maritime boundary was more controversial in the *Ghana/Côte d'Ivoire* case. In this case, the Parties agreed on the position of the land boundary terminus, which is BP 55. Nonetheless, they disagreed on the starting point for their maritime boundary. In this regard, Ghana maintained that BP 55 'is located some 150 metres from the low water line on the coast'; and that it 'must be connected to the provisional equidistance line through a point 24 on the low water line.'[778] According to Ghana,

[772] ibid, [171].

[773] ibid, [187]. Specifically, the position of the land boundary terminus is 21° 38′ 40.2″N, 89° 09′ 20.0″E (WGS-84). ibid, [188].

[774] ibid, [274].

[775] ibid, [275]. See also the *Guyana v Suriname* arbitral award, 30 *RIAA* 90, [323].

[776] The *Bangladesh v India* arbitral award, [276].

[777] The *Bangladesh/Myanmar* case, 48, [157].

[778] Presentation by Brillembourg, ITLOS/PV.17/C23/2/Rev.1, 14.

this can be made 'by 1 connecting BP 55 to the coastline by means of the shortest distance'.[779] In so doing, Chana claimed that: 'BP 55 remains the true starting point of the maritime boundary.'[780] However, Côte d'Ivoire proposed extending the direction of the land boundary between BP 54 via BP 55 until it reaches the low-water line at 'point Ω'.[781] In this connection, it claimed that: 'Unlike boundary post 55, point Ω is located on the low-water mark and is thus appropriate for the construction of the provisional equidistance line.'[782]

On this issue, the ITLOS Special Chamber noted that point Ω is not situated at the low-water line according to chart BA 1383.[783] Furthermore, the Tribunal was not persuaded by the argument of Ghana.[784] The Special Chamber thus decided in favour of extending the direction of the land boundary from BP 54 to BP 55 until it reaches the low-water line. Accordingly, the starting point for the maritime boundary is situated at 05° 05′ 23.2″ N and 03° 06′21.2″ W.[785] It seems that this point is not remote from point Ω, which is situated at 05° 05′ 24.9″ N and 03° 06′ 21.4″ W.[786]

B. Analysis of State Practice

i. Starting Point of Maritime Boundaries

It is almost self-evident that the intersection of the land boundary with the coast becomes the starting point of maritime boundaries between States with adjacent coasts. In some cases, however, a problem may arise regarding the identification of that starting point. One of the difficulties may be the change of position of a river flowing into the sea which constitutes the frontier between States.[787] This problem did arise in the course of negotiations between the United States and Mexico. The Rio Grande, which is the frontier between the United States and Mexico and whose mouth constitutes the starting point for any maritime boundaries, changed over time. Consequently, the starting point of maritime boundaries also changed, thus creating a problem of instability.[788] The instability of the course of the river caused friction between the two countries.[789]

[779] ibid, 15.
[780] ibid.
[781] The *Ghana/Côte d'Ivoire* case, [2017] ITLOS Rep [352].
[782] Rejoinder of Côte d'Ivoire, 54.
[783] The *Ghana/Côte d'Ivoire* case, [2017] ITLOS Rep [352].
[784] ibid, [354].
[785] ibid, [356].
[786] Counter-Memorial of Côte d'Ivoire, 176, [7.27].
[787] Concerning this issue, see in particular Caflisch, 'Règles générales du droit des cours d'eau internationaux,' 80–87.
[788] The mouth of the Rio Grande had migrated approximately 1.5 miles north and south along the coast over the last 120 years. Report by Smith and Colson in *IMB*, vol I, 429.
[789] The United States and Mexico faced the same problem regarding the Colorado river, which forms their frontier.

In 1970, the Parties concluded a treaty which removed the uncertainties regarding the sovereignty over several land tracts and islands in and near the river.[790] With respect to maritime delimitation, a fixed point was established seaward of the mouth of the Rio Grande. This point is situated approximately 2,000 feet seaward from the coast. From this point, according to the equidistance method, the maritime boundary extends into the Gulf of Mexico for 12 miles.[791] Regarding the spaces landward of that point, the 1970 Treaty accepted that the location of the maritime boundary in the Gulf may move according to the change of the location of the river mouth.[792] Thus, in the segment landward of that point, a boundary line was drawn linking a 'floating' initial boundary point with a fixed point situated about 2,000 feet offshore. In other words, the Parties overcame a potential problem of the meandering mouth of the Rio Grande by creating a flexible boundary in the landward segment and by fixing a starting point for the maritime boundary in the ocean.

Another difficulty concerns the change of the *thalweg* of a river which divides States as a land boundary. A change in a *thalweg* may occur even though the position of the river itself has not changed. Brazil and French Guyana had to deal with such a problem when establishing a maritime boundary. The frontier between Brazil and French Guyana ran along the *thalweg* from the mouth of the Oyapock to the source of the Kerindioutou. However, the *thalweg* moved over time. In the course of negotiations held in 1979, the Parties thus had to determine, first of all, a starting point of the maritime boundary to be established.[793] After the negotiation, in 1981, the Parties concluded a treaty establishing a single maritime boundary, which provides that the starting point of the single maritime boundary is at the intersection of the boundary in the bay of Oyapock, which had been established during the Fifth Conference of the Mixed Commission formed by the two countries, and the outer limit of the bay, established during the Sixth Conference of that Commission.[794]

ii. Prolongation of a Land Boundary

In State practice, the method for the prolongation of land boundaries is rarely used. Only a few instances can be quoted. For instance, the northern single

[790] Treaty to Resolve Pending Boundary Differences and Maintain the Rio Grande and Colorado River as the International Boundary. The Treaty dealt with the problem regarding the Colorado river as well.

[791] Art V. In 1976, the Parties agreed to extend the maritime boundary from the terminal point fixed in 1970 to the 200 miles limit for the delimitation of their EEZs and continental shelves. Report by Smith and Colson in *IMB*, vol I, 430.

[792] ibid, 428 and 434. In fact, Article V(A) of the 1970 Treaty provides that: 'The international maritime boundary in the Gulf of Mexico shall begin at the centre of the mouth of the Rio Grande, *wherever it may be located*' (emphasis added). For the text of the agreement, see ibid, 438–43.

[793] Caflisch, 'Règles générales du droit des cours d'eau internationaux' 89–90; D Bardonnet, 'Frontières terrestres et frontières maritimes' (1989) 35 *AFDI* 11.

[794] Art 1(3). Text in *IMB*, vol I, 782–83.

maritime boundary between Senegal and Gambia is clearly the prolongation of their land boundary, which follows the parallel of latitude 13°35'36"North.[795] Furthermore, the territorial sea boundary between Turkey and the former Soviet Union might be an approximate prolongation of the general direction of the last segment of the land boundary.[796] In addition, there are some instances in which a Party supports the idea of prolonging the land boundary in negotiations. For instance, it is reported that, in the course of the negotiations between the United States and Canada, the latter insisted on the prolongation of the land boundary with the United States as being a maritime boundary in the Beaufort Sea. By contrast, the United States favoured the application of the equidistance method.[797] It is also suggested that Venezuela advocated the prolongation of the land boundary in the course of negotiations with Colombia regarding the delimitation in the Gulf of Venezuela. Colombia supported the equidistance method, however.[798] In neither case have maritime boundaries been established as of yet.

C. Summary

The above analysis may be summarised in three points.

First, land boundaries indicate a starting point for maritime boundaries between States with adjacent coasts. In this sense, the land boundary affects maritime boundaries.

Secondly, where a land boundary meets a coast at something other than a right angle, the prolongation of the land boundary would create an inequitable result. Accordingly, except for the case where a land boundary crosses a coast at a right angle, the prolongation of the land boundary would lead to iniquity. Furthermore, where a land boundary crosses a coast at a right angle, such a line coincides with an equidistance line. Moreover, as pointed out earlier, in a certain geographical situation described in Figure 2,[799] a line of prolongation of the land boundary would create inequitable results. For that reason, the method of prolongation of a land boundary remains unusual in both case law and State practice.

Thirdly, the instability of coastline at the terminus of the land boundary may create a difficulty in maritime delimitation between States with adjacent coasts. To address this issue, the ICJ, in the *Costa Rica v Nicaragua* case, established a mobile line connecting a fixed point at sea and the starting-point on the coast.

[795] Text in ibid, 854–55.
[796] Report by Scovazzi in ibid, vol II, 1683.
[797] KL Lawson, 'Delimiting Continental Shelf Boundaries in the Arctic: The United States-Canada Beaufort Sea Boundary' (1981) 22 *Virginia Journal of International Law* 221 (see in particular 241–43); Bardonnet, 'Frontières terrestres et frontières maritimes' 26.
[798] ibid, 30.
[799] See ch 2, s I of this book.

In State practice, the United States and Mexico adopted the same solution in the 1970 Treaty. The creation of a mobile line in the short offshore segment seems to be a useful way to minimise the impact of future changes of the coastline on maritime boundary.

IX. PRESENCE OF ICE

A. Analysis of the Case Law: The *Jan Mayen* Case

The *Jan Mayen* case is the unique example in which the problem of drift ice is at issue in connection with access to marine resources. In that case, the Parties agreed that a 40 per cent cover of drift ice renders ordinary navigation and all fishing activity impossible during part of the year. Denmark thus argued that the median line proposed by Norway would in effect leave Denmark with only 10 per cent of the waters available for fishing.[800] When the ice cover is most extensive, however, there is no capelin or any other fishable species. The Court thus considered that the presence of ice did not materially affect the access to migratory fishery resources in the southern part of the area of overlapping claims.[801] This implies that, where the presence of ice materially affects the access to marine resources, this factor should be taken into account as a special/relevant circumstance.

B. Analysis of State Practice

There is but one text which considers the presence of ice. In the 1973 Agreement between Canada and Denmark (Greenland), an equidistance line was slightly modified in favour of Denmark because of the potential fluctuations of the ice-fringed coast of Greenland.[802] On the other hand, large quantities of sea ice found in the Denmark Strait did not influence the location of the single maritime boundary drawn in the 1997 Agreement between Denmark and Iceland.[803]

C. Summary

Apart from the *Jan Mayen* case, the issue of ice has been rarely discussed in the jurisprudence concerning maritime delimitation. However, the *Jan Mayen* judgment appears to imply that the presence of ice may be at issue when

[800] [1993] ICJ Rep 72, [77]. See also the Reply submitted by Denmark, vol I, 169–70.

[801] [1993] ICJ Rep 73, [78].

[802] B Kwiatkowska, 'Economic and Environmental Considerations' in *IMB*, vol I, 102. Report by Alexander in ibid, 375.

[803] Report by Anderson, ibid, vol IV, 2945.

considering the access to marine resources. In any case the issue of the presence of ice may arise only in a particular geographical context, such as maritime delimitation in the polar region.

X. CONCLUSIONS

This chapter examined various geographical factors to be taken into account in the process of maritime delimitations. The above considerations reveal the following conclusions.

First, the configuration of the coast is a primary factor to be considered in the process of maritime delimitation. Specifically opposite or adjacent coasts, concavity or convexity of toasts and the general direction of coastlines have been discussed in the jurisprudence concerning maritime delimitation. As the ICJ stressed in the *North Sea Continental Shelf* cases, '[t]here can never be any question of completely refashioning nature.' Even so, considerations of geographical factors are subject to a large discretion of an international court or tribunal. In considering the configuration of the coast, for instance, several interpretations may be possible according to the scale of the map or micro- or macro-geography. Thus an international court or tribunal may exercise large discretion when identifying the concavity or convexity of relevant coasts but thereby run the risk of subjectivity. The same would be true of the determination of the general direction of the coasts.

Secondly, (dis)proportionality can be regarded as a crucial element in the sense that it was taken into account in almost all cases concerning maritime delimitations. In the jurisprudence, it is established that the disproportionality test is applied at the third and final stage of maritime delimitations. The function of the disproportionality test is to check the equitableness of the delimitation line, avoiding a significant disproportionality. The checking of the equitableness of maritime boundary can only be approximate. In contrast, there appears to be limited State practice in this matter. Thus it is argued that the concept of (dis)proportionality is the product of a 'judge-made-law'.

Thirdly, the presence of islands constitutes an important geographical factor that needs serious consideration in the process of maritime delimitation. An essential issue that arises in this context concerns legal effect given to maritime features. In this regard, it is possible to identify four patterns: (i) full effect, (ii) no effect, (iii) partial (or half) effect, and (iv) enclave solution. Yet it is difficult to specify a general rule with respect to the legal effect given to these features in the jurisprudence. State practice tends to give partial effects to maritime features 'on the wrong side'. Where offshore features exist on one side only, it is likely that only partial effect would be given to them. Furthermore, detached maritime features are likely to be given full effect in applying the equidistance method. However, it must be stressed that this is merely a general trend of State practice.

Fourthly, the selection of base points is of critical importance in constructing a provisional equidistance line. Where base points selected by the Parties might produce distorting effects, an international court or tribunal may select other points for the purpose of maritime delimitation. As demonstrated in the *Libya/Malta* and *Qatar v Bahrain* cases, straight baselines drawn by the Parties may not be used by the ICJ when constructing a provisional equidistance line at the first stage of maritime delimitations. In State practice as well, there are comparatively many instances where straight baselines did not influence the maritime delimitation.

Fifthly, the role of geological and geomorphological factors remains modest in the jurisprudence concerning maritime delimitation within 200 nautical miles. Likewise these factors did not influence the location of maritime boundaries in a majority of the agreements. As in the case of Okinawa Trough, however, exceptionally the geological and geomorphological factors may be a crucial element in maritime delimitations.

Sixthly, States can take account of the presence of third-States in a flexible manner, by fixing the tri-point by agreement or leaving the delimitation with third States open. However, the influence of third-States on maritime delimitation creates challenges in international adjudication. The central issue in this regard is whether Article 59 of the ICJ Statute would be adequate to protect the rights of third States in the area to be delimited. In the *Cameroon v Nigeria* case (Merits), the Court accepted that Article 59 may not be sufficient to protect legal rights of third States.[804] In the *Nicaragua v Colombia* and *Costa Rica v Nicaragua* cases, however, the Court seems to relay on the principle *res inter alios acta* and Article 59 of the ICJ Statute. Thus the jurisprudence seems to be in flux on this matter.

Seventhly, normally the starting-point of the adjacent maritime boundary is the end-point of the land boundary. An international court or tribunal encounters a challenge where the relevant coasts are highly unstable. In this regard, it is notable that the ICJ, in the *Costa Rica v Nicaragua* case, established a mobile boundary connecting a fixed point at sea and the point on solid land on Costa Rica's coast. Interestingly, a similar solution was adopted in the 1970 Convention between the United States and Mexico. The construction of a mobile boundary provides a useful option in response to serious instability of the relevant coasts.

Lastly, in both State practice and the jurisprudence, the presence of ice was at issue in relation to the delimitation with Greenland. However, its influence on the location of maritime boundaries remains modest.

[804] Judgment, [2002] ICJ Rep 421, [238].

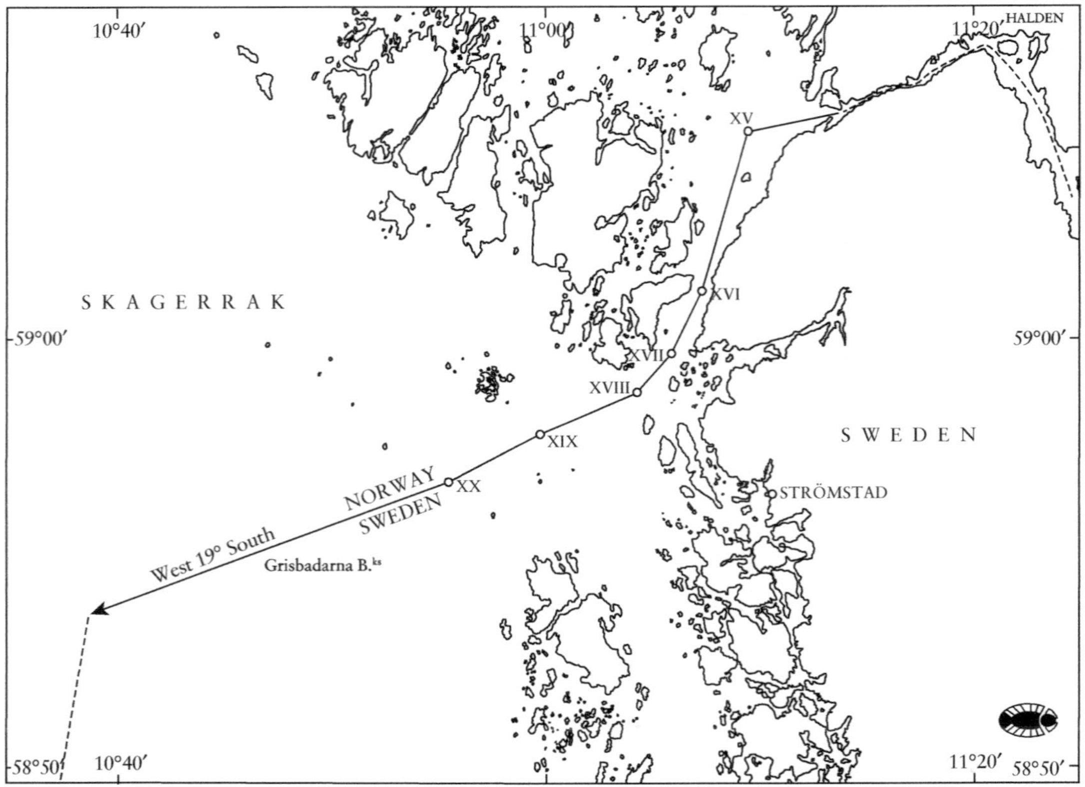

Illustration 1 The *Grisbadarna* Case

Source: G Francalanci and T Scovazzi (eds), Lines in the Sea (Dordrecht, Nijhoff, 1994) 199.

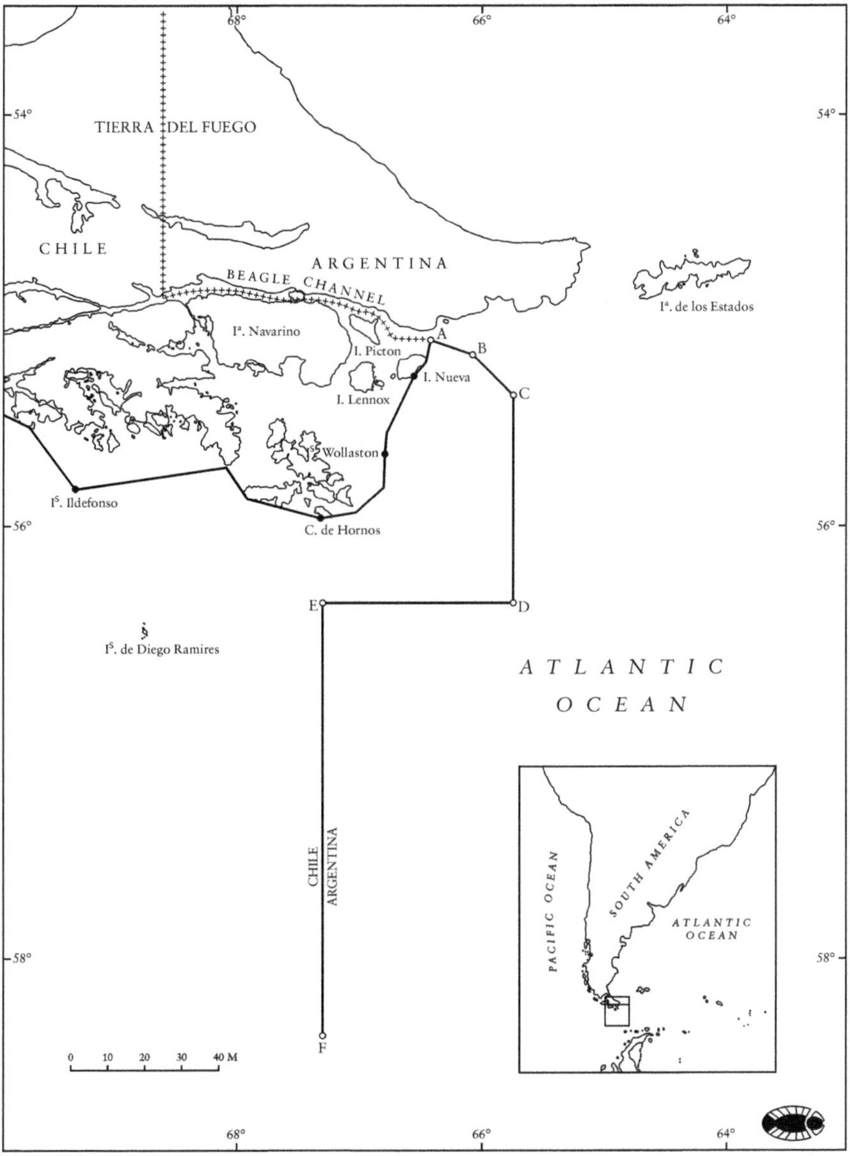

Illustration 2 Argentina/Chile, Beagle Channel

Source: G Francalanci and T Scovazzi (eds), *Lines in the Sea* (Dordrecht, Nijhoff, 1994) 227.

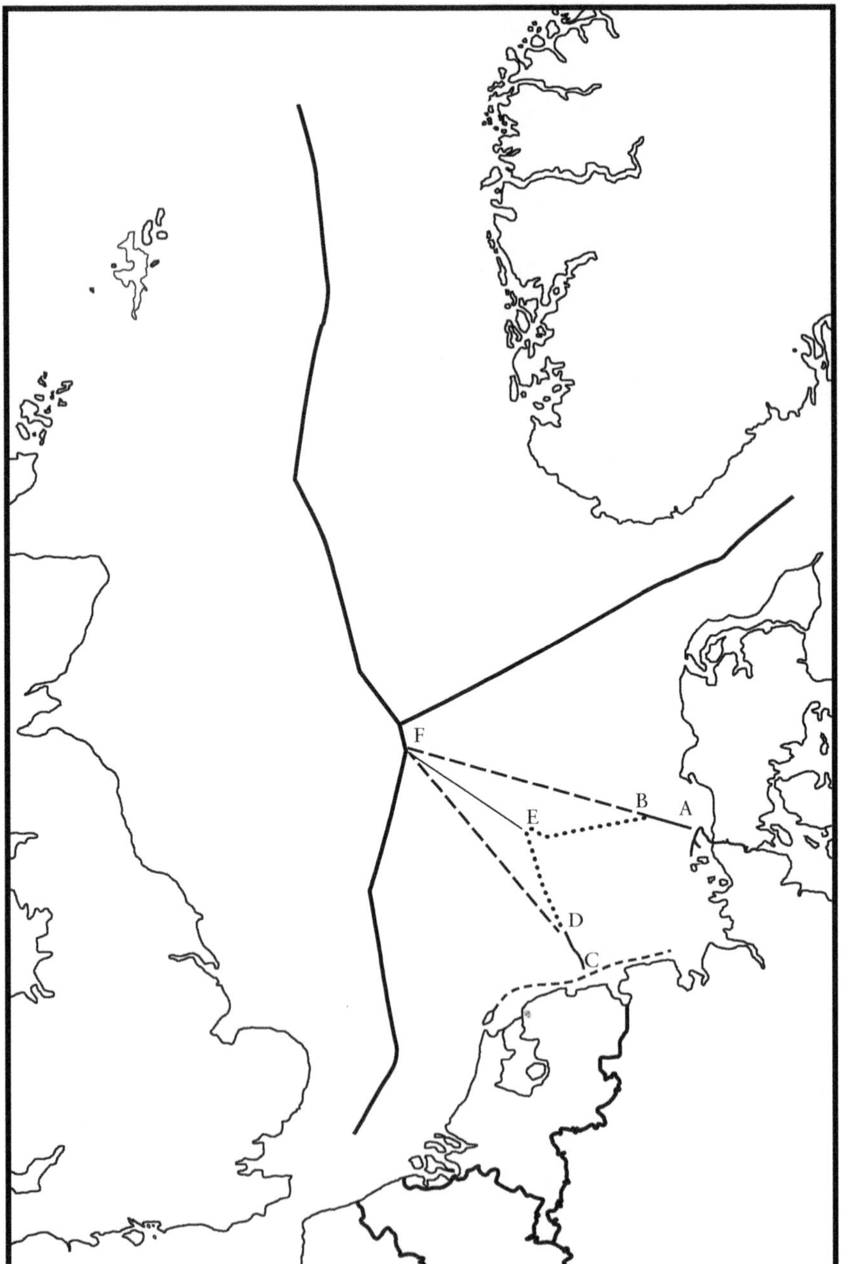

Illustration 3 The *North Sea Continental Shelf* Cases
Source: Map No. 3 annexed to the Judgment, [1969] ICJ Rep 16.

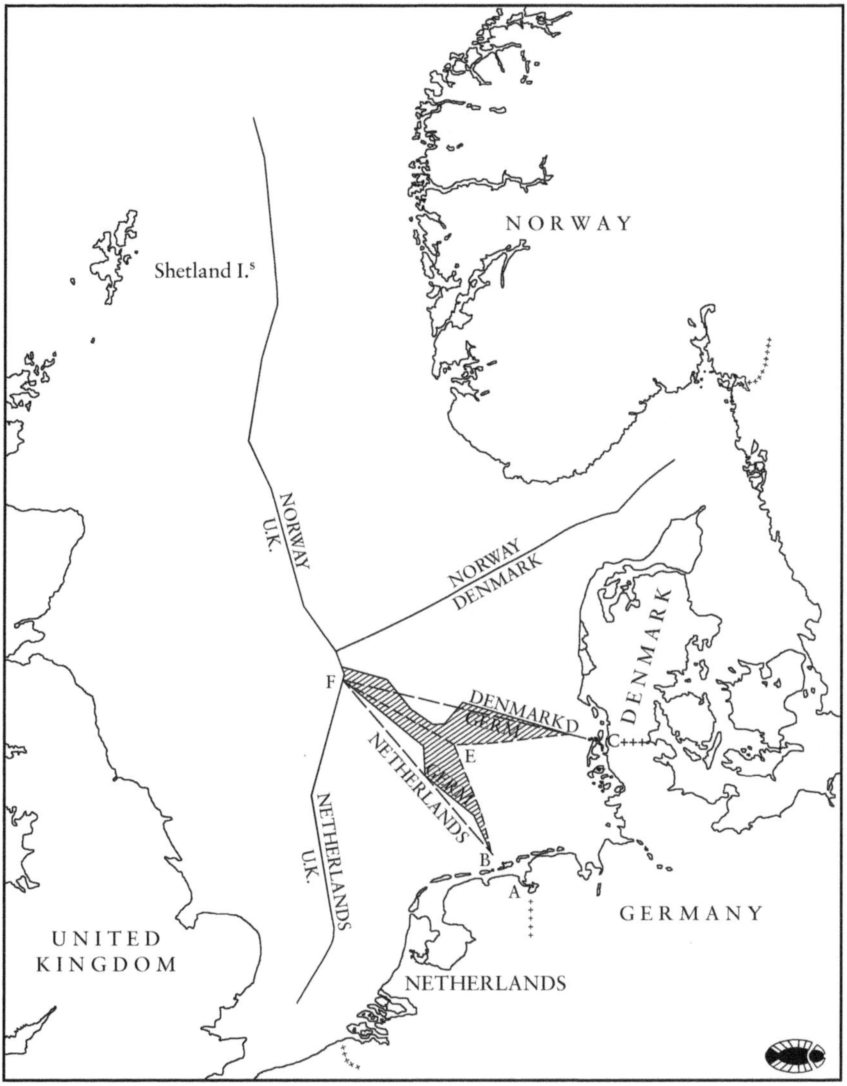

Illustration 4 Continental Shelf Boundary between the Netherlands and the Federal Republic Germany and between the Latter and Denmark

Source: G Francalanci and T Scovazzi (eds), *Lines in the Sea* (Dordrecht, Nijhoff, 1994) 237.

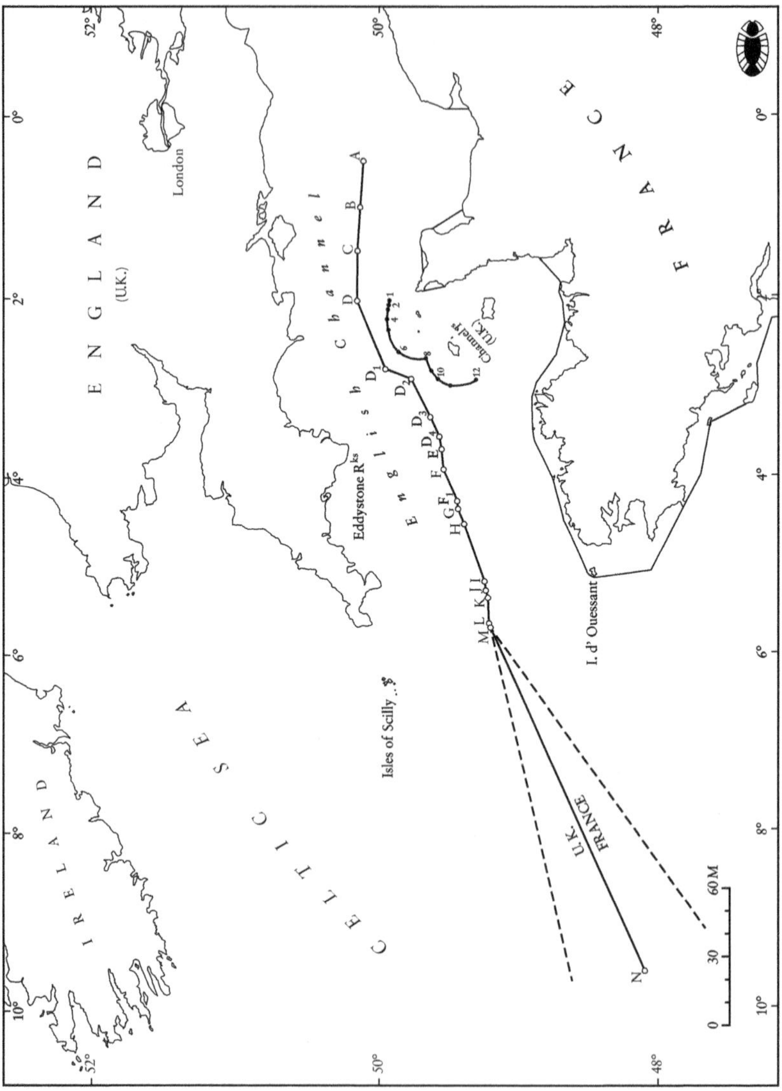

Illustration 5 The *Anglo-French Continental Shelf* Case

Source: G Francalanci and T Scovazzi (eds), *Lines in the Sea* (Dordrecht, Nijhoff, 1994) 239.

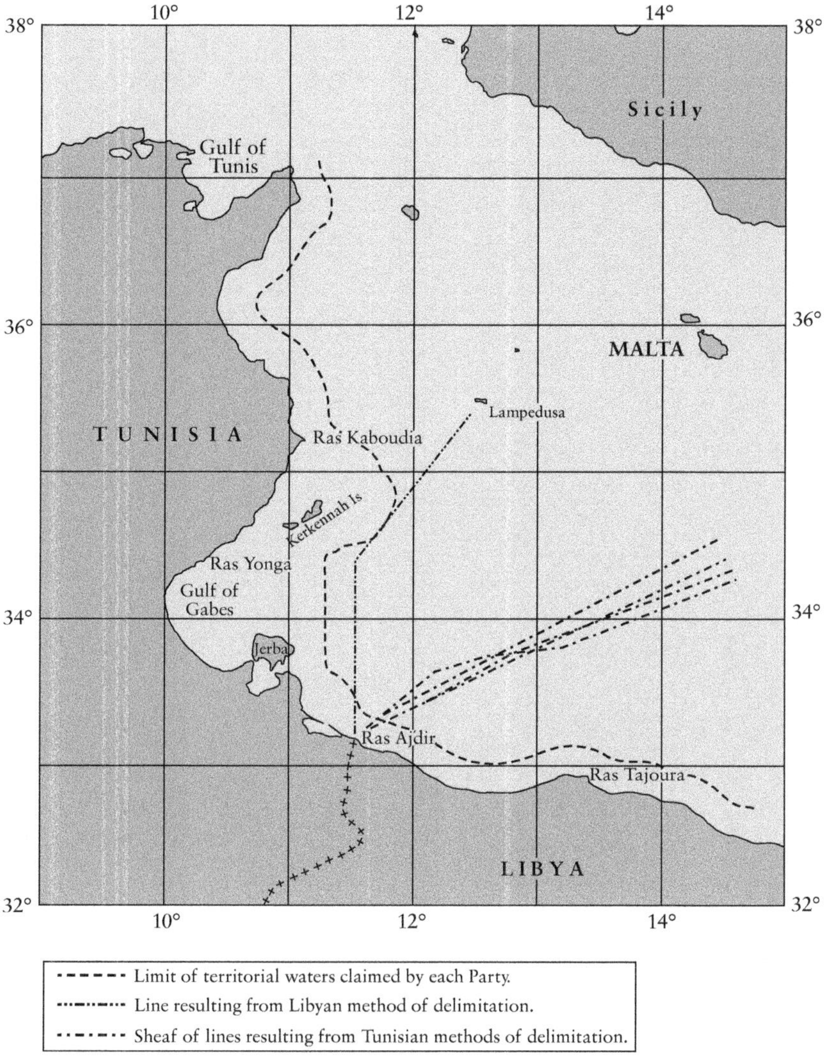

Illustration 6 The *Tunisia/Libya* Case (1)

Source: Map No. 2 annexed to the Judgment, [1982] ICJ Rep 81.

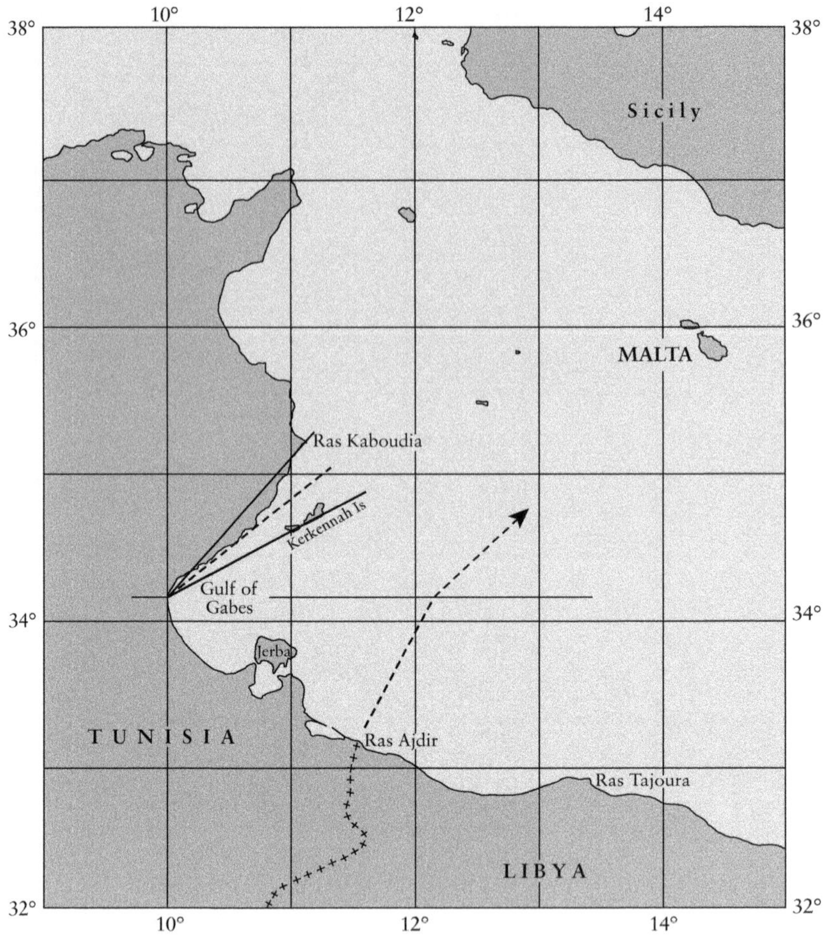

Illustration 7 The *Tunisia/Libya* Case (2)

Source: Map No. 3 annexed to the Judgment, [1982] ICJ Rep 90.

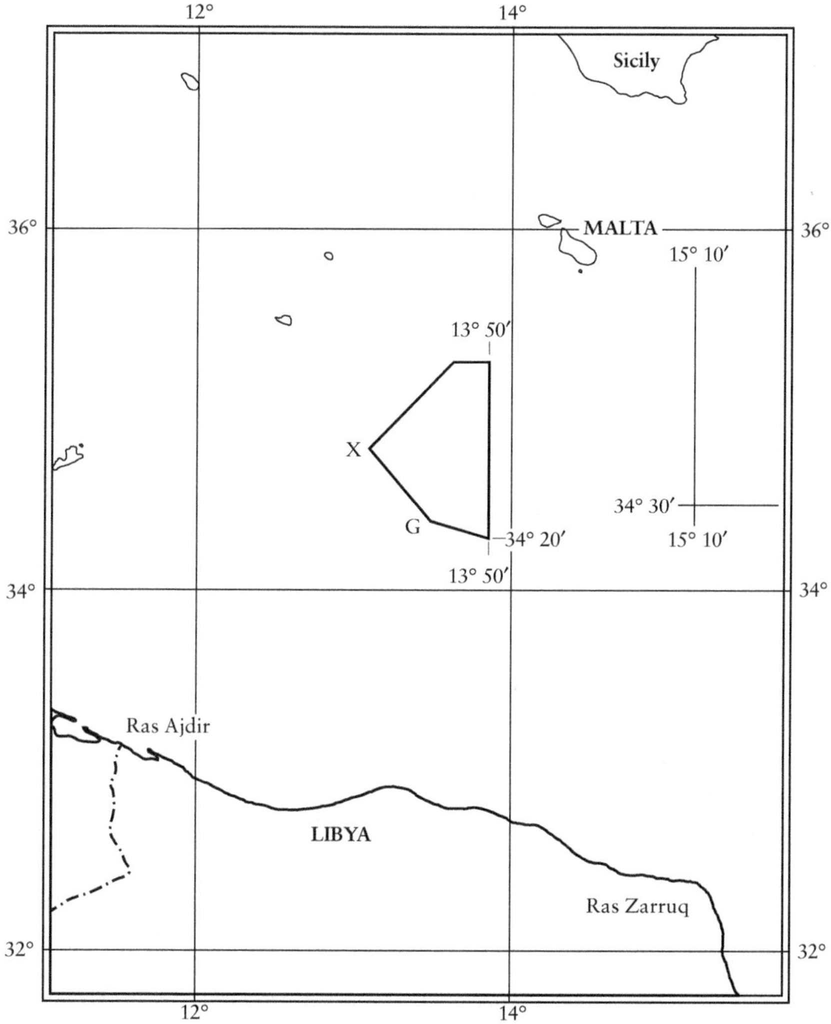

Illustration 8 The *Libya/Malta* Case (1)

Source: Map No. 2 annexed to the Judgment, [1985] ICJ Rep 27.

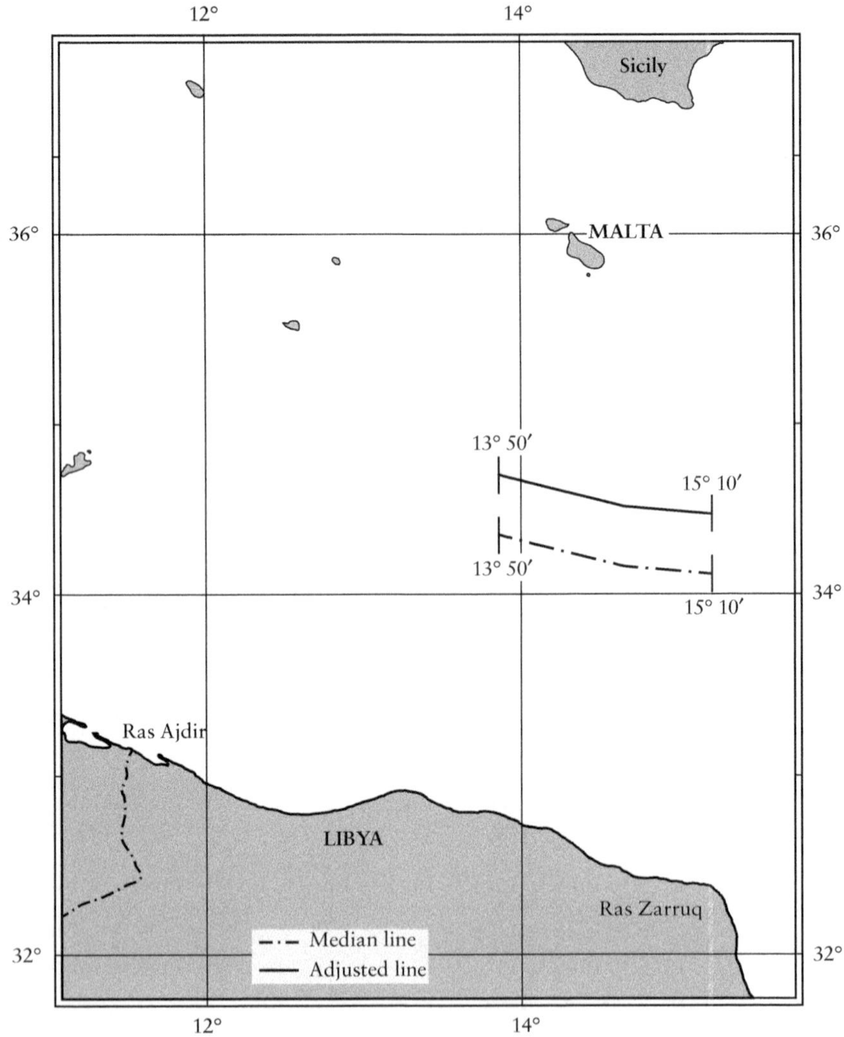

Illustration 9 The *Libya/Malta* Case (2)
Source: Map No. 3 annexed to the Judgment, [1985] ICJ Rep 54.

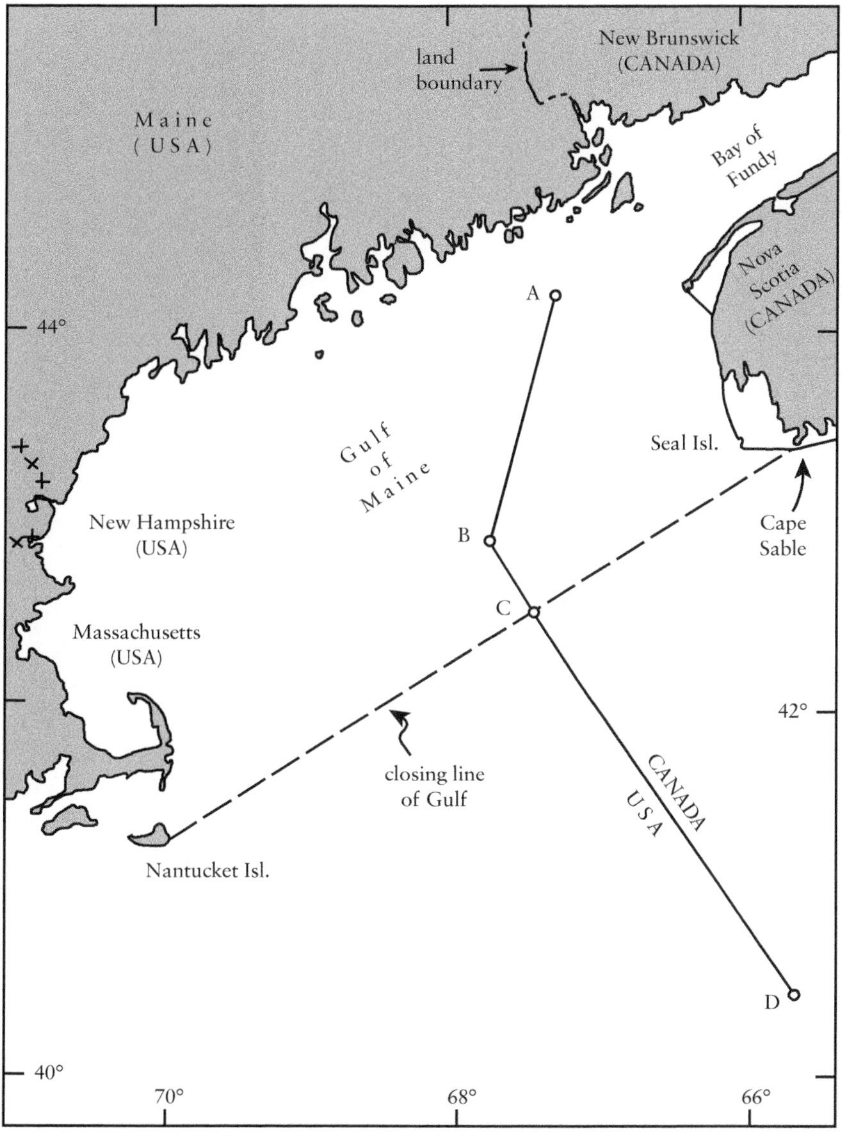

Illustration 10 The *Gulf of Maine* Case

Source: L Caflisch, 'The Delimitation of Maritime Spaces between States with Opposite or Adjacent Coast' in R-J Dupuy and D Vignes (eds), *A Handbook on the New Law of the Sea* (Dordrecht, Nijhoff, 1991), 453.

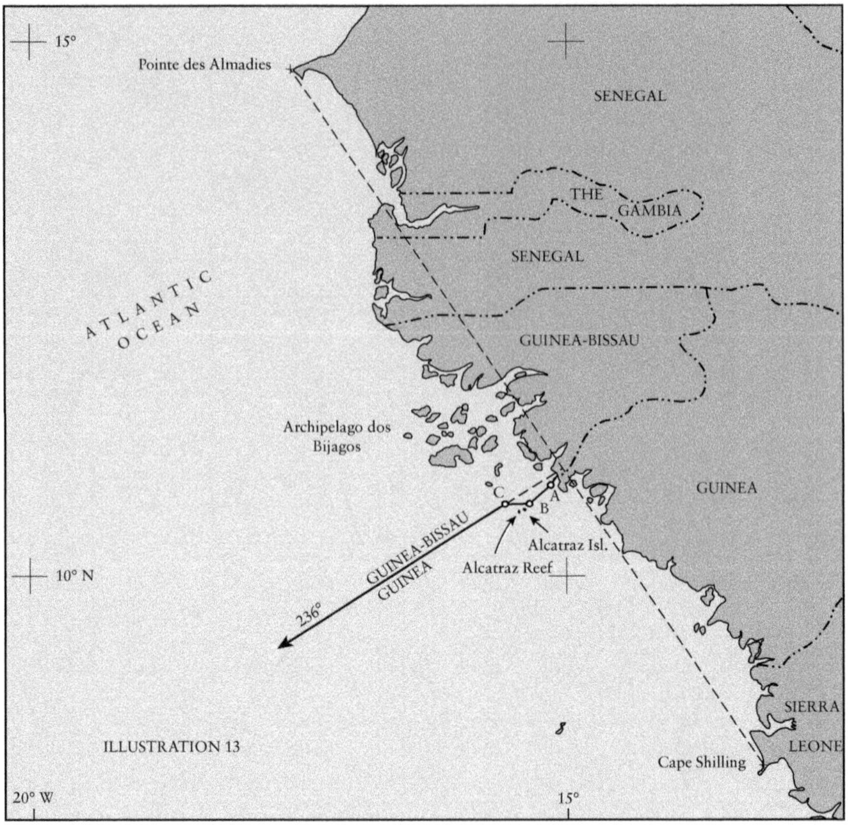

Illustration 11 The *Guinea/Guinea-Bissau* Case

Source: L Caflisch, 'The Delimitation of Maritime Spaces between States with Opposite or Adjacent Coast' in R-J Dupuy and D Vignes (eds), *A Handbook on the New Law of the Sea* (Dordrecht, Nijhoff, 1991).

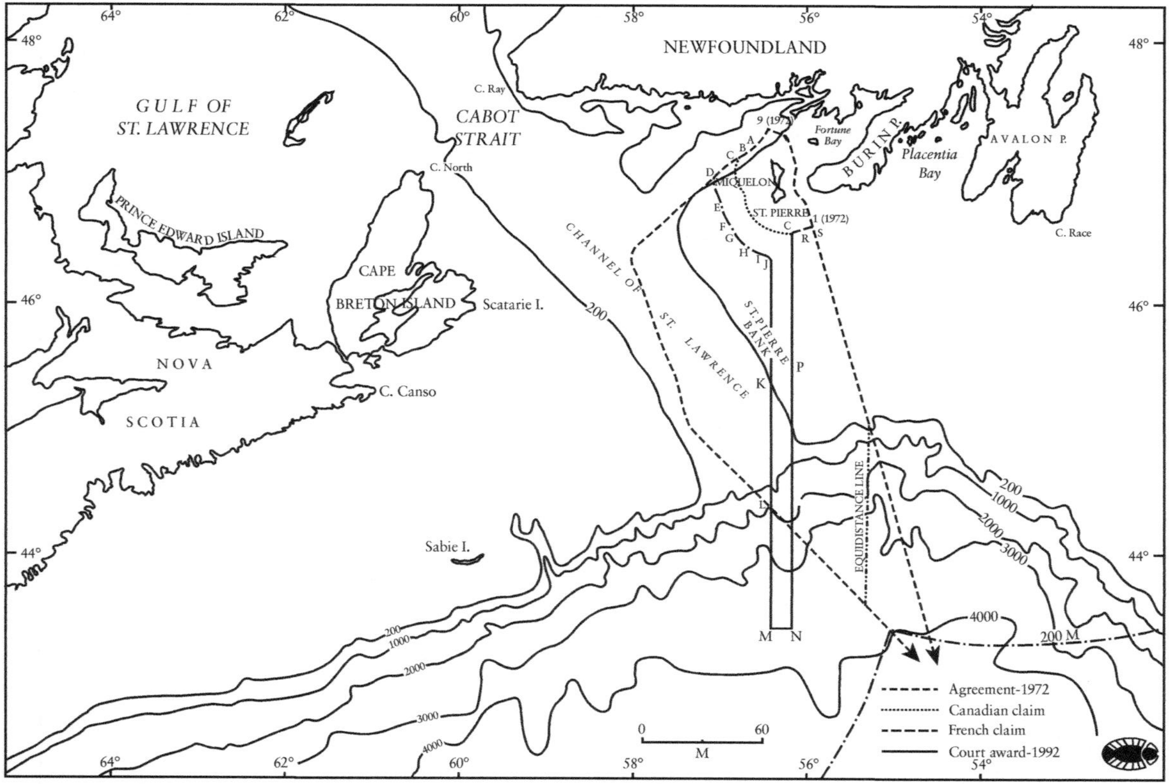

Illustration 12 The *St Pierre and Miquelon* Case

Source: G Francalanci and T Scovazzi (eds), *Lines in the Sea* (Dordrecht, Nijhoff, 1994) 253.

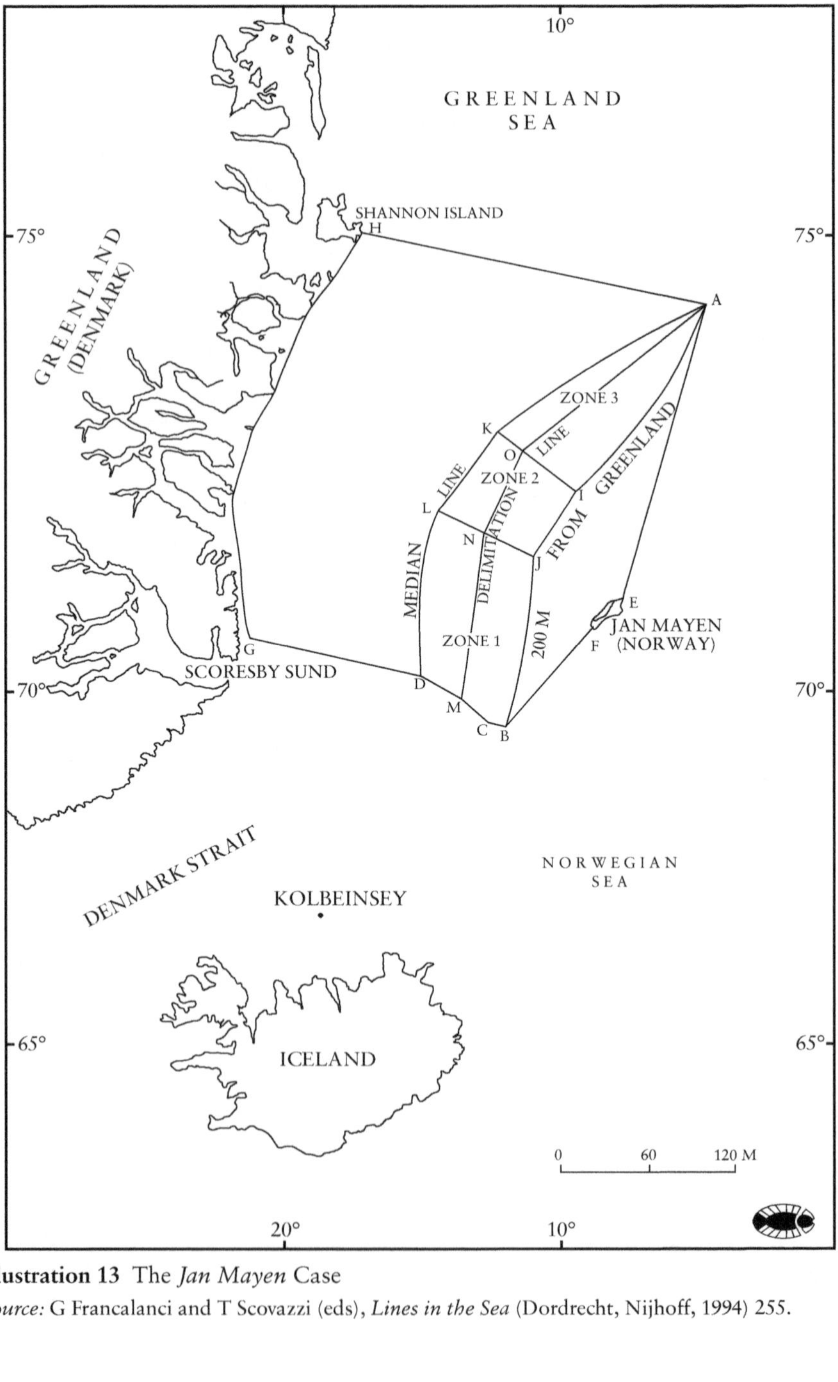

Illustration 13 The *Jan Mayen* Case

Source: G Francalanci and T Scovazzi (eds), *Lines in the Sea* (Dordrecht, Nijhoff, 1994) 255.

The international maritime boundary line

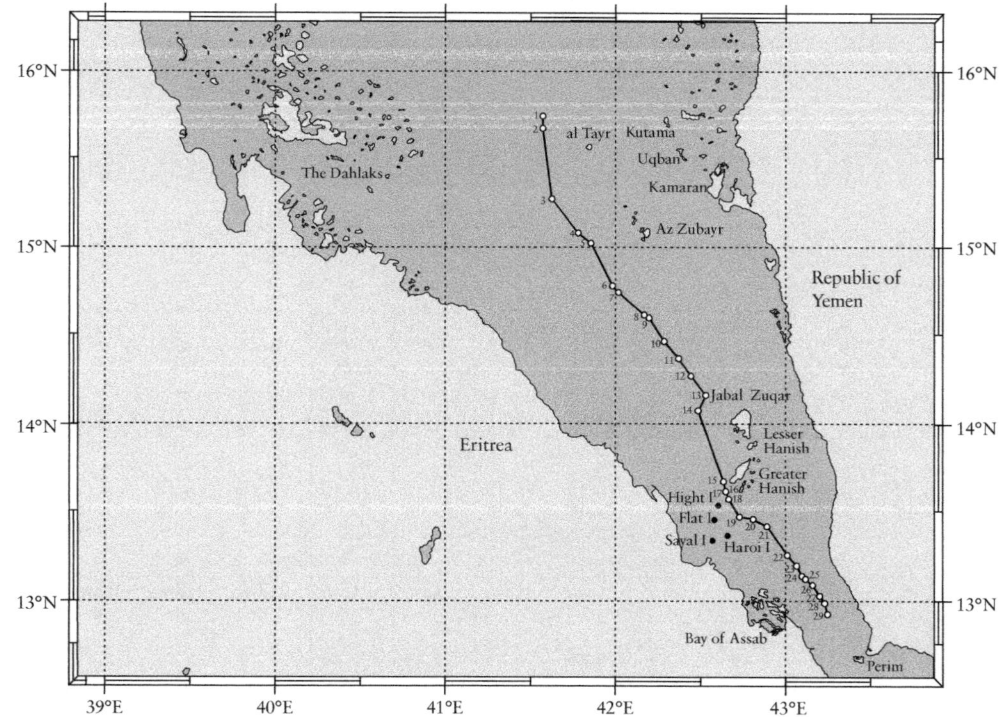

Illustration 14 The *Eritrea/Yemen* Case

Source: Y Tanaka, 'Reflections on the Eritrea/Yemen Arbitration of 17 December 1999 (Second Phase: Maritime Delimitation)' (2001) 48 *NILR* 225. (Figure drawn by the author on the basis of the figure annexed to the award, www.pca-cpa.org/chart3.)

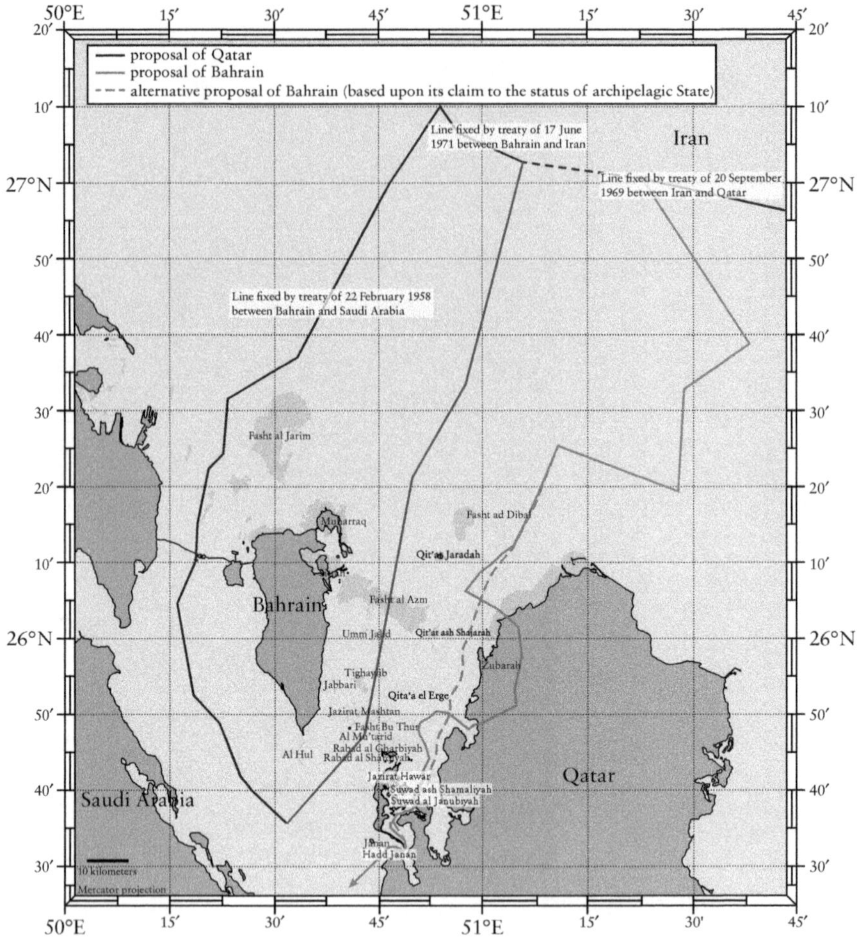

Illustration 15 Lines Proposed by Qatar and Bahrain in the *Qatar v Bahrain* Case (Merits)

Source: Sketch-map No. 2 annexed to the Judgment, [2001] ICJ Rep 92.

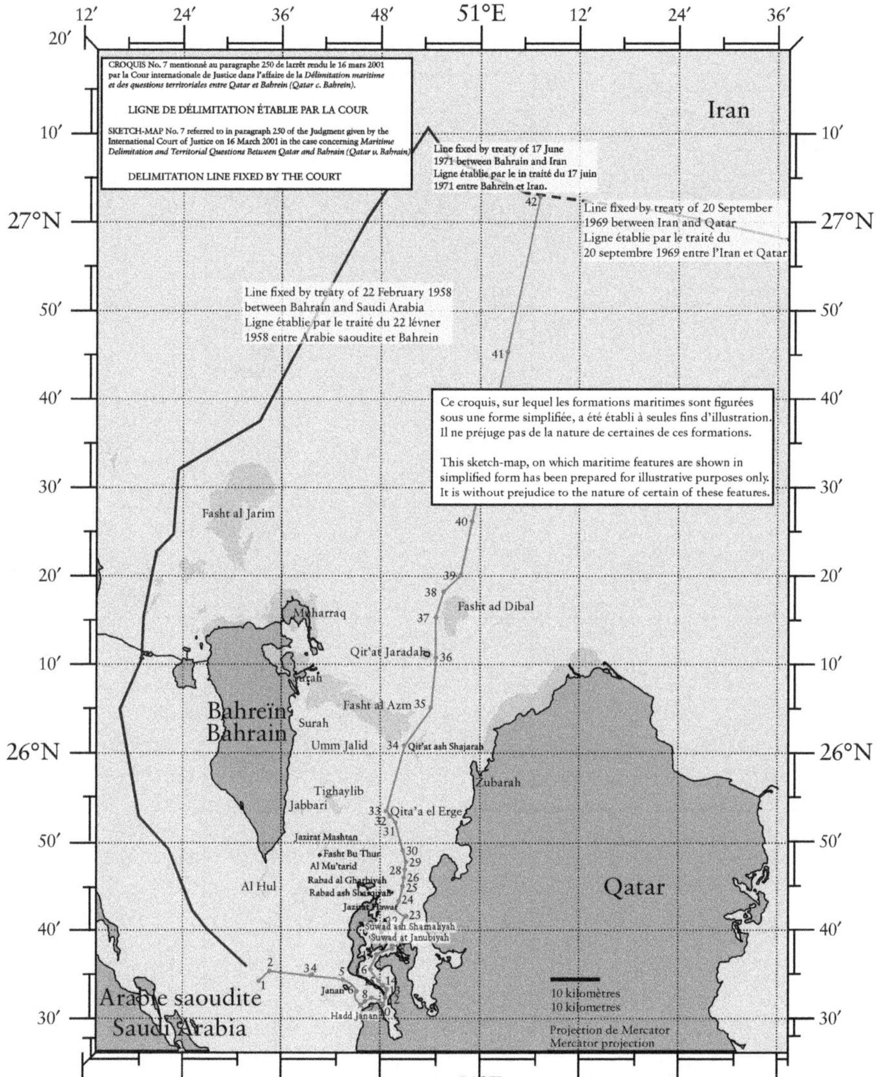

Illustration 16 Delimitation Line Fixed by the ICJ in the *Qatar v Bahrain* Case (Merits)
Source: Sketch-map No. 7 annexed to the Judgment, Merits, which is found inside the back cover of the volume of [2001] ICJ Rep.

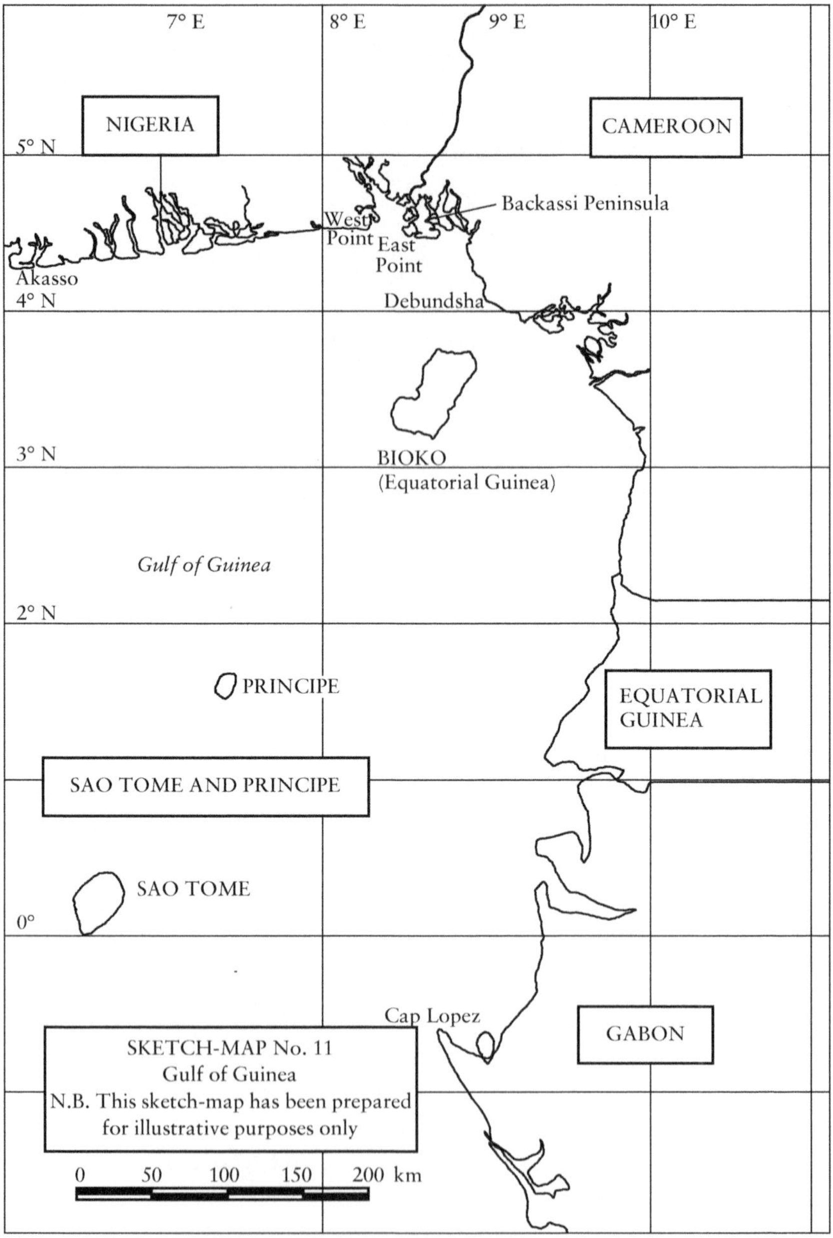

Illustration 17 Gulf of Guinea

Source: Sketch-map No. 11 annexed to the Judgment, [2002] ICJ Rep 444.

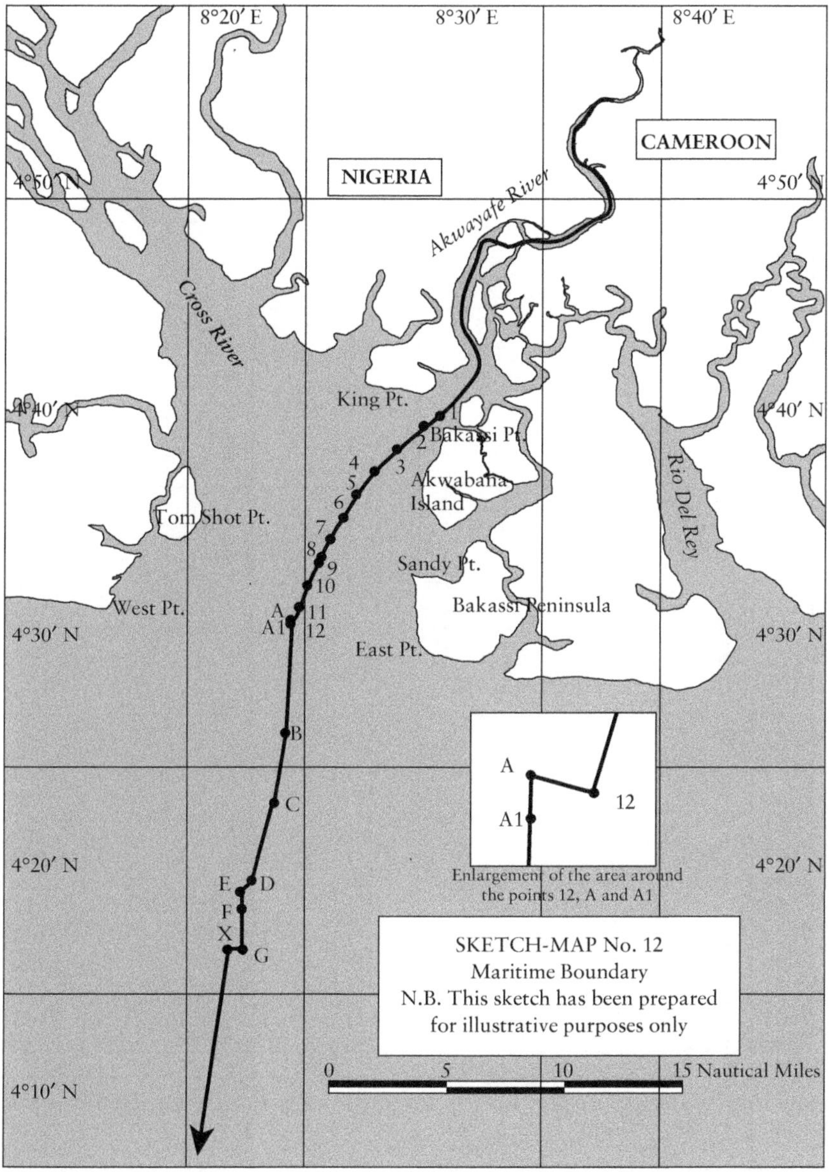

Illustration 18 Delimitation Line Fixed by the ICJ in the *Cameroon v Nigeria* Case (Merits)

Source: Sketch-map No. 12 annexed to the Judgment, [2002] ICJ Rep 449.

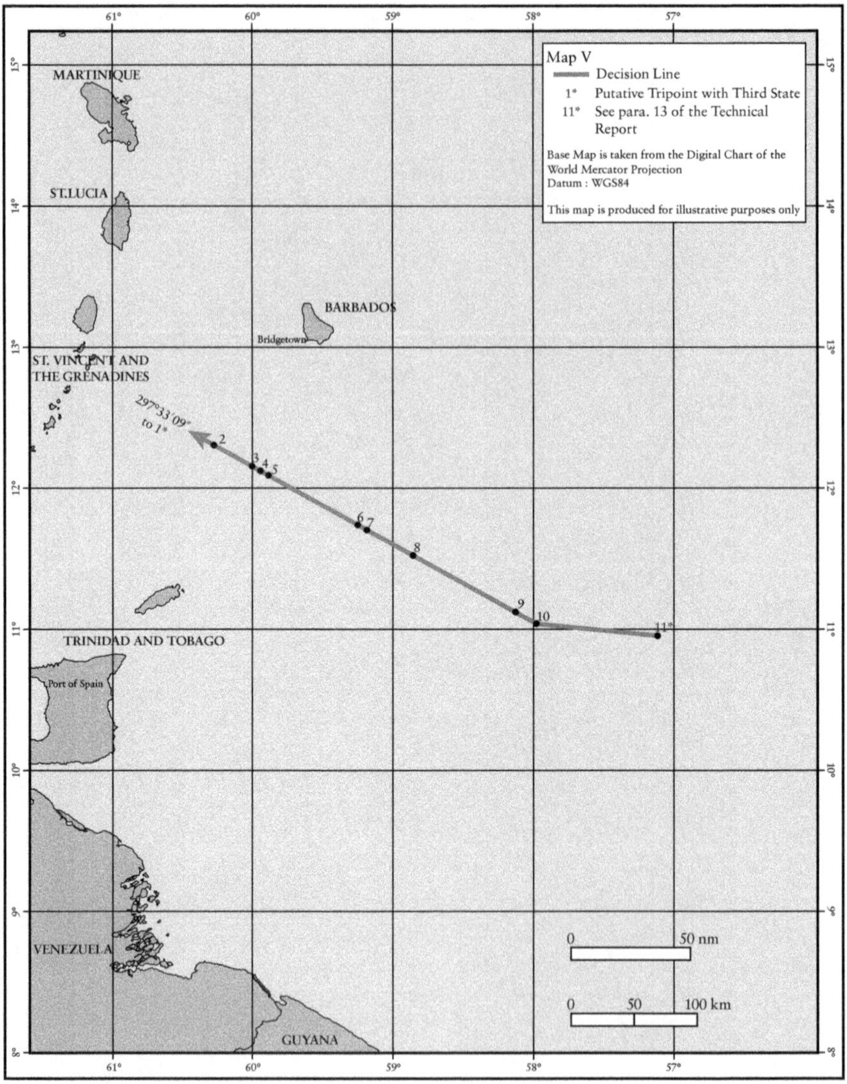

Illustration 19 Delimitation Line Established by the Arbitral Tribunal in the *Barbados v Trinidad and Tobago* Case

Source: Map V annexed to the arbitral award of 11 April 2006, [380], available at: https://pca-cpa.org/en/cases/104/ Reproduced with permission of the Permanent Court of Arbitration (copyright holder).

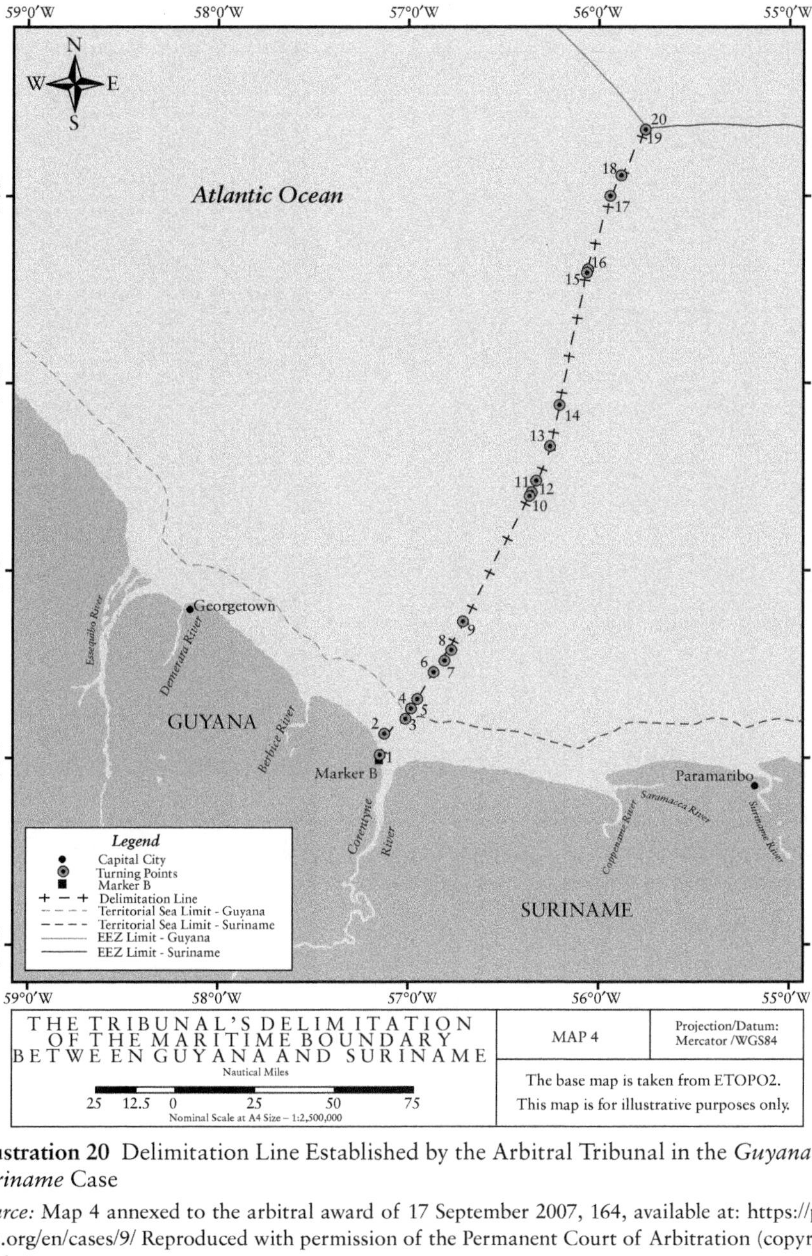

Illustration 20 Delimitation Line Established by the Arbitral Tribunal in the *Guyana v Suriname* Case

Source: Map 4 annexed to the arbitral award of 17 September 2007, 164, available at: https://pca-cpa.org/en/cases/9/ Reproduced with permission of the Permanent Court of Arbitration (copyright holder).

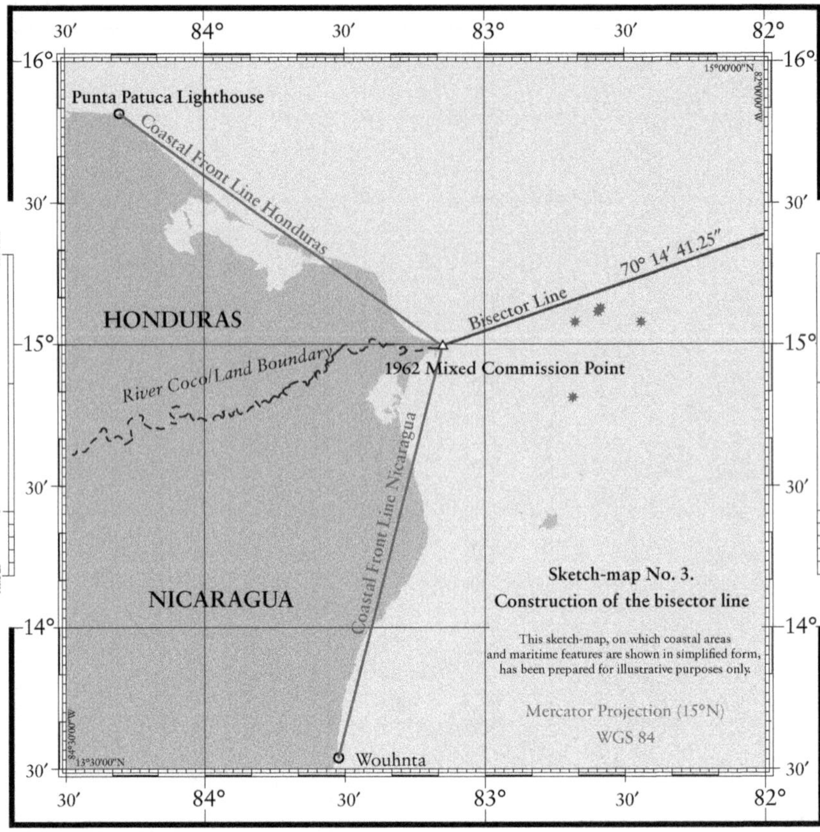

Illustration 21 Bisector Line Established by the ICJ in the *Nicaragua v Honduras* Case
Source: Sketch-map No. 3 annexed to the judgment, [2007] ICJ Rep 750.

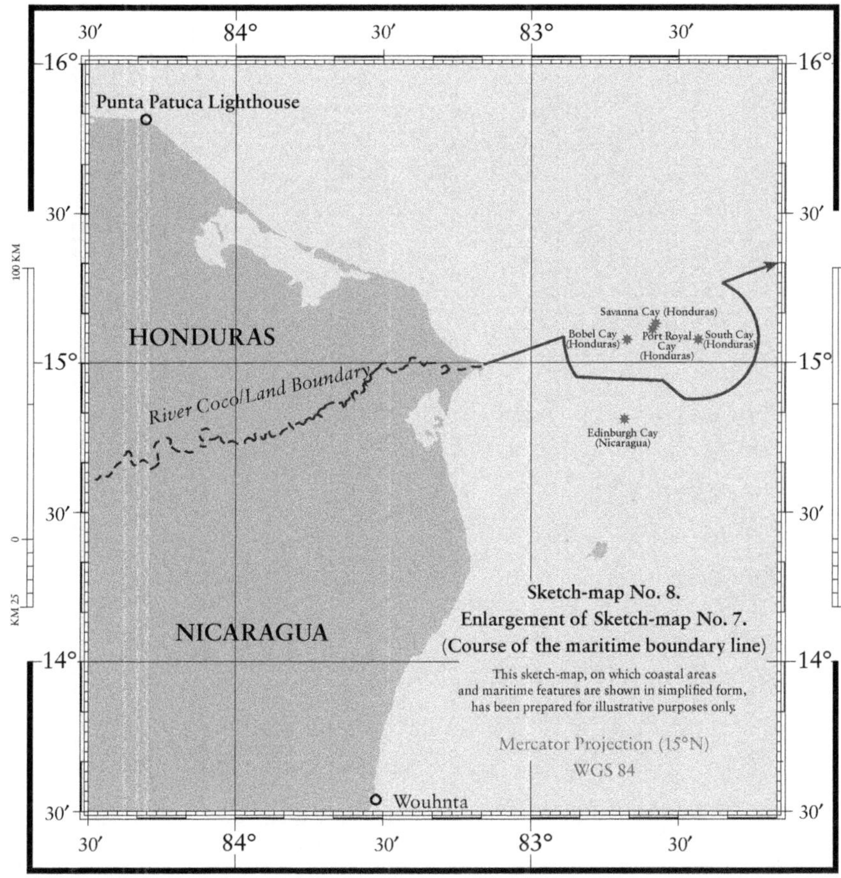

Illustration 22 Delimitation Line Established by the ICJ in the *Nicaragua v Honduras* Case

Source: Sketch-map No. 8 annexed to the judgment, [2007] ICJ Rep 762.

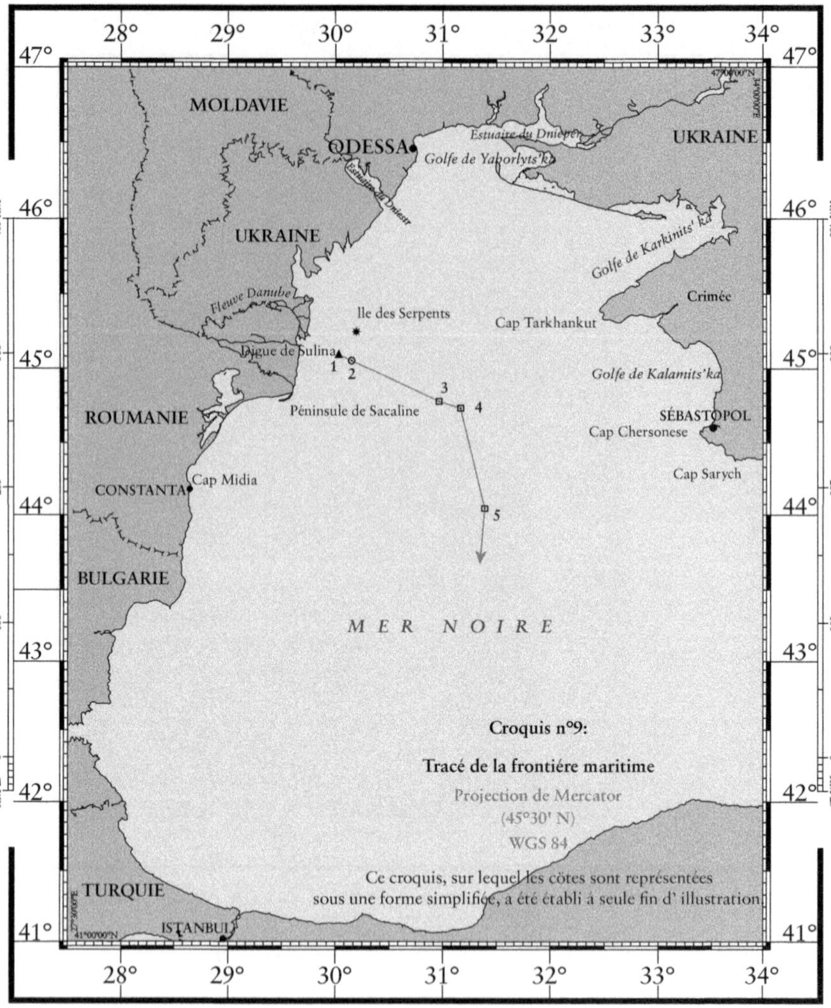

Illustration 23 Delimitation Line Established by the ICJ in the *Black Sea* Case
Source: Sketch-map No. 9 annexed to the judgment, [2009] ICJ Rep 133.

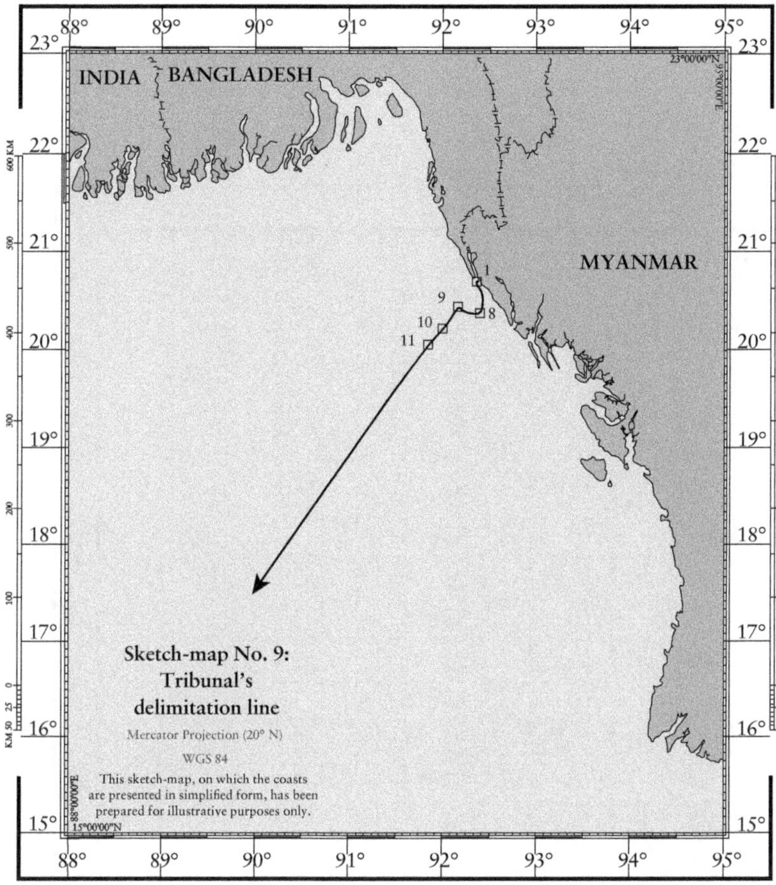

Illustration 24 Delimitation Line Established by ITLOS in the *Bangladesh/Myanmar* Case

Source: Sketch-map No. 9 annexed to the judgment, [2012] ITLOS Rep 129.

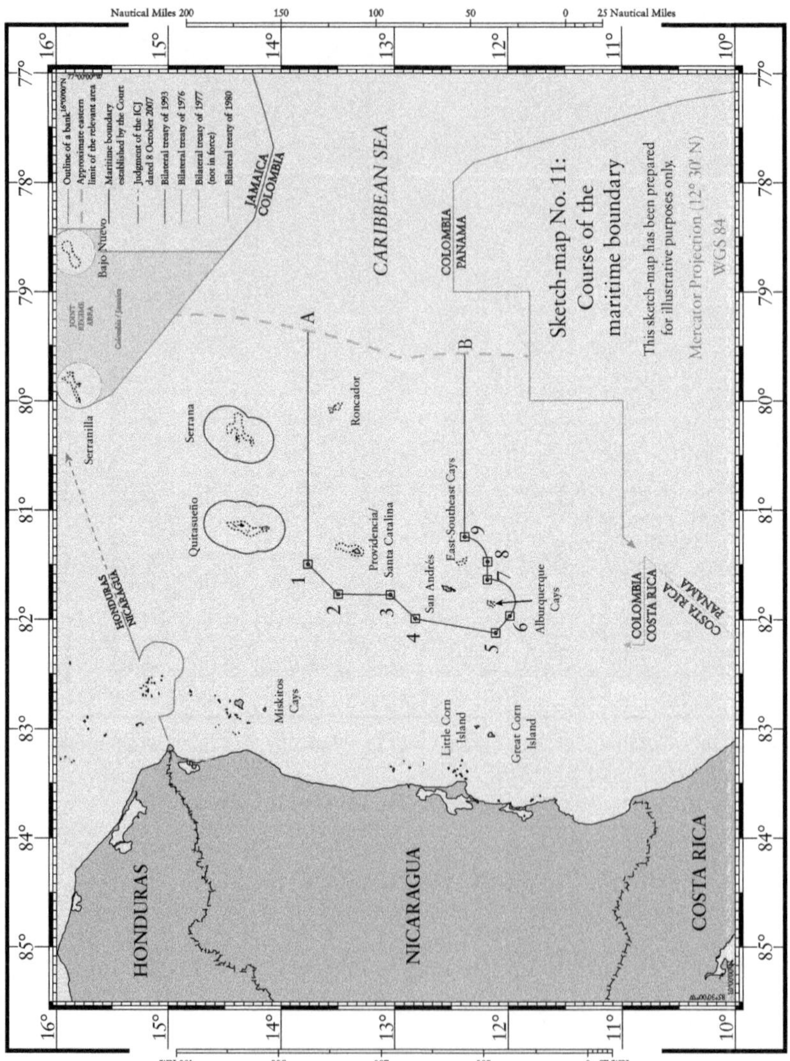

Illustration 25 Delimitation Line Established by the ICJ in the *Nicaragua v Colombia* Case

Source: Sketch-map No. 11 annexed to the judgment, [2012] ICJ Rep 714.

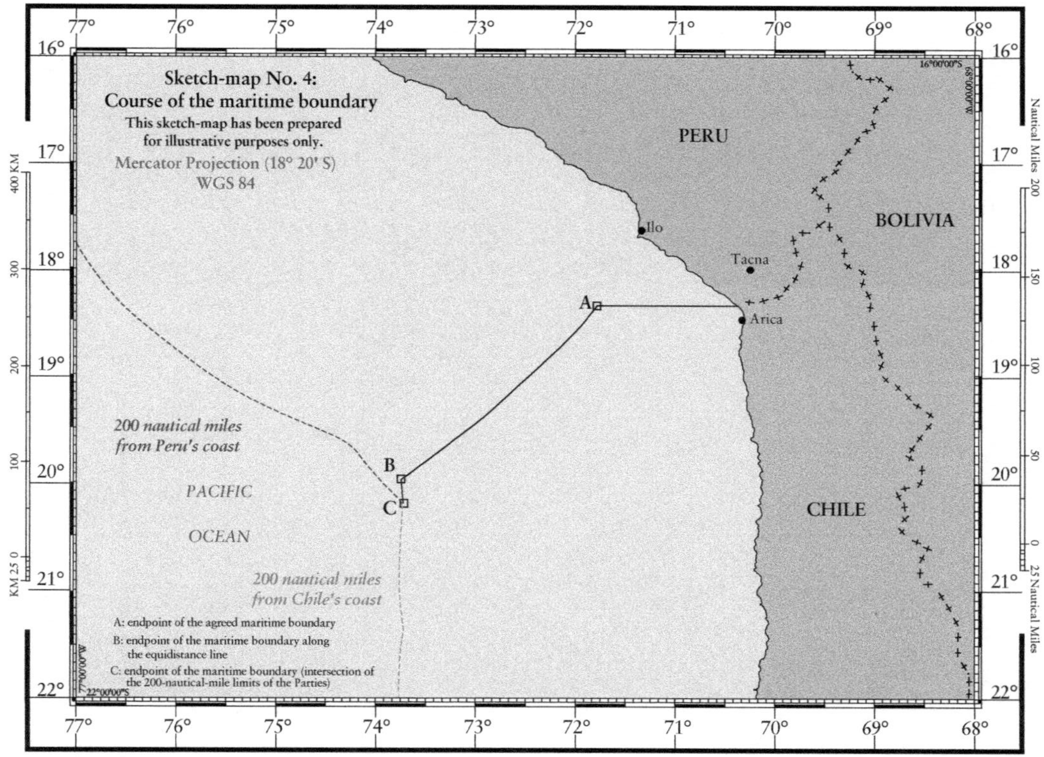

Illustration 26 Delimitation Line Established by the ICJ in the *Peru v Chile* Case

Source: Sketch-map No. 4 annexed to the judgment, [2014] ICJ Rep 70.

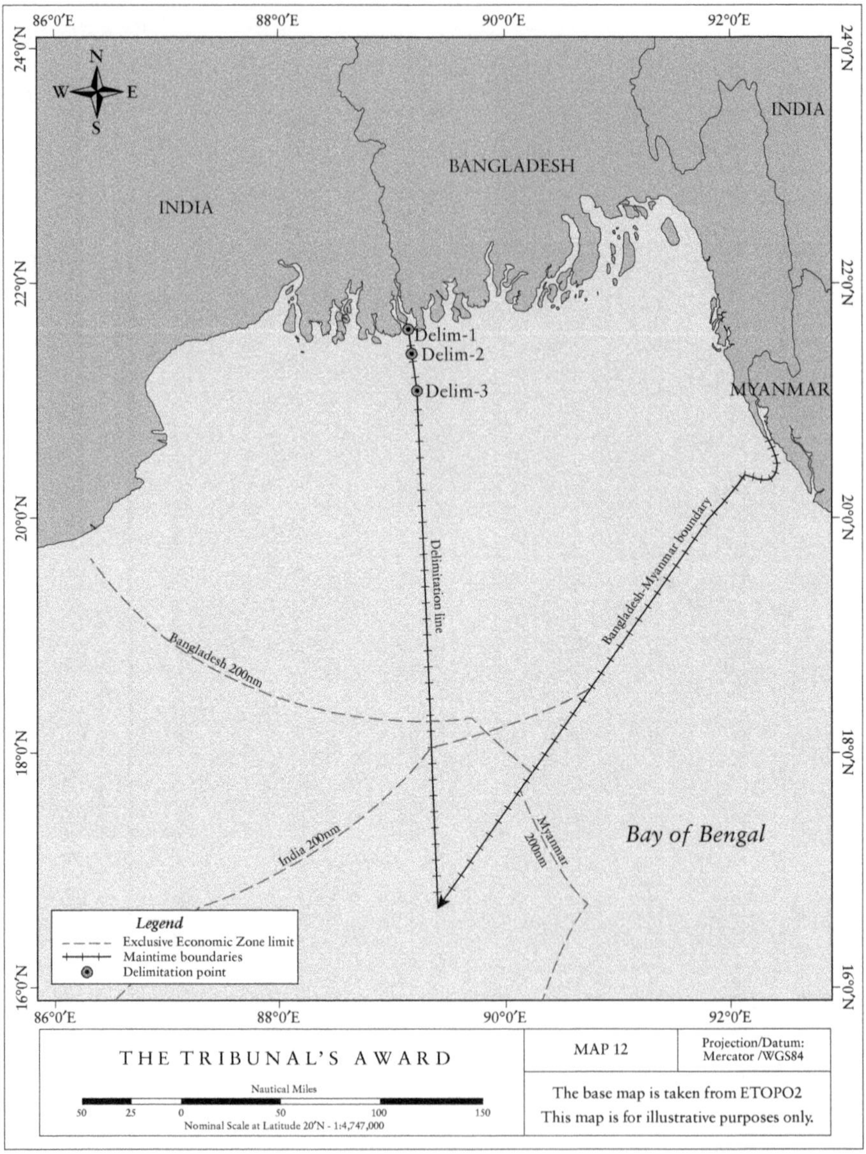

Illustration 27 Delimitation line established by the Annex VII Arbitral Tribunal in the *Bangladesh v India* Case

Source: Map 9 attached to the arbitral award of 7 July 2014, 163 available at: https://pca-cpa.org/en/cases/18/ Reproduced with permission of the Permanent Court of Arbitration (copyright holder).

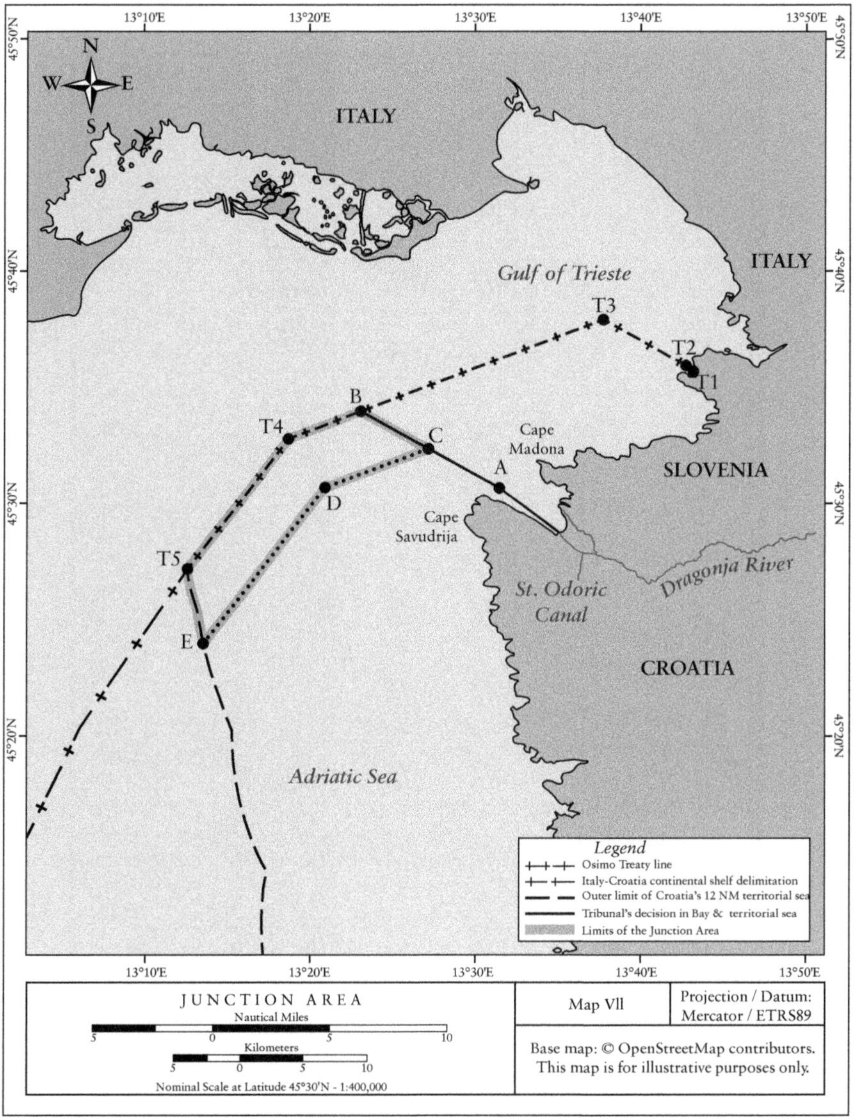

Illustration 28 Delimitation Line Established by the Arbitral Tribunal in the *Croatia/Slovenia* Case

Source: Map VII annexed to the arbitral award of 29 June 2017, 347, available at: https://pca-cpa.org/en/cases/3/ Reproduced with permission of the Permanent Court of Arbitration (copyright holder).

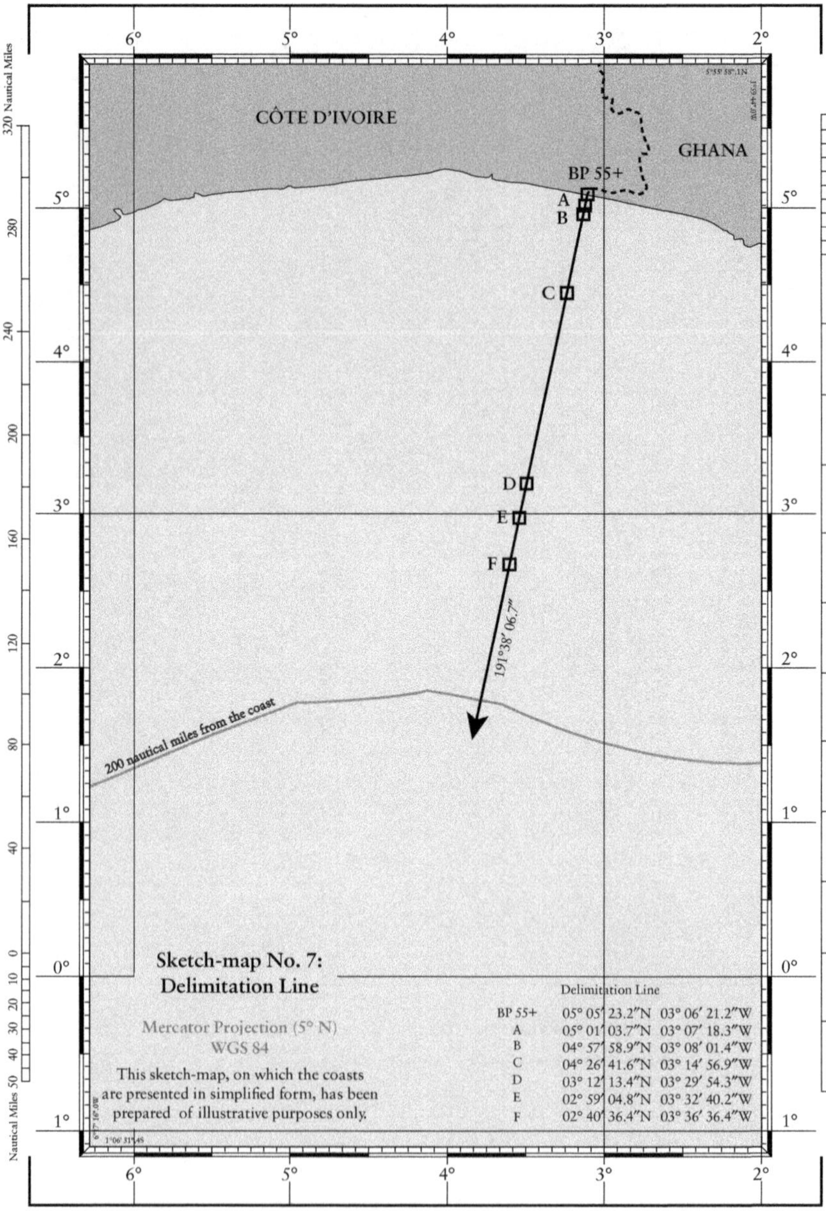

Illustration 29 Delimitation line established by the ITLOS Special Chamber in the *Ghana/Côte d'Ivoire* Case

Source: Sketch-map No. 7 annexed to the judgment, p 150, available at: https://www.itlos.org/fileadmin/itlos/documents/cases/case_no.23_merits/C23_Judgment_23.09.2017_corr.pdf.

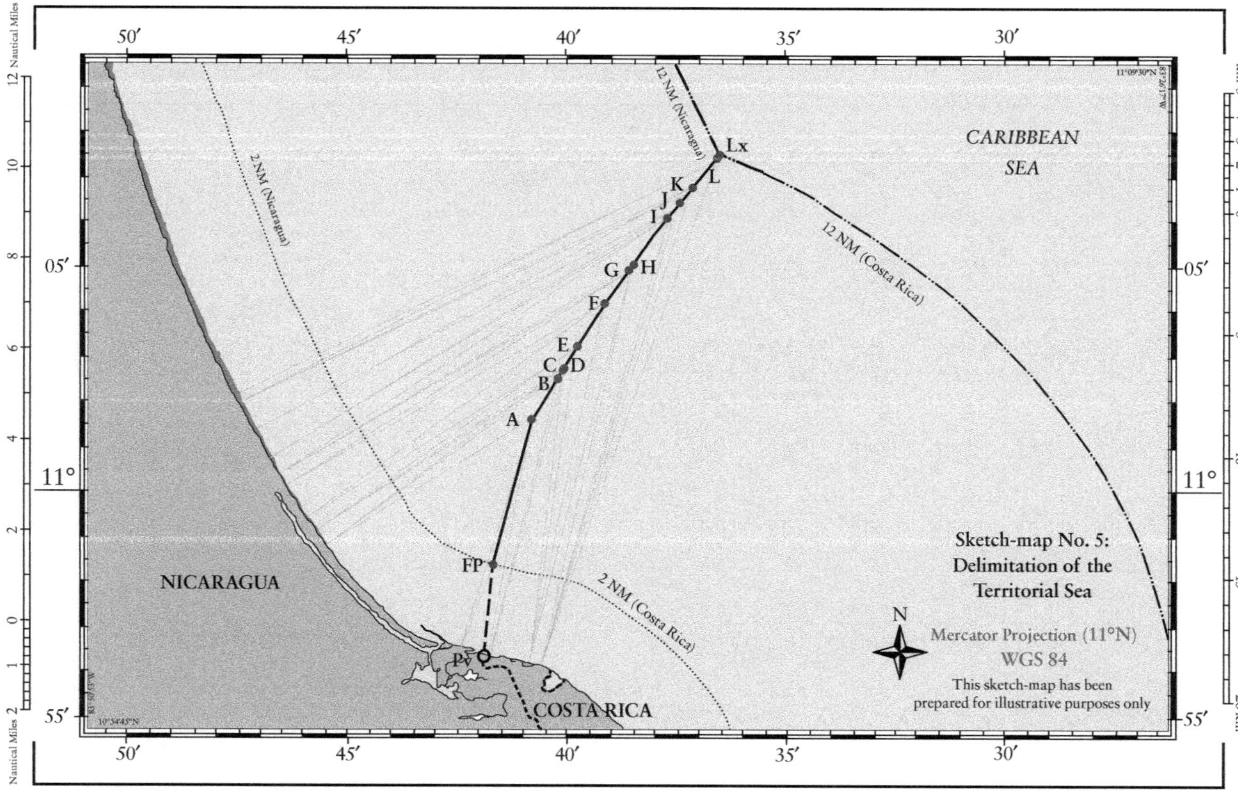

Illustration 30 Territorial Sea Boundary Established by the ICJ in the *Costa Rica v Nicaragua* Case

Source: Sketch-map No. 5 annexed to the judgment, p 43, available at: http://www.icj-cij.org/en/case/157.

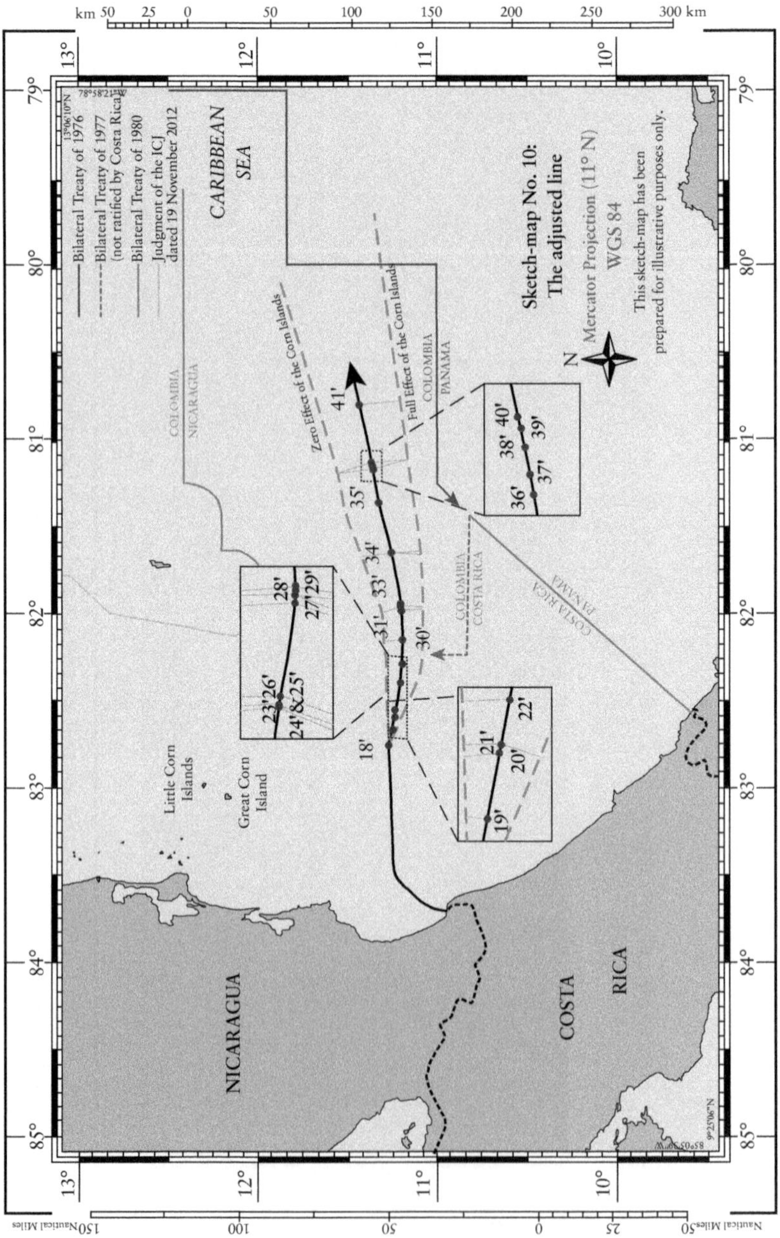

Illustration 31 The Adjusted Line Established by the ICJ in the *Costa Rica v Nicaragua* Case

Source: Sketch-map No. 10 annexed to the judgment, p 62, available at: http://www.icj-cij.org/en/case/157.

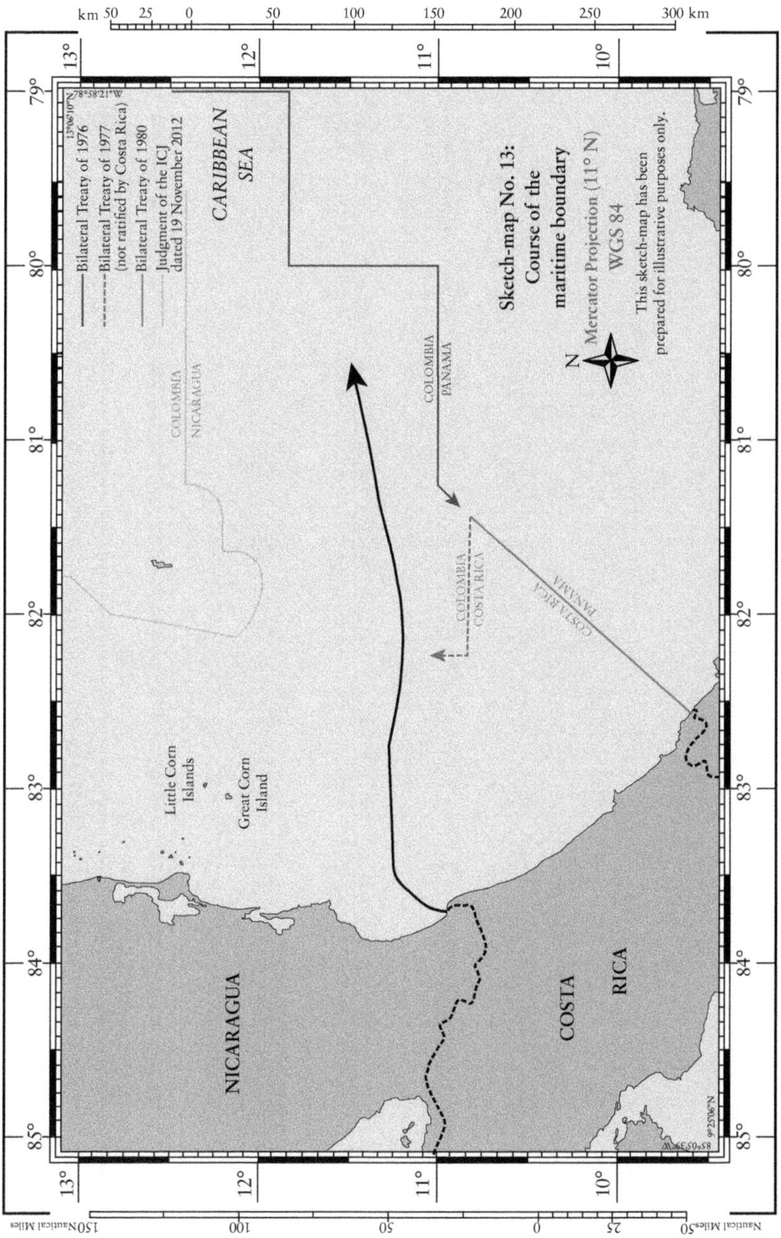

Illustration 32 Delimitation Line Established by the ICJ in the *Costa Rica v Nicaragua* Case

Source: Sketch-map No. 13 annexed to the judgment, p 68, available at: http://www.icj-cij.org/en/case/157.

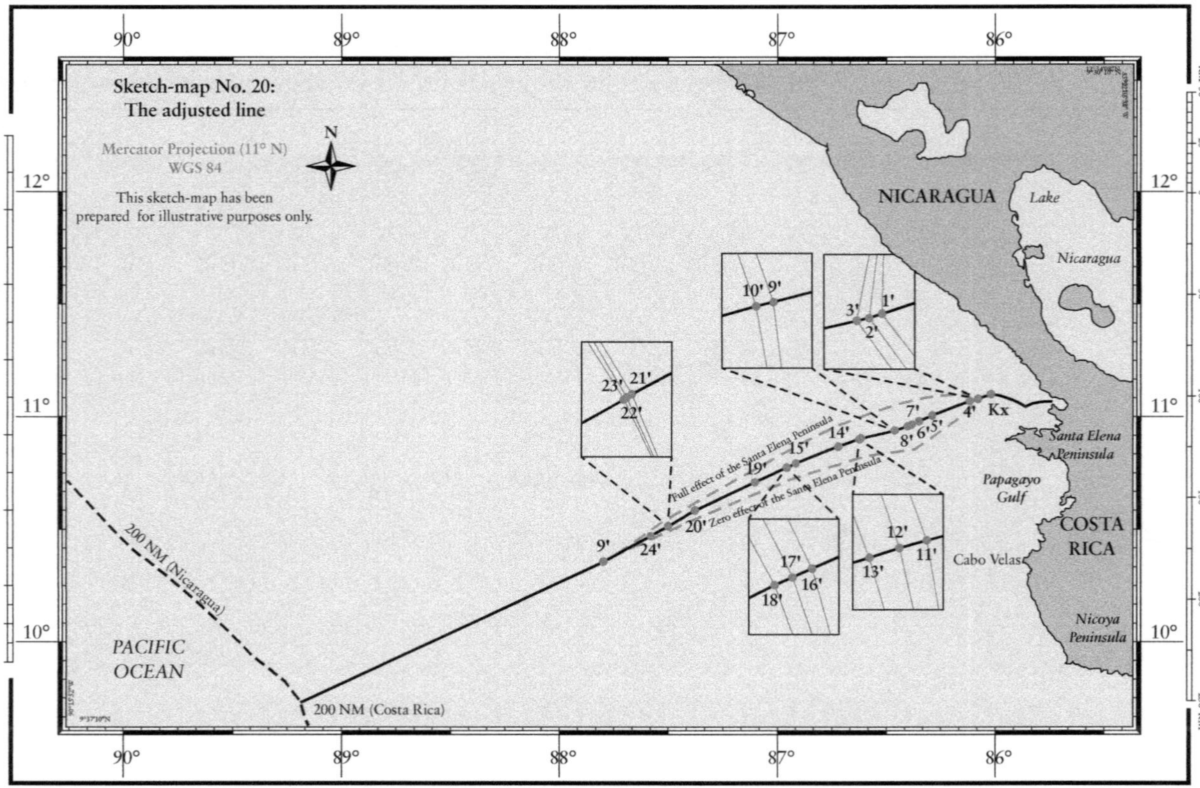

Illustration 33 The Adjusted Line Established by the ICJ in the *Costa Rica v Nicaragua* Case

Source: Sketch-map No. 20 annexed to the judgment, p 89, available at: http://www.icj-cij.org/en/case/157.

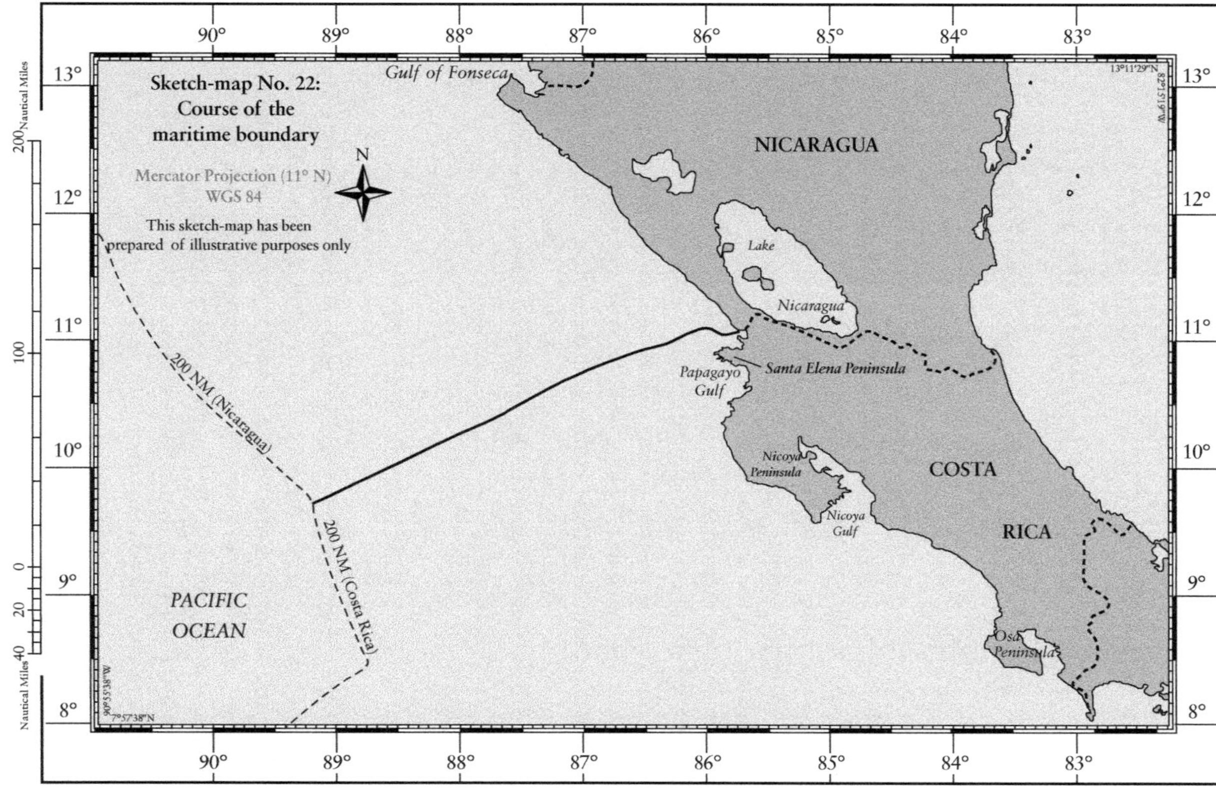

Illustration 34 Delimitation Line Established by the ICJ in the *Costa Rica v Nicaragua* Case

Source: Sketch-map No.22 annexed to the judgment, p 93, available at: http://www.icj-cij.org/en/case/157.

8

Flexibility in the Law of Maritime Delimitation II: Non-Geographical Factors

THE NEXT QUESTION to be considered is the influence of non-geographical factors upon maritime boundaries. In this respect, two points should be noted. First, in this category, factors are often interrelated. For instance, economic factors and the conduct of the Parties often overlap, since the conduct of States mainly concerns economic activities, such as fisheries and the exploration and exploitation of non-renewable resources. Furthermore, economic activities also relate to historic rights. In addition, historic rights often concern traditional livelihood or cultural factors. Considerations of security and navigation, in turn, are often connected, for security in the ocean cannot be separated from the navigation by vessels. Secondly, considering that some non-geographical factors overlap in reality, it is difficult to identify the precise effect of each of them when analysing State practice. Therefore, it should be stressed that, as in an earlier section in this chapter, the analysis solely identifies a general trend in State practice.

I. ECONOMIC FACTORS

In this section, 'economic factors' are divided into two categories. The first relates to the existence of natural resources, such as oil, gas and fish. These may be called economic factors in a strict sense. Another category pertains to socio-economic factors, such as States' economic dependency on natural resources and national economic wealth. In international adjudication, States often invoke these two types of economic factors jointly, for they are interrelated. Accordingly, it is relevant to consider them at the same time.

A. Analysis of the Case Law

i. Arguments in the Context of Continental Shelf Delimitations

a. Economic Factors in the ICJ Jurisprudence

In the *North Sea Continental Shelf* cases of 1969, the Federal Republic of Germany claimed a 'just and equitable share' of the continental shelf by referring to natural resources. On this point, on 25 October 1969, Judge Jessup asked the Parties whether the actual or probable location of known or potential resources on the continental shelf would be one of the criteria for determining a 'just and equitable share'.[1] The Agent of the Federal Republic of Germany replied, on 4 November, that: '[E]conomically exploitable resources of considerable importance, located in areas where the boundary is disputed or yet undetermined may, under the principle of the just and equitable share, be taken into account in determining the allocation of areas to one or the other State.'[2] As already indicated, however, the ICJ rejected this argument, as the concept of a 'just and equitable share' was inconsistent with the basic idea of entitlement to the continental shelf.[3] This does not mean, however, that the Court disregarded the existence of natural resources in the process of delimitation. In the operative part of its judgment, the Court indicated that '*so far as known or readily ascertainable*, the physical and geological structure, and *natural resources*, of the continental shelf areas involved' constituted factors to be taken into account in a negotiation.[4] This phrase appears to suggest that the Court considered the presence of natural resources as being a relevant circumstance.[5]

In the 1982 *Tunisia/Libya* case, economic factors produced a sharp dispute between the Parties. Tunisia invoked its relative poverty *vis-à-vis* Libya, attributing it to the absence of natural resources. Furthermore, it contended that the fishing resources derived from its claimed 'historic rights' necessarily had to be taken into account.[6] Libya argued that the presence or absence of oil or gas in the continental shelf areas appertaining to either Party should play an important role. For the rest, Libya asked the Court to dismiss as irrelevant Tunisia's argument of economic poverty.[7] In short, while Tunisia based itself on socio-economic factors, Libya involved economic factors in a strict sense, ie, the existence of natural resources in the disputed area. In this regard, the Court held that:

> [T]hese economic considerations cannot be taken into account for the delimitation of the continental shelf areas appertaining to each Party. They are virtually extraneous

[1] Verbatim Record 1968, Pleadings, Oral Arguments and Documents, *North Sea Continental Shelf* Cases, vol II, 65.

[2] Reply by Jaenicke, ibid, 164.

[3] [1969] ICJ Rep 22, [20]. See also the Separate Opinion of Judge Ammoun, ibid, 149, [53].

[4] Emphasis added. ibid, 54, [101 (D)–(2)].

[5] See also Separate Opinion of Judge Bustamante y Rivero, [1969] ICJ Rep 60, [5].

[6] The arguments concerning historic rights will be examined in s III of this chapter.

[7] [1982] ICJ Rep 77, [106].

> factors since they are variables which unpredictable national fortune or calamity, as the case may be, might at any time cause to tilt the scale one way or the other. A country might be poor today and become rich tomorrow as a result of an event such as the discovery of a valuable economic resource.[8]

Although the Court used the words 'economic considerations' in a general way, the above sentences only seem to concern the socio-economic factor, invoked by Tunisia, of the poverty or wealth of a country. Indeed, with respect to the existence of oil and gas deposits in the disputed area, the Court regarded them as being relevant circumstances, by stating that:

> As to the presence of oil-wells in an area to be delimited, it may, depending on the facts, be an element to be taken into account in the process of weighing all relevant factors to achieve an equitable result.[9]

Natural resources did not, however, come into play in the process of delimitation.[10]

The Court, in the *Libya/Malta* case, also dealt with the economic issue. In that case, Malta asked the Court to consider the absence of energy resources on the island, Malta's requirements as a developing island country, and the range of its established fishing activity.[11] Malta also contended that:

> The investigations so far carried out suggest that the most promising areas for the discovery and production of oil lie in or near the regions of Malta's southern equidistance line. Although there are also other cogent reasons, this is the fundamental reality which underlies Malta's opposition to Libya's assertion of rights north of that equidistance line.[12]

However, the Court rejected the above arguments by stating that:

> The Court does not however consider that a delimitation should be influenced by the relative economic position of the two States in question, in such a way that the area of continental shelf regarded as appertaining to the less rich of the two States would be somewhat increased in order to compensate for its inferiority in economic resources. Such considerations are totally unrelated to the underlying intention of the applicable rules of international law. It is clear that neither the rules determining the validity of legal entitlement to the continental shelf, nor those concerning delimitation between

[8] ibid, 77, [107]. However, Bowett questioned the Court's view, by saying that it is unlikely that a radical shift in economic fortunes will occur as between two neighbouring States over a short period. DW Bowett, 'The Economic Factor in Maritime Delimitation Cases' in *International Law at the Time of its Codification: Essays in Honour of Roberto Ago*, vol II (Milan, Giuffrè, 1987) 60.

[9] [1982] ICJ Rep 77–78, [107].

[10] Although the delimitation line in the first sector follows the *de facto* line of concessions, it may be said that the principal factor considered was the conduct of the Parties, not the presence of natural resources.

[11] Memorial of Malta, vol I, 478–85, [222–34]. By contrast, Libya contended that these arguments were invalid. Counter-Memorial of Libya, vol II, 59–71. See also presentation by Lucchini, Pleadings, vol IV, 133–35.

[12] Memorial of Malta, vol I, 401, [4]. Furthermore, Lauterpacht, Counsel for the Government of Malta, stated that 'the economic considerations which Malta invokes cannot in any way be described as changing or ephemeral.' Reply by Lauterpacht, Verbatim Record 1984, Oral Argument *(concluded)*, Correspondence vol IV, 318.

> neighbouring countries, leave room for any considerations of economic development of the States in question.[13]

With respect to natural resources, the Court expressed a different view, however:

> The natural resources of the continental shelf under delimitation 'so far as known or readily ascertainable' might well constitute relevant circumstances which it would be reasonable to take into account in a delimitation, as the Court stated in the North Sea Continental Shelf cases (ICJ Reports 1969, p 54, para 101 (D) (2)). Those resources are the essential objective envisaged by States when they put forward claims to sea-bed areas containing them.[14]

When drawing a continental shelf boundary, however, it was based solely on geographical factors, and economic considerations played no role in the judgment since little information had been given relating to natural resources.[15]

b. Economic Factors in the *Anglo-French Continental Shelf* Arbitration

In the *Anglo-French* Continental Shelf arbitration, socio-economic and political circumstances were at issue with respect to the Channel Islands. The United Kingdom invoked such circumstances in order to stress the importance of those territories.[16] In its view, the Channel Islands were to be given full effect by means of an equidistance line on account of their socio-economic importance. The Court of Arbitration, while accepting that the equitable considerations invoked by the United Kingdom carried a certain weight,[17] drew only a 12-mile radius around the islands. Consequently, it may be said that the weight attributed to the circumstances claimed by the United Kingdom was minimal.[18]

ii. Arguments in the Context of Single/Coincident Maritime Boundaries

a. Economic Factors in the ICJ Jurisprudence

As the Chamber of the ICJ itself accepted, the fishery resources in Georges Bank were at the heart of the *Gulf of Maine* dispute.[19] In its arguments, Canada laid great emphasis on socio-economic factors. According to Canada, these resources were vital to the people of Nova Scotia, while the economy of New England in the United States showed no comparable dependence.[20] Any single maritime boundary should safeguard vital interests of the coastal communities of the region in question. By contrast, the United States asserted

[13] [1985] ICJ Rep 41, [50].
[14] ibid.
[15] ibid.
[16] The *Anglo-French Continental Shelf* arbitral award, (1980) 18 *RIAA* 84–85, [171–73].
[17] ibid, 93, [198].
[18] Bowett, 'The Economic Factor in Maritime Delimitation Cases' 50.
[19] [1984] ICJ Rep 340, [232].
[20] Counter-Memorial of Canada, vol III, 112, [318]; 129, [355].

that the law of maritime delimitation had rejected the relevance of economic dependence and relative wealth because of their variable and unpredictable character. Furthermore, according to the United States, Canada's contentions in this regard were incomplete and factually misleading.[21] At the same time, the United States alleged that its monopoly over the Georges Bank fishery and other activities, including defence and scientific research, could not be disregarded when drawing a single maritime boundary in the area.[22]

The Chamber, however, discarded both arguments for three reasons. The first reason was related to the political and economic character of fishing and other activities, including oil exploration, scientific research and common defence. In the Chamber's view, to evaluate those activities would require an examination of valid considerations of a political and economic character. However, the Chamber was 'bound by its Statute, and required by the Parties, not to take a decision *ex aequo et bono*, but to achieve a result on the basis of law.'[23] Accordingly, such political and economic considerations are not proper for a judicial organ such as the Chamber. Secondly, in the Chamber's view, for the purposes of the delimitation of single maritime boundaries, the criteria to be applied were essentially to be determined in relation to the geographical features of the area. Only once the Chamber had envisaged a delimitation line on the basis of these criteria could other factors come into play.[24] Thirdly, according to the Chamber,

> there is no reason to consider *de jure* that the delimitation which the Chamber has now to carry out within the areas of overlapping apparent as between the respective exclusive fishery zones must result in each Party's enjoying an access to the regional fishing resources which will be equal to the access it previously enjoyed *de facto*.[25]

Consequently, it concluded that: '[T]he respective scale of activities connected with fishing – or navigation, defense or, for the matter, petroleum exploration and exploitation – cannot be taken into account as a relevant circumstance or, if the term is preferred, as an equitable criterion to be applied in determining the delimitation line.'[26]

The Chamber thus established a single maritime boundary by using neutral criteria and a geometrical method. No economic or socioeconomic factors intervened in the operational stage of the delimitation. Nevertheless, the Chamber did consider economic and socio-economic factors at the verification stage when testing the equitableness of the boundary established. While 'ineligible for consideration as criteria to be applied in the delimitation process itself',

[21] Counter-Memorial of the United States, vol IV, 6, [9]; 142, [342].
[22] Memorial of the United States, vol II, 113–14, [298–99]. See also Counter-Memorial of the United States, vol IV, 134–35, [321–28].
[23] [1984] ICJ Rep 278, [59].
[24] ibid.
[25] ibid, 342, [236].
[26] ibid, [237].

the Chamber stated, '[socioeconomic factors] may – as indicated in Section II, paragraph 59, above – be relevant to assessment of the equitable character of a delimitation first established on the basis of criteria borrowed from physical and political geography.'[27] The Chamber in effect verified whether the result would be 'radically inequitable' or entail 'catastrophic repercussions for the livelihood and economic well-being of the population of the countries concerned'[28] and came up with negative answers.[29] Yet, the test was limited merely to checking whether that test would lead to a 'radically inequitable' result.

In the *Jan Mayen* case, however, the ICJ changed its approach. In this case, both Parties emphasised the importance of their interest in capelin fishing.[30] With respect to the delimitation of the FZ, the ICJ examined whether any shift in or adjustment of a provisionally drawn median line would be required to ensure equitable access to the capelin fishery resources. In the Court's view, the median line would have been too far west for Denmark to be assured of equitable access to the capelin stock, so that the median line had to be adjusted or shifted eastward.[31] Accordingly, southernmost zone 1, which corresponded essentially to the principal fishing area, was divided into two parts of equal extent, so as to allow both Parties to enjoy equitable access.[32] By considering fishing during the delimitation process, the present judgment went in a new direction, giving economic factors a more important role.[33]

This change may be explained by two reasons. First, the Court was not requested to draw a single maritime boundary, but to create a boundary for the continental shelf and one for the FZ, which would coincide. If the case had been one of establishing a single maritime boundary, the weight of the issue of access to fishery resources would have been reduced by the application of neutral criteria which is based on purely geographical factors.[34] A second reason may be the fact that the general pattern of seasonal migration of the capelin could be identified. According to data submitted to the Court, the fishable capelin was centred in the southern part of the area of overlapping claims from July to September.[35]

[27] ibid, 340, [232].

[28] ibid, 342, [237].

[29] ibid, 343–44, [238–41].

[30] [1993] ICJ Rep 70, [73]. In fact, both Parties provided detailed data relating to fishing by their nationals. See in particular, Memorial submitted by Denmark, 48–51, [180–89]; Counter-Memorial Submitted by Norway, 40–49, [132–56]; Reply submitted by Denmark, 38–69, [101–73]; Rejoinder submitted by Norway, 27–48, [87–119].

[31] [1993] ICJ Rep 72, [76].

[32] ibid, 79–81, [92].

[33] This judgment is in clear contrast especially with the Chamber's view in the *Gulf of Maine* case. See [1984] ICJ Rep 342, [236].

[34] See R Churchill, 'The Greenland-Jan Mayen Case and Its Significance for the International Law of Maritime Boundary Delimitation' (1994) 9 *IJMCL* 27.

[35] [1993] ICJ Rep 72, [76]; Memorial submitted by Denmark, vol I, 50, [183]; Counter-Memorial submitted by Norway, vol I, 'Pattern of Location of Norwegian Capelin Catches in the Jan Mayen Area' 45–46.

The Court's reasoning creates at least two issues, however. First, what is meant by 'equitable' access?[36] In fact it is questionable whether the area's equal division guarantees equitable 'access'. Secondly, the division into two equal parts is nothing but so-called 'distributive justice', which had been rejected ever since the *North Sea Continental Shelf* cases.[37] In this respect, the Court's approach in the present case shows a clear contrast with earlier instances.[38] In subsequent cases, however, economic factors have been rarely considered by the Court when establishing maritime boundaries. The ICJ, in the *Peru v Chile* case, examined biology in the area of the maritime boundary, but only in the context of the determination of the extent of an agreed maritime boundary.[39] Therefore, it may be said that the *Jan Mayen* judgment is exceptional.

b. Economic Factors in Arbitral Awards

The relevance of economic factors was also at issue in arbitration concerning maritime delimitations. In the *Guinea/Guinea-Bissau* case, both Parties invoked factors relating to their economy, their lack of resources and their development plans, maritime transport, fishing, petroleum resources etc. It appears that their arguments related to socio-economic considerations rather than economic factors in a strict sense.[40] The Arbitral Tribunal touched on the socio-economic circumstances invoked by the Parties at the verification stage. Although showing some sympathy for the economic difficulties of the Parties, the Tribunal did not consider these circumstances as relevant:

> [T]his Tribunal has not, … acquired the conviction that economic problems constitute permanent circumstances to be taken into account for purposes of delimitation. As the Tribunal can be concerned only with a contemporary evaluation, it would be neither just nor equitable to base a delimitation on the evaluation of data which changes in relation to factors that are sometimes uncertain.[41]

This reasoning is a re-run of the *Tunisia/Libya* judgment. Furthermore, the Tribunal explicitly stated that it had no power to compensate for the economic

[36] Separate Opinion of Judge Oda, [1993] ICJ Rep 115, [94].

[37] Yet the Court in the present case, confirmed the view expressed by it in the *North Sea Continental Shelf* cases. ibid, 66–67, [64]. In any case, this question was already examined in ch 1 of this book.

[38] Separate Opinion of Judge Schwebel, [1993] ICJ Rep 120. In addition, regarding socio-economic factors, although Denmark had requested the Court to consider them in the delimitation, the Court clearly rejected this argument on the basis of its *dictum* in the *Libya/Malta* judgment. Memorial submitted by Denmark, vol I, 97–101, [302–13]; [1993] ICJ Rep 74, [80]. But, it should be noted that several Judges consider socio-economic factors as relevant. Separate Opinion of Judge Weeramantry, ibid, 267–69, [209–18]; Dissenting Opinion of Judge ad hoc Fischer, ibid, 309–10, [14]; Separate Opinion of Judge Ajibola, ibid, 301; Separate Opinion of Judge Oda, ibid, 116, [98].

[39] [2014] ICJ Rep 42–45, [104–11]. See s II of this chapter.

[40] The *Guinea/Guinea-Bissau* arbitral award, (1986) 25 *ILM* 301, [121].

[41] ibid, [122].

inequalities of States by modifying a delimitation accordingly. In its view, economic preoccupations called for cooperation, not delimitation.[42]

The negative attitude toward economic factors was echoed in the *St Pierre and Miquelon* case. As the Arbitral Tribunal itself accepted, access to and control of fisheries were central to the dispute. However, economic factors concerning fisheries were not taken into account when drawing the delimitation line since the Tribunal was neither requested nor authorised to apportion resources on the basis of need or other economic factors.[43] At the same time, the Tribunal noted that it was duty-bound to ensure that the result was not 'radically inequitable',[44] for arbitrators could not close their eyes to the impact of fishing rights and practices on the economic well-being of the people. Having applied the fisheries test, it concluded that the proposed delimitation line would not have a radical impact on existing fishing patterns in the area.[45] Obviously, the test of what is 'radically inequitable' echoes the findings in the *Gulf of Maine* case.

In the *Eritrea/Yemen* arbitration (Second Stage), both Parties stressed the importance of economic factors, including fishing. The arguments by the Parties can be divided into five subjects: (i) fishing in general, (ii) the location of fishing areas, (iii) the economic dependency of the Parties on fishing, (iv) consumption of fish by the populations of the Parties, and (v) the effect of fishing practices on the lines of delimitation proposed by the Parties.[46] On the basis of those considerations, each Party advanced the argument that essentially the delimitation line proposed by it would not alter the existing situation and historical practices, and consequently, would not have a catastrophic effect on local fishermen or on the local or national economy of the other Party, or a negative effect on the regional diet of the population of the other Party.[47] In so doing, they assumed that no solution could be equitable which would be inconsistent with long usage, which would create the danger of a catastrophic result on the local economy of one of the Parties, or which would fail to take into account the need to minimise detrimental effects on fishing communities, and the economic dislocation of States whose nationals had habitually fished in the relevant area.[48] As will be explained below, however, the Arbitral Tribunal did not accept the relevance of those factors for the present delimitation.

First, regarding fishing in general, Eritrea alleged that the Eritrean fishing industry was substantial before the civil war, and that, since the end of that war, serious efforts were underway to re-establish its fishing economy. Thus, in its view, it was a mistake to consider that the Eritrean fisheries were, as Yemen argued, to a large extent dependent on Eritrean freshwater fisheries. Furthermore, Eritrea

[42] ibid, [123].
[43] The *St Pierre and Miquelon* arbitral award, (1992) 31 *ILM* 1173, [83].
[44] ibid, [84].
[45] ibid, [85].
[46] The *Eritrea/Yemen* arbitral award (the Second Phase), (2001) 22 *RIAA* 346, [48].
[47] ibid, 346–347, [49].
[48] ibid, 347, [51].

contended that, since Yemen's fishing industry did not rely significantly on the Red Sea, it was in no way dependent for protection on the particular delimitation line proposed by Yemen.[49] By contrast, Yemen asserted that Yemeni nationals had long dominated fishing activities in the Red Sea, and that they had been of much greater significance in the past than those of Eritrea.[50] While confirming that fishing, fishermen, and fisheries were, and remain, of importance to each Party in the present case, the Tribunal, however, rejected the above arguments by stating that: '[T]he fishing practices of the Parties from time to time are not germane to the task of arriving at a line of delimitation.'[51]

Secondly, concerning economic dependency on fishing, Eritrea argued that the existing fisheries practices of its nationals should not be restricted by the delimitation to be effected. Furthermore, it stressed the significance of the future development of its fisheries.[52] Yemen alleged that its fishermen had always depended on the Red Sea fisheries and this fishing activity had long constituted an important part not only of Yemen's overall national economy but also of the regional economy of the Tihama region along the Red Sea coast.[53] Nevertheless, the Tribunal did not admit these arguments since 'it is not possible or necessary for the Tribunal to reach a conclusion that either Eritrea or Yemen is economically dependent on fishing to such an extent as to suggest any particular line of delimitation.'[54]

Thirdly, with respect to the location of fishing areas, Eritrea alleged that fishing in the Red Sea was dominated by Eritrean artisanal fishermen who caught their fish around the Dahlaks, along the Eritrean coast, around the Mohabbakahs, the Haycocks, and South West Rocks, as well as in the waters around the Zuqar-Hanish group of 'mid-sea islands', while Yemen fishermen had hardly, if at all, relied on those waters.[55] By contrast, Yemen argued that its artisanal and traditional fishermen had long fished in the waters around Jabal al-Tayr and the Zubayr group, the Zuqar-Hanish group, and in the deep waters west of Greater Hanish and around the Mohabbakahs, the Haycocks and the South-West Rocks.[56] In this regard, the Tribunal held that Eritrean fishermen had fished not only in and around the Dahlak archipelago and on inshore waters along the Eritrean coastline but also in and around the Hanish and Zuquar Islands as well as the deep waters to the west of the mid-sea islands and around the Mohabbakahs, the Haycocks and South West Rocks. At the same time, it accepted that Yemeni fishermen had operated as far north as the Dahlak archipelago, Jabal al-Tayr and the Zubayr group, and as far west as the Mohabbakahs, the Haycocks and South West Rocks. Those conclusions

[49] ibid, [52].
[50] ibid, [53].
[51] ibid, 350, [62–63].
[52] ibid, 348, [54].
[53] ibid, [55].
[54] ibid, 350, [64].
[55] ibid, 348, [56].
[56] ibid, 348–49, [57].

were already implied by the Tribunal's concern for maintenance of the traditional fishing regime 'in the region' as a whole, 'including free access and enjoyment for the fishermen of both Eritrea and Yemen' in the first phase of the Award on Sovereignty.[57]

Fourthly, both Parties alleged that their nationals consumed far more fish than those of the other Party.[58] Yet the Tribunal rejected the arguments of both sides, holding that the evidence on this matter was conflicting and uncertain. Thus, it concluded that there was no significant reason for accepting or rejecting the arguments of either Party as to the line of delimitation proposed by itself or by the other Party.[59]

Finally, regarding the effect of fishing on the delimitation lines proposed by it, each Party asserted that while the line proposed by itself would correctly reflect existing practice, the line proposed by the other Party would deprive its nationals of an important resource. However, the Tribunal ruled that it found no significant reason related to fishing for accepting or rejecting the arguments of either Party on the line of delimitation proposed by itself or by its opponent. The Tribunal thus concluded that: 'Neither Party has succeeded in demonstrating that the line of delimitation proposed by the other would produce a catastrophic or inequitable effect on the fishing activity of its nationals or detrimental effects on fishing communities and economic dislocation of its nationals.'[60]

In summary, according to the Tribunal, arguments regarding economic and socio-economic considerations had little significance in drawing the single maritime boundary. In fact, the line drawn by the Tribunal was based in essence on equidistance. Neither economic nor socio-economic factors affected its course. Nor were those circumstances taken into account even as a test of equitability. Consequently, it may be said that the role of economic factors was minimised in the present case.

Later on, economic factors were discussed in two arbitral awards. In the *Barbados v Trinidad and Tobago* case, Barbados based its claim on three core factual submissions: (i) a centuries-old history of Barbadian artisanal fishing in the waters off Tobago, (ii) critical dependence of Barbadian fisherfolk on the maintenance of access to that fishery, and (iii) non-dependence of Trinidad and Tobago's fisherfolk on fishery.[61] However, the Tribunal declined the claim since it was unable to conclude that any of the three core factual circumstances invoked

[57] ibid, 351, [65–69].
[58] ibid, 349, [58].
[59] ibid, 351–52, [70–71].
[60] ibid, 352, [72]. See also [73].
[61] The *Barbados v Trinidad and Tobago* case. (2007) 27 *RIAA* 217–218, [250]; Memorial of Barbados, 16–33, [36–73]; Reply of Barbados, 177–213, [351–421]; Presentation by Professor Reisman, 17 October 2005, 107; Presentation by Sir Henry Forde, ibid, 108–126; Presentation by Mr Fietta, 18 October 2005, 4–14.

by Barbados have been proved.[62] In this connection, the Arbitral Tribunal generally stated that:

> Resource-related criteria have been treated more cautiously by the decisions of international courts and tribunals, which have not generally applied this factor as a relevant circumstance.[63]

In the *Bangladesh v India* case, Bangladesh submitted that its people depend heavily on fish from the Bay of Bengal.[64] However, the Annex VII Arbitral Tribunal declined this submission because of the absence of sufficient evidence in this matter.[65]

c. Economic Factors in the ITLOS Jurisprudence

The issue of economic factors was discussed in the *Ghana/Côte d'Ivoire* case before ITLOS. In this case, Côte d'Ivoire invoked the location and distribution of hydrocarbon resources as a relevant circumstance. In this connection, the ITLOS Special Chamber took the view that only in extreme situations may considerations other than geographical ones become relevant. The *Ghana/Côte d'Ivoire* case is not such a case, however.[66] According to the Special Chamber, 'extreme situations' refer to the situation which is 'likely to entail catastrophic repercussions for the livelihood and economic well-being of the population of the countries concerned.'[67] This is the situation stated by the Chamber of the ICJ in the *Gulf of Main* case. Following the Chamber's view, the role of non-geographical factors, including economic factors, will be highly limited. Indeed, the Chamber in the *Ghana/Côte d'Ivoire* case did not consider the location of maritime mineral resources as a relevant circumstance.[68]

B. Analysis of State Practice

i. Agreements Regarding Delimitations of Continental Shelf

According to our research, the *direct* impact of mineral resources on the location of boundaries remains modest, even though their existence may provide an impetus for delimitation negotiations. In fact, there are but few conventions

[62] The *Barbados v Trinidad and Tobago* arbitral award, (2007) 27 *RIAA* 221, [265].
[63] ibid, 214, [241].
[64] Bangladesh's Memorial, 104, [6.63].
[65] *Bay of Bengal Maritime Boundary Arbitration between Bangladesh and India* (Bangladesh v India), Award, 7 July 2014, [424].
[66] *Dispute Concerning Delimitation of the Maritime Boundary between Ghana and Côte d'Ivoire in the Atlantic Ocean (Ghana/Côte d'Ivoire)*, [2017] ITLOS Rep (not yet reported), [453].
[67] ibid. In this regard, the Chamber relied on the *dictum* of the *Gulf of Maine* case. [1984] ICJ Rep 342, [237].
[68] The *Ghana/Côte d'Ivoire* case, [2017] ITLOS Rep [453–55].

in which the existence of mineral resources *directly* influenced the location of the boundary of a continental shelf. Exceptionally, in the 1969 Agreement between Qatar and the United Arab Emirates (Abu Dhabi), the boundary line was drawn so as to coincide with the location of the al-Bunduq oilfield at Point B.[69] Furthermore, the Parties agreed that that field was to be developed by Abu Dhabi Marine Areas, Ltd and that all revenues were to be divided equally.[70] As a similar instance, attention may also be drawn to the 1958 Agreement between Bahrain and Saudi Arabia. The dispute over the Fashat Abu-Sa'fah field was the impetus for negotiations for the establishment of a continental shelf boundary. Thus approximately 1/3 of the boundary was delimited so as to coincide with the limits of the field.[71] Consequently, the Agreement places the Fashat Abu-Sa'fah field entirely on Saudi Arabia's side. Yet Article 2 of the 1958 Agreement provides that Bahrain is entitled, under Article 2, to share equally in all petroleum revenues arising from the field.[72] In addition, it has been presumed that mineral resources were considered in the 1968 Agreement between Italy and the former Yugoslavia.[73]

There were some cases where discoveries of oil or gas reservoirs prevented agreements from entering into force. In 1965, for example, Iran and Saudi Arabia established a boundary based on equidistance. The 1965 Agreement was, however, never ratified, since the Iranian concessionaire discovered a petroleum deposit situated largely on Saudi Arabia's side of the boundary established in the Agreement. Thus, a new Agreement of 1968 established a boundary line in such a way as to apportion that deposit in an equitable manner.[74] In addition, it is reported that the 1976 Agreements between Portugal and Spain relating to the delimitation of the territorial sea and the continental shelf did not enter into force due to the discovery of gas deposits.[75] Finally, it has been said that the course of the boundary in the 1971 Agreement between Italy and Tunisia was influenced by the limits of the FZ claimed by Tunisia in 1963.[76]

ii. Agreements Regarding Single Maritime Boundaries

Regarding the drawing of single maritime boundaries, both mineral and fisheries resources are at issue.

[69] AA El-Hakim, *The Middle Eastern States and the Law of the Sea* (Manchester, MUP, 1979) 98.

[70] Art (7) of the 1969 Agreement. Text in: *IMB*, vol II, 1547–48.

[71] Report by Pietrowski, Jr in ibid, 1490–91.

[72] This does not infringe the right of sovereignty or that of administration of Saudi Arabia over that area (Art 2). For the text, see ibid, 1495–97.

[73] Report by Scovazzi and Francalanci in ibid, 1629.

[74] Report by Pietrowski in ibid, 1520–21.

[75] Report by Anderson in ibid, 1793.

[76] The Tunisian FZ was recognised in 1963, 1971 and 1976 fishing agreements between the same Parties. Nevertheless, the last fishing agreement expired in 1979, and Italy declared that the FZ of Tunisia was part of the high seas. Report by Scovazzi and Francalanci in ibid, 1614–15.

a. Fisheries Resources

The direct influence of fisheries resources on the localisation of boundaries has been limited, despite the fact that fisheries issues may constitute a leitmotiv for negotiations regarding maritime delimitation. Indeed, only a small number of conventions have considered fisheries resources for determining the location of boundaries. A serious impact of fisheries resources will be found in some agreements.

A typical example is the 1988 Agreement between Sweden and the former Soviet Union. In the negotiation between Sweden and the former USSR regarding the delimitation of the continental shelf, and of the Swedish FZ and the Soviet EEZ, fisheries were a vital issue. On 13 January 1988, this question was resolved by the Agreement on the Principles for Delimitation of the Sea Areas in the Baltic Sea. The Agreement provides that, during a period of 20 years after the line had been established, Sweden shall allow the Soviet Union, in its part of the previously disputed zone, an annual quota of 18,000 tons; and conversely, the Soviet Union shall allow Sweden an annual quota of 6000 tons on the Soviet side of the disputed zone.[77] On 18 April 1988, the final single maritime boundary was established by attributing 75 per cent of the disputed area to Sweden and 25 per cent to the USSR. Reportedly, for the former USSR, the fisheries arrangement in the Agreement of 13 January 1988 was an important condition for accepting a 25/75 per cent division of the disputed area.[78]

Furthermore, in 1980, Norway signed an agreement concerning fishery and continental shelf questions with Iceland, accepting Iceland's full 200-mile EEZ. It has been suggested that Iceland's dependence upon fisheries was a reason for Norway to accept Iceland's full 200-mile EEZ.[79] Following the recommendation by a Conciliation Commission, Iceland and Norway agreed in the Agreement of 1981 that the delimitation line of the continental shelf shall coincide with the delimitation line for the Parties' economic zone.[80] Moreover, it is suggested that access to fish stocks influenced the location of delimitation lines in the 1997 Agreement between Denmark and Iceland,[81] the Additional Protocol of 1997 between Iceland and Norway[82] and the 1997 Additional Protocol between

[77] Report by Franckx in ibid, vol II, 2060–61. Text in ibid, 2067–75.

[78] Regarding the negotiation of this Agreement, see Report by Franckx in ibid, 2057–65; Alex G Oude Elferink, *The Law of Maritime Boundary Delimitation: A Case Study of the Russian Federation* (Dordrecht, Nijhoff, 1994) 200–19 (in particular, 212). In addition, it should not be forgotten that the effect of the island of Gotland was also an important issue. That island was given a 75% effect.

[79] Report by Anderson in *IMB*, vol II, 1757. At the same time, security considerations might have affected the concessions made by Norway.

[80] Art 1. Agreement on the Continental shelf between Iceland and Jan Mayen. Text in ibid, vol II, 1762–65.

[81] Report by Anderson in ibid, vol IV, 2945. Text in ibid, 2951–53.

[82] Iceland's overwhelming dependence upon fisheries was also accepted in the Additional Protocol of 1997. Report by Anderson in ibid, vol IV, 2905. Text in ibid, 2910–11.

Denmark and Norway, respectively.[83] Finally, it may be presumed that, in the 1989 Agreement between Poland and Sweden, part of the boundary was created on the basis of fisheries considerations.[84]

b. Mineral Resources

Usually, the *direct* influence of mineral resources on the localisation of delimitation has also been slight. Yet, in some cases, such an influence could be identified. For instance, it is suggested that in the 1978 Agreement between the Netherlands (Antilles) and Venezuela, the boundary was drawn so as to preserve the jurisdiction of the Netherlands on the west side of Aruba, which had potential hydrocarbon deposits.[85] Furthermore, in the 1989 Agreement between Trinidad and Tobago and Venezuela, the equidistance line was modified in the Columbus Channel and in the southeastern sector for the purpose of preserving the integrity of the existing oil fields and concessions.[86] In addition, it is suggested that, in the Agreement between Burma and India of 1986, potential fields of natural gas or petroleum might have influenced the location of the boundary.[87]

iii. Three Flexible Solutions in State Practice

The above observation shows that in both the delimitation of the continental shelf and the drawing of a single maritime boundary, the *direct* influence of economic factors has been limited in treaty practice, although such factors may constitute a leitmotiv for concluding delimitation agreements.[88] It is not suggested, however, that economic factors have been totally ignored in agreements on maritime delimitation. As will be indicated below, State practice has adopted flexible solutions in this field. In this regard, three solutions merit being highlighted: common deposit clause and unitisation, joint development, and combination of a maritime delimitation agreement and a fishery agreement.

a. Common Deposit Clause

The first solution has been achieved by including a common deposit clause. That clause relates to transboundary mineral resources, including petroleum.

[83] Report by Anderson, ibid, 2915. Text in ibid, 2919.

[84] Report by Franckx in ibid, vol II, 2079.

[85] B Kwiatkowska, 'Economic and Environmental Considerations' in ibid, vol I, 91; Report by Nweihed in ibid, vol I, 620.

[86] Report by Nweihed in ibid, 665.

[87] Report by Cooper in ibid, vol II, 1331.

[88] As of 1993, Kwiatkowska identified only 27 agreements taking into account economic factors, ie, mineral resources, fisheries, and general economies out of over 130 instances. Kwiatkowska, 'Economic and Environmental Considerations' 111.

Since petroleum is liquid, if the stresses at one point of the area are different from those at another point, the petroleum will move until the different stresses are equalised. Accordingly, when a Party exploits a single petroleum reservoir, such exploitation will interfere with the neighbouring State's right to the petroleum in the reservoir by causing it to flow from one side of the boundary to the other.[89] In order to avoid such situations, many conventions creating maritime boundaries contain a 'common deposit clause', or 'mineral deposit clause'.[90] A typical example of such a clause is Article 4 of the 1965 Agreement between Norway and the United Kingdom Relating to the Delimitation of the Continental Shelf:

> If any single geological petroleum structure or petroleum field, or any single geological structure or field of any other mineral deposit, including sand or gravel, extends across the dividing line and the part of such structure or field which is situated on one side of the dividing line is exploitable, wholly or in part, from the other side of the dividing line, the Contracting Parties shall, in consultation with the licensees, if any, seek to reach agreement as to the manner in which the structure or field shall be most effectively exploited and the manner in which the proceeds deriving therefrom shall be apportioned.[91]

The above-quoted clause in essence forwards the idea of 'unitisation' that requires the Parties to cooperate with each other in the exploration or exploitation of transboundary mineral resources.[92] Unitisation seeks to permit the efficient development of the entire transboundary deposit as a unity and avoid wasteful duplication of effort to drain the deposit on the two sides of the boundary.[93] Unitisation is provided in comparatively many maritime delimitation agreements, such as: the 2006 Agreement between Denmark (Greenland) and Norway (Svalbard),[94] the 2009 Agreement between Albania and Greece,[95] the 2007 Agreement between Norway and the Russian Federation,[96] the 2010 Treaty between Grenada and Trinidad and Tobago,[97] the 2010 Agreement

[89] C Robson, 'Transboundary Petroleum Reservoirs: Legal Issues and Solutions' in GH Blake et al (eds), *The Peaceful Management of Transboundary Resources* (Dordrecht, Nijhoff, 1995) 5; R Lagoni, 'Oil and Gas Deposits Across National Frontiers' (1979) 73 *AJIL* 217.

[90] In fact, approximately 50 agreements concerning maritime boundaries contain common deposit clauses. For a detailed examination of common deposit clauses, see Kwiatkowska, 'Economic and Environmental Considerations' 86–90. See also by the same writer, 'Resource, Navigational and Environmental Factors in Equitable Maritime Boundary Delimitation Practice' in *IMB*, vol V, 3228; DM McRae and C Yacouba, 'The Legal Regime of Maritime Boundary Agreement' in ibid, 3291–93.

[91] Text in: *IMB*, vol II, 1886.

[92] Mouton voiced the same idea in his lecture at the Hague Academy of International Law in 1954. MW Mouton, 'The Continental Shelf' (1954) 85 *RCADI* 421. For examples of treaties providing unitisation, see Appendix, s VI of this book.

[93] Report by Smith, *IMB*, vol VII, 4650.

[94] Art 2. Text in ibid, vol VI, 4529.

[95] Art 3. Text in ibid, 4470.

[96] Art 3. Text in ibid, 4485.

[97] Art VII. Text in ibid, vol VII, 4716.

between Cyprus and Israel,[98] the 2010 Treaty between Norway and the Russian Federation,[99] the 2012 Agreement between the Cook Island and Kiribati,[100] the 2012 Agreement between the Cook Islands and Niue,[101] the 2012 Agreement between Kiribati and Marshall Islands,[102] the 2012 Agreement between Kiribati and Nauru,[103] the 2012 Agreement between Kiribati and Tuvalu, and[104] the 2012 Agreement between Marshall Islands and Nauru.[105] In some cases, States concluded a unitisation agreement for the exploitation of hydrocarbon or gas reservoirs. By way of example, the United Kingdom and Norway concluded the Frigg Reservoir Agreement in 1976 on the basis of such a clause.[106] Similar examples include: the 1965 Agreement between the Netherlands and the United Kingdom,[107] the 2005 Framework Agreement between Norway and the United Kingdom,[108] the 2007 and 2010 Agreements between Trinidad and Tobago and Venezuela,[109] the 2008 Agreement between Norway and Iceland, and[110] the 2012 Agreement between Mexico and the United States.[111]

In other agreements, the exploitation of single transboundary petroleum reservoirs is explicitly forbidden unless the Parties agree otherwise. For instance, Article 2 of the 1974 Agreement between Iran and the United Arab Emirates (Dubai) prescribes that, if single petroleum or other mineral deposits can be exploited wholly or in part, '(a) No well shall be drilled on either side of the Boundary line as set out in Article (1) so that any producing section thereof is less than 125 meters from the said Boundary line, except by mutual agreement

[98] Art 2. Text in ibid, 5100.

[99] Art 5(2). Text in ibid, 5189. See also, I Fodchenko, 'Legal Aspects of the Russian-Norwegian Model for Cross-Border Utilization in the Barents Sea and Arctic Ocean' (2018) 49 *ODIL* 262.

[100] Art 3. Text in *IMB*, vol VII, 4855.

[101] Art 3. Text in (2014) 82 *Law of the Sea Bulletin* 51; *IMB*, vol VII, 4866.

[102] Art 3. Text in *IMB*, vol VII, 4877.

[103] Art 3. Text in ibid, 4889.

[104] Art 3. Text in (2014) 83 *Law of the Sea Bulletin* 37; *IMB*, vol VII, 4911.

[105] Art 3. Text in *IMB*, vol VII, 4922.

[106] Text in ibid, vol V, 3951; *Treaty Series,* No 113 (1977) Cmnd 7043. For an analysis of the Agreement, see JC Woodliffe, 'International Unitization of an Offshore Gas Field' (1977) 26 *ICLQ* 338; WT Onorato, 'Joint Development of Seabed Hydrocarbon Resources: An Overview of Precedents in the North Sea' (1981) 6 *Energy* 1311; Robson, 'Transboundary Petroleum Reservoirs' 9–12. Owing to the elaborate provisions relating to the mechanisms for the exploitation and co-ordination of the activities of exploitation by the States' respective licensees, that Agreement will provide a useful model for the exploitation of transboundary mineral resources. Robson, ibid, 19.

[107] Agreement between the Government of the Kingdom of the Netherlands and the Government of the United Kingdom of Great Britain and Northern Ireland relating to the exploitation of single geological structures extending across the dividing line on the continental shelf under the North Sea, 6 October 1965. Entered into force 23 December 1966. The text is available at: www.un.org/Depts/los/LEGISLATIONANDTREATIES/PDFFILES/TREATIES/NLD-GBR1965GS.PDF.

[108] Text in *IMB*, vol VII, 5219.

[109] Text in ibid, 4656 and 4674.

[110] The 2008 Agreement establishes comprehensive procedures of energy cooperation concerning transboundary hydrocarbon deposits situated along previously delimited maritime boundaries between Iceland and Norway. Report by Fife, ibid, 5130–31. Text in ibid, 5135.

[111] Text in *IMB*, vol VII, 4625.

between the two Governments.'[112] The 2008 Agreement between Iceland and Norway provides another example.[113]

The validity of common mineral deposits clauses has been confirmed by the Arbitral Tribunal in the *Eritrea/Yemen* arbitration of 1999, stating that:

> [H]aving regard to the maritime boundary established by this Award, the Parties are bound to inform one another and to consult one another on any oil and gas and other mineral resources that may be discovered that straddle the single maritime boundary between them or that line in its immediate vicinity. Moreover, the historical connections between the people concerned, and the friendly relations of the Parties that have been restored since the Tribunal's rendering of its Award on Sovereignty, together with the body of State practice in the exploitation of resources that straddle maritime boundaries, import that Eritrea and Yemen should give every consideration to the shared or joint or unitised exploitation of any such resources.[114]

Owing to the liquidity of petroleum, the idea of unitisation of the common mineral deposit is reasonable when exploiting single transboundary petroleum reservoirs.[115] By inserting common deposit clauses, it will be possible both to create maritime boundaries and to resolve the problem of transboundary mineral resources.

b. Joint Development

The second solution is to establish a regime of joint development. The concept of 'joint development' has not been uniformly understood.[116] In this study, 'joint development' is defined as an inter-governmental agreement purported to

[112] Text in *IMB*, vol II, 1538.

[113] Art 1. Text in ibid, vol VII, 5135.

[114] The *Eritrea/Yemen* arbitral award (The Second Phase), (2001) 22 *RIAA* 356, [86].

[115] In this connection, a question which arises is whether a State may unilaterally develop transboundary resources without the agreement of its neighbours. Considering that unilateral development may jeopardise the profits of neighbours, the answer would have to be negative. In fact, such a development would be contrary to equity and to the spirit of Arts 74(3) and 83(3) of the LOSC which state that: 'Pending agreement as provided for in para 1, the States concerned in a spirit of understanding and co-operation, shall make every effort to enter into provisional arrangements of a practical nature and, during this transitional period, not to jeopardize or hamper the reaching of the final agreement.' Under those provisions, thus, it may be said that there is an obligation to refrain from unilateral development, where an irreparable damage to the natural resources might occur. Other writers take the same view from the angle of customary law. Lagoni, 'Oil and Gas Deposits Across National Frontiers' 235; WT Onorato, 'Apportionment of an International Common Petroleum Deposit' (1977) 26 *ICLQ*, 327; DM Ong, 'Joint Development of Common Offshore Oil and Gas Deposits: "Mere" State Practice or Customary International Law?' (1999) 93 *AJIL* 799; M Miyoshi, 'The Basic Concept of Joint Development of Hydrocarbon Resources on the Continental Shelf With Special Reference to the Discussions at the East-West Centre Workshops on the South-East Asian Seas' (1988) 3 *IJECL* 10.

[116] On this point, see Miyoshi, ibid, 5–6; G Zhiguo, 'Legal Aspects of Joint Development in International Law' in MK Atmadja, TA Mensah and BH Oxman (eds), *Sustainable Development an Preservation of the Oceans: The Challenges of UNCLOS and Agenda 21, Proceedings of the Law of the Sea Institute 29th Annual Conference in, 1995* (Honolulu, University of Hawaii, 1997) 631–33.

establish joint exploration and/or exploitation of living or non-living resources in a designated zone.[117] Such a regime may be provisional or permanent.[118] These agreements fall into two categories.[119]

The first category relates to areas where maritime boundaries are being established. In such areas, there have been some agreements in which the Parties have established a joint development zone straddling a delimitation line. Regarding fisheries resources, for instance, the 1978 Agreement on the Delimitation of Marine and Submarine Areas and Maritime Cooperation between the Dominican Republic and Colombia established a common scientific research and fishing zone, which was bisected by a single maritime boundary.[120] Such common fisheries zones were also set up in other instruments, such as the 1973 Agreement between Argentina and Uruguay Relating to the Delimitation of the River Plate and the Maritime Boundary,[121] the 1986 Agreement between France and Italy,[122] the 1983 Agreement between Italy and Yugoslavia,[123] and the 1999 Agreement between the United Kingdom and Denmark (Faroe Islands).[124]

[117] The British Institute of International and Comparative Law defines joint development as 'an agreement between two States to develop so as to share jointly in agreed proportions by inter-State cooperation and national measures the offshore oil and gas in a designated zone of the seabed and subsoil of the continental shelf to which both or either of the participating States are entitled in international law. Where the States recognise an EEZ the foregoing definition can be amended to extend also to the agreement jointly to develop overlapping EEZs.' H Fox et al (ed), *Joint Development of Offshore Oil and Gas: A Model Agreement for States for Joint Development with Explanatory Commentary* (London, British Institute of International and Comparative Law, 1989) 45.

[118] Some writers characterise joint development as a provisional nature. For instance, Zhiguo, 'Legal Aspects of Joint Development in International Law' 639. However, regarding the first category of joint development, ie, joint development in areas where maritime boundaries are being established, such a régime could be permanent one.

[119] Miyoshi, 'The Basic Concept of Joint Development' 3. The purpose of this sub-division is not to analyse each and every regime of joint development, but only to present typical examples briefly. Regarding the studies on joint development in general, see in particular, M Miyoshi, 'The Joint Development of Offshore Oil and Gas in Relation to Maritime Boundary Delimitation' *Maritime Briefing*, vol 2 (University of Durham, International Boundaries Research Unit, 1999) 1. This article includes many illustrations regarding joint development zones in State practice. See also, by the same author, 'Some Comments on the Legal Aspects of Precedents for Joint Development' (1981) 6 *Energy* 1359; RW Smith, 'Joint (Development) Zones: A Review of Past Practice and Thoughts on the Future' in MK Atmadja et al, *Sustainable Development an Preservation of the Oceans*, 645–62; D Colson, 'The Legal Regime of Maritime Boundary Agreement' in *IMB*, vol I, 54–60; Ong, 'Joint Development of Common Offshore Oil and Gas Deposits' 771–804; MJ Valencia, 'Taming Troubled Waters: Joint Development of Oil and Mineral Resources in Overlapping Claim Areas' (1986) 23 *San Diego Law Review* 661; I Brownlie, 'Legal Status of Natural Resources in International Law (Some Aspects)' (1979) 162 *RCADI* 289; McRae and Yacouba, 'The Legal Regime of Maritime Boundary Agreement' 3293–95. Moreover in 1989, British Institute of International and Comparative Law adopted 'A Model Agreement for States for Joint Development.' Fox et al, *Joint Development of Offshore Oil and Gas*, 387–416.

[120] Art III. Text in *IMB*, vol I, 488–90.

[121] Art 73. Text in ibid, 764–66.

[122] Art 2. Text in ibid, vol II, 1578–80.

[123] Report by Scovazzi and Francalanci in ibid, 1641.

[124] Art 5. Report by Anderson with the text of the Agreement in ibid, vol IV, 2955–77. See also CR Symmons, *Ireland and the Law of the Sea*, 2nd edn (Dublin, Round Hall Sweet & Maxwell Dublin, 2000) 337–39.

With respect to mineral resources, the 1981 Agreement between Norway and Iceland provides a typical example of a joint development zone. Considering Iceland's total dependence upon imports of hydrocarbon products and the very low hydrocarbon potential of the continental shelf of Iceland, the Conciliation Commission, in 1981, recommended the adoption of a joint development agreement covering essentially the entire area offering any significant prospect of hydrocarbon production.[125] Following the recommendation, Norway and Iceland agreed, in 1981, to establish a joint development zone straddling the single maritime boundary between the Parties.[126] To the north of the delimitation line, Iceland was to be entitled to participate with a share of 25 per cent in the petroleum production by virtue of Article 5, while, to the south of that line, Norway was to be entitled to participate in that production to the same extent in accordance with Article 6.[127] Such a joint development zone was also set up by the 1974 Agreement between France and Spain Concerning the Delimitation of the Continental Shelf in the Bay of Biscay.[128]

Furthermore, it is suggested that Tunisia and Libya signed agreements concerning the creation of a joint venture for oil exploration and exploitation in the Gulf of Gabes, and the financing of joint projects.[129] The agreed-upon zone appears to be divided into two parts by the continental shelf boundary indicated in the *Tunisia/Libya* judgment of 1982. With respect to the northwest part of the joint exploration zone, a joint Tunisian/Libyan exploration company was to be established in order to explore the gas-field. Concerning the southeast part of the joint exploration zone, which corresponds to the El Bouri oilfields on the Libyan continental shelf, Tunisia was to receive 10 per cent of the income from future production by separate agreement.[130]

More recently, Australia and Timor-Leste created the Greater Sunrise Special Regime for joint development of the Greater Sunrise gas fields in the 2018 Treaty between Australia and the Democratic Republic of Timor-Leste Establishing Their Maritime Boundaries in the Timor Sea.[131] Australia and Timor-Leste

[125] Report and Recommendations to the Governments of Iceland and Norway of the Conciliation Commission on the Continental Shelf Area between Iceland and Jan Mayen (1981) 20 *ILM* 826. For analysis of the joint development in some detail, see W Østreng, 'Reaching Agreement on International Exploitation of Ocean Mineral Resources with Special Reference to the Joint Development Area between Jan Mayen and Iceland' (1985) 10 *Energy* 555; see also RR Churchill, 'Maritime Delimitation in the Jan Mayen Area' (1985) 9 *Marine Policy* 16.

[126] Text in *IMB*, vol II, 1762–65.

[127] On the other hand, the costs of the survey in that zone were borne by Norway (Art 3). ibid, 1763. The extent of participation rights were clarified by the 2008 Agreed Minutes. For the text of the Minutes, see *IMB*, vol VII, 5141.

[128] Text in ibid, 1732–33.

[129] Report by Scovazzi in ibid, 1664; Fox et al, *Joint Development of Offshore Oil and Gas*, 63–65. The official texts of the agreements concerning joint development are not publicly available. Miyoshi points to the fact that the agreed scheme is similar to the proposition by Judge ad hoc Evensen in the *Tunisia/Libya* case of 1982. Miyoshi, 'The Joint Development of Offshore Oil and Gas' 36.

[130] Fox et al, *Joint Development of Offshore Oil and Gas* 64.

[131] The electronic text is available at: http://dfat.gov.au/geo/timor-leste/Documents/treaty-maritime-arrangements-australia-timor-leste.pdf.

agreed to share upstream revenue, meaning revenue derived directly from the upstream exploitation of Petroleum produced in the Greater Sunrise Fields: (a) in the ratio of 30 per cent to Australia and 70 per cent to Timor-Leste in the event that the Greater Sunrise Fields are developed by means of a Pipeline to Timor-Leste; or (b) in the ratio of 20 per cent to Australia and 80 per cent to Timor-Leste in the event that the Greater Sunrise Fields are developed by means of a Pipeline to Australia.[132] In this regard, the *Timor-Leste/Australia* Conciliation Commission significantly assisted the Parties to facilitate a decision on the development concept for Greater Sunrise, inter alia, by elaborating draft framework agreements.[133] The creation of joint development regime for Greater Sunrise, independent of the establishment of a seabed boundary, merits particular attention since it can provide a flexible solution, facilitating the agreement on the establishment of maritime boundaries.

Moreover, concerning both living and non-living resources, a joint development zone was established by the 1993 Agreement between Senegal and Guinea-Bissau.[134] Resources produced from the exploitation of that zone were to be shared in proportions of 50:50 regarding fishery resources, and, regarding resources of the continental shelf, 85 per cent to Senegal and 15 per cent to Guinea-Bissau pursuant to Article 2. For the exploitation of the zone, an International Agency, which has wide-ranging functions, was established by virtue of Article 4. According to Article 6 of the 1995 Protocol of Agreement, the Agency was to hold exclusive mineral or oil titles and fishing rights in that zone.[135]

Finally, as a special case, Bahrain and Saudi Arabia agreed equally to share oil revenues from the Fashat Abu-Sa'fah field in the 1958 Agreement creating a continental shelf boundary.[136] The 1969 Agreement between Qatar and the United Arab Emirates (Abu Dhabi) furnishes another example.[137]

The second category of joint development schemes relates to areas where delimitation was not or could not be effected.[138] In such areas, the Parties preferred, in some cases, to create joint development zones without drawing a delimitation line. An example is the joint development zone created in the 1974 Agreement between Japan and South Korea. In the East China Sea, the

[132] Annex B, Article 2(2).

[133] *Report and Recommendations on the Compulsory Conciliation Commission between Timor-Leste and Australia on the Timor Sea*, 9 May 2018, [279], available at: https://pca-cpa.org/en/cases/132/.

[134] Text in *IMB*, vol III, 2257–59.

[135] The competence of the Agency is defined in detail in the Protocol of Agreement Relating to the Organization and Operation of the Agency for Management and Co-operation between the Republic of Senegal and the Republic of Guinea-Bissau of 1995. For the text, ibid, pp 2260–78.

[136] Report by Pietrowski, Jr, *IMB*, vol II, 1490. See also IT Gault, 'Offshore Boundary Delimitation in the Arabian/Persian Gulf' in DM Johnston and PM Saunders (eds), *Ocean Boundary Making: Regional Issues and Developments* (London, Croom Helm, 1988) 212–14.

[137] Text in: *IMB*, vol II, 1547–48.

[138] The examination of the rights and obligation of States in undelimited areas falls outside scope of this book. On this subject, see British Institute of International and Comparative Law, *Report on the Obligations of States under Articles 73(3) and 83(3) of UNCLOS in respect of Undelimited Maritime Areas* (London, British Institute of International and Comparative Law, 2016).

continental shelf claims of the Parties overlapped considerably. As already indicated, while South Korea based its claim on the concept of natural prolongation, Japan insisted on the equidistance line as a boundary. In search of a breakthrough, both Parties agreed on joint development in the overlapping area.[139] According to the 1974 Agreement, in the joint development of the southern part of the continental shelf adjacent to the two countries, each Party shall authorise one or more concessionaires with respect to each subzone in accordance with Article IV. Concessionaires of both Parties shall be entitled to an equal share of natural resources extracted in the Joint Development Zone. Expenses for exploration and exploitation of natural resources shall be shared equally between the concessionaires of both Parties pursuant to Article IX. Furthermore, the Japan–South Korea Joint Commission was established as a means of consultation on matters concerning the implementation of the Agreement by virtue of Article XXIV(1). While all resolutions, recommendations and other decisions of the Commission shall be made only by agreement between the national sections under Article XXIV(3), the Parties shall respect to the extent possible recommendations made by the Commission in accordance with Article XXV(2). This Agreement remains in force for 50 years under Article XXXI(2). It should be stressed that nothing in this Agreement prejudices the position of the respective Parties with respect to the delimitation of the continental shelf under Article XXVIII.[140]

Another illustrative example is the joint development zone established in the 2001 Treaty between Nigeria and São Tomé and Principe. This Treaty created a joint development zone of around 34,540 square kilometres for the primary purpose of exploiting and sharing petroleum. Resources are to be shared between the two countries in the proportions 60 per cent for Nigeria and 40 per cent for São Tomé and Principe pursuant to Articles 3 and 18.[141] Interestingly, 'Special Regime Area' was established in the Joint Development Zone. Nigeria has the exclusive right to administer the Special regime Area and exercises jurisdiction over it, including the right to exploit and develop its resources for its own benefit.[142] It would seem to follow that the Treaty created a dual regime governing the exploitation of petroleum and other natural resources.

The joint development area between Malaysia and Thailand in the Gulf of Thailand also merits mention.[143] Due to mutual interest in the oil and gas

[139] For a detailed analysis of this Agreement, see M Miyoshi, 'The Japan-South Korea Agreement on Joint Development of the Continental Shelf' (1985) 10 *Energy* 545; CH Park, 'Joint Development of Mineral Resources in Disputed Waters: The Case of Japan and South Korea in the East China Sea' (1981) 6 *Energy* 1335; C Mizukami, *Nippon to Kaiyōhō* (Japan and the Law of the Sea in Japanese (Tokyo, Yūshindō, 1995)) 119–34.

[140] Text in *IMB*, vol I, 1073–89.

[141] For an analysis of this Treaty, see Report by Daniel, *IMB*, vol V, 3638–82.

[142] Appendix of the 2001 Treaty, ibid, 3681.

[143] Regarding that joint development Agreement in some detail, see DM Ong, 'The 1979 and 1990 Malaysia-Thailand Joint Development Agreements: A Model for International Legal Co-operation in Common Offshore petroleum Deposits?' (1999) 14 *IJMCL* 207.

potential of that area, the claims of the two States over the continental shelf overlapped. Having failed to establish a continental shelf boundary, the Parties, in 1979, determined to carry out exploitation in the overlapping area jointly through mutual cooperation.[144] In so doing, a joint authority was to assume all rights and responsibilities for the exploration and exploitation of the non-living natural resources of the sea-bed and subsoil in the overlapping area.[145] Furthermore, it 'shall exercise on behalf of both Parties all the powers necessary for, incidental to or connected with the discharge of its functions relating to the exploration and exploitation of the non-living natural resources of the sea-bed and subsoil in the joint development area' pursuant to Article III(4). The regime is to remain in force for 50 years. The creation of the joint development area does not mean, however, that a delimitation in the area becomes unnecessary. Rather, both Parties clearly agreed to continue to seek to resolve the delimitation of the boundary of the continental shelf in the Gulf of Thailand under Article II.[146]

In the Red Sea, the 1974 Agreement between Saudi Arabia and Sudan established a common zone for joint exploitation of the natural resources of the sea-bed and subsoil.[147] In that zone, both Governments have equal sovereign rights over all natural resources under Article V. To ensure the prompt and efficient exploitation of natural resources in the common zone, the strongly-powered Joint Commission was established under Article VII.[148] Three treaties, that is, the 1992 Memorandum of Understanding between Malaysia and Vietnam,[149] the 1993 Agreement between Colombia and Jamaica[150] and the 1995 Joint Declaration on Cooperation Over Offshore Activities in the South West Atlantic between Argentina and the United Kingdom,[151] furnish other examples of joint exploitation. It seems that joint development can provide a useful devise to facilitate the provisional utilisation of the disputed marine areas.

[144] RR Bundy, 'Natural Resource Development (Oil and Gas) and Boundary Disputes' in Blake, *The Peaceful Management of Transboundary Resources*, 31–33; D Ong, 'Southeast Asian State Practice on the Joint Development of Offshore Oil and Gas Deposits' in ibid, 77–79.

[145] Article III (2) of the 1979 Memorandum of Understanding.

[146] Text in *IMB*, vol I, 1107–10. The 1979 Memorandum of Understanding merely determined the broad framework for joint development. It was not until 1990 that the Parties agreed to transform the 1970 Memorandum of Understanding into a full-fledged Joint Development Agreement. See Agreement between Malaysia and Thailand on the Constitution and Other Matters Relating to the Establishment of the Malaysia-Thailand Joint Authority, ibid, 1111–23.

[147] 952 *United Nations Treaty Series* 198–200.

[148] It is empowered to undertake the studies concerning the exploration and the exploitation of the natural resources, to consider and decide on the applications for licenses and concessions and to organise the supervision of the exploitation, etc (Art VII).

[149] Text in *IMB*, vol III, 2341–44.

[150] Text in ibid, 2200–04.

[151] Text in (1996) 35 *ILM* 301. See also RR Churchill, 'Falkland Islands – Maritime Jurisdiction and Co-operative Arrangements with Argentina' (1997) 46 *ICLQ* 463.

c. Combination of a Maritime Delimitation Agreement and a Fishery Agreement

As for a third solution, combination of a maritime boundary agreement and a fishery agreement merits mention. An example is provided by the maritime boundary between the People's Republic of China and Viet Nam in the Gulf of Tonkin.[152] Fisheries constituted an important cross-boundary resource issue in the Gulf of Tonkin. Thus the Agreement on Fishery Co-Operation in the Gulf of Tonkin was both signed and ratified on the same day as the boundary agreement between People's Republic of China and Viet Nam.[153] Article 3 of the fishery agreement created the Common Fishery Zone 30.5 nautical miles on either side of the maritime boundary southward of 20° North latitude to the closing line of the Gulf of Tonkin. In addition, Article 12 of the fishery agreement established 'the buffer zone' adjacent to the territorial sea in order to avoid disputes caused by illegal entry by mistake of small fishing boats of one Party into the territorial sea of the other.

Another example on this matter is provided by the 2010 Treaty between Norway and the Russian Federation. After some 40 years' negotiation, the Agreement could establish a single maritime boundary between Norway and the Russian Federation in the Barents Sea and the Arctic Ocean.[154] The Preamble of the Agreement explicitly refers to 'the special economic significance of the living resources of the Barents Sea to Norway and the Russian Federation'. Thus Article 4(1) of the Agreement makes clear that: 'The fishing opportunities of either Party shall not be adversely affected by the conclusion of the present Treaty.' To this end, the Parties are obliged to 'pursue close cooperation in the sphere of fisheries' in accordance with Article 4(2). Furthermore, Article 1 of Annex I stipulates that the 1975 and 1976 Fisheries Agreements are to continue to stay in force for 15 years after the entry into force of the 2010 Agreement.[155]

C. Summary

The above considerations seem to reveal the three conclusions.

First, with respect to socio-economic factors, including differences in economic wealth, the case law consistently refused to take them into account

[152] Agreement on the Delimitation of the territorial Seas, Exclusive Economic Zones and Continental Shelves in the Beibu Gulf [Gulf of Tonkin] between the People's Republic of China and the Socialist Republic of Vietnam. Singed on 25 December 2000. Entered into force 30 June 2004. Text in *IMB*, vol V, 3755.

[153] Report by TL McDorman, ibid, 3748. Further, see Zou Keyuan, 'The Sino-Vietnamese Agreement on Maritime Boundary Delimitation in the Gulf of Tonkin' (2005) 36 *ODIL* 13; Nguyen Hong Thao, 'Maritime Delimitation and Fishery Cooperation in the Tonkin Gulf' (2005) 36 *ODIL* 25. The text of the agreement was reproduced in ibid, 35 et seq.

[154] Report by Rikf Eubar Fjfe, *IMB*, vol VII, 5167.

[155] Further, see ibid, 5175 et seq.

when establishing maritime boundaries. In the *Gulf of Maine* case, the Chamber of the ICJ considered socio-economic factors at the verification stage.[156] Even so, these elements played only a secondary role in testing whether the established boundaries produced 'radically inequitable' results. Economic wealth depends on a variety of political, social and economic circumstances, and there is no legal reason for adjusting such economic imbalances in the context of maritime delimitation. Furthermore, it is difficult to find objective criteria for reflecting the difference of economic wealth in delimitation areas. Accordingly, as the case law suggests, it would be relevant to take a restrictive view in considering socio-economic factors.

Secondly, it is true that some judgments have accepted the relevance of natural resources in the process of maritime delimitation. Considering that the real interest behind the institution of the continental shelf and EEZ/FZ is natural resources, it is arguable that, 'so far as known or readily ascertainable', the international tribunals take natural resources into account when creating maritime boundaries.[157] Apart from the *Jan Mayen* case, however, no judgment concerning the delimitation of the continental shelf or single maritime boundaries has taken the presence of natural resources into account, at least at the operational stage. It can be observed that the influence of economic factor remains modest in the jurisprudence regarding maritime delimitations, despite the fact that the areas to be delimited are 'resource-oriented zones'.[158]

Thirdly, in State practice, usually economic factors have not *directly* affected the location of boundaries of either continental shelves or single maritime boundaries. Although there were some agreements for which economic considerations have played a decisive role, they remain a minority. Nevertheless, it is worth noting that, in some agreements, States resolved economic issues in a flexible manner. In this regard, three solutions can be identified:

- to insert common deposit clauses;
- the establishment of joint development regimes; and
- combination of a maritime delimitation agreement and a fisheries agreement or arrangement.

In particular, the creation of joint development regimes can be regarded as a provisional arrangement provided by Articles 74(3) and 83(3) of the LOSC.[159]

[156] [1984] ICJ Rep 340, [232]; 342–44, [237–41].

[157] Some writers favour taking economic factors into account. See, for instance, Kwiatkowska, 'Economic and Environmental Considerations' 106–9; Bowett, 'The Economic Factor in Maritime Delimitation Cases' 58–63; D Attard, *The Exclusive Economic Zone in International Law* (Oxford, Clarendon Press, 1987) 267; F Orrego Vicuña, *The Exclusive Economic Zone: Regime and Legal Nature Under International Law* (Cambridge University Press, 1989) 221–22.

[158] See also T Cottier, *Equitable Principles of Maritime Delimitation: The Quest for Distributive Justice in International Law* (Cambridge University Press, 2015) 559–67.

[159] See also ch 3, s II of this book.

II. CONDUCT OF THE PARTIES

A. Analysis of the Case Law

The conduct of the Parties may generate two issues. The first issue is whether the conduct of the Parties will affect the location of maritime boundaries as a relevant circumstance and the second is whether the conduct provides any evidence to prove the existence of *modus vivendi* or *de facto* boundary.[160]

i. Arguments in the Context of Continental Shelf Delimitations

The *Tunisia/Libya* case raised the issue of the existence of *modus vivendi* or *de facto* boundary. In that case, the ICJ examined the relevance of four 'alleged maritime limits resulting from the conduct of the State concerned'.

The first line to be examined in this context was the ZV (Zénith vertical) 45° line claimed by Tunisia as limiting the area of its historic rights over sedentary and other fisheries since time immemorial.[161] The ZV 45° line was implied in the 1904 Tunisian Instruction and was expressly mentioned in the 1951 Decree. On this point, the Court concluded that the claim to the line was a mere unilateral act, and, thus, not opposable to Libya even as an inchoate maritime boundary between the two countries.[162]

The second line was one claimed by Libya and running northward, in the general direction of the land boundary established by the 1910 Convention. The line was based on Libya's petroleum legislation. In the Court's view, such laws were purely internal acts and were hardly considered even as a unilateral claim for lateral maritime boundaries with Tunisia. Accordingly, the Court found that the Libyan line was not opposable to Tunisia. In short, neither the ZV 45° line nor the Libyan line could be taken into consideration.[163]

Thirdly, the Court considered a line perpendicular to the coast at the border point. The line was drawn from Ras Ajdir based on a proposal made by Italy in 1914 for a delimitation line between Libyan and Tunisian sponge-banks. This line, which runs in an angle of approximately 26° to the meridian, became a sort of tacit *modus vivendi;* furthermore, the Italian authorities established two eight-mile buffer zones at the two ends of the Libyan coast. Both Parties recognised that a *de facto* compromise or provisional solution had been

[160] In this connection, the issues of estoppel or acquiescence may arise. The issues are, however, beyond the scope of this study since the doctrines of estoppel or acquiescence are not issues specific to the law of maritime delimitation, but general issues of international law. Evans takes the same view. MD Evans, *Relevant Circumstances and Maritime Delimitation* (Oxford, Clarendon Press, 1989) 217–18.

[161] The term 'Zénith Vertical' appears to mean a measurement of the true geographical north, likely to be used by mariners as a means of establishing their true location by a sun-sight. Counter-Memorial of Libya, vol II, 192, n 2.

[162] [1982] ICJ Rep 67–68, [88–90].

[163] ibid, 68–69, [91–92].

achieved by means of the buffer zone.[164] Although the Court considered that the existence of such a *modus vivendi* fell short of proving the existence of a recognised maritime boundary between the Parties, it nevertheless stated that:

> [I]n view of the absence of agreed and clearly specified maritime boundaries, the respect for the tacit *modus vivendi*, which was never formally contested by either side throughout a long period of time, could warrant its acceptance as a historical justification for the choice of the method for the delimitation of the continental shelf between the two States, to the extent that the historic rights claimed by Tunisia could not in any event be opposable to Libya east of the *modus vivendi* line.[165]

The fourth and the most important line is a *de facto* line drawn from Ras Ajdir at an angle of some 26° east of north, which resulted from concessions for the offshore exploration and exploitation of oil and gas granted by both Parties. The Court attached great importance to that line, stating that:

> This line of adjoining concessions, which was tacitly respected for a number of years, and which approximately corresponds furthermore to the line perpendicular to the coast at the frontier point which had in the past been observed as a *de facto* maritime limit, does appear to the Court to constitute a circumstance of great relevance for the delimitation.[166]

It was the *de facto* line which effectively governed the delimitation in the first segment to be delimited.

The line addressed by the Court is not one based on a tacit agreement between the Parties, or on estoppel, but on 'what method of delimitation would ensure an equitable result.'[167] According to the Court, 'it is evident that the Court must take into account whatever indicia are available of the line or lines which the Parties themselves may have considered equitable or acted upon as such – if only as an interim solution affecting part only of the area to be delimited.'[168] In the Court's view, the fact that that line was drawn by each of the two States separately for the purpose of delimiting the eastward and westward boundaries of petroleum concessions had great relevance.[169] Furthermore, the 26° line coincided with the *modus vivendi* line perpendicular to the coast. Hence the Court found that the former line was 'neither arbitrary nor without precedent in the relations between the two States.'[170] Consequently, on the basis of the *de facto* 26° concession line, which ran approximately perpendicular to the coast at the point where the land boundary between Tunisia and Libya abuts on the sea, the ICJ established the continental shelf boundary in the first sector. That solution is, however, open to challenge on some points.

[164] ibid, 70, [93–94].
[165] ibid, 70–71, [95].
[166] ibid, 71, [96].
[167] ibid, 84, [118].
[168] ibid.
[169] ibid.
[170] ibid, 84–85, [119].

First, theoretically, the Court's approach may be viewed as giving too much weight to the conduct of the Parties. But it entails the risk of introducing the idea of effectiveness or occupation into the law of maritime delimitation. The rights over the continental shelf are attributed to the coastal State *ipso facto* and *ab initio*. Accordingly, the idea of effectiveness would be incompatible with the fundamental character of legal rights over the continental shelf.

Secondly, by giving excessive weight to the conduct of the Parties, unilateral acts of occupation on the continental shelf may be encouraged.[171] It would be absurd if a State's restraint in its activity in an area claimed by another State were penalised by implying that it had consented to that claim.[172]

Thirdly, the Court attached importance to the fact that Libya suggested the 26° line in the context of negotiations.[173] Yet this hardly provides any evidence that Libya accepted the *de facto* line as a continental shelf boundary. In fact, while acceptance of the 26° line and the other lines might have been suggested in the course of negotiation, Libya stated that the 26° line 'was at no time accepted by Libya as the legal line of delimitation of the areas of the continental shelf appertaining *de jure* to Libya.'[174] The above observations thus cast doubt on the Court's reliance on the conduct of the Parties, at least on some points.[175]

ii. Arguments in the Context of Single/Coincident Maritime Boundaries

a. The Conduct of the Parties in the ICJ Jurisprudence

The issue of the conduct of the parties was raised in several cases before the ICJ. In the *Gulf of Maine* case, Canada relied on the conduct of the Parties in the context of the delimitation of the continental shelf proper and, *inter alia*, that of Geroges Bank at two levels.[176] First, based on the *Tunisia/Libya* case, Canada asserted the existence of a *modus vivendi* or of a *de facto* boundary based on the coincidence between the Canadian equidistance line

[171] P Weil, *Perspective du droit de la délimitation maritime* (Paris, Pedone, 1988) 100. In this respect, Kolb pointed to another problem. In his view, if tribunals start to adopt provisional lines as final solutions accepted by the parties or as equitable solutions imposed by the tribunal, States may in future refuse to have recourse to such lines, for fear of subsequently being bound by them on a definitive basis; this would have the effect of exacerbating disputes rather than reducing their scope. R Kolb, *Case Law on Equitable Maritime Delimitation: Digest and Commentaries* (The Hague, Brill/Nijhoff, 2003) 183.

[172] MB Feldman, 'The Tunisia-Libya Continental Shelf Case: Geographic Justice or Judicial Compromise?' (1983) 77 *AJIL* 234.

[173] [1982] ICJ Rep 84, [118].

[174] Counter-Memorial of Libya, vol II, 163, [43]. The Court itself referred to Libya's view. [1982] ICJ Rep 84, [118].

[175] ED Brown, 'The Tunisia-Libya Continental Shelf Case: A Missed Opportunity' (1983) *Marine Policy* 153.

[176] [1984] ICJ Rep 304, [128]. In addition, Canada also invoked the doctrine of acquiescence and estoppel in this context. ibid, 304–7, [129–36]. For the reason already explained in the opening of this subsection, however, the argument concerning acquiescence and estoppel is excluded from the scope of in this study. In any case, Canada's argument concerning acquiescence and estoppel was rejected by the Chamber. ibid, 307–10, [137–48].

(the 'strict equidistance line') and the United States 'BLM line', which was respected by the two Parties and by numerous oil companies from 1965 to 1972.[177] By contrast, the United States denied the very existence of the 'BLM line'.[178] The Chamber did not accept the Canadian arguments, stressing the difference between the *Tunisia/Libya* dispute and the present case. First, according to the Chamber, the Court, in the *Tunisia/Libya* case 'took special account of the conduct of the Powers formerly responsible for the external affairs of Tunisia (France) and of Tripolitanis (Italy), which it found amounted to a *modus vivendi*, and which the two States continued to respect when, after becoming independent, they began to grant petroleum concessions'. Secondly, in the Chamber's view, the period between 1965 and 1972 was too brief to produce the legal effect of instituting a *modus vivendi*.[179] The Chamber thus concluded that no *modus vivendi* or *de facto* boundary existed in the *Gulf of Maine* area. The Chamber's view presents a clear contrast with the *Tunisia/Libya* judgment, which had attached great importance to the conduct of the Parties. The difference may consist in the fact that the conduct of the Parties in the *Gulf of Maine* dispute did not provide unequivocal evidence for a *de facto* line as it had done in the *Tunisia/Libya* case.

Subsequently, the conduct of the Parties was discussed in the *Jan Mayen* case. Denmark had contended that the conduct of the Parties was a highly relevant factor in the choice of the appropriate method of delimitation, where such conduct had indicated some particular method as being likely to produce an equitable result. Denmark relied on the maritime delimitation between Norway and Iceland, and on an internal limit established by Norway between the economic zone of mainland Norway and the fishery protection zone of Bear Island, which is a part of Norway. According to Denmark, in those instances, Norway accepted that Jan Mayen *vis-à-vis* Iceland, and Bear Island *vis-à-vis* mainland Norway, not only could not have a delimitation effected by a median line but that the line should not cut into the 200-mile zones of Iceland and mainland Norway.[180]

The contention of Denmark was not accepted by the ICJ for two reasons. First, the Danish argument on Bear Island was irrelevant because that island is situated in a region unrelated to the area of overlapping claims to be delimited. Secondly, although the agreement between Iceland and Norway concerned Jan Mayen itself, the Court considered it irrelevant as well:

> In the particular case of maritime delimitation, international law does not prescribe, with a view to reaching an equitable solution, the adoption of a single method for the delimitation of the maritime spaces on all sides of an island, or for the whole of the

[177] ibid, 310, [149]. See also the rejoinder by Bowett (Canada), Verbatim Record 1984, Oral Arguments *(concluded)*; Correspondence, vol VII, 108–9. For the location of the BLM line, see Figure 21 in Pleadings, Maps, Charts and Illustrations, vol VIII, 167.

[178] [1984] ICJ Rep 310, [149]. See also the rejoinder by Robinson (the United States), Verbatim Record 1984, Oral Arguments *(concluded)*; Correspondence, vol VII, 155–56.

[179] [1984] ICJ Rep 310–11, [150–51].

[180] [1993] ICJ Rep 75–76, [82–83].

coastal front of a particular State, rather than, if desired, varying systems of delimitation for the various parts of the coast. *The conduct of the Parties will in many cases therefore have no influence on such a delimitation.*[181]

It should be pointed out that the 'conduct of the Parties' in the above quotation means the conduct relating to delimitation methods *vis-à-vis* other States in the same region, and not a *modus vivendi* or a *de facto* line. On this point, the meaning of 'the conduct of the Parties' is different from that used in the *Tunisia/Libya* case.

In the *Qatar v Bahrain* case, the relevance of the line dividing the sea-bed of the two States, which was described in the British decision of 23 December 1947, created a sharp dispute between the Parties. The British decision had been adopted within the context of the emerging legal continental shelf doctrine.[182] On the one hand, Qatar asked the ICJ to draw the single maritime boundary 'with due regard to the line dividing the sea-bed of the two States' described in the above British decision.[183] On this point, it alleged that 'it cannot be said that the Court is faced with a purely *de novo* maritime delimitation, since in a part of the relevant maritime area a line dividing the seabed between the Parties had already been drawn in 1947 by the British authorities.'[184] In Qatar's view, 'the 1947 line in itself constitutes a special circumstance insofar as it was drawn in order to permit each of the two interested States actually to exercise its inherent right over the sea-bed.'[185] At the same time, Qatar did *not* contend that the 1947 line was to be automatically regarded as the boundary line to be delimited between the maritime areas pertaining to Qatar and those pertaining to Bahrain. In fact, the British decision drew a line enclaving the Hawar Islands. Yet Qatar insisted that the third part of the 1947 line had to be disregarded for two reasons: Qatar's sovereignty over the Hawar islands and a third State's rights at the entrance of the Dawhat Salwah.[186]

Bahrain contested the relevance of the 1947 line for the following reasons: (i) The letters of 23 December 1947 did not constitute a 'decision' binding Bahrain and Qatar. (ii) The 1947 line was not based exclusively on legal criteria. (iii) The 1947 line related exclusively to the delimitation of the continental shelf and expressly did not purport to delimit the superjacent waters. (iv) The concepts and rules by reference to which the 1947 line had been drawn did not meet the requirements of contemporary law. Indeed, the notion of the EEZ, unknown in 1947, brought about a fundamental change in the theory of the continental shelf.

[181] Emphasis added. ibid, 77, [86].

[182] Memorial submitted by Qatar, 215. Regarding the background and contents of the British decision, see ibid, 218–14. According to Qatar's explanation, the 1947 line was not a strict or true median line, but a line in accordance with equitable principles. ibid, 224.

[183] The *Qatar v Bahrain* case (Merits), [2001] ICJ Rep 49, [31]; presentation by Quéneudec, Verbatim Record, CR 2000/10, [43].

[184] Memorial submitted by Qatar, 247.

[185] ibid, 261. See also, 261–62.

[186] ibid, 253–58.

(v) The 1947 line did not rest on any known or identifiable legal grounds. (vi) The 1947 line had no relevance in light of the supervening extension of the territorial seas of both countries from three to 12 miles. (vii) The 1947 line had no relevance as a source of 'historic rights'.[187]

The ICJ held that the 1947 line could not be considered to have direct relevance for the present delimitation process for two reasons. First, neither Party had accepted it as a binding decision and they invoked only parts of it to support their arguments. Secondly, while the British decision only concerned the division of the sea-bed between the Parties, the delimitation to be effected in the present case was mainly a combined delimitation of the continental shelf and the EEZ.[188] This appears to suggest that, in the delimitation of single maritime boundaries, theoretically at least, existing sea-bed lines would not have any influence since they concern the sea-bed alone.

The relevance of the oil concessions of the Parties was also disputed in the *Cameroon v Nigeria* case (Merits). Nigeria contended that State practice concerning oil concessions was of the highest relevance to delimitation and the Court cannot redistribute such oil concessions between Parties to the delimitation.[189] According to Nigeria, there was a clear and consistent pattern of mutual acquiescence in the oil activities and practice in their respective maritime areas.[190] However, Cameroon contested that the existence of oil concessions has never been accorded particular significance in the law of maritime delimitation and that State practice did not support Nigeria's arguments.[191] According to Cameroon, the limited significance of oil concessions in the law of maritime delimitation accorded with the essential nature of the concept of the continental shelf, over which coastal States have an inherent right which does not depend on its being exercised. In Cameroon's view, the granting of oil concessions is a unilateral *fait accompli*, and not a legal fact that is opposable to other States. Furthermore, according to Cameroon, there were areas of overlap in the concessions granted by Cameroon, Equatorial Guinea and Nigeria; thus, there could be no question of a *de facto* line in the area further south of point G since Cameroon had refrained from granting any concession there.[192]

Having reviewed precedents, the Court rejected the relevance of oil concessions and oil wells in maritime delimitation in the following terms:

> Overall, it follows from the jurisprudence that, although the existence of an express or tacit agreement between the parties on the sitting of their respective oil concessions

[187] Counter-Memorial submitted by Bahrain, paras 552–86. See also, presentation by Weil, Counsel of Bahrain, Verbatim Record, CR 2000/16, [125–62].

[188] Judgment, [2001] ICJ Rep113–14, [239–40].

[189] Counter-Memorial of Nigeria, 581–87, [21.24–21.31]; presentation by Crawford, Counsel of Nigeria, Verbatim Record, CR 2002/20, 56–58, [23–28].

[190] Rejoinder of Nigeria, Part IV, Ch 10, [10.19].

[191] Reply of Cameroon, 427–30, [9.96–9.117]; presentation by Pellet, Counsel of Cameroon, 18–31, [3–42].

[192] The *Cameroon v Nigeria* case (Merits), [2002] ICJ Rep 438–39, [283]. See also Reply of Cameroon, 427–30, [9.96–9.117]; presentation by Kamto, Verbatim Record, CR 2002/7, 18–26, [3–24] and 32, [45].

> may indicate a consensus on the maritime areas to which they are entitled, oil concessions and oil wells are not in themselves to be considered as relevant circumstances justifying the adjustment or shifting of the provisional delimitation line. Only if they are based on express or tacit agreement between the parties may they be taken into account. In the present case there is no agreement between the parties regarding oil concessions.[193]

In the *Black Sea* case, Ukraine contended that Romania's activities or lack of them are incompatible with the position taken by Romania in the proceedings before the Court. Ukraine further asserted that its oil related activities and fishing activities are consistent with its delimitation line.[194] Romania rejected the relevance of State activities in the *Romania/Ukraine* dispute.[195] By relaying on the *dictum* expressed by the Arbitral Tribunal in the *Barbados v Trinidad and Tobago* arbitration,[196] the Court held that it does not see any particular role for the State activities in the present maritime delimitation. By referring to the *dictum* of the *Gulf of Maine* case,[197] the Court also stated that there is no evidence that any delimitation line other than that claimed by Ukraine would be likely to entail catastrophic repercussions for the livelihood and economic well-being of the population. Thus the Court refused to admit the Ukraine's argument.[198]

In the *Nicaragua v Colombia* case, Colombia submitted that it has for many decades regulated fishing activities, conducted scientific exploration and conducted naval patrols throughout the area to the east of the 82nd meridian, whereas there is no evidence of any significant Nicaraguan activity there until recent times.[199] However, the ICJ declined the Colombia's submission since the Court, in its Judgment of 2007, had already held that the 1928 Treaty did not fix the 82nd meridian as a maritime boundary between the Parties.[200] In this connection, the Court made the following statement:

> While it cannot be ruled out that conduct might need to be taken into account as a relevant circumstance in an appropriate case, the jurisprudence of the Court and of arbitral tribunals shows that conduct will not normally have such an effect.[201]

It thus held that the conduct of the Parties was not a relevant circumstance in this case.[202]

193 Judgment, [2002] ICJ Rep 447–48, [304].
194 [2009] ICJ Rep 123–24, [189–91]; Counter-Memorial Submitted by Ukraine, 212–19, [8.39–8.65].
195 [2009] ICJ Rep 124–25, [193–96]; Reply Submitted by Romania, 246–69, [7.1–7.63].
196 The *Barbados v Trinidad and Tobago* arbitral award, (2007) 27 *RIAA* 214, [241].
197 [1984] ICJ Rep 342, [237].
198 [2009] ICJ Rep 125–26, [198].
199 [2012] ICJ Rep 704, [217]. See also Counter-Memorial of Colombia, 11 November 2008, 371–77, [8.77–8.93].
200 [2007] ICJ Rep 869, [120].
201 [2012] ICJ Rep 705, [220].
202 ibid.

The second issue, ie, the existence of a *de facto* boundary, was raised in the *Nicaragua v Honduras* and *Peru v Chile* cases. In the *Nicaragua v Honduras* case, the ICJ examined the existence of a '*de facto* boundary based on the tacit agreement of the Parties' at the 15th parallel.[203] On this issue, the Court made the following general statement:

> Evidence of a tacit legal agreement must be compelling. The establishment of a permanent maritime boundary is a matter of grave importance and agreement is not easily to be presumed. ... Even if there had been a provisional line found convenient for a period of time, this is to be distinguished from an international boundary.[204]

In this connection, the Court noted that from 1961 to1977, the 15th parallel appeared to have had some relevance in the conduct of the Parties. In fact, it observed that during this period, several oil concessions were granted by the Parties indicating the 15th parallel as their northern and southern limits, that the 15th parallel divided the respective fishing areas of the two States, and that the 15th parallel was also perceived by some fishermen as a line dividing maritime areas under the jurisdiction of the Parties. Nonetheless, the Court considered that: '[T]hese events, spanning a short period of time, are not sufficient for the Court to conclude that there was a legally established international maritime boundary between the two States.'[205] It further pointed to the fact that in the Note of the Honduran Minister for Foreign Affairs dated 3 May 1982, Honduras concurred with the Nicaraguan Foreign Ministry that 'the maritime border between Honduras and Nicaragua has not been legally delimited' and proposed that the Parties at least come to a 'temporary' arrangement about the boundary so as to avoid further boundary incidents.[206] The Court thus concluded that: '[T]here was no tacit agreement in effect between the Parties in 1982 – nor *a fortiori* at any subsequent date – of a nature to establish a legally binding maritime boundary.'[207]

In the *Peru v Chile* case, the conduct of the Parties constituted a crucial issue when determining the existence of an agreed maritime boundary and its extent. Focusing on the terms of the 1954 Special Maritime Frontier Zone Agreement, the ICJ held that the terms acknowledged in a binding international agreement that a maritime along a parallel boundary already existed between the Parties.[208] In this connection, the Court stated that:

> The 1954 Special Maritime Frontier Zone Agreement does not indicate when and by what means that boundary was agreed upon. The Parties' express acknowledgment of its existence can only reflect a tacit agreement which they had reached earlier.

[203] For an analysis of this issue, see also Y Tanaka, 'Reflections on Maritime Delimitation in the *Nicaragua/Honduras* Case' (2008) 68 *ZaöRV/Heidelberg Journal of International Law* 903, 909–10.

[204] [2007] ICJ Rep 735, [253].

[205] ibid, 736, [256].

[206] ibid, 736–37, [257]. See also 680, [56].

[207] ibid, 736–37, [257–58].

[208] [2014] ICJ Rep 38–39, [90–91].

> In this connection, the Court has already mentioned that certain elements of the 1947 Proclamations and the 1952 Santiago Declaration suggested *an evolving understanding* between the Parties concerning their maritime boundary.... In this case, the Court has before it an Agreement which makes clear that the maritime boundary along a parallel already existed between the Parties. The 1954 Agreement is decisive in this respect. That Agreement cements the tacit agreement.[209]

However, the content of an 'evolving understanding' is not wholly unambiguous. In this regard, the Court held that in the 1952 Santiago Declaration, Chile and Peru had not agreed to establish a lateral maritime boundary.[210] If this is the case, the tacit agreement has been formulated in the short period between 1952 and 1954. Yet, the Court offered scant explanation of how and when the tacit agreement could be formulated.[211] Thus some doubt can be expressed regarding whether 'compelling' evidence existed to establish the tacit agreement.[212]

In this connection, another issue arises with regard to the extent of the boundary. The Court noted that the species which were being taken in the early 1950s were generally to be found within a range of 60 nautical miles from the coast.[213] It also considered that the evidence at its disposal did not allow it to conclude that the agreed maritime boundary along the parallel extended beyond 80 nautical miles from its starting-point.[214] The later practice subsequent to 1954 did not lead the Court to change the conclusion.[215] It thus ruled that it extended up to Point A situated at a distance of 80 nautical miles up to (Point A) along the parallel from its starting-point of the single maritime boundary, namely, the intersection of the parallel of latitude passing through Boundary Marker No. 1 with the low-water line.[216] As the ICJ itself admitted, however, 'the all-purpose nature of the maritime boundary ... means that evidence concerning fisheries activity, in itself, cannot be determinative of the extent of that boundary.'[217] If this is the case, it would be hard to fix the extent of the agreed boundary on the basis of fisheries activity. In this connection, the Court added that:

> [T]he fisheries activity provides *some support* for the view that the Parties, at the time when they acknowledged the existence of an agreed maritime boundary between them, were unlikely to have considered that it extended all the way to the 200-nautical-mile limit.[218]

[209] Emphasis added. *Maritime Dispute (Peru v Chile)*, [2014] ICJ Rep 38–39, [91].
[210] ibid, 31, [70].
[211] According to Judge Owada, the ICJ declared the existence of a tacit agreement 'in an almost Delphic manner'. Separate Opinion of Judge Owada, ibid, 88, [8].
[212] T Scovazzi, 'Maritime Dispute (Peru v Chile), 2008' in PW Almeida and J-M Sorel, *Latin America and the International Court of Justice: Contributions to International Law* (London, Routledge, 2017) 243.
[213] The *Peru v Chile* case, [2014] ICJ Rep 44, [108].
[214] ibid, 47, [117].
[215] ibid, 57, [149].
[216] ibid, 58, [151] and 61, [176].
[217] ibid, 45, [111].
[218] Emphasis added. ibid.

Yet, 'some support' of the fishing activity alone is inadequate to prove that the agreed boundary stops exactly at 80 nautical miles from the coast.[219] In fact, Judge Sebutinde stated her misgivings that: '[T]his finding of the Court rests on dangerously weak and speculative grounds.'[220] Likewise Judge Tomka also stated that: 'In my view, there is insufficient evidence to conclude that the agreed maritime boundary extends only to 80 nautical miles.'[221] Overall it may have to be admitted that the Court's reasoning on this matter is highly debatable.[222]

b. The Conduct of the Parties in Arbitral Awards

In the *St Pierre and Miquelon* arbitration, Canada relied on two examples of conduct. The first form of conduct related to Declarations exchanged between the King of Great Britain and the King of France, when signing the 1783 Treaty of Versailles. Article IV of the 1783 Treaty of Versailles stipulated that the islands of St Pierre and Miquelon were ceded to France. The Declarations exchanged provided that possessions of St Pierre and Miquelon were not to become an object of jealousy. Canada alleged that these provisions were still in force and restricted France's rights to maritime areas beyond territorial waters. By contrast, France rejected Canada's argument.[223] The Arbitral Tribunal dismissed Canada's view: 'The stipulation that the islands will not become "an object of jealousy" between the Parties cannot plausibly be interpreted to mean that the legal rights of France under contemporary international law must be denied because of "jealousy".'[224]

The second example of conduct invoked by Canada was the 1972 *Relevé de Conclusions,* under which France would accept a reduced shelf area off St Pierre and Miquelon in return for Canadian concessions to French companies to exploit oil and gas in the Canadian shelf.[225] On this point, the Court held that no conclusions might be derived from the Relevé for two reasons: the 1972 *Relevé* referred only to the continental shelf and was not relevant to the all-purpose single maritime boundary; and the *Relevé* never became a binding

[219] In this regard, Judge Owada considered that: 'Logically there should be no reason why the line should stop at 80 nautical miles, rather than extending to the 200-nautical-mile limit, as each of the Parties claimed in the Santiago Declaration.' Separate Opinion of Judge Owada, ibid, 93, [24].

[220] Dissenting Opinion of Judge Sebutinde, ibid, 120, [14]. See also Declaration of Judge Skotnikov, ibid, 99, [6].

[221] Declaration of President Tomka, ibid, 75, [3]. Judges Xue, Gaja, Bhandari and Judge ad hoc Orrego Vicuña considered that the maritime boundary extends along the parallel for 200 nautical miles from the continental coasts of Peru and Chile. Joint Dissenting Opinion of Judges Xue, Gaja, Bhandari and Judge ad hoc Orrego Vicuña, ibid, 108–09, [35]. See also S Fietta and R Cleverly, *A Practitioner's Guide to Maritime Boundary Delimitation* (Oxford University Press, 2016) 547.

[222] Scovazzi, 'Maritime Dispute (Peru v Chile), 2008' 244–45.

[223] The *St Pierre and Miquelon* arbitral award, (1992) 31 *ILM* 1166, [53–54].

[224] ibid, [55].

[225] ibid, 1175, [90]. France used the *Relevé* during the *Anglo-French Continental Shelf* arbitration of 1977. See also DW Bowett, 'The Canada-France Arbitration Concerning the Delimitation of the Maritime Areas of St Pierre et Miquelon' in *Hacia Un Nuevo Orden Internacional Y Europeo, Estudios En Homenaje Al Profesor Don Manuel Diez De Velasco* (Madrid, Tecnos, 1993) 132.

agreement between the Parties.[226] Thus, the conduct of the Parties played no role in the award of 1992.

In the *Eritrea/Yemen* arbitration, the relevance of petroleum agreements was disputed between the Parties. In this context, the Arbitral Tribunal, in the first stage of the arbitration on sovereignty, had concluded that:

> The offshore petroleum contracts entered into by Yemen, and by Ethiopia and Eritrea, fail to establish or significantly strengthen the claims of either party to sovereignty over the disputed island. Those contracts however lend a measure of support to a median line between the opposite coasts of Eritrea and Yemen, drawn without regard to the islands, dividing the respective jurisdiction of the Parties.[227]

On the basis of this *dictum*, Eritrea thought that the Tribunal's Award provided support for its 'historic median line'. Yemen contended that, although it had introduced maps drawn by Petroconsultants as evidence of its sovereignty over the disputed islands, it did not do so to show maritime boundaries. Furthermore, according to Yemen, those maps included mistakes. In addition, referring to paragraph 412 of the Award on Sovereignty, Yemen recalled the Tribunal's holding according to which the concessions were 'issued with commercial considerations in mind and without particular regard to the existence of the Islands.'[228]

The Tribunal accepted that it should take into account, *inter alia,* the *dictum* expressed at the first stage of the Award regarding the question of territorial sovereignty. However, it was not suggested that the maritime boundary to be established by it should be drawn throughout its length entirely without regard to the islands whose sovereignty had been determined. Nor did it say that the boundary should follow Eritrea's 'historic median line'. The Tribunal thus concluded that:

> The concession lines were drawn without regard to uninhabited, volcanic islands when their sovereignty was indeterminate. Those lines can hardly be taken as governing once that sovereignty has been determined. While initial weight is to be given to the mainland coasts and their island fringes, some weight is to be or may be accorded to the islands, certainly in respect of their territorial waters.[229]

Thus, unlike what had occurred in the *Tunisia/Libya* case, the petroleum agreements provided no *modus vivendi* and had little influence upon the maritime boundary. At the same time, it is worth noting that the Tribunal found that there was an obligation for the Parties to give every consideration to the shared or joint or unitised exploitation of any mineral resources.[230] In short, according to

[226] The *St Pierre and Miquelon* arbitral award, (1992) 31 *ILM*, [91].

[227] This passage was quoted in the *Eritrea/Yemen* case (The Second Phase), 22 *RIAA* 353, [78]. The disputed islands included all the islands and islets disputed between the Parties, such as Jabal al-Tayr, the Zubayer group, the Haycocks and the Mohabbakahs. On this point, see the award regarding sovereignty, (2001) 40 *ILM* 914, para 90. See also [527].

[228] The *Eritrea/Yemen* arbitral award (The Second Phase), 22 *RIAA* 353–54, [79–80].

[229] ibid, 354–55, [83].

[230] ibid, 356, [86].

the Tribunal, the petroleum agreements were not relevant circumstances in the context of maritime delimitation but generated a need for cooperation between the Parties.

In the *Barbados v Trinidad and Tobago* case, Barbados contended that Trinidad and Tobago was prevented from claiming an adjustment of the equidistance lien to the north because Trinidad and Tobago had consistently recognised and acquiesced in Barbados' exercise of sovereignty in the area. However, this argument was not supported by the Arbitral Tribunal. According to the Tribunal,

> Seismic surveys sporadically authorised, oil concessions in the area and patrolling, while relevant do not offer sufficient evidence to establish estoppel or acquiescence on the part of Trinidad and Tobago. Nor, on the other hand, is there proof of any significant activity by Trinidad and Tobago relevant to the exercise of its own claimed jurisdiction north of the equidistance line.[231]

For the Tribunal,

> Trinidad and Tobago's argument to the effect that, as held by the International Court of Justice in *Cameroon v. Nigeria* (I.C.J. Reports 2002, p. 303), oil wells are not in themselves to be considered as relevant circumstances, unless based on express or tacit agreement between the parties, finds application in this context.[232]

The Tribunal therefore held that the activities of either Party, or the responses of each Party to the activities of the other, themselves did not constitute a factor that must be taken into account in the drawing of an equitable delimitation line.[233]

The *dictum* of the *Barbados v Trinidad and Tobago* arbitral award was supported by the Arbitral Tribunal in the *Guyana v Suriname* case. In this case, the question of the relevance of the conduct of the Parties was raised with regard to the shifting of the provisional equidistance line. Guyana argued that the oil concessions reflected a *de facto* pattern of acceptance that the line extending from Point 61 on a bearing of approximately N34E has long been treated as reflecting an equidistance line which divides the parties' maritime spaces.[234] However, Suriname countered that: '[T]he conduct of the parties to a maritime boundary dispute, in particular one that concerns a single maritime boundary, is generally not relevant to the maritime delimitation.'[235] After examining the jurisprudence on this subject, the Tribunal held that:

> The cases reveal a marked reluctance of international courts and tribunals to accord significance to the oil practice of the parties in the determination of the delimitation line.[236]

[231] The *Barbados v Trinidad and Tobago* arbitral award, (2013) 27 *RIAA* 241, [363].
[232] ibid, [364].
[233] ibid, 242, [366].
[234] Guyana Memorial, vol I, 88–89, [7.34].
[235] Suriname Counter Memorial, vol I, 51, [4.37].
[236] The *Guyana v Suriname* arbitral award, 30 *RIAA*, 108, [390].

In fact, the Tribunal, in the *Guyana v Suriname* case, found 'no evidence of any agreement between the Parties regarding such practice'.[237] The Tribunal thus concluded that: '[T]he oil practice of the parties cannot be taken into account in the delimitation of the maritime boundary in this case.'[238]

c. The Conduction of the Parties in the ITLOS Jurisprudence

The issue of the conduct of the Parties was discussed in two cases before ITLOS, that is, the *Bangladesh/Myanmar* and *Ghana/Côte d'Ivoire* cases.

An issue at point in the *Bangladesh/Myanmar* case related to the existence of a tacit or *de facto* agreement with regard to the boundary of the territorial sea. In this regard, the value of affidavits submitted by Bangladesh was at issue. Bangladesh contended that the affidavits from fishermen and the naval officers demonstrated the existence of a tacit or *de facto* agreed line.[239] In approaching this issue, ITLOS relied on the *dictum* of the ICJ in the *Nicaragua v Honduras* case:

> [W]itness statements produced in the form of affidavits should be treated with caution. In assessing such affidavits the Court must take into account a number of factors. These would include whether they were made by State officials or by private persons not interested in the outcome of the proceedings and whether a particular affidavit attests to the existence of facts or represents only an opinion as regards certain events.[240]

Referring to the *dictum*, ITLOS considered that the affidavits submitted by Bangladesh did not provide convincing evidence to support the existence of an agreement between the Parties on the delimitation of their territorial seas.[241] Furthermore, the Tribunal reviewed the statement of the Minister of Foreign Affairs of Myanmar of 19 November 1985 and the note verbale of 16 January of 2008 addressed by the Ministry of Foreign Affairs of Myanmar to the ministry of Foreign Affairs of Bangladesh. By referring to the *dictum* of the ICJ in the *Nicaragua v Honduras* case, ie, '[e]vidence of a tacit legal agreement must be compelling', the Tribunal then found that the instruments did not indicate a tacit or *de facto* agreement. It thus denied the existence of such an agreement.[242]

The *Ghana/Côte d'Ivoire* case raised two issues regarding the conduct of the Parties. The first was whether, as Ghana claimed, a tacit agreement on a common maritime boundary between the Parties exists.[243] In this regard, Ghana invoked

[237] ibid.

[238] ibid.

[239] [2012] ITLOS Rep 37, [101-103]. See also Bangladesh's Memorial, vol I, 64, [5.19].

[240] [2007] ICJ Rep 731, [244]. See also Dissenting Opinion of Judge Lucky on the *Bangladesh/Myanmar* case. [2012] ITLOS Rep 261.

[241] The *Bangladesh/Myanmar* case, Judgment, ibid, 40, [115].

[242] ibid, 41, [116-18].

[243] Ghana called the tacit agreement the 'customary equidistance boundary'. Ghana's Memorial, vol I, 29, [3.3].

multiple factors, such as: oil activities, legislation of the Parties, representation to international institutions, bilateral exchanges and negotiations.[244] According to the ITLOS Special Chamber, 'the oil practice, no matter how consistent it may be, cannot in itself establish the existence of a tacit agreement on a maritime boundary.'[245] Furthermore, 'evidence relating solely to the specific purpose of oil activities in the seabed and subsoil is of limited value in proving the existence of an all-purpose boundary which delimits not only the seabed and subsoil but also superjacent water columns.'[246] Accordingly, the Special Chamber did not admit the existence of a tacit agreement between the Parties.[247]

The second issue was whether the conduct of the Parties can constitute a relevant circumstance requiring an adjustment of the provisional equidistance line. Ghana maintained that the consistent practice of the Parties in respect of the boundary for five decades would constitute a relevant circumstance justifying a modest adjustment of the provisional equidistance line to conform the customary boundary line.[248] For the Special Chamber, however, Ghana's argument appeared to be an attempt to revive a tacit maritime boundary that was rejected by the Chamber. Hence the Chamber declined Ghana's argument.[249]

B. Analysis of State Practice

i. Agreements Regarding Continental Shelf Delimitations

In general, it is difficult to identify a clear influence of the conduct of the Parties on the process of maritime delimitation. A notable example in this matter is the 1971 Agreement between Denmark and the Federal Republic of Germany. Denmark had issued licenses to certain companies in areas which fell to Denmark according to the equidistance method. In 1969, as explained already, the ICJ denied the obligatory character of that method. Pursuant to the *North Sea Continental Shelf* judgment, Denmark and the FRG thus concluded an agreement without having recourse to equidistance (see Illustration 4). In this connection, Danish licenses already granted to companies presented a problem. In order to avoid conflicts, the 1971 Agreement was established in an 'irregular' way so as to leave some Danish licensees undisturbed on the Danish side of the line. Accordingly, between Points S2 and S5, the boundary curves southward around areas provisionally drilled by Danish licensees. Furthermore, under Article 4 of that Agreement, the Danish licensees in the area designated in

[244] ibid, 29–87, [3.1–3.120].
[245] The *Ghana/Côte d'Ivoire* case, [2017] ITLOS Rep [215].
[246] ibid, [226].
[247] ibid, [228].
[248] Ghana's Memorial, 147, [5.93]; Ghana's Reply, 110–17, [3.78–3.93].
[249] The *Ghana/Côte d'Ivoire* case, [2017] ITLOS Rep [478–79].

Annex 2 had a right to acquire a German license within one year after the Agreement came into force.[250]

ii. Agreements Regarding Single Maritime Boundaries

The conduct of the Parties affected the delimitation line drawn in the 1988 Agreement between Denmark and the German Democratic Republic. In the vicinity of Bornholm, Denmark had already issued licenses for the exploration and exploitation of hydrocarbons. It is suggested that the Agreement was negotiated in such a way as to keep the areas for which Danish licenses had already been issued on the Danish side of the boundary.[251] Furthermore, the single maritime boundary established in the 2000 Treaty between Nigeria and Equatorial Guinea largely reflects concession practice of the parties. In fact, the northeast side of the delimitation line corresponds to the northern limit of Equatorial Guinea's concession practice except for the 'cut-out' around Nigeria's Ekanga–1 well. On the southwest side of the single maritime boundary, the line corresponds to the limits of Nigeria's concession practice in this area.[252] Overall, however, the influence of the conduct of the Parties has been slight in treaties concerning single maritime boundaries.

C. Summary

The above survey of case law and State practice yields the following conclusions.

First, where an agreed boundary exists, there is no need to effectuate maritime delimitations. Thus the examination of the existence of an agreed maritime boundary is of critical importance. When examining the existence of a *modus vivendi* or a *de facto* line, however, the conduct of the Parties may become an element to be taken into account by an international court or tribunal.[253] In this connection, the ICJ in the *Nicaragua v Honduras* case required a 'compelling' evidence to accept the existence of an agreed boundary. Given the importance of a permanent maritime boundary, the Court seemed to take a rigid approach to this matter.

[250] Lagoni, 'Oil and Gas Deposits Across National Frontiers' 241–42. See also the report by Anderson in *IMB*, vol II, 1802–3. For the text of the Agreement, see *ibid*, 1809–13. But, Annex 2 of that Agreement is not included. It was a reproduced in the Office for Ocean Affairs and the Law of the Sea, United Nations, *The Law of the Sea: Maritime Boundary Agreements (1970–1984)* (New York, NY, United Nations, 1987) 69. In addition, Art 4 of the 1971 Agreement between the Netherlands and the FRG provides that the Dutch concessionaires were to be granted licenses under German law to explore for and extract mineral oil and natural gas within one year from the date of entry into force of the Agreement. Text in *IMB*, vol II, 1844–48.

[251] At the same time, it should be noted that proportionality and economic significance were taken into account in the Adler Grund area. But, the relationship between these factors was unclear. Report by Franckx in *IMB*, vol II, 2089 and 2092.

[252] Report by Colson in ibid, vol IV, 2662.

[253] See also Evans, *Relevant Circumstances and Maritime Delimitation* 221.

Secondly, while the conduct of the Parties may not be a priori precluded from the scope of relevant circumstances at the second stage of maritime delimitation, the judicial practice suggests that the conduct of the Parties usually plays only a modest role for the purpose of maritime delimitation.

Thirdly, the influence of the conduct of the Parties is very limited in State practice. Indeed, seabed concessions play little, if any, role for the delimitation of continental shelves or the tracing of single maritime boundaries.

III. HISTORIC RIGHTS

The LOSC contains no definition on the concept of 'historic rights' and 'historic title'. In this regard, the Annex VII Arbitral Tribunal in the *South China Sea* arbitration (merits) clarified the concept of 'historic rights' and 'historic title' as follows:

> The term 'historic rights' is general in nature and can describe any rights that a State may possess that would not normally arise under the general rules of international law, absent particular historical circumstances. Historic rights may include sovereignty, but may equally include more limited rights, such as fishing rights or rights of access, that fall well short of a claim of sovereignty. 'Historic title', in contrast, is used specifically to refer to historic sovereignty to land or maritime areas.[254]

With respect to the delimitation of the territorial sea, both Article 12 of the Geneva Convention on the Territorial Sea and the Contiguous Zone and Article 15 of the LOSC include 'historic titles' in a category of special circumstances. Regarding the delimitation of the continental shelf and the EEZ, however, no mention was made of such titles in Articles 74(1) and 83(1) of the LOSC. Here a question arises whether historic titles and/or historic rights may be regarded as a relevant circumstance in the delimitation of the continental shelf or EEZ.

A. Analysis of the Case Law

i. Arguments in the Context of Continental Shelf Delimitations

A leading case on this subject is the *Tunisia/Libya* case. In that case, Tunisia claimed historic rights which derived from long-established sedentary fishing

[254] PCA Case No. 2013–19, the *South China Sea* arbitration (Merits), Award of 12 July 2016, [225], available at: https://pca-cpa.org/en/cases/. See also Zou Keyuan, 'China's U-Shaped Line in the South China Sea Revisited' (2012) 43 *ODIL* 241; CR Symmons, *Historic Waters in the Law of the Sea: A Modern Re-appraisal* (Nijhoff, Leiden, 2008) 5. For an analysis of the concept of historic rights in the *South China Sea* arbitration (Merits), see Y Tanaka, 'Reflections on Historic Rights in the South China Sea Arbitration (Merits)' (2017) 32 *The International Journal of Marine and Coastal Law* 458; CR Symmons, 'Historic Rights in the Light of the Award in the South China Sea Arbitration: What Remains of the Doctrine Now?' in S Jayakumar et al (eds), *The South China Sea Arbitration: The Legal Dimension* (Cheltenham, Edward Elgar, 2018) 101.

activities in the bed and waters of the Mediterranean off its coasts. According to Tunisia, the long-established interests and activities of its population, coupled with at least the tacit toleration and recognition by third States, resulted in the acquisition by Tunisia of historic rights over a substantial area of sea-bed. Accordingly, Tunisia claimed that the delimitation of the continental shelf between itself and Libya should not encroach at any point upon the area within which it possessed such historic rights.[255] Libya contested the Tunisian arguments since, insofar as the area claimed might overlap with the natural prolongation of Libya, the fishing practice of one State could not prevail over the inherent rights of another State over the natural prolongation of its land territory.[256]

The ICJ discussed the issue in general terms giving, at first sight, a positive answer: 'Historic titles must enjoy respect and be preserved as they have always been by long usage.'[257] Furthermore, it noted that: '[T]he question of Tunisia's historic rights may be relevant for the decision in the present case in a number of ways.'[258] In the operational stage of the delimitation, however, the Court did not consider it necessary to decide on the validity of Tunisian historic rights with regard to Libya, since the line indicated by the Court left Tunisia in full possession of the area covered by such rights.[259]

Some members of the Court discussed the validity of the historic rights claim more thoroughly. Judge Oda criticised the concept from the angle of legislative history. In his view, the Court had failed to recognise the fact that at the 1958 Conference the question of historic title had been taken up in connection with the delimitation of the territorial sea, not with that of the continental shelf.[260] According to Judge Oda,

> [i]t is ..., very important to note that even at the 1958 Conference there was no suggestion that this exception to the median line method of territorial-sea delimitation should be applied to the case of the delimitation of the continental shelf, and no argument in favour of such an idea was ever put forward at UNCLOS III.

[255] Judgment, [1982] ICJ Rep 72, [98]. For the Tunisian claims regarding historic rights, see also Memorial of Tunisia, 73–111; Reply of Tunisia, 12–20; Plaidoire by R-J Dupuy, Verbatim Record 1981, Pleadings, Oral Arguments, Documents, vol IV, 457–85.

[256] Judgment, [1982] ICJ Rep 72, [98]. See also Counter-Memorial of Libya, 182–216, [92–179]; Reply of Libya, 113–24.

[257] [1982] ICJ Rep 73, [100]. In this respect, Kolb considered that historic rights were not an ordinary relevant circumstance in the sense that historic rights were the basis of a prescriptive title which in principle might result in the attribution of the area in question to one of the States in dispute. In his view, while an ordinary relevant circumstances is of a 'relative' or 'dispositive' nature, historic rights concern relevant circumstances that are 'absolute' or 'dispositive' in its nature. In any case, the effect of such historic rights on a delimitation line is similar to the effect of an ordinary relevant circumstance: there will simply be a requirement for the line not to encroach upon historic waters. Kolb, *Case Law on Equitable Maritime Delimitation* 184.

[258] The *Tunisia/Libya* case, [1982] ICJ Rep 75, [102].

[259] ibid, 86, [121].

[260] Dissenting Opinion of Judge Oda, ibid, 210, [87].

> Thus it may be assumed that historic title by reason of longstanding practice of sedentary fisheries might justify some deviation in the line of the delimitation of the territorial sea, but otherwise historic title would not have any impact on delimitation of the continental shelf. This is not incompatible with the principle that any historic fishing right based on long-standing practice should be respected whatever the status of the submerged areas under the new régime.[261]

By contrast, Judge Jiménez de Aréchaga thought that historic rights may be relevant for the delimitation of a continental shelf. First, with respect to the criticism based on the legislative history, he considered that the explanation was simple. In his view,

> [i]t is not that historic rights are irrelevant or unimportant for shelf delimitation, but that there are, in this case, besides the historic factor, other special circumstances equally relevant. Consequently, the historic factor is included in the wider formula of 'special circumstances', as the *travaux préparatoires* of 1958 indicate, and is undoubtedly contained within the broad terms of the Special Agreement: the relevant circumstances which characterize the area.[262]

With respect to the objection based on the *ab initio* character of the rights over the continental shelf, Judge Jiménez de Aréchaga discarded it by stating that:

> A new legal concept, consisting in the notion introduced in 1958 that continental shelf rights are inherent or '*ab initio*' cannot by itself have the effect of abolishing or denying acquired and existing rights. That would be contrary to elementary legal notions and to basic principles of intertemporal law. It would be absurd to contend that the Truman Proclamation or the 1958 Convention abolished or disregarded pre-existing rights over the continental shelf, when, on the contrary, they embodied or assimilated those rights into the new doctrine.[263]

The two different views highlight the difficulties of the question. On the one hand, as already held in the *Grisbadarna* case, it is an objective of the law to preserve historic rights grown from long usage. In fact, States will not regard a line disregarding their historic rights as equitable. But, as with seabed concessions, the concept of historic rights creates a theoretical difficulty: the incompatibility between that concept and the basic nature of the continental shelf. The former is based on acquisition, while the latter relates to rights *ipso facto* and *ab initio*. The right of a coastal State over the continental shelf exists without any act of acquisition. It would seem to follow that the two notions are incompatible. Hence, the Court has to face the difficult question of the compatibility between the *Grisbadarna* rule and the concept of the continental shelf.

[261] ibid, 211, [88].
[262] Separate Opinion of Judge Jiménez de Aréchaga, ibid, 123, [80].
[263] ibid, 123–24, [82].

ii. Arguments in the Context of Single/Coincident Maritime Boundaries

a. Historic Rights in the ICJ Jurisprudence

In the ICJ jurisprudence concerning the delimitation of single/coincident maritime boundaries, the issues of historic rights arose in the *Gulf of Maine* and *Qatar v Bahrain* cases. In the *Gulf of Maine* case, the United States asserted that the activities pursued by the United States and its nationals since the country's independence and even before constituted a decisive factor. Such activities included not only fishing and its conservation, but also other maritime activities concerning navigational assistance, rescue, research, defence, etc.[264] The Chamber of the ICJ thought that such a claim was somewhat akin to the 'invocation of historic rights', although that expression was not used in the arguments of the United States.[265] However, the Chamber discarded the United States' arguments. According to the Chamber, until very recently, the areas in question were part of the high seas and were open to the fishermen not only of the United States and Canada, but also of other countries. Furthermore, after the creation of the 200-mile FZs, the situation radically altered, and third States and their nationals found themselves deprived of any right of access to the sea areas within those zones. The Chamber concluded that whatever preferential situation the United States may previously have enjoyed, this cannot constitute in itself a valid ground for incorporating into its own exclusive fishery zone any area which, in law, has become part of Canada.[266]

In the *Qatar v Bahrain* case, the ICJ dealt with the question of whether Bahrain's historic rights over pearling banks could be considered a relevant circumstance in the delimitation of the northern sector. Bahrain maintained that the pearling banks, many of which were situated to the north of the Qatar peninsula, appertained to Bahrain since time immemorial, and that Bahrain had consistently exercised jurisdiction and control over them.[267] According to Bahrain, its historic rights over these banks were thus relevant to the delimitation of the maritime boundary in accordance with equitable principles and could not be ignored in carrying out the delimitation.[268] By contrast, in denying Bahrain's exclusive rights over the exploitation of the pearling banks, Qatar maintained that these fisheries had always been considered as common to all tribes along the shores of the Gulf.[269] Furthermore, Qatar alleged that Bahrain's claim had lost its relevance since the pearl fisheries had ceased to exist over half a century ago.[270]

[264] [1984] ICJ Rep 340–41, [233].
[265] ibid.
[266] ibid, 341–42, [235].
[267] Memorial submitted by Bahrain, 257; presentation by Reisman, Counsel of Bahrain, Verbatim Record, CR 2000/15, [55–58]; Judgment, [2001] ICJ Rep 112, [235].
[268] Memorial submitted by Bahrain, 274. See also, 283–84.
[269] Counter-Memorial submitted by Qatar, 282–88.
[270] ibid, 277–78; presentation by Salmon, Counsel of Qatar, Verbatim Record, CR 2000/10, [2–4]; Judgment, [2001] ICJ Rep 112, [235].

In this respect, the Court first confirmed the fact that the pearling industry effectively ceased to exist a considerable time ago. Furthermore, it held that, from the evidence submitted to it, it was clear that pearling was traditionally considered as a right which was common to the coastal populations. Moreover, in the Court's view, even if pearling had been carried out by a group of fishermen from one State only, this never seemed to have led to the recognition of an exclusive *quasi*-territorial right to the fishing grounds themselves or to the superjacent waters. Consequently, the Court rejected the argument that pearling constituted a special circumstance justifying an eastward shift of the equidistance line.[271] The rejection of Bahrain's historic rights relied on the facts of the case, and the Court did not express, in a general way, views relating to the relevance of historic rights in maritime delimitations.

b. Historic Rights in Arbitral Awards

The influence of historic rights on maritime delimitation was discussed in two arbitral awards. In the *Eritrea/Yemen* award regarding sovereignty, the Arbitral Tribunal had found that:

> such sovereignty [over various Islands] is not inimical to, but rather entails, the perpetuation of the traditional fishing regime in the region. This existing regime has operated, as the evidence presented to the Tribunal amply testifies, around the Hanish and Zuqar Islands and the islands of Jabal al-Tayr and Zubayr group.[272]

Furthermore, in paragraph vi of the operative part of the award, the Tribunal determined that: '[T]he sovereignty found to lie within Yemen entails the perpetuation of the traditional fishing regime in the region, including free access and enjoyment for the fishermen of both Eritrea and Yemen.'[273]

Eritrea argued that these findings entailed the establishment of a joint resource zone.[274] Eritrea thus proposed 'the joint resource area boxes' around the mid-sea islands.[275] Yemen opposed Eritrea's arguments. In its view, it was clear from paragraph 526 of the Award on Sovereignty that it was Yemen which ensured the preservation of the traditional fishing regime. In other words, Yemen's sovereignty over the islands concerned was not conditional. Moreover, the applicable law, that is, equitable principles, does not encompass the creation or modalities of 'joint resource zones' around Yemen's islands.[276] In addition, the Parties had already established a framework for addressing the modalities of their fishing activities in the Red Sea with their 1994 and 1998 Agreements. In short, according to Yemen, the perpetuation of the traditional fishing regime

[271] ibid, [236].
[272] The *Eritrea/Yemen* arbitral award (First Phase), (2001) 22 *RIAA* 330, [526].
[273] ibid, [527 (iv)].
[274] The *Eritrea/Yemen* arbitral award (The Second Phase), (2001) 22 *RIAA* 356, [89].
[275] ibid, 341, [27–28].
[276] Annex II, Yemen's Answer to Judge Schwebel's Question Put to Yemen on Tuesday, 13 July 1999.

is not synonymous with the rights and obligations of the Parties to be determined by the drawing of a single maritime boundary.[277]

In considering this issue, the Arbitral Tribunal first specified the contents of the traditional fishing regime. In this respect, it stated that sovereignty of Yemen over the Jabal al-Tayr, the Zubayr group and the Zuqar-Hanish group was subject to the Islamic legal concepts of the region, according to which all humans have an inherent right to sustain their nutritional needs through fishing from coast to coast, with free access to fish on either side, and to trade the surplus.[278] According to the Tribunal '[t]he traditional fishing regime is not an entitlement in common to resources nor is it a shored right in them. Rather, it entitles both Eritrean and Yemeni fishermen to engage in artisanal fishing around the islands which, in its Award on Sovereignty, the Tribunal attributed to Yemen.'[279] In so doing, there must be free access to and from the islands concerned, including unimpeded passage through waters. The entitlement to enter the relevant ports, and to sell and market the fish there, was also an integral element of the traditional regime.[280] By contrast, the extraction of guano or minerals did not form part of the traditional fishing regime.[281] In addition, that regime did not extend to large-scale commercial or industrial fishing nor to fishing by nationals of third States in the Red Sea, whether small-scale or industrial.[282]

The Tribunal then turned to the question regarding the effect of such a traditional fishing regime on maritime delimitation. On this point, it stated that such a regime operated throughout the waters beyond the territorial seas of each of the Parties, and also in their territorial waters and ports.[283] 'Accordingly', it continued, 'it does not depend, either for its existence or for its protection upon the drawing of an international boundary by this Tribunal.'[284] Thus, the course of the maritime boundary was not conditioned by the findings of the traditional fishing regimes in the Award on Sovereignty.[285] Furthermore, the Tribunal held that no further joint agreement was legally necessary to maintain a regime based on mutual freedom and the absence of unilaterally imposed

[277] Transcript, Day 6, 13 July 1999, 88, quoted in ibid.

[278] Regarding the concept of Islamic international law, see M Khadduri, 'International Law, Islamic' in R Bernhardt (ed), *Encyclopaedia of Public International Law*, vol 6 (Amsterdam, North-Holland, 1983) 227; AS El-Kosheri, 'History of the Law of Nations, Regional Developments: Islam' ibid, vol 7, 222–30. While questioning the Tribunal's argument relying on the Islamic law, Nuno Sérgio Marques Antunes pointed out that one primary concern of the Tribunal was not to disturb the socio-economic reality of the community of fishermen. Nuno Sérgio Marques Antunes, 'The 1999 Eritrea-Yemen Maritime Delimitation Award and the Development of International Law' (2001) 50 *ICLQ* 307. Regarding problems of the Tribunal's argument relating to the Islamic law, see also G Distefano, 'La sentence arbitrale du 17 décembre 1999 sur la délimitation des frontière maritimes entre l'Erythrée et le Yémen: quelques observations complémentaires' (2000) *AFDI* 261 and 272.

[279] The *Eritrea/Yemen* case (The Second Phase), 22 *RIAA* 359, [103].

[280] ibid, 360, [107].

[281] ibid, 359, [104].

[282] ibid, 360, [106].

[283] ibid, 361, [109].

[284] ibid, [110].

[285] ibid.

conditions.[286] Consequently, the *Eritrea/Yemen* arbitration did not rely on the traditional fishing regime when drawing the delimitation line.

In the *Barbados v Trinidad and Tobago* case, Barbados maintained that the provisional equidistance line should be adjusted in light of traditional fishing by Barbadian fisherfolk. However, Barbados' claim was rejected by the Annex VII Arbitral Tribunal. In this regard, the Tribunal clearly stated that:

> Determining an international maritime boundary between two States on the basis of traditional fishing on the high seas by nationals of one of those States is altogether exceptional. Support for such a principle in customary and conventional international law is largely lacking. Support is most notably found in speculations of the late eminent jurist, Sir Gerald Fitzmaurice, and in the singular circumstances of the judgment of the International Court of Justice in the *Jan Mayen* case (I.C.J. Reports 1993, p. 38). That is insufficient to establish a rule of international law.[287]

Historic fishing rights were also invoked by Slovenia in the *Croatia/Slovenia* arbitration. In this regard, Slovenia stressed that: '[I]ts fishing activities far south of the equidistance line.'[288] More generally, Slovenia claimed that: '[T]he historic entitlements that Slovenia exercised as part of the SFRY before independence extended throughout the SFRY's territorial sea, including in the northern Adriatic.'[289] The Arbitral Tribunal, in its arbitral award of 2017, denied the existence of historic titles that would warrant a departure from the equidistance line.[290] Yet the Tribunal provided no further detail on this matter.

B. Analysis of State Practice

In general, the importance of historic fishing rights in the context of maritime delimitations remains unclear. It is suggested, however, that, in the 1978 exchange of notes effecting agreement on the provisional maritime boundary between the United States and Mexico, the fishing banks traditionally used by US fishermen in the Pacific Ocean influenced the decision by the United States to use all existing islands for generating an equidistance line, thereby bringing Cortez and Tanner banks under US jurisdiction.[291]

In this connection, it is worth noting that the problem of traditional fishing rights may be resolved without adjusting the maritime boundaries. For instance, in the 1976 Agreement between India and Sri Lanka relating to the Gulf of Manaar and the Bay of Bengal, the question of the historic fishing rights claimed

[286] ibid, [111].
[287] The *Barbados v Trinidad and Tobago* arbitral award, (2001) 22 *RIAA* 222–23, [269].
[288] PCA Case No. 2012-04. *In the Matter of an Arbitration under the Arbitration Agreement between the Government of the Republic of Croatia and the Government of the Republic of Slovenia,* 29 June 2017. Final Award, [958].
[289] ibid, [956].
[290] ibid, [1011].
[291] Report by Smith and Colson in *IMB*, vol I, 430.

by Sri Lanka on Wedge Bank, located 25 miles southwest of Cape Comorin in India, was settled by an exchange of letters, on the day which the Agreement was signed, without adjusting the boundary. The letters stated that Sri Lankan fishermen were entitled to fish on Wedge Bank for three years from the time of India's proclamation of its EEZ, and that India agreed to provide annually to Sri Lanka 2,000 tons of fish for a period of five years with effect from the date of cessation of the fishing activity by Sri Lankan vessels on Wedge Bank.[292] Furthermore, the 1981 Memorandum of Understanding between Indonesia and Australia Concerning the Implementation of a Provisional Fisheries Surveillance and Enforcement Arrangement provided that the latter would not affect traditional fishing by Indonesian traditional fishermen in accordance with the 1974 Memorandum.[293] In addition, the 2001 treaty between Honduras and the United Kingdom (Cayman Islands) created a special fishing area within the Honduran EEZ delimited by the established maritime boundary with a view to allowing Cayman fishermen to continue the historic fishing in the area of the Misteriosa and Rosario Banks.[294]

C. Summary

On the basis of the above considerations, three points can be made.

First, the ICJ, in the *Tunisia/Libya* case, regarded historic rights as relevant. Yet the question of how to take them into account is difficult to answer, since the consideration of historic rights produces theoretical difficulties regarding the incompatibility with the *ipso facto* and *ab initio* nature of continental shelf rights.

Secondly, the Arbitral Tribunal in the *Eritrea/Yemen* case did not take the traditional fishing regime into account on the grounds that free access to fishing, which is the essence of that regime, was not dependent on maritime delimitation. Thus the Tribunal shows another possible solution, separating traditional fishing regimes from maritime delimitations. If, as the Tribunal indicated, free access to natural resources was to be the real interest which underlies historic rights, such interest could be protected by an agreement ensuring such access independently of maritime delimitation.

Thirdly, it is notable that to resolve the problem of historic rights, the 1976 Agreement between India and Sri Lanka instituted a transitory period for

[292] Text in ibid, vol II, 1426–29.

[293] ibid, 1239. According to the 1974 Memorandum of Understanding between Australia and Indonesia Regarding the Operation of Indonesian Traditional Fishermen in Areas of the Australian Exclusive Fishing Zone and Continental Shelf, 'traditional fishermen' means the fishermen who have traditionally taken fish and sedentary organisms in Australian waters by methods which have been the tradition over decades of time. ibid.

[294] Art 3. Text in ibid, vol V, 3571. See also Report by CL Contreras and M Woold, ibid, 3566; Kwiatkowska, 'Resource, Navigational and Environmental Factors' 3234.

fisheries and attributed a certain amount of fish to the other State involved without adjusting the delimitation line. This solution may provide useful guidance in practice.

IV. SECURITY INTERESTS

A. Analysis of the Case Law

i. Arguments in the Context of Continental Shelf Delimitations

a. Security Interests in the *Anglo-French Continental Shelf* Case

In the *Anglo-French Continental Shelf* case, the French Government had contended that: '[A]lthough the allocation of the intervening area of the continental shelf of the United Kingdom would not theoretically affect the legal status of its superjacent waters and airspace, the vital interests of the French Republic in the security and defense of its territory could not fail to be put in doubt.'[295] In France's view, if the whole Hurd Deep Fault zone were to be attributed to the United Kingdom, 'this would involve serious inconveniences and risks for French submarines stationed at Cherbourg as well as [affect] the French Republic's military supervision of the approaches to its territory.'[296] By contrast, the United Kingdom argued that such security considerations might equally be urged in favour of a continuous continental shelf between the British mainland and the Channel Islands. In its view, zonal defence arrangements 'have little or nothing to do with national frontiers, and much less with continental shelf boundaries.'[297] The Court of Arbitration had this to say:

> [T]he weight of such considerations in this region is, in any event, somewhat diminished by the very particular character of the English Channel as a major route of international maritime navigation serving ports outside the territories of either of the Parties. Consequently, they cannot be regarded by the Court as exercising a decisive influence on the delimitation of the boundary in the present case. *They may support and strengthen, but they cannot negative, any conclusions that are already indicated by the geographical, political and legal circumstances of the region which the Court has identified.*[298]

The phrase 'they may support and strengthen' shows that the Court of Arbitration did not rule out the possibility of security considerations being relevant circumstances. However, the above quotation as a whole clearly shows that such considerations are subsidiary in character.

[295] The *Anglo-French Continental Shelf* arbitral award, 18 *RIAA* 80, [161].
[296] ibid.
[297] ibid, 85, [175].
[298] Emphasis added. ibid, 90, [188].

b. Security Interests in the ICJ Jurisprudence

In the *Libya/Malta* case, the ICJ took a different view on this matter. In that case, Malta had referred to the 'equitable consideration' of security and defence as supporting the validity of the equidistance method. On this point, E Lauterpacht, Counsel for Malta, stated that:

> [T]he identification of a boundary line in the area of the Rift Zone would entitle Libya to place massive oil rigs equipped with helicopter pads within a few minutes' flying time of Malta. Malta would be confronted by the prospect of constant foreign ship and aircraft movement close to its shores but not subject to its regulation, supervision or control (see III, pp 335–36). Such a situation, I argued, would be unacceptable anywhere else.[299]

He continued,

> If the presence of rigs and the activity associated with them on the shelf of one State threaten the security of opposite or adjacent States, it is reasonable that matters should be so regulated that the risk, or potential for risk, to each should bear upon each equally. The risk is a function of distance or proximity. It follows therefore that a line which is equidistant from the two States either equally reduces or equally generates the risk for each, depending upon how you look at it.[300]

Libya contested Malta's arguments by declaring that there were no facts bearing out Malta's assertion. According to Libya, security interests played a secondary role and were not apt to overrule or outweigh the relevant circumstances of the case.[301]

With respect to this issue, the Court, on the one hand, expressed a certain degree of sympathy to Malta's arguments by stating that:

> Security considerations are of course not unrelated to the concept of the continental shelf. They were referred to when this legal concept of first emerged, particularly in the Truman Proclamation.[302]

[299] Reply by Lauterpacht, Verbatim Record 1984, Oral Argument *(concluded)*, Correspondence vol IV, 321.

[300] ibid, 322. Furthermore in its Memorial, Malta stated that: 'The distance criterion, ..., is a reflection of the rule that all coastal States have a lateral reach of jurisdiction. Such an apron of jurisdiction is a necessary attribute of national security. The equidistant method thus gives effect to the logic that Malta's need for security is no less than that of Libya.' Memorial of Malta, vol I, 444, [149]. In Malta's view, '[t]he impact upon the security, or sense of security of a State, is related not to geology, geomorphology, bathymetry or natural prolongation, but to simple consideration of distance'. Counter-Memorial of Malta, vol. I. 329, [210].

[301] Counter-Memorial of Libya, vol II, 73–74, [3.39]. See also the statement by Lucchini, Verbatim Record 1984, Oral Argument *(concluded)*, Correspondence vol IV, 136–39.

[302] [1985] ICJ Rep 42, [51]. Indeed, the Truman Proclamation stated that 'self-protection compels the coastal nation to keep close watch over activities off its shores which are of the nature necessary for utilisation of these resources.' Nevertheless, it is doubtful whether the above phrase directly concerns security interests in a military sense or relates to a general interest in controlling the offshore activities. In any event, the above reason played no role in the promotion of the institution of the continental shelf. Evans, *Relevant Circumstances and Maritime Delimitation* 172.

However, the Court pointed out that:

> [I]n the present case neither Party has raised the question whether the law at present attributes to the coastal State particular competences in the military field over its continental shelf, including competence over the placing of military devices. In any event, the delimitation which will result from the application of the present Judgment is, …, not so near to the coast of either Party as to make questions of security a particular consideration in the present case.[303]

While security factors were thus considered as a relevant circumstance, they did not affect the location of the continental shelf boundary. It is of interest to note that the Court considered security considerations to be a matter of distance. Yet it remains unclear how important the distance between the coast and the boundary line should be.

ii. Arguments in the Context of Single/Coincident Maritime Boundaries

a. Security Interests in the ICJ Jurisprudence

The relevance of security interests was discussed in a series of cases before the ICJ. In the *Gulf of Maine* case, the United States asked the Chamber to consider its 'dominance' in the Gulf, including defence, on the basis of the *Anglo-French Continental Shelf* case.[304] Canada objected that, as with lines for fisheries or the safety of navigation, ad hoc operational lines for purposes of military cooperation were not, in State practice, accorded legal significance for drawing general jurisdictional boundaries. Accordingly, the general concept of the United States' 'dominance' in the Gulf of Maine area was incapable of suggesting any principle of division.[305] The Chamber refused to take defence factors into account for reasons similar to those which lead it to discard economic and socio-economic factors.[306] In the Chamber's view, since its judgment was not to be a decision rendered *ex aequo et bono*, and since a single maritime boundary had to be drawn essentially on the basis of geographical features of the area concerned, security factors were not relevant.

In the *Jan Mayen* case, Norway had argued that: '[T]he drawing of a boundary closer to one State than to another would imply an inequitable displacement of the possibility of the former State to protect interests which require protection.'[307] The Court discarded Norway's argument since the boundary to be established was not sufficiently near Jan Mayen's coast to create a security

[303] [1985] ICJ Rep 42, [51].

[304] Submissions in Memorial of the United States, vol II, 126. See also ibid, 87, [224] and 99, [259].

[305] Counter-Memorial of Canada, vol III, 170, [452–54].

[306] [1984] ICJ Rep 342, [237].

[307] [1993] ICJ Rep 74, [81]; Counter-Memorial submitted by Norway, vol I, 162–64, [561–66]; Rejoinder submitted by Norway, 161–62, [541–46].

problem.[308] It will be noted that the ICJ considered, once again, security issues on the basis of distance from the coast. This is a rerun of the *dictum* in the *Libya/Malta* judgment. But the rejection of Norway's contention does not mean that the Court refused to treat security considerations as relevant circumstances. On the contrary, basing itself on the *dictum* of the *Libya/Malta* case, it accepted that such considerations were relevant to the delimitation of all maritime zones, but it did not indicate how to take them into account and merely referred to the *Libya/Malta* case.[309]

In the *Qatar v Bahrain* case, Qatar contested the proposed boundaries by Bahrain on the basis of security considerations. According to Qatar, Bahraini line in the southern sector was drawn so close to Qatar's coast that it would certainly create serious problems concerning Qatar's security interests.[310] Bahrain did not contest the fact that security was one of factors to be taken into account in effecting an equitable result. However, it argued that in no case had a court or tribunal 'reshaped' geography for security reason.[311] The ICJ did not touch on security interests in that case. When examining the nature of Fasht al Azm, however, the Court held that if Fasht al Azm was to be regarded as part of the Sitrah Island, a possible equidistance line would place the boundary disproportionately close to Qatar's mainland coast.[312] In so stating, the Court might have implicitly considered security interests.

In the *Nicaragua v Honduras* case, Nicaragua referred to a number of factors, including security considerations, in order to demonstrate the equitable character of its own proposed bisector line.[313] Nonetheless, Nicaragua's claim was not supported by the ICJ.[314]

Security interests were also discussed in the *Black Sea* case. While Romania asserted that Ukraine's delimitation line runs unreasonably close to the Romanian coast, encroaching on its security interests,[315] Ukraine argued that its delimitation line does not compromise any Romanian security interests.[316] According to the Court, as stated in the *Libya/Malta* judgment,[317] legitimate security consideration may play a role in the maritime delimitation. However, the Court took

[308] [1993] ICJ Rep 74–75, [81].
[309] ibid, 75, [81].
[310] Counter-Memorial submitted by Qatar, 230–31.
[311] Reply submitted by Bahrain, [305]; presentation by Weil, Counsel of Bahrain, Verbatim Record, CR 2000/15, [42–45].
[312] Judgment, [2001] ICJ Rep 104, [218].
[313] Judgment, [2007] ICJ Rep 748, [291]. See also Memorial of Nicaragua, vol I, 134–36, [22–25]; counter-memorial of Nicaragua, vol I, 184–85, [9.26-27]; presentation by Brownlie, Verbatim Record, CR 2007/2, 47–8, [163–71]. By contrast, Honduras argued that: '[E]ven in the *United Kingdom v France* case, where some very strong real security-based arguments were made, this factor was not applied by the arbitral tribunal and it has never been taken into account by the Court [ICJ].' Presentation by Colson, Verbatim Record, CR 2007/14, 14, [10].
[314] Judgment, [2007] ICJ Rep 748, [292].
[315] Judgment, [2009] ICJ Rep 127, [202]; Reply Submitted by Romania, 303, [9.39].
[316] [2009] ICJ Rep 127–28, [203]; Counter-Memorial Submitted by Ukraine, 248, [10.26–10.27]; Rejoinder Submitted by Ukraine, 146–47, [8.26].
[317] [1985] ICJ Rep 42, [51]. See also [1993] ICJ Rep 74–75, [81].

the view that the provisional equidistance line constructed by the Court in the present case fully respects the legitimate security interests of either Party. The Court thus held that there is no need to adjust the equidistance line on the basis of the security considerations.[318]

In the *Nicaragua v Colombia* case, the ICJ recognised that legitimate security concerns might be a relevant consideration if a maritime delimitation was effected particularly near to the coast of a State.[319] It thus stated that it would 'bear this consideration in mind in determining what adjustment to make to the provisional median line or in what way that line should be shifted.'[320] In addition, the Court noted that the Nicaraguan proposal to enclave Colombian islands facing Nicaraguan territory would 'produce a disorderly pattern of several distinct Colombian enclaves within a maritime space which otherwise pertained to Nicaragua with unfortunate consequences for the orderly management of maritime resources, *policing and the public order of the oceans in general*, all of which would be better served by a simpler and more coherent division of the relevant area.'[321] In so stating, the Court seemed to enlarge the concept of security including 'policing' and 'the public order of the oceans in general'.[322] Nonetheless, it remained less clear to what extent those elements were taken into account when adjusting the provisional medial line in the *Nicaragua v Colombia* case.

b. Security Interests in Arbitral Awards

In the context of arbitration, three cases merit discussion. The first is the *Guinea/Guinea-Bissau* case. In this case, the Parties invoked security considerations by linking them to economic circumstances. On this point, the Arbitral Tribunal held that security circumstances were not without interest.[323] Accordingly, as in the *Libya/Malta* judgment, the Tribunal accepted that security factors might be relevant circumstances. But it also held that they would not affect the conclusion already reached by it:

> However, the implications that this circumstance might have had were avoided by the fact that, in its proposed solution, the Tribunal has taken care to ensure that each State controls the maritime territories situated opposite its coasts and in their vicinity. The Tribunal has constantly been guided by its concern to find an equitable solution. Its prime objective has been to avoid that either Party, for one reason or another,

[318] [2009] ICJ Rep 128, [204].

[319] Judgment, [2012] ICJ Rep 706, [222].

[320] ibid.

[321] Emphasis added. ibid,708, [230].

[322] M Evans, 'Relevant Circumstances' in Alex G Oude Elferink, T Henriksen and SV Busch (eds), *Maritime Boundary Delimitation: The Case Law Is It consistent and Practicable?* (Cambridge University Press, 2018) 257.

[323] The *Guinea/Guinea-Bissau* arbitral award, (1986) 25 *ILM* 302, [124].

> should see rights exercised opposite its coast or in the immediate vicinity thereof, which could prevent the exercise of its own right to development or compromise its security.[324]

In this quotation, the words 'immediate vicinity' appear to refer to distance from the coast. Yet it remains unclear how closely a boundary may approach another State. Indeed, the boundary line runs 2.25 miles above the Guinean Island of Alcatraz. It would be doubtful whether an area 2.25 miles from the coast of Alcatraz Island is not 'immediate vicinity'.[325]

The second case that deserves consideration is the second phase of the *Eritrea/Yemen* arbitration. In this case, Yemen advanced security as a relevant circumstance. The question of security arose especially in connection with the narrow waters separating the Hanish group from the Eritrean coast. According to Yemen, this concern automatically pointed to reliance on the equidistance method.[326] When drawing a median line in the area concerned, the Tribunal did not, however, take security into account.[327]

The third case to be examined is the *Croatia/Slovenia* arbitration. In this case, Slovenia claimed that under Articles 19 and 25(2) of the LOSC, 'territorial sea sovereignty is closely linked with coastal State security interests.'[328] Referring to the *Libya/Malta* and *Jan Mayen* cases, Slovenia also argued that the ICJ recognised security interests as a potentially relevant circumstance for delimitation.[329] In response, Croatia countered that Slovenia's reliance on case law is irrelevant to the delimitation of the territorial sea.[330] As explained earlier, the Arbitral Tribunal established the territorial sea boundary by adjusting an equidistance line. In this connection, the Tribunal considered the 'boxing in' effect resulting from the geographic configuration as a special circumstance that calls for the adjustment of an equidistance line.[331] Yet, it offered scant explanation with regard to the relevance of security interests in the delimitation of the territorial sea.

B. Analysis of State Practice

It is difficult to assess the influence of security considerations upon maritime boundaries since they are almost never mentioned in the text of agreements.

[324] ibid.

[325] Evans states that there may be some distinction between the weight of security factors appertaining to the mainland of a State and that attributed to such factors with respect to small islands. Evans, *Relevant Circumstances and Maritime Delimitation*, 177.

[326] The *Eritrea/Yemen* arbitral award (the Second Phase), 22 *RIAA* 340, [21].

[327] As explained above, it should be noted that the delimitation line drew by the Tribunal was not identical to a median line proposed by Yemen.

[328] The *Croatia/Slovenia* arbitral award, [985].

[329] ibid, [985].

[330] ibid, [988].

[331] ibid, [1012–14]. See also chapter 5, s XVI of this book.

In fact, there is little evidence that maritime boundaries were established so as to reflect security interests.[332] An instance where security factors were taken into account is the 1988 Agreement between Sweden and the former Soviet Union establishing a single maritime boundary in the Baltic Sea. In the course of the negotiations, Sweden argued that full effect should be given to Island of Gotland, while the former Soviet Union proposed disregarding the island. It is suggested that strategic considerations influenced the firm position taken by the Swedish Government, since Gotland played a crucial role in the national defence system of Sweden. The problem was resolved by giving the island a 75 per cent effect.[333]

A second example is provided by the 1985 Agreement between North Korea and the former Soviet Union creating a territorial sea boundary in the region of Peter the Great Bay. The region to be delimited was strategically important to the former Soviet Union, as the largest of the four Soviet naval units was based inside the bay at Vladivostok. Accordingly, it has been said that the former Soviet Union attempted to win as much territorial sea as possible on its side, dividing the delimitation area in its favour.[334]

In addition, security considerations might have affected the 1980 Agreement between Norway (Jan Mayen) and Iceland. A base at Keflavik in Iceland, which was created by an agreement between the latter and the United States, is of vital importance to NATO for the surveillance of the entire Norwegian Sea. If Norway claimed an EEZ disregarding Icelandic interests, Iceland could have resigned from NATO and denounced the Keflavik Agreement with the United States. This would have created problems for NATO as well as for Norway. Thus, in addition to Iceland's dependence upon fisheries, it is reported that security considerations influenced Norway's concession in favour of Iceland accepting its full 200-mile economic zone.[335]

There are also agreements creating maritime boundaries in the areas of great value for national security, but it appears that security factors did not *directly* affect the locations of boundaries. For instance, in the 1986 Agreement between France and Italy, the Parties agreed to create a territorial sea boundary in the Mouths of Bonifacio. This area has great strategic importance since, under the 1972 Treaty between Italy and the United States, an American base for nuclear submarines was established on the island of La Maddalena, at the southeast entrance of the Mouths of Bonifacio.[336] This being the case, military navigation in the Mouths may have exercised an important impact on the negotiations.[337] Yet the established territorial sea boundary was one of simplified equidistance, and, consequently, the influence of security considerations remains obscure.

[332] BH Oxman, 'Political, Strategic, and Historical Considerations' in *IMB*, vol I, 22 and 24.
[333] Report by Franckx in ibid, vol II, 2058–59.
[334] Report by Park in ibid, vol I, 1136.
[335] Østreng, 'Reaching Agreement on International Exploitation of Ocean Mineral Resources,' 563–65.
[336] The text of the treaty is not public. Report by Scovazzi and Francalanci in *IMB*, vol II, 1572.
[337] ibid.

With respect to the Strait of Hormuz, which is of great strategic importance,[338] it is said that the security of that seaway was considered in the 1974 Agreement between Iran and Oman drawing a continental shelf boundary. Yet the boundary line is almost equidistant: thus the influence of security remains unclear.[339] Furthermore, the 1976 Agreement between Cuba and Mexico established a single maritime boundary in the Yucatan Channel, which is one of the most important strategic straits in the western hemisphere. Security considerations did not, however, directly influence the location of the boundary line, which result from applying the equidistance method.[340] Regarding those agreements, although security factors may have been considered in the negotiations, there is little evidence that such considerations had a specific influence upon the end result.

All in all, it can be said that, at least, the *direct* effect of security factors upon maritime boundaries has been hard to identify in most agreements. It is not suggested, however, that they played no role in determining the location of maritime boundaries. In fact, security is one of the elements accounting for disputes over marine areas. Furthermore, as one writer indicates, defence ministries are often consulted when governments determine the position of maritime boundaries. In some cases, the navy is the primary internal source of charts and technical data concerning maritime spaces. Accordingly, it may be presumed that the acceptability of maritime boundaries could be reviewed from a security perspective.[341]

C. Summary

On the basis of the above survey, two observations can be made.

First, in *Libya/Malta, Guinea/Guinea-Bissau*, *Jan Mayen*, *Black Sea*, and *Nicaragua v Colombia*, cases, the ICJ and arbitral tribunal expressly confirmed that security considerations may be relevant to maritime delimitations.[342] Nevertheless, such considerations did not directly affect the location of

[338] For the background of the East-West rivalry for the domination of the region, see A Razavi, *Continental Shelf Delimitation and Related Maritime Issues in the Persian Gulf* (The Hague, Nijhoff, 1997) 157–59. For an analysis of the situation in the Strait of Hormuz within the broader context of the economic and strategic interests of East and West, see RK Ramazani, *International Straits of the World. The Persian Gulf and the Strait of Hormuz* (Alphen aan den Rijn, Sijthoff and Noordhoff, 1979).

[339] Report by R Pietrowski, Jr in *IMB*, vol II, 1504. On 7 March 1974, prior to signing the Agreement, Iran and Oman issued a joint communiqué expressing a joint desire for co-operation in order to ensure the freedom of passage through the Strait of Hormuz. Razavi, *Continental Shelf Delimitation*, 159.

[340] Report by Nweihed in *IMB*, vol I, 566.

[341] Oxman, 'Political, Strategic, and Historical Considerations' 22.

[342] Some writers also consider security factors to be relevant circumstances. Bowett, 'The Economic Factor in Maritime Delimitation Cases' 58–59; Attard, *The Exclusive Economic Zone in International Law* 270–71.

maritime boundaries, since the boundaries involved were not sufficiently close to the coasts of the Parties. As demonstrated in the *Libya/Malta* and the *Jan Mayen* cases, the ICJ appeared to have appraised such elements on the basis of distance from the coast.[343] Yet none of the cases clarified the question of how close a boundary may approach a State. Thus it is difficult to indicate any objective standard of how is it possible to take security factors into account in the process of maritime delimitation, even though they might be regarded as relevant.

Secondly, it is true that all States enjoy the freedom of navigation in EEZ/FZs and in the waters above the continental shelf. However, freedom of navigation is exercisable 'subject to the relevant provisions of this Convention'. Accordingly, unlike navigation in the high seas, such freedom could be restricted by coastal States. Furthermore, Article 58(3) of the LOSC prescribes that, in exercising their rights, States shall have due regard to the rights and duties of the coastal State and shall comply with the laws and regulations adopted by that State in accordance with the provisions of this Convention and other rules of international law. Therefore, it is easy to understand that States prefer to avoid situations where a navigational route of great strategic relevance will come under the jurisdiction of another coastal State. Nonetheless, it is hard to find evidence that maritime boundaries were established so as to reflect security interests in State practice.

V. NAVIGATIONAL INTERESTS

A. Analysis of the Case Law

i. Arguments in the Context of Continental Shelf Delimitations

a. Navigational Interests in the *Anglo-French Continental Shelf* Case

Theoretically, navigation has little relationship to the institution of the continental shelf. As with Article 3 of the 1958 Convention on the Continental Shelf, Article 78(1) of the LOSC stipulates that: 'The rights of the coastal State over the continental shelf do not affect the legal status of the superjacent waters or of the air space above those waters.'[344] Accordingly, the institution of the

[343] In addition, Judge Jiménez de Aréchaga indicated in the *Tunisia/Libya* case that there was 'an immediate and almost instinctive rejection by all coastal States of the possibility that foreign States, or foreign companies or individuals, might appear in front of their coasts.' Separate Opinion of Judge Jiménez de Aréchaga in the *Tunisia/Libya* case, [1982] ICJ Rep 121, [72].

[344] Art 78(2) of the UN Convention on the Law of the Sea provides: 'The exercise of the rights of the coastal State over the continental shelf must not infringe or result in any unjustifiable interference with navigation and other rights and freedoms of other States as provided for in this Convention.'

continental shelf per se does not concern navigation, which takes place on or in the superjacent waters. However, it is not unheard of that navigational interests are invoked by Parties before international courts and tribunals.[345] An example is the *Anglo-French Continental Shelf* case. In this case, France stressed that: '[T]he sea areas in question [the Channel Islands region] constitute a maritime route which is not only militarily but economically of vital interest to the French Republic, since they serve important commercial ports, such as Dunkerque, Le Havre, Antifer and La Basse Seine.'[346] However, the United Kingdom resisted the French arguments in two ways. First, as was the case for the French Republic's preoccupations concerning security interests, the French arguments did not take account of the legal protection provided by Articles 3 to 5 of the Geneva Convention on the Continental Shelf. Secondly, they ignored the fact that the areas in question to the north and northwest of the Channel Islands constituted an international channel of navigation of major importance. According to the United Kingdom, the traffic on this route is not exclusively or even predominantly British or French, and no delimitation of the continental shelf between France and the United Kingdom would change this situation.[347] The Court of Arbitration observed that the weight of considerations regarding navigation was diminished since the English Channel was a major route of international maritime navigation. In the view of the Court, such navigational and security interests could not, accordingly, have a decisive influence on the delimitation of the continental shelf.[348]

b. Navigational Interests in the *Libya/Malta* Case

In the *Libya/Malta* case, Libya touched on the presence of navigable channels as a 'factor which in a given case might prove to be relevant, although perhaps in a subsidiary role'.[349] The ICJ did not, however, allude to navigational interests in its judgment.

[345] It is true that in the *travaux préparatoires* of the Geneva Convention on the Continental Shelf, the ILC included navigational channels as a category of special circumstances. While accepting the rule of equidistance as the general rule, the ILC in 1953, referred to navigable channels as factors justifying a departure from the equidistance line. (1953) 2 *YILC* 216, [82]. Furthermore in 1956, the ILC repeated the same view in the commentary to draft Art 72 regarding delimitation of the continental shelf. (1956) 2 *YILC* 300. This view was criticised, however. In fact, Francois, the *Rapporteur*, objected that questions of navigation was irrelevant for delimiting the continental shelf. (1953) 2 *YILC* 129, [55]; 134, [53].

[346] The *Anglo-French Continental Shelf* arbitral award, 18 *RIAA* 80, [162].

[347] ibid, 86, [176].

[348] ibid, 90, [188]. On this point, Evans believes that where a particular route has a special importance to one party, not matched by its relevance to another, this could amount to a relevant circumstance. Evans, *Relevant Circumstances and Maritime Delimitation*, 181.

[349] Counter-Memorial of Libya, vol II, 144, [6.08].

ii. Arguments in the Context of the Territorial Sea and Single Maritime Boundaries

a. Navigational Interests in the ICJ Jurisprudence

Navigational interests were invoked by the Parties in the *Gulf of Maine* and *Qatar v Bahrain* cases. In the *Gulf of Maine* case, the United States asked the Chamber of the ICJ to consider the activities pursued by it and its nationals. Such activities included not only fishing but other maritime activities such as navigational assistance, rescue, research, defence, etc.[350] As outlined elsewhere in this book, however, the Chamber refused to consider those factors as relevant, except in the extreme case of 'catastrophic repercussions'.[351]

In the *Qatar v Bahrain* case, navigational factors did not directly affect the location of maritime boundaries. According to the delimitation line drawn by the ICJ, however, Qatar's maritime zones situated to the south of the Hawar Islands and those situated to the north of those islands are connected only by the channel separating the Hawar islands from the peninsula. As this channel is narrow and shallow, it is unsuitable for navigation. Hence, the Court emphasised that the waters lying between the Hawar Islands and the other Bahraini islands were not Bahrain's internal waters, but her territorial sea. Consequently, it held, unanimously, that Qatari vessels should enjoy in these waters the right of innocent passage accorded by customary international law.[352] Although this is a truism, it is conceivable that the Court stressed the right of innocent passage owing to the peculiar geographical situation of the Hawar Islands area.[353]

In the *Nicaragua v Honduras* case, Nicaragua argued that the bisector method would produce an equitable result with regard to, inter alia, 'equitable access to the main navigable channel in the adjacent coastal areas'.[354] However, the ICJ did not consider that the factors claimed by Nicaragua, including navigational factor, as 'legally determinative for the purposes of the delimitation to be effected'.[355] Instead, the Court focused on 'the geographical configuration of the coast' and 'the geomorphological features of the area where the endpoint of the land boundary is located'.[356]

350 [1984] ICJ Rep 340–41, [233].
351 ibid, 342, [236].
352 Judgment, [2001] ICJ Rep 109, [223].
353 See also Kwiatkowska, 'Resource, Navigational and Environmental Factors' 3239–41.
354 [2007] ICJ Rep 747–78, [291]. See also presentation by Brownlie, Verbatim Record, CR 2007/2, 48–50, [172–76]. Honduras countered that 'equitable access to the main navigable channel in the adjacent coastal areas' did not constitute a relevant circumstances partly because 'the freedom of navigation beyond the territorial sea and the right of innocent passage in the territorial sea are guaranteed' under the LOSC. See presentation by Colson, Verbatim Record, CR 2007/14, 14, [12].
355 [2007] ICJ Rep 748, [292].
356 ibid.

b. Navigational Interests in Arbitral Awards

Navigational interests were discussed in four arbitral awards. First, in the *Guinea/Guinea-Bissau* case, Guinea-Bissau referred to its particular interest concerning future free access to the part of Buba by the Orango channel and the Rio Grande estuary.[357] On this point, no mention was made by the Arbitral Tribunal. In any event, the delimitation line indicated by the Tribunal allows for free access through the Orango Channel.[358]

Secondly, in the *Eritrea/Yemen* case (the Second Phase), Eritrea objected to the enclave solution proposed for the South-West Rocks and the Haycocks by Yemen on the basis of navigational interests. According to Eritrea, such a solution would have placed the western main shipping channel between Haycocks and South-West Rocks in Yemeni territorial waters, although the eastern main channel, east of Zuqar, was already located in those waters. Consequently, acceptance of Yemen's proposal would have included both main shipping channels in Yemen's territorial waters, which was unacceptable to Eritrea.[359] The Arbitral Tribunal upheld Eritrea's solution since it avoided the creation of awkward enclaves in the vicinity of a major international shipping route.[360] Furthermore, in the part of that route located in the overlapping territorial seas areas in the southern sector, the Tribunal, 'mindful of the simplicity desirable in the neighbourhood of a main shipping lane', drew a delimitation line which would follow this passage directly and independently of Yemeni and Eritrean islands.[361] It thus appears that the Tribunal took navigational factors into account in several parts of the delimitation line.[362]

Thirdly, in the *Guyana v Suriname* case, there was disagreement between the Parties as to whether navigational considerations can constitute a special circumstance.[363] When considering the 10° Line as the territorial sea boundary, Suriname maintained that navigational considerations, namely the control of shipping by the coastal State, are special circumstances for the purposes of Article 15 of the LOSC.[364] However, Guyana countered that there is very limited judicial authority for the proposition that navigational requirements can be treated as a special circumstance 'having so decisive an effect' as that argued for by Suriname.[365] The Arbitral Tribunal, in its Award of 2007, made it clear that: 'Navigational interests have been found to constitute such special

[357] The *Guinea/Guinea-Bissau* arbitral award, (1986) 25 *ILM* 301, [121].

[358] ibid, 298, [111(a)]. Evans, *Relevant Circumstances and Maritime Delimitation*, 182.

[359] The *Eritrea/Yemen* arbitral award (The Second Phase), 22 *RIAA* 340–41, [26].

[360] ibid, 364, [125]. See also, 370, [155].

[361] ibid, 364, [128].

[362] See also Kwiatkowska, 'Resource, Navigational and Environmental Factors' 3237–38.

[363] The *Guiana/Suriname* arbitral award, 30 *RIAA* 83, [300].

[364] ibid, 77, [283]. See also Suriname Counter-Memorial, vol I, 103–04, [6.51–6.52]; Suriname Rejoinder, vol I, 119, [3.265].

[365] The *Guiana/Suriname* arbitral award, 30 *RIAA* 81–82, [294]. See also Guyana Reply, vol I, 112, [6.26].

circumstances.'[366] It thus concluded that special circumstances of navigation may justify deviation from the median line and that the predecessors of the Parties agreed upon a N10°E delimitation line for the reason that all of the Corentyne River was to be Suriname's territory and that the 10° Line provided appropriate access through Suriname's territorial sea to the western channel of the Corentyne River.[367]

Finally, the *Croatia/Slovenia* case provides a unique precedent that the Arbitral Tribunal created a Junction Area to secure Slovenia's interest of navigation. Both Croatia and Slovenia agreed that for the purposes of the arbitral proceedings there are no proclaimed EEZ in the Adriatic Sea.[368] As the Tribunal observed, there is no place where Slovenia's territorial sea is immediately adjacent to an area in which the applicable legal regime preserves the freedoms of navigation and overflight referred to in Article 87 of the LSOC.[369] Here a concern arose with regard to rights of access from the high seas to Slovenia and from Slovenia to the high seas for ships and aircraft.[370] In response, the Tribunal established the Junction Area as approximately 2.5 nautical miles wide (see Illustration 28).[371] The 'Junction Area' connects the Slovenian territorial sea with the area that is beyond the 12-nautical mile-territorial sea limits of Croatia and Italy.[372] In this connection, the Tribunal made clear that in the 'Junction Area', 'the ships and aircraft enjoy essentially the same rights of access to and from Slovenia as they enjoy on the high seas'.[373]

B. Analysis of State Practice

i. Agreements Regarding Territorial Sea Delimitations

It may well be that navigational interests relate to the territorial sea rather than to the continental shelf or the EEZ. Indeed, more concern about protection of navigation can be found in agreements delimiting territorial seas, witness the following texts: 1932 Agreement between Denmark and Sweden,[374] 1973 Agreement between Indonesia and Singapore,[375] 1975 Agreement between

[366] The *Guiana/Suriname* arbitral award, 30 *RIAA* 84, [304].
[367] ibid, 85, [306].
[368] The *Croatia/Slovenia* arbitral award, [1015].
[369] ibid, [1078].
[370] ibid, [1066].
[371] ibid, [1083].
[372] ibid.
[373] ibid, [1081].
[374] Report by Franckx in *IMB*, vol II, 1933.
[375] Point 2 lies about 1/2 a nautical mile inside the Indonesian archipelagic baseline owing to the deep-draft tanker route around that particular point. Report by Park in ibid, vol I, 1050. Furthermore, Park indicated that the Parties' immediate concern was the safety of navigation in the Straits of Malacca and Singapore rather than extension of their territorial sea boundary around Singapore. ibid, 1052.

Italy and Yugoslavia in the Gulf of Trieste,[376] 1986 Agreement between France and Italy in the Straits of Bonifacio,[377] Joint Declaration by the United Kingdom and France made on the occasion of the signature of the 1988 Agreement Relating to the Delimitation of the Territorial Sea in the Straits of Dover.[378] Furthermore, while drawing a single maritime boundary, the 1984 Treaty of Peace and Friendship between Argentina and Chile places an obligation upon Argentina to 'maintain, at all times and under any circumstances, the right of ships of all flags to navigate expeditiously and without obstacles through its jurisdictional waters toward and away from the Straits of Magellan.'[379]

ii. Agreements Regarding Continental Shelf Delimitations and Single Maritime Boundaries

Few agreements take navigational interest into account when determining the location of a continental shelf boundary. Exceptionally, Jagota suggested that the boundary established in the 1978 Agreement between India and Thailand on the basis of equidistance was slightly adjusted to simplify the boundary line for the convenience of navigation.[380] Yet the available charts and sailing directions do not show why such an adjustment was needed.[381]

As with the delimitation of the continental shelf, little attention has been drawn to navigational interests in agreements drawing single maritime boundaries. Exceptionally, however, navigation played an important role in the 1989 Agreement between the German Democratic Republic and Poland.[382] In the Baltic Sea, the navigational approaches to the Polish ports of Szczecin and Swinoujscie, which were the so-called western and northern approaches adjacent to the coast of the German Democratic Republic, were, and still are, of vital interest for Poland. Accordingly, the 1989 Agreement establishes boundaries for the territorial sea and single maritime boundaries allowing ships to sail to Polish ports from the western side of the Oder Bank without entering the territorial waters of the German Democratic Republic.[383] In so doing, the delimitation

[376] In the waters of the Gulf of Trieste, both Parties claimed the central part of the Gulf as their own territorial limit. On this point, Mr Rumor, Italian Minister for Foreign Affairs, stated that: 'This state of affairs is now clearly resolved with the defining of the separation of the waters in such a way as to include in Italian waters a part of those sounding-depths from which we are today excluded, thus allowing the passage of big tonnage ships without necessarily passing through waters under Yugoslav control.' (1976) 2 *Italian Yearbook of International Law* 423.

[377] Reports by Scovazzi and Francalanci in *IMB*, vol II, 1573.

[378] For the text of the Agreement in ibid, 1754.

[379] Art 10. For the text of the Agreement in ibid, vol I, 736.

[380] SP Jagota, *Maritime Boundary* (Dordrecht, Nijhoff, 1985) 80.

[381] Report by Prescott in *IMB*, vol II, 1436.

[382] After the unification of Germany, Germany and Poland confirmed the 1989 agreement in question. See Treaty between the Federal Republic of Germany and Poland Concerning the Confirmation of the Frontier Existing between Them. ibid, 2027–28.

[383] Report by Franckx in ibid, 2012–14.

lines preserve secure access to Swinoujscie and Szczecin for Poland.[384] Furthermore, it is suggested that, in the 1996 Agreement between Estonia and Latvia, navigational interests influenced the location of the boundary line in more than one area.[385] Moreover, it is assumed that the motivation behind the maritime boundary established in 2008 between Qatar and Saudi Arabia is to allow Saudi Arabia deep water access from her coast in this region to the north of the Qatar-United Arab Emirates boundary where deeper water exists.[386]

Furthermore, there are agreements containing specific clauses to protect navigational interests. For instance, the 1978 Agreement between the Netherlands (Antilles) and Venezuela made detailed provisions on the right of transit passage.[387] The 1990 Agreement between Trinidad and Tobago and Venezuela specifies the right of transit passage and innocent passage in the strait concerned.[388] In addition, the 1976 Agreement between Colombia and Panama,[389] the 1973 Agreement between Argentina and Uruguay,[390] and the 1976 Agreement between India and the Maldives[391] contain general clauses confirming the freedoms of navigation and overflight.

C. Summary

The above survey reveals two points.

First, in State practice, normally navigational interests do not affect the location of the continental shelf and single maritime boundaries. It can be observed that in State practice, navigational interests have been considered in the context of the delimitation of territorial seas rather than in connection with the continental shelf or the establishment of single maritime boundaries. If navigational interests did not directly influence the location of maritime boundary, however, it is possible to insert a specific clause to protect these interests in a maritime delimitation agreement.

Secondly, the judicial practice suggests that navigational interests had little impact on the delimitation of the continental shelf. In the context of the

[384] Kwiatkowska, 'Economic and Environmental Considerations' 100. In this respect, Art 5 of the 1989 Agreement stipulates that: '1. The entire northern approach to the ports of Szczecin and Swijoujscie and the places of anchorage are all located in the territorial sea of the People's Republic of Poland or the high seas respectively. 2. The part of the northern approach to the ports of Szczecin and Swinoujscie situated to the east of the outer boundary of the territorial sea of the German Democratic Republic, ..., do not form part of the continental shelf, the fishing zone and, possibly, of the exclusive economic zone of the German Democratic Republic.' For the text of the 1989 Agreement, see *IMB*, vol II, 2020–22.

[385] Report by Franckx in ibid, vol IV, 3004.

[386] Report by Carleton, ibid, vol VI, 4417-18.

[387] Art 4. Text in ibid, 631.

[388] Art 6. Text in ibid, 685.

[389] Art 4. Text in ibid, 532.

[390] Art 72. Text in ibid, 764.

[391] Art 4. Text in ibid, vol II, 1397.

territorial sea delimitations and single maritime boundaries, however, there may be scope to consider that in appropriate cases, navigational interests may be regarded as a special/relevant circumstance.

VI. ENVIRONMENTAL FACTORS

A. Analysis of the Case Law

The case law has paid little attention to environmental concerns. However, the *Gulf of Maine* case was an exception in that a Party relied on environmental factors to justify an equitable maritime boundary.[392] In that case, both the United States and Canada agreed that the sea-bed of the Gulf constituted a single and uniform-looking continental shelf. Regarding the water column, however, there was disagreement between the Parties.[393] On the one hand, the United States argued that in the Gulf of Maine, there were three ecological regimes divided by natural boundaries; the most important and clearly apparent of which was the Northeast Channel. On that ground, the United States contended that the Northeast Channel must be seen as a natural boundary which can serve as a basis for drawing a single maritime boundary.[394] On the other hand, Canada emphasised the overall unity of the water column. According to Canada, thus, there was no natural boundary resulting from the marine environment within the delimitation area, or at least up to the southwestern limit of that area.[395]

The Chamber of the ICJ discarded the ecological criterion proposed by the United States for two reasons. The first was the impossibility of discerning stable natural boundaries. According to the Chamber, there were no factors sufficiently important, evident and conclusive to draw a single, incontrovertible natural boundary.[396] The second and more important reason was that such an ecological criterion was inconsistent with the Chamber's view that the single maritime boundary had to be drawn on the basis of 'neutral criteria'. The natural boundary suggested by the United States was based solely on the ecosystem of the water column. However, an ecological factor related only to the superjacent waters, was contrary to the idea of applying neutral criteria. In fact, the

[392] DA Colson, 'Environmental Factors: Are They Relevant to Delimitation?' in ED Brown and RR Churchill (eds), *The UN Convention on the Law of the Sea: Impact and Implementation, Proceedings, Law of the Sea Institute Nineteenth Annual Conference* (Honolulu, Law of the Sea Institute, 1987) 218–24.

[393] [1984] ICJ Rep 275, [50].

[394] ibid, 276, [51–52]. See also the Memorial of the United States, vol II, 112–13, [292–96].

[395] ICJ Reports 1984, pp 275–76, para 50. See also the Counter-Memorial of Canada, vol III: 'Chapter III: The Offshore Environment' 60–89, [168–320].

[396] [1984] ICJ Rep 277, [56].

Chamber stated that an ecological criterion 'could scarcely be adapted also to a delimitation which had not only to divide a volume of water but had also to effect a division of the underlying continental shelf, in respect of which the criterion in question could not be appropriate.'[397]

Insofar as the application of neutral criteria is concerned, ecological criteria will not, therefore, be applicable to the drawing of single maritime boundaries. This will not, however, exclude the possibility of considering, at the verification stage, whether a boundary entails catastrophic repercussions for the marine environment.

B. Analysis of State Practice

Usually environmental factors have played little, if any, role in agreements concerning maritime delimitations.[398] Although in some instances, such factors were mentioned in the course of negotiations, they did not affect such delimitations. For instance, Venezuela expressed its ecological concerns by Decree No 1069 of 23 August 1972 which declared a wildlife sanctuary on the Aves Island as well as in its territorial sea and continental shelf.[399] Although it is reported that Venezuela voiced these elements in the course of the negotiations, environmental factors did not directly influence the location of Venezuela's single maritime boundaries with France (Guadeloupe and Martinique),[400] the Netherlands (Antilles)[401] and the United States (Puerto Rico and the Virgin Islands).[402] Environmental issues were in evidence in the negotiation leading to the 2009 Treaty between Indonesia and Singapore with regard to the delimitation of the territorial sea. However, the territorial sea boundary was established by applying the equidistance method.[403]

There are, however, several agreements containing provisions on the protection of the marine environment.[404] In the context of the delimitation of the continental shelf, for instance, Article 3 of the 1977 Agreement between Greece and Italy states that: 'The Contracting Parties shall adopt all possible measures to ensure that the exploration of their respective zones of the continental shelf and the mining of its natural resources do not adversely affect the ecological balance or other legitimate uses of the sea.'[405] The 1974 Agreement between

[397] ibid, 327, [193].
[398] Kwiatkowska reached the same conclusion. 'Economic and Environmental Considerations' 101.
[399] Aves is the only place in the Eastern Caribbean, where the green turtle returns to spawn. Report by Nweihed in *IMB*, vol I, 606.
[400] ibid.
[401] ibid, 620.
[402] ibid, 695.
[403] Report by Schofield, McDorman and Arsana, ibid, vol VII, 4815 and 4818.
[404] See also McRae and Yacouba, 'The Legal Regime of Maritime Boundary Agreement' 3295–96.
[405] Text in *IMB*, vol II, 1598.

Italy and Spain[406] and the 1974 Agreement between France and Spain[407] furnish similar examples. These Agreements place the protection of the marine environment in the context of the development of the natural resources of the continental shelf.

In the context of the single maritime boundary, Article 48 of the 1973 Agreement between Argentina and Uruguay provides that:

> Each Party agrees to protect and preserve the aquatic environment and, in particular, to prevent its pollution, establishing standards and adopting appropriate measures in conformity with applicable international agreements and in consonance, when applicable, with the guidelines and recommendations of international technical organizations.[408]

Furthermore, Article 7 of the 1980 Agreement between Indonesia and Papua New Guinea obliged the Parties to coordinate their policies in accordance with international law on the protection of the marine environment and the conduct of marine research in their respective exclusive economic zones or fishing zones.[409] Moreover, Article 3 of the 1993 Agreement between Colombia and Jamaica stipulates that, in the Joint Regime Area, the Parties will carry out activities relating to the protection and preservation of the marine environment on a joint basis agreed by both Parties.[410] In addition, cooperation in marine environmental protection is provided in agreements, such as: the 1978 Agreement between the Dominican Republic and Colombia,[411] the 1979 Agreement between the Dominican Republic and Venezuela,[412] the 1989 Agreement between Papua New Guinea and the Solomon Islands,[413] the 1990 Agreement between Trinidad and Tobago and Venezuela,[414] the 1999 Agreement between Denmark (Faroe Islands) and the United Kingdom,[415] the 2006 Treaty between Micronesia and Marshall Islands,[416] the 2006 Treaty between Micronesia and Palau,[417] the 2010 Treaty between Grenada and Trinidad and Tobago,[418] the 2011 Agreement between Comoros and Tanzania,[419] and the 2012 Agreement between Comoros and Seychelles.[420] Interestingly, the 2010 Treaty between Norway and the Russian Federation places an explicit obligation upon the Parties to apply the

[406] Art 5. Text in ibid, 1607.
[407] Art 7. Text in ibid, 1728.
[408] ibid, vol I, 764.
[409] ibid, 1045.
[410] ibid, vol III, 2200.
[411] Art IV and V. Text in ibid, vol I, 488.
[412] Art 5. Text in ibid, 588.
[413] Art 5. Text in ibid, 1162.
[414] Art 9. Text in ibid, vol I, 685.
[415] Art 6(a) and (d). Text in ibid, vol IV, 2970.
[416] Art 6. Text in ibid, vol VI, 4325.
[417] Art 5. Text in ibid, vol VI, 4357.
[418] Art V. Text in ibid, vol VII, 4716.
[419] Art 4. For the text of the Agreement, see ibid, 5066.
[420] Art 4. Text in ibid, 5046.

precautionary approach widely to conservation of shared fish stocks, including straddling fish stocks 'in order to protect the living marine resources and preserve marine environment'.[421]

As demonstrated by the Deepwater Horizon incident, safety and environmental considerations are of critical importance in the exploration and exploitation of marine natural resources. In this connection, the 2012 Agreement between Mexico and the United States merits mention. This Agreement provides for the unitisation of hydrocarbon resources crossing a maritime boundary. Article 19(1) of the Agreement obliges the Parties to 'adopt, where appropriate, common safety and environmental standards and requirements applicable to activity contemplated under this Agreement'. Furthermore, the Agreement provides a joint inspection to achieve compliance with applicable safety and environmental standards in accordance with Article 18.[422]

In this context, particular attention must be paid to the 2018 Timor Sea Treaty between Australia and Timor-Leste. This treaty established a Special Regime Area for the Greater Sunrise Fields.[423] Article 6(2) of the Treaty provides that the Special Regime Area is regulated by the Designated Authority in accordance with Good Oilfield Practice, having regard to relevant factors including, inter alia, 'environmental protection, which calls for the adoption of methods and processes that minimise the impact of the Petroleum operations on the environment'.

C. Summary

The above survey can be summarised in three points.

First, in both case law and State practice, the role of environmental factors remains a modest one. On this point, the trends of case law and State practice do coincide.

Secondly, insofar as a neutral criterion is applicable to the drawing of single maritime boundaries, there may be little room to take environmental factors into account.[424] As with the geological and geomorphological factors, the concept of a natural boundary based on ecological systems will be inconsistent with the legal title provided by the distance criterion. Accordingly, in the case law, the concept of a natural boundary will be theoretically rejected.

Thirdly, in State practice, the obligation to cooperate in marine environmental protection is increasingly provided in maritime delimitation treaties. It appears that the Parties regard environmental protection as a matter of cooperation

[421] Art 4(3). Text in ibid, 5189.
[422] Text in ibid, 4625.
[423] Annexes B and C of the Timor Sea Treaty.
[424] See also Cottier, *Equitable Principles of Maritime Delimitation*, 471.

rather than of delimitation per se. This seems to be a reasonable approach. In fact, marine pollution may spread beyond maritime boundaries. Furthermore, marine species and ecosystems may straddle man-made maritime boundaries. Hence one can argue that international cooperation is a prerequisite to protect the marine environment.[425]

VII. TRADITIONAL LIVELIHOOD

A. Analysis of the Case Law

Usually, traditional livelihood or cultural factors were not at issue in the case law, but there is an exception. In the *Jan Mayen* dispute, Denmark contended that the attachment of the people of Greenland to their land and the surrounding sea made it difficult to accept that the sea area within the 200-mile zone off their coast should be curtailed in deference to the interests of the people of a remote and highly developed industrial State.[426] Yet the ICJ did not consider such factors, relying on the reason used for rejecting socio-economic factors.[427]

B. Analysis of State Practice

Exceptionally, in some agreements, the Parties pay attention to the livelihood of traditional inhabitants. In this connection, the 1978 Torres Strait Agreement between Australia and Papua New Guinea provides an interesting example. Under Article 10, that Agreement creates a protected zone in order to 'acknowledge and protect the traditional way of life and livelihood of the traditional inhabitants including their traditional fishing and free movement'. Furthermore, Article 11 of that Agreement stipulates that 'each Party shall continue to permit free movement and the performance of lawful traditional activities in and in the vicinity of the Protected Zone by the traditional inhabitants of the other Party'. Moreover, pursuant to Article 12, traditional customary rights of the traditional inhabitants of one Party shall be permitted by the other Party on the same conditions applying to its own traditional inhabitants.[428] The 1989 Agreement between Papua New Guinea and the Solomon Islands establishes a special area. This purports to acknowledge and protect the traditional life and

425 See also The *MOX Plant* case (Ireland v United Kingdom), Provisional Measures, ITLOS Case No. 10, [2001] ITLOS Rep 110, [82].

426 [1993] ICJ Rep 73, [79].

427 ibid, 74, [80].

428 For the text of the Agreement, see *IMB*, vol I, 937–75.

livelihood of the traditional inhabitants living in that area, including the rights of free movement, fishing and other lawful traditional activities.[429]

VIII. CONCLUSIONS

This chapter examined the role of non-geographical factors in the jurisprudence and State practice concerning maritime delimitations. The above considerations appear to reveal the following conclusions.

First, the influence of economic factor remains modest in the jurisprudence regarding maritime delimitations, even though they are not *a priori* precluded from the scope of relevant circumstances. Similarly, normally economic factors have not *directly* affected the location of maritime boundaries established by agreement between relevant States. To this extent, it can be observed that the trends of case law and State practice coincide. In this connection, it is of particular interest to note that States took account of economic factors in a flexible manner by inserting common deposit clauses or by establishing joint development regimes or by combining a maritime delimitation agreement to a fishery agreement. The flexible solutions seem to provide useful options when considering economic factors in the process of maritime delimitation.

Secondly, the conduct of the Parties plays only a modest role in the jurisprudence and State practice concerning maritime delimitations. As shown by the *Tunisia/Libya* judgment, however, this factor may influence the location of maritime boundaries when the conduct of the Parties can prove the existence of a *modus vivendi* or a *de facto* line, or an agreement to apply a particular method. Furthermore, as demonstrated in the *Peru v Chile* case, the conduct of the Parties may be taken into account when determining the extent of the existence of an agreed maritime boundary.

Thirdly, considerations of historic rights remain exceptional in the jurisprudence regarding maritime delimitations. In State practice, as the 1976 Agreement between India and Sri Lanka demonstrated, the question of traditional fishing rights may be resolved without adjusting the maritime boundaries.

Fourthly, while security interests were not precluded from the scope of relevant circumstances in the jurisprudence, the influence of these interests on the location of maritime boundaries remains less clear. The ICJ, in the *Libya/Malta* and the *Jan Mayen* cases, examined security interests on the basis of distance from the coast. Yet there is no objective standard for judging how close a boundary may approach a State. The direct influence of security factors also remains somewhat unclear in State practice.

Fifthly, as typically shown in the *Eritrea/Yemen (the Second Phase)* and *Guyana v Suriname* cases, navigational interests may be regarded as a special/relevant

[429] Art 7. Text in ibid, 1162–65.

circumstance in the context of the territorial sea delimitations and single maritime boundaries. In State practice, it can be observed that navigational interests have been considered particularly in relation to the delimitation of territorial seas.

Sixthly, normally environmental factors have played little, if any, role in the jurisprudence concerning maritime delimitations. However, cooperation in marine environmental protection is provided in comparatively recent treaties concerning maritime delimitations. In State practice, it may be said that environmental factors are considered as a matter of international cooperation, rather than an element of maritime delimitation.

Seventhly, apart from the *Jan Mayen* case, traditional livelihood was not discussed in the jurisprudence. In State practice, this factor was considered only in some exceptional treaties regarding maritime delimitations.

Part III

Balance between Predictability and Flexibility in the Law of Maritime Delimitation

9

Legal Framework Reconciling Predictability and Flexibility in the Law of Maritime Delimitation

I. TENSION BETWEEN PREDICTABILITY AND FLEXIBILITY IN THE LAW OF MARITIME DELIMITATION

THE BALANCE BETWEEN predictability and flexibility is difficult to achieve in every domain of law. It will differ according to the legal field under consideration. Thus, the balance between predictability and flexibility should be judged case-by-case in each field of law, *in specie* the law of maritime delimitation.

As noted, the concept of equity, which underlies equitable principles, is at the core of the law of maritime delimitation. That concept requires individualism. As Charles De Visscher points out, 'l'équité se caractérise essentiellement comme une expression individualisée de la justice.'[1] Yet an over-individualism based on equity hampers the formation of predictable rules. Furthermore, the concept of equity requires flexibility. By having recourse to that concept, thus, States or international courts and tribunals would have a large discretion.[2] Nevertheless, such flexibility may, if excessive, result in voiding the law of maritime delimitation of their contents. As Schachter stated, '[i]f the rules were so flexible as to afford complete discretion to the parties or to the judge, we would not have law or decisions based on law.'[3] The same would be true of the law of maritime delimitation.

In short, the individualistic and flexible character of equity makes it difficult to formulate its contents. As Schachter indicates, '[n]o concept of international law resists precise definition more than the notion of equity.'[4] A certain degree of predictability is essential in the law of maritime delimitation, however. Indeed,

[1] Furthermore, Charles De Visscher, *De l'équité dans le règlement arbitral ou judiciaire des litiges de droit international public* (Paris, Pedone, 1972) 7; R Kolb, *La bonne foi en droit international public: Contribution à l' étude des principes généraux de droit* (Paris, PUF, 2000) 109. Regarding the origin and history of the notion of equity, see ibid, 101–5.

[2] In this connection, Brownlie states that 'the most significant role of "equitable principles" is to confer a wider discretion on tribunals.' I Brownlie, 'Legal Status of Natural Resources in International Law (Some Aspects)' (1979) 162 *RCADI* 288. See also 287.

[3] O Schachter, *International Law in Theory and Practice* (Dordrecht, Nijhoff, 1991) 34.

[4] ibid, 55.

as Jennings says, '[a] law the application of which is wholly unpredictable is a contradiction in terms.'[5] Accordingly, the difficulty arises as to how it is possible to formulate predictable rules governing maritime delimitation. As pointed out earlier, it may be said that the difficulty of the law of maritime delimitation resides in the tension between the two contrasting elements of predictability and flexibility.

The tension between predictability and flexibility creates an acute problem *when a maritime delimitation is entrusted to international courts and tribunals.* Obviously, it is important that a method of delimitation and relevant circumstances should be, to a certain extent, predictable. As shown in Part Two, however, the geographical and non-geographical factors to be considered by the courts are different in each and every case. Furthermore, owing to the diversity of State practice, it appears to be inconceivable that there will always be pre-defined rules concerning various relevant circumstances. Even so, international courts and tribunals have to apply them without losing sight of the postulate of predictability.

As discussed in chapter five, in a broad perspective, it can be observed that the law of maritime delimitation is moving in a direction from co-existence of the two different approaches to unification of the approach under the three-stage approach, and from emphasis on flexibility to the enhancement of predictability. As ITLOS stated in the *Bangladesh/Myanmar* case, '[o]ver time, the absence of a settled method of delimitation prompted increased interest in enhancing the objectivity and predictability of the process.'[6]

In the present writer's view, the requirement of predictability is particularly valuable in the law of maritime delimitation. As Judge Sørensen stated in the *North Sea Continental Shelf* cases, the rules of international law should be so framed and constructed as to reduce causes of disagreement and dispute to a minimum. The clearer the rule, and the more automatic its application, the less the seed of discord that will be sown.[7] This is particularly true of maritime delimitations. Considering that there are still many areas where maritime delimitation disputes may arise, predictable rules will be a prerequisite to prevent potential disputes on this matter. Furthermore, arguably these rules may provide a criterion limiting exaggerated unilateral claims by coastal States in an area where a maritime delimitation line is not yet drawn. Given that equidistance is the only predictable method of drawing an initial line to be tested for equity, it can provide an objective starting point for discussion.[8]

[5] Sir Robert Jennings, 'The Judicial Function and the Rule of Law in International Relations' in *International Law at the Time of Its Codification, Essays in Honour of Roberto Ago* (Milan, Giuffrè, 1987) 144.

[6] The *Bangladesh/Myanmar* case, [2012] ITLOS Rep 65, [228].

[7] Dissenting Opinion of Judge ad hoc Sørensen, [1969] ICJ Rep 256. Furthermore in the article published in 1976, Akehurst stated that: 'Although it is desirable that rules of law should be just, it is perhaps even more desirable that they should be certain, clear and predictable.' M Akehurst, 'Equity and General Principles of Law' (1976) 25 *ICLQ* 809.

[8] In this connection, Scovazzi stated that: '[t]he only way to determine the equity of a solution is to start by drawing the equidistance line and then evaluate whether the resulting solution is equitable

By incorporating the equidistance method, the corrective-equity or three-stage approach will enhance predictability as a requirement of law in the international community.[9] Nonetheless, the application of the corrective-equity or three-stage approach does not completely guarantee the predictability and objectivity of the process of maritime delimitation. Regardless of predictability at the methodological level, it appears that the law of maritime delimitation is still fluid in some respects. In particular, two issues need further consideration.

The first issue relates to the clarification of relevant circumstances. According to the three-stage approach, the location of maritime boundaries is to be determined by the consideration of relevant circumstances. Hence the role of these circumstances is of critical importance in the process of maritime delimitation. Yet the concept of relevant circumstances needs further clarification with regard to the scope of these circumstances and the balance to be established between them.

The second issue pertains to the *manner* of the application of the three-stage approach. Despite the predictability at the methodological level, unfortunately the manner of the application of that approach in the jurisprudence has not always been predictable and transparent.

Examining the two issues, chapter nine considers the current stage of the law of maritime delimitation. Following section I, section II makes a general observation on the general trend of the case law in the field of maritime delimitation. Section III addresses the scope and balance of relevant circumstances. Section IV moves on to examine the problems with the application of the three-stage approach, before offering the conclusions in section V.

II. GENERAL OBSERVATION

When considering the trend of the law of maritime delimitation, two general observations can be made: the predominance of geographical factors over non-geographical factors and the formation of rules for adjudication, detached from State practice.

or not.' Scovazzi, 'The Evolution of International Law of the Sea' 200. For the same view, Vœlckel, 'Aperçu de quelques problèmes techniques' 693: G Guillaume, 'Les accords de délimitation maritime passé par la France' in *Colloque de Rouen, Pérspectives du droit de la mer à l'issue de la 3e conférence des Nations Unies* (Paris, Pedone, 1984) 282. Furthermore, it will be recalled that in UNCLOS I, Kennedy, a representative of the United Kingdom, had already expressed the same view. *Conférence des Nations Unies sur le droit de la mer, Documents officiel,* vol VI, 1958, 112. In this connection, one may recall the equiratio method. When recoursing to the equiratio method, it is necessary, first, to determine a ratio to be applied. The problem is how it is possible to decide on such a ratio. As there is no objective criterion for determining a ratio, it must be decided by negotiations between the Parties concerned. Contrary to the equidistance method, thus, the equiratio method could not provide a predictable starting point in a true sense.

[9] Bedjaoui expressly stated that: 'Ils [les principes équitables] ne constituent pas une forme d'équité autonome, indépendante de la règle de droit et substituable à celle-ci, mais bien une équité *correctrice* intervenant de manière endogène pour éviter que la règle de *droit* n'aboutisse à un résultat inéquitable dans son application à un cas concret.' M Bedjaoui, 'L'«énigme» des «principes équitables» dans le droit des délimitations maritimes' (1990) 17 *Revista española de derecho international* 384.

Figure 7

	1969 ICJ	1977 Arbitration	1982 ICJ	1984 ICJ	1985 Arbitration	1985 ICJ	1992 Arbitration	1993 ICJ	1999 Arbitration	2001 ICJ
Coastal Geography	C	C	C	C	C	C	C	C	C	C
Proportionality	C	C	CV	C	CV	C/CV	CV	C	CV	N
Islands	–	En/H/F	No/H	H	No/P	–	No/P/F	F	No/P/F	No/F
Geology/ Geomorphology	C	N	N	N	N	N	N	–	–	–
Basepoints/baseline	–	–	N	–	–	C	–	N	C	C
Third States	–	N	C	–	C	C	–	–	C	C
Land Boundary	–	–	C	N	C	–	–	–	–	C
Economic Factors	–	C	N	CV	N	N	CV	C	N	–
Conduct of the Parties	–	–	C	N	–	–	–	N	N	N
Historic Rights	–	–	N	–	–	–	–	–	N	N
Security	–	N	–	N	N	N	–	N	N	–
Environment	–	–	–	N	–	–	–	–	–	–
Traditional Livelihood	–	–	–	–	–	–	–	N	–	–
Navigation	–	N	–	N	–	–	–	–	C	N

C, Considered; CV, considered at the stage of verification; N, not considered; En, enclavement; H, Half-effect; P, partial effect; F, full effect; No, no effect; -, not discussed

To specify the cases, see Figure 3 in chapter five.

A. General Trend of the Case Law

The judicial practice demonstrates that international courts and tribunals attach more importance to geographical than to non-geographical factors (see Figure 7). In this regard, Judge Oda in the *Qatar v Bahrain* case already pointed out that:

> The geography of the areas concerned has played a very important role in the drawing of maritime boundaries ever since the International Law Commission first dealt with the law of the sea. Rarely has any other factor been considered to affect this determination and consensus has been reached under Art 6 of the 1958 Convention on the Continental Shelf that the concept of geographical equity lies at the heart of the criterion of equitable considerations.[10]

[10] Separate Opinion of Judge Oda, [2001] ICJ Rep 140, [37]. Willis also stated that: 'One can state with confidence that geography will always prevail over non-geographical factors in the event of a conflict.' LA Willis, 'From Precedent to precedent: The Triumph of Pragmatism in the Law of Maritime Boundaries' (1986) 24 *CYIL* 55. See also T Scovazzi, 'The Evolution of International Law of the Sea: New issues, New Challenges' (2000) 286 *RCADI* 199.

2002	2006	2007	2007	2009	2012	2012	2014	2014	2017	2017	2018
ICJ	Arbitration	Arbitration	ICJ	ICJ	ITLOS	ICJ	ICJ	Arbitration	Arbitration	ITLOS	ICJ
C	C	C	C	C	C	C	C	C	C	C	C
N	C/CV	CV	–	CV	CV	C/CV	CV	CV	–	CV	CV
N	–	–	F/En	F/No/En	F/No	En/P	–	–	–	–	H
–	–	–	C	–	N	–	–	–	–	C	–
–	–	–	C	C	C	C	C	C	C	C	C
C	C	–	C	C	C	N	–	–	C	–	C
C	–	–	–	–	–	–	–	C	C	C	C
–	–	–	–	–	–	N	C	N	–	N	–
N	–	N	N	N	–	N	C	–	N	N	–
–	N	–	N	–	–	–	–	–	N	–	–
–	–	–	N	N	–	C	–	–	N	–	–
–	–	–	–	–	–	–	–	–	–	–	–
–	–	–	–	–	–	–	–	–	–	–	–
–	–	C	N	–	–	–	–	–	C	–	–

The Annex VII Arbitration Tribunal, in the *Barbados v Trinidad and Tobago* case, also noted that:

> Resource-related criteria have been treated more cautiously by the decisions of international courts and tribunals, which have not generally applied this factor as a relevant circumstance.[11]

More recently, the ITLOS Special Chamber, in the *Ghana/Côte d'Ivoire* case, ruled that:

> In assessing the international jurisprudence, the Special Chamber wishes to emphasize that such jurisprudence, at least in principle, favours maritime delimitation which is based on geographical considerations. Only in extreme situations … may considerations other than geographical ones become relevant.[12]

According to the Chamber, 'extreme situations' refer to the situation which is 'likely to entail catastrophic repercussions for the livelihood and economic

[11] (2007) 27 *RIAA* 214, [241].

[12] *Dispute Concerning Delimitation of the Maritime Boundary between Ghana and Côte d'Ivoire in the Atlantic Ocean (Ghana/Côte d'Ivoire)*, Judgment, [2017] ITLOS Rep [453].

well-being of the population of the countries concerned'.[13] In accordance with the *dictum* of the Chamber, the role of non-geographical factors is to be highly limited in the process of maritime delimitations.

Overall it may be said that that maritime delimitation is effected by international courts and tribunals based primarily on geographical considerations.[14] In particular, the modest role played by economic factors shows that maritime delimitation relates to the conflicts over how much maritime space coastal States can obtain on account of geographical factors, regardless of their economic importance. In that sense, it may be said that maritime delimitation is, in essence, of a *spatial* rather than that of an *economic* nature.[15]

However, it is not suggested that non-geographical factors are completely disregarded by international courts and tribunals. As discussed in chapter eight, in some cases, navigational and security interests were taken into account by international courts and tribunals, even though their precise impacts upon the location of maritime boundaries remained less clear.[16] In the *Jan Mayen* case, an economic factor, that is, equitable access to fish stocks, exceptionally influenced the location of the maritime boundary.[17] Furthermore, as typically shown in the *Peru v Chile* case, the conduct of the Parties may be relevant when examining the existence of an agreed boundary and its extent.[18] Thus it must be stressed that non-geographical factors are not *a priori* precluded in the jurisprudence concerning maritime delimitation.

B. Formation of the Case Law of Maritime Delimitation

Another remarkable feature of the law of maritime delimitation concerns the formation of the case law distinguished from State practice. As commenters have indicated, the law of maritime delimitation can be regarded as a product of a 'judge-made law'.[19] In this connection, two issues arise: the formation of the

[13] ibid, [453]. In this regard, the Chamber relied on the *dictum* of the *Gulf of Maine* case, [1984] ICJ Rep 342, [237].

[14] On this point, Judge Guillaume stated that: 'Such a result [an equitable result] may be achieved by first identifying the equidistance line, then correcting that line to take into account special circumstances or relevant factors, which are both *essentially geographical in nature*' (emphasis added). Speech by His Excellency Judge Gilbert Guillaume, President of the International Court of Justice, to the Sixth Committee of the General Assembly of the United Nations, 31 October 2001, 8–9.

[15] Weil reached a similar conclusion. Dissenting Opinion of Mr Weil in the *St Pierre and Miquelon* case, case (1992) 31 *ILM* 1209, [30]. This view was also echoed by Cottier. T Cottier, *Equitable Principles of Maritime Delimitation: The Quest for Distributive Justice in International Law* (Cambridge University Press, 2015) 458.

[16] See ch 8, ss IV and V of this book.

[17] See ch 8, s I of this book.

[18] See ch 8, s II of this book.

[19] P Weil, 'Le droit international en quête de son identité. Cours général de droit international public' (1992-VI) 237 *RCADI* 143. Weil's observation continues to remain valid today. See also Alex G Oude Elferink, T Henriksen, and SV Busch, 'The Judiciary and the Law of Maritime

case law through 'institutional circularity' and the difference between the case law and State practice.

As for the first issue, it can be observed that in the jurisprudence concerning maritime delimitation, an international court or tribunal tends to rely primarily on its own precedents or jurisprudence of another court or tribunal when deciding its approach and the effect given to relevant circumstances in a specific case.[20] One may take the three-stage approach as an example. The three-stage approach provides a structural framework for the process of maritime delimitation. When deciding the application of that approach to a specific case, an international court or tribunal has merely relied on the jurisprudence in this field. As explained earlier, the three-stage approach was, for the first time, clearly formulated by the ICJ in the *Black Sea* case.[21] In this regard, the Court relied only on its own precedents, ie, the *Libya/Malta* and *Nicaragua v Honduras* cases.[22] No State practice was examined by the Court. Nor did the Court furnish any other legal basis for the application of the three-stage approach. Subsequently, the ICJ, in the *Nicaragua v Colombia* case, held that it

> has made clear on *a number of occasions* that the methodology which it will normally employ when called upon to effect a delimitation between overlapping continental shelf and exclusive economic zone entitlements involves proceeding in three stages ....[23]

In the above passage, however, the Court referred to the *Libya/Malta* and *Black Sea* cases only.[24] In the *Peru v Chile* case, the ICJ relied only on the *Black Sea* and *Nicaragua v Colombia* cases when it decided to apply the three-stage method,[25] and the reference to the *Libya/Malta* case was omitted. In the *Bangladesh/Myanmar* case, ITLOS decided to apply the three-stage approach because 'jurisprudence has developed in favour of the equidistance/relevant circumstances method.'[26] Likewise the ITLOS Special Chamber applied the three-stage approach in the *Ghana/Côte d'Ivoire* case since 'the international jurisprudence concerning the delimitation of maritime spaces in principle favours the equidistance/relevant circumstances methodology.'[27] Furthermore, referring to the *Nicaragua v Honduras* case, the Annex VII Arbitral Tribunal, in the *Bangladesh v India* case, ruled that: '[E]quidistance/relevant circumstances method is preferable

Delimitation: Setting the Stage' in Alex G Oude Elferink, T Henriksen and SV Busch (eds), *Maritime Boundary Delimitation: The Case Law Is It consistent and Practicable?* (Cambridge University Press, 2018) 3.

[20] cf P von Mühlendahl, *L'équidistance dans la délimitation des frontière maritimes: étude de la jurisprudence internationale* (Paris, Pedone, 2016) 226–29.

[21] See ch 5, s XI of this book.

[22] [2009] ICJ Rep101, [116].

[23] Emphasis added. [2012] ICJ Rep 695, [190].

[24] ibid.

[25] [2014] ICJ Rep 65, [180].

[26] [2012] ITLOS Rep 67, [238].

[27] [2017] ITLOS Rep [289].

unless, [...], there are "factors which make the application of the equidistance method inappropriate".'[28] Subsequently, the ICJ, in the *Costa Rica v Nicaragua* case, referred to its own precedent, that is, the *Black Sea* case, and to the *Bangladesh/Myanmar* case of ITLOS and the *Bangladesh v India* case of the Annex VII Arbitral Tribunal, when applying the three-stage method.[29]

Overall it can be observed that the three-stage approach has been formulated through 'institutional circularity'. The judicial practice contributes to consolidating the normative status of the three-stage approach in the jurisprudence concerning maritime delimitation. It also prevents the fragmentation of international law by maintaining consistency with the jurisprudence. At the same time, caution must be taken in noting that the development of a rule of international law through institutional circularity may entail the risk of detaching the rule from actual State practice.[30] This point will lead to the second issue, that is, the formulation of the case law distinguished from State practice.

Regarding some relevant circumstances, there is a certain degree of difference between the case law and State practice. A typical example is the concept of proportionality. As discussed already, the large role of proportionality as an operational rule or as a test of equitableness cannot be explained from the viewpoints of State practice and *opinio juris*. The same is true of the effect to be given to islands. Since there is no customary law on the subject, the effect attributable to islands was to be determined, case by case, at the discretion of international tribunals. On this point, the courts have developed the 'half effect' solution regarding offshore islands. In State practice, however, there are only a few agreements giving half effect to offshore islands. In this sense, it would seem that the courts' solutions of giving half effect to offshore islands are a novelty in this field different from State practice.

All in all it may have to be admitted that international courts and tribunals have developed special rules within the framework of case law, independently of State practice.[31] It may not be unreasonable to consider the courts' solutions as a result of 'judicial creativity'. This provides an interesting insight into the role of courts in international law-making. According to Article 38(1) of the Statute of the ICJ, judicial decisions are merely subsidiary means for the determination of rules of law. In maritime delimitation, however, it is safe to say that the ICJ,

[28] The *Bangladesh v India* arbitral award, [345].

[29] [2018] ICJ Rep [135].

[30] Further, see Y Tanaka, 'The Impacts of the ITLOS Jurisprudence on the Development of International Law' in International Tribunal for the Law of the Sea, *The Contribution of the International Tribunal for the Law of the Sea to the Rule of Law: 1996–2016* (Leiden, Brill/Nijhoff, 2017) 161, 166–67.

[31] In an article published in 1981, Jennings said that: '[T]he law of continental shelf boundaries outside the parties to the 1958 Convention, is pure judge-made law. The supposition that the principles emerged from practice is a pure fiction.' RY Jennings, 'What Is International Law and How Do We Tell It When We See It?' (1981) 37 *ASDI* 68. Lucchini/Vœlckel and Churchill/Lowe also took a similar view. L Lucchini and M Vœlckel, *Droit de la mer,* tome 2, *Délimitation* (Paris, Pedone, 1996) 200; RR Churchill and AV Lowe, *The Law of the Sea*, 3rd edn (Manchester, MUP, 1999) 185.

ITLOS and arbitral tribunals have been creating and developing the law of maritime delimitation.[32] The significant role of judicial creativity in the nature of maritime delimitation may be explained by at least two reasons.

First, to achieve equitable results, there is a need to take various geographical and non-geographical factors into account. Yet, since one cannot expect there to be specific rules regarding each and every factor to be considered, international courts and tribunals often face potential lacunae in the law. Consequently, in their decisions, international courts and tribunals need to develop rules regarding the effect to be attributed to those factors in the framework of equitable principles.[33] If this were not done, they could not render decisions, and the customary law of maritime delimitation would never progress.[34] In that sense, the distinction between resort to equity as an application of the law and as a creation of law is a delicate matter.[35]

Secondly, the Parties to a treaty seldom explain in the latter why and to what extent a certain relevant circumstance was taken into account when drawing a maritime boundary. For this very reason, it is difficult to find evidence of *opinio juris* in State practice. It may be said that there is an inherent difficulty in identifying customary rules in the field of maritime delimitation. Hence, it is hardly surprising that international courts and tribunals have to rely mainly on judge-made law in this particular field.[36]

[32] Weil, *Perspectives du droit de la délimitation maritime* 13. See also P Cahier, 'Les sources du droit relatif à la délimitation du plateau continental' in *Le droit international au service de la paix, de la justice et du développement, Mélanges Michel Virally* (Paris, Pedone, 1991) 175–82.

[33] Orrego Vicuña argues that: 'Judge-made law by means of the application of equity has been the natural consequence of not having States fill the framework of international law with specific general rules in the matter either through conventions or customary law.' F Orrego Vicuña, 'The Role of the International Court of Justice and Other Tribunals in the Development of the Law of Maritime Delimitation' in AHA Soons (ed), *Implementation of the Law of the Sea Convention Through International Institutions* (Honolulu, University Hawaii, The Law of the Sea Institute, 1990) 606. See also Lucchini and Vœlckel, *Droit de la mer*, 201.

[34] Even when there is a lacunae in the law, this does not necessarily lead to *non liquet*. Traditionally, international tribunals refrain from declaring *non liquet*. The Courts attempt to fill the gaps by referring to general principles of international law, general principles of law applied by civilised nations, teleological interpretation, and equity. For an analysis of specific solutions, see T Sugihara, 'Some Observations on the *Non Liquet* Problem in International Adjudication' (in Japanese) (1978) 24 *The Hokkaido Law Review* 151. See also Sir Gerald Fitzmaurice, 'The Problem of *Non-Liquet*: Prolegomena to a Restatement' in *La communauté internationale, Mélanges offerts à Charles Rousseau* (Paris, Pedone, 1974) 99.

[35] P Reuter, 'Quelques réflexions sur l'équité en droit international' reprinted in his monograph, *Le développement de l'ordre juridique international, Ecrits de droit international* (Paris, Economica, 1995) 26.

[36] It might be argued that such a difficulty is a question of degree. It may be true that some elements of judicial creativity would be inevitable for judicial decisions in customary law, since it includes, more or less, ambiguity. Even so, however, it appears that the degree of judicial creativity in the field of maritime delimitation is quantitatively very large. For instance, in a domain where specific rules are well-established as customary law, such as diplomatic law, there would be little room for judicial creativity. But in the field of maritime delimitation, such specific rules are relatively rare. Furthermore, in this particular field, the international courts and tribunals have to draw an equitable boundary taking all relevant circumstances into account. Owing to the diversity of relevant circumstances in a quantitative sense, a relatively large degree of judicial creativity would come into play.

At the same time, it should be stressed that that creativity takes place in the framework of law, not *ex aequo et bono*. In this sense, criticism of an *excessive* subjectivity in judgments relating to maritime delimitation, which had been voiced by members of the ICJ themselves, cannot be underestimated.[37] In fact, as pointed to in relevant parts of this book, it is undeniable that there is legal obscurity underlying the courts' reasoning for reading their solutions. It is true that more or less the same problem arises in any other type of case since a certain degree of subjectivity cannot be avoided because judges are human. In that sense, the problem of subjectivity is not necessarily built only into the law of maritime delimitation. Even so, however, it should not be forgotten that the removal of excessive subjectivity is one of the most important conditions for ensuring the validity and respect of judgments relating to maritime delimitation. There appears to be room to make efforts for limiting the margin of subjectivity in the actual decisions in this field.

III. ASSESSMENT OF RELEVANT CIRCUMSTANCES

As pointed out earlier, the consideration of relevant circumstances is of critical importance since, according to the three-stage approach, the location of maritime boundaries is to be determined by considering these circumstances. In this regard, two issues must be examined: the scope of the relevant circumstances and the balance to be established between them.

A. Scope of Relevant Circumstances

i. Two Hypotheses

a. Relevant Circumstances in the Broadest Sense

Theoretically, it is possible to identify two hypotheses relating to the identification of relevant circumstances. In the first hypothesis, the categories of relevant circumstances are open-ended. Thus, the concept of relevant circumstances would include an infinite variety of factors. For instance, Judge Weeramantry, in the *Jan Mayen* case, stated that:

> No complete list [of relevant circumstances] can be made, if for no other reason than that each case is unique and one can never foretell what circumstances may surface

[37] In particular, Judge Oda's view in the *Jan Mayen* case will be recalled, according to which judgments regarding maritime delimitation may be rendered only as decisions according to *ex aequo et bono*. Separate Opinion of Judge Oda in the *Jan Mayen* case, [1993] ICJ Rep 113, [85]. In addition, referring to the *Libya/Malta* case, he considers the Court's judgment as a decision *ex aequo et bono*, even though the Court never expressly said as much. ibid, 113, [86]; See also, ibid, 114, [88]. Rosenne also points to a similar problem. S Rosenne, 'Equitable Principles and the Compulsory Jurisdiction

> or achieve importance in the unknown disputes of the future. Moreover, each item – such as state conduct or national security – is infinitely variable and, more often than not, is itself a conglomerate of factors which themselves need to be assessed and evaluated.[38]

This view appears to echo the view of the Court in the *North Sea Continental Shelf* cases: 'In fact, there is no legal limit to the considerations which States may take account of for the purpose of making sure that they apply equitable procedures.'[39] It should be noted, however, that the ICJ, in that case, was addressing States involved in a negotiation process. In international decisions, such an enlarged concept of relevant circumstances carries the risk of bringing the judgment close to a conciliation procedure on account of an uncontrolled proliferation of relevant circumstances.[40] In fact, the ICJ, in the *Libya/Malta* case, held that: '[A]lthough there may be no legal limit to the considerations which States may take account of, this can hardly be true for a court applying equitable procedures.'[41] As discussed already, the international courts and tribunals do not attribute legal relevance to every circumstance invoked by the Parties. Regarding non-geographical factors, in particular, their relevance is not often accepted in the case law. It thus appears that the case law attempts to avoid the unbridled proliferation of relevant circumstances.

b. Relevant Circumstances in the Narrowest Sense

The second hypothesis to be envisioned is that it is necessary to limit the extent of the relevant circumstances. The narrowest view may be that taken by Weil. In his view, only circumstances which play a role in the establishment of legal title are relevant to maritime delimitation.[42] According to Weil, the concept of proportionality cannot therefore be regarded as a relevant circumstance, since it has no relationship to the legal title resulting from the distance criterion.[43] For the same reason, economic factors are theoretically excluded from the list of relevant circumstances.[44] Furthermore, Weil refuses to consider ambiguous elements as relevant circumstances. For instance, the general configurations of the coasts or special geographical features are not to be regarded as relevant circumstances because of their ambiguity. In his view, even the distinction

of International Tribunals' in *Festschrift für Rudolf Bindschedler* (Bern, Stämpfli, 1980) 407–25 (in particular, 424).

[38] Separate Opinion of Judge Weeramantry, [1993] ICJ Rep 261–62, [182]. It appears that Judges Oda and Ajibola also considered relevant circumstances in a large sense. Separate Opinion of Judge Oda, ibid, 116, [98]; Separate Opinion of Judge Ajibola, ibid, 301.

[39] [1969] ICJ Rep 50, [93].

[40] Dissenting Opinion of Arbitrator Weil in the *St Pierre and Miquelon* case (1992) 31 *ILM* 1212, [36]. See also Dissenting Opinion of Judge Gros in the *Tunisia/Libya* case, [1982] ICJ Rep 156, [24].

[41] [1985] ICJ Rep 40, [48].

[42] P Weil, *Perspectives du droit de la délimitation maritime* (Paris, Pedone, 1988) 228–29.

[43] ibid, 258.

[44] ibid, 274.

between opposite and adjacent coasts cannot be considered a circumstance carrying any real weight since, more often than not, the distinction is hard to make.[45] Moreover, in Weil's view, even geographical circumstances, including the presence of islands, may not be a valid factor to correct equidistance lines. According to him, nature and geography have completed their task once the equidistance line is established in the first stage, and they have no place in a second stage. It is absurd to correct the equidistance line on the basis of geographical circumstances since equidistance lines are themselves the products of geography.[46] Consequently, Weil argues that the category of relevant circumstances boils down to just one: The distance of the delimitation line from the coasts.[47]

It appears, however, that that view is too extreme to support. The first and the most important question one may ask is why relevant circumstances should have to be connected to the legal title over maritime spaces. There is no legal ground to justify a restrictive interpretation of the concept of relevant circumstances by connecting them to the legal title. In fact, international courts and tribunals have never taken such a restrictive view.[48] According to Weil's approach, there are no relevant circumstances in maritime delimitation. The distance of the delimitation line from the coasts, which is the only circumstance considered relevant by that author, is not a relevant circumstance, but the legal title itself. Secondly, since a certain degree of ambiguity is inevitable when considering possible factors, the rejection of their relevance on the mere basis of their vagueness is difficult to support. Thirdly, as the international courts and tribunals have indicated, it is undeniable that certain special geographical features, including the presence of islands, may produce distorting effects. Accordingly, it is not unreasonable to hold that equidistance may be modified to take account of geographical circumstances. In fact, as Weil accepts, the case law giving relevance to those factors is well established.

ii. The Attempt to Establish a Legal Framework of Relevant Circumstances

While there is no limit to relevant circumstances in negotiations, that is not true before international courts and tribunals. As they are organs of adjudication, the relevance of circumstances must be judged on the basis of international law. The boundless proliferation of relevant circumstances would open up a risk of assimilating judgments based on law to those rendered *ex aequo et bono*. Accordingly, it is conceivable that there will be an inherent limit regarding

[45] ibid, 260–64.
[46] ibid, 249.
[47] ibid, 284.
[48] B Kwiatkowska, 'Economic and Environmental Considerations in Maritime Boundary Delimitations' in JI Charney and LM Alexander (eds), *International Maritime Boundaries* (Dordrecht, Nijhoff, 1993) vol I, 107.

the scope of relevant circumstances in the case law. However, the too narrow concept of relevant circumstances disregards its function in the jurisprudence. Accordingly, the proper scope of relevant circumstances should be identified in the middle between the two hypotheses. In this regard, the ICJ's view in the *Libya/Malta* case is noteworthy:

> For a court, although there is assuredly no closed list of considerations, *it is evident that only those that are pertinent to the institution of the continental shelf as it has developed within the law, and to the application of equitable principles to its delimitation, will qualify for inclusion*. Otherwise, the legal concept of continental shelf could itself be fundamentally changed by the introduction of considerations strange to its nature.[49]

The above language reveals that certain factors can be regarded as relevant circumstances insofar as they are pertinent to the institution of the continental shelf. The same would be true for the EEZ/FZ. On this point, Judge Ranjeva in the *Jan Mayen* case expressed a similar view in different terms:

> [I]t is important to specify that it is in relation to the rights of the Parties over their maritime spaces that these circumstances can – or, sometimes, should – be taken into account in a delimitation operation. Hence, special or relevant circumstances appear as facts which affect the rights of States over their maritime spaces as recognized in positive law, either in their entirety or in the exercise of the powers relating thereto.[50]

On the basis of the above *dicta*, it appears to be possible to suggest at least three criteria:

The first criterion is whether the relevant circumstances should be relevant to correct inequitable results when the equidistance method is resorted to. The configuration of the coasts, such as concavity and convexity, and the presence of islands are typical examples.

The second criterion is whether the factors in issue affect rights over the maritime spaces involved. The relevant circumstances should be pertinent to the maritime space concerned. In other words, they are factors which underlie the legal rights of coastal States over marine spaces. Thus, economic factors may be justifiably regarded as relevant, since the legal rights over the continental shelf and the EEZ pertain mainly to exploration and the exploitation of natural resources. Other factors may also be considered as relevant circumstances if they affect legal rights over the maritime institutions. For instance, the conduct of the Parties may be taken into account when it affects legal rights over a maritime zone by proving the existence of *de facto* lines.

The third criterion is whether the circumstances in question do not run counter to the legal title of distance. They should not be contrary to the legal title.

[49] Emphasis added. The *Libya/Malta* case, [1985] ICJ Rep 40, [48].
[50] Declaration of Judge Ranjeva, [1993] ICJ Rep 88.

Accordingly, so far as maritime space within 200 miles is concerned, geological and geomorphological factors cannot be regarded as relevant, since, in the present-day international law of the sea, each coastal State has equal legal title over that space, regardless of the configuration of the sea-bed, on the basis of distance from the relevant baselines.[51] For the same reason, the concept of ecological boundaries is not tenable.

It is true that the above criteria cannot eliminate all ambiguities, as the decision on what 'affects' legal rights must be made on a case-by-case basis. Even so, at least the criteria will provide a legal framework which could prevent an anarchic proliferation of relevant circumstances.

B. Balancing Relevant Circumstances

The second issue to be examined is the balancing of relevant circumstances. The question of interest here is how, if there are more than two special/relevant circumstances, they should be balanced.[52] This question must be examined in State practice and case law.

i. The Balancing of Relevant Circumstances in State Practice

It is highly difficult to establish how relevant circumstances were balanced in negotiations for the drawing of maritime boundaries since, in many cases, the details of negotiations are shrouded in secrecy. In reality, it will be impossible to extrapolate any criterion for balancing different relevant circumstances from State practice. The balancing problem becomes particularly difficult where geographical and non-geographical factors are involved at the same time.

The balancing of relevant circumstances gives rise to serious problems particularly when drawing single maritime boundaries. Indeed, as the factors to be taken into account may be different for the seabed and superjacent waters, the boundary of a continental shelf and an EEZ/FZ may differ.[53] Thus, the question of how to handle the different factors related to the sea-bed and the superjacent waters does arise in the context of single maritime boundaries. In State practice, there is a clear trend in favour of single maritime boundaries.[54] However, there are some instances where the difficulties of balancing factors relating to the seabed and the superjacent waters make it difficult to establish single maritime boundaries.

[51] R Kolb, *Case Law on Equitable Maritime Delimitation: Digest and Commentaries* (The Hague, Brill/Nijhoff, 2003) 333.

[52] M Miyoshi, *Considerations of Equity in the Settlement of Territorial and Boundary Disputes* (Dordrecht, Nijhoff, 1993) 201–03.

[53] See above, ch 1, s II.

[54] See Appendix.

A typical example of separate maritime boundaries is provided by the Torres Strait Treaty of 1978.[55] This Treaty establishes four different boundaries: (1) a seabed jurisdiction boundary, (2) a fisheries jurisdiction boundary, (3) a single maritime boundary for both the seabed and fisheries, and (4) a protected-zone boundary. Special attention should be drawn to the fact that a fisheries jurisdiction boundary is established in front of Papua New Guinea, separating it from a seabed jurisdiction boundary. Boundaries for the seabed and the superjacent waters were thus separated. It has been said that the critical issue in the negotiations was the living resources of the area offered to the inhabitants of the Australian islands. In addition, the islanders' feeling that they had been cut from Australia by a single maritime boundary also had to be taken into account. A separate fisheries jurisdiction boundary was thus drawn so as to avoid establishing Australian-inhabited enclaves north of the single maritime boundary between the two States.[56] Consequently, in the 'top hat' area, where the two types of jurisdiction diverge, Australia exercises fisheries jurisdiction, while Papua New Guinea has seabed jurisdiction. Moreover, it should be noted that the seabed boundary runs beyond 200 miles from the relevant basepoints because of the geomorphological configuration of the area. The Torres Strait Treaty presents an example of a flexible solution establishing four types of delimitation lines for different purposes. According to Burmester, who was a member of the Australian negotiating team, it was unlikely that an agreement would have been acceptable if the delimitation had been approached from the angle of drawing a single maritime boundary.[57] This special agreement may be regarded as a consequence of the complex political, economic and social situation in the area.

Another example on this matter is the 1997 Perth Treaty between Australia and Indonesia for the Timor and Arafura Sea.[58] That Treaty is unique in that

[55] The precise title is: Treaty between Australia and the Independent State of Papua New Guinea Concerning Sovereignty and Maritime Boundaries in the Area between the Two Countries, Including the Area Known as Torres Strait, and Related Matters. The text is included in Charney and Alexander, *IMB*, vol I, 937–75. Regarding this Treaty, see Report by Choon-ho Park, ibid, 930–34; H Burmester, 'The Torres Strait Treaty: Ocean Boundary Delimitation by Agreement' (1982) 76 *AJIL* 321; and D Renton, 'The Torres Strait Treaty After 15 Years: Some Observations from a Papua New Guinea Perspective' in J Crawford and DR Rothwell, (eds), *The Law of the Sea in the Asian Pacific Region* (Dordrecht, Kluwer, 1995) 171.

[56] Burmester, 'The Torres Strait Treaty' 337.

[57] ibid, 332.

[58] Even though the Perth Treaty has never entered into force, according to the *Timor-Leste/Australia* Conciliation Commission, its provisions are observed in practice by the governments of Australia and Indonesia. *Report and Recommendations on the Compulsory Conciliation Commission between Timor-Leste and Australia on the Timor Sea*, 9 May 2018, [30]. For an analysis of the Treaty in some detail, see M Herriman and M Tsamenyi, 'The 1997 Australia-Indonesia Maritime Boundary Treaty: A Secure Legal Regime for Offshore Resource Development?' (1998) 29 *ODIL* 361; V Prescott, 'Current Legal Developments, Australia/Indonesia' (1997) 12 *IJMCL* 533; Report by Prescott, *IMB*, vol IV, 2697.

it draws two continental shelf and EEZ boundaries, which do not coincide.[59] In so doing, the Perth Treaty produces an area where the EEZ appertaining to the First Party (Indonesia) overlaps the continental shelf of the Second Party (Australia). Article 7 of the Treaty attempts to explain the rights enjoyed by each Party and the arrangements to resolve potential conflicts arising from the overlap. In essence, while Indonesia enjoys sovereign rights regarding the water column in the overlap, Australia has sovereign rights relating to the seabed in that area. It is conceivable that the Parties failed to reach an agreement to establish a single maritime boundary owing to the divergent factors relevant for the seabed and the superjacent waters. The Perth Treaty represents, however, conceptual and practical difficulties on some points. Article 7 stipulates that '(a) the First Party may exercise exclusive economic zone sovereign rights and jurisdiction provided for in the 1982 Convention in relation to the water column; (b) the Second Party may exercise continental shelf sovereign rights and jurisdiction provided for in the 1982 Convention in relation to the seabed.'[60] Yet the reference to the exclusive economic zone in (a) of that Article signals a misunderstanding of the concept of the EEZ. The EEZ is not a legal regime which concerns solely the water column, but associates the seabed, superjacent waters and airspace above it. The idea that the EEZ relates only to the water column perhaps incorrectly assumes that jurisdiction over activities in the superjacent waters can be isolated from those associated with the seabed.[61] Accordingly, the 'EEZ' referred in that Treaty is no longer the EEZ stated in the LOSC but, perhaps, a sort of FZ.

ii. The Balancing Relevant Circumstances in the Case Law

In the jurisprudence concerning maritime delimitation, as noted, there is a clear trend that geographical factors prevail over non-geographical factors. Accordingly, in most cases, the problem of balancing relevant circumstances tends to be as a rule avoided by restricting the relevant circumstances to one or two geographical factors. It is not suggested, however, that problems of balancing relevant circumstances will never arise. The *Eritrea/Yemen* case is an example. In this case, the Arbitral Tribunal drew a single maritime boundary on the basis of geographical factors, including coastal configuration, proportionality, islands, baseline and the presence of third States and one non-geographical factor, that

[59] Regarding continental shelf boundary, the Perth Treaty reaffirmed in its preamble, the seabed boundaries established in the 1971 and 1972 Agreements between the same Parties. On the other hand in the area to the west of Point A25 specified in those Agreements, the 1997 Treaty established a new seabed boundary line (Art 1). In addition, the 1989 Agreement concerning the Zone of Cooperation is also reaffirmed in that Treaty (Preamble).

[60] For the text of the Treaty, see Prescott, 'Current Legal Developments, Australia/Indonesia' 535–47; Herriman and Tsamenyi, 'The 1997 Australia-Indonesia Maritime Boundary Treaty' 382–93.

[61] ibid, 364.

is, navigation.[62] There was no clash between geographical factors. Yet attention should be drawn to the fact that, in the southern part of the boundary, Yemeni and Eritrean islands were ignored to preserve the simplicity desirable in the neighbourhood of a main shipping lane. In other words, the consideration of a navigational element had priority over the islands concerned. However, the Arbitral Tribunal did not explain why navigational factors should be given such preference. It appears that the Court's solution was motivated by the simplicity and practicality of the delimitation line, and it is difficult to extract from this case any legal criterion for balancing geographical and non-geographical factors.

Another example on this matter is provided by the *Jan Mayen* case. In this case, two relevant circumstances – proportionality and equitable access to fishing resources – were at issue in zone 1. While the consideration of proportionality related to both the continental shelf and FZ delimitations, equitable access to fishing only pertained to the FZ. On this point, a problem did arise regarding the balance between two factors. Nevertheless, the Court divided the zone into two equal parts without explaining the relationship between the two factors.[63] As pointed out already, the only explanation may be that a specific adjustment to fishery requirements was made to make them coincide with the consideration of proportionality. It may be said that the question of balancing relevant circumstances may be more serious when it comes to coincident maritime boundaries. In this respect, Judge Oda, in the *Jan Mayen* case, stated that:

> [I]f a single maritime delimitation for the continental shelf and the exclusive economic zone is to be effected by the Court in response to a joint request by the parties in dispute, then the parties have to agree which factors or elements relevant to either the exclusive economic zone or the continental shelf (or, in other words, relevant to either fishery resources or mineral resources), are to be given priority. The Court is not competent even as an arbitrator to decide the priority of either the exclusive economic zone or the continental shelf unless expressly requested to do so by the parties.[64]

The above view points to the danger that the Court's discretion will arbitrarily extend not only to the identification of relevant circumstances, but also to their proper balancing. Obviously, that concern is not without interest. In reality, however, it will be difficult to expect that the Parties would agree on priorities regarding factors to be taken into account. In most cases, the factors and importance given to them by the Parties have been different. To resolve disputes over differences regarding relevant circumstances is at the heart of the maritime delimitation cases. Thus, it is inevitable that the international courts and

[62] Regarding the process of delimitation, see ch 5, s V of this book.
[63] Regarding the process of delimitation, see ch 5, s IV of this book.
[64] Separate Opinion of Judge Oda, [1993] ICJ Rep 114, [89].

tribunals should identify relevant circumstances. If this is the case, it will be reasonable to consider that the international courts and tribunals are also entitled to determine the balance between the relevant circumstances.

Concerning geographical factors, there are few clashes. The real question is the reconciliation of geographical and non-geographical factors, and between different non-geographical factors, especially economic ones. Regarding the latter, Judge Oda stated that:

> If the marine resources constitute a factor to be taken into account, it is unthinkable to draw a single maritime boundary without having a clear idea as to which particular circumstances ought to predominate (ie, those relating either to the exclusive economic zone or the continental shelf.)[65]

While Judge Oda's view is worthy of note, the case law is insufficient to provide any criterion for determining such a hierarchy. The only conclusion justified by it is that that priority shall be judged by international tribunals on a case-by-case basis. Given the fact that international courts and tribunals have relied mainly on geographical factors, it may be said that normally the latter will be considered first in the process of maritime delimitation. [66]

IV. PROBLEMS WITH THE APPLICATION OF THE THREE-STAGE APPROACH

As pointed out in chapter five,[67] presently the application of the three-stage approach becomes an orthodox approach in the law of maritime delimitation. Nonetheless, the three-stage approach leaves some room for discussion with regard to *the manner* in which this approach is applied. In this regard, three problems must be examined.

A. Problems with the First Stage of Maritime Delimitation: Subjectivity in the Construction of a Provisional Equidistance Line

A first issue is whether, at the first stage of maritime delimitations, the equidistance method is applied by an international court or tribunal in a scientific

[65] ibid, 117, [99].

[66] When indicating the 'fundamental norm', the Chamber of the ICJ, in the *Gulf of Maine* case, stated that 'with regard to the geographic configuration of the area and other relevant circumstances.' [1984] ICJ Rep 300, [112]. In this phrase, the accent lies on the 'geographic configuration' as distinct from 'other relevant circumstances'. On this point, see LH Legault and B Hankey, 'From Sea to Seabed' (1985) 79 *AJIL* 971; LA Willis, 'From Precedent to precedent: The Triumph of Pragmatism in the Law of Maritime Boundaries' (1986) 24 *CYIL* 55.

[67] See ch 5, s XIX of this book.

manner. As a matter of theory, inputs of data representing two coasts mechanically compute an equidistance line, that is, a line every point of which is equidistant from the nearest points on those coasts.[68] This is called a strict equidistance line. To secure the inherent value of predictability at the first stage of maritime delimitations, that stage must rest on a strict equidistance line. This point was echoed by the ICJ itself in the *Black Sea* case:

> In keeping with its settled jurisprudence on maritime delimitation, the first stage of the Court's approach is to establish the provisional equidistance line. At this initial stage of the construction of the provisional equidistance line the Court is not yet concerned with any relevant circumstances that may obtain and the line is plotted on strictly geometrical criteria on the basis of objective data.[69]

In the same case, however, the Court went to add that:

> In [...] the delimitation of the maritime areas involving two or more States, the Court should not base itself solely on the choice of base points made by one of those Parties. The Court must, when delimiting the continental shelf and exclusive economic zones, select base points by reference to the physical geography of the relevant coasts.[70]

The Court's view was echoed by ITLOS in the *Bangladesh/Myanmar* case.[71]

In judicial practice, more often than not, the equidistance line has been constructed on the basis of base points selected by judges.[72] In the *Libya/Malta* case, for instance, the ICJ did not take account of Filfla in the calculation of the provisional median (equidistance) line between Malta and Libya, even though Filfla was included in Maltese baselines.[73] Likewise the ICJ, in the *Black Sea* case, ignored Serpents' Island when constructing a provisional equidistance line.[74] However, the question whether that Island should be ignored seems to be an issue at the second stage of maritime delimitations.[75] In the *Bangladesh/Myanmar* case, ITLOS excluded St Martin's Island as the source of any base point since 'the selection of a base point on St Martin's Island would result in a line that blocks the seaward projection from Myanmar's coast.'[76] Yet the Tribunal's consideration relates to a matter of relevant circumstances at the

[68] CG Lathrop, 'The Provisional Equidistance Line: Charting a Course between Objectivity and Subjectivity?' in Alex G Oude Elferink, T Henriksen, and SV Busch, *Maritime Boundary Delimitation: The Case Law Is It Consistent and Predictable?* (Cambridge University Press, 2018) 211.

[69] [2009] ICJ Rep 101, [118].

[70] ibid, 108, [137]. See also the *Libya/Malta* case, [1985] ICJ Rep 48, [64].

[71] The *Bangladesh/Myanmar* case, [2012] ITLOS Rep 81, [264].

[72] ibid, 210.

[73] [1985] ICJ Rep 48, [64].

[74] [2009] ICJ Rep 103-104, [149].

[75] D McRae, 'The Applicable Law: The Geneva Convention on the Continental Shelf, the LOSC, and Customary International Law' in Oude Elferink, Henriksen, and Busch, *Maritime Boundary Delimitation*, 103.

[76] [2012] ITLOS Rep 73, [265].

second stage of maritime delimitations.[77] The treatment of base points was also at issue in the *Peru v Chile* case. In this case, the ICJ held that:

> For the purpose of constructing a provisional equidistance line, only those points on the Peruvian coast which are more than 80 nautical miles from Point A can be matched with points at an equivalent distance on the Chilean coast.[78]

The only justification of the Court's selection of base points was to link its provisional line to Point A of the agreed boundary. As a consequence, the Peruvian coast which lies within an 80-nautical-mile radius from Point A was ignored. Even though the Court called the constructed line the 'provisional equidistance line', that line is not related to a strict equidistance line.[79]

The judicial practice demonstrates that at the first stage of the delimitation process, consideration of equity already comes into play in an international court's selecting relevant base points for drawing a provisional equidistance line.[80] A reason may be that an international court or tribunal might be able to avoid the critique of subjectivity which often emerged at the second stage, by creeping considerations of equity into the process of construction of a provisional equidistance line at the first stage of maritime delimitations.[81] Yet this approach blurs the distinction between the first and second stages of maritime delimitation.[82] The intrinsic value of the equidistance method consists in its scientific character. Given that selection of base points by judges is not free from subjectivity,[83] however, judge-selected base points may entail the risk of undermining the value of predictability at the first stage of maritime delimitation.[84] To this extent, it may have to be admitted that the construction of a provisional equidistance line is not free from elements of subjectivity and unpredictability.

B. Problems with the Second Stage of Maritime Delimitation: The Manner of an Adjustment of the Provisional Equidistance Line

The next issue pertains to the manner of an adjustment of a provisional equidistance line at the second stage of maritime delimitation. An excessive departure

[77] Alex G Oude Elferink, 'International Law and Negotiation and Adjudicated maritime Boundaries: A Complex Relationship' (2015) 18 *German Yearbook of International Law*, 252.

[78] [2014] ICJ Rep 66, [185].

[79] Oude Elferink, 'International Law and Negotiation and Adjudicated maritime Boundaries' 253–55; CG Lathrop, 'The Provisional Equidistance Line' in Oude Elferink, Henriksen, and Busch, *Maritime Boundary Delimitation*, 219.

[80] ibid, 215 et seq.

[81] ibid, 220.

[82] ibid, 214

[83] ibid, 211.

[84] Commentators gave their misgivings about the risk. See Y Tanaka, 'The Mirage of Predictability in the Law of Maritime Delimitation: A Comparative Analysis of the Bangladesh v Myanmar and Nicaragua v Colombia Cases' (2014) 113 *The Journal of International Law and Diplomacy* 14-15; Nuno Marques Antunes and Vasco Becker-Weinberg, 'Entitlement to Maritime Zones and Their

from a provisional equidistance line runs the serious risk of undermining the predictability of the law of maritime delimitation and eventually damaging the confidence of States in judicial settlement of maritime delimitation disputes.[85] The question with an adjustment of a provisional equidistance line has already appeared in the *Libya/Malta* case. As pointed out earlier, the legal basis for shifting the equidistance line by 18' northward in that case remains less clear.[86] A similar problem arose in more recent cases.

In the *Bangladesh/Myanmar* case, for instance, ITLOS considered that the concavity of the coast of Bangladesh was a relevant circumstance which required an adjustment of the provisional equidistance line.[87] Accordingly, from point 11(X), the Tribunal adjusted the provisional equidistance line so as that that line follows a geodetic line starting at an azimuth of 215°.[88] Nonetheless, the 215° azimuth line is the line advocated by Bangladesh on the basis of the angle-bisector method and that method was clearly rejected by ITLOS itself. The revival of the 215° azimuth line at the second stage of the delimitation process is a contradiction which is hard to justify.[89] In addition, ITLOS offered scant explanation why the adjusted delimitation line should follow the 215°, not, for instance, 214° or 216°, azimuth line. Nor was there any explanation how the 215° azimuth line was to be constructed.[90] Overall there are some doubts as to whether the delimitation line drawn by ITLOS can be considered as an adjusted equidistance line.[91]

The *Bangladesh v India* case also raised a similar problem. From point Prov-3, the Annex VII Arbitral Tribunal adjusted the provisional equidistance line to a geodetic line with an initial azimuth of 177° 30′ 00″.[92] Yet, the Tribunal offered scant explanation about the legal basis for selecting an azimuth of 177° 30′ 00″.[93] As noted, the azimuth chosen by the majority is similar to the azimuth of the bisector line proposed by Bangladesh which was rejected by the Tribunal,

Delimitation: In the Doldrums of Uncertainty and Unpredictability' in Oude Elferink, Henriksen, and Busch, *Maritime Boundary Delimitation*, 81 and 90; Lathrop, 'The Provisional Equidistance Line' 210–11; McRae, 'The Applicable Law' 111 and 115.

[85] The Colombian Government was dissatisfied with the *Nicaragua v. Colombia* judgment and, on 27 November 2012, Colombia denounced the 1948 American Treaty on Pacific Settlement (Pact of Bogotá) in which the States Parties to the Treaty accepted the compulsory jurisdiction of the ICJ (Article XXXI). www.oas.org/juridico/english/sigs/a-42.html#Colombia. In this regard, see Naomi Burke, 'Nicaragua v Colombia at the ICJ: Better the Devil You Don't?' (2013) 2 *Cambridge Journal of International and Comparative Law* 322–23.

[86] See ch 4, s IV of this book.

[87] [2012] ITLOS Rep 92, [297]; 98, [323–24].

[88] ibid, 100, [334]; 101, [340]. See also ch 5, s XII of this book.

[89] Declaration of Judge Wolfrum, [2012] ITLOS Rep 139; Separate Opinion of Judge Cot, ibid, 189.

[90] Separate Opinion of Judge Gao, ibid, 208–09, [39] and 212, [50]. See also Dissenting Opinion of Judge Lucky, ibid, 283.

[91] Separate Opinion of Judge Cot, ibid, 191–92.

[92] The *Bangladesh v India* arbitral award, [478].

[93] Concurring and Dissenting Opinion of Dr PS Rao in the *Bangladesh v India* arbitral award, [21].

that is, an azimuth of 180°.[94] As a consequence, the azimuth of the bisector line was *de facto* re-introduced at the second stage of maritime delimitation, even though it was rejected by the Tribunal itself. In this regard, Judge Rao gave his misgivings that the re-introduction of the azimuth of the bisector line is 'arbitrary and intrinsically runs counter to the majority's own reasoning which effectively rejected a bisector as a matter of law.'[95]

The question regarding the adjustment of a provisional equidistance line was also raised in the *Nicaragua v Colombia* case. In this case, the ICJ ruled that, in the western part of the relevant area, the disparity in coastal length is so marked as to justify a significant shift. When shifting the provisional median line eastwards, it constructed a line each point on which is three times as far from the controlling base point on the Nicaraguan islands as it is from the controlling base point on the Colombian islands. Thus, the 'weighted line' was constructed using a 3:1 ratio between the Nicaraguan and Colombian base points.[96] Nonetheless, the legal ground of the 3:1 ratio is less clear. Indeed, the ratio of the lengths of the relevant coasts is approximately 1:8.2 in favour of Nicaragua. In this regard, there may be scope to consider the question whether there is any relationship between the ratio of coastal lengths of each party which is 8:1 and the 3:1 ratio for the adjustment. An explanation may be that the effect of the provisional median line was to cut Nicaragua off from some three quarters of the area into which its coast projects.[97] Even so, a question arises as to whether the weighted line can be considered as a shifting of the provisional median line or a reconstruction of a new line by a 3:1 ratio between the base points of the Parties.[98] Furthermore, as explained earlier, the ICJ drew two horizontal lines along lines of latitude from points 1 and 9. Nonetheless, it is problematic that there is no linkage between the provisionally drawn equidistance line and these two horizontal lines. This point was criticised by Judge Abraham, stating that:

> [I]t is difficult to regard these two horizontal lines as a mere 'adjustment' or even 'shifting' of the provisional line. With the exception of the starting-point of the first line, those lines are actually entirely unrelated to the provisional line.[99]

Furthermore, Judge Xue noted that in the northern part, the Court used the parallel of latitude and enclaving Quitasueño and Serrana and that in the southern part, the Court constructed a maritime boundary along the parallel of

[94] ibid, [9] and [22].
[95] ibid, [9].
[96] The *Nicaragua v Colombia* case, [2012] ICJ Rep 709-10, [233–35].
[97] ibid, [215].
[98] Declaration of Judge Xue in the *Nicaragua v Colombia* case. [2012] ICJ Rep 748, [5].
[99] Separate Opinion of Judge Abraham in the *Nicaragua v Colombia* case, ibid, 738, [32]. See also Declaration of Judge Xue, ibid, 750, [13].

latitude till the 200-nautical-mile limit of Nicaragua.[100] In this regard, Judge Xue gave her misgivings that:

> The boundary in these two sections is apparently drawn by different methods – enclaving and latitude line. It is hard to justify them as 'adjustment of' or 'shifting from' the provisional median line, if the latter does not mean total departure.[101]

As Judges Abraham and Xue pointedly observed, it appears that these two horizontal lines are essentially creative lines, not an adjustment or shift of the provisionally drawn equidistance line. If this is the case, this may entail the serious risk of equating maritime delimitations on the basis of international law by the Court with a decision *ex aequo et bono*.[102]

As demonstrated by the *Bangladesh/Myanmar*, *Bangladesh v India*, and *Nicaragua v Colombia* cases, the manner of adjustment of a provisional equidistance line may be a matter for debate. An excessive departure from a provisional equidistance line may run the serious risk of undermining the predictability of the law of maritime delimitation and eventually damaging the confidence of States in judicial settlement of maritime delimitation disputes.[103] Therefore, it must be stressed that adjustment at the second stage of maritime delimitation must rest on clear reasoning and a more objective method. It will also require a sufficient degree of approximation to a provisional equidistance line.[104]

C. Problems with the Third Stage of Maritime Delimitations: Subjectivity in the Application of the Disproportionality Test

The third and last stage of maritime delimitations is the disproportionality test. That test aims to check the equitableness of maritime boundaries. The question of interest here is whether the disproportionality test contributes to enhancing the predictability of the law of maritime delimitation. The answer is no. In this regard, at least four problems must be noted.[105]

[100] Declaration of Judge Xue, ibid, 748, [7].

[101] ibid, [8]. See also P von Mühlendahl, *L'équidistance dans la délimitation des frontière* maritimes 224–25, [355].

[102] Tanaka, 'Reflections on the Territorial and Maritime Disputes between Nicaragua and Colombia' 920–21.

[103] The Colombian Government was dissatisfied with the *Nicaragua v Colombia* judgment and, on 27 November 2012, Colombia denounced the 1948 American Treaty on Pacific Settlement (Pact of Bogotá) in which the States Parties to the Treaty accepted the compulsory jurisdiction of the ICJ (Article XXXI). www.oas.org/juridico/english/sigs/a-42.html#Colombia. In this regard, see Naomi Burke, 'Nicaragua v Colombia at the ICJ: Better the Devil You Don't?' (2013) 2 *Cambridge Journal of International and Comparative Law* 322–23.

[104] In this regard, Judge Gao argued that adjustment must be carried out within legal, geographical, scientific and mathematical limits. Separate Opinion of Judge Gao in the *Bangladesh/Myanmar* case. [2012] ITLOS Rep 215–16, [58].

[105] The author highlighted the problem with the disproportionality test in: Y Tanaka, 'Disproportionality Test' in Oude Elferink, Henriksen, and Busch, *Maritime Boundary Delimitation* 314–16.

The first and the most serious problem is that there is no objective criterion to define the relevant coasts and areas and to calculate their lengths and surfaces.[106] In order to calculate the lengths of relevant coasts, it is necessary to define the coasts to be evaluated. More often than not, however, the definition of what are the relevant coasts is itself a disputable point; international courts and tribunals have failed to come up with any objective criterion. Nor is there any criterion for calculating the lengths of the relevant coasts. That calculation may be complicated by the presence of islands.[107] It is also difficult to define relevant areas, especially where legal titles of third States may be at issue. Indeed, the ICJ, in the *Costa Rica v Nicaragua* case, however, admitted the difficulty in precisely identifying relevant areas, stating that:

> [T]he attribution of some maritime space to a third State will affect the part of the relevant area that appertains to each Party. Since the maritime space appertaining to third States cannot be identified in the present proceedings, it is impossible for the Court to calculate precisely the part of the relevant area of each Party.[108]

Thus, the concept of proportionality is far from being objective when it comes to determining and calculating relevant coasts and areas. Practical difficulties in calculating relevant coasts and maritime zones may also arise in the process of negotiations concerning maritime delimitation. In 1971, for example, two agreements between Denmark and the FRG, and between the latter and the Netherlands were concluded pursuant to the *North Sea Continental Shelf* judgment. The latter indicated proportionality as a factor to be considered in the negotiations. Nevertheless, Jaenicke pointed out that the Parties had experienced difficulties in calculating coasts or maritime areas and regarding the weight to be accorded to such calculations in determining the boundary of the continental shelf.[109] Overall it is difficult to disagree with the observation of Higgins that: 'The concept of proportionality in maritime delimitation remains, for me, full of uncertainties and problems.'[110]

The second problem relates to the excessive subjectivity with regard to the evaluation of (dis)proportionality between the coastal lengths and maritime areas appertaining to each party. In the jurisprudence in this field, there is no objective standard for determining disproportion between the ratio of the

[106] M Vœlckel, 'Aperçu de quelques problèmes techniques concernant la délimitation des frontières maritimes' (1979) 25 *AFDI* 706.

[107] R Ida, 'The Role of Proportionality in Maritime Delimitation Revisited: The Origin and Meaning of the Principle from the Early Decisions of the Court' in N Ando et al (eds), *Liber Amicorum Judge Shigeru Oda* (The Hague, Kluwer, 2002) 101.

[108] [2018] ICJ Rep [164].

[109] G Jaenicke, 'The Role of Proportionality in the Delimitation of maritime Zones' in A Bos and H Siblesz (eds), *Realism in Law-Making, Essays on International Law in Honour of Willem Riphagem* (Dodrecht, Nijhoff, 1986) 58, note 15.

[110] R Higgins, *Problems and Process: International Law and How We Use It* (Clarendon Press Oxford 1994) 230; Kolb, *Case Law on Equitable Maritime Delimitation*, 197.

relevant coastal lengths and maritime areas belonging to each party.[111] According to the ICJ, the disproportionality test is a means of checking whether there is a 'significant' disproportionality in the ratios between the maritime areas which would fall to one party or other by virtue of the delimitation line arrived at after the second stage of the delimitation process, and the lengths of their respective coasts.[112] However, the adjective 'significant' is too vague to be very useful.[113] By way of example, in the *Nicaragua v Colombia* case, the ratio of maritime areas was 1 (Colombia): 3.44 (Nicaragua), even though the ratio of coastal length was 1 (Colombia): 8.2 (Nicaragua). Accordingly, the ratio of coastal length is more than twice as great as that of maritime areas. Nonetheless, the ICJ considered that the 'disproportionality' test was met. If this is not disproportionate, what is the meaning of the 'disproportionality' test?[114] Furthermore, in some cases, the ICJ ruled that the disproportionality test was met, without presenting any specific figures of the relevant coastal lengths and maritime areas accorded to each party. The disproportionality test without calculation of the ratio of the coastal length and the maritime area is merely legal impressionism. To date, there is no single case where an international court or tribunal admitted the existence of disproportion between the ratio of coastal lengths and the ratio for maritime areas appertaining to the Parties.[115] It is difficult to resist the temptation to submit that, at the second stage of maritime delimitation, the maritime boundary was already established in such a way as to pass the disproportionality test.[116] If this is the case, the distinction between the second and third stages of maritime delimitation appears to be thin.

Thirdly, as Judge Oda pointedly observed, (dis)proportionality cannot determine any concrete delimitation line since the number of lines capable of producing the same proportion is limitless.[117] Accordingly, the role of the disproportionality test is limited to check the equitableness of the maritime boundary established by a court or tribunal only in a *retrospective* manner.

[111] For statistics on the proportionality test, see S Fietta and R Cleverly, *A Practitioner's Guide to Maritime Boundary Delimitation* (Oxford University Press Oxford 2016) 605–06. See also A Pellet and B Samson, 'La delimitation des espaces marins' in M Forteau and J-M Thouvenin (eds), *Traité de droit international de la mer* (Paris, Pedone, 2017) 608.

[112] [2009] ICJ Rep 99, [110].

[113] According to Evans, the concept of proportionality is a means to demonstrate that 'the delimitation line settled upon [...] has an equitable "feel" to it.' M Evans, 'Maritime Boundary Delimitation: Where Do We Go From Here?' in D Freestone, R Barnes and D Ong (eds), *The Law of the Sea: Progress and Prospects* (Oxford University Press, Oxford, 2006) 155.

[114] MD Evans, 'Maritime Boundary Delimitation: Whatever Next?' in J Barrett and R Barnes (eds), *Law of the Sea: UNCLOS as a Living Treaty* (British Institute of International and Comparative Law London 2016) 62.

[115] P von Mühlendahl, *L'équidistance dans la délimitation des frontières maritimes* 330, [521]; Tanaka, 'Disproportionality Test' 315.

[116] ibid., 315–16.

[117] Dissenting Opinion of Judge Oda, [1982] ICJ Rep 258, [162]; H Thirlway, *The Law and Procedure of the International Court of Justice: Fifty Years of Jurisprudence*, vol I (Oxford University Press Oxford 2013) 500–01.

Given that it cannot objectively constrain discretion of judges in the adjustment of the provisional equidistance line, it is open to the question as to whether the disproportionality test can contribute to enhancing the transparency and objectiveness of the process of maritime delimitation.

Fourthly, it cannot pass unnoticed that the concept of (dis)proportionality entails the risk of blurring the distinction between delimitation and apportionment. It is true that the importance of this distinction was repeatedly highlighted by the ICJ.[118] Given that the very idea of 'ratios' necessarily entails that of shares,[119] however, the disproportionality test raises a serious concern that the process of maritime delimitation may be transformed to 'apportionment' or 'award of a just and equitable share' of marine spaces which was rejected by the Court itself.[120]

All in all, it may have to be admitted that the application of the disproportionality test is far from being objective. Thus some commentators denied the role of that test in the process of maritime delimitation. For instance, Evans proposed as an option that: '[P]roportionality should no longer play any formal role in the process of maritime boundary delimitation conducted on the basis of international law.'[121] McRae also argued that: 'In fact, if relevant circumstances have been fully assessed, there might be no need for a further disproportionality test.'[122] Given that the three-stage approach is increasingly consolidated, however, it seems unlikely that a court or a tribunal would remove the disproportionality test in the jurisprudence concerning maritime delimitation. As a more moderate option, a court or tribunal should limit the application of the disproportionality test to the situations where a provisional equidistance line would create the cut-off effect by a markedly concave or convex coastline, even though relevant coasts are comparative in length.[123] Indeed, this was the original role of (dis)proportionality in the law of maritime delimitation.[124]

V. CONCLUSIONS

It is significant that international courts and tribunals increasingly stress the need for predictability and transparency in the law. The emphasis on

[118] See for instance, [1969] ICJ Rep 22, [18]; [1982] ICJ Rep 60, [71]; [1985] ICJ Rep 40, [46]; [1993] ICJ Rep 67, [64].

[119] HWA Thirlway, *The Law and Procedure of the International Court of Justice: Fifty Years of Jurisprudence*, vol I (Oxford University Press, Oxford, 2013) 500. See also the *Nicaragua v Colombia* case, [2012] ICJ Rep 696, [193].

[120] Tanaka, 'Disproportionality Test' 316.

[121] Evans, 'Maritime Boundary Delimitation: Where Do We Go From Here?,' 156. P von Mühlendahl also took the same view. P von Mühlendahl, *L'équidistance dans la délimitation des frontières maritimes* 332, [525] and 336, [526].

[122] McRae, 'The Applicable Law' 114.

[123] Tanaka, 'Disproportionality Test' 318; Fietta and Cleverly, *A Practitioner's Guide to Maritime Boundary Delimitation*, 608.

[124] Tanaka, 'Disproportionality Test' 294. See also ch 7, s III of this book.

predictability and transparency is reflected in the application of the three-stage approach to maritime delimitations. The important advantage of the three-stage approach is that it has a certain degree of predictability by incorporating an objective method of delimitation, that is, the equidistance method, into the legal domain. Under this approach, a consideration of equity may come into play at a second stage, but only in cases in which equidistance lines provisionally drawn produce inequitable results. To this extent, the three-stage approach makes it possible to reduce the subjectivity and unpredictability of the law of maritime delimitation. The adoption of this approach can be regarded as a positive development of the law. However, the application of the three-stage approach is not free from the risk of subjectivity in three respects.

First, international courts and tribunals can exercise their discretion when selecting relevant basepoints for constructing a provisional equidistance line. Thus, at this stage, consideration of equity may already come into play.

Secondly, it could be contended that the general direction of case law reveals a predominance of geographical over non-geographical factors. Yet, there is no established rule concerning legal effects given to relevant circumstances. Accordingly, it is unpredictable to what extent an international court or tribunal would attribute effect to geological factors, such as islands. Where multiple relevant circumstances exist, balancing these circumstances is a matter of subjective appreciation of international courts and tribunals. A crucial issue that arises in this regard concerns the *manner* of the shift or adjustment of a provisional equidistance line. As demonstrated by the *Bangladesh/Myanmar, Bangladesh v India* and *Nicaragua v Colombia* cases, the manner of adjustment of a provisional equidistance line by an international court or tribunal is totally unpredictable since it lacks adequate legal reasoning. An excessive departure from a provisional equidistance line runs the serious risk of undermining the predictability of the law of maritime delimitation and eventually damaging the confidence of States in judicial settlement of maritime delimitation disputes.

Thirdly, it is argued that the disproportionality test contains four major problems:

- lack of any objective criterion for calculating the lengths of relevant coasts and relevant areas;
- lack of any objective criterion for evaluating (dis)proportionality between the coastal lengths and maritime areas appertaining to each Party;
- inability to determine any concrete delimitation line since the number of lines capable of producing the same proportion is limitless; and
- risk of making the distinction between delimitation and apportionment unclear.

Owing to the problems, it is open to debate whether the disproportionality test can contribute to enhancing predictability and objectiveness of the law of maritime delimitation.

In conclusion, regardless of predictability at the methodological level, it appears that the law of maritime delimitation is still fluid in some respects. In particular, excessive creativity and imagination of an international court in adjusting a provisional equidistance line may significantly undermine the predictability of the law of maritime delimitation. If this is the case, only a mirage of predictability would remain in the legal desert.[125]

[125] Tanaka, 'The Mirage' 29.

10

General Conclusion

THIS STUDY HAS considered more than 100 years of the law of maritime delimitation in the perspective of a possible reconciliation between predictability and flexibility. In this respect, it has purported to clarify the essence of the law of maritime delimitation and to present a framework for it. For that purpose, we focused on three aspects: the evolution of the law of maritime delimitation, the comparative study of case law and State practice, and a legal framework for reconciling predictability and flexibility in the law. These considerations lead to the following conclusions.

(1) The history of the law of maritime delimitation shows a constant and probably unavoidable recourse to the concept of equity or equitable principles, and at the same time a vacillation between two contrasting approaches: The result-oriented equity approach (ie, *l'équité créatrice*) and the corrective-equity approach (ie, *l'équité correctrice*). According to the former, no method of delimitation is prescribed by law, and equity is the sole parameter prescribed. For the latter, the equidistance method is applied at the first stage, and a shift of the equidistance line should be subsequently envisaged if relevant circumstances warrant it. While the result-oriented equity approach purports to maintain maximum flexibility, the corrective-equity approach stresses predictability. In that sense, it could be contended that the essential issue of the law of maritime delimitation consists in the tension between these two conceptions. This is why the quest for a legal framework reconciling predictability and flexibility has become essential.

(2) It is true that the essence of equity, which is at the heart of the law in this field, is individualism and flexibility. In fact, owing to the diversity of geographical and other elements, flexibility is indispensable for drawing equitable delimitation lines. Nevertheless, the law of maritime delimitation is not a simple mosaic of ad hoc considerations concerning relevant circumstances. Since a law which is wholly unpredictable is a contradiction in terms, predictability is essential in the law of maritime delimitation as well. This is why predictability should be enhanced. Hence the transformation from 'equity as mere judicial discretion' to 'structured or controlled equity' is of particular importance.[1] In this regard,

[1] P Weil, 'Le droit international en quête de son identité, Cours général de droit international public' (1992) 237 *RCADI* 254. In this lecture, Weil considered the notion of equity in recent ICJ judgments as changing the process from 'une juridisation sauvage de l'équité' to 'une juridisation sage de l'équité.' ibid, 245–60.

it is easy enough to agree with the view of Judge Gros in the *Gulf of Maine* case: 'Controlled equity as a procedure for applying the law would contribute to the proper functioning of international justice; equity left, without any objective elements of control, to the wisdom of the judge reminds us that equity was once measured by "the Chancellor's foot".'[2]

(3) Before the end of the twentieth century, two different approaches co-existed in the law of maritime delimitation. Regarding delimitation between States with opposite coasts, international courts and tribunals have applied the corrective-equity approach. With respect to delimitations between States with adjacent coasts, the case law has been less favourable to the equidistance method, even though this may not necessarily mean that the corrective-equity approach has been rejected altogether in a situation of adjacency. However, currently there is a general trend, 'unless there are compelling reasons' not to do so, for international courts and tribunals to apply the three-stage approach, a variation of the corrective-equity approach, to all types of maritime delimitations at the conventional and customary law levels. Viewed from a broad perspective, the law of maritime delimitation thus moves from *co-existence of the two different approaches to a unified approach based on corrective-equity*. This is an important step toward the unification of the approaches to maritime delimitation.

(4) By its very nature, the result-oriented equity approach runs the risk of producing legal impressionism by blurring the distinction between decisions based on equitable principles and those taken *ex aequo et bono*. By contrast, the corrective-equity approach or three-stage approach maintains a higher degree of predictability by proceeding from a predictable method, that is, equidistance. Indeed, the sole method that would seem to ensure totally predictable results is equidistance. In this sense, the three-stage approach provides a better framework for balancing predictability and flexibility.

(5) However, it is not suggested that the law of maritime delimitation could acquire a sufficient degree of predictability. The value of the three-stage approach may be undermined by three elements:

- subjectivity in selection of base points for drawing a provisional equidistance line;
- imaginary adjustment of the provisional equidistance line; and
- subjectivity in the application of the disproportionality test.

Given that the intrinsic value of the equidistance method consists in its scientific character, it is argued that consideration of equity should not come into play in

[2] [1984] ICJ Rep 386, [41]. Jennings also stated that: 'A structured and predictable system of equitable procedures is an essential framework for the only kind of equity that a court of law that has not been given competence to decide *ex aequo et bono*, may properly contemplate.' Sir Robert Jennings, 'Equity and Equitable Principles' (1986) 42 *ASDI* 38.

selecting relevant base points for drawing a provisional equidistance line; and that the first stage of maritime delimitation should be clearly distinguished from the second stage. Furthermore, an excessive departure from a provisional equidistance line may ruin the first stage of maritime delimitation. An adjustment of a provisional equidistance line at the second stage of maritime delimitation is not unlimited and the final boundary should have a sufficient degree of approximation to a provisional equidistance line. Owing to the lack of the objective criteria, it appears that the application of the disproportionality test at the third stage does not contribute to enhancing predictability and objectiveness of the law of maritime delimitation. If it is hard to abolish the disproportionality test, as an alternative, the application of that test should be limited to the situations where a provisional equidistance line would create the cut-off effect by a markedly concave or convex coastline, even though relevant coasts are comparative in length.

(6) The delimitation of the continental shelf beyond 200 nautical miles creates novel challenges in the law of maritime delimitation. In particular, four issues merit highlighting:

- the relationship between the function of the CLCS and that of an international court or tribunal;
- the identification of overlapping entitlements to the continental shelf beyond 200 nautical miles;
- the relationship between the natural prolongation and the distance criterion; and
- the methodology of delimitation.

The jurisprudence suggests that delimitation is distinct from delineation and that the lack of recommendations by the CLCS do not always constitute a barre to prevent the delimitation of the continental shelf beyond 200 nautical miles by an international court or tribunal. In this connection, it must be noted that the existence of overlapping entitlements should be a prerequisite for an international court or tribunal to effect maritime delimitation. Yet, there is no guarantee that a court or tribunal can always identify the overlapping entitlement to the continental shelf beyond 200 nautical miles. This is particularly true when parties dispute the existence of overlapping entitlement. Where there is 'significant uncertainty' as to the existence of a continental margin in the area concerned, great caution will be needed for a court or tribunal in deciding whether or not the delimitation of the continental shelf beyond 200 nautical miles should be effected. With regard to the methodology of delimitation, as pointed out in chapter five, international tribunals took the view that the same approach is to apply to the delimitation of the continental shelf, irrespective of whether the continental shelf to be delimited lies within or beyond 200 nautical miles. If the same approach is applicable to the adjacent delimitation of the continental shelf beyond 200 nautical miles, however, it appears that the application of that approach to delimitation between States with opposite coasts may not be free from difficulty.

(7) The law of maritime delimitation is still developing. But the essence of the law of maritime delimitation remains the same: *the concept of equity and the reconciliation between the predictability and the flexibility of the law*. Hence, the law of maritime delimitation should undertake to harmonise the two requirements. Given that the sound balance between predictability and flexibility should be a crucial issue in the legal field, the law of maritime delimitation may provide an interesting case study of the legal philosophy concerning the classical dilemma.

Appendix

State Practice Regarding Maritime Delimitation

1. This research is based mainly on the following sources:

- *International Maritime Boundaries*, 7 volumes (Brill/Nijhoff and American Society of International Law, Dordrecht/Leiden/Boston). Volumes I, II (1993) and III (1998) were edited by JI Charney and LM Alexander; volume IV (2002) was edited by JI Charney and RW Smith; volumes V (2005) and VI (2011) were edited by DA Colson and RW Smith; volume VII (2016) was edited by CG Lathrop. Hereafter quoted as *IMB*.
- United Nations, *Law of the Sea Bulletin*.
- 'Current Developments' in *International Journal of Marine and Coastal Law*.

Data on the entry into force relies primarily on *IMB*. Information was also provided by Permanent Missions in Geneva for relevant States and Ministries of Foreign Affairs. The author wishes to thank the Missions and Ministries of Foreign Affairs for the relevant information on this subject.

2. Distinction between adjacency and oppositeness in this survey follows the interpretation expressed in the *Anglo-French Continental Shelf* award.

Abbreviations

AC	adjacent coasts
OC	opposite coasts
AC/OC	mixed figure of adjacent and opposite coasts
ED	the equidistance method was used
p	a part of the delimitation line is an equidistance line
*	methods other than the equidistance were used
#	treaties drawing a territorial sea boundary which delimit, at the same time, continental shelves and/or EEZ
+	delimitation of the continental shelf beyond 200 nautical miles

–	not entered into force
†	agreements following decisions of the ICJ
FRG	Federal Republic of Germany
GDR	German Democratic Republic

I. DELIMITATION OF TERRITORIAL SEA

Parties	Signature/Entered into force	Method	Configuration
#Norway-Soviet Union[1]	1957/1957	*	AC/OC
Poland-Soviet Union[2]	1958/1958	ED	AC
Cyprus-United Kingdom (Akrotiri, Dhekelia)[3]	1960/1960	ED(p)	AC
#Guinea-Bissau-Senegal[4]	1960/see footnote	*	AC
Mexico-United States[5]	1970/1972	ED (Art V)	AC
Indonesia-Malaysia[6]	1970/1971	ED (Art I)	OC
Canada-France (St Pierre and Miquelon)[7]	1972/1972	ED (Annex, p)	OC
Indonesia-Singapore[8]	1973/1974	ED(p)	OC
Turkey-Soviet Union[9]	1973/1975	*	AC

(continued)

[1] Text in *IMB,* vol II, 1786. This agreement was replaced by the 2007 Agreement between the Russian Federation and the kingdom of Norway on the Maritime delimitation in the Varangerfjord Area.

[2] Text in ibid, 2051.

[3] The 1960 Agreement established four territorial sea boundaries between Dhekelia (UK) and Cyprus and between the latter and Akrotiri (UK). Territorial sea boundaries between Dhekelia and Cyprus are equidistance lines. Those between Akrotiri and Cyprus are modified or partly equidistance lines. Text in ibid, 1564.

[4] The 1960 Agreement between France and Portugal established a straight line running at 240° as the boundary for the territorial sea, contiguous zone, and continental shelf. Later, however, a dispute arose as to whether that Agreement had any force of law for Guinea-Bissau and Senegal. On 31 July 1989, the Arbitral Tribunal held that that Agreement did have force of law between the Parties. For Exchange of Notes between France and Portugal of 26 April 1960, ibid, vol I, 872.

[5] As the United States claimed a three-mile territorial sea and 12-mile contiguous zone at that time, for the United States, the boundaries established by the agreement were for both the territorial sea and the contiguous zone. Text in ibid, 438.

[6] Text in ibid, 1035.

[7] Text in ibid, 396.

[8] Text in ibid, 1055.

[9] The territorial sea boundary might be an approximate prolongation of the general direction of the last course of the land boundary. Report by Scovazzi in ibid, vol II, 1683. For the text of the Protocols between Turkey and USSR, ibid, 1686.

(Continued)

Parties	Signature/Entered into force	Method	Configuration
Cameroon-Nigeria[10]	1975/1975	*	AC
France-Spain[11]	1974/1975	ED	AC
FRG-GDR[12]	1974/1975	*	AC/OC
Italy-Yugoslavia[13]	1975/1977	ED	AC
#Kenya-Tanzania[14]	1976/1976	ED	AC/OC
Portugal-Spain[15]	1976/–	*	AC
Malaysia-Thailand[16]	1979/1982	ED	AC
#Burma (Myanmar)-Thailand[17]	1980/1982	ED (Art I)	AC/OC
#France-Monaco[18]	1984/1985	*	AC
North Korea-Soviet Union[19]	1985/unknown	*	AC
France-Italy[20]	1986/1989	ED(p)	AC/OC
#Mozambique-Tanzania[21]	1988/–	ED (Art III)	AC
#Poland-FRG[22]	1989/1989	*	AC

(continued)

[10] The territorial sea boundary is a negotiated line. For the text of the Maroua Declaration, ibid, vol I, 846.

[11] Text in ibid, vol II, 1727.

[12] For the German Democratic Republic, the delimitation line constituted a territorial sea boundary. On the other hand, in the Federal Republic of Germany's side, over half of the boundary lies outside its territorial sea. Thus, the boundary is more than a territorial sea boundary. In any event, owing to the unification of the two Germanys, the boundary line is no longer operative. Report by Franckx in Charney and Alexander, ibid, vol II, 1998. For the Protocol between the Federal Republic of Germany and the German Democratic Republic, ibid, 2004.

[13] The territorial sea boundary is an equidistance line, with some slight effect give to straight baselines. Report by Scovazzi in ibid, 1639 and 1643. For the text of the Agreement, ibid, 1646.

[14] For Exchange of Notes between Tanzania and Kenya, *IMB*, vol I, 881.

[15] The Agreement established two territorial sea boundaries off the western and southern coasts, respectively. The boundaries are approximately perpendicular to the general direction of the coasts. Both lines follow a parallel of latitude and a meridian of longitude. Report by Anderson, ibid, vol II, 1794. Text in ibid, 1797.

[16] Text in ibid, vol I, 1096.

[17] Text in ibid, vol II, 1350.

[18] The boundary line is a pragmatic line considering the peculiar geographic situation of Monaco. Text in ibid, 1588.

[19] The territorial sea boundary is a negotiated line. In addition, according to Park, it may be safely assumed that the 1985 agreement had entered into force on or before the 22 January 1986, when the continental shelf agreement, which refers to the 1985 Agreement, was concluded between the Parties. In 1990, the Parties signed another agreement to substantiate the river-boundary defined in the 1985 Agreement. Report by Park, ibid, 1135 and 1138. Text in ibid, vol I, 1142.

[20] Text in ibid, vol II, 1578.

[21] Text in ibid, vol I, 898–902. Subsequently the Agreement was replaced by the 2011 Agreement.

[22] The territorial sea boundary is a pragmatic line taking navigational interests into account. Report by Frankx, ibid, vol II, 2008 and 2012. At the same time, the 1989 Agreement also established a single maritime boundary. Text in ibid, 2020.

(Continued)

Parties	Signature/Entered into force	Method	Configuration
Belgium-France[23]	1990/1993	ED	AC
North Korea-Soviet Union[24]	1990/unknown	*	AC
Iraq-Kuwait[25]	1993/1993	ED(p)	OC
Malaysia (Johor)-Singapore[26]	1995/1995	*	OC
Israel-Jordan[27]	1996/1996	ED (Art 1)	AC
Belgium-The Netherlands[28]	1996/1999	ED (Art 2)	AC
Turkey-Bulgaria[29]	1997/1998	unclear	AC
Lithuania-Russia[30]	1997/2003	ED	AC
#Latvia-Lithuania[31]	1999/–	ED	AC
Bosnia-Herzegovina-Croatia[32]	1999/provisionally in force only	ED (Art 4)	AC/OC
#China-Viet Nam (Gulf of Tonkin)[33]	2000/2004	*	AC/OC

(continued)

[23] Text in ibid, 1898.

[24] This Agreement supplements the 1985 Agreement between North Korea and the USSR regarding the territorial sea boundary. It does not change the original boundary. According to Park, it is assumed that the 1990 Agreement came into force not long after the signing of the Agreement, although the precise date is unknown. Report by Park, ibid, vol III, 2299. Text in ibid, 2302.

[25] The boundary was established by an Iraqi-Kuwaiti Boundary Demarcation Commission according to UN Security Council Resolution 687. For the first four miles, the boundary follows the low-water springs line along the coast of Kuwait. It then follows an equidistance line between the two coasts of the Parties. Report by LM Alexander and RF Pietrowski, Jr, ibid, 2387. Regarding Final Report on the Demarcation of the International Boundary between Iraq and Kuwait by the United Nations Iraq-Kuwait Boundary Demarcation Commission, ibid, 2397.

[26] The delimitation method is at the centre of the deep-water channel. Report by McDorman, ibid, 2348. Text in ibid, 2351.

[27] Text in ibid, 2460.

[28] Text in (1997) 12 *IJMCL* 552; (2000) 42 *Law of the Sea Bulletin* 172; *IMB*, vol IV, 2936.

[29] The 1997 Agreement was reproduced in (1998) 38 *Law of the Sea Bulletin* 62. Yet, map is not available. The Parties agreed to establish a common navigation sector in the Begendic/Rezovo Bay (Art 2(2)).

[30] See *IMB*, vol V, 4009. Frankx pointed out that the delimitation of the territorial sea was based on the principle of equidistance. E Frankx, 'Current Legal Developments: New Maritime Boundaries Concluded in the Eastern Baltic Sea Since 1998' (2001) 16 *IJMCL* 650. For the text of the Agreement, ibid, 655. But the English text is based on the unofficial translation. On the same day, Lithuania and Russia concluded the Agreement regarding the delimitation of their EEZ and continental shelf.

[31] According to Frankx, the delimitation of the territorial sea was guided by the principle of equidistance. ibid, 653. Text in ibid, 657; *IMB*, vol IV, 3125. See also Franckx, 'Maritime Delimitation in the Baltic Sea' 440.

[32] Text in ibid, vol IV, 2891.

[33] The delimitation line serves as the boundary for the territorial sea, the EEZ and continental shelf. Text in 2336 *UNTS* 179; (2005) 56 *Law of the Sea Bulletin* 137; *IMB*, vol VII, 4842.

(Continued)

Parties	Signature/Entered into force	Method	Configuration
France-UK (Jersey)[34]	2000/2004	ED	OC
#Angola-Namibia[35]	2002/unknown	*	AC
#Oman-Yemen[36]	2003/2004	ED	AC
# Estonia-Russian Federation[37]	2005/–	ED (Art 1)	AC
#Benin-Nigeria[38]	2006/–	ED(p)	AC
#Norway-Russian Federation[39]	2007/2008	*	AC/OC
Jordan-Saudi Arabia[40]	2007/2010	ED	AC
#Qatar-Saudi Arabia[41]	2008/2008	*	AC
#Albania-Greece[42]	2009/–	ED (Art 1)	AC/OC
Indonesia-Singapore[43]	2009/2010	ED	OC

(continued)

[34] Text in ibid, vol IV, 2991. The Agreement entered into force on 1 January 2004. See www.marineregions.org/documents/6138.pdf.

[35] For the text of unofficial text of the treaty, see *IMB*, vol V, 3719. It seems that the maritime boundary serves as the boundary for the territorial sea, the EEZ and the continental shelf.

[36] Text in ibid, 3909. The maritime boundary separates the territorial sea, the EEZ and the continental shelf. The boundary joining Points 1 to 5 is a median line. Report by Prescott, ibid, 3905.

[37] Text in ibid, vol VI, 4582. After having been signed by both Parties, the Russian Federation withdrew its signature. ibid, 4569; 4571–72; E Franckx, 'Maritime Delimitation in the Baltic Sea: What Has Already Been Accomplished?' (2012) 6 *International Journal on Marine Navigation and Safety of Sea Transportation*, 441. The amended land and maritime boundary treaties were signed in Moscow on 18 February 2014. A Lott, 'The Estonian-Russian Territorial Sea Boundary Delimitation in the Gulf of Finland' (2017) 32 *IJMCL*, 488. The treaties have not been ratified yet. The Estonian Parliament's Press Release *Riigikogu*, 18 May 2017, available at: www.riigikogu.ee/en/press-releases/foreign-affairs-committee-en/mihkelson-estonia-cannot-accused-stalling-ratification-border-treaty-estonia-russia/.

[38] Text in: *IMB*, vol VI, 4266. The Treaty provides for a single, all purpose boundary. Report by Daniel, ibid, 4258.

[39] Text in *IMB*, vol VI, 4485.

[40] The maritime boundary is approximately four nautical miles in length. Jordan only claims a three-nautical-miles territorial sea, while Saudi Arabia claims a twelve-nautical-mile territorial sea. Report by Carleton, ibid, vol VII, 5106 and 5108. Accordingly, the boundary is the territorial sea boundary for Saudi Arabia. It can be presumed that the boundary up to three nautical miles is the territorial sea boundary and the remaining part of the boundary is the continental shelf boundary for Jordan. Text in ibid, 5110; (2010) 74 *Law of the Sea Bulletin* 69.

[41] For the text of Joint Minutes, see *IMB*, vol VI, 4424.

[42] Text in ibid, 4470. It can be considered that the boundary delimits the territorial sea and the continental shelf. Report by Scovazzi, Papanicolopulu and Francalanci, ibid, 4464–65. The Albanian Constitutional Court declared that the Agreement constituted a violation of the Constitution of Albania. K Cenaj, 'Albania-Greece Agreement on Setting Maritime Boundaries, According to International Law' (2015) 4 *Academic Journal of Interdisciplinary Studies* 147.

[43] Text in 2713 *UNTS*, 163; (2011) 75 *Law of the Sea Bulletin*, 21; *IMB*, vol VII, 4823.

(Continued)

Parties	Signature/Entered into force	Method	Configuration
#The Bahamas-Cuba[44]	2011/2012	ED	OC
Indonesia-Singapore[45]	2014/2017	*	OC
Total			45
Total number only for delimitation of territorial sea: 28			

II. DELIMITATION OF CONTINENTAL SHELF

Parties	Signature/Entered into force	Method	Configuration
Trinidad and Tobago-Venezuela[46]	1942/1942	*	OC
Norway-Soviet Union[47]	1957/1957	*	AC/OC
Bahrain-Saudi Arabia[48]	1958/1958	ED(p) AC/OC	AC/OC
Guinea-Bissau-Senegal[49]	1960/see footnote	*	AC
The Netherlands-FRG[50]	1964/1965	ED	AC
Norway-United Kingdom[51]	1965/1965	ED (Art I)	OC

(continued)

[44] Text in (2013) 79 *Law of the Sea Bulletin*, 19; *IMB*, vol VII, 4729.

[45] Text in *IMB*, vol VII, 4835. It appears that the maritime boundary is a negotiated line. ibid, 4831.

[46] It is conceivable that this treaty was subsumed by a new agreement of 1989 regarding both the legal regime and the position of the line wherever a discrepancy may arise. Report by Nweihed in ibid, vol I, 659. For the text of the Agreement, ibid, 670–73.

[47] The agreement also delimits territorial seas. Both States claimed an EEZ of 200 n.m. Report by Anderson, ibid, vol II, 1784. Text in ibid, 1786.

[48] Text in ibid, 1495–97. Saudi Arabia claimed an EEZ of unspecified breadth in 1974. Report by Pietrowski, Jr, ibid, 1493. On the other hand, Bahrain has not claimed an FZ A Razovi, *Continental Shelf Delimitation and Related maritime Issues in the Persian Gulf* (The Hague, Nijhoff, 1997) 103.

[49] In 1989, the Arbitral Tribunal confirmed the force of that Agreement between the Parties. *IMB*, vol I, 872.

[50] In 1977, both States claimed FZs of 200 miles. But no boundary agreement has been concluded. Report by Anderson in ibid, vol II, 1839. Text in ibid, 1841.

[51] Text in ibid, 1885. Norway established a 200-mile EEZ in 1977, and in the same year, the UK claimed a 200-mile FZ But, no boundary agreement has been concluded. Report by Anderson, ibid, 1883. Royal Decree of 17 December 1976 relating to the establishment of the Economic Zone of Norway provides that: 'Where the economic zone is adjacent to the area of jurisdiction of another State, the limit shall be drawn according to agreement.' United Nations, Division for Ocean Affairs and the Law of the Sea, Office of Legal Affairs, *The Law of the Sea: National Legislation on the Exclusive Economic Zone* (New York, 1993) 261.

(Continued)

Parties	Signature/Entered into force	Method	Configuration
Denmark-FRG (Baltic Sea)[52]	1965/1966	ED (Protocol)	OC
Denmark-FRG (The North Sea)[53]	1965/1966	ED (Art I)	OC
Denmark-Norway[54]	1965/1966	ED (Art I)	AC/OC
Denmark-United Kingdom[55]	1966/1967	ED (Art I)	OC
Denmark-The Netherlands[56]	1966/1967	ED	OC
Iran-Saudi Arabia[57]	1968/1969	ED(p)	OC
Norway-Sweden[58]	1968/1969	ED(Art I)	AC/OC
Italy-Yugoslavia[59]	1968/1970	ED(p)	OC
Poland-GDR[60]	1968/1969	ED(Art I)	AC
Indonesia-Malaysia[61]	1969/1969	ED	OC
		ED(p)	AC/OC

(continued)

[52] Both States claimed 200-mile FZs. Report by Franckx in *IMB*, vol II, 1921. The same is true for the 1971 agreement between the same parties. Text in ibid, 1923.

[53] Text in ibid, 1807.

[54] Norway established an EEZ and Denmark claimed an FZ. The dispute regarding maritime delimitation was resolved in the judgment of the ICJ in 1993.

[55] The 1966 Agreement was replaced by a new agreement of 1971. For the text of the 1966 Agreement, *ibid,* vol II, 1831; For the text of the 1971 Agreement, ibid, 1833.

[56] Following the decision in the *North Sea Continental Shelf* cases, Denmark and the Netherlands terminated the 1966 Agreement by means of a bilateral declaration contained in a trilateral Protocol on 28 January 1971. Termination took effect on 7 December 1972. Report by Anderson in ibid, vol III, 2497. For the text of 1966 Agreement, ibid, 2505.

[57] In the Persian Gulf, Iran claimed an FZ up to the equidistance line or to established continental shelf boundaries. On the other hand, Saudi Arabia claimed an FZ of unspecified breadth. Report by Pietrowski, *IMB*, vol II, 1523. For the text of the Agreement, ibid, 1526.

[58] Text in ibid, 1876. Norway claimed a 200-mile EEZ in 1977. Sweden claimed its FZ of 200 miles in 1978. But, no new boundary agreement was concluded. Report by Anderson, ibid, 1874. The limit of the EEZ established by Sweden follows the boundaries previously agreed upon with Norway for the continental shelf. ibid, vol III, 2532.

[59] The equidistant continental shelf boundary is modified in the area of small islands which are given reduced effects. Text in ibid, vol II, 1634.

[60] This agreement was replaced by the 1989 Agreement. For the text of the 1968 Agreement, ibid, 2018. For the text of the 1989 Agreement, ibid, 2020.

[61] Text in ibid, vol I, 1025–27. The 1969 Agreement established three continental shelf boundaries. In the Malacca Strait and Western South China Sea, where coastal geography is in opposite relation, continental shelf boundaries were drawn using the equidistance method. In the Eastern South China Sea area, where coastal geography represents somewhat a mixed feature between opposite and adjacent relations, a continental shelf boundary partly follows an equidistance line.

(Continued)

Parties	Signature/Entered into force	Method	Configuration
Iran-Qatar[62]	1969/1970	ED	OC
Bahrain-Iran[63]	1971/1972	ED	OC
Denmark-FRG (North Sea)[64]	1971/1972	*	AC
Denmark-United Kingdom[65]	1971/1972	ED (Art I)	OC
The Netherlands-FRG[66]	1971/1972	*	AC
United Kingdom-FRG[67]	1971/1972	ED	OC

(continued)

Furthermore in 1980, both States claimed their 200-mile EEZs. Report by Park, ibid, 1023. Act No 5 of 18 October 1983 on the Indonesian Exclusive Economic Zone provides that so long as a delimitation agreement between Indonesia State is concerned, and no special conditions need be considered, the boundary line of the EEZ of Indonesia and that of the other State shall be the median line or line which is equidistant from the baselines of the Indonesian territorial sea or the outermost points of Indonesia and the baselines of the territorial sea or outermost points of the other States, except if an agreement has been reached with the said State on a provisional arrangement of the boundaries of the Indonesian Exclusive Economic Zone (para 2 of Art 3). United Nations, *The Law of the Sea: National Legislation on the Exclusive Economic Zone*, 142. No provision likewise was included in the Malaysian EEZ Act of 1984. ibid, 186.

[62] Text in *IMB*, vol II, 1516. Iran claimed its FZ in the Persian Gulf up to established continental shelf boundaries at the equidistance line. Qatar claimed an EEZ to the equidistance line or to boundaries delimited with neighbouring States. Report by Pietrowski, Jr, ibid, 1514. On the other hand, Art 4 explicitly provides that: 'Nothing in this Agreement shall affect the status of the superjacent waters or airspace above any part of the continental shelf.'

[63] Later, Iran claimed an FZ in the Persian Gulf coextensive with its continental shelf jurisdiction. Report by Pietrowski, Jr, ibid, 1483. Text in ibid, 1487.

[64] After the *North Sea Continental Shelf* judgment, the Parties drew a pragmatic line as a continental shelf boundary. Both States claimed 200-mile FZs in the North Sea. Report by Anderson, ibid, vol II, 1805. For the text of the Agreement, ibid, 1809. The Danish EEZ created in 1996 followed the established boundary with Germany on the continental shelf. ibid, vol III, 2531.

[65] Text in ibid, vol II, 1833. The 1971 Agreement Replaced one signed on 3 March 1966. The 1966 Agreement also used the equidistance method. While both States claimed their FZs of 200 miles, no boundary agreement has been concluded for the FZ Report by Anderson, ibid, 1829. On this point, however, the Danish EEZ established in 1996 followed the established boundary with the United Kingdom on the continental shelf. The 1996 Pollution Regulations of the United Kingdom followed the same line. ibid, vol III, 2530.

[66] After the *North Sea Continental Shelf* judgment, the Parties drew a pragmatic line as a continental shelf boundary. Text in ibid, vol II, 1844. In 1977, both States extended fishery limits to 200 miles. But no boundary agreement has been concluded. Report by Anderson, ibid, 1839. The EEZ of the Netherlands followed the same established boundary. The German Proclamation of an EEZ included the coordinates agreed on for the boundary of the continental shelf. ibid, vol III, 2530.

[67] Text in ibid, vol II, 1856. The equidistance method was used. In so doing, however, the FRG's coast was disregarded and the coasts of Denmark and the Netherlands were used. Report by Anderson, ibid, 1853. In addition, while both States claimed FZs of the maximum 200 miles in 1977, no agreement has been concluded. ibid, 1854. The German EEZ listed the three points defined in Art 1 of the 1971 Agreement as part of the perimeter of the EEZ in question. The Pollution Zone of the United Kingdom also followed the agreed boundary. ibid, vol III, 2530.

(Continued)

Parties	Signature/Entered into force	Method	Configuration
Indonesia-Thailand (Malacca Strait Andaman Sea)[68]	1971/1973	ED	OC
Italy-Tunisia[69]	1971/1978	ED(Art I, p)	OC
Australia-Indonesia (Timor and Arafura Seas)[70]	1972/1973	*	OC
Finland-Sweden[71]	1972/1973	ED (Art I)	OC
Australia-Indonesia (Timor and Arafura Seas)[72]	1973/1974	ED	AC
Iran-Oman[73]	1974/1975	ED	OC

(continued)

[68] Text in ibid, vol II, 1462. In 1981, Thailand claimed a 200-mile EEZ Report by V Prescott, *ibid*, vol II, 1459. The 1981 Royal Proclamation establishing the EEZ of Thailand simply provides that: 'In any case where the exclusive economic zone of the Kingdom of Thailand is adjacent or opposite to the exclusive economic zone of another coastal State, the Government of the Kingdom of Thailand is prepared to enter into negotiations with the coastal State concerned with a view to delimiting their respective economic zone.' United Nations, *The Law of the Sea: National Legislation on the Exclusive Economic Zone*, 354.

[69] Text in *IMB*, vol II, 1621–25. The continental shelf boundary of equidistance is modified in the areas around the islands of Pantelleria, Lampione, Lampedusa and Linosa, by giving reduced effects to those islands.

[70] The delimitation line was drawn in the zone between an equidistance line and the axis of the Timor Trough to the north. Report by Prescott in ibid, 1211–12. Text in ibid, 1215. Later, the continental shelf boundary established in 1972 was extended westwards in the Perth Treaty of 1997.

[71] Text in ibid, 1954. While referring to the median line, Art 1 of the 1972 Agreement states that the continental shelf boundary shall in principle be a median line. At the same time, it refers to special circumstances which would justify departures from that principle. In fact, the boundary in the Åland area departures from the equidistance line. In addition, Sweden claimed a 200-mile FZ Report by Franckx, ibid, vol II, 1949 and 1952. The 1992 Act of Sweden provides that in the absence of an agreement of delimitation, the Swedish EEZ may not extend beyond the midline in relation to the other State (Art 1). United Nations, Division for Ocean Affairs and the Law of the Sea, Office of Legal Affairs, *Current Developments in State Practice,* No IV (New York, United Nations) 118.

[72] By virtue of Art 7, the seabed boundary lines referred to in Art 3 of the 1973 Agreement and in Art 4 of the 1971 Agreement are used for the boundaries of the territorial seas and exclusive fishing zones. Text in *IMB*, vol II, 1225.

[73] Text in ibid, 1508. Iran extended its FZ in the Gulf of Oman to the equidistance line boundary with the UAE and Oman in 1977. Report by Pietrowski, Jr, ibid, vol II, 1506. In this respect, Art 19 of the 1993 Act on the Marine Areas of the Islamic Republic of Iran in the Persian Gulf and the Oman Sea provides that the limits of the exclusive economic zone and the continental shelf, unless otherwise determined in accordance with bilateral agreements, shall be an equidistance line. United Nations, *Current Developments in State Practice,* No IV. 67. Oman claimed a 200-mile EEZ in 1981, stating that the outer limits of the territorial sea, exclusive economic zone and continental shelf

(Continued)

Parties	Signature/Entered into force	Method	Configuration
France-Spain[74]	1974/1975	ED (Art 2, p)	AC/OC
Italy-Spain[75]	1974/1978	ED (Art. I.)	OC
Indonesia-Thailand (Andaman Sea)[76]	1975/1978	*	OC
Mauritania-Morocco[77]	1976/1976	*	AC
Portugal-Spain[78]	1976/–	*	AC
Greece-Italy[79]	1977/1980	ED (Art I)	OC
Norway-United Kingdom[80]	1978/1980	ED (preamble)	AC
India-Thailand[81]	1978/1978	ED	OC

(continued)

shall be (measured up to) the median line (so that) every point on it is equidistant from the nearest points on the baselines. United Nations, *The Law of the Sea: National Legislation on the Exclusive Economic Zone* 262.

[74] As stipulated in Art 2(1)(b) of the 1974 Agreement, the first segment of the continental shelf boundary was equidistance between the normal baselines. Yet, the boundary of outer segment is not equidistant taking proportionality into account. Both France and Spain claimed their EEZ in 1976–78. According to Anderson, while the French Government considers the continental shelf boundary to be suitable as a single maritime boundary, Spain takes a different view. Report by Anderson, *IMB,* vol II, 1720. Text in ibid, 1728.

[75] Text in ibid, 1607.

[76] The continental shelf boundary is a negotiated line. Report by Prescott, ibid, 1468. Text in ibid, 1471.

[77] The agreement mainly concerned the land boundary, and the maritime boundary was an adjunct to the latter. The boundary is a straight line following 24° parallel north. As the land boundary between Morocco and Mauritania was abandoned, however, the effectiveness of the maritime boundary is doubtful at present. Report by Adede, ibid, vol I, 885. Text in ibid, 889.

[78] Text in ibid, vol II, 1798. The Agreement established two territorial sea boundaries off the western and southern coasts, respectively. The boundaries are approximately perpendicular to the general direction of the coasts. Both lines follow a parallel of latitude and a meridian of longitude. Report by Anderson, ibid, 1794. Portugal established an EEZ in 1977, and Spain did likewise in 1977/1978. ibid, 1795. According to Act No 33/77 of 28 May 1977 of Portugal regarding the juridical status of the Portuguese Territorial Sea and the EEZ, without any agreement, the limits of the EEZ shall not extend beyond the median line and equidistance line (Art 2(2)). United Nations, *Current Developments in State Practice,* No IV, 284. Spanish Act No 15/1978 on the Economic Zone also defined the same article (Art 2(1)). ibid, 347.

[79] Text in *IMB,* vol II, 1598.

[80] Text in ibid, 1887. Norway established a 200-mile EEZ in 1977, and in the same year, the UK claimed a 200-mile FZ But, no boundary agreement has been concluded. Report by Anderson, *ibid,* 1883. Royal Decree of 17 December 1976 relating to the establishment of the Economic Zone of Norway provides that: 'Where the economic zone is adjacent to the area of jurisdiction of another State, the limit shall be drawn according to agreement.' United Nations, *The Law of the Sea: National Legislation on the Exclusive Economic Zone*, 261.

[81] Text in *IMB,* vol II, 1440. India claimed a 200-mile EEZ in 1977. Report by Prescott, ibid, 1438. Thailand did likewise in 1981. While an Act of Thailand includes no provision on the delimitation of an EEZ, Indian Act No 80 of 28 May 1976 defined that, pending an agreement of delimitation

(Continued)

Parties	Signature/Entered into force	Method	Configuration
Malaysia-Thailand[82]	1979/1982	ED	AC
France-United Kingdom[83]	1982/1983	ED	OC
France-Monaco[84]	1984/1985	*	AC
Libya-Malta[85]†	1986/1987	ED	OC
Tunisia-Libya[86]†	1988/1989	*	AC/OC
Belgium-France[87]	1990/1993	*	AC
France-United Kingdom[88]	1991/1992	ED	OC
Albania-Italy[89]	1992/1999	ED (Art 1)	OC

(continued)

and unless any other provisional arrangements are agreed to between them, the maritime boundaries between India State shall not extend beyond the equidistance line (Art 9(1)). United Nations, *The Law of the Sea: National Legislation on the Exclusive Economic Zone*, 137.

[82] Text in *IMB*, vol II, 1105. Thailand claimed a 200-mile EEZ in 1981, and Malaysia did likewise in 1984. Report by Park, ibid, 1102. As with the Act of Thailand, no article on the delimitation of the EEZ was provided in Act No 311 of 1984 of Malaysia. United Nations, *The Law of the Sea: National Legislation on the Exclusive Economic Zone* 186.

[83] Text in *IMB*, vol II, 1750. Later, the 1988 Agreement transformed part of the continental shelf in the Strait of Dover into a territorial sea boundary following the extension of the territorial sea of the United Kingdom with effect from 1 October 1987. Report by Anderson, ibid, 1736. For the text of the 1988 Agreement, ibid, 1752. By Agreement of 21 and 27 March 1990, points 13 and 14 of the 1982 Agreement was corrected because of a material error. ibid, 1743; E Decaux, 'Chronique de plateau continental et des delimitations' (1991) 5 *Espaces et ressources maritimes* 78.

[84] According to Scovazzi, the convention is intended to establish an all-purpose delimitation, and the boundary will remain the same when parties claim their EEZ Report by Scovazzi in *IMB*, vol II, 1583. At present, the boundary established by the convention is for the continental shelf, for neither party has claimed an EEZ In addition, this agreement also delimits territorial seas between the parties. Text in ibid, 1588.

[85] Following the decision in the *Libya/Malta* case, the Parties drew a continental shelf boundary. As explained in the text of this study, the ICJ adjusted an equidistance line provisionally drawn to the north. Text in ibid, 1661.

[86] The continental shelf boundary was drawn following the decision in the *Tunisia/Libya* case. Later, the Parties established a joint exploitation zone, which is bisected by the boundary. Text in ibid, 1679.

[87] While Belgium claimed a 200-mile FZ, France declared a 200-mile EEZ Both States are bound by the common fisheries policy of European Union. Report by Anderson, ibid, vol II, 1895. Text in ibid, 1899.

[88] Text in ibid, vol III, 2466. The Preamble of the 1991 agreement refers to the application of the same methods as were illustrated for the definition of the boundary line between points 1 and 14. ibid, 2466. As the boundary line between points 1 and 14 was fixed using the equidistance method in the 1982 agreement, 'the same methods' referred to in the 1991 agreement appear to equate to the equidistance method. Information regarding entering into force of the Agreement was given by Foreign and Commonwealth Office in the United Kingdom.

[89] Text in *IMB*, vol III, 2453. The year of entering into force was provided by the Permanent Mission of Italy in Geneva.

(Continued)

Parties	Signature/Entered into force	Method	Configuration
India-Thailand[90]	1993/–	ED	OC
Belgium-The Netherlands[91]	1996/1999	ED	AC
United States-Mexico[92]	2000/2001	ED	OC
+Barbados-France (Guadeloupe and Martinique)[93]	2009/–	ED	AC
Indonesia-Viet Nam[94]	2003/2007	*	OC
Albania-Greece[95]	2009/–	ED (Art 1)	AC/OC
Norway-Russian Federation[96]	2007/2008	ED (p)	AC/OC
+Denmark (Faroes)-Iceland-Norway[97]	2006/2006	*	OC
+Denmark (Greenland)-Iceland[98]	2013/2013	*	OC
Total			53

[90] Text in ibid, 2380. According to the Ministry of Foreign Affairs of Thailand, the 1993 Agreement has not been ratified yet. The present Agreement extends the boundary drawn by the 1978 Agreement to the tri-junction between three countries in the Andaman See, ie, India, Thailand and Myanmar. The tri-junction was fixed on the same day as the signature to the present Agreement. Report by Prescott, ibid, 2377.

[91] The date of entering into force was provided by the Permanent Mission of the Netherlands to the Office of the United Nations in Geneva. Text in: (2000) 42 *Law of the Sea Bulletin* 170; (1997) 12 *IJMCL* 552; *IMB*, vol IV, 2938–39. Strictly speaking, an equidistance line has been slightly shifted to the east of the established continental shelf boundary. Alex G Oude Elferink, 'Current Legal Developments: Belgium/The Netherlands' (1997) 12 *IJMCL* 548. In addition, Art 2 of the 1996 Agreement stipulates that if one of the Parties decides to establish an EEZ, the continental shelf boundary shall be used for its lateral delimitation.

[92] Text in (2001) 44 *Law of the Sea Bulletin* 71; *IMB*, vol IV, 2629. This treaty purports to delimit a continental shelf beyond 200 nm from the respective baselines. Furthermore, Smith indicated that no method of delimitation other than the equidistance method was ever tabled. ibid, 2623 and 2625.

[93] Text in ibid, vol VI, 4229. Under Art 3.1 of the Agreement, if the continental shelf of Barbados and that of France overlap beyond 200 nautical miles, the line joining points 7–9 serves as the boundary.

[94] Text in (2008) 67 *Law of the Sea Bulletin* 39; *IMB*, vol VI, 4313. While the boundary line reflects an equidistance line at the western end, it departs from the equidistance line throughout most its length stretching to the east. The substantial difference in relevant coastal lengths may be taken into account. Report by McDorman and Schofield, ibid, 4307 and 4309.

[95] Text in *IMB*, vol VI, 4470. See also note 42.

[96] Text in ibid, 4485. Points 4, 5 and 6 are equidistant points. Report by M Wood, ibid, 4482.

[97] For the text of the Agreed Minutes, ibid, 4546. The Agreed Minutes concerns the future delimitation of the continental shelf beyond 200 nautical miles.

[98] For the text of the Agreed Minutes, see ibid, vol VII, 5269.

III. SINGLE MARITIME BOUNDARIES

A. Treaties on the Continental Shelf which Coincide with EEZ/FZ Boundary Established Afterwards

Parties	Signature/Entered into force	Method	Configuration
Finland-USSR[99]	1965/1966	ED (Art 2, 3)	OC
The Netherlands-United Kingdom[100]	1965/1966	ED	AC/OC
Finland-USSR[101]	1967/1968	ED (Art 1)	OC
Qatar-United Arab Emirates (Abu Dhabi)[102]	1969/1969	ED(p)	AC
Poland-Soviet Union[103]	1969/1970	ED	AC
Denmark-FRG.[104]	1971/1972	*	AC
Australia-Indonesia[105]	1971/1973	ED (Art 4)	AC/OC
Canada-Denmark (Greenland)[106]	1973/1974	ED (Art I)	OC

(continued)

[99] Text in ibid, vol II, 1966–69. The equidistance line was not measured from the basepoints used for the delimitation of the territorial sea, but from the outer limit of the territorial sea. Report by Franckx, ibid, 1963. By the 1985 agreement, entered into force in 1986, the continental shelf boundary was transformed into the single maritime boundary for the EEZ and continental shelf. ibid, 1995–96. The same is true for the continental shelf boundary established by the 1967 Agreement between the same Parties.

[100] For the text of the Agreement, ibid, vol II, 1866. The Exchange of Notes of 2013 confirmed that the continental shelf boundary would also be the boundary of the EEZ between the two States. For the text of the Exchange of Notes, ibid, vol VII, 5208.

[101] For the text of the Agreement, ibid, vol II, 1977.

[102] For the text of the Agreement, ibid, 1547. In 1974, Qatar claimed an EEZ The Declaration of 2 June 1974 provided that the outer limits of these areas shall be the outer limits of the continental prolongation of the State of Qatar or the median line. In 1980, UAE claimed an EEZ. The Declaration of 25 July 1980 stated that the outer limit of the EEZ shall be determined in accordance with the provisions of the agreements concluded by the Emirates members of the Union in connexion with their continental shelf. United Nations, *The Law of the Sea: National Legislation on the Exclusive Economic Zone*, 287 and 384. It would seem that the 1969 continental shelf boundary is used for the boundary of their EEZs.

[103] Text in *IMB*, vol II, 2052. The boundary was transformed into a single maritime boundary for the EEZ, FZ and continental shelf by the 1985 agreement. ibid, 2054–56.

[104] Text in ibid, 1924. The agreement was only for the delimitation of the continental shelf. But, Denmark established a 200-mile FZ in 1976 and Germany in 1978. According to Franckx, this line also delimits the fishery zone. Report by Franckx in *ibid,* 1918.

[105] Text in ibid, 1202. By the 1973 agreement, the boundary of the continental shelf drawn in 1971 will also be used for the boundary of the territorial sea and FZ (Art 7). The seabed boundary will also be used for the boundary of the territorial sea until the outer limit of 12 miles. Report by Prescott, ibid, vol II, 1220 and 1227.

[106] Text in ibid, vol I, 380. The boundary has been extended, *de facto,* to divide fisheries zones. Indeed, Canada claimed a 200-mile FZ in 1976, and Denmark did likewise in 1980. Report by Alexander, ibid, 377–78. The equidistance line is partly modified. On 5 April 2004, Canada and

(Continued)

Parties	Signature/Entered into force	Method	Configuration
India-Indonesia[107]	1974/1974	ED	OC
Iran-United Arab Emirates (Dubai)[108]	1974/–	ED(p)	OC
Japan-South Korea[109]	1974/1978	ED(p)	OC
India-Indonesia[110]	1977/1977	ED	AC/OC
Sweden-GDR.[111]	1978/1978	ED (Art I)	OC
Turkey-Soviet Union[112]	1978/1981	ED	AC/OC
Burma (Myanmar)-Thailand[113]	1980/1982	ED (Art I0	AC/OC
Ireland-United Kingdom[114]	1988/1990	ED(p)	AC/OC

(continued)

Denmark exchanged notes and modified the median line coordinates set out in Art II of the 1973 Agreement. Exchange of Notes Constituting an Agreement to Amend the Agreement between the Government of Canada and the Government of the Kingdom of Denmark Relating to the Delimitation of the Continental Shelf Between Greenland and Canada Done at Ottawa on 17 December 1973. The text is available at: www.treaty-accord.gc.ca/text-texte.aspx?id=104991. Entered into force 16 December 2009.

[107] Text in ibid, vol II, 1369. According to Prescott, although not stated in the agreement, the two countries decided that when they had claimed their EEZs, the seabed boundary would also separate those zones. Report by Prescott, *ibid,* 1364. India established the EEZ in 1977, and Indonesia claimed it in 1980.

[108] Text in ibid, 1538. Although the continental shelf boundary is not a strict equidistance line, it is generally equidistant from the respective mainlands. In its eastern portion, the boundary follows the 12-mile arc drawn around the Iranian island of Sirri. Iran claimed an FZ out to the established continental shelf boundary or an equidistance line in the Gulf. The UAE declared an EEZ to the agreed continental shelf boundary or to the median line. Alexander points out that the continental shelf boundary also divides the FZ/EEZ boundary. ibid, vol II, 1534. See also AAEl-Hakim, *The Middle Eastern States and the Law of the Sea* (Manchester, MUP, 1979) 103.

[109] Text in *IMB*, vol I, 1063. The continental shelf boundary is basically an equidistance line, but with slight modification, especially in the Western Channel of the Korea Strait for technical reasons. Report by Park, ibid, 1061. The EEZ boundary drawn in the 1998 Agreement between Japan and South Korea regarding fisheries coincides with the continental shelf boundary.

[110] Text in ibid, vol II, 1376. According to Prescott, both countries later decided that when they had claimed their EEZs, the seabed boundary would also separate them. Report by Prescott, ibid, 1372.

[111] Text in ibid, 2036. Under the Protocol of 1978, both parties agreed that the boundary established shall also form the boundary of the fishing zone of the two States. ibid, 2038. In addition, because of the unification of the Federal Republic of Germany and the German Democratic Republic on 3 October 1990, the parties to this boundary agreement became the Federal Republic of Germany and Sweden.

[112] By the 1987 'Exchange of Notes on the Delimitation of the Exclusive Economic Zones in the Black Sea', the parties agreed that the boundary of the continental shelf was also valid regarding their EEZ boundary. For the text, ibid, 1706.

[113] Text in ibid, 1350. Art 1 provided that if Thailand claimed an EEZ, the western part would also separate the EEZ of each country. Burma had claimed an EEZ in 1977 and Thailand in 1981. Report by Prescott, ibid, 1347 and 1351. This agreement also delimits the territorial sea.

[114] Text in ibid, 1774. This Agreement established two continental shelf boundaries. They follow medians and parallels. In accordance with commentaries, the established boundaries partly follow

(Continued)

Parties	Signature/Entered into force	Method	Configuration
Belgium-United Kingdom[115]	1991/1993	*	OC
Ireland-United Kingdom[116]	1992/1993	*	OC
Total			18

B. Delimitation of the EEZ/Continental Shelf Boundary (Single Maritime Boundary)

i. Treaties Both for the Continental Shelf and EEZ/FZ

Parties	Signature/Entered into force	Method	Configuration
Chile-Peru[117]	1951/1954	*	AC
Ecuador-Peru[118]	1952/1975	*	AC
Brazil-Uruguay[119]	1972/1975	*	AC

(continued)

modified equidistance lines. On this point, see CR Symmons, 'The UK/Ireland Continental Shelf Agreement 1988: A Model for Compromise in Maritime Delimitation' *International Boundaries Research Unit, Conference Proceedings 1989*, 395; C Lysaght, 'The Agreement on the Delimitation of the Continental Shelf between Ireland and the United Kingdom' (1990) 3 *Irish Studies in International Affairs* 97. The 1988 Agreement was amended by the 2013 Agreement in order to establish a single maritime boundary between the EEZ of Ireland and the United Kingdom and those parts of their continental shelves lying within 200 nautical miles of their respective baselines. Report by Anderson, *IMB*, vol VII, 5151.

115 The delimitation method is a pragmatic one. Report by DH Anderson, ibid, vol II, 1907. For the text of the Agreement, ibid, 1909–12. The Exchanges of Notes of 2013 confirmed that the continental shelf boundary would also be the boundary of the EEZ between the two States. For the text of the Exchanges of Notes, ibid, vol VII, 5256.

116 For the text of the Protocol, ibid, vol III, 2495. The 1992 protocol extended the continental shelf boundary previously agreed in 1988 by approximately 10 miles to the north northwest. The boundary is a pragmatic line. Report by Anderson, ibid, 2487. The 1992 Protocol was amended by the 2013 Agreement in order to establish a single maritime boundary between the EEZ of Ireland and the United Kingdom and those parts of their continental shelves lying within 200 nautical miles of their respective baselines. Report by Anderson, *IMB*, vol VII, 5151. The 2013 Agreement entered into force on 31 March 2014.

117 Text in ibid, vol I, 799. However, the ICJ, in its judgment of 2014, ruled that no-all purpose maritime boundary between Chile and Peru had previously been delimited by any international agreement between the States up to the 200 nautical mile from their coasts. See ch 5, s XIV of this book. See also Report by Klein, *IMB*, vol VII, 4749 et seq.

118 Text in *IMB*, vol I, 815. The delimitation line runs along the parallel of latitude drawn from the point at which the land frontier between the Parties reaches the sea. Report by Jiménez de Aréchaga, ibid, 797. However, Peru has claimed that the agreement was not intended to be delimitation agreement. Report by Otero, ibid, vol VII, 4770.

119 Text in ibid, vol I, 791. The method used was a rhumb line nearly perpendicular the general direction of the coast. Substantially the same result is given as a true or strict equidistance line. ibid, 785.

(Continued)

Parties	Signature/Entered into force	Method	Configuration
Argentina-Uruguay[120]	1973/1974	ED (Art 70)	AC
Australia-Indonesia[121]	1973/1974	ED	AC
Colombia-Ecuador[122]	1975/1975	*	AC
The Gambia-Senegal[123]	1975/1976	*	AC
Kenya-Tanzania[124]	1976/1976	*	AC
India-Sri Lanka[125] (Gulf of Manaar and Bay of Bengal)	1976/1976	ED	AC/OC
Cuba-Mexico[126]	1976/1976	ED (Art I)	AC/OC
Colombia-Panama[127]	1976/1977	ED (Art I, p)	AC/OC
India-Maldives[128]	1976/1978	ED	AC/OC
Cuba-United States[129]	1977/Applied provisionally	ED	OC

(continued)

[120] Text in ibid, 764–76. Both Parties claimed a 200-mile territorial sea. Yet, Jiménez de Aréchaga considered that in the light of the developments in the Law of the Sea, the boundary line may be considered as a single maritime boundary dividing both the EEZ and continental shelf. Report by Jiménez de Aréchaga, ibid, 759. On the other hand, United States Department of State categorised the 1973 Agreement into the continental shelf boundary agreement. US Department of States, *Limits in the Seas,* No. 64, 24 October 1975, 2. Art 70 of the 1973 Agreement stipulates that the lateral maritime boundary begins at the midpoint of the baseline consisting of an imaginary straight line that joins Punta del Este (Uruguay) and Punta Rasa del Cabo San Antonio (Argentina). According to Jiménez de Aréchaga, by drawing a closing line at the mouth of the Rio de la Plata, the waters behind that line are internal waters. If this is the case, the single maritime boundary only begins seaward of the closing line.

[121] Text in *IMB*, vol II, 1225.

[122] Text in ibid, vol I, 815. The maritime boundary extends the land frontier along a parallel of latitude. ibid, 812.

[123] Text in ibid, 854. The maritime boundary is a straight line following the parallel of latitude 13° 35′ 36″N and is an extension of the land boundary. Both States claimed the 200-mile EEZ Adede considered this as an all-purpose boundary, Report by Adede, ibid, 850–51.

[124] For the text of the Exchange of Notes between Tanzania and Kenya, ibid, 881. The maritime boundary in the eastern segment runs along a line of latitude, while the territorial sea boundary is an equidistance line. The second sector of boundary established by this agreement divides the 50-mile territorial sea of Tanzania and a 200-mile EEZ of Kenya. At present, both States have established a 200-mile EEZ. Adede considers this as an all-purpose boundary. Report by Adede, ibid, 876.

[125] Text in ibid, vol II, 1426.

[126] Text in ibid, vol I, 575.

[127] Text in ibid, 532. The Agreement established two maritime boundaries in the Caribbean Sea and Pacific Ocean, respectively. The coastal geography concerned changes from adjacency to opposite. While the equidistance method is applied in the adjacent coasts, it is not in the case of opposite coasts.

[128] Text in ibid, vol II, 1397.

[129] Text in ibid, vol I, 423. The Agreement entered into force provisionally 1 January 1978. The maritime boundary runs between two equidistance lines, one using only low-water line basepoints and one using straight (construction) basepoints. Report by Smith, ibid, 420. The Parties agreed to

(Continued)

Parties	Signature/Entered into force	Method	Configuration
Cuba-Haiti[130]	1977/1978	ED (Art I)	OC
Colombia-Costa Rica[131]	1977/–	*	AC
Mexico-United States[132]	1978/1997	ED	AC/OC
Colombia-Dominican Republic[133]	1978/1979	ED (Art I)	OC
Venezuela-The Netherlands (Antilles)[134]	1978/1978	ED(p)	AC/OC
Colombia-Haiti[135]	1978/1979	ED (Art I)	OC
Venezuela-United States[136] (Puerto Rico and Virgin Islands)	1978/1980	ED	OC
Denmark (Faroe Islands)-Norway[137]	1979/1980	ED (Art 1, 2)	OC
Dominican Republic-Venezuela[138]	1979/1982	ED	OC
Tonga-France (Wallis and Futuna)[139]	1980/1980	ED (Art I)	AC/OC

(continued)

apply the terms of this Agreement provisionally from 1 January 1978, for a period of two years in accordance with Art V. Every two years beginning in 1979 the Parties have exchanged diplomatic notes to continue provisional application. Report by Roach, ibid, vol VII, 4607 et seq. According to US Department of States, as of 2 January 2019, the Agreement is listed in 'Treaties Pending in the Senate.' See www.state.gov/s/l/treaty/pending/.

[130] Text in ibid, vol I, 560. Art 1 of the 1977 Agreement refers to 'the principle of equidistance or equity.' ibid, 561. Legault and Hankey regard the agreed boundary as a modified equidistance line. ibid, 232.

[131] Text in ibid, vol I, 806. Costa Rica did not ratify the 1977 Treaty. See *Maritime Delimitation in the Caribbean Sea and the Pacific Ocean* (*Costa Rica v Nicaragua*), Judgment, [2018] ICJ Rep (not yet reported), [57] and [131].

[132] Text in ibid, 444. By a 1976 exchange of notes, the Parties agreed to establish a *provisional* boundary according to the equidistance method. The 1978 Agreement contains the line identical to the one found in the 1976 exchange of notes. Along the eastern coast, its configuration changes from adjacent to opposite coasts. On the western side, the configuration is one of adjacency. On both sides, the equidistance method was adopted. Report by Smith and Colson, ibid, 433–32. The 1978 Agreement has entered into force in 1997. ibid, vol IV, 2619.

[133] Text in *IMB*, vol I, 488.

[134] Text in ibid, 631. The maritime boundaries may be divided into four sectors. Sector D is a true equidistance line. A Line between Point 5 to Point 6 in sector B is an equidistance. A line from Point 8 to Point 10 in sector B is nearly an equidistance as well. However, the delimitation line in other parts deviates from equidistance.

[135] Text in ibid, 500.

[136] Text in ibid, 701.

[137] Text in ibid, vol II, 1717.

[138] Text in ibid, vol I, 588.

[139] Text in ibid, 1016.

(Continued)

Parties	Signature/Entered into force	Method	Configuration
France (Reunion)-Mauritius[140]	1980/1980	ED (Preamble)	AC/OC
Costa Rica-Panama[141]	1980/1982	ED (Art I)	AC
Indonesia-Papua New Guinea[142]	1980/1982	ED	AC
Venezuela-France (Guadeloupe and Martinique)[143]	1980/1983	ED	OC
Cook Islands-United States[144] (American Samoa)	1980/1983	ED	OC
New Zealand (Tokekau)-United States (American Samoa)[145]	1980/1983	ED	OC
France (Martinique)-Saint Lucia[146]	1981/1981	ED (Art I)	AC/OC
Brazil-France(French Guiana)[147]	1981/1981	*	AC
Australia-France (New Caledonia)[148]	1982/1983	ED	OC
France (Kerguelen Islands)[149]	1982/1983	ED	OC
United Kingdom (Pitcairn)-France (French Polynesia)[150]	1983/1984	ED (Art I)	OC
Fiji-France (New Caledonia, Wallis and Futuna)[151]	1983/1984	ED (Art I)	OC

(continued)

[140] Text in ibid, vol II, 1360.

[141] Text in ibid, vol I, 547. The 1980 Agreement drew two maritime boundaries in the Caribbean Sea and Pacific Ocean, respectively. Art I of the Agreement explicitly refers to the equidistance method. But maritime boundaries are partly modified.

[142] Text in ibid, 1045.

[143] Text in ibid, 613. The Parties identified two probable triple equidistant points, ie, a point for Aves-Martinique-Dominica and a point for Aves-Martinique-Saint Lucia. The final boundary runs midway between the respective meridians of these two points. This is an equidistant meridian between two triple equidistant meridians.

[144] Text in ibid, 991.

[145] Text in ibid, 1131.

[146] Text in ibid, 599.

[147] Text in ibid, 782. The delimitation method is defined by the loxodoromic curve of the true azimuth 41 degrees, 30 minutes (Art 1).

[148] Text in ibid, 911.

[149] Text in ibid, vol II, 1192.

[150] Text in ibid, vol I, 1009.

[151] Text in ibid, 1000; 1597 *UNTS*, 339. Annex I B of the Convention was modified on 8 November 1990. See Décret n° 91–156 du 8 février 1991 portant publication de l'avenant portant modification de la convention du 19 janvier 1983 entre le Gouvernement de la République française et le Gouvernement de Fidji relative à la délimitation de leur zone économique, signé à Suva le 8 novembre 1990. *Journal officiel* du 10 février 1991, 2095.

(Continued)

Parties	Signature/Entered into force	Method	Configuration
Argentina-Chile[152]	1984/1985	*	AC
Denmark-Sweden[153]	1984/1985	ED (Art I)	OC
Colombia-Costa Rica[154]	1984/2001	*	OC
France-Monaco[155]	1984/1985	*	AC
Costa Rica-Ecuador[156]	1985/–	ED (Art I)	OC
Poland-Soviet Union[157]	1985/1986	ED	AC
Colombia-Honduras[158]	1986/1999	*	OC
North Korea-Soviet Union[159]	1986/obscure	ED(p)	AC
Burma (Myanmar)-India[160]	1986/1987	ED(p)	OC

(continued)

[152] Text in *IMB*, vol I, 736.

[153] Text in ibid, vol II, 1939. As mentioned in Art 1, the delimitation line was drawn based on equidistance. Yet in the southern segment of the boundary in Kattegat, the equidistance line is dramatically simplified taking navigation and fishing elements into account. Report by Franckx, ibid, 1935–36.

[154] Jiménez de Aréchaga states that the delimitation line is an equidistance drawn to and from points located by their latitude and longitude. Report by Eduardo Jiménez de Aréchaga, ibid, vol I, 803. Yet it appears that that line is different from an equidistance line indicated in the map by *International Maritime Boundaries*. Thus, it may be difficult to regard the maritime boundary drawn in the 1984 Agreement as an equidistance line. In addition, the text reprinted on pp 806 to 808 in *International Maritime Boundaries* is not the text of the 1984 Agreement, but that of the 1977 Agreement. Thus, the author was provided the text of the 1984 Agreement by the Permanent Mission of Colombia in Geneva.

[155] Text in *IMB*, vol II, 1588. The boundary line is a pragmatic line considering a peculiar geographic situation of Monaco. Beyond the territorial seas, the Agreement is intended to establish a single maritime boundary, although neither France (in the Mediterranean) nor Monaco has claimed their EEZs. Report by Scovazzi, ibid, 1583.

[156] Text in ibid, vol I, 825–28. Art I of the 1985 Agreement clearly provides that maritime areas concerned shall be delimited by a geodesic line equidistant between the two countries in that sector where their seas overlap, although the maritime boundary deviates partly from an equidistance line indicated by *IMB*, vol I, 825. The 1985 Agreement has not entered into force since Costa Rica did not ratify it, while Ecuador did so in 1990. The information was provided by the Permanent Mission of Ecuador in Geneva. On 21 April 2014, another agreement on maritime delimitation was concluded.

[157] Text in ibid, vol II, 2054. The 1985 Agreement replaces the 1958 Protocol and 1969 Agreement although it totally relied on those previous agreements.

[158] Text in ibid, vol I, 517. The date of entering into force was provided by the Permanent Mission of Colombia in Geneva.

[159] Text in ibid, 1152. The delimitation line may be divided into two segments (Point 1 to Point 2; Point 2 to Point 3). While the first half of the first segment deviates from an equidistance line, the second segment and the second half of the first are generally equidistant. See Report by Park and map, ibid, 1151. On the other hand, Elferink indicates that the first segment is an equidistance line measured from the straight baselines claimed by North Korea and the Soviet Union. Furthermore, the second segment is equidistant from the *South Korean* and Russian coasts. Alex G Oude Elferink, *The Law of Maritime Boundary Delimitation: A Case Study of the Russian Federation* (Dordrecht, Nijhoff, 1994) 321–22.

[160] Text in *IMB*, vol II, 1338.

(Continued)

Parties	Signature/Entered into force	Method	Configuration
Dominican Republic-France[161] (Guadeloupe and Martinique)	1987/1988	ED(p)	AC/OC
Sweden-Soviet Union[162]	1988/1988	ED	OC
Mozambique-Tanzania[163]	1988/–	ED (Art IV p)	AC
Australia-Solomon Islands[164]	1988/1989	ED	OC
Denmark-GDR.[165]	1988/1989	ED(p)	OC
Poland-FRG.[166]	1989/1989	*	AC
Poland-Sweden[167]	1989/1989	ED	OC
Trinidad and Tobago-Venezuela[168]	1989/1991	ED(p)	AC/OC
Papua New Guinea-Solomon Islands[169]	1989/–	ED(p)	OC

(continued)

[161] Text in ibid, vol I, 714.

[162] Text in ibid, vol II, 2073. In the course of negotiations, first, two equidistance lines were proposed. One was a line giving Gotland full effect and the other is a line measured from mainlands of the Parties. Then, the area overlapped two equidistance lines was divided in a 75–25% ratio to the advantage of Sweden. Although this is a political compromise, it remains true that the equidistance method was used at the first stage of delimitation. Accordingly, it may be possible to say that the agreed boundary is a modified equidistance line. Report by Franckx, ibid, 2063.

[163] Text in ibid, vol I, 898. This is an all-purpose boundary for the internal waters, territorial sea, and EEZ Report by Adede, ibid, 894. According to the Permanent Mission of the United Republic of Tanzania in Geneva, the Agreement has not entered into force. Subsequently the Agreement was replaced by the 2011 Agreement.

[164] Text in ibid, 983. The date of entering into force was provided by the Ministry of Foreign Affairs and Trade of Australia.

[165] Text in ibid, vol II, 2094. The established boundary is an equidistance line. Yet in the Alder Grund area, the boundary deviates from an equidistance. It is suggested that proportionality was taken into account in drawing the boundary in this area. Report by Frankx, ibid, 2091.

[166] Text in ibid, vol II, 2020. The Agreement was concluded between Poland and German Democratic Republic. Owing to the unification of Germany in 1990, the General Republic of Germany ceased to exist. Yet the 1989 agreement was confirmed by the 1990 treaty, entered into force in 1992, between the Federal Republic of Germany and the Republic of Poland concerning the confirmation of the frontier existing between them. For the text of the 1990 treaty, *ibid,* 2027. The established boundary is a pragmatic line taking navigational factors into account. This agreement also delimits territorial seas between the parties. In addition, it replaced a boundary of continental shelf established by the 1968 agreement.

[167] Text in ibid, 2085. In the first segment (point A to halfway between Points D–E), the established boundary is an equidistance line. In the second segment (halfway between Points D–E, Point F), the line was modified by giving 75% effect to Swedish Island of Gotland. Report by Franckx, ibid, 2081.

[168] Text in ibid, vol I, 670. This agreement subsumed the 1942 agreement between the parties, which was the oldest one relating to the delimitation of the seabed.

[169] Text in ibid, 1162. For an analysis of the instrument, see V Prescott, 'Papua New Guinea-Solomon Islands Maritime Boundary' (1994) 11 *Ocean Yearbook* 179.

(Continued)

Parties	Signature/Entered into force	Method	Configuration
France (New Caledonia)-Solomon Islands[170]	1990/1990	ED (Art I)	OC
Cook Islands-France[171]	1990/1990	ED (Art I)	OC
United States-Soviet Union[172]	1990/1990	*	AC/OC
Trinidad and Tobago-Venezuela[173]	1990/1991	ED(p)	AC
United Kingdom (British Virgin Islands)-United States (Puerto Rico and the US Virgin Islands)[174]	1993/1995	ED (Preamble)	OC
United Kingdom (Anguilla)-United States (US Virgin Islands)[175]	1993/1995	ED (Preamble)	OC
Cape Verde-Senegal[176]	1993/1994	*	OC
Colombia-Jamaica[177]	1993/1994	ED(p)	OC
Cuba-Jamaica[178]	1994/1995	ED (Art 1)	OC
Finland-Sweden (Bogskär Area)[179]	1994/1995	*	OC
Denmark(Greenland)-Norway (Jan Mayen)[180]†	1995/1995	ED	OC

(continued)

[170] Text in *IMB*, vol I, 1172.

[171] Text in ibid, 1180.

[172] Text in *ibid,* 454. The maritime boundary was drawn on the basis of the 1867 Convention between the Parties. Report by Verville, ibid, 451. The 1990 Agreement between United States and Soviet Union created three special areas that lie beyond 200 nautical miles from one party but within the 200 nautical miles from another party yet on the side of the former party of the boundary line.

[173] Text in ibid, 685.

[174] Text in ibid, vol III, 2167.

[175] Text in ibid, 2177.

[176] Text in ibid, 2287; www.un.org/Depts/los/LEGISLATIONANDTREATIES/STATEFILES/CPV.htm. Art 1 explicitly provides that the boundary is a median line. However, the boundary drawn in reality is different from an equidistance line. It is unclear whether this line may be regarded as a modified equidistance line or not. See map, *IMB*, vol III, 2286.

[177] Text in ibid, 2200. The 1993 Agreement established a joint regime as well.

[178] Text in ibid, 2214.

[179] Text in ibid, 2553. The established boundary is a pragmatic line.

[180] Text in ibid, 2524. The Agreement was concluded following the decision in the *Jan Mayen* case. The Parties slightly adjusted three of four points indicated by the ICJ. Report by Anderson, ibid, 2519.

(Continued)

Parties	Signature/Entered into force	Method	Configuration
France (St Martin and St Barthelemy)-United Kingdom(Anguilla)[181]	1996/1997	ED (Art 1)	OC
France (Guadeloupe)-United Kingdom (Montserrat)[182]	1996/1997	ED (Art 1)	OC
Dominican Republic-United Kingdom (Turks and Caicos Islands)[183]	1996/–	*	OC
Estonia-Latvia[184]	1996/1996	ED(p)	AC/OC
Estonia-Finland[185]	1996/1997	ED	OC
Niue-United States (American Samoa)[186]	1997/2014	ED (Preamble)	AC/OC
Denmark(Greenland)-Iceland[187]	1997/1998	ED (Art 1)	OC
Iceland-Norway[188]	1997/1998	*	OC

(continued)

[181] Text in ibid, 2224. Information regarding the entering into force of the Agreement was provided by the Foreign and Commonwealth Office in the United Kingdom. See also ibid, vol V, 3562.

[182] Text in ibid, vol III, 2232–33. Information regarding the entering into force of the Agreement was provided by the Foreign and Commonwealth Office in the United Kingdom. See also ibid, vol V, 3563.

[183] Text in ibid, vol III, 2242. The established boundary is a pragmatic line. Report by Anderson, ibid, 2239. See also US Department of States, *Limits in the Seas*, No. 130, 31 January 2014, 6.

[184] In addition to the single maritime boundary, the agreement also delimits the territorial sea between the parties. Text in (1999) 39 *Law of the Sea Bulletin* 28; *IMB*, vol IV, 3014. For short analysis, see Report by Franckx, ibid, 2995; (1997) 12 *IJMCL* 365. Although a lack of information makes it difficult to point to a method applied to the maritime boundary, so far as the base of an annexed map is concerned in essence, the boundary inside the Gulf of Riga appears not to coincide with an equidistance line. On the other hand, outside the Gulf of Riga, the established boundary is a line perpendicular to the eastern closing line of the Gulf. ibid, 369. It may be said that that line might be a sort of an equidistance line.

[185] The boundary is based on the former maritime boundary between Finland and the former Soviet Union. In 1965 and 1967, Finland and the former Soviet Union reached an agreement for drawing a boundary for their continental shelves. Later, the continental shelf boundaries were transformed into a single maritime boundary for the EEZ and the continental shelf by the 1985 agreement, which entered into force in 1986. Regarding the 1985 agreement, *IMB*, vol II, 1995. For the 1996 agreement, ibid, 369 and 375; (1999) 39 *Law of the Sea Bulletin* 33; Report by Franckx, *IMB*, vol IV, 3038–39.

[186] Text in (1997) 35 *Law of the Sea Bulletin* 104; *IMB*, vol IV, 2680. See also ibid, vol VII, 4839.

[187] The different baselines used by Denmark and Iceland to measure a median line produced an overlapping area of 11, 500 square kilometres. The area was divided by a percentage ratio of 7:3 in favour of Iceland. Alex G Oude Elferink, 'Current Legal Developments: Denmark/ Iceland/Norway' (1998) 13 *IJMCL* 608. For the text of the Agreement, ibid, 613; (1999) 39 *Law of the Sea Bulletin* 35; *IMB*, vol IV, 2951. The year of entering into force was provided by the Ministry of Foreign Affairs of Denmark.

[188] For the text of the Agreement, Oude Elferink, 'Current Legal Developments: Denmark/ Iceland/ Norway' 616; (2000) 43 *Law of the Sea Bulletin* 109; *IMB*, vol IV, 2910–11. The maritime boundary is a pragmatic line. Report by Anderson, ibid, 2906.

(Continued)

Parties	Signature/Entered into force	Method	Configuration
Denmark-Norway[189]	1997/1998	*	OC
Lithuania-Russia[190]	1997/2003	ED	AC
Thailand-Vietnam[191]	1997/1997	*	OC
Turkey-Bulgaria[192]	1997/1998	ED(p)	AC
Japan-South Korea[193]	1998/1999	ED(p)	OC
Estonia-Sweden[194]	1998/2000	ED	OC

(continued)

[189] The year of entering into force was provided by the Ministry of Foreign Affairs of Denmark and the Permanent Mission of Norway in Geneva. For the text of the Agreement, (2000) 43 *Law of the Sea Bulletin* 111; Oude Elferink, 'Current Legal Developments: Denmark/ Iceland/Norway' 615; *IMB*, vol IV, 2919. The maritime boundary is a pragmatic line. Report by Anderson, ibid, 2916.

[190] Text in (1998) 13 *IJMCL* 282. Yet the English text is based on the inauthentic text unexpectedly published by a Lithuanian newspaper. Unofficial translation of the text was also available in: *IMB*, vol IV, 3073. See also ibid, vol V, 4009. For a short analysis of the Agreement, see E Franckx, 'Two More Maritime Boundary Agreements Concluded in the Eastern Baltic Sea in 1997' 278–80.

[191] Text in (1999) 39 *Law of the Sea Bulletin* 23; *IMB*, vol IV, 2692. Art 1(5) of that Agreement provides that the continental shelf boundary determined in Art 1(1) shall also constitute the boundary of the EEZ between the Parties. According to the Ambassador of Vietnam, Nguyen Quy Binh, the equidistance method was not used in the course of negotiations because of the dispute regarding the legitimacy of the Parties' baselines. By contrast, the Department of Treaties and Legal Affairs of Thailand is of the view that the delimitation method used is a modified equidistance method. Fax dated 21 March 2001. In this regard, McDorman indicated that the maritime boundary was a negotiated solution that divided the disputed area by giving Thailand two-thirds and Vietnam one-third of the area. Report by McDorman, ibid, vol IV, 2688.

[192] Text in *IMB*, vol IV, 2879–86. The 1997 Agreement was also Reproduced, (1998) 38 *Law of the Sea Bulletin* 62. The date of entering into force was provided by the Permanent Missions of Turkey and Bulgaria in Geneva. According to the Bulgarian explanation, the equidistance method was used in combination with another method. Yuksel Inan suggested that the maritime boundary was based on a simplified equidistant line. Report by Yuksel Inan, *IMB*, vol IV, 2874.

[193] The text of the 1998 Agreement was provided by the Ministry of Foreign Affairs in Japan. The 1998 Agreement is a new agreement establishing EEZ boundary, which coincides with the existing continental shelf boundary. Thus, we will list the 1998 Agreement distinguishing from the 1974 Agreement, even though the delimitation line drawn in 1998 coincides with the 1974 continental shelf boundary.

[194] Following the dissolution of the Soviet Union, Estonia and Sweden concluded a new Agreement on the Delimitation of the Maritime Zones in the Baltic Sea in 1998. The 1998 Agreement establishes in principle, the same maritime boundary drawn by the 1988 Agreement between Sweden and the Soviet Union. But contrary to the 1988 Agreement, which delimited a Swedish fishery zone and Soviet EEZ, the 1998 Agreement delimits the EEZs of both Sweden and Estonia. Sweden established its EEZ in 1992, and Estonia did so in 1993. Regarding the analysis relating to the 1998 Agreement, see Alex G Oude Elferink, 'Current Legal Developments: Delimitation of Maritime Zones Between Estonia and Sweden' (1999) 14 *IJMCL* 299; by the same author, 'The 1998 Estonia-Sweden Maritime Boundary Agreement: Lessons to be Learned in the Area of Continuity and/or Succession of States' (2000) 31 *ODIL* 269. The text of the Agreement was reproduced in ibid, 282–83; *IMB*, vol IV, 3105; (2003) 52 *Law of the Sea Bulletin* 48. Date of entering into force was provided by the Permanent Mission of Sweden in Geneva.

(Continued)

Parties	Signature/Entered into force	Method	Configuration
United Kingdom-Denmark (Faroe Islands)[195]	1999/1999	ED(p)	OC
Latvia-Lithuania[196]	1999/–	ED	AC
Equatorial Guinea-São Tomé and Príncipe[197]	1999/provisionally in force	ED (Preamble)	OC
Nigeria-Equatorial Guinea[198]	2000/2002	*	AC/OC
Saudi Arabia-Yemen[199]	2000/2000	*	AC
Oman-Pakistan[200]	2000/2000	ED (Art 2)	OC
China-Viet Nam[201]	2000/2004	*	AC/OC
France-Seychelles[202]	2001/2001	ED (Art 1)	AC/OC
Gabon-São Tomé and Principe[203]	2001/unknown	ED (Art 2)	OC
Honduras-UK[204]	2001/2002	ED	AC/OC

(continued)

[195] Information regarding the entering into force of the Agreement was provided by the Foreign and Commonwealth Office in the United Kingdom. Text in: (1999) 41 *Law of the Sea Bulletin* 58; *IMB*, vol IV, 2970. The maritime boundary was based primarily upon the equidistance method. Report by Anderson, ibid, 2964–65 and 2967. The 1999 Agreement was supplemented by the 2012 Protocol. *IMB*, vol VII, 5279.

[196] Franckx pointed out that the boundary is a line perpendicular to the general direction of the coast. Franckx, 'Current Legal Developments: New Maritime Boundaries Concluded in the Eastern Baltic Sea Since 1998' 653. It could be said that this is an equidistance line. For the analysis and the text of the Agreement, Report by Franckx, *IMB*, vol IV, 3125. See also Franckx, 'Maritime Delimitation in the Baltic Sea' 440. According to data base of the Ministry of Foreign Affairs of Latvia, the Agreement has not entered into force. The data base is available at: www.mfa.gov.lv/en/policy/bilateral-agreements.

[197] Text in (2001) 47 *Law of the Sea Bulletin* 39; *IMB*, vol IV, 2654.

[198] Text in (2001) 45 *Law of the Sea Bulletin* 68; *IMB*, vol IV, 2666. According to the Embassy of Nigeria, the delimitation line is not strictly based on the equidistance method. A letter from the Embassy of Nigeria in Switzerland. The Agreement entered into force on 3 April 2002. ibid, vol V, 3623.

[199] According to DOALOS, the line Represents a single maritime boundary for all maritime zones since there is no indication to the contrary and the line appears to go beyond 12 nautical miles. Email received on 30 October 2002. For the text of the Agreement, *IMB*, vol IV, 2807. Furthermore, Colson suggested that the maritime boundary was not based on the equidistance method. Report by Colson, *IMB*, vol VI, 2803.

[200] Text in (2003) 50 *Law of the Sea Bulletin*, 39; *IMB*, vol IV, 2818.

[201] The delimitation line serves as the boundary for the territorial sea, the EEZ and continental shelf. Text in 2336 *UNTS* 179; (2005) 56 *Law of the Sea Bulletin* 137; *IMB*, vol VII, 4842.

[202] Text in (2001) 47 *Law of the Sea Bulletin* 42; *IMB*, vol V, 3792.

[203] Text in (2003) 50 *Law of the Sea Bulletin* 65; *IMB*, vol V, 3691.

[204] Text in (2002) 49 *Law of the Sea Bulletin* 60. Date of entering into force was provided by the Foreign and Commonwealth Office in the UK. Nuno Marques Antunes suggested that the maritime boundary was an equidistance line with some modifications. Nuno Marques Antunes, *Towards the Conceptualisation of Maritime Delimitation: Legal and Technical Aspects of a Political Process* (Leiden, Brill/Nijhoff, 2003) 579. Contreras and Wood considered that the maritime boundary was 'essentially a pragmatic line, being a simplified and adjusted median line'. Report by Contreras and Wood, *IMB*, vol V, 3568.

(Continued)

Parties	Signature/Entered into force	Method	Configuration
Tanzania-Seychelles[205]	2002/2002	ED (Art 1)	OC
Angola-Namibia[206]	2002/ unknown	*	AC
Cyprus-Egypt[207]	2003/2004	ED (Art 1)	OC
France (Wallis and Futuna)-New Zealand (Tokelau)[208]	2003/2003	ED (Art 1)	OC
Cape Verde-Mauritania[209]	2003/–	ED (Art 1, p)	OC
Oman-Yemen[210]	2003/2004	ED (p)	AC/OC
Cyprus-Egypt[211]	2003/2004	ED (Art 1)	OC
+Australia-New Zealand[212]	2004/2006	ED (p)	OC
Honduras-Mexico[213]	2005/2006	ED	AC
France (Reunion)-Madagascar[214]	2005/2007	ED (Preamble)	OC
Estonia-Russian Federation[215]	2005/–	ED (Art 1)	AC
Denmark (Greenland)-Norway (Svalbard)[216]	2006/2006	ED (Art 1)	OC
Benin-Nigeria[217]	2006/–	ED(p)	AC
Micronesia-Marshall Islands[218]	2006/2015	ED	OC

(continued)

[205] Text in (2002) 49 *Law of the Sea Bulletin* 56; *IMB*, vol V, 3802. Date of entering into force was provided by the Ministry of Foreign Affairs in Seychelles.

[206] For the text of unofficial text of the treaty, *IMB*, vol V, 3719. The maritime boundary runs the parallel of 17° 15' latitude south. This line is not so very different from an equidistance line. Report by Daniel, ibid, 3715.

[207] Text in (2003) 52 *Law of the Sea Bulletin* 45; *IMB*, vol V, 3924. See also ibid, vol VI, 4433.

[208] Text in *IMB*, vol VI, 4346.

[209] Text in ibid, vol V, 3702. While Art 1 of the Treaty provides that the maritime boundary between the Parties is a median line, the line deviates from an equidistance line in the southern sector. Report by Daniel, ibid, 3698.

[210] Text in ibid, 3909. The maritime boundary separates the territorial sea, the EEZ and the continental shelf. The boundary joining Points 1 to 5 is a median line. From Point 5, however, the boundary departs from an equidistance line. Report by Prescott, ibid, 3905–6.

[211] Text in: (2003) 52 *Law of the Sea Bulletin* 45; *IMB*, vol. V, 3924. See also www.un.org/Depts/los/LEGISLATIONANDTREATIES/STATEFILES/EGY.htm.

[212] The 2004 Treaty established maritime boundaries for the EEZ and the continental shelf beyond 200 nautical miles. While the EEZ boundary was determined by equidistance, its role is limited in the delimitation of the continental shelf beyond 200 nautical miles. Report by Fyfe and French, *IMB*, vol V, 3764. For the text of the Treaty, ibid, 3768. See also, ibid, vol VI, 4300.

[213] Text in (2007) 65 *Law of the Sea Bulletin* 33; *IMB*, vol VI, 4210.

[214] Text in *IMB*, 4412.

[215] Text in ibid, 4582.

[216] Text in ibid, 4529.

[217] Text in ibid, 4266.

[218] Text in ibid, 4325. According to the National Oceanic Resource Management Authority of the Federated States of Micronesia, the Treaty came into force on 24 July 2015. See www.norma.fm/press-releases/federated-states-of-micronesia-registers-its-maritime-treaties-with-the-united-nations-secretariat/.

(Continued)

Parties	Signature/Entered into force	Method	Configuration
Micronesia-Palau[219]	2006/–	ED (Art 2)	OC
Cyprus-Lebanon[220]	2007/–	ED (Art 1)	OC
Denmark (The Faroes)-Iceland[221]	2007/2008	ED (Art 1)	OC
Mauritius-Seychelles[222]	2008/2008	ED (Art 1)	AC/OC
Barbados-France (Guadeloupe and Martinique)[223]	2009/–	ED	AC
Qatar-Saudi Arabia[224]	2008/2008	*	AC
Grenada-Trinidad and Tobago[225]	2010/2010	ED	OC
The Bahamas-Cuba[226]	2011/2012	ED	OC
Cuba-Honduras[227]	2012/2013	*	OC
Ecuador-Peru[228]	2011/2011	*	AC
+Kenya-Tanzania[229]	2009/2009	*	AC
Mozambique-Tanzania[230]	2011/–	ED(p)	AC
Cook Island-Kiribati[231]	2012/2014	ED (Art 1)	AC/OC
Cook Island-Niue[232]	2012/2013	ED (Art 1)	OC
Kiribati-Marshall Islands[233]	2012/–	ED (Art 1)	OC

(continued)

[219] Text in *IMB*, vol VI, 4357.

[220] Text in ibid, 4452. While Cyprus has ratified the Agreement of 2007, Lebanon has not ratified it yet. Report by Srebro et al, ibid, vol VII, 5092.

[221] Text in ibid, vol. VI, 4561. The Agreement also provides for a 'Special Area' where fishing vessels of the Faroes and Iceland may fish. Report by Wood, ibid, 4553.

[222] Text in ibid, 4398; (2009) 69 *Law of the Sea Bulletin* 106.

[223] Text in *IMB*, vol. VI, 4229.

[224] For the text of Joint Minutes, ibid, 4424. This boundary is an all purpose maritime boundary. However, the resources below the seabed between this boundary and the Abu Dubai-Qatar line remain under the control and ownership of Qatar. Report by Carleton, ibid, 4419.

[225] Text in (2010) 73 *Law of the Sea Bulletin* 43; *IMB*, vol VII, 4716.

[226] Text in (2013) 79 *Law of the Sea Bulletin* 19; *IMB*, vol VII, 4729.

[227] Text in ibid, vol VII, 4741. The maritime boundary is essentially a pragmatic line. ibid, 4738.

[228] For the text of the Exchange of Notes, (2011) 76 *Law of the Sea Bulletin* 30; *IMB*, vol VII, 4776. The maritime boundary follows the parallel of latitude. ibid, 4773.

[229] The 2009 Agreement limited the effect of the 1976 Agreement to the maritime boundary up to 12 nautical miles. It then established the maritime boundary delimiting the EEZ and continental shelf, including areas of continental shelf beyond 200 nautical miles. Report by Pratt, ibid, 4781 et seq. Text in ibid, 4788; (2009) 70 *Law of the Sea Bulletin* 54. The maritime boundary follows the parallel of latitude. *IMB*, vol VII, 4784.

[230] Although the 2011 Agreement is a new agreement, it is essentially an update of the 1988 Agreement. Report by Pratt, ibid, 4796. For the text of the Agreement, ibid, 4800.

[231] Text in ibid, 4855; (2015) 85 *Law of the Sea Bulletin* 35.

[232] Text in (2014) 82 *Law of the Sea Bulletin* 51; *IMB*, vol VII, 4866.

[233] Text in *IMB*, vol VII, 4877.

(Continued)

Parties	Signature/Entered into force	Method	Configuration
Kiribati-Nauru[234]	2012/–	ED (Art 1)	OC
Kiribati-New Zealand (Tokelau)[235]	2012/–	ED (Art 1)	OC
Kiribati-Tuvalu[236]	2012/–	ED	OC
Marshall Island-Nauru[237]	2012/–	ED (Art 1)	OC
+Kiribati-United States[238]	2013/–	ED	OC
Micronesia-United States (Guam)[239]	2014/–	ED	OC
Comoros-Mozambique[240]	2011/2012	ED (Art 1)	OC
Comoros-Seychelles[241]	2012/–	ED (Art 2)	OC
Comoros-Tanzania[242]	2011/–	ED (Art 1)	OC
Cyprus-Israel[243]	2010/2011	ED (Art 1)	OC
+Norway-Russian Federation[244]	2010/2011	ED (p)	AC
Ecuador-Costa Rica[245]	2014/2016	ED	OC
Saudi Arabia-Egypt[246]	2016/2017	ED	OC

[234] Text in ibid, 4889.

[235] Text in ibid, 4900.

[236] Text in (2014) 83 *Law of the Sea Bulletin* 37; *IMB*, vol VII, 4911.

[237] Text in *IMB*, vol VII, 4922.

[238] Text in ibid, 4942. Even though not stated in the text of the treaty, the coordinates reflect an agreement by the parties to extend the maritime boundary by 1 nautical mile beyond 200 nautical miles at three of the six terminal points. Report by Baumert and Melchior, ibid, 4938.

[239] Text in ibid, 4969.

[240] Text in ibid, 5025.

[241] Text in ibid, 5046.

[242] Text in ibid, 5066.

[243] Text in ibid, 5100; (2011) 75 *Law of the Sea Bulletin* 27.

[244] Text in (2012) 74 *Law of the Sea Bulletin* 24; *IMB*, vol VII, 5189. The 2010 Treaty established maritime boundaries for the EEZ and the continental shelf beyond 200 nautical miles. The Agreement created the 'Special Area' which lies beyond 200 nautical miles from the Russian coast, but within 200 nautical miles from the Norwegian coast (Art 3). For a detailed analysis of the 2010 Agreement, see Report by Fife, ibid, 5167. T Henriksen and G Ulfstein, 'Maritime Delimitation in the Arctic: The Barents Sea Treaty' (2011) 42 *ODIL*, 1; Ø Jensen, 'Treaty between Norway and the Russian Federation Concerning Maritime Delimitation and Cooperation in the Barents Sea and the Arctic Ocean' (2011) 26 *IJMCL*, 151; I Fondchenko, 'Legal Aspects of the Russian-Norwegian Model for Cross-Border Unitization in the Barents Sea and Arctic Ocean' (2018) 49 *ODIL* 262.

[245] Text in: (2017) 93 *Law of the Sea Bulletin* 16. Under Art 1, the Ecuadorian EEZ and continental shelf of the Galapagos Archipelago and the Costa Rican EEZ and continental shelf of Isla del Coco shall be delimited in the Pacific Ocean 'by the geodetic lines that pass through points equidistant from two countries ….'

[246] Text in: (2017) 94 *Law of the Sea Bulletin* 17. According to *Sovereign Limits*, the maritime boundary generally follows an equidistance line. See https://sovereignlimits.com/boundaries/egypt-saudi-arabia.

ii. Treaty on Delimitation of the EEZ which Coincides with Delimitation Line of Continental Shelf Established Afterwards

Iceland-Norway (Jan Mayen)[247]	1980/1980	*	OC

iii. Treaty on Delimitation of Fishery Zone which was Transformed into Single Maritime Boundary Including Seabed

Finland-Soviet Union[248]	1980/1980	ED (Art 2)	OC
Total			132

Total of Agreements regarding Single Maritime Boundary (1 + 2): 150.

IV. TREATIES WHICH ESTABLISHED SEPARATE MARITIME BOUNDARIES FOR THE SEABED AND THE SUPERJACENT WATERS

Australia-Papua New Guinea[249]	1978/1985	OC
Australia-Indonesia[250]	1981/1982	OC
Australia-Indonesia[251]	1997/–	OC
Australia-Timor-Leste[252]	2018/–	OC
Total		4

[247] The 1980 Agreement established an EEZ boundary following a 200-mile line measured from Iceland's basepoints for fisheries purpose. But the question of the continental shelf was submitted to a Conciliation Commission. Following the recommendation of this Conciliation Commission, the 1981 agreement on the Continental Shelf provides that the continental shelf in the area between Iceland and Jan Mayen shall coincide with the delimitation for the Parties' economic zones (Art 1). For the text of the 1981 Agreement, *IMB*, vol II, 1762.

[248] By the 1985 agreement, entered into force in 1986, the fishery zone boundary was transformed into a single maritime boundary for the EEZ and the continental shelf. For the text of the 1985 Agreement, ibid, 1995.

[249] Text in ibid, vol I, 937.

[250] For Memorandum of Understanding between Indonesia and Australia, ibid, vol II, 1238.

[251] The 1997 Perth Treaty between Australia and Indonesia for the Timor and Arafura Sea created an area where the Indonesia's EEZ overlaps the Australia's continental shelf. For the text and analysis regarding the Agreement, V Prescott, 'Current Legal Developments: Australia/Indonesia' (1997) 12 *IJMCL* 5337; Report by Prescott in *IMB*, vol IV, 2697. For the text of the Agreement, see also (1997) 35 *Law of the Sea Bulletin* 107; (1997) 36 *ILM* 1055. Even though the Perth Treaty has never entered into force, it is submitted that its provisions are observed by Australia and Indonesia in practice. *Report and Recommendations on the Compulsory Conciliation Commission between Timor-Leste and Australia on the Timor Sea* (hereafter the Conciliation Report of 2018), 9 May 2018, [30], available at: https://pca-cpa.org/en/cases/132/.

[252] Treaty between Australia and the Democratic Republic of Timor-Leste Establishing Their Maritime Boundaries in the Timor Sea. The southern boundary is a single maritime boundary (From points TA-5 to TA-10). The eastern and western lateral boundaries are the continental shelf boundary only (from points TA-1 to TA-5, and TA-10 to TA-13). The text was reproduced as Annex 28 to the Conciliation Report of 2018. The *Timor-Leste/Australia* Conciliation Commission significantly affected the establishment of maritime boundaries in the Timor Sea. See Y Tanaka, 'Maritime Delimitation by Conciliation,' (2018) 36 *Australian Year Book of International Law* (forthcoming).

V. TREATIES WHICH FIXED TRI-JUNCTION

Indonesia-Malaysia-Thailand[253]	1971/1973	*
India-Maldives-Sri Lanka[254]	1976/1976	ED (Art I)
India-Indonesia-Thailand[255]	1978/1979	*
Poland-Sweden-Soviet Union[256]	1989/1990	ED
India-Myanmar-Thailand[257]	1993/1995	ED (Art 1)
Estonia-Latvia-Sweden[258]	1997/1998	ED
Estonia-Finland-Sweden[259]	2001/2001	ED
Kiribati-Marshall Islands-Nauru[260]	2012/–	ED (Art 1)
Comoros-Seychelles-Tanzania[261]	2012/–	ED
Total		9

VI. SPECIAL TYPES OF TREATY RELATING TO MARITIME DELIMITATION

A. Treaties which Established Special Regimes in Areas where Delimitation was Not or Could Not be Effected

Parties	Signature/Entered into force	Regime
Japan-South Korea[262]	1974/1978	Joint Development Zone
Saudi Arabia-Soudan[263]	1974/1974	Common Zone

(continued)

[253] Text in *IMB*, vol II, 1452.
[254] Text in ibid, 1407.
[255] Text in ibid, 1386. Prescott indicates that the tri-junction was fixed on the basis of the equidistance. Report by Prescott, ibid, 1382. But, according to a map annexed in International Maritime Boundaries, that point deviates from an equidistant tri-junction point.
[256] Text in ibid, 2103.
[257] Text in ibid, vol V, 3782.
[258] For a short analysis regarding this tri-point Agreement, Franckx, 'Two More Maritime Boundary Agreements Concluded in the Eastern Baltic Sea in 1997' 277–78; for the text of the Agreement, ibid, 281; (1999) 39 *Law of the Sea Bulletin* 25; *IMB*, vol IV, 3056. According to Estonian Mission in Geneva, the tri-point is based on equidistance.
[259] For the text of the Agreement, *IMB*, vol IV, 3138; (2003) 50 *Law of the Sea Bulletin* 68; Frankx, 'Current Legal Developments: New Maritime Boundaries Concluded in the Eastern Baltic Sea Since 1998' 659. See also E Frankx, 'New Maritime Boundaries Concluded in the Eastern Baltic Sea Since 1998 (*bis*)' (2002) 17 *IJMCL* 263.
[260] Text in *IMB*, vol VII, 4933.
[261] The agreed tripoint between Comoros, Seychelles, and Tanzania (Point T) is equidistant from the nearest points on the baselines of all three States. Report by Pratt, ibid, 5042. Text in ibid, 5056.
[262] Text in ibid, vol I, 1073.
[263] Text in (1982) 952 *UNTS* 198.

(Continued)

Parties	Signature/Entered into force	Regime
Malaysia-Thailand[264]	1979/1982	Joint Development Area
Cambodia-Vietnam[265]	1982/1982	Joint Development Historical Water Zone
Yemen Arab Republic-People's Democratic Republic of Yemen[266]	1988/1989	Joint Development Area
Australia-Indonesia (Timor Gap)[267]	1989/1991	Cooperation Zone
Malaysia-Vietnam[268]	1992/1992	Joint Exploration and Exploitation of Petroleum
Guinea-Bissau -Senegal[269]	1993/1995	Joint Development Zone
Japan-China[270]	1997/2000	Joint Fishery Zone
Japan-South Korea[271]	1998/1999	Joint Provisional Fishery Zone
Nigeria-São Tomé and Principe[272]	2001/2003	Joint Development of Petroleum and other Resources
Angola-Republic of Congo[273]	2001/–	Unitisation
Nigeria-Equatorial Guinea[274]	2002/2002	Unitisation
Australia-East Timor[275]	2002/2003	Arrangements for the Exploration and Exploitation of Petroleum in the Timor Sea
Australia-East Timor[276]	2002/2003	Joint Development Zone
Australia-East Timor[277]	2003/2007	Unitisation of the Sunrise/ Troubadour Fields

(continued)

[264] Text in *IMB*, vol I, 1107. In 1990, they concluded the Agreement on the Constitution and Other Matters Relating to the Establishment of the Malaysia-Thailand Joint Authority. Text in ibid, 1111.

[265] Text in ibid, vol III, 2364.

[266] For this Agreement, WT Onorato, 'Joint Development in the International Petroleum Sector: the Yemeni Variant' (1990) 39 *ICLQ* 653. In 1990, the two countries were unified.

[267] Text in *IMB*, vol I, 1256. The Timor Gap Treaty terminated on 1 June 2000, through an Exchange of Letters between the respective Ministries of Foreign Affairs. Letter by Permanent Mission of Indonesia to the United Nations in Geneva dated 26 October 2000.

[268] For Memorandum of Understanding between Malaysia and Vietnam, ibid, vol III, 2341.

[269] Text in ibid, 2257.

[270] The text of the Agreement was provided by the Ministry of Foreign Affairs in Japan.

[271] The text of the Agreement was provided by the Ministry of Foreign Affairs in Japan. The EEZ boundary drawn in the 1998 Agreement coincides with the continental shelf boundary between Japan and South Korea drawn in 1974.

[272] Text in (2003) 50 *Law of the Sea Bulletin* 42; *IMB*, vol V, 3649.

[273] Text in *IMB*, vol V, 4288.

[274] This is a Protocol in Implementation of Art 6.2 of the 2002 Treaty between Nigeria and Equatorial Guinea. The Protocol creates unitization arrangements to enable the hydrocarbons in the Ekanga 'cut-out' to be developed in a commercially feasible manner. Report by Smith, ibid, 3624.

[275] Exchange of Notes Constituting an Agreement between East Timor and Australia. Text in *IMB*, vol V, 3821.

[276] Text in ibid, 3829.

[277] Text in ibid, 3872. See also *IMB*, vol VI, 4366.

(Continued)

Parties	Signature/Entered into force	Regime
Guyana-Barbados[278]	2003/2004	Co-operation Zone
Angola-Republic of Congo[279]	2007/2008	Common Interest Zone
Total		18

B. Treaties which Established Special Types of Delimitation Line

Parties	Signature/Entered into force	Type of line
India-Sri Lanka[280]	1974/1974	Historic Waters
Australia-Papua New Guinea[281]	1978/1985	Several Types
Australia-Indonesia[282]	1981/1982	Provisional Fisheries Surveillance Line
France-UK (Guernsey)[283]	1992/1992	Fisheries Control Line
Kuwait-Saudi Arabia[284]	2000/2001	Partitioning line
Tunisia-Algeria[285]	2002/2003	Provisional Arrangements
Australia-East Timor[286]	2006/2007	Provisional Arrangements
Qatar-Saudi Arabia[287]	2001/2001	Delimitation of the Dawhat Salwa (a Bay)
Indonesia-Philippines[288]	2014/–	EEZ (superjacent waters only)
Total		9

[278] The 2003 Treaty establishes a provisional arrangement pursuant to Art 74(3) of the LOSC. For the text of the Treaty, (2004) 55 *Law of the Sea Bulletin* 36; *IMB*, vol V, 3587. See also Report by Dundas, ibid, 3578.

[279] Text in *IMB*, vol VI, 4277.

[280] Text in ibid, vol II, 1416.

[281] Text in ibid, vol I, 937. This treaty deals with four sets of maritime boundaries; the territorial sea, continental shelf, fishery zone and protected zone for the Torres Strait.

[282] For the text of the Memorandum of Understanding between Indonesia and Australia, ibid, vol II, 1238.

[283] For the text of the Exchange of Notes, ibid, vol III, 2479.

[284] Text in ibi*d*, vol IV, 2837; (2001) 46 *Law of the Sea Bulletin* 84.

[285] This is an agreement on provisional arrangements for the delimitation of the maritime boundaries between Tunisia and Algeria. For the text of the Agreement, (2003) 52 *Law of the Sea Bulletin* 41; *IMB*, vol V, 3935.

[286] The 2006 Treaty, referred to as the CMATS agreement, seeks to resolve the outstanding issues concerning Greater Sunrise Unitization and postpones for an extended period the rights of the Parties to pursue maritime boundary claims. Report by Smith, *IMB*, vol VI, 4369. For the text of the Treaty, ibid, 4375.

[287] The agreed boundary is a simplified equidistance line. Report by Colson and Vohrer, *IMB*, vol VII, 5076. For the text of Minutes between the Parties, ibid, 5079.

[288] The Agreement relates to the EEZ delimitation only, without prejudice to continental shelf delimitation between the Parties (Art I(3)). The boundary line is a modified equidistance line.

C. Other Types

Parties	Signature Entered into force	Purpose
Netherlands-United Kingdom[289]	1965/1966	Unification of mineral resources
Norway-United Kingdom[290]	1976/1977	Exploitation of the Figg Field Reservoir
Norway-United Kingdom[291]	1979/1981	Exploitation of the Murchison Field Reservoir
Norway-United Kingdom[292]	1979/1981	Exploitation of the Statfjord Field Feservoir
Finland-USSR[293]	1985/1986	Change an existing continental shelf boundary into single maritime boundaries
France (Wallis and Futuna)-Tuvalu[294]	1985/1985	An interim arrangement
France-United Kingdom[295]	1988/1989	Change an existing continental shelf boundary into a territorial sea boundary
FRG.-Poland[296]	1990/1992	Confirmation of the frontier existing between FRG and Poland after the unification of FRG and GDR.

(continued)

Report by Schofield and Arsana, ibid, vol VII, 4947 and 4956. For the text of the Agreement, ibid, 4959. Indonesia ratified the Agreement in 2017. See www.straitstimes.com/asia/se-asia/indonesia-philippines-sea-border-pact-ratified. As of July 2018, however, the Agreement remained pending in the Foreign Relations Committee at the Senate of the Philippines. See www.senate.gov.ph/17th_congress/treaties_17thcongress.asp.

[289] The Agreement relates to the exploitation of single geological structures extending across the dividing line on the continental shelf under the North Sea. The text of the Agreement is available at: www.un.org/Depts/los/LEGISLATIONANDTREATIES/PDFFILES/TREATIES/NLD-GBR1965GS.PDF.

[290] Text in *IMB*, vol V, 3951.

[291] Text in ibid, 3970.

[292] Text in ibid, 3987.

[293] Text in ibid, vol II, 1995.

[294] For the text of the Exchange of Notes, 1506 *UNTS* 35; *IMB*, vol VI, 4337. The Exchange of Notes creates and interim arrangement acknowledging the principle of the equidistant line as a reference limit. Report by McDorman and Schofield, ibid, 4330.

[295] Text in ibid, 1752.

[296] Text in ibid, vol II, 2027.

(Continued)

Parties	Signature Entered into force	Purpose
UK (Pitcairn)-France (Polynesia)[297]	1992 and 1993/1993	Change previously concluded boundary into that of two EEZs
Turkey-Georgia[298]	1997/1999	Confirmation of the frontier existing between Soviet Union and Turkey
Australia-East Timor Transitional Administration[299]	2000/2000	Confirmation of the Timor Gap treaty
Cambodia-Thailand[300]	2001/2001	Agreement-to-agree respecting the overlapping maritime claims of the two states in the Gulf of Thailand
The Netherlands-United Kingdom[301]	2004/2006	Amendment of the previous agreement
Canada-Denmark[302]	2004/2009	Amendment of the previous agreement
Belgium-United Kingdom[303]	2005/2006	Amendment of the previous agreement
Norway-United Kingdom[304]	2005/2007	Cross-boundary cooperation

(continued)

[297] The 1984 Agreement separated the French economic zone around French Polynesia from the British fishing zone of the British Pitcairn Territory. As the United Kingdom proclaimed an EEZ around Pitcairn in 1992, the status of the area was changed. The Exchange of Notes between the Parties, which was proposed by the United Kingdom in 1992 and accepted by France in 1993, provides that the delimitation line drawn in 1984 becomes the boundary of the two EEZs. Report by Prescott, ibid, vol III, 2295.

[298] Text in ibid, vol IV, 2867.

[299] For the text of the Memorandum of Understanding between the Government of Australia and UNTAET, acting on behalf of East Timor on Arrangements relating to the Timor Gap Treaty, ibid, 2766–95. Later on, Timor Sea Arrangement was concluded. For the text of this arrangement, see (2001) 47 *Law of the Sea Bulletin* 45; (2002) 17 *IJMCL* 106; For an analysis regarding the Timor Sea Arrangement, see DM Ong, 'The New Timor Sea Arrangement 2001: Is Joint Development of Common Offshore Oil and Gas Deposits Mandated under International Law?' (2002) 17 *IJMCL* 79.

[300] This is a Memorandum of Understanding. The text in *IMB*, vol V, 3743.

[301] The Exchange of Notes amends the Agreement of 6 October 1965, as amended by the Protocol of 25 November 1971. Report by Whomersley, ibid, vol VI, 4494. For the text of the Exchange of Notes, ibid, 4497.

[302] Exchange of Notes Constituting an Agreement to Amend the Agreement between the Government of Canada and the Government of the Kingdom of Denmark Relating to the Delimitation of the Continental Shelf Between Greenland and Canada Done at Ottawa on 17 December 1973. The text is available at: www.treaty-accord.gc.ca/text-texte.aspx?id=104991. Entered into force 16 December 2009. See also note 106.

[303] For the text of the Exchange of Notes, ibid, 4509; (2008) 66 *Law of the Sea Bulletin* 96.

[304] Text in *IMB*, vol VII, 5219. Under Art 1.1, this Agreement applies to 'cross-boundary cooperation' between the Parties with regard to petroleum activities.

(Continued)

Parties	Signature Entered into force	Purpose
Trinidad and Tobago-Venezuela[305]	2007/2010	Unitisation of hydrocarbon resources
Iceland-Norway[306]	2008/2011	Unitisation of hydrocarbon resources
Iceland-Norway[307]	2008/2008	Clarifications of Participation Rights Participation Rights
Iceland-Norway[308]	2008/2011	Unitisation of hydrocarbon resource
Denmark-United Kingdom[309]	2009/2009	Change previously concluded boundary into that of two EEZs
Norway-United Kingdom[310]	2009/2009	Change previously concluded boundary into that of two EEZs
Trinidad and Tobago-Venezuela[311]	2010/2010	Unitisation of hydrocarbon resources
France-United Kingdom[312]	2011/2014	Change previously concluded boundary into that of two EEZs
Mexico-United States[313]	2012/2014	Unitisation of hydrocarbon resource
Colombia-Ecuador[314]	2012/2012	Land boundary terminus
Denmark (Faroe Islands)-United Kingdom[315]	2012/2014	Supplements to the 1999 Agreement

(continued)

[305] Text in ibid, 4656. Under Art 2.1, '[t]his Treaty establishes the general legal framework under which any hydrocarbon reservoir that extends across the Delimitation line' between the Parties.

[306] The 2008 Agreement establishes comprehensive procedures of energy cooperation concerning transboundary hydrocarbon deposits situated along previously delimited maritime boundaries between Iceland and Norway. Report by Fife, *ibid*, 5130. Text in ibid, 5135.

[307] Text in ibid, 5141.

[308] The 2008 Agreement establishes comprehensive procedures of energy cooperation concerning transboundary hydrocarbon deposits situated along previously delimited maritime boundaries between Iceland and Norway. Report by Fife, ibid, 5130–31. Text in ibid, 5135.

[309] Text in ibid, vol VI, 4491.

[310] For the text of the Exchange of Notes, ibid, 4503.

[311] Text in ibid, vol VII, 4674. Under Art 1(1), '[t]his Agreement establishes legal principles and procedures which shall govern the exploitation and development of the Hydrocarbon Reservoirs within the Unit Area of the Loran-Manatee Field as a single Unit.'

[312] See Report by Whomersley, ibid, 5116. Text in ibid, 5119.

[313] For the text of the Agreement, ibid, 4625. This is an agreement providing for the unitization of hydrocarbon resources that cross a maritime boundary. Report by Sullivan, ibid, 4613.

[314] Text in ibid, 4767.

[315] The 2012 Protocol seeks to facilitate the declarations of EEZs around the United Kingdom and the Faroe Islands. Report by Whomersley, ibid, 5275.

(Continued)

Parties	Signature Entered into force	Purpose
Ireland-United Kingdom[316]	2013/2014	Change previously concluded boundary into that of two EEZs
Netherlands-United Kingdom[317]	2013/2014	Change previously concluded boundary into that of two EEZs
Ireland-United Kingdom[318]	2013/2014	Change previously concluded boundary into that of two EEZs
Belgium-United Kingdom[319]	2013/2016	Change previously concluded boundary into that of two EEZs
Micronesia-Papua New Guinea[320]	2015/–	Amendment of the previous agreement
Total		32

Total of Agreements Relating to Maritime Boundaries (including Joint Development Regime and Special Types of Delimitation Line): 303

[316] Text in ibid, 5163.
[317] For the text of the Exchange of Notes, ibid, 5208.
[318] Text in ibid, 5163.
[319] For the text of the Exchanges of Notes, ibid, 5256. The Exchanges of Notes entered into force on 12 February 2016. See https://assets.publishing.service.gov.uk/government/uploads/system/uploads/attachment_data/file/504731/TS_14.2016_Cm_9224_EoL_Belg_Cont_Shelf_WEB.pdf.
[320] The full title is: Amendment to the Treaty between the Federated States of Micronesia and the Independent State of Papua New Guinea Concerning Maritime Boundaries and Cooperation on Related Matters. The text is available at: www.un.org/Depts/los/LEGISLATIONANDTREATIES/PDFFILES/FSM-PNG.pdf. The original treaty was signed on 29 July 1991. Yet, the status of the original treaty of 1991 seems to remain unknown. In this regard, the study of the US Department of States merely stated that: 'Papua New Guinea has an undelimited boundary with the Federated States of Micronesia.' US Department of States, *Limits in the Seas,* No. 138, 23 May 2014, 6.

Addendums: It is reported that in 2017, Saint Lucia signed maritime delimitation agreements with Barbados and with Saint Vincent and the Grenadines, respectively. See www.stlucianewsonline.com/press-release-saint-lucia-signs-maritime-boundary-delimitation-agreements-with-barbados-and-saint-vincent-and-the-grenadines/; http://thecommonwealth.org/media/news/maritime-treaty-success-barbados-st-lucia-and-st-vincent-and-grenadines. In 2018, Denmark and Poland reached an agreement on maritime boundary in the Baltic Sea. See http://um.dk/en/news/NewsDisplayPage/?newsID=B359C775-6EED-43E1-9AF1-5E2D9300B4CF. At the time of writing, the text of the agreement was unknown.

Selected Bibliography

I. THE CASE LAW

The *Alaska Boundary* Case (1903 U.K/USA), (1966) 15 Reports of International Arbitral Awards (RIAA) 491.

The *Grisbadarna* Case (1909 Norway/Sweden), (1961) 11 RIAA 155.

Norwegian Fisheries case (*The United Kingdom v Norway,* 1951), [1951] ICJ Rep 116.

The *North Sea Continental Shelf* Cases, Judgment, [1969] ICJ Rep 3.

The *Beagle Channel* Case (1977, Argentina/Chili), (1978) 17 ILM, 634–679; (1979) 52 ILR 93.

The *Anglo-French Continental Shelf* Case (1977), 18 RIAA 3.

The *Anglo-French Continental Shelf* Case (1978, interpretation of the decision of 30 June 1977), 18 RIAA 271.

The *Aegean Sea Continental Shelf* Case (Jurisdiction of the Court) *(Greece v Turkey),* [1978] ICJ Rep 3.

The *Tunisia/Libya* Case (Application by Malta for Permission to Intervene) Judgment, [1981] ICJ Rep 3.

The *Tunisia/Libya* Case, Judgment, [1982] ICJ Rep 18.

The *Gulf of Maine* Case, Judgment, [1984] ICJ Rep 246.

The *Libya/Malta Case* (Application by Italy for Permission to Intervene), Judgment, [1984] ICJ Rep 3.

The *Libya/Malta* Case, Judgment, [1985] ICJ Rep 13.

The *Guinea/Guinea-Bissau* Case (1985), (1990) 19 RIAA 149; (1985) 89 RGDIP 484; (1986) 25 ILM 251.

The *Guinea-Bissau v Senegal* Case (1989), (1990) 94 RGDIP 204.

The *St Pierre and Miquelon* Case (France/Canada), (1992), (1997) 21 RIAA 265; (1992) 31 ILM 1145.

The *Land, Island and Maritime Frontier Dispute* Case *(Application by Nicaragua for Permission to Intervene)*, Order, [1990] ICJ Rep 92.

The *Land, Island and Maritime Frontier Dispute* Case *(Application by Nicaragua for Permission to Intervene)*, Judgment, [1992] ICJ Rep 351.

The *Jan Mayen* Case, Judgment, [1993] ICJ Rep 38.

The *Libya/Chad* case, [1994] ICJ Rep 6.

The *Eritrea/Yemen* Case (Second Stage), (2001) 22 RIAA 335; (2001) 40 ILM 983.

The *Land and Maritime Boundary* Case *(Cameroon v Nigeria: Application by Equatorial Guinea for Permission to Intervene)*, ICJ Judgment, [1999] ICJ Rep 1029.

The *Qatar v Bahrain* Case (Merits), [2001] ICJ Rep 40.

The *Cameroon v Nigeria* Case (Merits), [2002] ICJ Rep 303.

The *Barbados v Trinidad and Tobago* Case (2006), (2007) 27 RIAA 147

The *Guyana v Suriname* Case (2007), (2013) 30 RIAA 1.

The *Nicaragua v Honduras* Case, [2007] ICJ Rep 659.

The *Black Sea* Case, [2009] ICJ Rep 61.

The *Bangladesh/Myanmar* Case, [2012] ITLOS Rep 4.

The *Nicaragua v Colombia* Case, [2012] ICJ Rep 624.

The *Chile v Peru* Case, [2014] ICJ Rep 3.

The *Bangladesh v India* Case (2014), available at: https://pca-cpa.org/en/cases/.

The *Croatia/ Slovenia* Case (2017), available at: https://pca-cpa.org/en/cases/.

The *Ghana/Côte d'Ivoire* Case, [2017] ITLOS Rep (not yet reported), available at: www.itlos.org/en/cases/list-of-cases/case-no-23/.

The *Costa Rica v Nicaragua* Case, [2018] ICJ Rep (not yet reported), available at: www.icj-cij.org/en/contentious-cases.

The *Somalia v Kenya* case (Preliminary Objections), [2017] ICJ Rep 3.

II. DOCUMENTS AND COLLECTIONS

A. League of Nations

League of Nations, *Acts of the Conference for the Codification of International Law*, Meetings of the Committees, vol III, Territorial Waters, 1930.

League of Nations Treaty Series, vol 2, 1920–1921.

——, vol 30, 1924–1925.

B. United Nations

i International Law Commission

Discussions and Documents relating to territorial sea and continental shelf delimitations in Yearbook of the International Law Commission (*YILC*) from 1950 to 1956, especially:

Régime of the High Seas: Report by Mr. François (A/CN/.4/17), in 67th-69th Meetings, *YILC* (1950), 216–239.

Régime of the High Seas: Report by Mr. François (A/CN/.4/42), in 114th-131st Meetings, *YILC*, vol I (1951), 274–411.

'Draft Articles on the Continental Shelf and Related Subjects', Report of the International Law Commission to the General Assembly, A/1858, *YILC*, vol II (1951), 141–143.

Régime of the Territorial Sea (A/CN.4/53), in 171st–172nd Meetings, *YILC*, vol I (1952), 180–191.

Document A/CN.4/61/Add. 1. Additif au deuxième rapport de MJPA François, JPA François, *YILC*, vol II (1953) 75–79.

Document A/CN.4/71 and Add. 1–2, Information and Observation Submitted by Governments regarding the Question of the Delimitation of the Territorial Sea of Two Adjacent States, *YILC*, vol II (1953), 79–89.

Régime of the High Seas (A/CN.4/60), 204th-205th Meetings, *YILC*, vol I (1953), 124–136.

Report of the International Law Commission to the General Assembly, A/2456, *YILC*, vol II (1953), 212–217.

Régime of the territorial sea (A/CN.4/53, A/CN.4/61 and Add. 1, A/CN.4/71 and Add. 1 and 2, A/CN.4/77), 261st-262nd Meetings, *YILC*, vol I (1954), 96–107.

Document A/CN.4/77, Régime of the Territorial Sea, Troisième rapport de JPA François, *YILC*, vol II (1954), 1–6.

Report of the International Law Commission to the General Assembly, A/2693, *YILC*, vol II (1954), 153–163.

Report of the International Law Commission to the General Assembly, A/3159, *YILC*, vol II (1956), 265–277 (Territorial Seas); 295–301 (Continental Shelf).

C. UNCLOS I and III

United Nations Conference on the Law of the Sea, *Official Records*, vol III, First Committee: Territorial Sea and Contiguous Zone (Geneva, 1958).

United Nations Conference on the Law of the Sea, *Official Records*, vol VI, Fourth Committee: Continental Shelf, (Geneva, 1958).

UNCLOS III, *Official Records*, vol IX.

D. Institut de Droit International

Règle adoptées par l'Institut de Droit international, à Paris, le 31 mars 1894, sur la définition et le régime de la mer territoriale, (1904) 20 *Annuaire de l'Institut de Droit international* 341–344.

Projet de règlement international de navigation fluviale, Institut de droit international, Wehberg, H., *Tableau général des résolutions (1873–1956)* (Bâle, Editions juridiques et socilogiques S.A., 1957) 70–81.

E. International Law Association

'Rules Relating to Territorial Waters', *Report of the Seventeenth Conference* (Brussels, 1895) 114–116.

'La mer territoriale Proje de Convention internationale (commenté par article)' *Report of the Thirty-First Conference Held at the Palace of Justice* vol 2, (*Buenos* Aires, 1923) 93–106.

'Draft Convention on the Law of Maritime Jurisdiction in Time of Peace' *Report of the 33rd Conference* (Stockholm, 1924) 262–265.

'Amended Draft Convention: Law of Maritime Jurisdiction in Time of Peace' *Report of the 33rd Conference* (Stockholm, 1924) 285–288.

'Rules concerning the Extent of Littoral Waters and Concerning Powers Exercised Therein by the Littoral State' of 1926, adopted by the Japanese Association of International Law and the Japanese branch of the ILA (in Japanese and in English), (1926) 25 *The Journal of International Law and Diplomacy* 608–609; 634–636.

F. Harvard Law School

Draft Convention on Territorial Waters, Drafts of Conventions Prepared in Anticipation of the First Conference on the Codification of International Law, Harvard Law School, *Supplement to* (1929) 23 (Special Number) *AJIL* 243–289.

G. Collections Regarding Agreements on Maritime Delimitation

US Department of State, Office of the Geographer, *Limits in the Seas*, since 1970.

Charney, JI et al (eds), *International Maritime Boundaries*, 7 vols (Dordrecht, Brill/Nijhoff, 1993, 1998, 2002, 2005, 2011, 2016).

United Nations office for Ocean Affairs and the Law of the Sea, *The Law of the Sea: Maritime Boundary Agreements (1942–1969)* (United Nations, New York, 1991).

——, *The Law of the Sea: Maritime Boundary Agreements (1970–1984)* (United Nations, New York, 1987).

——, *The Law of the Sea: Maritime Boundary Agreements (1985–1991)* (United Nations, New York, 1992).

H. Other Collections and Documents

(1841–1842) 30 *British and Foreign State Papers*

(1845–1846) 34 *British and Foreign State Papers*

(1869) 54 *British and Foreign State Papers*

(1892–1893) 85 *British and Foreign State Papers*

(1937) 135 *British and Foreign State Papers*
De Cesari, P, Migliorino, L, Scovazzi, T, Tavazzani, N, Treves, T, Trombetta-Panigadi, F (eds), *Index of Multilateral Treaties on the Law of the Sea* (Milan, Giuffrè, 1985).
De Martens, GF, *Nouveau Recueil Général de Traités*, 2ème série, vol 4 (1879).
——, vol 32 (1905).
Moore, JB, *A Digest of International Law*, vol I (Washington, Government Printing Office, 1906).
Research Centre for International Law, University of Cambridge, *International Boundary Cases: The Continental Shelf*, 2 vols (Cambridge, Grotius Publications Limited, 1992).
Rosenne, S (ed), *League of Nations Committee of Experts for the Progressive Codification of International Law 1925–1928*, vol II (New York, Oceana Publications, 1972).
United Nations Office for Ocean Affairs and the Law of the Sea, *National Legislation on the Continental Shelf* (New York, United Nations, 1989).
——, *National Legislation on the Exclusive Economic Zone* (New York, United Nations, 1993).
——, *Current Developments in States Practice*, vols I–IV (New York United Nations, 1987, 1989, 1992, 1995).
Whiteman, MM, *Digest of International Law*, vol 4 (Washington, Department of State Publication, 1965).

III. MONOGRAPHS AND ARTICLES

Acikgonul, YE, 'Equitable Delimitation of Maritime Boundaries: The Uncontested Supremacy of Coastal Geography in Case Law' (2017) 31 *Ocean Yearbook* 173–96.
Adede, AO, 'Toward the Formulation of Delimitation of Sea Boundaries between States with Adjacent or Opposite Coasts' (1979) 19 *Virginia Journal of International Law* 207–55.
——, *The System for Settlement of Disputes under the United Nations Convention on the Law of the Sea* (Dordrecht, Nijhoff, 1987).
Ahnish, FA, *The International Law of Maritime Boundaries and the Practice of States in the Mediterranean Sea* (Oxford, Clarendon Press, 1993).
Akehurst, M, 'Equity and General Principles of Law' (1976) 25 *ICLQ* 801–25.
Al-Enazy, AH, 'The International Boundary Treaty (Treaty of Jeddah) Concluded Between the Kingdom of Saudi Arabia and the Yemeni Republic on June 12, 2000' (2002) 96 *AJIL* 161–73.
Alexander, LM, 'Baseline Delimitation and Maritime Boundaries' (1982–83) 23 *Virginia Journal of International Law* 503–36.
——, 'The Delimitation of Maritime Boundaries' (1986) 5 *Political Geography Quarterly* 19–24.
——, 'Delimiting Continental Shelf Boundaries' in T Grigalunas and LC Hanson (eds), *Continental Shelf, Resources, Boundaries, and Management* (Kingston, RI, University of Rhode Island, 1986) 43–48.
Alexiades, P, 'The Search for a Panacea for Maritime Boundary Settlement: Equity or Equidistance?' (1985) 14 *Thesaurus Acroasium* 811–28.
Allot, P, 'Power Sharing in the Law of the Sea' (1983) 77 *AJIL* 1–30.
Amin, SH, 'Law of the Continental Shelf Delimitation: the Gulf Example' (1980) 27 *NILR* 335–46.
——, 'Customary Rules of Delimitation of the Continental Shelf: the Gulf Practice' (1980) 11 *Journal of Maritime Law and Commerce* 509–26.
Anderson, DH, 'Maritime Delimitation: A View of British Practice' (1988) 12 *Marine Policy* 231–40.
——, 'Developments in Maritime Boundary Law and Practice' in DA Colson and RW Smith (eds), *International Maritime Boundaries*, vol V (Leiden Brill/Nijhoff, 2005) 3197–3222.
——, 'Delimitation of the Maritime Boundary in the Bay of Bengal (Bangladesh/Myanmar. Case No. 16' (2012) 106 *AJIL* 817–24.
Antinori, CM, 'The Bering Sea: A Maritime Delimitation Dispute between the United States and the Soviet Union' (1987) 18 *ODIL* 1–47.

Antonio Pastor Palomar, 'La qualification juridique des formations maritimes dans l'arrêt du 16 mars 2001 (Affaire Qatar/Bahreïn)' (2002) 106 *RGDIP* 329–56.

Apollis, G, *Les frontières maritimes en droit international: mutations et perspectives* (Montpellier, Faculté de droit et des sciences *économiques*, 1979).

——, *L'emprise maritime de l'Etat côtier* (Paris, Pedone, 1981).

Árnadóttir, S, 'Termination of Maritime Boundaries due to a Fundamental Change of Circumstances' (2016) 32 *Utrecht Journal of International and European Law* 94–111.

Ascensio, H, 'Chronique du plateau continental et des délimitations' (1999–2000) 13 *Collection Espaces et resources maritimes* 117–26.

Ascensio, H and Bonucci, N, 'Chronique du plateau continental et des délimitations' (1995) 9 *Collection espaces et resources maritimes* 82–91.

Attard, D, *The Exclusive Economic Zone in International Law* (Oxford, Clarendon Press, 1987).

Auburn, FM, 'The North Sea Continental Shelf Boundary Settlement' (1974/1975) 16 *Archiv des Völkerrechts* 28–36.

Bardonnet, D, 'Equité et frontières terrestres' in *Le droit international: unité et diversité, Mélanges offerts à Paul Reuter* (Paris, Pedone, 1981) 35–74.

——, 'Frontières terrestres et frontières maritimes' (1989) 35 *AFDI* 1–64.

Barvender-Coyle, P, 'The Emerging Legal Principles and Equitable Criteria Governing the Delimitation of Maritime Boundaries between States' (1988) 19 *ODIL* 171–227.

Baldet-Ladan, G, 'Le traité concernant la délimitation du plateau continental conclu entre les Etats-Unis et le Mexique le 9 juin 2000' (2000) 5 *Annuaire du droit de la mer* 45–54.

Basset, PG, 'Australia's maritime boundaries' (1984) 55 *Australian Foreign Affairs Record* 186–91.

Beauchamp, KP, 'The Management Function of Ocean Boundaries' (1986) 23 *San Diego Law Review* 611–60.

Beazley, PB, 'Maritime Boundaries: A Geographical and Technical Perspective' in ED Brown and RR Churchill (eds), *The UN Convention on the Law of the Sea: Impact and Implementation, Proceedings of the 19th Annual Conference of the Law of the Sea Institute* (Honolulu, University of Hawaii, 1987) 319–39.

——, *Maritime Limits and Baselines: A Guide to their Delimitation*, 2nd edn (London, The Hydrographic Society, 1978).

——, 'Developments in Maritime Delimitation' (1986) 39 *Hydrographic Journal* 5–9.

——, 'Maritime Boundaries: A Geographical and Technical Perspective' in ED Brown and RR Churchill (eds), *The UN Convention on the Law of the Sea: Impact and Implementation* (Honolulu, University of Hawaii, 1987) 319–39.

——, 'Technical Considerations in Maritime Boundary Delimitations' in IJ Charney and LM Alexander, *International Maritime Boundaries*, vol I (Dordrecht, Nijhoff, 1993) 243–62.

Becker-Weinberg, V, *Joint Development of Hydrocarbon Deposits in the Law of the Sea* (Heidelberg, Springer, 2014).

Bedjaoui, M, 'L'«énigme» des «principes équitables» dans le droit des délimitations maritimes' (1990) 42 *Revista Española de Derecho Internacional* 367–88.

Ben Achour, Y, 'L'affaire du plateau continental tunisio-libyen (analyse empirique)' (1983) 110 *Journal du droit international* 247–92.

Blake, GJ (ed), *Maritime Boundaries and Ocean Resources* (London and Sydney, Croom Helm, 1987).

—— (ed), *Maritime Boundaries. World Boundaries Series*, vol 5 (London, New York, Routledge, 1994).

Blake, GH et al (eds), *The Peaceful Management of Transboundary Resources* (Dordrecht, Nijhoff, 1995).

Blake, GH, Pratt, MA and Schofield, CH (eds), *Boundaries and Energy: Problems and Prospect* (Kluwer Law International, 1998).

Blecher, MD, 'Equitable Delimitation of the Continental Shelf' (1979) 73 *AJIL* 60–88.

Blum, YZ, 'Historic Rights' in R Bernhardt (ed), *Encyclopaedia of Public International Law*, vol 2, (Amsterdam, Elsevier, 1995) 710–15.

Bluntschli, J, *Le droit international codifié*, traduit par MC Lardy (Paris, Librairie Guillaumin, 1881).

Boggs, SW, 'Delimitation of the Territorial Sea' (1930) 24 *AJIL* 541–55.

——, 'Problems of Water-Boundary Definition: Median Lines and International Boundaries Through Territorial Waters,' (1937) 27 *The Geographical Review* 445–56. (The article was reproduced in the next book written by the same author: *International Boundaries. A Study of Boundary Functions and Problems* (New York, Columbia University Press, 1949)) 176–92.

——, 'Delimitation of Seaward Areas under National Jurisdiction' (1951) 45 *AJIL* 240–66.

Bonafé, BI, 'Maritime Delimitation in the Indian Ocean' (2017) 111 *AJIL* 725–31.

Bonfils, H, *Manuel de droit international public (droit des gens)*, 4e éd (Paris, Librairie nouvelle de droit et de jurisprudence, 1905).

Bouchez, LJ, 'The North Sea Continental Shelf Cases' (1969) *JMLC* 113–21.

——, 'Some Reflections on the 1982 Convention on the Law of the Sea and the Delimitation of the Continental Shelf and Exclusive Economic Zone' in E Hey and AW Koers (eds), *The International Law of the Sea: Issues of Implementation in Indonesia* (Rijswijk, Netherlands Institute of Transport, 1984) 37–49.

Bowett, DW, 'The Arbitration between the United Kingdom and France concerning the Continental Shelf Boundary in the English Channel and South-Western Approaches' (1978) 49 *BYIL* 1–29.

——, *The Legal Regime of Islands in International Law* (Dobbs Ferry, NY; Alphen aan den Rijn, 1979).

——, 'The Economic Factor in Maritime Delimitation Cases' in *International Law at the Time of Its Codification, Essays in Honour of Roberto Ago*, vol II (Milan, Giuffrè, 1987) 45–63.

——, 'The Canada-France Arbitration Concerning the Delimitation of the Maritime Areas of St Pierre et Miquelon' in *Hacia un naevo orden international y europeo, Mélanges M. Diéz de Velasco* (Madrid, 1993) 123–36.

——, 'Islands' in R Bernhardt (ed), *Encyclopaedia of Public International Law*, vol 2, (Amsterdam, Elsevier, 1995) 1455–58.

Briscoe, J, 'Islands in Maritime Boundary Delimitation' (1989) 7 *Ocean Yearbook* 14–41.

——, 'The Use of Islands in International Maritime Boundary Delimitation' in G Dorinda, Dalmeyer and Louis de Vorsey (eds), *Rights to Oceanic Resources: Deciding and Drawing Maritime Boundaries* (Dordrecht, 1989) 115–48.

British Institute of International and Comparative Law, *Report on the Obligations of States under Articles 73(3) and 83(3) of UNCLOS in respect of Undelimited Maritime Areas* (London, British Institute of International and Comparative Law, 2016).

Brown, ED, *The Legal Regime of Hydrospace* (London, Stevens Sons, 1971).

——, 'The Continental Shelf and the Exclusive Economic Zone: The Problem of Delimitation at UNCLOS III' (1977) 4 *Maritime Policy and Management* 377–408.

——, 'Rockall and the Limits of National Jurisdiction of the UK: Part 1' (1978) 2 *Marine Policy* 181–211.

——, 'Rockall and the Limits of National Jurisdiction of the UK: Part 2' (1978) 2 *Marine Policy* 275–303.

——, 'The Anglo-French Continental Shelf Case' (1979) 16 *San Diego Law Review* 461–530.

——, 'Delimitation of Offshore Areas: Hard Labour and Bitter Fruits at UNCLOS III' (1981) 5 *Marine Policy* 172–84.

——, 'The Tunisia-Libya Continental Shelf Case' (1983) 7 *Marine Policy* 142–62.

——, *The International Law of the Sea*, 2 vols (Aldershot, Dartmouth, 1994).

Brownlie, I, 'Legal Status of Natural Resources in International Law (Some Aspects)' (1979) 162 *RCADI* 289–93.

——, 'The Sources of the Law Governing Maritime Delimitation', in *International Law in an Evolving World, Liber Amicorum in Tribute to Professor Eduardo Jiménez de Aréchaga* (Montevideo, Fundacion de Cultura Universitaria, 1994) 733–44.

Burke, N, 'Nicaragua v Colombia at the ICJ: Better the Devil You Don't?' (2013) 2 *Cambridge Journal of International and Comparative Law* 314–26.

Burmester, H, 'The Torres Strait Treaty: Ocean Boundary Delimitation by Agreement' (1982) 76 *AJIL* 321–49.

Burney, US, 'International Court of Justice Defines Maritime Boundary Between Peru and Chile' (2014) 18 *ASIL Insights*, available at: www.asil.org/insights/year/2014.

Busch, SV, *Establishing Continental Shelf Limits Beyond 200 Nautical Miles by the Coastal State: A Right of Involvement for Other States?* (Leiden, Brill/Nijhoff, 2016).

Caflisch, L, 'Les zones maritimes sous juridiction nationale, leurs limites et leur délimitation' (1980) 84 *RGDIP* 68–119.

——, 'La délimitation des espaces marins entre Etats dont les côtes se font face ou sont adjacentes' in R-J Dupuy and D Vignes (eds), *Traité du nouveau droit de la mer* (Paris, Economica, 1985) 374–440.

——, 'Maritime Boundaries, Delimitation', in *Encyclopaedia of Public International Law*, vol 11 (Amsterdam, Elsevier, 1989) 212–19.

——, 'Règles générales du droit des cours d'eau internationaux' (1989) 219 *RCADI* 13–225 (in particular, 62–103).

——, 'Essai d'une typologie des frontières' (1990) 63 *Relation internationales* 265–93.

——, 'The Delimitation of Maritime Spaces between States with Opposite or Adjacent Coast' in R-J Dupuy and D Vignes (eds), *A Handbook on the New Law of the Sea* (Dordrecht, Nijhoff, 1991) 425–99.

Cahier, P, 'Les sources du droit relatif à la délimitation du plateau continental' in *Le droit international au service de la paix, de la justice et du développement, Mélanges Michel Virally* (Paris, Pedone, 1991) 175–82.

Carleton, CM, 'The Evolution of the Maritime Boundary – The UK Experience in the Southern North Sea and Channel' (1992) 7 *IJMCL* 99–122.

——, 'The Maritime Boundary Agreements Between the United Kingdom and the United States' (1994) 9 *IJMCL* 253–60.

Castellano, L, 'La ligne maritime unique' in *Mémoire de D.E.S.* (IUHEI, 1995) 1–68.

Cazala, J, 'Retour sur le méthodes de délimitation juridictionnelle d'espaces maritimes mises en œuvre dans quelques affaires récentes' (2008) 54 *AFDI* 411–27.

Cenaj, K, 'Albania-Greece Agreement on Setting Maritime Boundaries, According to International Law' (2015) 4 *Academic Journal of Interdisciplinary Studies* 143–48.

Chai, JKT, 'The Problem of Continental Shelf Delimitation in Relation to Small Islands' (1978) 15 *The Annals of the Chinese Society of International Law* 20–44.

Charney, JI, 'The Delimitation of Lateral Seaward Boundaries in a Domestic Context' (1981) 75 *AJIL* 28–68.

——, 'Ocean Boundaries between Nations: A Theory for Progress' (1984) 78 *AJIL* 582–606.

——, 'The Delimitation of Ocean Boundaries' (1987) 18 *ODIL* 497–531.

——, 'Progress in International Maritime Delimitation Law' (1994) 88 *AJIL* 227–56.

——, 'Central East Asian Maritime Boundaries and the Law of the Sea' (1995) 89 *AJIL* 724–49.

——, 'International Maritime Boundaries for the Continental Shelf: The Relevance of Natural Prolongation' in N Ando et al (eds), *Liber Amicorum Judge Shigeru Oda* (The Hague, Kluwer, 2002) 1011–29.

Chaturvedi, SC, 'The North Sea Continental Shelf Cases Analysed' (1973) 13 *Indian Journal of International Law* 481–93.

Chemillier-Gendreau, M, 'La signification des principes équitables dans le droit international contemporain' (1981–1982) 16 *Revue belge de droit international* 509–35.

Chinkin, CM, *Third Parties in International Law* (Oxford, Clarendon Press, 1993).

——, 'Third-Party Intervention before the International Court of Justice' (1986) 80 *AJIL* 495–531.

Chiu, H, 'The Problem of Delimitating the Maritime Boundary between the Exclusive Economic Zone and the Continental Shelf of Opposite States' in *Essays in Honour of Wang Tieya* (The Hague, Nijhoff, 1993) 181–90.

Christie, DR, 'From the Shoals of Ras Kaboudia to the Shores of Tripoli: The Tunisia/Libya Continental Shelf Boundary Delimitation' (1983) 13 *Georgia Journal of International and Comparative Law* 1–30.

Chu, H, 'Some Problems Concerning the Application of the Delimitation of Maritime Boundaries Provisions of the 1982 United Nations Convention on the Law of the Sea' (1984) 4 *Chinese Yearbook of International Law* 66–86.

——, 'Some Problems concerning the Application of the Delimitation of Maritime Boundary Provisions in the 1982 United Nations Convention on the Law of the Sea between Adjacent and Opposite States' (1985) 9 *Maryland Journal of International Law and Trade* 1–17.

Chuanxiang Sun, 'Comments on the Tree-stage Approach of Maritime Delimitation' in MH Nordquist, JN Moore, and R Long (eds), *Challenges of the Changing Arctic; Continental Shelf, Navigation, and Fisheries* (Leiden, Brill/Nijhoff, 2014) 613–36.

Churchill, RR, 'Maritime Delimitation in the Jan Mayen Area' (1985) 9 *Marine Policy* 16–38.

——, 'Fisheries Issues in Maritime Boundary Delimitation' (1993) 17 *Marine Policy* 44–57.

——, 'The Greenland-Jan Mayen Case and Its Significance for the International law of Maritime Delimitation' (1994) 9 *IJMCL* 1–29.

——, 'The Role of the International Court of Justice in Maritime Boundary' in Alex G Oude Elferink and DR Rothwell (eds), *Oceans Management in the 21st Century: Institutional Frameworks and Responses* (Leiden, Nijhoff, 2004) 125–42.

——, 'Dispute Settlement under the UN Convention on the Law of the Sea: Survey for 2007' (2008) 23 *IJMCL* 601–42.

——, 'The *Bangladesh/Myanmar* Case: Continuity and Novelty in the Law of Maritime Boundary Delimitation' (2012) 1 *Cambridge Journal of International and Comparative law* 137–52.

Churchill, RR and Lowe, AV, *The Law of the Sea*, 3rd edn (Manchester, Manchester University Press, 1999).

Ciciriello, MC, 'The Effect of Islands on the Delimitation of Marine Areas' in B Vukas (ed), *Essays on the New Law of the Sea*, vol 2 (Zagreb, Sveucilisna naklada Liber, 1990) 7–38.

Clain, LE, 'Gulf of Maine: A Disappointing First in the Delimitation of a Single Maritime Boundary' (1985) 25 *Virginia Journal of International Law* 521–620.

Colliard, CA, 'Principes et règles de droit international applicables en matière de délimitation maritime. Analyse de la "jurisprudence" de la Cour internationale de Justice' in *International Law at the Time of Its Codification, Essays in Honour of Roberto Ago*, vol II (Milan, Giuffrè, 1987) 87–105.

Collier, JG, 'Intervention in the International Court: A Slight Breakthrough' (1991) 50 *Cambridge Law Journal* 216–18.

Collins, EJ and Rogoff, M, 'The International Law of Maritime Boundary Delimitation' (1982) 34 *Maine Law Review* 1–62.

Colson, DA, 'The United Kingdom–France Continental Shelf Arbitration' (1978) 72 *AJIL* 95–112.

——, 'Environmental Factors: Are they Relevant to Delimitation?' in ED Brown and RR Churchill (eds), *The UN Convention on the Law of the Sea: Impact and Implementation, Proceedings of the 19th Annual Conference of the Law of the Sea Institute* (Honolulu, 1987, Law of the Sea Institute) 218–24.

——, 'The Delimitation of the Outer Continental Shelf Between Neighboring States' (2003) 97 *AJIL* 91–107.

Combacau, J, *Le droit international de la mer* (Paris, PUF, 1985).

Conforti, B, 'L'arrêt de la Cour internationale de Justice dans l'affaire de la délimitation du plateau continental entre la Libye et Malte' (1986) 90 *RGDIP* 313–43.

——, 'La délimitation et les méthodes pratiques: équité, délimitation et critères de délimitation' in D Pharand and V Leanza *Le plateau continental et la zone économique exclusive* (Dordrecht, Nijhoff, 1993) 55–56.

Cooper, J, 'Delimitation of the Maritime Boundary in the Gulf of Maine Area' (1986) 16 *ODIL* 59–90.

Costi, A, 'L'arrêt de la Cour internationale de Justice dans l'affaire du golfe du Maine (Canada c. Etats-Unis d'Amérique)' (1985) 2 *Revue québécoise de droit international* 323–70.

Cottier, T, *Equitable Principles of Maritime Delimitation: The Quest for Distributive Justice in International Law* (Cambridge University Press, 2015).

Currie, J 'Maritime Boundary Delimitation in a Federal Domestic Setting: The Newfoundland and Labrador v Nova Scotia Arbitration' (2007) 17 *LJIL* 155–70.

Curtis, L, 'The Gulf of Maine Case: Major Implications for Maritime Boundary Delimitation' (1985) 14 *Thesaurus Acroasium* 829–42.

Dallmeyer, DG and Devorsey, L (eds), *Right to Oceanic Resources: Deciding and Drawing Maritime Boundaries* (Dordrecht, Nijhoff, 1989).

Danelius, H, 'The Law of the Sea: A Swedish Point of View' (1980) 36 *Revue égiptienne de droit international* 35–49.

David, E, 'La sentence arbitrale du 14 février 1985 sur la délimitation de la frontière maritime Guinée-Guinée Bissau' (1985) 31 *AFDI* 350–89.

Decaux, E, 'L'arrêt de la Cour internationale de Justice dans l'affaire du plateau continental (Tunisie/Libye): arrêt du 24 février 1982' (1982) 28 *AFDI* 357–91.

——, 'L'arrêt de la Cour internationale de Justice à fin d'intervention dans l'affaire du plateau continental entre la Libye et Malte, arrêt du 21 mars 1984' (1984) 30 *AFDI* 282–303.

——, 'L'arrêt de la Chambre de la Cour internationale de Justice sur l'affaire de la délimitation de la frontière maritime dans le golfe du Maine (Canada/Etats-Unis): arrêt du 12 octobre 1984' (1984) 30 *AFDI* 304–39.

——, 'L'arrêt de la Cour internationale de Justice sur la demande en révision et interprétation de l'arrêt du 24 février 1982 en l'affaire du plateau continental (Tunisie/Libye): arrêt du 10 décembre 1985' (1985) 31 *AFDI* 324–49.

——, 'L'arrêt de la Cour internationale de Justice dans l'affaire du plateau continental (Libye/Malte), arrêt du 3 juin 1985' (1985) 31 *AFDI* 294–323.

——, 'L'intervention' in *La juridiction internationale permanente*, Société française pour le droit international, Colloque de Lyon (Paris, Pedone, 1987) 219–55.

——, 'L'accord anglo-irlandais de delimitation du plateau continental' (1990) 36 *AFDI* 757–76.

——, 'L'affaire de la délimitation maritime dans la région située entre le Groenland et Jan Mayen (Danemark c. Norvège) Arrêt de la C.I.J. du 14 juin 1993' (1993) 39 *AFDI* 495–513.

——, 'Chronique du plateau continental et des délimitations' (1991) 5 *Collection espaces et resources maritimes* 75–87.

——, 'Chronique du plateau continental et des délimitations' (1992) 6 *Collection espaces et resources maritimes* 113–22.

——, 'Chronique du plateau continental et des délimitations', (1993) 7 *Collection espaces et ressources maritimes* 102–10.

——, 'Affaire de la délimitation maritime et des questions territoriales entre Qatar et Bahreïn, fond, arrêt du 16 mars 2001 (Qatar c Bahreïn)' (2001) 47 *AFDI* 177–240.

Degan, V-D, 'Equitable Principle in Maritime Delimitations' in *International Law at the Time of Its Codification, Essays in Honour of Roberto Ago*, vol II (Milan, Giuffrè, 1987) 107–37.

——, 'La raison, l'équité et le droit dans les délimitations maritimes' (1999–2000) 13 *Collection espaces et resources maritimes* 101–16.

De Hoogh, AJ, 'Intervention under Article 62 of the Statute and the Quest for Incidental Jurisdiction without the Consent of the Principal Parties' (1993) 6 *LJIL* 17–46.

Delabie, ML, 'Le fragile équilibre entre prévisibilité juridique et opportunité judiciaire en matière de délimitation maritime: l'arrêt de la Court internationale de Justice du 19 november 2012 dans l'affaire du *Différend territorial et maritime (Nicaragua c Colombie)*' (2012) 58 *AFDI* 223–52.

De La Fayette, L, 'The Award in the Canada-France Maritime Boundary Arbitration' (1993) 8 *IJMCL* 77–103.

Delbrück, J, 'Proportionality' in R Bernhardt (ed), *Encyclopaedia of Public International Law*, vol 3, (Amsterdam, Elsevier, 1997) 1140–44.

Delin, L, 'Shall Islands Be Taken into Account when Drawing the Median Line According to Art. 6 of the Convention on the Continental Shelf?' (1971) 41 *Nordisk tidsskrift for international ret* 205–19.

De Martens, F, *Traité de droit international public* (Paris, A Marescq Aine, 1883).

Despagnet, F, *Cours de droit international public* (Paris, Librarie de la société du Recueil général des lois et des arrêts, 1903).

Despeux, G, *Droit de la délimitation maritime: Commentaire de quelques décisions plutoniennes*, (Frankfurt am Main, Peter Lang, Schriften zum internationalen und zum öffentlichen recht, Band 40, 2000).

De Visscher, Ch, *De l'équité dans le réglement arbitral ou judiciaire des litiges de droit international public* (Paris, Pedone, 1972).

De Vorsey, L and De Vorsey, MC, 'The World Court Decision in the Canada-United States Gulf of Maine Seaward Boundary Dispute: A Perspective from Historical Geography' (1986) 18 *Case Western Reserve Journal of International Law* 415–42.

Diplia, H, *Le régime juridique des îles dans le droit international de la mer* (Paris, PUF, 1984).

——, 'Les règles de droit international en matière de délimitation fluviales: remise en question?' (1985) 89 *RGDIP* 589–624.

——, 'L'arrêt de la Cour internationale du Justice en l'affaire de la délimitation maritime dans la région située entre le Groenland et Jan Mayen' (1994) 98 *RGDIP* 899–930.

Distefano, G, 'La sentence arbitrale du 17 décembre 1999 sur la délimitation des frontières maritimes entre l'Erythrée et le Yémen: Quelques observations complémentaires' (2000) 46 *AFDI* 255–84.

——, 'L'arrêt de la C.I.J. du 16 mars 2001 dans l'affaire de la délimitation entre Qatar et Bahreïn' (2001) 34 *Revue belge de droit international* 357–410.

Dobelle, J-F, 'Le différend entre l'Erythrée et le Yémen: la sentence arbitrale du 17 décembre 1999 sur la délimitation des frontières maritimes' (1999) 45 *AFDI* 554–63.

——, 'Les accords franco-britaniques relatifs à la baie de Granville du 4 juillet 2000' (2000) 5 *Annuaire du droit de la mer* 9–33.

Doussis, E, 'Intérêt juridique et intervention devant la Court internationale de Justice' (2001) *RGDIP* 55–91.

Dundas, CW, 'Current Legal Developments: Dominica; Maritime Boundary Delimitation Agreement with France' (1989) 4 *IJECL* 288–93.

Dupont, P-E and Solomou, A, 'Provisional Measures in Maritime Delimitation Cases' in J Crawford, A Koroma, S Mahmoudi and A Pellet (eds), *The International Legal Order: Current Needs and Possible Responses* (Leiden, Brill/Nijhoff, 2017) 312–33.

Dupuy, R-J and Vignes, D, *A Handbook on the New Law of the Sea* (Dordrecht, Nijhoff, 2 vols, 1991).

Dzurek, DJ, 'Deciphering the North Korean-Soviet (Russian) Maritime Boundary Agreements' (1992) 23 *ODIL* 31–54.

——, 'Maritime Agreements and Oil Exploration in the Gulf of Thailand' in GH Blake, MA Pratt, and CH Schofield (eds), *Boundaries and Energy: Problems and Prospects* (The Hague, Kluwer Law International, 1998) 117–35.

——, 'Southeast Asian Offshore Oil Disputes' (1994) 11 *Ocean Yearbook* 157–78.

El-Hakim, A, *The Middle Eastern States and the Law of the Sea* (Manchester, Manchester University Press, 1979).

Elias, TO, 'The Limits of the Right of Intervention in a Case before the International Court of Justice' in *Völkerrecht als Rechtsordnung, Internationale Gerichtsbarkeit Menschenrechte, Festschrift für Hermann Mosler* (Berlin, Springer, 1983) 159–72.

Ely, N, 'Seabed Boundaries between Coastal States: The Effect to Be Given Islets as 'Special Circumstances'' (1972) 6 *International Lawyer* 219–36.

Ely, N and Pietrowski, RF, 'Boundaries of Seabed Jurisdiction Off the Pacific Coast of Asia' (1975) 8 *Natural Resources Lawyer* 611–29.

Emanuelli, C, 'La délimitation des espaces maritimes entre le Canada et les Etats-Unis dans le golfe du Maine' (1982–1983) 28 *McGill Law Journal* 335–77.

Eustache, F, 'L'affaire du plateau continental de la mer du Nord devant la Cour internationale de Justice (arrêt du 20 février 1969)' (1970) 74 *RGDIP* 590–639.

Eustis, FA III, 'Method and Basis of Seaward Delimitation of Continental Shelf Jurisdiction' (1976) 17 *Virginia Journal of International Law* 107–30.

Evans, MD, *Relevant Circumstances and Maritime Delimitation* (Oxford, Clarendon Press, 1987).
——, 'Maritime Delimitation and Expanding Categories of Relevant Circumstances' (1991) 40 *ICLQ* 1–33.
——, 'Case Concerning the Land, Island and Maritime Frontier Dispute (El Salvador/Honduras): Nicaraguan Intervention' (1992) 41 *ICLQ* 896–906.
——, 'Delimitation and the Common Maritime Boundary' (1993) 64 *BYIL* 283–332.
——, 'Case Concerning Maritime Delimitation in the Area between Greenland and Jan Mayen (Denmark v Norway)' (1994) 43 *ICLQ* 697–704.
——, 'Less than an Ocean Apart: The St. Pierre and Miquelon and Jan Mayen Islands and the Delimitation of Maritime Zones' (1994) 43 *ICLQ* 678–96.
——, 'Maritime Delimitation after Denmark v Norway: Back to the Future?' in GS Goodwin-Gill and S Talmon (eds), *The Reality of International Law, Essays in Honour of Ian Brownlie* (Oxford, Clarendon Press, 1999) 153–76.
——, 'The Maritime Delimitation Between Eritrea and Yemen' (2001) 14 *LJIL* 141–70.
——, 'Case Concerning Maritime Delimitation and Territorial Questions Between Qatar and Bahrain (Qatar v Bahrain)' (2002) 51 *ICLQ* 709–18.
——, 'Maritime Boundary Delimitation' in D Rothwell, Alex G Oude Elferink, K Scott and T Stephens (eds), *Oxford Handbook on the Law of the Sea* (Oxford University Press, 2015) 254–79.
——, 'Maritime Boundary Delimitation: Whatever Next' in J Barrett and R Barnes (eds), *Law of the Sea: UNCLOS as a Living Treaty* (London, British Institute of International and Comparative Law, 2016) 41–79.
Evensen, J, 'La délimitation entre la Norvège et l'Islande du plateau continental dans le secteur de Jan Mayen' (1981) 27 *AFDI* 711–38.
——, 'The Delimitation of Exclusive Economic Zones and Continental Shelves as Highlighted by the I.C.J.' in L Rozakis and CA Stephanou (eds), *The New Law of the Sea* (Athens and Amsterdam, North-Holland, 1983) 107–54.
Fattal, A, *Les conférences des Nations Unies et la Convention de Genève du 29 avril 1958 sur la mer territoriale et la zone contiguë* (Beyrouth, Librairie du Liban, 1968).
Feldman, MB, 'The Tunisia-Libya Continental Shelf Case: Geographic Justice or Judicial Compromise?' (1983) 77 *AJIL* 219–38.
Feldman, MB and Colson, D, 'The Maritime Boundaries of the United States' (1981) 75 *AJIL* 729–63.
Feulner, GR, 'Delimitation of Continental Shelf Jurisdiction Between States: The Effect of Physical Irregularities in the Natural Continental Shelf' (1976) 17 *Virginia Journal of International Law* 77–105.
Fiedmann, W, 'The North Sea Continental Shelf Cases-A Critique' (1970) 64 *AJIL* 229–40.
Fietta, S, 'Guyana/Suriname: Award: UN Convention on the Law of the Sea Annex VII Arbitral Tribunal, September 17, 2007' (2008) 101 *AJIL* 119–28.
Fietta, S and Cleverly, R, *A Practitioner's Guide to Maritime Boundary Delimitation* (Oxford University Press, 2016).
Fitzmaurice, G, *The Law and Procedure of the International Court of Justice* (Cambridge, Grotius Publications Limited, vol II, 1986).
Fodchenko, I, 'Legal Aspects of the Russian-Norwegian Model for Cross-Border Unitization in the Barents Sea and Arctic Ocean' (2018) 49 *ODIL* 262–75.
Foighel, I, 'The North Sea Continental Shelf Case' (1969) 39 *Nordisk Tidsskrift for International Ret* 109–27.
Francalanci, G, 'La ligne d'équidistance' in D Pharand and V Leanza, *Le plateau continental et la zone économique exclusive* (Dordrecht, Nijhoff, 1993) 57–62.
Francalanci, G, Romano, D and Scovazzi, T (eds), *Atlas of the Straight Baselines* (Milan, Giuffrè, 1986).
Francis, A, 'Treaty between the Republic of Trinidad and Tobago and the Republic of Venezuela on the Delimitation of the Marine and Submarine Areas: An Analysis' (1991) 6 *IJMCL* 169–98.

Frank, T, 'Fairness in the International Legal and Institutional System: General Course on Public International Law' (1993) 240 *RCADI* 9–498 (in particular, 62–97).

Franckx, E, 'The 1989 Maritime Boundary Delimitation Agreement Between the GDR and Poland' (1989) 4 *IJECL* 237–51.

——, 'First Trijunction Point Agreed upon in the Baltic Between Poland, Sweden and U.S.S.R' (1990) 5 *IJECL* 394–97.

——, 'European Community (EC) Maritime Zones: The Delimitation Aspect' (1992) 23 *ODIL* 239–58.

——, 'Maritime Boundary Agreements: The Case of Belgium' (1992) 25 *RBDI* 390–447.

——, 'Frontières maritimes dans la mer Baltique: passé, present et future' (1995) 9 *Collection espaces et resources maritimes* 92–115.

——, 'Finland and Sweden Complete Their Maritime Boundary in the Baltic Sea' (1996) 27 *ODIL* 291–314.

——, 'Current Legal Developments: Finland-Sweden Delimitation Agreement' (1996) 11 *IJMCL* 394–400.

——, 'Current Legal Developments: Two New Maritime Boundary Delimitation Agreements in the Eastern Baltic Sea' (1997) 12 *IJMCL* 365–76.

——, 'Two More Maritime Boundary Agreements Concluded in the Eastern Baltic Sea in 1997' (1998) 13 *IJMCL* 274–83.

——, '"New" Soviet Delimitation Agreements with its Neighbors in the Baltic Sea' (1998) 19 *ODIL* 143–58.

——, 'Maritime Boundaries in the Baltic Sea' in GH Blake, MA Pratt and CH Schofield (eds), *Boundaries and Energy: Problems and Prospects* (The Hague, Kluwer Law International, 1998) 275–95.

——, 'Current Legal Developments: Delimitation of Maritime Zones between Estonia and Sweden' (1999) 14 *IJMCL* 299–308.

——, 'The 1998 Estonia-Sweden Maritime Boundary Agreement: Lessons to be Learned in the Area of Continuity and/or Succession of States' (2000) 31 *ODIL* 269–84.

——, 'New Maritime Boundaries Concluded in the Eastern Baltic Sea Since 1998 (*bis*)' (2002) 17 *IJMCL* 263–66.

——, Maritime Delimitation in the Baltic Sea: What Has Already Been Accomplished?' (2012) 6 *International Journal on Marine Navigation and Safety of Sea Transportation* 437–42.

Gao, J, 'A Note on the Nicaragua v Colombia Case' (2013) 44 *ODIL* 219–34.

Gehrana, V, 'Maritime Delimitation: Dispute Amongst Peru and Chile: International Court of Justice, 2008–2014' (2014) 26 *Florida Journal of International Law* 331–46.

Geslin, A, 'La jurisprudence du Tribunal international du droit de la mer en matière de délimitations maritimes' in G Le Floch (ed), *Les 20 ans du Tribunal International du droit de la mer* (Paris, Pedone, 2018) 207–21.

Gherari, H, *Le différend tunisio-libyen relatif à la délimitation du plateau continental devant la Cour internationale de Justice* (Thèse Université de Paris I, 1974).

Gidel, G, *Le droit international de la mer* (reprint, Paris, Librairie Edouard Duchemin, 1981).

Gilas, J, 'Equitable Principles of the Delimitation of Continental Shelf' (1991–1992) *PYIL* 61–69.

Giraudeau, G, 'La Remarque entée en sène du TIDM dans le contentieux de la délimitation maritime: L'arrêt du 14 mars 2012 relatif au différend entre le Bangladesh et le Myanmar dans le Golfe du Bengal' (2012) 17 *Annuaire du droit de la mer* 93–118.

Gold, E (ed), *A New Law of the Sea for the Caribbean: An Examination of Marine Law and Policy Issues in the Lesser Antilles* (New York, Springer-Verlag, 1988).

Goldie, LFE, 'A Lexicographical Controversy: The Word 'Adjacent' in Article 1 of the Continental Shelf Convention' (1972) 66 *AJIL* 829–35.

——, 'The International Court of Justice's "Natural Prolongation" and the Continental Shelf Problem of Islands' (1973) 4 *NYIL* 237–61.

Gounaris, E, 'The Delimitation of the Continental Shelf of Islands: Some Observations' (1980) 33 *Revue hellénique de droit international* 111–19.

——, 'The Delimitation of the Continental Shelf of Jan Mayen' (1983) 21 *Archiv des Vökerrechts* 492–501.
——, 'The extension and Delimitation of Sea Areas under the Sovereignty, Sovereign Rights and Jurisdiction of Coastal States' in B Vukas (ed), *Essays on the New Law of the Sea* (Zagreb, Sveucilisna Naklada Liber, 1985) 85–98.
——, 'The Delimitation of the Sea Areas in the International Law' (1991) 17 *Thesaurus Acroasium* 295–313.
Greenfield, J, *China's Practice in the Law of the Sea* (Oxford, Clarendon Press, 1992).
Greig, DW, 'Third-Party Rights and Intervention Before the International Court' (1992) 32 *Virginia Journal of International Law* 285–376.
Grisel, E, 'The Lateral Boundaries of the Continental Shelf and the Judgment of the International Court of Justice in the North Sea Continental Shelf Cases' (1970) 64 *AJIL* 562–93.
Gutteridge, J, 'The 1958 Convention on the Continental Shelf' (1959) *BYIL* 102–23.
Guyomar, G, *Commentaire du règlement de la Cour internationale de Justice* (Paris, Pedone, 1983).
Hambro, E, 'Intervention under Article 36 of the Statute of the International Court of Justice' (1975) 14 *Communicazioni e Studi*, 387–400.
Hamman, DB, 'The Single Maritime Boundary: A Solution for Maritime Delimitation between Namibia and South Africa?' (1995) 10 *IJMCL* 369–96.
Hao Duy Phan, 'Conduct of Parties in Disputed Maritime Areas: the Guyana v Suriname Case' (2014) 54 *Indian Journal of International Law* 487–504.
Hedberg, HD, 'A Critique of Boundary Provisions in the Law of the Sea' (1983) 12 *ODIL* 337–42.
Helali, MSE, 'Chronique de jurisprudence internationale: sentence du 17 décembre 1999' (2000) 104 *RGDIP* 511–14.
Henriksen, T and Ulfstein, G, 'Maritime Delimitation in the Arctic: The Barents Sea Treaty' (2011) 42 *ODIL* 1–21
Herman, LL, 'The Court Giveth and the Court Taketh Away: An Analysis of the Tunisia-Libya Continental Shelf Case' (1984) 33 *ICLQ* 825–58.
Hershey, AS, *Essentials of International Public Law* (New York, The MacMillan Company, 1912).
Higgins, R, *Problems and Process: International Law and How We Use It* (Oxford, Clarendon Press, 1994) 228–36.
Highet, K, 'The Use of Geophysical Factors in the Delimitation of Maritime Boundaries' in JI Charney and LM Alexander (eds), *International Maritime Boundaries*, vol 1 (Dordrecht, Boston, London, Nijhoff, 1993) 163–202.
Hodgson, RD, 'Islands: Normal and Special Circumstances' in *Law of the Sea: The Emerging Regime of the Oceans, Proceedings of the Law of the Sea Institute 8th Annual Conference* (Honolulu, Law of the Sea Institute 1973) 137–99.
——, 'The Delimitation of Maritime Boundaries between Opposite and Adjacent States Through the Economic Zone and the Continental Shelf: Selected State Practice in Zones of Special Jurisdictions' in A Clingan Thomas Jr (ed), *Law of the Sea: State Practice in Zones of Special Jurisdiction* (Honolulu: Law of the Sea Institute, 1982) 280–316.
——, 'The Tunisio-Libyan Continental Shelf Case' (1984) 16 *Case Western Reserve Journal of International Law* 1–37.
Hodgson, RD and Cooper, EJ, 'The Technical Delimitation of a Modern Equidistant Boundary' (1976) 3 *ODIL* 361–88.
Hodgson, RD and Robert WS, 'Boundaries of the Economic Zone' in EL Miles and JK Gamble (eds), *Law of the Sea: Conference Outcomes and Problems of Implementation, Proceedings of the tenth Annual Conference of the Law of the Sea Institute* (Honolulu, Law of the Sea Institute, 1976) 183–206.
Hodgson, RD and Smith, RW, 'Boundary Issues Created by Extended National Marine Jurisdictions' (1979) 69 *Geographic Review* 423–33.
Hosni, SM, 'The Partition of the Neutral Zone' (1966) 60 *AJIL* 735–49.
Hsu, RTS, 'A Rational Approach to Maritime Boundary Delimitation' (1983) 13 *ODIL* 103–13.

Huang Yao and Liao Xuexia, 'Natural Prolongation and Delimitation of the Continental Shelf Beyond 200 nm: Implications of the *Bangladesh/Myanmar* Case' (2014) 4 *Asian Journal of International Law* 281–307.

Hughes, V, 'Nova Scotia-Newfoundland Dispute over Offshore Areas: The Delimitation Phase' (2002) 40 *CYIL* 373–417.

Hungdah Chiu, 'The Problem of Delimiting the Maritime Zone Between China (Mainland and Taiwan) and Japan' in N Ando et al (eds), *Liber Amicorum Judge Shigeru Oda* (The Hague, Kluwer, 2002) 1031–35.

Hutchinson, DN, 'The Seaward Limit to Continental Shelf Jurisdiction in International Law' (1985) 56 *BYIL* 111–88.

——, 'The Concept of Natural Prolongation in the Jurisprudence Concerning Delimitation of Continental Shelf Areas' (1984) 55 *BYIL* 133–87.

Hyun Jung Kim, 'La délimitation de la frontière maritime dans le golfe du Bengale: courir deux lièvres à la fois avec succès dans le règlement de la délimitation maritime' (2012) 58 *AFDI* 453–69.

——, 'Natural Prolongation: A Living Myth in the Regime of the Continental Shelf?' (2014) 45 *ODIL* 374–88.

Ida, R, 'La notion de la proportionalité dans les conflits récents sur la délimitation maritime – Le principe de la proportionnalité en droit international' (in Japanese), (1989) 124 *Kyoto Law Review* 81–110.

——, 'The Role of Proportionality in Maritime Delimitation Revisited: The Origin and Meaning of the Principle from the Early Decisions of the Court' in N Ando et al (eds), *Liber Amicorum Judge Shigeru Oda* (The Hague, Kluwer, 2002) 1037–53.

Iguchi, T, 'Recent Trends and Development of International Law Regarding the Maritime Delimitation between States: Significance of the Introduction of Principle of "Equity"' (in Japanese), (1994) 13 *Tokai Law Review* 33–124.

Infante-Caffi, MT, 'Peru v Chile: the International Court of Justice Decides on the Status of the Maritime Boundary' (2014) 13 *CJIL* 741–62.

——, 'The Decision on the Maritime Boundary between Chile and Peru: International Law Revisited' in Lilian del Castillo (ed), *Law of the Sea, from Grotius to the International Tribunal for the Law of the Sea, Liber Amicorum Judge Hugo Caminos* (Leiden, Brill/Nijhoff, 2015) 529–44.

Irwin, PC, 'Settlement of Maritime Boundaries Disputes: An Analysis of the Law of the Sea Negotiations' (1980) 8 *ODIL* 105–48.

Jacovides, AJ, 'Three Aspects of the Law of the Sea: Islands, Delimitation and Dispute Settlement' (1979) 3 *Marine Policy* 278–88.

Jaenicke, G, 'The Delimitation of the Continental Shelf on the Basis of the "Natural Prolongation Concept"' in EL Miles and S Allen (eds), *The Law of the Sea and Ocean Development Issues in the Pacific Basin, Proceedings of the 15th Annual Conference of the Law of the Sea Institute* (Honolulu, Law of the Sea Institute, 1983) 457–560.

——, 'The Role of Proportionality in the Delimitation of Maritime Zones' in A Bos and H Siblesz (eds), *Realism in Law-Making: Essays in International Law in Honour of Willem Riphagen* (Dordrecht, Nijhoff, 1986) 51–69.

——, 'North Sea Continental Shelf Cases' in R Bernhardt (ed), *Encyclopaedia of Public International Law* (Amsterdam, Elsevier, 1997) 657–60.

Jagota, SP, 'Maritime Boundary' (1981) 171 *RCADI* 81–223.

——, *Maritime Boundary* (Dordrecht, Nijhoff, 1985).

Janis, MW, 'Equity in International Law' in R Bernhardt (ed), *Encyclopaedia of Public International Law*, vol 2 (Amsterdam, Elsevier, 1995) 109–12.

Jayaraman, K, *Legal Regime of Islands* (New Delhi, Marwah Publications, 1982).

Jayewardene, HW, *The Regime of Islands in International Law* (Dordrecht, Nijhoff, 1990).

Jennings, RY, 'The Limits of Continental Shelf Jurisdiction: Some Possible Implications of the North Sea Case Judgment' (1969) 18 *ICLQ* 819–32.

——, 'Equity and Equitable Principles' (1986) 42 *ASDI* 27–38.

——, 'The Principles governing Marine Boundaries' in *Staat und Völkerrechtsordnung: Festschrift für Karl Doehring* (Berlin, Springer, 1989) 397–408.

Jensen, Ø, 'Treaty Between Norway and the Russian Federation Concerning Maritime Delimitation and Cooperation in the Barents Sea and the Arctic Ocean' (2011) 26 *IJMCL* 151–68.

——, 'Maritime Boundary Delimitation Beyond 200 Nautical Miles: The International Judiciary and the Commission on the Limits of the Continental Shelf' (2015) 84 *NJIL* 580–604.

Jessup, PC, 'Intervention in the International Court' (1981) 75 *AJIL* 903–09.

Jiménez de Aréchaga, E, 'Intervention under Article 62 of the Statute of the International Court of Justice' in *Völkerrecht als Rechtsordnung, Internationale Gerichtsbarkeit Menschenrechte, Festschrift für Hermann Mosler* (Berlin, Springer, 1983) 453–65.

——, 'The Concept of Equity in Maritime Delimitation' in *International Law at the Time of Its Codification, Essays in Honour of Roberto Ago*, vol II (Milan, Giuffrè, 1987) 229–39.

Johnson, DHN, 'The North Sea Continental Shelf Cases' (1969) 3 *International Relations* 522–40.

——, *The Theory and History of Ocean Boundary-Making* (Kingston, Montreal, McGill Queen's University Press, 1988).

Johnston, DM, and Saunders, PM (eds), *Ocean Boundary Making: Regional Issues and Developments* (London, Croom Helm, 1988).

Johnston, DM, and Valencia, MJ, *Pacific Ocean Boundary Problems: Status and Solutions* (Dordrecht, Nijhoff, 1991).

Josette, Beer-Gabel, 'Variations sur la notion de frontière maritime' in *Droit de la mer, Etudes dédiées au Doyen Claude-Albert Colliard* (Paris, Pedone, 1992) 11–35.

Jouannet, E, 'L'impossible protection des droits du tiers par la Cour international de justice dans les affaires de délimitation maritime' in *La mer et son droit, Mélanges offerts à Laurent Lucchini et Jean-Pierre Quéneudec* (Paris, Pedone, 2003) 315–41.

Kamga, MK, *Délimitation maritime sur la côte atlantique africaine* (Bruxelles, Bruyant, 2006).

Kamto, M, 'L'affaire de la délimitation maritime Guinée/Guinée-Bissau' (1985) 41 *Revue égiptienne de droit international* 73–147.

——, 'Considérations actuelles sur la méthode de délimitation maritime devant la Cour international de Justice: De charybde en scylla?' in J Crawford, A Koroma, S Mahmoudi and A Pellet (eds), *The International Legal Order: Current Needs and Possible Responses* (Leiden, Brill/Nijhoff, 2017) 383–420.

Kanehara, A, 'Equitable Principle of Continental Shelf Delimitation–from the Viewpoint of a Process of Customary International Law Formation (1) (2) (3)' (in Japanese), (1988) 101 *Kokka Gakkai Zassi (The Journal of the Association of Political and Social Sciences)* 493–559; 601–48; 766–821.

Kapoor, DC, 'The Delimitation of Exclusive Economic Zones' (1977) 4 *Maritime Policy and Management* 255–63.

Kapoor, DC and Kerr, JA, *A Guide to Maritime Boundary Delimitation* (Toronto, Carswell, 1986).

Karl, DE, 'Islands and the Delimitation of the Continental Shelf: A Framework for Analysis' (1977) 71 *AJIL* 642–73.

Kaye, S, 'The Torres Strait Treaty: A Decade in Perspective' (1994) 9 *IJMCL* 311–36.

Kays, S and Rothwell, DR, 'Australia's Antarctic Maritime Claims and Boundaries' (1995) 26 *ODIL* 195–226.

Kingue, N, 'La sentence du 14 février 1985 du tribunal d'arbitrage dans l'affaire de la délimitation de la frontière maritime entre la Guinée et la Guinée-Bissau' (1987) 91 *RGDIP* 45–82.

Kittichaisaree, K, *The Law of the Sea and Maritime Boundary Delimitation in South-East Asia* (Oxford, Oxford University Press, 1987).

Kohen, MG, 'La requête à fin d'intervention du Nicaragua dans l'affaire du différend frontalier terrestre, insulaire et maritime (El Salvador/Honduras). L'ordonnance de la Cour du 28 février 1990 et l'arrêt de la chambre du 13 septembre 1990' (1990) 36 *AFDI* 341–67.

Kolb R, 'L'interprétation de l'article 121, paragraphe 3, de la convention de Montego Bay sur le droit de la mer: les «Rochers qui ne se prêtent pas à l'habitation humaine ou à une vie économique propre…»' (1994) 40 *AFDI* 876–909.

——, *La bonne foi en droit international public: Contribution à l'étude des principes généraux de droit*, (Paris, PUF, 2000) 99–111 (in particular).
——, *Jurisprudence sur les délimitations maritimes selon l'équité* (The Hague, Brill/Nijhoff, 2003).
——, 'Note commentée: l'affaire de la délimitation maritime et des questions territoriales entre Qatar et Bahreïn (fond), arrêt de la Cour internationale de Justice du 16 mars 2001' (2001) 9 *Aftican Yearbook of International Law* 301–63.
Kunoy, B, 'The Admissibility of a Plea to an International Adjudicative Forum to Delimit the Outer Continental Shelf Prior to the Adoption of Final Recommendations by the Commission on the Limits of the Continental Shelf' (2010) 25 *IJMCL* 237–70.
——, 'The Delimitation of an Indicative Area of overlapping Entitlement to the Outer Continental Shelf' (2012) 83 *BYI*, 61–81.
——, 'Agreed Minutes on the Delimitation of the Continental Shelf Beyond 200 Nautical Miles between Greenland and Iceland in the Irminger Sea' (2013) 12 *CJIL* 125–42.
——, 'Le tracé d'une frontière dans la zone située au-delà de 200 milles marins en l'absence de recommandations de la commission du plateau continental' (2015) 61 *AFDI* 35–71.
Kuwahara, T, *International Law of the Sea* (in Japanese) (Tokyo, Kokusai Shoin, 1992).
——, *Introduction to International Law of the Sea* (in Japanese) (Tokyo, Sinzansha, 2002).
Kwiatkowska, B, 'The ICJ Doctrine of Equitable Principles Applicable to Maritime Boundary Delimitation and Its Impact on the International Law of the Sea' in *Forty Years International Court of Justice: Jurisdiction, Equity and Equality* (Utrecht, 1988) 121–58.
——, *The 200 mile Exclusive Economic Zone in the New Law of the Sea* (Dordrecht, Nijhoff, 1989).
——, 'Judge Sigeru Oda's Opinions in Law-of-the-Sea Cases: Equitable Maritime Boundary Delimitation' (1993) 36 *GYIL* 225–94.
——, 'Economic and Environmental Considerations in Maritime Boundary Delimitations' in JI Charney and LM Alexander (eds), *International Maritime Boundaries*, vol 1 (Dordrecht, Nijhoff, 1993) 75–113.
——, 'Equitable Maritime Boundary Delimitation: As Exemplified in the Work of the World Court during the Presidency of Sir Robert Yewdall Jennings' in V Lowe and M Fitzmaurice (eds), *Fifty Years of the International Court of Justice, Essays in Honour of Sir Robert Jennings* (Cambridge University Press, 1996) 264–92.
——, 'The Eritrea-Yemen Arbitration: Landmark Progress in the Acquisition of Territorial Sovereignty and Equitable Maritime Boundary Delimitation' (2001) 32 *ODIL* 1–25.
——, 'The Qatar v Bahrain Maritime Delimitation and Territorial Questions Case' (2002) 33 *ODIL* 227–62.
——, 'Resource, Navigational and Environmental Factors in Equitable Maritime Boundary Delimitation' in DA Colson and RW Smith (eds), *International Maritime Boundaries*, vol V (Leiden, Brill/Nijhoff, 2005) 3223–44.
——, 'The 2006 Barbados/Trinidad and Tobago Award: a Landmark in Compulsory Jurisdiction and Equitable Maritime Boundary Delimitation' (2007) 22 *IJMCL* 7–60.
——, 'Barbados/Trinidad and Tobago: Award on Jurisdiction and Merits: UN Convention on the Law of the Sea Annex VII Arbitral Tribunal, April 11, 2006' (2007) 101 *AJIL* 149–57.
Kwiatkowska, B and Soons, AHA, 'Entitlement to Maritime Areas of Rocks Which Cannot Sustain Human Habitation or Economic Life of Their Own' (1990) 21 *NYIL* 139–81.
Lagoni, R, 'Oil and Gas Deposits Across National Frontiers' (1979) 73 *AJIL* 215–43.
——, 'Interim Measures Pending Maritime Delimitation Agreements' (1984) 78 *AJIL*, 345–68.
Lando, M, 'Judicial Uncertainties Concerning Territorial Sea Delimitation under Article 15 of the United Nations Convention on the Law of the Sea' (2017) 66 *ICLQ* 589–623.
——, 'Delimiting the Continental Shelf Beyond 200 Nautical Miles at the International Court of Justice: The Nicaragua v Colombia Cases' (2017) 16 *CJIL* 137–73.
——, *Maritime Delimitation as a Judicial Process* (Cambridge University Press, 2019).
Lang, J, *Le plateau continental de la mer du Nord: arrêt de la Cour internationale de Justice, 20 février 1969* (Paris, Librairie générale de droit et de jurisprudence, 1970).

Langeraar, W, 'Delimitation of Continental Shelf Areas: A New Approach' (1986) 17 *Journal of Maritime Law and Commerce* 389–406.

——, 'Maritime Delimitation: The Equiratio Method – A New Approach' (1986) 10 *Marine Policy* 3–18.

Lapodoth, R, 'Equity in International Law' (1987) 22 *Israel Law Review* 161–83.

Laraba, A, 'La délimitation des espaces marins' (1978) 15 *Revue algérienne des sciences juridiques, éonomiques et politiques* 265–91.

Lathrop, C, 'Tripoint Issues in Maritime Boundary Delimitation' in DA Colson and RW Smith (eds), *International Maritime Boundaries*, vol V (Leiden Nijhoff, 2005) 3305–75.

——, 'Continental Shelf Delimitation Beyond 200 Nautical Miles: Approaches Taken by Coastal States before the Commission on the Limits of the Continental Shelf' in DA Colson and RW Smith (eds), *International Maritime Boundaries*, vol VI (Leiden Nijhoff, 2011) 4139–60.

Lauterpacht, E, 'Equity, Evasion, Equivocation and Evolution in International Law' *Proceedings and Committee Reports of the American Branch of the ILA* (1977–1978) 1–15.

Laveissier, J, 'Les îles et la détermination des frontières maritimes' in (1985) 14 *Thesaurus Acroasium, National and International Boundaries* 79–99.

Lawson, KL, 'Delimiting Continental Shelf Boundaries in the Arctic: The United States-Canada Beaufort Sea Boundary' (1981) 22 *Virginia Journal of International Law* 221–46.

Leanza, U, 'The Delimitation of the Continental Shelf of the Mediterranean Sea' (1993) 8 *IJMCL* 373–94.

Leanza, U and Sico, L (eds), *Mediterranean Continental Shelf: Delimitations and Regimes*, 2 vols, (New York, Oceana Publications, 1988).

Legault, LH, 'A Line for All Uses: The Gulf of Maine Boundary Revisited' (1984–1985) 40 *International Journal* 461–77.

Legault, LH and Hankey, B, 'From Sea to Seabed: The Single Maritime Boundary in the Gulf of Maine Case' (1985) 79 *AJIL* 961–91.

Legault, LH and Hankey, B, 'Method, Oppositeness and Adjacency, and Proportionality in Maritime Boundary Delimitation' in JI Charney and LM Alexander (eds), *International Maritime Boundaries*, vol 1 (Dordrecht, Nijhoff, 1993) 203–42.

Legault, LH and McRae, DM, 'The Gulf of Maine Case' (1984) 22 *CYIL* 267–90.

Leigh, M, 'Intervening in Judicial Proceedings, Intervention of Article 62 of the Statute of the International Court of Justice' (1981) 75 *AJIL* 949–52.

Licari, T, 'Intervention under Article 62 of the Statute of the International Court of Justice' (1982) 8 *Brooklyn Journal of International Law* 267–87.

Llanos Mardones, HI, *The Delimitation of Maritime Areas between Adjacent States in the Southeastern Pacific Region* (Geneva, Thesis, IUHEI, 1996).

Lloyd, S, 'Natural Prolongation: Have the Rumours of Its Demise Been Greatly Exaggerated?' (1991) 3 *African Journal of International and Comparative Law* 558–72.

Lott, A, 'The Estonian-Russian Territorial Sea Boundary Delimitation in the Gulf of Finland' (2017) 32 *IJMCL* 484–509.

Lowe, V, 'The Role of Equity in International Law' (1988–1989) 12 *Australian YearBook of International Law* 54–81.

Lucchini, L and Voelckel, M, *Droit de la mer: Délimitation*, tome 2, vol 1 (Paris, Pedone, 1996).

Lumb, RD, 'The Delimitation of Maritime Boundaries in the Timor Sea' (1981) 7 *Australian Yearbook of International Law* 72–86.

Lysaght, C, 'The Agreement on the Delimitation of the Continental Shelf Between Ireland and the United Kingdom' (1990) 3 *Irish Studies in International Affairs* 81–109.

MacDonald, CG, *Iran, Saudi Arabia, and the Law of the Sea* (Westport Connecticut, Greenwood Press, 1980).

MacDonald, R and Hughes, V, 'Intervention before the International Court of Justice' (1993) 5 *African Journal of International and Comparative Law* 1–33.

MacDougal, MS, 'The Evolution of Maritime Boundary Law' in TA Grigalunas and LC Hanson (eds), *Continental Shelf, Resources, Boundaries, and Management* (Kingston, RI, University of Rhode Island, 1986) 74–80.

McGinley, GP, 'Intervention in the International Court: The Libya/Malta Continental Shelf Case' (1985) 34 *ICLQ* 671–94.

Madakou, A, 'Intervention Before the International Court of Justice' *Mémoire de D.E.S.* (Geneva, IUHEI, 1988) 1–99.

Magnússon, BM, 'Judgment in the Dispute Concerning Delimitation of the Maritime Boundary between Bangladesh and Myanmar in the Bay of Bengal (14 March 2012)' (2012) 27 *IJMCL* 623–33.

——, 'Is There a Temporal Relationship between the Delineation and the Delimitation of the Continental Shelf beyond 200 Nautical Miles?' (2013) 28 *IJMCL* 465–83.

——, 'Outer Continental Shelf Boundary Agreements' (2013) 62 *ICLQ* 345–72.

——, 'The Rejection of a Theoretical Beauty: The Foot of the Continental Slope in Maritime Boundary Delimitations Beyond 200 Nautical Miles' (2014) 45 *ODIL* 41–52.

——, *The Continental Shelf Beyond 200 Nautical Miles: Delineation, Delimitation and Dispute Settlement* (Leiden, Brill/Nijhoff, 2015).

——, 'The Grey Areas in the Bay of Bengal' (2016) 57 *Indian Journal of International Law* 41–58.

Mani, VS, 'Towards Codification of the Legal Regime of Islands' (1986) *Indian Yearbook of International Affairs* 53–105.

Manin, PH, 'Le juge international et la règle générale: réflexions à partir des arrêts rendus par la C.I.J. dans l'affaire du plateau continental de la mer du Nord (1969) et dans l'affaire des pêcheries (1974)' (1976) *RGDIP* 7–54.

Manner, EJ, 'Some Basic Viewpoints on Delimitation of Marine Areas between Neighbouring States' in Ocean Association of Japan, *Proceedings of the 5th International Ocean Symposium: The Frontier of the Seas: the Problems of Delimitation*, 1980 (Tokyo, Ocean Association of Japan, 1981) 1–17.

——, 'Settlement of Sea Boundary Disputes According to the Provisions of the 1982 Law of the Sea Convention' in J Makarczyk, (ed), *Etudes de droit international en l'honneur du juge Manfred Lacks* (The Hague, Nijhoff, 1984) 625–43.

Mariateresa Garrido Villareal, 'The *Bay of Bengal Case* and the Effect of Island in the Delimitation of Maritime Boundaries' in Juan Carlos Sainz-Borgo et al (eds), *Liber Amicorum in Honour of a Modern Renaissance Man: His Excellency Guðmundur Eiríksson* (San José, Universal Law Publishing, 2017) 125–40.

Marsh, JE, 'The Boundary Provisions of the New United Nations Convention on the Law of the Sea' in *National and International Boundaries* (1985) 14 *Thesaurus Acroasium*, Thessaloniki 229–69.

Marston, G, 'St. Pierre-Miquelon Arbitration: Canada-France Maritime Delimitation Award' (1993) 17 *Marine Policy* 155–70.

Mbaye, K, 'L'intérêt pour agir devant la Cour internationale de Justice' (1988) 209 *RCADI* 223–345.

McDorman, TL, 'The Canada-France Maritime Boundary Case: Drawing a Line Around St. Pierre and Miquelon' (1990) 84 *AJIL* 157–89.

——, 'The Libya-Malta Case: Opposite States Confront the Court' (1986) 24 *CYIL* 335–67.

McDorman, TL, Saunders, PM and Vanderzwaag, DL, 'The Gulf of Maine Boundary: Dropping Anchor or Setting a Course?' (1985) 9 *Marine Policy* 90–107.

McDougal, MS and Burke, WT, *The Public Order of the Oceans: A Contemporary International Law of the Sea* (Dordrecht, Nijhoff, 1985).

McHugh, P, 'International Law: Delimitation of Maritime Boundaries' (1985) 25 *Natural Resources Journal* 1025–38.

McLlarky, 'Guinea/Guinea-Bissau: Disputes Concerning Delimitation of Maritime Boundary, February 14, 1985' (1987) 11 *Maryland Journal of International Law* 93–121.

McRae, DM, 'Delimitation of the Continental Shelf between the United Kingdom and France: The Channel Arbitration' (1977) 15 *CYIL* 173–97.
——, 'Proportionality and the Gulf of Maine Maritime Boundary Dispute' (1981) 19 *CYIL* 287–301.
——, 'The Single Maritime Boundary: Problems in Theory and Practice' in ED Brown and RR Churchill (eds), *The UN Convention on the Law of the Sea: Impact and Implementation* (Honolulu: Law of the Sea Institute, 1987) 225–34.
McRae, DM and Yacouba, C, 'The Legal Regime of Maritime Boundary Agreement' in DA Colson and RW Smith (eds), *International Maritime Boundaries*, vol V (Leiden, Brill/Njhoff, 2005) 3281–3304.
Meese, R, 'Délimitations maritimes: règlement juridictionnel et conciliation internationale' (1998) 3 *Annuaire du droit de la mer* 161–87.
Mendelson, M, 'The Curious Case of *Qatar* v *Bahrain* in the International Court of Justice' (2001) 72 *BYIL* 183–211.
——, 'On the Quasi-Normative Effect of Maritime Boundary Agreements' in N Ando et al (eds), *Liber Amicorum Judge Shigeru Oda* (The Hague, Kluwer, 2002) 1069–86.
Mensah, T, 'The Role of Peaceful Dispute Settlement in Contemporary Ocean Policy and Law' in D Vidas and W Østreng (eds), *Order for the Oceans at the Turn of the Century* (The Hague, Kluwer, 1999) 81–94.
——, 'Delimitation of the Continental Shelf: The Methodology' in Juan Carlos Sainz-Borgo et al (eds), *Liber Amicorum in Honour of a Modern Renaissance Man: His Excellency Guðmundur Eiríksson* (San José, Universal Law Publishing, 2017) 31–49.
Merrills, JG, 'The United Kingdom-France Continental Shelf Arbitration' (1980) 10 *California Western International Law Journal* 314–64.
Miller, JT, 'Intervention in Proceedings before the International Court of Justice' in L Gross (ed), *The Future of the International Court of Justice*, vol II (New York, Oceana) 550–71.
Mishra, R, 'The "Grey Area" in the Northern Bay of Bengal: A Note on a Functional Cooperative Solution' (2016) 47 *ODIL* 29–39.
Miyoshi, M, 'The Role of Equitable Principles in the Delimitation of Maritime Boundaries' in Ocean Association of Japan, *Proceedings of the 5th International Ocean Symposium: The Frontier of the Seas: the Problems of Delimitation* (1980, Tokyo, Ocean Association of Japan, 1981) 42–46.
——, 'Transition of Legal Principles on Delimitation of Continental Shelf'(in Japanese) (1982) 5 *Kaiyoho to Kaiyoseisaku (Law of the Sea and Ocean Policy)*, Ministry of Foreign Affairs, Japan 39–59.
——, 'Delimitation of Continental Shelf and Exclusive Economic Zone' (in Japanese) (1983) 6 *Kaiyoho to Kaiyoseisaku (Law of the Sea and Ocean Policy)*, Ministry of Foreign Affairs, Japan 65–73.
——, 'The Japan-South Korea Agreement on Joint Development of the Continental Shelf' (1985) 10 *Energy* 545–53.
——, 'The Basic Concept of Joint Development of Hydrocarbon Resources on the Continental Shelf With Special Reference to the Discussions at the East-West Centre Workshops on the South-East Asian Seas' (1988) 3 *IJECL* 1–18.
——, 'Reflections on Rules Regarding Continental Shelf Delimitation' (in Japanese) in *New Order of the Law of the Sea, In tribute to Professor Hideo Takabayashi* (Tokyo, Toshindo, 1993) 161–95.
——, *Considerations of Equity in the Settlement of Territorial and Boundary Disputes* (Dordrecht, Nijhoff, 1993).
——, 'Is Joint Development Possible in the South China Sea?' in MK Atmadja, TA Mensah and BH Oxman (eds), *Sustainable Development and Preservation of the Oceans: The Challenges of UNCLOS and Agenda 21, Proceedings of the Law of the Sea Institute 29th Annual Conference in 1995* (Honolulu, University of Hawaii, 1997) 610–28.
——, 'International Maritime Boundaries and Joint Development: A Quest for a Multilateral Approach' in GH Blake, MA Pratt and CH Schofield (eds), *Boundaries and Energy: Problems and Prospects* (The Hague, Kluwer Law International, 1998) 453–71.

——, 'The Joint Development of Offshore Oil and Gas in Relation to Maritime Boundary Delimitation' *Maritime Briefing*, vol 2 (International Boundaries Research Unit, University of Durham, 1999) 1–53.

——, 'Joint Development Under the United Nations Convention on the Law of the Sea: A Reevaluation' (in Japanese) (2002) 75 *Hogakukenkyu* 87–104.

——, 'Considerations of Equity in Maritime Boundary Cases Before the International Court of Justice' in N Ando et al (eds), *Liber Amicorum Judge Shigeru Oda* (The Hague, Kluwer, 2002) 1087–1101.

Miyoshi, M and Valencia, MJ, 'Southeast Asian Seas: Joint Development of Hydrocarbons in Overlapping Claim Area?' (1986) 16 *ODIL* 211–54.

Mizukami, C, *Japan and the Law of the Sea* (in Japanese) (Yushindo, 1995).

——, 'Delimitation of the Exclusive Economic Zone (1), (2)' (in Japanese) (2000) 24 *The Hiroshima Law Journal* 1–19; 1–24.

Mizuta, S, 'The Relationship between the Delimitation of the Continental Shelf and the Exclusive Economic Zone under the United Nations Convention on the Law of the Sea' (in Japanese) (2000) 44 *Sophia Law Review* 99–131.

Mohd. Talaat El Ghoneimy, 'The Legal Status of the Saudi-Kuwaiti Neutral Zone' (1966) 15 *ICLQ* 690–717.

Monconduit, F, 'Affaire du plateau continental de la mer du Nord: République fédérale d'Allemagne *c.* Danemark; République fédérale d'Allemagne *c.* Pays-Bas: arrêt du 20 février 1969' (1969) 15 *AFDI* 213–44.

Morelli, G, 'Fonction et objet de l'intervention dans le procès international' in J Makarczyk (ed), *Etudes de droit international en l'honneur du Juge Manfred Lachs* (The Hague, Nijhoff, 1984) 403–08.

Mossop, J, *The Continental Shelf Beyond 200 Nautical Miles: Rights and Responsibilities* (Oxford University Press, 2016).

Murphy, SD, 'International Law Relating to Islands' (2017) 386 *RCADI* 21–265.

Nabil a Hilmy, 'Article 6 of the Geneva Convention on the Continental Shelf 1958 in the Law of the Sea' (1977) *Thesaurus Acroasium* 505–10.

Nandan, SN, and Rosenne, S, (eds), *United Nations Convention on the Law of the Sea 1982: A Commentary*, vol II (Dordrecht, Nijhoff, 1993).

Ndiaye, TM, 'Le juge et la délimitation maritime: mode d'emploi' in JM Van Dyke, SP Broder, S Lee, and J-H Paik (eds), *Governing Ocean Resources: New Challenges and Emerging Regimes, A Tribute to Judge Choon-Ho Park* (Leiden, Nijhoff, 2013) 139–61.

——, 'The Judge, Maritime Delimitation and the Grey Areas' (2015) 55 *Indian Journal of International Law* 493–533.

Nelson, LDM, 'The North Sea Continental Shelf Cases and Law-Making Conventions' (1972) 35 *Modern Law Review* 52–56.

——, 'The Role of Equity in the Delimitation of Maritime Boundaries' (1990) 84 *AJIL* 837–58.

——, 'The Settlement of Disputes Arising From Conflicting Outer Continental Shelf Claims' (2009) 24 *IJMCL* 409–22.

Nguyen Hong Thao, 'Le premier accord de délimitation des frontières maritimes au Viêt-Nam' (1996) 1 *Annuaire du droit de la mer* 259–70.

——, 'Maritime Delimitation and Fishery Cooperation in the Tonkin Gulf' (2005) 36 *ODIL* 25–44.

Nuno Sérgio Marques Antunes, 'The 1999 *Eritrea-Yemen* Maritime Delimitation Award and the Development of International Law' (2001) 50 *ICLQ* 299–344.

——, *Towards the Conceptualisation of Maritime Delimitation: Legal and Technical Aspects of a Political Process* (Leiden, Nijhoff, 2003).

——, 'Some Thoughts on the Technical Input in Maritime Delimitation' in DA Colson and RW Smith (eds), *International Maritime Boundaries*, vol V (Leiden, Brill/Nijhoff, 2005) 3377–98.

Nweihed, KG, 'EZ (Uneasy) Delimitation in the Semi-enclosed Caribbean Sea: Recent Agreements Between Venezuela and Her Neighbors' (1980) 8 *ODIL* 1–33.

O'Connell, DPO in IA Shearer (ed), *The International Law of the Sea*, 2 vols (Oxford, Clarendon Press, 1984).
Oda, S, 'Boundary of the Continental Shelf' (1968) 12 *The Japanese Annual of International Law* 264–84.
——, 'The Delimitation of the Continental Shelf in Southeast Asia and the Far East' (1973) 1 *Ocean Management* 327–46.
——, 'Intervention in the International Court of Justice' in *Völkerrecht als Rechtsordnung, Internationale Gerichtsbarkeit Menschenrechte, Festschrift für Hermann Mosler* (Berlin, Springer, 1983) 629–48.
——, *Commentary on the United Nations Convention on the Law of the Sea* (in Japanese), vol 1 (Tokyo, Yuhikaku, 1985).
——, 'Delimitation of a Single Maritime Boundary' in *International Law at the Time of Its Codification, Essays in Honour of Roberto Ago*, vol II (Milan, Giuffrè, 1987) 349–62.
——, 'The International Court of Justice Viewed from the Bench (1976–1993)' (1993) 244 *RCADI* 9–190.
Olorundami, F, 'Objectivity versus Subjectivity in the Context of the ICJ's Three-stage Methodology of Maritime Boundary Delimitation' (2017) 32 *IJMCL* 36–53.
Ong, DM, 'Joint Development of Common Offshore Oil and Gas Deposits: 'Mere' State Practice or Customary International Law?' (1999) 93 *AJIL* 771–804.
——, 'The Legal Status of the 1989 Australia-Indonesia Timor Gap Treaty Following the End of Indonesian Rule in East Timor' (2000) 31 *NYIL* 67–129.
——, 'The New Timor Sea Arrangement 2001: Is Joint Development of Common Offshore Oil and Gas Deposits Mandated under International Law?' (2002) 17 *IJMCL* 79–122.
Onorato, WT, 'Apportionment of an International Common Petroleum Deposit' (1968) 17 *ICLQ* 85–102.
——, 'Apportionment of an International Common Petroleum Deposit' (1977) 26 *ICLQ* 324–37.
——, 'Joint Development of Seabed Hydrocarbon Resources: An Overview of Precedents in the North Sea' (1981) 6 *Energy* 1311–24.
Oppenheim, L, *International Law*, vol I, Peace (London, Longmans, 1905).
Orrego Vicuña, F, 'The Contribution of the Exclusive Economic Zone to the Law of Maritime Delimitation' (1988) 31 *GYIL* 120–37.
——, *The Exclusive Economic Zone: Regime and Legal Nature Under International Law* (Cambridge, Cambridge University Press, 1989).
——, 'International Law Issues in the Judgment of the International Court of Justice in the Peru-Chile Maritime Dispute Case' in Lilian del Castillo (ed), *Law of the Sea, from Grotius to the International Tribunal for the Law of the Sea: Liber Amicorum Judge Hugo Caminos* (Leiden, Brill, 2015) 563–82.
Ossintsev, VF, 'Peaceful Settlement of Disputes Concerning Maritime Boundary Delimitation' (1988) *Soviet Yearbook of Maritime Law* 26–32.
Østreng, W, 'Reaching Agreement on International Exploitation of Ocean Mineral Resources (with Special Reference to the Joint Development Area Between Jan Mayen and Iceland)' (1985) 10 *Energy* 555–71.
Oude Elferink, Alex G, *The Law of Maritime Boundary Delimitation: A Case Study of the Russian Federation* (Dordrecht, Nijhoff, 1994).
——, 'The Law and Politics of the Maritime Boundary Delimitations of the Russian Federation: Part 1', (1996) 11 *IJMCL* 533–69.
——, 'The Law and Politics of the Maritime Boundary Delimitations of the Russian Federation: Part 2', (1997) 12 *IJMCL* 5–35.
——, 'Current Legal Development: Belgium/The Netherlands; Delimitation of Maritime Zones' (1997) 12 *IJMCL* 548–53.
——, 'Current Legal Developments: Denmark/Iceland/Norway; Bilateral Agreements on the Delimitation of the Continental Shelf and Fishery Zones' (1998) 13 *IJMCL* 607–16.

——, 'The Impact of the Law of the Sea Convention on the Delimitation of Maritime Boundaries' in D Vidas and W Østreng (eds), *Order for the Oceans at the Turn of the Century* (The Hague, Kluwer, 1999) 457–69.

——, '"Openness" and Article 76 of the Law of the Sea Convention: The Process Does not Need to be Adjusted' (2009) 40 *ODIL* 36–50.

——, *The Delimitation of the Continental Shelf between Denmark, Germany and the Netherlands: Arguing Law, Practicing Politics?* (Cambridge University Press, 2013).

——, 'ITLOS's Approach to the Delimitation of the Continental Shelf beyond 200 Nautical Miles in the Bangladesh/Myanmar Case: Theoretical and Practical Difficulties' in R Wolfrum, M Seršić, and T Šošić (eds), *Contemporary Developments in International Law: Essays in Honour of Budislav Vukas* (Leiden, Nijhoff, 2015) 230–49.

——, 'International Law and Negotiated and Adjudicated Maritime Boundaries: A Complex Relationship' (2015) 58 *German Yearbook of International Law* 231–64.

Oude Elferink, Alex G and Rothwell, DR, *The Law of the Sea and Polar Maritime Delimitation and Jurisdiction* (The Hague, Kluwer, 2001).

Oude Elferink, Alex G, Henriksen, T and Busch, SV (eds), *Maritime Boundary Delimitation: The Case Law Is It Consistent and Predictable?* (Cambridge University Press, 2018).

Padwa, DJ, 'Submarine Boundaries' (1960) 9 *ICLQ* 628–53.

Paik, JH, 'A Single Boundary for the Continental Shelf and the Exclusive Economic Zone' (1989) *Korean Journal of Comparative Law* 39–98.

——, 'The Grey Area in the Bay of Bengal Case' in MH Nordquist, JN Moore and R Long (eds), *International Marine Economy: Law and Policy* (Leiden, Brill/Nijhoff, 2017) 271–81.

Park, CH, 'Oil Under Troubled Waters: The Northeast Asia Sea-Bed Controversy' (1973) 14 *Harvard International Law Journal* 212–60.

——, 'Joint Development of Mineral Resources in Disputed Waters: The Case of Japan and South Korea in the East China Sea' (1981) 6 *Energy* 1335–54.

——, *East Asia and the Law of the Sea* (Seoul, Seoul National University Press, 1983).

——, 'River and Maritime Boundary Problems Between North Korea and Russia in the Tumen and the Sea of Japan' (1993) 5 *The Korean Journal of Defense Analysis* 65–97.

Park, CH and Park, JK, *The Law of the Sea: Problems from the East Asian Perspective* (Honolulu, The Law of the Sea Institute, University of Hawaii, 1987).

Pazarci, H, *La délimitation du plateau continental et les îles* (Ankara, Faculté des Sciences Politiques de l'Université d'Ankara, 1982).

Pedersen, T, 'Denmark's Policies Toward the Svalbard Area' (2009) 40 *ODIL* 319–32.

Pellet, A, 'Land and Maritime Tripoints in International Jurisprudence' in H, Hestermeyer et al (eds), *Coexistence, Cooperation and Solidarity, Liber Amicorum Rüdiger Wolfrum* (Leiden, Nijhoff, 2011) 245–63.

Pellet, A and Samson, B, 'La délimitation des espaces marins' in M Forteau and J-M Thouvenin (eds), *Traité de droit international de la mer* (Paris, Pedone, 2017) 565–623.

Peters, P and Tanja, GJ, 'Lateral Delimitation of Continental Shelf and Exclusive Economic Zone' (1984) 86 *Diritto Mrittimo*, 463–77.

Pharand, D and Leanza, U, *The Continental Shelf and Exclusive Economic Zone* (Dordrecht, Boston, London, Nijhoff, 1993).

Pietrowski Jr, RF, 'Legal Perspective on the Guinea/Guinea-Bissau Dispute' in TA Grigalunas, and LC Hanson (eds), *Continental Shelf, Resources, Boundaries and Management* (University of Rhode Island, 1986) 69–73.

Pirotte, O, 'La notion d'équité dans la jurisprudence récente de la Cour internationale de Justice' (1973) 77 *RGDIP* 92–135.

Plant, G, 'Maritime Delimitation and Territorial Questions Between Qatar and Bahrain (Qatar v Bahrain)' (2002) 96 *AJIL* 198–210.

Platzöder, R and Verlaan, P (eds), *The Baltic Sea: New Development in National Policies and International Cooperation* (Dordrecht, Kluwer Law International, 1996).

Politakis, GP, 'The French-Canadian Arbitration around St. Pierre and Miquelon: Unmasked Opportunism and the Triumph of the Unexpected' (1993) 8 *IJMCL* 105–34.

——, 'The 1993 Jan Mayen Judgment: The End of Illusions?' (1994) 41 *NILR* 1–31.

Poulantzas, MN, 'The Chambers of the I.C.J. and the Judicial Settlement of Disputes: The Delimitation of the Maritime Boundary in the Gulf of Maine Area Case' (1985) 63 *Revue de droit international de sciences diplomatiques et politiques* 323–28.

Pratt, M, 'Commentary: Case Concerning Territorial and Maritime Dispute between Nicaragua and Honduras in the Caribbean Sea (Nicaragua v Honduras' (2007) 2 *Hague Justice Journal* 34–38.

Prescott, JRV, 'Existing and Potential Maritime Claims in the Southwest Pacific Ocean' (1980) 2 *Ocean Yearbook* 317–45.

——, *Maritime Political Boundaries of the World* (London, Methuen, 1985).

——, *Australia's Maritime Boundaries* (Canberra, Department of International Relations, The Australian National University, 1985).

——, 'Delimitation of Marine Boundaries by Baselines' (1986) 8 *Marine Policy Reports* 1–5.

——, 'The Papua New Guinea-Solomon Islands Maritime Boundary' (1994) 11 *Ocean Yearbook*, 179–92.

——, 'The Problems of Completing Maritime Boundary Delimitation between Australia and Indonesia' (1995) 10 *IJMCL* 389–96.

——, 'Current Legal Developments: Treaty between the Government of Australia and the Government of the Republic of Indonesia Establishing an Exclusive Economic Zone Boundary and Certain Seabed Boundaries' (1997) 12 *IJMCL* 533–47.

Prescott, JRV and Schofield, C, *Maritime Political Boundaries of the World*, 2nd edn (Leiden, Brill/Nijhoff, 2005).

Prescott, JRV and Triggs, G, 'Islands and Rocks and Their Role in Maritime Delimitation' in DA Colson and RW Smith (eds), *International Maritime Boundaries*, vol V (Leiden Brill/Nijhoff, 2005) 3245–80.

Pulvenis, J-F, 'La mer des Caraïbes' (1980) 84 *RGDIP* 310–27.

Quéneudec, J-P, 'L'affaire de la délimitation du plateau continental entre la France et le Royaume-Uni' (1979) 83 *RGDIP* 53–103.

——, 'Note sur l'arrêt de la Cour international de Justice relatif à la délimitation du plateau continental entre la Tunisie et la Libye' (1981) 27 *AFDI* 203–12.

Quintana, JJ, 'The Intervention by Nicaragua in the Case between El Salvador and Honduras before an Ad Hoc Chamber of the International Court of Justice' (1991) 38 *NILR* 199–208.

Razavi, A, *Continental Shelf Delimitation and Related Maritime Issues in the Persian Gulf* (Dordrecht, Nijhoff, 1997).

Reisman, WM, 'Eritrea-Yemen Arbitration (Award, Phase II: Maritime Delimitation)' (2000) 94 *AJIL* 721–36.

Reisman, WM and Westerman, GS, *Straight Baselines in International Maritime Boundary Delimitation* (New York, St Martin's Press, 1992).

Reynaud, A, *Les différends du plateau continental de la mer du Nord devant la Cour internationale de Justice: la volonté, la nature et le droit* (Paris, 1975).

——, *Le plateau continental de la France* (Paris, Librairie Générale de Droit et de Jurisprudence, 1984).

Renton, D, 'The Torres Strait Treaty After 15 Years: Some Observations from a Papua New Guinea Perspective' in J Crawford and DR Rothwell (eds), *The Law of the Sea in the Asian Pacific Region* (Dordrecht, Kluwer, 1995) 171–80.

Reuter, P, 'Une ligne unique de délimitation des espaces maritimes?' in *Mélanges: George Perrin* (Lausanne, Diffusion Payot, 1984) 251–67.

Rhee, SM, 'Equitable Solutions to the Maritime Boundary Dispute between the United States and Canada in the Gulf of Maine' (1981) 75 *AJIL* 591–628.

——, 'Sea Boundary Delimitation between States before World War II' (1982) 76 *AJIL* 555–88.

Richardson, EL, 'Jan Mayen in Perspective' (1988) 82 *AJIL* 443–58.

Ridi, N, 'Precarious Finality – Reflections on Res Judicata and the Question of the Delimitation of the Continental Shelf Case' (2018) 31 *LJIL* 383–401.

Rigaldies, F, 'La délimitation du plateau continental entre Etats voisins' (1976) 14 *CYIL* 116–74.

——, 'L'affaire de la délimitation du plateau continental entre la République française et le Royaume-Uni de Grande-Bretagne et d'Irlande du Nord' (1979) 106 *Journal du droit international* 506–31.

Rivier, A, *Principes du droit des gens* (Paris, Librairie de droit et de jurisprudence, vol I, 1896).

Roach, JA and Smith, RT, 'Straight Baselines: The Need for a Universally Applied Norm' (2000) 31 *ODIL* 47–80.

Robinson, DR, Colson, DA and Rashkow, BC, 'Some Perspectives on Adjudicating before the World Court: The Gulf of Maine Case' (1985) 79 *AJIL* 578–97.

Rodgers, WD, Beat, JA, and Wolf, C, 'Application of El Salvador to Intervention in the Jurisdiction and Admissibility Phase of Nicaragua v United States' (1984) 78 *AJIL* 929–36.

Romualdo Bermejo, 'Les principes equitables et les délimitations des zones maritimes: analyse des affaires Tunisie/Jamahiriya arabe libyenne et du Golfe du Maine' (1988) 1 *Hague Yearbook of International Law* 59–110.

Rosenne, S, 'Some Procedural Aspects of the English Channel Continental Shelf Arbitration' in *Essays in Honour of Erik Castrén* (Helsinki, 1979) 96–115.

——, 'Equitable Principles and the Compulsory Jurisdiction of International Tribunals' in *Festschrift für Rudolf Bindschedler* (Bern, Stämpfli, 1980).

——, *Procedure in the International Court: A Commentary on the 1978 Rules of the International Court of Justice* (The Hague, Nijhoff, 1983).

——, *The Law and Practice of the International Court* (Dordrecht, Nijhoff, 1985).

——, 'Some Reflections on Intervention in the International Court of Justice' (1987) 34 *NILR* 75–90.

——, 'Reflections on International Arbitration and Litigation in the International Court of Justice' (1987) 9 *Forum International* 3–21.

——, *Intervention in the International Court of Justice* (Dordrecht, Nijhoff, 1993).

Rothpfeffer, T, 'Equity in the North Sea Continental Shelf Cases: A Case Study in the Legal Reasoning of the International Court of Justice' (1972) 42 *Nordisk tidsskrift for international ret* 81–137.

Roubertou, A, 'Carte marine et délimitations maritimes' (1993) 1 *Revue de l'Indemer* (Paris) 25–26.

Rozakis, CL, 'Compromises of States' Interests and their Repercussions upon the Rules on the Delimitation of the Continental Shelf: From the Truman Proclamation to the 1982 Convention on the Law of the Sea' in CL Rozkis and CA Stephanou (eds), *The New Law of the Sea* (Amsterdam, North-Holland, 1983) 155–83.

Ruiz-Fabri, H, 'Sur la délimitation des espaces maritimes entre le Canada et la France, sentence arbitrale du 10 juin 1992' (1993) 97 *RGDIP* 67–106.

Ryan, KW and White, MW, 'The Torres Strait Treaty' (1981) 7 *Australian Yearbook of International Law* 87–113.

Sarzo, M, '*Res Judicata*, Jurisdiction *Ratione Materiae* and Legal Reasoning in the Dispute between Nicaragua and Colombia before the International Court of Justice' (2017) 16 *The Law and Practice of International Courts and Tribunals* 224–44.

Schachter, O, 'International Law in Theory and Practice: General Course in Public International Law' (1982) 178 *RCADI* 9–396 (in particular, pp 74–90).

Shalowitz, AL, *Shore and Sea Boundaries* 2 vols (Washington, Department of Commerce, 1962–64).

Sharma, S, 'The Single Maritime Boundary Regime and the Relationship between the Continental Shelf and the EEZ' (1987) 2 *IJECL* 203–27.

Schneider, J, 'The Gulf of Maine Case: The Nature of an Equitable Result' (1985) 79 *AJIL* 539–77.

Schofield, C, Telesetsk, A and Lee, S, 'A Tribunal Navigating Complex Waters: Implications of the *Bay of Bengal Case*' (2013) 44 *ODIL* 363–88.

Schofield, C, 'Seeking Lines in the Sea: Progress and Challenges in the Delimitation of Maritime Boundaries over the Past 50 Years' in HN Sheiber, N Oral and Moon-Sang Kwon (eds), *Ocean Law Debates: The 50 Year Legacy and Emerging Issues for the Years Ahead* (Leiden, Brill/Nijhoff, 2018) 135–57.

Scovazzi, T, 'L'affaire de la délimitation des espaces maritimes entre le Canada et la France: exagérer, mesurer ou nécessiter?' (1992) 6 *Collection espaces et ressources maritimes*, 61–83.

——, 'The Establishment of Straight Baselines Systems: The Rules and the Practice' in D Vidas, and W Østreng (eds), *Order for the Oceans at the Turn of the Century* (The Hague, Kluwer, 1999) 445–56.

——, 'The Evolution of International Law of the Sea: New issues, New Challenges' (2000) 286 *RCADI* 39–243.

——, 'Maritime Dispute (Peru v Chile), 2008' in PW Almeida and J-M Sorel, *Latin America and the International Court of Justice: Contributions to International Law* (London, Routledge, 2017) 237–49.

Seifi, J, 'Nicaragua Granted Permission to Intervene in the (El Salvador/Honduras) Land, Island and Maritime Frontier Case' (1991) 6 *IJECL* 253–63.

Serita, K, 'Islands and the Delimitation of the Continental Shelf' (in Japanese) (1980) 30 *Kobe Law Journal* 351–93.

——, *Possession of Islands and Delimitation of the Exclusive Economic Zone* (in Japanese) (Tokyo, Yushindo, 1999).

Shah, R, 'Bangladesh-Myanmar ITLOS Verdict:Precedence for India?' (2013) 37 *Strategic Analysis* 178–85.

Sharma, SP, 'The Relevance of Economic Factors to the Law of Maritime Delimitation between Neighbouring States' in ED Brown and RR Churchill (eds), *The UN Convention on the Law of the Sea: Impact and Implementations*, Proceedings Law of the Sea Institute Nineteenth Annual Conference, (Honolulu, Law of the Sea Institute, 1987) 248–65.

Shaw, MN, 'Case concerning the Land, Island and Maritime Frontier Dispute (El Salvador/Honduras: Nicaragua Intervening), Judgment of 11 September 1992' (1993) 42 *ICLQ* 929–37.

Shelley, AF, 'Law of the Sea: Delimitation of the Gulf of Maine: Case concerning Delimitation of the Maritime Boundary in the Gulf of Maine Area (Canada v United States)' (1985) 26 *Harvard International Law Journal* 646–54.

Shihata, Ibrahim FI and Onorato, WT, 'Joint Development of International Petroleum Resources in Undefined and Disputed Areas' in GH Blake, MA Pratt and CH Schofield (eds), *Boundaries and Energy: Problems and Prospects* (The Hague, Kluwer Law International, 1998) 433–51.

Sholanke, OO, 'Delimiting the Territorial Sea between Nigeria and Cameroon: A Rational Approach' (1993) 42 *ICLQ* 398–411.

Singh, N, *The Role and Record of the International Court of Justice* (Dordrecht, Nijhoff, 1989).

Skrk, M, 'The 1987 Law of Yugoslavia on the Coastal Sea and the Continental Shelf' (1989) 20 *ODIL* 501–14.

Slim, H, 'Les arrêts de la Cour internationale de Justice du 24–2–1982 et du 10–12–1985 dans l'affaire du plateau continental (Tunisie/Jamahiriya arabe libyenne)' (1986) 21 *Etudes internationales* 97–148.

Smith, RW, 'The Maritime Boundaries of the United States' (1981) 71 *Geographical Review* 395–410.

——, 'A Geographical Primer to Maritime Boundary Making' (1982) 12 *ODIL* 1–22.

——, 'A Geographical Primer to Maritime Boundary-Making' in EL Miles and A Scott, *The Law of the Sea and Ocean Development Issues in the Pacific Basin, Proceedings of Fifteenth Annual Conference of the Law of the Sea Institute in 1981* (Honolulu, University of Hawaii, 1983) 526–46.

——, 'Joint (Development) Zones: A Review of Past Practice and Thoughts on the Future' in MK Atmadja, TA Mensah and BH Oxman (eds), *Sustainable Development and Preservation of the Oceans: The Challenges of UNCLOS and Agenda 21, Proceedings of the Law of the Sea Institute 29th Annual Conference in 1995* (Honolulu, University of Hawaii, 1997) 645–62.

Sohn, LB, 'The Role of Equity in the Jurisprudence of the International Court of Justice' in *Mélanges: Georges Perrin* (Lausanne, Diffusion Payot, 1984) 303–12.

Soons, AHA, 'The Effects of a Rising Sea Level on Maritime Limits and Boundaries' (1990) 37 *NILR* 207–32.

Sperduti, G, 'L'intervention de l'Etat tiers dans le procès international: une nouvelle orientation' (1985) 31 *AFDI* 286–93.

——, 'Notes sur l'intervention dans le procès international', in *International Law at the Time of Its Codification, Essays in Honour of Roberto Ago*, vol III (Milan, Giuffrè, 1987) 429–42.

Stanczyk, J, 'Permissibility of Intervention under Article 62 of the Statute before the International Court' (1987) 16 *PYIL* 121–42.

Suk Kyoon Kim, 'Maritime Boundary Negotiations between China and Korea: The Factors at Stake' (2017) 32 *IJMCL* 69–94.

Sun Pyo Kim, *Maritime Delimitation and Interim Arrangements in North East Asia* (Leiden, Brill, 2004).

Symmons, CR, *The Maritime Zones of Islands in International Law* (The Hague, Nijhoff, 1979).

——, 'British Off-Shore Continental Shelf and Fishery Limit Boundaries: An Analysis of Overlapping Zones' (1979) 28 *ICLQ* 703–33.

——, 'The Rockall Dispute Deepens: An Analysis of Recent Danish and Icelandic Actions' (1986) 35 *ICLQ* 344–73.

——, 'The Outstanding Maritime Boundary Problems Between Ireland and the United Kingdom' in ED Brown and RR Churchill (eds), *The UN Convention on the Law of the Sea: Impact and Implementation* (Honolulu, The Law of the Sea Institute, University of Hawaii, 1987) 235–47.

——, 'The UK/Ireland Continental Shelf Agreement 1988: A Model for Compromise in Maritime Delimitation' in *International Boundaries and Boundary Conflict Resolution, Proceedings of the IBRU Conference held at the University of Durham 14–17 September 1989* (International Boundaries Research Unit, University of Durham, 1989) 387–412.

——, *Ireland and the Law of the Sea*, 2nd edn (Dublin, The Round Hall Press, 2000).

——, 'The 1992 Protocol to the 1988 Anglo-Irish Agreement on the Continental Shelf' (1993) 42 *ICLQ* 970–75.

——, The Background to the Imposition of the Straight Baseline System Around the Irish Coast: An Interesting Episode in Anglo-Irish Legal Relations' (1998) 13 *IJMCL* 47–69.

Symonides, J, 'Delimitation of Maritime Areas between the States with Opposite or Adjacent Coasts' (1984) 12 *PYIL* 19–46.

——, 'The Legal Status of Islands in the New Law of the Sea' (1987) 65 *Revue de droit international* 161–80.

Tanaka, Y, 'Reflections on Single Maritime Boundaries between Continental Shelf and EEZ/FZ' (in Japanese) (1997) 121 *The Hitotsubasi Review* 105–21.

——, 'Review of the Case concerning Maritime Delimitation between Greenland and Jan Mayen in 1993' (1999) 24 *Hitotsubashi Journal of Social Sciences* 1–31.

——, 'Reflections on the Eritrea/Yemen Arbitration of 17 December 1999 (Second Phase: Maritime Delimitation)' (2001) 48 *NILR* 197–225.

——, 'Reflections on the Concept of Proportionality in the Law of Maritime Delimitation' (2001) 16 *IJMCL* 433–63.

——, 'Reflections on Maritime Delimitation in the *Qatar/Bahrain* Case of 16 March 2001 (Merits)' (2003) 52 *ICLQ* 53–80.

——, 'Reflections on Maritime Delimitation in the *Cameroon/Nigeria* Case' (2004) 53 *ICLQ* 369–406.

——, 'Award of the Arbitral Tribunal Constituted Pursuant to Article 287, and in Accordance with Annex VII, of the UN Convention on the Law of the Sea: the Barbados and the Trinidad and Tobago Case (11 April 2006)' (2006) 21 *IJMCL* 523–34.

——, 'Barbados/Trinidad and Tobago Maritime Delimitation' (2007) 2 *Hague Justice Journal* 54–57.

——, 'The *Guyana/Suriname* Arbitration: A Commentary' (2007) 2 *Hague Justice Journal* 28–33.

——, 'Case Concerning the Territorial and Maritime Disputes between Nicaragua and Honduras in the Caribbean Sea' (2008) 23 *The International Journal of Marine and Coastal Law* 327–46.

——, 'Reflections on Maritime Delimitation in the *Nicaragua/Honduras* Case' (2008) 68 *ZaöRV/Heidelberg Journal of International Law* 903–37.

——, 'Reflections on Maritime Delimitation in the *Romania/Ukraine* Case before the International Court of Justice (2009) 56 *NILR* 397–427.
——, 'Reflections on the Territorial and Maritime Dispute between Nicaragua and Colombia before the International Court of Justice' (2013) 26 *LJIL* 909–31.
——, 'The Mirage of Predictability in the Law of Maritime Delimitation' (2014) 113 *The International Journal of Law and Diplomacy* 1–29.
——, 'Unilateral Exploration and Exploitation of Natural Resources in Disputed Areas: A Note on the *Ghana/Côte d'Ivoire* Order of 25 April 2015 before the Special Chamber of ITLOS' (2015) 46 *ODIL* 315–30.
——, 'The Impacts of the ITLOS Jurisprudence on the Development of International Law' in International Tribunal for the Law of the Sea, *The Contribution of the International Tribunal for the Law of the Sea to the Rule of Law: 1996–2016* (Leiden, Brill/Nijhoff, 2017) 161–78.
——, 'Article 74: Delimitation of the Exclusive Economic Zone between States with Opposite or Adjacent Coasts' in A Prölss (ed), *The United Nations Convention on the Law of the Sea: A Commentary*, (Oxford, Hart Publishing, 2017) 563–583.
——, 'Article 83: Delimitation of the Continental Shelf between States with Opposite or Adjacent Coasts,' in A Prölss (ed), *The United Nations Convention on the Law of the Sea: A Commentary*, (Oxford, Hart Publishing, 2017) 651–666.
——, 'The Disproportionality Test in the Law of Maritime Delimitation' in Alex G Oude Elferink, T Henriksen and SV Busch (eds) *Maritime Boundary Delimitation: The Case Law Is It Consistent and Practicable?* (Cambridge University Press, 2018) 291–318.
——, 'Maritime Boundary Delimitation by Conciliation' (2018) 36 *Australian Year Book of International Law* (forthcoming).
Tanja, G, *The Legal Delimitation of International Maritime Boundaries* (The Hague, Kluwer Law Publishers, 1990).
Thamsborg, M, 'Geodetic Hydrography as Related to Maritime Boundary Problems' (1974) 51 *International Hydrographic Review* 157–73.
Thirlway, HWA, 'The Law and Procedure of the International Court of Justice: Part Five' (1994) 64 *BYIL* 1–54.
——, 'The Law and Procedure of the International Court of Justice: Part Six' (1995) 65 *BYIL* 1–102.
Touzé, S, 'Affaire relative à la Délimitation maritime en mer Noire (Roumanie c. Ukraine): une clarification didactique de la règle de l'équidistance circonstances pertinentes' (2009) 55 *AFDI* 221–51.
Treves, T, 'La limite extérieure du plateau continental. Evolution récente de la pratique' (1989) 35 *AFDI* 724–35.
——, 'Codification du droit international et pratique des Etats dans le droit de la mer' (1990) 223 *RCADI* 9–302.
——, (ed), *The Law of the Sea: The European Union and Its Member States* (The Hague, Nijhoff, 1997).
——, 'New Trends in the Settlement of Disputes and the Law of the Sea Convention,' in HN Scheiber (ed), *Law of the Sea: The Common Heritage and Emerging Challenges* (The Hague, Nijhoff, 2000), 61–86.
——, 'Law and Science in the Interpretation of the Law of the Sea Convention: Article 76 Between the Law of the Sea Tribunal and the Commission on the Limits of the Continental Shelf' (2012) 3 *Journal of International Dispute Settlement* 483–91.
Trost, RH, *The Contested Maritime and Territorial Boundaries of Malaysia: An International Law Perspective* (The Hague, Kluwer Law International, 1998).
Twiss, T, *The Law of Nations Considered as Independent Political Communities* (Oxford, Clarendon Press, 1861).
United Nations Office of Ocean Affaires and the Law of the Sea, *Law of the Sea: Regime of Islands* (New York, United Nations, 1988).
——, *Baselines: National Legislation With Illustrative Maps* (New York, United Nations, 1989).
——, *Handbook on the Delimitation of Maritime Boundaries* (New York, United Nations, 2000).

United States Department of State, *Limits in the Seas, No. 106: Developing Standard Guidelines for Evaluating Straight Baselines* (1987) 1–37.

Usman, A, 'The Timor Gap in the Delimitation of the Continental Shelf Boundary Between Indonesia and Australia' (1986) 14 *The Indonesian Quarterly* 375–92.

Valencia, MJ, 'Taming Troubled Waters: Joint Development of Oil and Mineral Resources in Overlapping Claim Areas' (1986) 23 *San Diego Law Review* 661–84.

Van Dyke, JM, 'The Role of Islands in Delimiting Maritime Zones: The Case of the Aegean Sea' (1990) 8 *Ocean Yearbook* 44–69.

——, 'Uninhabited Islands: Their Impact on the Ownership of the Oceans' Resources' (1983) 12 *ODIL* 265–300.

Vega-Barbosa, G, 'The Admissibility of Outer Continental Shelf Delimitation Claims Before the ICJ Absent a Recommendation by the CLCS' (2017) *ODIL* 103–17.

Virally, M, 'L'équité dans le droit: à propos des problèmes de délimitation maritime' in *International Law of the Time of Its Codification, Essays in Honour of Roberto Ago*, vol II (Milan, Giuffrè, 1987) 523–34.

Virzijl, JHW, *International Law in Historical Perspective*, Part III, State Territory (Leyden, Sijthoff and Noordhoff, 1970).

Vœlckel, M, 'Les lignes de base dans la Convention de Genève sur la mer territoriale' (1973) 19 *AFDI* 820–36.

——, 'Aperçu de quelques problèmes techniques concernant la délimitation des frontières maritimes' (1979) 25 *AFDI* 293–711.

——, 'Les cartes marines dans la convention de Montego Bay,' in Institut de droit économique de la mer, Monaco, *Droit de la mer, Etudes dédiées au Doyen Claude-Albert Colliard* (Paris, Pedone, 1992) 93–107.

von Mühlendahl, P, *L'équidistance dans la délimitation des frontières maritimes: étude de la jurisprudence internationale* (Paris, Pedone, 2016).

——, 'Tiny Land Features in Recent Maritime Delimitation Case Law' (2016) 31 *IJMCL* 1–31.

Vukas, B, 'The Law of the Sea Convention and Sea Boundaries Delimitation' in *Essays on the New Law of the Sea* (Zagreb, Sveucilisna naklada Liber, 1985) 147–85.

——, 'Possible Role of the International Tribunal for the Law of the Sea in Interpretation and Progressive Development of the Law of the Sea' in D Vidas and W Østreng (eds), *Order for the Oceans at the Turn of the Century* (The Hague, Kluwer, 1999) 95–104.

Walsh, F, 'Guinea/Guinea Bissau case Study: Leading to a "compromise d'arbitrage"' in TA Grigalunas and LC Hanson (eds), *Continental Shelf, Resources, Boundaries, and Management* (Kingston, RI, University of Rhode Island, 1986) 64–69.

Warr, CG (ed), *International Boundaries and Boundary Conflict Resolution, Proceedings of the 1989 IBRU Conference* (International Boundaries Research Unit (IBRU), University of Durham, UK, 1989).

Weckel, P, 'CIJ: Arrêt du 16 mars 2001 (fond)' (2001) 105 *RGDIP* 443–47.

Weil, P, *Perspectives du droit de la délimitation maritime* (Paris, Pedone, 1988).

——, *The Law of Maritime Delimitation-Reflections* (Cambridge, 1989).

——, 'La technique 'comme partie intégrante du droit international': à propos des méthodes de délimitation des juridictions maritimes' in *Etudes offertes à Claude-Albert Colliard* (Paris, Pedone, 1984) 347–59.

——, 'A propos du droit coutumier en matière de délimitation maritime' in *International Law at the Time of Its Codification, Essays in Honour of Roberto Ago*, vol II (Milan, Giuffrè, 1987) 535–52.

——, 'Délimitation maritime et délimitation terrestre' in Dinsterin, Y (ed.), *International Law at a Time of Perplexity, Essays in Honour of Shabtai Rosenne* (Dordrecht, Kluwer, 1989) 1021–26.

——, 'Geographic Considerations in Maritime Delimitation' in JI Charney and LM Alexander (eds), *International Maritime Boundaries*, vol 1 (Dordrecht, Nijhoff, 1993) 115–30.

——, 'L'équité dans la jurisprudence de la Cour Internationale de Justice: Un mystère en voie de dissipation?' in V Lowe and M Fitzmaurice (eds), *Fifty Years of the International Court of Justice, Essays in Honour of Sir Robert Jennings* (Cambridge University Press, 1996) 121–44.

——, 'A propos de la double fonction des lignes de base dans le droit de la mer' in *Essays in Honour of Judge Taslim Olawale Elias* (Dordrecht, Nijhoff, 1992), 145–62. Reprinted in P Weil, *Écrits de droit international* (Paris, PUF, 2000) 279–99.

Westlake, J, *International Law Part I, Peace* (Cambridge, Cambridge University Press, 1904).

Willis, LA, 'From Precedent to Precedent: The Triumph of Pragmatism in the Law of Maritime Boundaries' (1986) 24 *CYIL* 3–60.

Wolfrum, R, 'The Delimitation of the Outer Continental Shelf: Procedural Considerations' in *Liber amicorum Jean-Pierre Cot, Le procès international* (Bruxelles, Bruylant, 2009) 349–66.

Xinjun Zhang, 'The ITLOS Judgment in the Bay of Bengal Case between Bangladesh and Myanmar' (2013) 12 *CJIL* 255–80.

Xuexia Liao, 'Evaluation of Scientific Evidence by International Courts and Tribunals in the Continental Shelf Delimitation Cases', (2017) 48 *ODIL* 136–57.

——, 'Is There a Hierarchical relationship between Natural Prolongation and Distance in the Continental Shelf Delimitation?' (2017) 32 *IJMCL* 1–37.

Yamamoto, S, *The Status of Islands in International Law* (in Japanese) (Tokyo, Ministry of Foreign Affairs in Japan, 1991).

Young, R, 'The Geneva Convention on the Continental Shelf: A First Impression' (1958) 52 *AJIL* 733–38.

——, 'Equitable Solutions for Offshore Boundaries: The 1968 Saudi Arabian-Iran Agreement' (1970) 64 *AJIL* 152–57.

Zeidman, SJ, 'Sittin'on the Dhaka the Bay: the Dispute Between Bangladesh and Myanmar and Its Implications for the International Tribunal for the Law of the Sea' (2012) 50 *Columbia Journal of Transnational Law* 442–89.

Zhen Wu, *Maritime Delimitation in the China Seas* (Geneva, Thesis, IUHEI, 1992).

Zhiguo, G, 'Legal Aspects of joint Development in International Law' in MK Atmadja, TA Mensah and BH Oxman (eds), *Sustainable Development and Preservation of the Oceans: The Challenges of UNCLOS and Agenda 21, Proceedings of the Law of the Sea Institute 29th Annual Conference in 1995* (Honolulu, University of Hawaii, 1997) 629–44.

Zoller, E, 'L'affaire de la délimitation du plateau continental entre la République française et le Royaume-Uni de Grande Bretagne et d'Irlande du Nord: Décision du 30 juin 1977' (1977) 23 *AFDI* 359–407.

——, 'Recherche sur les méthodes de délimitation du plateau continental: à propos de l'affaire Tunisie-Libye (Arrêt du 24 février 1982)' (1982) 86 *RGDIP* 645–78.

——, 'L'affaire de la délimitation des espaces maritimes entre le Canada et la République française (décision du 10 juin 1992)' (1992) 38 *AFDI* 480–500.

Zou Keyuan, 'The Sino-Vietnamese Agreement on Maritime Boundary Delimitation in the Gulf of Tonkin' (2005) 36 *ODIL* 13–24.

Index